DATE DUE

Women and Women's Issues

A Handbook
of Tests and Measures

CAROLE A. BEERE

Women and Women's Issues

A Handbook
of Tests and Measures

Jossey-Bass Publishers

San Francisco • Washington • London • 1979

WOMEN AND WOMEN'S ISSUES
A Handbook of Tests and Measures
by Carole A. Beere

Copyright © 1979 by: Jossey-Bass, Inc., Publishers
433 California Street
San Francisco, California 94104
&
Jossey-Bass Limited
28 Banner Street
London EC1Y 8QE

Library of Congress Cataloging in Publication Data

Beere, Carole A   1944-
    Women and women's issues.

    (The Jossey-Bass social and behavioral science
series)
    Bibliography: p.
    Includes index.
    1. Women's studies—Methodology—Handbooks, manuals,
etc. 2. Sex role—Testing—Handbooks, manuals, etc.
3. Social role—Testing—Handbooks, manuals, etc.
I. Title.
HQ1180.B43   301.41'2'018   79-88106
ISBN 0-87589-418-6

Manufactured in the United States of America

JACKET DESIGN BY WILLI BAUM

FIRST EDITION

Code 7923

The Jossey-Bass
Social and Behavioral Science Series

✠ ✠ ✠ ✠ ✠ ✠ ✠ ✠ ✠ ✠ ✠ ✠ ✠ ✠ ✠ ✠ ✠ ✠

441621

Preface

The acquisition of knowledge in any area of the behavioral sciences depends partly on the quality of the measuring instruments used to gather data. The study of women is no exception.

The study of women encompasses a broad variety of topics, including sex roles (often referred to as masculinity-femininity), sex stereotypes, women's roles (such as marital, parental, and employee roles), attitudes toward women, and topics pertinent to women (such as equal rights, abortion, and sexuality). Although research devoted specifically to women has been conducted for at least forty years, there has been a tremendous increase in the number of such studies in the last fifteen years. Much of this research has relied on paper-and-pencil measures or interview data to obtain information about the variables being studied. *Women and Women's Issues: A Handbook of Tests and Measures* is the first extensive and organized compilation of the measuring instruments used in research regarding women. The literature through 1977 was comprehensively searched to identify instruments that measure variables pertinent to women and women's issues. Included are paper-and-pencil and orally administered instruments that met one of the

ix

following four criteria: there had to be information regarding (1) the empirical or theoretical development of the instrument, (2) the instrument's reliability, or (3) the instrument's validity; or (4) the instrument must have been used by a variety of researchers. The search located the 235 instruments described in this volume.

The handbook is divided into two parts. Part One describes the process used to locate and screen instruments for inclusion, the format for describing the instruments, their organization, and the problems connected with them. Part Two presents descriptions of 235 instruments, organized into eleven chapters, with each chapter preceded by an overview. The instrument descriptions follow a standard format that provides the following information: title and author of the instrument, year in which it first appeared in the literature, a statement of the characteristics of respondents who have previously completed the instrument and of respondents who could reasonably be expected to complete it, a description of the instrument, information about the administration and scoring of the items, sample items, a description of the development of the instrument, information regarding its reliability and validity, some "notes and comments" about the instrument (including, for example, information regarding modifications and foreign language translations of the instrument, a list of variables that have previously been related to the scores, results from factor analytic studies, and evaluative comments), the source from which the complete instrument can be obtained, and a bibliography of the research studies in which the instrument was used.

The availability of this handbook will alleviate some of the problems previously encountered in conducting research in this area. It greatly reduces the time that a researcher must spend locating existing instruments. I hope that this time-saving feature will encourage researchers to use existing instruments, for repeated use will increase our knowledge of these instruments' psychometric properties, and the data gathered from successive applications can be used to refine and improve the instruments. This process should result in the development of instruments that are more reliable and more valid than most of those now being used. Furthermore, repeated use encourages more rapid growth of knowledge in the field. The comparison and integration of results from several studies are more valid if those studies used the same measuring instrument. I also hope that the convenient access to existing instruments will discourage researchers from constructing new instruments for their research—a frequent yet often nonproductive practice. Researchers often fail to devote sufficient attention to instrument development because their goals are usually to test hypotheses, *not* to develop instruments. As a result, the psychometric properties of such instruments are at best unknown and at worst unacceptable.

This book should encourage more research on women and issues pertaining to women since it provides easy access to measuring instruments and since the contents are likely to suggest innumerable studies to the potential researcher, including studies that focus on instrument development. In fact, a review of the contents indicates that there are essentially no instruments for many aspects of research on women and that existing instruments are often inadequate—they are obsolete, not enough is known about their psychometric properties, or their psychometric properties do not satisfy conventional standards. The development of new, quality instruments is clearly needed in many areas, and this book helps identify such areas.

It is apparent from the literature that researchers typically communicate insufficient information regarding the development and psychometric properties of the instruments used in their research. This omission is not surprising for journal articles: the costs of publishing articles are so high that all nonessential information is omitted, and information about the measuring instruments is often considered nonessential. Now, however, researchers who use an instrument described in this book can refer readers of their articles to published information about the instrument.

Given that the study of women spans many disciplines, this handbook will interest persons in a variety of fields, including psychology, sociology, anthropology, home economics, education, and communication. In essence, any behavioral scientist who is interested in the study of women or women's issues should find this book useful. It will help researchers identify appropriate instruments for their research; it will help consumers of research familiarize themselves with the instruments used in research and with the problems associated with them.

I view this book as a beginning in that it provides those engaged in research pertaining to women and women's issues with a clearinghouse for material on relevant instruments. I invite researchers to send me information about instruments included in this book as well as information about newly developed or previously developed instruments not included herein. I anticipate that the accumulation of this material will result in a second, more comprehensive, edition. And I hope that the prospect of a subsequent volume will encourage researchers who are developing new instruments to develop ones that have adequate reliability and established validity.

Women and Women's Issues could not have been completed without much help and support. My thanks to Central Michigan University for granting me a sabbatical leave to write the book and to the Faculty Research and Creative Endeavors Committee for providing the financial support for the project. Many individuals provided valuable assistance during the preparation of the book. I extend my sincere appreciation to Patricia Gugel, graduate student in psychology, who assisted with the literature search and located reliability and validity data for selected instruments; Mary Cannon and Julie Bizzis, who handled the tremendous amount of clerical work and typing associated with preparing the book; Doris Miller and Joy Pastucha, Central Michigan University reference librarians, who provided invaluable assistance in locating and obtaining needed reference materials; Thomas Miller, who always responded to my requests for help; and Daniel King and Lynda King, my colleagues, who read portions of the manuscript and provided valuable suggestions. To my children, Jonathan and Jennifer, who are too young to understand what I have been doing, thank you for tolerating my long working hours. My deepest gratitude and appreciation goes to Donald Beere, my husband and colleague, who read and reacted to the entire manuscript as it was being written, offered helpful suggestions, discussed ideas with me, and most of all, offered continuous support and encouragement.

Mount Pleasant, Michigan   Carole A. Beere
July 1979

Contents

The Author

Carole A. Beere is associate professor in the Department of Psychology at Central Michigan University, where she teaches psychological testing, statistics, and research design. Born in Chicago in 1944, Beere lived there until she went to Michigan State University, where she earned her bachelor's degree (1966) in business and mathematics. She was awarded a graduate fellowship from the U.S. Office of Education for study in the Department of Educational Psychology at Michigan State. While a graduate student, she was a research assistant on projects relating to the improvement of teaching. In 1969, she worked as a research consultant for the State of Michigan's Department of Education, evaluating state-funded compensatory education programs. Following the award of her doctor's degree (1970) in testing and research design, Beere became coordinator of the research data program for the state's Department of Education.

In 1971, Beere and her husband, Donald, a clinical psychologist, accepted faculty positions at Central Michigan University. Beere's professional interests include developing and teaching a "Sex Role Issues" course, conducting research in response to some of the problems raised in this book, and expanding her collection of scales that pertain to women. The author of a test for measuring young children's attitudes toward school, she has also had work published in *Psychology in the Schools.*

Beere's nonacademic interests focus primarily on her family, which includes two children, Jonathan and Jennifer. Since the births of her children, Beere has retained her full-time academic position and is experiencing, rather than researching, the problems of women's dual career-family roles. She serves as the board director of the daycare center that her children attend.

Women and Women's Issues

A Handbook
of Tests and Measures

1

　　　　　　　　　　

Organization
of the Handbook

　　　　　　　　　　　　　　　　　　　　

The foci of this book are *women and issues pertaining to women* and *measures.* What are issues pertaining to women? They are issues that apply to women because of their gender or because of the roles they occupy in society. In many instances, women's issues cannot be separated from men's issues. The definitions of, enactments of, and attitudes toward male and female roles are interdependent. Regardless of whether male and female roles are considered as coinciding, complementary, or disparate, they are typically thought of as having an impact on each other. The roles that females assume for themselves or presume for males generally have an impact—either directly or indirectly—on the roles that males can or are willing to assume. The converse is also true: The roles that males assume for themselves or presume for females generally have an impact on the roles that females can or are willing to assume. Thus, many of the issues considered here are more accurately described as sex role issues. The term *women* was chosen because issues that are unique to women have been included and, with two exceptions,* issues that are unique to men have generally

---

*The Podell Scale of Attitudes Regarding Family Role of Men (#122) measures attitudes regarding the place of occupational success in the role of husband and father. These roles have an impact on the role of women. A researcher could change the wording

1

been excluded. What are *measures*? As used here, the term *measures* includes paper-and-pencil and orally administered instruments designed to gather data in the conduct of research. Because measuring instruments are crucial to the conduct of research, anyone who is interested in producing or consuming research related to women's issues should be conversant with the measurement problems and procedures used in the discipline.

Locating and Screening the Instruments

The first step in preparing this book was to locate measuring instruments used in the study of women's issues. A five-pronged approach was used: (1) the publications of various abstracting services were searched; (2) books compiling, describing, or listing instruments used in the social sciences were checked; (3) page-by-page searches were conducted with selected journals; (4) notices were placed in professional publications inviting readers to submit relevant instruments; and (5) the bibliographies at the end of at least 3,000 articles were checked.

The search of published abstracts was by far the most productive step. Following are the sources and years searched: *Psychological Abstracts* (1927-1977), *Sociological Abstracts* (1952-1977), *Educational Resources Information Clearinghouse (ERIC)* (1966-1977), *Dissertation Abstracts* and *Dissertation Abstracts International* (1861-1977), *Current Index to Journals in Education* (1969-1977), *Women Studies Abstracts* (1972-1977), and *Journal Supplement Abstract Service* (1971-1977). Each search began with the initial volume of the publication. *Women Studies Abstracts* and *Journal Supplement Abstract Service* were searched in their entirety. The specific search terms listed below were used to identify potentially relevant publications in the other five sources.

Psychological Abstracts:

Attitude (and all related terms)	Marital Conflict	Role(s)
Chivalry	Marital Relations	Role Conflicts
Family	Marital Status	Role Expectations
Family Relations	Marriage	Role Perceptions
Family Structure	Marriage Attitudes	Sex Roles
Female	Masculinity	Social Movements
Femininity	Maternal	Stereotyped Attitudes
Housewives	Matriarchy	Stereotypes
Human	Mother	Wife (Wives)
Human Females	Mother-Child Relations	Woman
Marital	Parent(s)	Women's Liberation
	Parental Role	Movement

Sociological Abstracts:

Family	Male	Sex
Female	Marriage	Stereotype
Feminist	Masculinity	Wife
Homemakers	Mother	Woman
Housewives	Parent	

of the items to ask the same questions about the role of mother and wife. The Inventory of Masculine Values (#188) measures attitudes toward the masculine role. It is included because it parallels the Inventory of Feminine Values (#187).

Dissertation Abstracts and *Dissertation Abstracts International:*

Abortion	Homemakers	Maternal
Boy(s)	Homemaking	Mothers (and all related
Conjugal	Housewives	terms)
Familial	Husbands	Parent (and all related
Family (Families)	Male(s)	terms)
Female	Man (Men)	Sex (and all related
Feminine	Marital	terms)
Femininity	Marriage(s)	Spouse
Feminism	Married	Wife (Wives)
Gender	Masculine	Woman (Women)
Girl(s)	Masculinity	

ERIC and *Current Index to Journals in Education:*

Abortions	Identification (Psychologi-	Sex Discrimination
Contraception	cal)	Sex Roles
Family Attitudes	Marriage	Sex Stereotypes
Family Role	Mother Attitudes	Women's Studies
Feminism	Parent Attitudes	Working Women
Housewives	Parent Role	

The abstracts for all articles obtained from the searches were read. If the abstract revealed that the article was not a report of empirical research or it was written in a language other than English, the article was eliminated from further consideration; otherwise a copy of the article was obtained.

The following bibliography lists books that compile, describe, or list instruments used in research in the social sciences. Each of these books was scanned in order to identify potentially relevant instruments.

Bonjean, C. M., Hill, R. J., and McLemore, S. D. *Sociological Measurement: An Inventory of Scales and Indices.* San Francisco: Chandler, 1967.

Buros, O. K. *Tests in Print.* Highland Park, N.J.: Gryphon Press, 1961.

Buros, O. K. *Tests in Print II.* Highland Park, N.J.: Gryphon Press, 1974.

Chun, K. T., Cobb, S., and French, J. R. P., Jr. *Measures for Psychological Assessment: A Guide to 3,000 Original Sources and Their Applications.* Ann Arbor, Mich.: Survey Research Center of the Institute for Social Research, 1975.

Comrey, A. L., Backer, T. E., and Glaser, E. M. *A Sourcebook of Mental Health Measures.* Los Angeles: Human Interaction Research Institute, 1973.

Goldman, B. A., and Busch, J. C. *Directory of Unpublished Experimental Mental Measures.* Vol. 2. New York: Human Sciences Press, 1978.

Goldman, B. A., and Saunders, J. L. *Directory of Unpublished Experimental Mental Measures.* Vol. 1. New York: Behavioral Publications, 1974.

Johnson, O. G., and Bommarito, J. W. *Tests and Measurements in Child Development: Handbook I.* San Francisco: Jossey-Bass, 1971.

Johnson, O. G. *Tests and Measurements in Child Development: Handbook II.* San Francisco: Jossey-Bass, 1976.

Miller, D. C. *Handbook of Research Design and Social Measurement.* (2nd ed.) New York: McKay, 1970.

Robinson, J. P., Athanasiou, R., and Head, K. B. *Measures of Occupational Attitudes and Occupational Characteristics.* Ann Arbor: Institute for Social Research, University of Michigan, 1969.

Robinson, J. P., Rusk, J. G., and Head, K. B. *Measures of Political Attitudes.* Ann Arbor: Institute for Social Research, University of Michigan, 1968.

Robinson, J. P., and Shaver, P. R. *Measures of Social Psychological Attitudes.* (rev. ed.) Ann Arbor: Institute for Social Research, University of Michigan, 1973.

Shaw, M. E., and Wright, J. M. *Scales for the Measurement of Attitudes.* New York: McGraw-Hill, 1967.

Straus, M. A. *Family Measurement Techniques: Abstracts of Published Instruments, 1935-1965.* Minneapolis: University of Minnesota Press, 1969.

Walker, D. K. *Socioemotional Measures for Preschool and Kindergarten Children.* San Francisco: Jossey-Bass, 1973.

Four journals were identified as particularly relevant to sex roles and women's issues: *Psychology of Women Quarterly, Sex Roles, Signs,* and *Archives of Sexual Behavior.* Page-by-page searching was done beginning with the first issue of each journal and continuing through the last issue of 1977.

Two notices were published requesting that relevant instruments or other pertinent information be submitted. The following notice appeared in the *Division 35 Newsletter* (April 1978) published by the Division of the Psychology of Women, American Psychological Association: "WANTED: Information, validation studies, and copies of instruments or data-gathering procedures used in research about women, especially in the following areas: sex role stereotypes, marital roles, maternal roles, masculinity-femininity, and attitudes toward women or women's issues; for possible inclusion in a compendium of assessment procedures used in research about women." A comparable notice appeared in the June 1978 issue of the *APA Monitor,* a monthly newspaper sent to all members of the American Psychological Association. Unfortunately the notices did not elicit many responses. About ten letters were received and fewer than half of these produced relevant information. The last source for identifying instruments was the bibliographies accompanying articles that had been identified through prior searching. Between 3,000 and 4,000 bibliographies were scanned for articles that would help locate additional instruments or that were pertinent to instruments previously located.

As a result of the extensive search, more than 6,000 references were identified as possibly including relevant instruments. The majority of the references were journal articles; also included were books, doctoral dissertations, masters theses, ERIC documents, and convention papers. The description of the methods used to conduct each study was read, and a file was developed of all the measuring instruments used. Instruments measuring variables closely related to but still distinct from sex roles or women's issues were eliminated. For example, scales were eliminated if they measured (1) parental identification rather than sex role identification, (2) self-concept or self-esteem but not sex role self-concept, (3) feelings about one's own parents or marital partner (unless the instrument focused on parental or marital *roles*), and (4) measures of fear of success. Instruments that were intended to gather demographic or factual information about a respondent were also eliminated, as were behavioral observation measures and "instruments" consisting of a single item or single question. Finally, with one exception, instruments that were used in a masters thesis or doctoral dissertation but in no other reference were excluded.

As a result of the searching, scanning, and eliminating described above, a file listing over 800 instruments was compiled. The next step was to obtain a copy of each measuring instrument, because no instrument could be described or evaluated without being seen. Furthermore, no instrument was to be included in the book unless a potential user could obtain a copy of it. Obtaining a copy of the majority of instruments was not a problem. Either the complete instrument appeared in a journal article, a doctoral dissertation, or a masters thesis, or it was available from a commercial publisher. In some cases, however, the complete instrument could be obtained only by writing to its author. In such instances, a letter was sent to the author asking for a copy of the instrument and any other information pertinent to its development, reliability, or validity. An instrument was eliminated if no current address could be found for the author, if the author never responded to the request, or if the author could not or would not send the instrument.

After the measuring instruments that could not be obtained were eliminated, four criteria were established for determining which of the remaining instruments would be included: (1) the construction of the instrument must be empirically or theoretically based and must be explained, (2) data must be available regarding its reliability, (3) data must be available regarding its validity, and (4) it must have been used by a variety of researchers. Only one of the four criteria had to be satisfied in order for the instrument to be included in the book. Unfortunately, it was very common to find no information regarding development, reliability, or validity; as a result, only 235 instruments satisfied the criteria for inclusion.

Format for Instrument Descriptions

Detailed descriptions following a standard format were written for 220 of the instruments that met the criteria for inclusion; abridged descriptions were written for the remaining fifteen instruments, which yield numerous scores, only one of which is relevant to women's issues. Below is an explanation of each heading used in the standard format.

NUMBER AND TITLE: At the beginning of each instrument description is a number identifying its sequential position in the book. Whenever the instrument is referred to at other places in the book, it is identified by its title followed by its number in parentheses. The title given is that used by the author of the instrument unless the author did not formally title the scale. In those cases, a title was assigned. Generally assigned titles begin with the author's name. When there was more than one author, the authors' names are hyphenated in the assigned title.

AUTHOR(S): The authors are listed in the order in which they appear on the earliest publication describing the instrument. There are occasional exceptions to this when the more recent literature suggests that following this rule would be misleading. For example, Franck and Rosen published the earliest article describing a drawing completion test, but on the commercially available manual and in all later publications, the test is referred to as the Franck Drawing Completion Test (#11). Thus, only Kate Franck is listed as the author in this book as well.

DATE: The date given is the earliest date the instrument was mentioned in the literature. When it was determined that the instrument was actually used at an earlier date, the earlier date is noted in parentheses following the publication date. For example, for the Femininity Adjective Check List (#34), the date is given as "1959 (used 1955)," which means that the earliest reference in the literature was in 1959, but the test was actually used as early as 1955. Likewise, the date of a revision is noted in parentheses following the original date. Since all information was taken from literature written in English, some instruments may have appeared at an earlier date in foreign-language publications. This earlier use would not be noted.

VARIABLES: The variables named are those which the author of the instrument claimed or implied that the instrument measures. There are, of course, instances in which the instrument does not actually measure what the author claims it measures; and there are instances in which users of an instrument claim that it measures a variable different from that which the author intended it to measure.

TYPE OF INSTRUMENT: Included in the book are twenty-two different types of instruments. *Adjective checklists* provide a series of adjectives or adjective phrases. Respondents are directed to place a check mark next to each of the adjectives that apply to or describe a specified referent. *Adjective rating scales* are series of adjectives or adjective phrases, each accompanied by a rating scale. Respondents are directed to use the scales to rate a specified referent on each of the adjectives. An *alternate choice* instrument is a series of items, each of which is accompanied by two response options, which are something other than "true" and "false." A *checklist* is a list of items other than adjectives or adjective phrases. Respondents are directed to check all of the items that apply to a specified referent. A *forced choice* instrument presents pairs of items and asks the respondent to select one item from each pair. A *forced choice picture preference* instrument presents pairs of pictures and directs respondents to select one picture from each pair. A *Guttman scale* is an attitude measure that typically consists of about five or six statements. Respondents indicate which statements they agree with. Guttman scales are unique in that "a person with a more favorable attitude score than another person must also be just as favorable or more favorable in his response to every statement in the set than the other person" (Edwards, 1957, p. 172). A *multiple-choice* instrument includes a series of items, each of which is accompanied by more than two response options, though the number and wording of response options may vary from item to item. Respondents are directed to select one response option for each item. *Open-ended questions* are instruments in which the items do not have fixed response alternatives; the respondents may give any response rather than being restricted to selecting their response from a specified set of options. *Picture preference* instruments present respondents with pictured stimuli, and the respondents must choose from among the pictures. *Projective drawing* tasks require that respondents draw; *projective storytelling* tasks require that respondents tell a story either verbally or in writing. Both types of projective tasks involve relatively ambiguous stimuli and brief, somewhat vague instructions. Projective techniques are presumed to measure relatively covert or unconscious aspects of personality. Scoring generally involves judgment and low interscorer reliability may be a problem. *Ranking scales* require respondents to rank order a series of items. *Rating scales* require respondents to rate a specified referent on particular dimensions. *Semantic differential scales* include rating scales with the endpoints labeled with bipolar adjectives—for example, "large" on the left end of the scale and "small" on the right end. The respondent is directed to rate a concept on the series of bipolar adjective scales. *Sentence-completion* tasks require that respondents finish incomplete sentences. *Sorting* tasks require that respondents sort objects or pictures according to some specific criterion which they are given. A *story completion-fixed-response alternatives* task asks respondents to complete a story by filling in the blanks. The blanks must be filled in using words from a specific list. *Summated rating scales* contain a series of statements, each of which is accompanied by the same set of response alternatives. Most often there are four to six response options ranging from "strongly agree" to "strongly disagree." Scale scores are obtained by summing the scores assigned to the individual items. A *Thurstone attitude scale* consists of a series of statements. Respondents are directed to place a check mark next to each statement they endorse. The scale is constructed by using a panel of judges to determine the degree of favorability expressed in each statement. The judges' responses are used to select items for the scale and to determine scale values (scores) for each of the selected items. Overall scores reflect the median scale value of endorsed items. *Toy preference* tests present respondents with an array of toys and the respondents must choose among them. A *true-false* instrument consists of a series of items, each of which is accompanied by the two response alternatives "true" and "false."

DESCRIPTION: Included here is a description of item content, a statement indicating the length of the instrument, and a description of the response options.

PREVIOUSLY ADMINISTERED TO: A description is given of the respondents who have previously completed the instrument. The description is based on the studies listed in the bibliography following the instrument description. If no sex is specified, one can assume that both males and females have completed the instrument, and if no country is specified, one can assume that the respondents were from the United States.

APPROPRIATE FOR: The sex and ages of persons who could complete the instrument are given. For most instruments, the author does not provide this information, so a judgment was made regarding which groups the instrument is appropriate for; this judgment was based primarily on an examination of item content. Some instruments have previously been administered to a narrower age range than is recommended here; others have previously been administered to a broader age range. A recommendation that the instrument is appropriate for a particular group is not intended to imply that it is reliable or valid for that group; it merely means that the persons in the described group could reasonably be expected to respond to the items on the instrument.

ADMINISTRATION: The majority of instruments are self-administered; specific information on the administration of these instruments is not provided. The procedures for administering all other types of instruments are explained. The time required to complete them is also given here. (Generally, the author does not indicate the time required, and so it was estimated.)

SAMPLE ITEMS: Typically at least two representative sample items are given for an instrument. When the instrument includes several subscales, a sample item is given for each. If the instrument does not include a verbal item or if the items are all apparent from the test description, no sample item is provided.

SCORING: This section indicates whether scoring is objective, how the items are weighted, and the number and names of the scores obtained. If a more thorough description of the scoring would aid the potential user in understanding the instrument, additional information is given. Furthermore, for most instruments, the range of possible scores and the interpretation of the extreme scores is given.

DEVELOPMENT: The theoretical basis and/or the empirical procedures used to develop the instrument are explained. When no information is provided here, it means either that the author failed to report the procedures used to develop the instrument or there is neither an empirical nor theoretical basis for its development.

RELIABILITY: Data regarding test-retest, alternate form, split-half, and internal-consistency reliability are presented here. In addition, if item-total correlations or Guttman reproducibility coefficients are available, the data are reported here. The reliability data were gleaned from all the references in the bibliography except the dissertations. (In general, abstracts of dissertations rather than the dissertations themselves were relied on for information, and abstracts do not usually include reliability information. In those rare instances where the dissertation itself was consulted, reliability information was extracted.) When the statement "No data are provided" is made, it means that no information regarding the instrument's reliability is reported in any of the accompanying bibliographic references. (Of course, reliability information may have been overlooked in some of the dissertations.)

Note that the information presented here is pertinent to the instrument's reliability but is not necessarily supportive of its reliability; it may suggest that the instrument is, in fact, not sufficiently reliable. Furthermore, evidence pertaining to the reliability of the instrument for a particular group should not be generalized to another significantly different group.

VALIDITY: Data regarding criterion-related and construct validity are presented here. Evidence of the criterion-related validity was based on correlations obtained between scores on the instrument and scores on a criterion measure, which was often another instrument purported to measure the same variable. Typically the evidence regarding construct validity derived from the support or nonsupport of the hypotheses tested.

Content validity is generally a function of the development of the instrument. Therefore, content validity or lack of content validity can be inferred from the Development section for each instrument. Face validity is not a technical form of validity, so there was no attempt to assess the face validity of the instruments.

As was the case with reliability, the statement "No data are provided" means that no information regarding validity is reported in any of the accompanying bibliographic references. But, as was pointed out earlier, dissertation abstracts rather than complete dissertations were typically consulted, and validity data reported in the actual dissertations may have been overlooked.

It should be noted that information presented here is relevant to the instrument's validity but does not necessarily mean that the scale is valid; the data presented may indicate that the instrument is not valid. Furthermore, the fact that the instrument is or is not valid in a particular situation for a particular group of respondents does not mean that it is or is not valid for another group in a different situation.

NOTES AND COMMENTS: Included in this section is information that is relevant to the potential user but does not clearly belong under one of the other headings. For example, factor analysis can relate to both the reliability and validity of the instrument, so results from factor-analytic studies are reported here. Other examples of what might be included in this section are information regarding modifications of the instrument, a list of variables that have been related to the scores but do not provide evidence of validity, information regarding foreign-language translations, intercorrelations between subscores, evaluative comments, and references to other books that describe the instrument.

SOURCE: A copy of the complete instrument can be obtained from the sources listed here. When the word *See* is given, followed by an abbreviated reference, the complete reference is given in the bibliography that follows the source. Instruments that are available in the published literature are obviously free. Two options exist for obtaining an instrument that appears in a doctoral dissertation. If the dissertation is listed in *Dissertation Abstracts* or *Dissertation Abstracts International,* it can be purchased from University Microfilms International, P.O. Box 1346, Ann Arbor, Michigan 48106. Consult a recent copy of *Dissertation Abstracts International* for up-to-date prices and ordering information. Some dissertations can be borrowed through the interlibrary loan office of a college library. The masters theses referenced in this book can usually be borrowed through an interlibrary loan office. Instruments that are available from a document depository or a commercial publisher must be purchased. Check on prices before ordering, as orders must usually be prepaid. ERIC documents are often available in microfiche at college libraries; otherwise they can be purchased in microfiche or paper copy from the ERIC Document Reproduction Service, P.O. Box 190, Arlington, Virginia 22210. Instruments that are available from ETS Tests in Microfiche Collection can be purchased in microfiche from Educational Testing Service, Princeton, New Jersey 08540. Instruments that are available from their authors are sometimes free and sometimes a fee is charged. Only by writing to the author can one determine if a fee is presently being charged.

If an instrument is not available in its entirety in the published literature, and if the Notes and Comments section indicates that it is described in *Family Measurement Techniques* (Straus, 1969; Straus and Brown, 1978), then it is quite likely that the instrument is available from the National Auxiliary Publications Service of the American Society for Information Science, P.O. Box 3513, Grand Central Station, New York, New York 10017. Consult the appropriate edition of *Family Measurement Techniques* for information on how to order the instrument. Remember, however, that prices for reproductions may have increased since *Family Measurement Techniques* was published.

BIBLIOGRAPHY: Listed here are references for research studies in which the instrument was used. Dissertations, recent convention papers, books, journal articles, and ERIC documents are included. It would be absurd to claim that the bibliographies are complete, but hopefully they approach that. Occasionally in the description of an instrument, a journal article or book is cited that is *not* a report of the use of the instrument. The complete reference is given in the bibliography and preceded with an asterisk. If the bibliography accompanying the instrument includes only one reference, no reference citations are included in the text. One can assume that all information was gleaned from the one source. Whenever a dissertation is abstracted in *Dissertation Abstracts* or *Dissertation Abstracts International,* the bibliographical entry for the abstract is given in parentheses following the bibliographical entry for the dissertation. Citations in the text refer to dissertations by the date on the dissertation, not the date of the abstract. Whenever a research report is available through the ERIC Document Reproduction Service, the document number is given in parentheses following the bibliographic entry.

Organization of the Instruments

In order to facilitate locating instruments within this book, the descriptions have been divided into eleven chapters, each preceded by a brief overview of the contents and a summary of the significant problems associated with the instruments in that chapter. A completely pragmatic approach was used to organize the book. Measures of sex role adoption, preference, or orientation/identity were first grouped together. Two persons working independently sorted the remaining instruments into groups based primarily on an examination of their items and secondarily on the authors' claims as to what the instruments measure. Instruments that were classified differently by the two persons were discussed until consensus was achieved on how they ought to be classified. This process resulted in eleven classifications.

"Sex Roles" contains fifty-nine instruments that assess sex role adoption, sex role preference, and sex role orientation or identity. These are frequently referred to as measures of masculinity-femininity. This chapter is subdivided into thirty instruments appropriate for children and adolescents and twenty-nine appropriate for adults. "Sex Stereotypes" contains twenty-five instruments that assess perceptions of personality traits, occupations, and activities. "Sex Role Prescriptions" contains seven instruments that focus on personality traits and behaviors considered appropriate for males and for females. These instruments emphasize what should or ought to be true of persons of each gender. "Children's Sex Roles" contains eleven instruments pertaining to sex-typed behaviors or personality traits of children. "Gender Knowledge" contains five instruments that measure whether preschoolers know their own gender or can correctly classify other persons on the basis of gender. "Marital and Parental Roles" contains twenty-three instruments that measure attitudes toward marital roles, perceptions and feelings regarding one's own or one's parents' marital roles, marital task allocation, or marital power (including decision making). "Employee Roles" contains sixteen instruments relating to paid employment outside the home, including conditions under which a woman should work, the important features of jobs for women, perceptions of which jobs are open to women, comparisons between male and female workers, and the effects of males entering female-dominated professions. "Multiple Roles" contains twenty instruments pertaining to more than one role. The majority of the instruments concern the marital/parental role and the work role; thus most of them cut across the two preceding chapters. "Attitudes Toward Women's Issues" contains forty-one instruments, each of which measures attitudes toward a variety of issues. Many of the issues are relevant to other chapters as well. If an instrument measures attitudes toward a single issue, it is classified in the appropriate chapter; if it measures attitudes toward marital roles and work roles, it is classified in "Multiple Roles"; but if it measures attitudes toward a variety of issues, it is classified in this chapter. "Somatic and Sexual Issues" contains seventeen instruments pertaining to abortion, sexuality, menstruation, body perception, contraception, pregnancy, menopause, and somatic androgyny. Finally, there are eleven unclassified instruments relating to women's issues which are not appropriate to any of the other chapters.

The process used to classify the instruments ensured that each would be classified into one and only one chapter. Since many instruments measure more than one variable, a subject index was also prepared. The subject index lists each instrument under every variable that it measures. Thus, in order to locate a particular instrument, the reader should not restrict herself* to the instruments listed in the relevant section; the subject index should also be consulted. Furthermore, many instruments can be modified slightly to measure a variable different from what they were intended to measure. Of course, such modification means that an essentially new scale has been constructed and that its psychometric properties are unknown. Nevertheless, readers might find potentially useful

---

*Because the focus of this book is women and there is no generally accepted pronoun denoting *he* or *she*, the pronoun *she* will be used throughout this book.

instruments included in numerous sections of the book. An author index and a title index are provided to help the reader who is looking for a particular instrument or for an instrument by a particular author.

The descriptions of each instrument provide readers with enough information to know whether it is inappropriate for their needs; that is, an instrument can be eliminated from consideration based on reading the description given. However, no instrument should be selected for use solely on the basis of reading the description given here. A copy of the instrument should be obtained and carefully read, and the references listed at the end of the description should be consulted. Once a promising instrument has been identified, its author(s) should be contacted. Many instruments require that permission be obtained before they are used. Failure to obtain permission from the author or publisher is often a copyright violation. An additional benefit can be derived from contacting the author(s): Often they have new information that will affect the instrument's use, can supply an updated bibliography, or can supply the names of other researchers engaged in similar research using the instrument. Typically authors like to be apprised of who is using their instrument and what type of research is being conducted with it. Addresses of authors are not provided in this book because they are so quickly outdated. However, university librarians can assist in locating reference books that provide addresses for college and university faculty, for members of various professional associations, and for persons listed in biographical directories.

BIBLIOGRAPHY:

Edwards, A. L. *Techniques of Attitude Scale Construction.* New York: Appleton-Century-Crofts, 1957.

Straus, M. A. *Family Measurement Techniques: Abstracts of Published Instruments, 1935-1965.* Minneapolis: University of Minnesota Press, 1969.

Straus, M. A., and Brown, B. W. *Family Measurement Techniques: Abstracts of Published Instruments, 1935-1974.* Minneapolis: University of Minnesota Press, 1978.

2

████████████

Measurement
Problems

████████████████████████

There are numerous problems associated with the instruments used to conduct research relevant to women. Some of the problems became very apparent during the preparation of this book. Specifically, difficulties in locating complete instruments and complete information about them were frequently encountered. Many instruments had to be eliminated from consideration because copies of them could not be obtained. Whenever an instrument was not reproduced in its entirety in a journal article, doctoral dissertation, or masters thesis, and was not available from a commercial publisher or national depository, a letter was written to its author. Most authors were cooperative about sending a copy of their instrument. However, seventy-eight instruments were eliminated because the author never responded to the letter. Since none of those seventy-eight letters were returned as "undeliverable," one can assume that most of them reached the addressee. Therefore, it must be concluded that the authors no longer had a copy of the instrument or chose not to send it. Whichever is so, one must question the value of their research. Certainly no one can replicate their studies; furthermore, no one can really evaluate their research because the instrument on which it was based is not available for inspection.

Eighteen authors acknowledged the request for a copy of their instruments but neither sent the instrument nor indicated another source from which it could be obtained. These eighteen instruments are clearly unavailable for use in future research. The explanations for the refusals varied: Some indicated that they no longer had a copy of the instrument; others indicated that its quality was poor and it should not be used in further research. The former excuse highlights the need for a system of preserving instruments. The latter excuse causes one to wonder why data gathered with the instrument were ever published or presented at a convention, since the quality of the instrument should have been evaluated prior to the data gathering.

Letters to an additional twelve authors were returned as "undeliverable." Despite repeated attempts to obtain more current addresses for those twelve persons, no addresses were located. Similarly, no addresses, old or current, could be located for the authors of five scales. The implication is clear: if the author cannot be located to provide a copy of the instrument, there is no way to replicate or evaluate the quality of the research.

For those instruments that could be located, either from the literature or directly from the author, problems were often encountered in obtaining complete information. In fact, in some instances, no information at all was provided; the researcher simply reported that "a scale was used to measure . . . ." With such scant information, it is impossible to evaluate the research.

Even when some information was provided, the year in which the scale was used was rarely given. This may not be a serious omission in some research areas, but when the variables pertain to women's issues, it is a serious omission. There is reason to believe that sex role norms and attitudes toward women's issues have been changing in the past twenty years. An instrument that was validated in 1960 cannot be presumed valid today. The author must know when the instrument was first used, and it would require little space to report it; thus it seems inexcusable that it is omitted from the research reports. Similarly, the author knows how the instrument was developed, but a description of the development process is frequently omitted from the research report. Perhaps the information is not reported because the researcher simply combined a series of items and proclaimed them "a scale." Of course, it is always possible that a psychometrically sound procedure was employed in the development of the instrument, but in the absence of information one cannot draw that conclusion.

Evidence of the reliability and validity of an instrument was frequently omitted from the research report. This observation is consistent with Thomas's (1978, p. 4) observations. She reviewed ninety-six studies that used at least one measure of sex role and concluded that "little concern was evident for the reliability or validity of the instruments used, whether published, unpublished, or devised especially for that research project." Since little effort is required to compute the split-half reliability of an instrument, it is surprising that research reports do not routinely include this estimate of reliability. The expectation that test-retest reliability be computed for new instruments does not seem unreasonable. However, because researchers are usually most concerned about testing a hypothesis, they seem to overlook the need to establish the stability of the measure upon which their hypothesis test rests. They devote their time and resources toward their final goal and fail to realize that they cannot reach their final goal unless they use an instrument that is adequately reliable. For similar reasons researchers often overlook the need to establish the validity of the instrument. When validity data are presented in this book, they are usually based on the support or nonsupport of the hypothesis tested. Thus, the researcher probably knew nothing about the validity of the instrument until after the research was complete. Under these conditions, if the hypothesis was not supported, it is difficult to know whether the cause was a theoretical error or an invalid instrument.

The problems described above can be alleviated by researchers setting stricter standards for themselves. Instruments should not be used unless they have been well developed and have established reliability and validity. They can be made available to all researchers if their authors would submit them to the National Auxiliary Publications Service of the American Society for Information Science, P.O. Box 3513, Grand Central Station, New York, New York 10017 or ERIC Document Reproduction Service, P.O. Box 190, Arlington, Virginia 22210. If authors also deposited information pertaining to the development, reliability, and validity of their instruments, future researchers would have easy access to the information they need to determine the usefulness of selected instruments.

Not all the problems involved in measuring variables pertaining to women's issues can be so easily solved. Typically, the more knotty problems plague other research areas as well as research pertaining to women's issues. Some of these problems are very difficult, and their solutions will probably remain elusive for some time. Others can be at least partially solved through additional research for which there is already the technical capability. Problems pertaining to definitions can be solved relatively easily if scholars in the field reach consensus on terminology. Despite the varying level of difficulty associated with solving the problems, all must eventually be solved.

It is not unusual to find in the literature two instruments that purport to measure the same variable and yet are obviously measuring very different entities, as is demonstrated by a low correlation between scores from the two measures. Similarly it is not unusual to discover two instruments that purport to measure different variables and yet are very similar to each other. At least part of this inconsistency is attributable to the lack of standardized definitions for terms used in research related to women's issues. Terms such as *sex role adoption, sex role ideology, masculinity* and *femininity,* and *sex stereotypes* seem to have different connotations for different researchers. Because some of the inadequately defined terms have come into common usage fairly recently, there are still no generally agreed-upon definitions. Attempts have been made to define some of these terms in the following chapters. I hope these definitions will either gain general acceptance or will spur others to specify definitions that can gain general acceptance.

Lack of content validity is common in tests pertaining to women's issues. "Content validity involves essentially the systematic examination of the test content to determine whether it covers a representative sample of the behavior domain to be measured. . . . Content validity is built into a test from the outset through the choice of appropriate items" (Anastasi, 1976, p. 135). Thus to develop an instrument with content validity requires that one begin by specifying the domain to be assessed. This is rarely done in developing instruments pertaining to women's issues. Failure to specify a domain does not allow anyone to know to what domain the results are intended to apply. Some instruments measuring attitudes toward women's issues begin by specifying the domain as the platform planks advocated by various women's liberation organizations. Items are then developed to sample these platform planks. This procedure provides information on the domain to which results can be generalized. However, this systematic procedure is rare. More often, instruments are developed by initially constructing an item pool that is not tied to a particular content domain. As a result, it is difficult to know how to interpret scores. The failure to specify the content domain contributes to another problem described earlier: There may be a low correlation between scores from two instruments that both purport to measure attitudes toward women's issues. Even if the authors defined the variable similarly, they may have defined the content domain differently or they may have failed to define a content domain at all, and thus chose items that actually represent different, though undefined, content domains. This type of problem can best be avoided if the content domain is clearly specified before the instrument is developed and clearly communicated in the report of the research.

Frequently there are problems regarding the dimensionality of the underlying variable. For several of the instruments described in this book, the dimensionality has been extensively studied. Separate factor analyses have been performed on the responses from different groups of people, and the resulting factors have been compared with each other. The results are often ambiguous, and the conclusion must sometimes be drawn that different factors are needed to explain the variance in the different groups. Nevertheless, this is far better than simply assuming either that the instrument is unidimensional or that the same factors will apply to all groups. All too often, the factor structure and internal consistency of the instruments are not empirically tested, and the authors seem to assume that the instrument is unidimensional. They recommend an overall score be calculated for each respondent, yet an examination of the item content suggests that the variable is multidimensional. Since an examination of item content is not sufficient to establish the dimensionality of the instrument, and because it provides no evidence regarding the specific dimensions involved, empirical evidence of the dimensionality is clearly necessary. Given the ease with which computers can perform the analyses, this is not an unreasonable recommendation. Furthermore, the results of one factor analysis do not indicate whether the obtained factors apply to groups differing from the group on which the analysis was based. Different factors may be obtained for groups that differ in terms of sex, age, ethnic background, educational attainment, religion, race, and so on. Thus, it is further recommended that factor-analytic studies be conducted for groups similar to those with which the instrument will be used.

Because most instruments used to measure aspects of women's issues are self-reported, they present additional problems. Books are available to guide authors in writing good items; nevertheless, some instruments include many poor items. Items can be considered poor for numerous reasons, but the most common reasons encountered here are: the items contain more than a single idea, so that respondents may find themselves agreeing with one portion of an item and disagreeing with the other portion of the item; items are ambiguously phrased so that respondents may not all interpret the item identically; items are awkwardly phrased so that the respondents' attention is diverted to trying to understand the item rather than reacting to it; or all items on the instrument are phrased in the same direction (for example, all positively or all negatively), which encourages careless responding and an acquiescent response style. For example, if an instrument contains twenty-five items which are all phrased positively, then it seems very likely that after reacting positively to the first twenty items, the respondent is likely to become quite lax about reading the items. Acquiescence is the tendency to respond in the same direction (either affirmatively or negatively) to all of the items on an instrument, regardless of the specific content of the items. Kleinmuntz (1967, p. 250) has specifically stated: "A simple way of avoiding this effect of response style is to construct a balanced scoring key in which half the items are tallied for the answer 'true' and half for the answer 'false.' "

Self-report instruments are also plagued by problems resulting from their susceptibility to faking. *Faking* means that the respondent is consciously or unconsciously motivated to present a particular picture of herself, her attitudes, her perceptions, or her beliefs. One common type of faking is that the respondent endorses socially desirable responses rather than reporting honest responses. This is labeled as the social desirability response style. It seems logical that many of the instruments in this book are affected by these problems. Feminist organizations as well as the popular media have drawn attention to women's issues and have communicated that there is a "right" or "good" way to react to the issues. There has been considerable social pressure on people's attitudes. This pressure may have affected the verbalization of attitudes more than changing the actual attitudes. Many of the issues covered by these instruments are highly affective, emotionally charged issues. Respondents may have a vested interest in believing that their reactions to these issues reflect a particular perspective, regardless of whether that perspective is the one that they truly support. In other words, in order to maintain a certain self-concept, respondents may choose to answer the items in a particular direction. They are not trying to fool the researcher; they are trying to fool themselves. Stated differently, a person's true reaction may be either unconscious or unacceptable to her; thus she may respond to the items in terms of what she thinks she ought to believe. For example, if a woman has a need to believe that she is "feminine," she might respond to items on a sex role measure as she believes a "feminine" woman would respond. Problems of faking are exacerbated by the transparency of the items; that is, responses are easy to fake because the respondents can easily tell how their answers will be interpreted.

A serious problem with many instruments included here is that the behavioral correlates of the various scores are unknown. What does it mean if a person scores as highly feminine on a measure of sex role? What does it mean if a person expresses positive attitudes toward issues advocated by the feminist movement? What does it mean if a person accepts stereotypic views of men and women? If the results of studies employing these instruments are to have implications beyond just describing how people feel, then the behavioral correlates of the instruments must be known. If a woman scores as highly feminine on a sex role scale, will she inhibit the expression of her intellect in the presence of men? If a woman expresses positive attitudes toward abortion, will she be more likely to become pregnant out of wedlock? If a man accepts stereotypic views of men and women, will he be less likely to hire a woman for a professional or managerial job? Because of the problems of faking, the correlations between scores on the instruments and behavior may be low. If the correlations are low, should the scores on the measures be used to test hypotheses or to contribute to the formulation of theories? Or should attention be directed to the development of instruments that have predictable behavioral concomitants? At this time, these are essentially moot questions, because little research has been done on the behavioral correlates of scores on these instruments.

Many of the problems associated with measuring variables related to women's issues are attributable to misuse of instruments rather than problems inherent in the instruments themselves. When reliability and validity are reported, they are reported for a specific application of the instrument with a particular group of persons. Frequently users assume that the reliability and validity of the instrument generalize to all its applications and to all groups of persons. Any time an instrument is used with persons who differ in some significant way from the group on which reliability was calculated, one should reassess the instrument's reliability. An instrument that is reliable for eight-year-olds may not be reliable for six-year-olds; an instrument reliable for whites may not be reliable for blacks. Similarly, an instrument might be valid for one application but not for another: An instrument that can validly assess the sex role orientation of college students may not validly assess the sex role orientation of a noncollege group of comparable age. An instrument that can validly predict behavior in an academic setting may not validly predict behavior in an employment setting. Clearly, reliability and validity must be empirically demonstrated for the groups and applications for which it will be used. Similarly, when an instrument is modified, reliability and validity evidence accumulated for the original instrument cannot be presumed applicable to the modified one.

Just as one should not presume that the reliability and validity data based on one group can "transfer" to another group, one should not presume that an instrument developed using one group is appropriate for another group. Other than those instruments that were designed specifically for use with children, most instruments included here were developed using college students and may well have evolved differently had a noncollege sample been used. For example, instruments are often developed by selecting items that successfully differentiated between responses given by males and by females. Items that successfully differentiate between college males and college females may differ from items that successfully differentiate between employed males and employed females. Furthermore, many instruments were developed many years ago. Items that successfully differentiated between males and females in 1960 may not be the same items that successfully differentiate between males and females today. This does not imply that older instruments should be discarded; rather one should be aware that what the instrument is measuring today may be very different from what it measured when it was first used. If researchers wish the instrument to measure the same variable it originally measured, they must determine whether the items differentiate the same way today as they did when they were first used.

Researchers studying women's issues frequently overlook variables related to the conditions of administering the instrument. Too little is known about whether different responses are elicited by examiners of different sexes, whether the composition of the group in which the instrument is administered affects the responses given by individual members of the group, and whether the setting in which the instrument is administered affects responses. These are all issues that need to be empirically studied.

Obviously the problems associated with measuring variables pertaining to women's issues are numerous. Some can be solved fairly easily; some require extensive research; and some have plagued other areas of research where there has been little success in solving them. But if our knowledge of women's issues is to be based on reliable and valid information, then these problems, regardless of how difficult they are, must be tackled. Throughout this book, there are numerous suggestions for specific research that should be conducted. Hopefully some readers will take up the challenge and the instruments used in research regarding women and women's issues will be improved.

BIBLIOGRAPHY:

Anastasi, A. *Psychological Testing.* (4th ed.) New York: Macmillan, 1976.
Kleinmuntz, B. *Personality Measurement: An Introduction.* Homewood, Ill.: Dorsey Press, 1967.
Thomas, S. "Measurement of Sex Roles: What Are We Really Measuring?" Paper presented at the annual meeting of the National Council of Measurement in Education, Toronto, Canada, March 1978.

3

▦ ▦ ▦ ▦ ▦ ▦ ▦ ▦ ▦ ▦

Sex Roles

▦ ▦ ▦ ▦ ▦ ▦ ▦ ▦ ▦ ▦ ▦ ▦ ▦ ▦ ▦ ▦ ▦ ▦

Masculinity, femininity, androgyny, sex role preference, sex role adoption, sex role orientation, and *sex role identity* are all terms used to describe the variables measured by the instruments in this chapter. What do these terms mean? Are they interchangeable? Do they have clear, generally agreed-upon definitions? These are crucial questions because (1) it is absurd to evaluate an instrument unless one understands what it is intended to measure; (2) it is essentially impossible to select an appropriate criterion measure for validating the instrument unless one defines the variable it is intended to measure; and (3) one cannot select an instrument for future use without understanding the variable it measures.

A source of simple and brief definitions of psychological terms is the glossaries included in introductory psychology textbooks. The glossaries accompanying seventeen relatively new introductory books were consulted (ten were published in 1977 or 1978). The results were extremely disappointing. Over half of the glossaries did not even include a term related to those listed above; and only two glossaries defined any of the specific terms listed above. Obviously, introductory psychology textbooks are not a good source for defining these terms. Another reasonable source for locating definitions is a dictionary of psychological terms. In their *Comprehensive Dictionary of Psychological and Psychoanalytical Terms,* English and English (1958) include *masculinity* and *femininity. Masculinity* is defined as a "state or condition of an organism that manifests the characteristic appearance and behavior of a male" (p. 305); and *femininity* is defined as "the usual characteristics, taken collectively, of women." Unfortunately, these definitions are not particularly useful. In addition to being of nonparallel construction, the definitions are so broad as to be virtually useless. Are the "usual characteristics" that constitute femininity only those that are unique to women? Why is "appearance" an aspect of masculinity but not an aspect of femininity?

Perhaps the best place from which to extract definitions of the terms of interest here is the relevant professional literature—that is, publications that either theoretically or empirically deal with these constructs. The most commonly used and probably the oldest of these terms are *masculinity* and *femininity*. Surprisingly, however, these terms are essentially undefined even in the relevant professional literature. As Constantinople (1973, p. 390) pointed out in discussing these terms: "A search for definitions related to some theoretical position leads almost nowhere except to Freud . . . and Jung." In the absence of a theoretical definition of the terms, one is left to work backwards. Instead of positing a theoretical definition and determining whether the masculinity and femininity instruments actually measure that theoretical construct, one is forced to look at the instruments first and then describe what it is that they measure. Employing this procedure leads to the following definitions: *femininity* refers to the personality traits, interests, and behaviors that either are, or are believed to be, more characteristic of females than of males; similarly, *masculinity* refers to the personality traits, interests, and behaviors that either are, or are believed to be, more characteristic of males than of females. It must be stressed that this is not a theoretical definition; rather it is a definition based on the assumption that instruments purporting to measure masculinity and femininity do, in fact, measure these constructs.

Androgyny is an easier term to define; it refers to both masculinity and femininity. That is, an androgynous person is one who is characterized by both masculinity and femininity. It seems somewhat incongruous that the definition of this easily defined construct hinges on two essentially undefined terms.

The remaining four terms—*sex role preference, sex role adoption, sex role orientation,* and *sex role identity*—are easier to define because their definitions have been explicated in the literature. Lynn (1966, p. 469) defines *sex role preference* as "the desire to adopt the behavior associated with one sex or the other or the perception of such behavior as preferable or more desirable." His definition can reasonably be extended to include the desire to adopt personality traits and interests as well as behaviors. Thus, sex role preference refers to a preference or a desire to be a particular way; it does not necessarily mean that persons are, in fact, the way they desire to be. The way persons actually are, that is, the way they actually behave, reflects their *sex role adoption*. In other words, sex role adoption is "the overt behavior characteristic of a given sex" (Lynn, 1966, p. 470). The overt behaviors can be assumed to reflect personality traits and interests as well as other facets of the person. Furthermore, it is quite possible—though there appears to be no research to substantiate this—that sex role adoption is situation specific; that is, people's overt behaviors will vary according to the situation they are in, and those overt behaviors may sometimes be more characteristic of feminine behaviors and sometimes more characteristic of masculine behaviors. The definitions of *sex role orientation* and *sex role identity* seem to blend, as some authors have expressed a preference for one term and other authors seem to prefer the other. Both terms have been used to refer to "an underlying, and not necessarily conscious, perception of the maleness or femaleness of the self" (Biller and Borstelmann, 1967, p. 260). In essence then, sex role orientation or sex role identity is one aspect of self-concept. Though for most persons it is quite likely that there is a relationship between their sex role preference, adoption, and orientation/identity, it is unlikely that there is perfect congruence between these three aspects of sex role.

Masculinity, femininity, and androgyny can be the summary descriptors for labeling a person's sex role preference, adoption, or orientation/identity. For example, if one *prefers* the personality traits, interests, and behaviors that either are, or are believed to be, more characteristic of females than of males, that person would be characterized as having a feminine sex role preference. Similarly, if one *exhibits behaviors* that are, or are believed to be, more characteristic of females than of males, that person would be characterized as adopting a feminine sex role. And, if one *believes,* either consciously or unconsciously, that she has the personality traits, interests, and behaviors that are, or are believed to be, more characteristic of females than of males, that person would have a feminine sex role orientation or feminine sex role identity.

For each instrument in this chapter, a statement is made as to what variable it measures. The variable name reflects what the author claimed that the instrument measures. However, the variable name is often inconsistent with the definitions provided above. First, many instruments purport to measure masculinity and/or femininity. According to the definitions given above, one does not measure masculinity or femininity; rather one measures sex role preference, sex role adoption, or sex role orientation/identity and expresses the results in terms of masculinity or femininity. Second, many authors either disregarded or misunderstood the distinction between sex role preference, adoption, and orientation/identity. For example, Brown (1956), who authored the It Scale for Children (#17), claimed that it measures sex role preference; Biller (1968), on the other hand, claimed that the It Scale measures sex role orientation. And third, an examination of the item content for many instruments suggests that they are measuring more than one aspect of sex role. Because the authors often disregarded the distinction between sex role preference, adoption, and orientation/identity, it is nearly impossible for anyone, including the original authors, to classify their instruments into one of the three categories.

Given that masculinity and femininity are used to describe a person's sex role preference, adoption, or orientation/identity, can a person be simultaneously labeled as masculine and feminine? Older sex role instruments imply that the answer to this question is "no." Masculinity and femininity were conceptualized as opposite ends of a continuum; that is, they were considered bipolar. Much like short and tall are not used to describe the same person, masculine and feminine could not be used to describe the same person. Until recently this issue was not even considered in the literature, yet it is apparent that the bipolar nature of masculinity-femininity was assumed. As Constantinople (1973, p. 392) pointed out: "In M-F [masculinity-femininity] test construction, the assumption of bipolarity is evident in at least three ways: (a) The dependence on biological sex alone as the appropriate criterion for an item's M-F relevance, since item selection is usually based solely on its ability to discriminate the responses of the two sexes; (b) the implication that the opposite of a masculine response is necessarily indicative of femininity, especially in tests where only two options are provided; and (c) the use of a single M-F score which is based on the algebraic summation of M and F responses and places the individual somewhere on a single bipolar dimension." If an instrument is constructed to yield only one score, then a person cannot possibly score high on both masculinity and femininity, and theoretical formulations derived from data collected using the instrument must conceive of masculinity-femininity as bipolar. Thus, the assumption that masculinity and femininity are bipolar leads to the construction of instruments that treat them as bipolar. This, in turn, leads to theoretical formulations that conceive of masculinity and femininity as bipolar.

More recent conceptions of masculinity and femininity suggest that they are not opposite ends of a single continuum; rather, they are two separate—though not necessarily uncorrelated—continua. Just as people can be tall and thin or tall and fat, people can be feminine and masculine or feminine and not masculine in their sex role preference, adoption, or orientation/identity. There seems to be general agreement among those who believe that masculinity and femininity are two separate continua that a person who is high on both masculinity and femininity should be labeled as androgynous; a person who scores high on masculinity and low on femininity should be labeled as masculine; a person who scores high on femininity and low on masculinity should be labeled as feminine; and a person who scores low on both should be labeled as undifferentiated (Spence, Helmreich, and Stapp, 1974). It seems logical that the theoretical formulations derived from instruments that treat masculinity and femininity as two separate continua are likely to be different from the theoretical formulations that treat them as the ends of a single continuum.

The problems associated with dimensionality of the constructs measured by sex role instruments are indeed complex. The authors of instruments that yield a single score, usually labeled "masculinity-femininity," apparently assume that the construct being measured is unidimensional. The authors of instruments that yield one score labeled "masculinity" and one score labeled "femininity" apparently assume that the construct being measured is bidimensional. Some authors differentiate between sex role adoption, sex role preference, and sex role orientation/identity; other authors do not. Clearly there is confusion about what construct(s) is being measured with sex role instruments, and until that confusion is cleared up, it is difficult to talk about whether the construct(s) is unidimensional or multidimensional. If the construct is considered to be masculinity-femininity, then one must question whether it is reasonable to believe that it is a unidimensional construct, as some authors assume. Logic and empiricism both suggest that it is not a unidimensional construct. On logical grounds, it is difficult to accept that all of the personality traits, interests, and behaviors included on masculinity-femininity measures can be represented by a unidimensional construct, and it is difficult to ignore that sex role preference is probably a different factor than sex role adoption, which is probably different from sex role orientation/identity. On empirical grounds, prior factor-analytic studies (Engel, 1962, 1966; Lunneborg, 1972; Lunneborg and Lunneborg, 1970) have shown that many factors are necessary to account for the variance on traditional masculinity-femininity instruments. If the underlying constructs of sex role instruments are considered to be masculinity and femininity, then one must question whether each of those constructs is logically unidimensional. Again, the answer is probably "no," but research is needed to determine the veracity of this assumption. Of course one can argue that the underlying constructs are not masculinity and femininity but are really sex role adoption, sex role preference, and sex role orientation/identity. If these are the constructs, are they each unidimensional (as is assumed by those who assign one overall score), bidimensional (as is assumed by those who assign one score for masculinity and one score for femininity), or multidimensional? The confusion apparent in this discussion reflects the confusion that exists in the literature.

Questions regarding the definitions of the variables, whether masculinity and femininity are one or two continua, and whether the underlying variables are uni- or multidimensional all pose problems for the measurement of sex roles. But these are not all of the problems one will encounter in dealing with sex role measures. All too often, authors and users of sex role instruments ignore the potential effects of other variables, such as race, age, socioeconomic class, cultural background, and educational attainment. Since the original definitions of masculinity and femininity concerned what is, or what is believed to be, more characteristic of one sex than the other, it is unreasonable to assume that a particular sex role instrument applies equally to persons of different races, ages, socioeconomic classes, cultural backgrounds, and educational attainment. What is considered feminine for persons from one cultural background may not be considered feminine for persons from a different cultural background. Though this may seem obvious, it is essentially ignored by most authors and users of sex role instruments. The development of these instruments has relied primarily on data gathered from college students. However, without empirical evidence, there is no basis for assuming that college students' conceptions of what is characteristic of one sex would generalize to a noncollege population. A closely related problem concerns the year in which an instrument is used. There is little doubt that what is more characteristic of one sex changes over time. And yet, some very old measures of sex role are still in use today. For example, the Attitude Interest Analysis Test (#31), which was published in 1936, is still being used, yet the items that successfully differentiated between males and females in 1936 may not be the same items that would differentiate between males and females if the test were constructed today. Clearly instruments that have been developed more recently are more likely to reflect current conceptions of what characterizes femininity and masculinity.

Because of all the problems associated with sex role measurement, the interpretation of scores is very difficult and probably often erroneous. If masculinity and femininity are on two separate continua, then how is it possible to interpret scores from an instrument constructed on the assumption that they form a single continuum? If sex role measures are, in fact, multidimensional, then how does one interpret a score that cuts across factors in some undetermined way? Furthermore, sex role measures do not represent a systematic sample from some content domain. As a result, it is impossible to know to what domain the results can generalize. Score interpretation is further complicated by the unknown effects of social desirability. To what extent do responses reflect the respondent's conscious or unconscious need to give socially desirable responses? Though the development of some instruments has taken account of the social desirability factor, all too often it is ignored. Also ignored have been the behavioral correlates of scores on sex role measures. Occasionally researchers have looked at the behavioral concomitants of high and low scores on a particular sex role instrument, but this has definitely been the exception rather than the rule. Given the seriousness and quantity of problems involved in interpreting scores from sex role instruments, it cannot be stressed too strongly that extreme care must be taken in drawing any conclusions based on these instruments. No instrument yields sufficiently unambiguous scores that any decision or judgments should be made about a particular individual based on results from the instrument. Certainly no judgments of an evaluative nature should ever be based on scores from sex role instruments that presently exist; that is, the idea that it is "good" for a woman to score in the feminine range on a sex role instrument and "bad" for her to score in the masculine range must be assiduously avoided.

Despite the problems that exist with measures of sex role preference, adoption, and orientation/identity, there are numerous instruments that purport to measure these variables. Included here are thirty instruments intended for use with children and adolescents and fourteen intended for use with adults. In addition, abridged information is provided for fifteen instruments that yield a profile of scores, with at least one score pertaining to a variable relevant to this chapter. The instruments are organized by the age level of the intended respondents, and those that are appropriate for children *and* adults are included in the children and adolescents section.

Though all the instruments included here are intended to measure sex role preference, adoption, and orientation/identity, they can also be used to measure sex role stereotypes and sex role prescriptions. By modifying the instructions to ask for perceptions of what is true of most women or men or the typical woman or man, the instruments can be used to assess sex role stereotypes. Similarly, by modifying the instructions to ask for beliefs about what ought to be true of women or men, the instruments can be used to assess sex role prescriptions. Of course, the reliability and validity of the modified instruments must be empirically determined.

BIBLIOGRAPHY:

Biller, H. B. "A Multiaspect Investigation of Masculine Development in Kindergarten-Age Boys." *Genetic Psychology Monographs,* 1968, *78,* 89-138.

Biller, H. B., and Borstelmann, L. J. "Masculine Development: An Integrative Review." *Merrill-Palmer Quarterly,* 1967, *13,* 253-294.

Brown, D. G. "Sex Role Preference in Young Children." *Psychological Monographs,* 1956, *70* (entire issue).

Constantinople, A. "Masculinity-Femininity: An Exception to a Famous Dictum?" *Psychological Bulletin,* 1973, *80,* 389-407.

Engel, I. M. "A Factor Analytic Study of Items from Five Masculinity-Femininity Tests." Unpublished doctoral dissertation, University of Michigan, 1962. (*Dissertation Abstracts,* 1962, *23*[1], 307-308.)

Engel, I. M. "A Factor-Analytic Study of Items from Five Masculinity-Femininity Tests." *Journal of Consulting Psychology,* 1966, *30,* 565.

English, H. B., and English, A. C. *A Comprehensive Dictionary of Psychological and Psychoanalytical Terms.* New York: McKay, 1958.

Lunneborg, P. W. "Dimensionality of M-F." *Journal of Clinical Psychology,* 1972, *28,* 313-317.

Lunneborg, P. W., and Lunneborg, C. E. "Factor Structure of M-F Scales and Items." *Journal of Clinical Psychology,* 1970, *26,* 360-366.

Lynn, D. B. "The Process of Learning Parental and Sex Role Identification." *Journal of Marriage and the Family,* 1966, *28,* 466-470.

Spence, J. T., Helmreich, R., and Stapp, J. "The Personal Attributes Questionnaire: A Measure of Sex Role Stereotypes and Masculinity-Femininity." *Journal Supplement Abstract Service Catalog of Selected Documents in Psychology,* 1974, *4,* 43-44.

Children and Adolescents

The following thirty instruments are appropriate for children and adolescents. Five of them can also be used with persons over age 21; some of them can be used with children as young as age 3. Most of the instruments focus on children's interests or behaviors. Three deserve particular mention. The oldest instrument is the Figure Drawing (#10), which first appeared in the literature as a measure of sex role orientation in 1948. The next oldest is the Franck Drawing Completion Test (#11), which first appeared in 1949. Despite their age, both instruments are still in use today. In fact, both are among the three most frequently used instruments. The most frequently used is the It Scale for Children (#17), which first appeared in the literature in 1956, so it too is a rather old instrument. Though many questions have been raised about the validity of the It Scale, especially for girls, it is still commonly used today, though the original form is often modified. Compared with instruments in some other chapters, much is known about those included here. Of the thirty instruments, there is some information pertaining to the development of twenty-five, some evidence relevant to the reliability of nineteen, and some information pertaining to the validity of all thirty.

The instruments in this section highlight some of the problems mentioned above regarding sex role measures. Eight are purported to measure masculinity-femininity, though it was pointed out that instruments should measure masculinity and femininity of a particular aspect of sex role. Furthermore, one could take issue with the variables that many of the other instruments purportedly measure, especially because the user may not label the variable the same as the author labeled it. Seventeen instruments treat masculinity and femininity as a bipolar dimension, though newer conceptions of the constructs suggest that they should be treated as two separate continua. None of the instruments treat the underlying variable as multidimensional. In fact, the authors essentially ignore the possibility of multidimensionality. Each instrument yields either a single masculinity-femininity score or one score reflecting masculinity and one score reflecting femininity. The development of most instruments follows the typical procedure of determining which items differentiate between males and females and keying the items in terms of the direction in which they differentiate; that is, items that are endorsed more frequently by males are scored as masculine and items that are endorsed more frequently by females are scored as feminine. Ten instruments were developed on the basis of which items actually elicited different responses from males and females. Nine were developed on the basis of sex stereotypes; that is, items that "judges" believed would be differentially associated with males and females were included. Thus, for nineteen instruments, sex differences—either real or stereotyped—served as the criterion for development. This focus on an empirical procedure for development highlights the lack of a theoretical foundation for sex role instruments.

A very common method for assessing sex roles in children focuses on their preferences for, or actual play behavior with, particular toys and/or games. Thirteen of the thirty instruments involve toys and/or games. The particular procedures vary. For example, the procedures include asking the child to select preferred toys from an array of toys, asking the child to make choices from successive pairs of toy pictures, and asking the child to check on a list the toys and games that are preferred. Generally, the instruments that use actual toys or pictures of toys include only common toys. However, often the toys are inadequately described so that it is impossible to know what was originally intended. For example, to say that a doll was one of the toys does not provide a potential user with enough information. Dolls range in size from a few inches tall to several feet tall; some are soft and some are solid; some can walk, talk, eat, and so on. Detailed descriptions of the toys are necessary to enable a researcher to use the same instrument that was originally used.

Some of these toy- and game-preference instruments are well developed. In selecting "masculine" and "feminine" toys, the authors controlled for color, general attractiveness, size, and manipulative potential of the toy. In the development of other instruments, these variables were apparently overlooked. When the variables are overlooked, problems arise in interpreting the findings. For example, if a large, bright-red fire engine, with numerous moving parts, detachable parts, and wheels is paired with a small, soft, drab doll, what is really being compared? Is a fire engine being compared with a doll? Or is a large toy being compared with a small toy? Or is a toy with moving parts being compared with a toy without moving parts? The results of a study by Goldberg and Lewis (1969) suggest that it is important to balance these variables across masculine and feminine toys. In an observational study with thirteen-month-old babies, they found that "toys which received the most attention were those that offered the most varied possibilities for manipulation" (p. 27). Another variable that has often been overlooked by users of toy- and game-preference instruments is the prior experiences of the children being tested. Does sibling constellation affect toy preferences? Does prior exposure to the toys affect toy preferences? These questions need to be empirically answered.

BIBLIOGRAPHY:

Goldberg, S., and Lewis, M. "Play Behavior in the Year-Old Infant: Early Sex Differences." *Child Development,* 1969, *40,* 21-32.

---

1. ACTIVITY PREFERENCE CHECK LIST

AUTHOR: Albert F. Angrilli

DATE: 1957

VARIABLE: Sex role preference

TYPE OF INSTRUMENT: Checklist

DESCRIPTION: The checklist consists of twenty-one activities that nursery school children are likely to engage in. The list includes typically masculine and typically feminine activities. The nursery school teacher is asked to check the four activities that the boy being rated is most likely to engage in when he is given a free choice of activities. The teacher is also asked to rank order the four activities checked.

PREVIOUSLY ADMINISTERED TO: Nursery school teachers who rated preschool boys from their classes

APPROPRIATE FOR: Rating ages 3-7

ADMINISTRATION: The teacher can complete the checklist for an individual child in about two or three minutes.

SAMPLE ITEMS: Dancing
Ball play (throwing and catching)
Stringing beads
Setting the table

SCORING: The score is equal to the number of masculine activities that the teacher checked.

DEVELOPMENT: A list of activities was prepared and submitted to "six competent authorities in the field of early childhood education" (Angrilli, 1957, p. 45), with instructions to indicate which activities were more masculine, which were more feminine, and which were questionable as to sex assignment. Items that were questionable were eliminated from the list.

RELIABILITY: No data are provided.

VALIDITY: Scores from the Activity Preference Check List, Figure Drawing (#10), and the Children's Behavior and Personality Rating Scale (#5) were available for thirty boys between the ages of four and five. There was not a significant correlation between the Figure Drawing and the Activity Preference Check List ($r = .11$), but there was a significant correlation between the Activity Preference Check List and the Children's Behavior and Personality Rating Scale ($r = .37$, $p < .05$) (Angrilli, 1957).

NOTES AND COMMENTS: Despite the age of the instrument, all activities listed are ones that children today are still likely to engage in. However, there is no evidence to indicate whether the sex typing of the activities is still accurate.

SOURCE: See Angrilli, 1957.

BIBLIOGRAPHY:

Angrilli, A. F. "A Study of the Psychosexual Identification of Pre-School Boys." Unpublished doctoral dissertation, New York University, 1957. (*Dissertation Abstracts*, 1958, *19* [4] , 874-875.)
Angrilli, A. F. "The Psychosexual Identification of Preschool Boys." *Journal of Genetic Psychology*, 1960, *97,* 329-340.

---

2. BILLER GAME PREFERENCE TEST

AUTHOR: Henry B. Biller

DATE: 1967

VARIABLE: Sex role preference

TYPE OF INSTRUMENT: Forced choice picture preference

DESCRIPTION: This test consists of eight drawings (3" x 5") of the same two boys engaged in playing a game. Four drawings show the boys playing a masculine game (archery, baseball, basketball, and football) and four show the boys playing a feminine game (hopscotch, jacks, dancing, and jump rope). The eight drawings are used to form sixteen pairs so that each masculine game is paired with each feminine game.

PREVIOUSLY ADMINISTERED TO: Ages 3-6

APPROPRIATE FOR: Ages 3-10

ADMINISTRATION: The instrument is individually administered. The child is shown a pair of pictures and asked to indicate which game she would like to play the most. The procedure is repeated for the sixteen pairs.

SCORING: One point is earned for each masculine choice. The maximum score is 16.

DEVELOPMENT: The games selected were "highly sex typed by Rosenberg and Sutton-Smith (1959) and pilot work indicated boys responded meaningfully to the pictures" (Biller, 1968, p. 105). No explanation of "meaningfully" was provided.

RELIABILITY: Using the data obtained from 186 kindergarten boys, Biller (1968) found the corrected split-half reliability to be .78.

VALIDITY: Biller (1968) predicted that the correlation between two measures of sex role preference would be higher than the correlations between a measure of sex role preference and measures of sex role orientation or adoption. Biller tested 186 kindergarten boys with five measures: two measures of sex role preference (Biller Game Preference Test and Group Toy Preference Test—#15); two measures of sex role orientation (It Scale for Children—#17)—and Figure Drawing—#10); and a measure of sex role adoption (Biller Sex Role Adoption Rating Scale—#3). The correlation between the two measures of sex role preference was .75. The correlations between the Biller Game Preference Test and each of the other measures was: It Scale for Children = .27; Figure Drawing = .07; Biller Sex Role Adoption Rating Scale = .20. As can be seen, Biller's prediction was supported.

NOTES AND COMMENTS: (1) If the scale is to be used with girls, the figures playing the games should be girls rather than boys.

(2) Some researchers have combined scores from the Biller Game Preference Test with scores on the Group Toy Preference Test (#15) to arrive at an overall sex role preference score (Biller, 1967, 1968, 1969b; Biller, Singer, and Fullerton, 1969; Flammer, 1971).

(3) Scores on the Biller Game Preference Test have been compared with other variables, including sex (Laosa and Brophy, 1971, 1972; Flammer, 1971); self-esteem (Flammer, 1971); parent identification (Flammer, 1971); birth order (Laosa and Brophy, 1971, 1972); father dominance (Biller, 1967, 1968, 1969b); father availability (Biller, 1967, 1968, 1969a); maternal encouragement of masculine behaviors (Biller, 1967, 1968, 1969a); intelligence (Biller, 1967, 1968); physique (Biller, 1967, 1968); creativity (Biller, Singer, and Fullerton, 1969); and socioeconomic status (Biller, Singer, and Fullerton, 1969).

SOURCE: See Biller, 1967 or 1968.

BIBLIOGRAPHY:

Biller, H. B. "An Exploratory Investigation of Masculine Development in Kindergarten-Age Boys." Unpublished doctoral dissertation, Duke University, 1967. (*Dissertation Abstracts,* 1968, *28*[10-B], 4290.)

Biller, H. B. "A Multiaspect Investigation of Masculine Development in Kindergarten-Age Boys." *Genetic Psychology Monographs,* 1968, *78,* 89-138.

Biller, H. B. "Father Absence, Maternal Encouragement, and Sex Role Development in Kindergarten-Age Boys." *Child Development*, 1969a, *40*, 539-546.

Biller, H. B. "Father Dominance and Sex Role Development in Kindergarten-Age Boys." *Developmental Psychology*, 1969b, *1*, 87-94.

Biller, H. B., Singer, D. L., and Fullerton, M. "Sex Role Development and Creative Potential in Kindergarten-Age Boys." *Developmental Psychology*, 1969, *1*, 291-296.

Brophy, J. E., and Laosa, L. M. "The Effect of a Male Teacher on the Sex Typing of Kindergarten Children." *Journal Supplement Abstract Service Catalog of Selected Documents in Psychology*, 1973, *3*, 44.

Flammer, D. P. "Self-Esteem, Parent Identification, and Sex Role Development in Pre-school-Age Boys and Girls." *Child Study Journal*, 1971, *2*, 39-45.

Laosa, L. M., and Brophy, J. E. "Effects of Sex and Birth Order on Sex Role Development and Intelligence in Kindergarten Children." Paper presented at 17th annual meeting of the Southwestern Psychological Association, San Antonio, Texas, April 1971. (ERIC Document Reproduction Service No. ED 053 403.)

Laosa, L. M., and Brophy, J. E. "Effects of Sex and Birth Order on Sex Role Development and Intelligence Among Kindergarten Children." *Developmental Psychology*, 1972, *6*, 409-415.

*Rosenberg, B. G., and Sutton-Smith, B. "The Measurement of Masculinity and Femininity in Children." *Child Development*, 1959, *30*, 373-380.

---

3. BILLER SEX ROLE ADOPTION RATING SCALE

AUTHOR: Henry B. Biller

DATE: 1967 (revised 1971)

VARIABLE: Sex role adoption

TYPE OF INSTRUMENT: Rating scale

DESCRIPTION: The 1967 rating scale consists of sixteen behavioral descriptions, nine characteristic of high masculinity and seven characteristic of low masculinity. Each item is to be rated on a five-point scale indicating the frequency of occurrence of the behavior. The response options are: very frequently, frequently, sometimes, seldom, never.

The 1971 rating scale consists of twenty items, ten characteristic of masculinity and ten characteristic of femininity. Response options are identical to the 1967 rating scale.

PREVIOUSLY ADMINISTERED TO: Teachers who rated children ages 3-14

APPROPRIATE FOR: Rating children ages 3-12

ADMINISTRATION: Raters are directed to rate each child independently in regard to each item and then to recheck their ratings by comparing children with one another.

SAMPLE ITEMS: (1967 rating scale) *High masculinity*: is active and energetic (on the move, plays hard)

Low masculinity: asks for help (acts helpless, wants someone to do things for him he could do himself)

SCORING: *1967 rating scale*: Items are objectively scored and equally weighted; total scores can range from 0 to 64.

1971 rating scale: Some users obtain separate scores on the masculinity and femininity items; other users obtain a single composite score; and still others find the difference between masculinity and femininity scores.

DEVELOPMENT: The development of this scale was based on pilot studies done by Biller. He asked adults to indicate what constitutes masculine behavior in boys between the ages of 4 and 7. Based on their responses, Biller concluded that most of the items used by Freedheim (1960) in combination with some additional items would be appropriate for rating masculinity in preschool boys.

RELIABILITY: *1967 rating scale*: In Biller's (1967) study, teachers rated kindergarten boys. The correlations between two teachers' ratings (based on total scores) ranged from .75 to .96. The median correlation was .91. Thompson and McCandless (1970) report percentages of agreement ranging from 72.5 to 89.3 percent for pairs of teachers who rated thirty-six boys.

Biller (1968a) computed split-half reliability of .89 using the scores for children who were rated by only one teacher. In another study, Biller (1969a) also had teachers rate kindergarten boys. The interrater reliability was .82.

Biller (1967, 1968a) reports item-total correlations ranging from .50 to .78. The median correlation was .60.

1971 rating scale: In Biller and Liebman's study (1971), teachers rated ninth-grade boys. Separate scores were computed for the masculinity and femininity items. On the masculinity items, interrater reliability was .82; on the femininity items, it was .77. In Flammer's study (1971), teachers rated preschoolers. Interrater reliability was .71.

VALIDITY: *1967 rating scale*: Biller (1968a) contends that sex role adoption is different from sex role orientation and sex role preference. Therefore, he states that the results from the Biller Sex Role Adoption Rating Scale should not be expected to correlate highly with measures of sex role orientation and preference. Based on data collected from 186 kindergarten boys, he reports a correlation of .16 with Figure Drawing (#10) (orientation); .11 with the It Scale for Children (#17) (orientation); .29 with the Group Toy Preference Test (#15) (preference); and .20 with the Biller Game Preference Test (#2) (preference).

Thompson and McCandless (1970) correlated the ratings assigned to thirty-six kindergarten boys with the scores the boys earned on the It Scale for Children (#17), a measure of sex role preference. The It Scale was administered using three different sets of instructions: standard, "It" concealed in an envelope, and "It" labeled as same sex as child. For black boys, the correlations between It Scale scores and rating scores were not significant for any of the instructions used. For white boys, significant correlations (r = .512 and .479, p < .001) were obtained between rating scores and It Scale scores for two of the three sets of instructions used.

NOTES AND COMMENTS: (1) Scores on the Biller Sex Role Adoption Rating Scale have been related to many other variables including age (LaVoie and Andrews, 1975; Piercy, 1976); sex (Flammer, 1971; Laosa and Brophy, 1971, 1972; LaVoie and Andrews, 1976); self-esteem (Flammer, 1971); parent identification (Flammer, 1971); birth order (Laosa and Brophy, 1971, 1972); father dominance and availability (Biller, 1967, 1968a, 1969a, 1969b); maternal encouragement of masculine behaviors (Biller, 1967, 1968a, 1969a); intelligence (Biller, 1967, 1968a; Piercy, 1976); and body build (Biller, 1967, 1968a; Biller and Liebman, 1971; LaVoie and Andrews, 1976).

(2) Newman (1976) modified the scale for use as a self-rating scale for adults.

(3) This scale is also described in *Tests and Measurements in Child Development: Handbook II* (Johnson, 1976, pp. 628-629) and in *Socioemotional Measures for Preschool and Kindergarten Children* (Walker, 1973, pp. 165-166).

SOURCE: For 1967 rating scale, see Biller, 1968a.

For 1971 rating scale, Henry Biller
Department of Psychology
University of Rhode Island
Kingston, Rhode Island 02881

BIBLIOGRAPHY:

Biller, H. B. "An Exploratory Investigation of Masculine Development in Kindergarten-Age Boys." Unpublished doctoral dissertation, Duke University, 1967. (*Dissertation Abstracts,* 1968, *28*[10-B], 4290.)

Biller, H. B. "A Multiaspect Investigation of Masculine Development in Kindergarten-Age Boys." *Genetic Psychology Monographs,* 1968a, *78,* 89-138.

Biller, H. B. "A Note on Father Absence and Masculine Development in Lower-Class Negro and White Boys." *Child Development,* 1968b, *39,* 1003-1006.

Biller, H. B. "Father Absence, Maternal Encouragement, and Sex Role Development in Kindergarten-Age Boys." *Child Development,* 1969a, *40,* 539-546.

Biller, H. B. "Father Dominance and Sex Role Development in Kindergarten-Age Boys." *Developmental Psychology,* 1969b, *1,* 87-94.

Biller, H. B., and Liebman, D. A. "Body Build, Sex Role Preference, and Sex Role Adoption in Junior High School Boys." *Journal of Genetic Psychology,* 1971, *118,* 81-86.

Flammer, D. P. "Self-Esteem, Parent Identification, and Sex Role Development in Preschool-Age Boys and Girls." *Child Study Journal,* 1971, *2,* 39-45.

*Freedheim, D. K. "An Investigation of Masculinity and Parental Role Patterns." Unpublished doctoral dissertation, Duke University, 1960. (*Dissertation Abstracts,* 1961, *21*[8], 2363.)

*Johnson, O. G. *Tests and Measurements in Child Development: Handbook II.* San Francisco: Jossey-Bass, 1976.

Laosa, L. M., and Brophy, J. E. "Effects of Sex and Birth Order on Sex Role Development and Intelligence in Kindergarten Children." Paper presented at 17th annual meeting of the Southwestern Psychological Association, San Antonio, Texas, April 1971. (ERIC Document Reproduction Service No. ED 053 403.)

Laosa, L. M., and Brophy, J. E. "Effects of Sex and Birth Order on Sex Role Development and Intelligence Among Kindergarten Children." *Developmental Psychology,* 1972, *6,* 409-415.

LaVoie, J. C., and Andrews, R. "Cognitive Determinants of Gender Identity and Constancy." Paper presented at 83rd annual meeting of the American Psychological Association, Chicago, September 1975.

LaVoie, J. C., and Andrews, R. "Facial Attractiveness, Physique, and Sex Role Identity in Young Children." *Developmental Psychology,* 1976, *12,* 550-551.

Montgomery, G. T., and Landers, W. F. "Transmission of Risk Taking Through Modeling at Two Age Levels." *Psychological Reports,* 1974, *34,* 1187-1196.

Newman, R. C., II. "Development and Standardization of Measures of Stereotypic Sex Role Concepts and of Sex Role Adoption in Adults." *Psychological Reports,* 1976, *39,* 623-630.

Piercy, P. A. "The Relationship of Cognitive Functioning to the Development of Sex Role in Black Male Children Ages Four to Ten." Unpublished doctoral dissertation, Adelphi University, 1976. (*Dissertation Abstracts International,* 1976, *37*[4-B], 1974.)

Thompson, N. L., Jr., and McCandless, B. R. "It Score Variations by Instructional Style." *Child Development,* 1970, *41,* 425-436.

*Walker, D. K. *Socioemotional Measures for Preschool and Kindergarten Children.* San Francisco: Jossey-Bass, 1973.

---

4. CHECKLIST OF GAMES AND PLAY ACTIVITIES

AUTHORS: B. G. Rosenberg and Brian Sutton-Smith

DATE: 1959 (revised 1964)

VARIABLES: Masculinity, femininity

TYPE OF INSTRUMENT: Checklist

DESCRIPTION: The original Checklist of Games and Play Activities is a list of 181 items, including 125 games with formal rules, 38 general activities and pastimes, and 18 dramatic play activities. The number of items actually used in administering the instrument depends on which version is being given.

PREVIOUSLY ADMINISTERED TO: Ages 8-12

APPROPRIATE FOR: Ages 8-12

ADMINISTRATION: The child is asked to indicate for each item whether she likes it or dislikes it. If the child is unfamiliar with an item, no response is to be given.

SAMPLE ITEMS: Bandits
Monopoly
"Name That Tune"
Knit

SCORING: The number of items scored depends on the version of the test being used. The 1959 version is scored on the responses to sixty-seven items, twenty-four of which are scored as masculine and forty-five of which are scored as feminine. The 1964 version is scored on the basis of fifty items, twenty-five of which are masculine and twenty-five of which are feminine.

Each child is given a score on masculinity and a score on femininity. The scores are based on only those items which the child indicates she likes doing. On the 1959 version, items are scored 3, 2, or 1, depending on the level of significance with which the item differentiated between boys and girls. The maximum score for masculinity is 56; the maximum score for femininity is 116. On the 1964 version, all items are scored 1; thus, the maximum score for masculinity is 25 and the maximum score for femininity is 25.

DEVELOPMENT: *1959 version:* Four hundred and two children in first through eighth grades were asked to list all the games they played. Using these lists and adding items from published game lists, a final list of 181 items was compiled. This list was given to 187 children in fourth through sixth grades, with instructions to indicate which games they liked and which games they disliked. Games they did not play were to be ignored. Games that were unknown to at least 50 percent of the children were eliminated from further analysis. The remaining 115 items were analyzed for male-female differences, and 67 items were found to differentiate between boys and girls. Items that differentiated at the .01 level were assigned scoring weights of 3; items that differentiated at the .05 level (but not at the .01 level) were assigned scoring weights of 2; and items that differentiated at the .10 level (but not at the .05 level) were assigned scoring weights of 1.

1964 version: The original list used in developing the 1959 version (less one item) was administered to 1,901 children in third through sixth grades with the same instructions described above. The data were analyzed as described above. It was found that twenty-five items differentiated in favor of boys at the .01 level and twenty-five differentiated in favor of girls at the .01 level. These fifty items constitute the masculinity-femininity scales.

RELIABILITY: No reliability data are provided.

VALIDITY: *1959 version:* Using the data from the children on which the instrument was developed, it was found that on the sex-appropriate measure,* 2 percent of the males and 10 percent of the females fell below the mean of the opposite sex. On the sex-inappropriate measure, 9 percent of the females and 7 percent of the males scored above the mean of the opposite sex. To cross-validate these findings, the lists were administered first to 165 children in the fourth through sixth grades and later to another 404 children in the fourth through sixth grades. The results for the first cross-validation sample were as follows: on the sex-appropriate scale, 4 percent of the males and 7 percent of the females fell below the mean of the opposite sex; on the sex-inappropriate scale, 2 percent of the females and 8 percent of the males fell above the mean of the opposite sex. The results for the second cross-validation sample were: on the sex-appropriate scale, 6 percent of the females and 5 percent of the males scored below the mean of the opposite sex; on the sex-inappropriate scale, 9 percent of the females and 8 percent of the males scored above the mean of the opposite sex (Rosenberg and Sutton-Smith, 1959).

*The masculinity score is the sex-appropriate measure for boys but the sex-inappropriate measure for girls.

For both cross-validation groups, it was found that the differences between the means for boys and girls were significant at the .001 level for masculinity and femininity scales (Rosenberg and Sutton-Smith, 1959). Purcell and Clifford (1966) also found significant differences in scores obtained by boys and girls.

1964 version: The instrument was cross-validated on four groups of children (n = 296, 557, 657, and 512) in the third through sixth grades. For all four groups, the difference between means of boys and girls was significant at the .001 level on both the masculinity and femininity measures. For the cross-validation groups, the percentages falling below the mean of the opposite sex on the sex-appropriate scale were 4 percent, 7 percent, 5 percent, and 9 percent for males, and 4 percent, 1 percent, 4 percent, and 1 percent for females. The percentages falling above the mean of the opposite sex on the sex-inappropriate scale were 2 percent, 2 percent, 5 percent, and 2 percent for males, and 6 percent, 6 percent, 11 percent, and 15 percent for females (Rosenberg and Sutton-Smith, 1964a).

NOTES AND COMMENTS: (1) There is a third "version" of the scale (Rosenberg and Sutton-Smith, 1960), which is similar to the 1959 version. The six masculine items and three feminine items that were scored 1 on the 1959 version are not scored on the "1960 version." In other words, the nine items that differentiated between boys and girls at the .10 level but not at the .05 level were not scored. Thus, the maximum score on masculinity is 50 and the maximum score on femininity is 113.

(2) Some users have modified the Checklist of Games and Play Activities. For example, Cowan (1972) adapted the instrument for use with blind children by including only those activities that blind children could participate in and by administering the checklist orally. DeLucia (1963) shortened the list of activities and presented them in a paired-comparison format. Walker (1964) and Biller and Zung (1972) shortened and altered the list of activities.

(3) Research findings suggest that scores on opposite-sex scales may be more effective measures of sex role identification (Rosenberg, Sutton-Smith, and Morgan, 1961). In other words, boys' femininity scores and girls' masculinity scores may be better indicators of sex role identification than boys' masculinity scores and girls' femininity scores.

(4) The greatest caution in using this instrument was written by its authors: "To continue to rely upon play data which accrued several decades ago as the basis for present prediction is highly questionable in view of the marked shift in masculine and feminine preferences" (Rosenberg and Sutton-Smith, 1960, p. 169). Clearly validation data obtained in the early 1960s cannot be presumed applicable today.

(5) Of the 181 items on the Checklist of Games and Play Activities, many are likely to be unfamiliar to children today.

SOURCE: For the 181-item checklist, see Sutton-Smith and Rosenberg, 1971.
For the 1959 version, see Rosenberg and Sutton-Smith, 1959.
For the 1964 version, see Rosenberg and Sutton-Smith, 1964a.

BIBLIOGRAPHY:

Biller, H. B., and Zung, B. "Perceived Maternal Control, Anxiety, and Opposite Sex Role Preference Among Elementary School Girls." *Journal of Psychology,* 1972, *81,* 85-88.

Cohen, S., and Gault, J. V. "Sex Role Orientation and Creativity in Young Females." *Home Economics Research Journal,* 1975, *3,* 280-285.

Cowan, M. K. "Sex Role Typing in the Blind Child as Measured by Play Activity Choices." *American Journal of Occupational Therapy,* 1972, *26,* 85-87.

DeLucia, L. A. "The Toy Preference Test: A Measure of Sex Role Identification." *Child Development,* 1963, *34,* 107-117.

Houston, H. S. "Familial Correlates of Sex Role Development in Boys: An Exploratory Study." *Personality: An International Journal,* 1970, *1,* 303-317.

Kaplar, J. E. "Creativity, Sex Role Preference, and Perception of Parents in Fifth-Grade Boys." Unpublished doctoral dissertation, University of Massachusetts, 1970. (*Dissertation Abstracts International,* 1970, *30*[12-B], 5689-5690.)

McGuire, L. S., Ryan, K. O., and Omenn, G. S. "Congenital Adrenal Hyperplasia: II. Cognitive and Behavioral Studies." *Behavior Genetics,* 1975, *5,* 175-188.

Purcell, K., and Clifford, E. "Binocular Rivalry and the Study of Identification in Asthmatic and Nonasthmatic Boys." *Journal of Consulting Psychology,* 1966, *30,* 388-394.

Rosenberg, B. G., and Sutton-Smith, B. "The Measurement of Masculinity and Femininity in Children." *Child Development,* 1959, *30,* 373-380.

Rosenberg, B. G., and Sutton-Smith, B. "A Revised Conception of Masculine-Feminine Differences in Play Activities." *Journal of Genetic Psychology,* 1960, *96,* 165-170.

Rosenberg, B. G., and Sutton-Smith, B. "The Measurement of Masculinity and Femininity in Children: An Extension and Revalidation." *Journal of Genetic Psychology,* 1964a, *104,* 259-264.

Rosenberg, B. G., and Sutton-Smith, B. "Ordinal Position and Sex Role Identification." *Genetic Psychology Monographs,* 1964b, *70,* 297-328.

Rosenberg, B. G., Sutton-Smith, B., and Morgan, E. E. "The Use of Opposite-Sex Scales as a Measure of Psychosexual Deviancy." *Journal of Consulting Psychology,* 1961, *25,* 221-225.

Schaffer, M. C. "Parent-Child Similarity in Psychological Differentiation." Unpublished doctoral dissertation, Purdue University, 1969. (*Dissertation Abstracts International,* 1969, *30*[4-B], 1888.)

Sutton-Smith, B., and Rosenberg, B. G. "Manifest Anxiety and Game Preference in Children." *Child Development,* 1960, *31,* 307-311.

Sutton-Smith, B., and Rosenberg, B. G. "Impulsivity and Sex Preference." *Journal of Genetic Psychology,* 1961, *98,* 187-192.

Sutton-Smith, B., and Rosenberg, B. G. "Sixty Years of Historical Change in the Game Preferences of American Children." In R. E. Herron and B. Sutton-Smith (Eds.), *Child's Play.* New York: Wiley, 1971.

Sutton-Smith, B., Rosenberg, B. G., and Morgan, E. F., Jr. "Historical Changes in the Freedom with Which Children Express Themselves in Personality Inventories." *Journal of Genetic Psychology,* 1961, *99,* 309-315.

Sutton-Smith, B., Rosenberg, B. G., and Morgan, E. F., Jr. "Development of Sex Differences in Play Choices During Preadolescence." *Child Development,* 1963, *34,* 119-126.

Walker, R. N. "Measuring Masculinity and Femininity by Children's Games Choices." *Child Development,* 1964, *35,* 961-971.

5. CHILDREN'S BEHAVIOR AND PERSONALITY RATING SCALE

AUTHOR: Albert F. Angrilli

DATE: 1957

VARIABLE: Sex role adoption

TYPE OF INSTRUMENT: Rating scale

DESCRIPTION: The scale consists of eight phrases referring to children's behavior. Each phrase is followed by five response options. The rater is to select the option that best describes the child's behavior.

PREVIOUSLY ADMINISTERED TO: Nursery school teachers who rated preschool boys from their classes

APPROPRIATE FOR: Rating ages 3-7

ADMINISTRATION: A teacher can complete the scale for an individual child in about three minutes.

SAMPLE ITEMS: Seeking of praise
• Never seeks praise
• Less than average seeking for praise
• Average
• More than average seeking for praise
• Constantly looking for praise
                    Degree of daring
• Fearless, rushes in, daredevil
• Takes more than average risk or chance
• Will take reasonable chances
• Somewhat hesitant to take chances
• Extremely fearful of risk

SCORING: The child's score is the sum of the ratings assigned on the eight items. A higher score indicates greater masculinity.

DEVELOPMENT: Kindergarten and nursery school teachers were asked to rate their students on twelve traits. The 101 boys and 95 girls they rated ranged in age from 3½ to 6½ years. The mean rating obtained for boys was compared with the mean rating obtained for girls on each of the items. The eight items on which girls and boys scored significantly different ($p < .05$) were retained for the scale.

RELIABILITY: No data are provided.

VALIDITY: Scores from the Children's Behavior and Personality Rating Scale along with scores from Figure Drawing (#10) and the Activity Preference Check List (#1) were available for thirty boys between the ages of 4 and 5. There was not a significant correlation between the Figure Drawing and the Children's Behavior and Personality Rating Scale (r = .05), but there was a significant correlation between the Children's Behavior and Personality Rating Scale and the Activity Preference Check List (r = .37, p < .05) (Angrilli, 1957).

SOURCE: See Angrilli, 1957.

BIBLIOGRAPHY:

Angrilli, A. F. "A Study of the Psychosexual Identification of Preschool Boys." Unpublished doctoral dissertation, New York University, 1957. (*Dissertation Abstracts,* 1958, *19*[4], 874-875.)
Angrilli, A. F. "The Psychosexual Identification of Preschool Boys." *Journal of Genetic Psychology,* 1960, *97,* 329-340.

---

6. EAGLY SEX ROLE IDENTIFICATION SCALE

AUTHOR: Alice H. Eagly

DATE: 1969

VARIABLE: Sex role identification

TYPE OF INSTRUMENT: Multiple choice

DESCRIPTION: The instrument consists of thirty questions concerning one's feelings, behavior, interests, and occupational goals. Each question is accompanied by five graded response options.

PREVIOUSLY ADMINISTERED TO: Grade 9

APPROPRIATE FOR: Ages 14-18

ADMINISTRATION: This instrument can be self-administered and can be completed in about fifteen minutes.

SAMPLE ITEMS: How frightening to you is the thought of being in an automobile accident?
• Very frightening
• Fairly frightening
• Slightly frightening
• Not very frightening
• Not at all frightening
                    Would you like to be a lawyer?
• Definitely yes

- Probably yes
- Undecided
- Probably no
- Definitely no

SCORING: Items are objectively scored and equally weighted. Total scores can range from 30 (very masculine) to 150 (very feminine).

DEVELOPMENT: Gough's Femininity Scale (#36) and a number of additional items were given to a sample of college students. The thirty items that best differentiated between males and females comprise this instrument.

RELIABILITY: Ninety-six male and 121 female ninth graders completed the scale. Corrected split-half reliability was .88 for both sexes together, .67 for males alone, and .45 for females alone.

VALIDITY: Based on the groups described above, the mean score for females ($\overline{X}$ = 111.9) was significantly higher than the mean score for males ($\overline{X}$ = 82.6, p < .01).

NOTES AND COMMENTS: (1) Eagly correlated scores for sex role identification with scores on a measure of susceptibility to influence. Because the correlation was only .19 for females, she suggests that the Eagly Sex Role Identification Scale may not be valid for females.

(2) The content, but not the format, of twenty-six out of the thirty items on the Eagly Sex Role Identification Scale is the same as items on the Gough Femininity Scale (#36).

SOURCE: Alice Eagly, Professor of Psychology
University of Massachusetts
Amherst, Massachusetts 01003

BIBLIOGRAPHY:

Eagly, A. H. "Sex Differences in the Relationship Between Self-Esteem and Susceptibility to Social Influence." *Journal of Personality,* 1969, *37,* 581-591.

---

7. FAULS-SMITH ACTIVITY PREFERENCE TEST

AUTHORS: Lydia Boyce Fauls and Walter D. Smith

DATE: 1956

VARIABLE: Masculinity-femininity

TYPE OF INSTRUMENT: Forced choice picture preference

DESCRIPTION: This test consists of three pairs of pictures (8½" x 11") with one member of the pair depicting a male-appropriate activity and the other depicting a female-appropriate activity. Baseball playing (masculine) is paired with doll playing (feminine); playing with toy cars and trucks (masculine) is paired with playing cooking (feminine); raking (masculine) is paired with sweeping (feminine). Each picture includes an adult female and an adult male. There are two forms of the test: in one form, a boy is the central figure in the picture; in the other form, a girl is the central figure.

PREVIOUSLY ADMINISTERED TO: Ages 4-5

APPROPRIATE FOR: Ages 3-6

ADMINISTRATION: The child is shown a pair of pictures in which the central figure in the pictures is the same sex as the child completing the test. The pictures are described by the investigator and the child is asked four questions: "Which of these do you do? Which do you like to do best? Which does mother want the boy [girl] to do? Which does daddy want the boy [girl] to do?" The procedure is repeated for the three pairs of pictures.

SCORING: Responses to the questions, "Which does mother want the boy [girl] to do?" and "Which does daddy want the boy [girl] to do?" provide the data for scoring perceptions of paternal and maternal preferences.

A masculine score is obtained by assigning 1 point for each choice of a male-appropriate activity. Perceptions of paternal and maternal preferences are scored in the same way. Sex appropriateness or inappropriateness is scored by assigning 1 point for each sex-appropriate choice. Sex-appropriateness scores are obtained in the same way for perceptions of maternal and paternal preferences. A parent-child agreement score is found by assigning 1 point whenever the child's response is identical to the child's perception of the parental response. This scoring is done for maternal-child agreement and paternal-child agreement. Thus, the test yields a total of eight scores (three masculinity, three sex-appropriateness, and two parent-child agreement), each of which has a maximum value of 3.

DEVELOPMENT: Pictures of activities were presented to twenty 3- and 4-year-old children who were asked to judge their sexual appropriateness for men, women, boys, and girls. The responses of these "judges" were used to select activities for the pictures included in the test.

RELIABILITY: No data are provided.

VALIDITY: Fauls and Smith report that boys chose male-appropriate activities significantly more often than girls, and girls chose female-appropriate activities significantly more often than boys.

NOTES AND COMMENTS: (1) The scale is extremely short, which is of concern particularly because there are no reliability data.

(2) The pictures are described, but they are not actually reproduced in Fauls and Smith (1956).

(3) The Sears Activity Preference Test (#25) is based on and closely related to this scale.

SOURCE: See Fauls and Smith, 1956.

BIBLIOGRAPHY:

Fauls, L. B., and Smith, W. D. "Sex Role Learning of Five-Year-Olds." *Journal of Genetic Psychology,* 1956, *89,* 105-117.

---

8. FELDMAN-NASH-CUTRONA SEX ROLE SELF-DESCRIPTION SCALE

AUTHORS: S. Shirley Feldman, Sharon C. Nash, and Carolyn Cutrona

DATE: 1977

VARIABLES: Masculinity, femininity

TYPE OF INSTRUMENT: Adjective rating scale

DESCRIPTION: The scale consists of fifteen adjectives: five masculine (brave, mean, leader, active, and strong), five feminine (kind, gentle, worried, warm-hearted, and sensitive), and five neutral. Each adjective is followed by a five-point rating scale ranging from "not at all like me" to "very much like me."

PREVIOUSLY ADMINISTERED TO: Ages 8-9 and 14-15

APPROPRIATE FOR: Ages 8 and older

ADMINISTRATION: The scale can be administered individually or in groups and can be completed in about three minutes.

SCORING: A masculinity score is obtained by taking the average of the ratings assigned to the five masculine adjectives. Similarly, a femininity score is obtained by taking the average of the ratings assigned to the five feminine items.

DEVELOPMENT: No information is provided.

RELIABILITY: No data are provided.

VALIDITY: The Feldman-Nash-Cutrona Sex Role Self-Description Scale and the Bem Sex Role Inventory (#32) were administered to thirty-two adolescents. "The intercorrelations across the two scales of the masculinity and femininity scores calculated separately for boys and girls were high, ranging from 0.70 to 0.86" (p. 7).
    For twenty-seven third graders, boys' masculinity scores averaged 3.5 and their femininity scores averaged 3.0; girls' masculinity scores averaged 3.3 and their femininity scores averaged 3.8. There are no data to indicate which, if any, of the differences are significant.

NOTES AND COMMENTS: (1) The format for this scale is similar to the Bem Sex Role Inventory (#32).

(2) No evidence is provided that the adjectives are correctly sex typed.

SOURCE: See Feldman, Nash, and Cutrona, 1977.

BIBLIOGRAPHY:

Feldman, S. S., Nash, S. C., and Cutrona, C. *Baby Responsiveness as a Sex-Stereotyped Behavior: A Developmental Study.* Rockville, Md.: National Institute of Mental Health, 1977. (ERIC Document Reproduction Service No. ED 139 503.)

---

9. FEMININITY INDEX

AUTHORS: Elizabeth Douvan and Joseph Adelson

DATE: 1966 (used 1955)

VARIABLE: Femininity

TYPE OF INSTRUMENT: Open-ended questions

DESCRIPTION: The Femininity Index consists of seven open-ended questions which allow for the expression of feminine interests and goals.

PREVIOUSLY ADMINISTERED TO: Females, grades 6-12

APPROPRIATE FOR: Females, ages 12-18

ADMINISTRATION: Questions and responses are oral.

SAMPLE ITEMS: If someone wanted to start a new club for girls like you, what things should the club do? What do you think girls like to do best?

We find that some girls have a kind of plan or picture of what they will do when they get out of school. What ideas have you about the way you want things to work out for you?

SCORING: For each of the questions, specific responses have been designated as "feminine." If the girl gives a feminine response to the item, she receives 1 point. Maximum score is 7.

DEVELOPMENT: No information is provided.

RELIABILITY: No data are provided.

VALIDITY: Douvan and Adelson (1966) report that the "data are rich with evidence that the index is, in fact, measuring an explicit preoccupation with femininity and future female goals" (p. 238). To substantiate this statement, they indicate that girls who score high (5, 6, or 7) on the Femininity Index are more interested in boys, are more concerned with being popular with boys, think more about marriage and family life, and have more specific and sophisticated ideas about marriage.

NOTES AND COMMENTS: (1) The scoring of this instrument follows very traditional, stereotypic conceptions of femininity.

(2) The questions on the Femininity Index were originally embedded in a lengthy interview schedule. Interviews lasted from one to four hours.

(3) Haft (1975) used the seven questions alone in a paper-and-pencil administration of the index. She related scores on the Femininity Index to scores on measures of body image, self-acceptance, and responses to menstruation.

SOURCE: See Douvan and Adelson, 1966, p. 461.

BIBLIOGRAPHY:

Douvan, E., and Adelson, J. *The Adolescent Experience.* New York: Wiley, 1966.
Haft, M. S. "An Exploratory Study of Early Adolescent Girls: Body Image, Self-Acceptance, Acceptance of 'Traditional Female Role,' and Response to Menstruation." Unpublished doctoral dissertation, Columbia University, 1973. (*Dissertation Abstracts International,* 1975, *35* [8-B], 4173-4174.)

---

10. FIGURE DRAWING

DATE: 1948

VARIABLE: Sex role identification

TYPE OF INSTRUMENT: Projective drawing

DESCRIPTION: There is some variability in the procedure. Typically the respondent is asked to draw a picture of a whole person. No other instructions are usually provided. When the picture is complete, the respondent is asked to draw a picture of a person who is of the opposite sex of the first person drawn. When both pictures are completed, the respondent is asked to indicate the sex of each person drawn.

PREVIOUSLY ADMINISTERED TO: Ages 3 and older; black adolescents; children in Mexico and Barbados; Jordanian and American college students; juvenile delinquents, sex offenders, neurotics, schizophrenics, retardates

APPROPRIATE FOR: Ages 3 and older

ADMINISTRATION: Usually the instrument is individually administered, although some researchers have administered it to groups of respondents.

SCORING: It is very common to score this instrument simply by noting the sex of the first figure drawn. It is also common to score the drawings on the basis of sexual differentiation as outlined by Swenson (1955). This latter system consists of a nine-point rating scale on which higher scores indicate greater sexual differentiation. Characteristics reflecting differentiation include the following: long versus short hair; rounded versus angular body contour; presence or absence of rounded hips and breasts; feminine versus masculine clothing; appropriateness of minor details such as eyelashes, earrings, or fuller lips on the female. An additional method of scoring takes into account the size of the figures drawn simply by measuring height and various other bodily proportions.

DEVELOPMENT: There is no information provided on how figure drawings, a commonly used projective assessment procedure, came to be used as a measure of sex role identification.

RELIABILITY: To estimate the reliability of Swenson's (1955) sexual differentiation scale, two independent judges rated fifty-eight sets of drawings. The interrater reliability coefficient was .84. A study by Donini (1967), which also used Swenson's scale, found that agreement between three independent raters was significantly different from chance (p < .001). The precise correlations were not provided.

Other studies used characteristics different from Swenson's to examine the degree of differentiation manifested in figure drawings. Reed (1957) reports interrater reliability coefficients ranging from .91 to .99; Saarni and Azara (1977) report an average interrater reliability of .77; Laosa and Brophy (1972) report agreement in judging the drawings of ninety-two out of ninety-three persons; Vroegh (1970) reports 90 percent agreement between at least two of three raters; Hassell and Smith (1975) scored drawings on two different dimensions: On one dimension they found 93 percent agreement between the judges; on the other dimension, they report 85 percent agreement between the judges.

VALIDITY: Several studies have found that males are more likely to draw same-sex figures than opposite-sex figures (Bieliauskas, 1960, 1974; Biller, 1968, 1969a; Biller and Borstelmann, 1965; Burton, 1972; Fellows and Cerbus, 1969; Fisher, 1960; Hammer and Kaplan, 1964; Jolles, 1952; Laosa and Brophy, 1972; Phelan, 1964; Saarni and Azara, 1977; Tolor and Tolor, 1974). Similarly many studies have found that females are more likely to draw same-sex figures than opposite-sex figures (Bieliauskas, 1960, 1974; Biller and Borstelmann, 1965; Burton, 1972; Fellows and Cerbus, 1969; Fisher, 1961; Hammer and Kaplan, 1964; Jolles, 1952; Laosa and Brophy, 1972; Tolor and Tolor, 1974).

Results of several studies have shown that male respondents draw same-sex figures first significantly more often than female respondents (Daoud, 1976; Granick and Smith, 1953; Heinrich and Triebe, 1972; Vroegh, 1970), whereas other studies have found that females draw same-sex figures first significantly more often than males (Weider and Noller, 1950, 1953).

From drawings obtained from children ages 7 to 15, Burton (1972) and Fellows and Cerbus (1969) found that both males and females tended to draw their same-sex figures larger than opposite figures. Weider and Noller (1950, 1953) reported that girls drew significantly larger same-sex figures than boys.

Other studies have provided evidence of the validity of figure drawings. After obtaining drawings from adolescent delinquent girls before and after a series of self-concept group sessions, James, Osborn, and Oetting (1967) found that nine of the twelve girls drew larger figures on the posttest (p < .01) than on the pretest. A greater proportion of inappropriately sex-typed boys, as measured by the Games and Activities Preference List (#12), drew opposite-sex figures first (p < .05; Lefkowitz, 1962). Hassell and Smith (1975) found that homosexual females both sexualize and embellish their female drawings significantly more than heterosexual females, whereas Roback, Langevin, and Zajac (1974) found no significant differences between homosexuals' and heterosexuals' drawings.

To determine whether degree of sexual differentiation on drawings reflects visual motor functioning capacity, ratings of drawings and Bender-Gestalt scores were correlated (Swenson, 1955). A correlation coefficient of .24 (nonsignificant) was obtained, suggesting that figure drawings are not a function of visual motor capacity.

Several correlational studies involving other measures of sex typing have been done. A consistent finding is that figure drawings and the It Scale for Children (#17) are significantly correlated (Biller, 1968, 1969a, 1969b; Biller and Borstelmann, 1965). Kettering (1965) obtained a significant correlation between sex of figure drawn and scores on the Franck Drawing Completion Test (#11), a measure of masculinity-femininity. Respondents who drew female figures first scored at the feminine end of the scale, and respondents who drew male figures first scored at the masculine end of the scale. Using data obtained from female psychotics, Reed (1957) found a negative correlation between height of the figure drawings and scores on the Franck Drawing Completion Test. Two studies (Granick and Smith, 1953; Reed, 1957) indicated no significant relationship between figure drawings and scores on the masculinity-femininity scale of the Minnesota Multiphasic Personality Inventory (MMPI) (#52). Gravitz (1969) also found no relationship between MMPI masculinity-femininity scores and figure drawings for female respondents. In males the correlation was opposite to what would be expected in that those with high masculinity-femininity scores, indicating feminine interest patterns, drew more same-sex figures than did those with low masculinity-femininity scores. In addition, Kokonis (1972a) found that sex of first figure drawn was not significantly related to Swenson's Sexual Differentiation Scale, Terman and Miles' Emotional-Ethical Attitudes Test, which is a subscale of the Attitude Interest Analysis Test (#31), or Krout and Tabin's Personal Preference Scale (#54), all of which are measures of sex role orientation.

NOTES AND COMMENTS: (1) Some researchers have varied the instructions to respondents. Darke and Geil (1948) directed respondents to "make the very best picture of a man" that they could; Lebovitz (1972) asked respondents to draw a picture of themselves after they completed the first two drawings; LeCorgne and Laosa (1976) directed persons to draw a male and a female; Grossman (1977) asked respondents to "draw a picture of the person you'd like to be" and then to designate the sex of the figure; Biller and Poey (1969) asked respondents to modify carbon copies of their own initial pair of drawings to increase sexual differentiation; Roback, Langevin, and Zajac (1974) asked respondents to produce two free-choice human figure drawings; and Tolor and Tolor (1974) asked respondents to draw only one figure and label it as boy, girl, man, or woman.

(2) A number of variables have been investigated in conjunction with the figure drawings, including father availability (Burton, 1972; Donini, 1967; Hetherington, 1972; LeCorgne and Laosa, 1976); parental dominance (Biller, 1969a; Kokonis, 1971, 1972a, 1973); perception of maternal salience (Biller, 1969b); birth order (Laosa and Brophy, 1972); intelligence (Biller and Borstelmann, 1965; Fisher, 1961; Kettering, 1965; Weider

and Noller, 1953); age (Fisher, 1961; Vroegh, 1970; Weider and Noller, 1953); socio-economic level (Weider and Noller, 1950); sex offenses (Hammer, 1954); gender abnormality (Money and Wang, 1966); creativity (Biller, Singer, and Fullerton, 1969); and stress (Goldstein, 1972).

(3) As described here, Figure Drawing is a procedure rather than a specific instrument. Researchers have referred to this procedure by different names, most often calling it the Draw-a-Person scale. However, typically the purpose and scoring of the Draw-a-Person differ from the purpose and scoring described here.

SOURCE: None is necessary.

BIBLIOGRAPHY:

Angrilli, A. F. "A Study of the Psychosexual Identification of Preschool Boys." Unpublished doctoral dissertation, New York University, 1957. (*Dissertation Abstracts,* 1958, *19*[4], 874-875.)

Angrilli, A. F. "The Psychosexual Identification of Preschool Boys." *Journal of Genetic Psychology,* 1960, *97,* 329-340.

Armstrong, R., and Hauck, P. "Sexual Identification and the First Figure Drawn." *Journal of Consulting Psychology,* 1961, *25,* 51-54.

Azimi, C. "Masculinity, Femininity, and Perception of Warmth and Saliency in Parent-Son Relationships." Unpublished doctoral dissertation, Michigan State University, 1964. (*Dissertation Abstracts,* 1964, *25*[4], 2608-2609.)

Bieliauskas, V. J. "Sexual Identification in Children's Drawings of Human Figure." *Journal of Clinical Psychology,* 1960, *16,* 42-44.

Bieliauskas, V. J. "A New Look at 'Masculine Protest.' " *Journal of Individual Psychology,* 1974, *30,* 92-97.

Biller, H. B. "A Multiaspect Investigation of Masculine Development in Kindergarten-Age Boys." *Genetic Psychology Monographs,* 1968, *78,* 89-138.

Biller, H. B. "Father Dominance and Sex Role Development in Kindergarten-Age Boys." *Developmental Psychology,* 1969a, *1,* 87-94.

Biller, H. B. "Maternal Salience and Feminine Development in Young Girls." *Proceedings of the 77th Annual Convention of the American Psychological Association,* 1969b, *4,* 259-260.

Biller, H. B., and Borstelmann, L. J. "Intellectual Level and Sex Role Development in Mentally Retarded Children." *American Journal of Mental Deficiency,* 1965, *70,* 443-447.

Biller, H. B., and Poey, K. "An Exploratory Comparison of Sex Role Related Behaviors in Schizophrenics and Nonschizophrenics." *Developmental Psychology,* 1969, *1,* 629.

Biller, H. B., Singer, D. L., and Fullerton, M. "Sex Role Development and Creative Potential in Kindergarten-Age Boys." *Developmental Psychology,* 1969, *1,* 291-296.

Brophy, J. E., and Laosa, L. M. "The Effect of a Male Teacher on the Sex Typing of Kindergarten Children." *Journal Supplement Abstract Service Catalog of Selected Documents in Psychology,* 1973, *3,* 44.

Brown, D. G., and Tolor, A. "Human Figure Drawings as Indicators of Sexual Identification and Inversion." *Perceptual and Motor Skills,* 1957, *7,* 199-211.

Burns, R. A. "The Effect of Father's Absence on the Development of the Masculine Identification of Boys in Residential Treatment." Unpublished doctoral dissertation,

St. Johns University, 1971. (*Dissertation Abstracts International,* 1972, *32*[7-B], 4179-4180.)

Burton, R. V. "Cross-Sex Identity in Barbados." *Developmental Psychology,* 1972, *6,* 365-374.

Butler, R. I., and Marcuse, F. L. "Sex Identification at Different Ages Using the Draw-A-Person Test." *Journal of Projective Techniques and Personality Assessment,* 1959, *23,* 299-302.

Clark, E. T. "Sex Role Preference in Mentally Retarded Females." *American Journal of Mental Deficiency,* 1963, *68,* 433-439.

Craddick, R. A. "The Self-Image in the Draw-A-Person Test and Self-Portrait Drawings." *Journal of Projective Techniques and Personality Assessment,* 1963, *27,* 288-291.

Daoud, F. S. "First-Drawn Pictures: A Cross-Cultural Investigation." *Journal of Personality Assessment,* 1976, *40,* 376-377.

Darke, R. A., and Geil, G. A. "Homosexual Activity, Relation of Degree and Role to the Goodenough Test and the Cornell Selectee Index." *Journal of Nervous and Mental Disease,* 1948, *108,* 217-240.

Datta, L., and Drake, A. K. "Examiner Sex and Sexual Differentiation in Preschool Children's Figure Drawings." *Journal of Projective Techniques and Personality Assessment,* 1968, *32,* 397-399.

Donini, G. P. "An Evaluation of Sex Role Identification Among Father-Absent and Father-Present Boys." *Psychology,* 1967, *4,* 13-16.

Eichler, L. S. " 'Feminine Narcissism': An Empirical Investigation." Unpublished doctoral dissertation, Boston University, 1973. (*Dissertation Abstracts International,* 1973, *33*[12-B], 6074-6075.)

Fellows, R., and Cerbus, G. "HTP and DCT Indicators of Sexual Identification in Children." *Journal of Projective Techniques and Personality Assessment,* 1969, *33,* 376-379.

Fisher, G. M. "Relationship Between Diagnosis of Neuropsychiatric Disorder, Sexual Deviation, and the Sex of the First-Drawn Figure." *Perceptual and Motor Skills,* 1959, *9,* 47-50.

Fisher, G. M. "Sexual Identification in Mentally Retarded Male Children and Adults." *American Journal of Mental Deficiency,* 1960, *65,* 42-45.

Fisher, G. M. "Sexual Identification in Mentally Subnormal Females." *American Journal of Mental Deficiency,* 1961, *66,* 266-269.

Fisher, S. "Right-Left Gradients in Body Image, Body Reactivity, and Perception." *Genetic Psychology Monographs,* 1960, *61,* 197-228.

Goldstein, H. S. "Gender Identity, Stress, and Psychological Differentiation in Figure-Drawing Choice." *Perceptual and Motor Skills,* 1972, *35,* 127-132.

Granick, S., and Smith, L. J. "Sex Sequence in the Draw-A-Person Test and Its Relation to the MMPI Masculinity-Femininity Scale." *Journal of Consulting Psychology,* 1953, *17,* 71-73.

Gravitz, M. A. "Direction of Psychosexual Interest and Figure Drawing Choice." *Journal of Clinical Psychology,* 1969, *25,* 311.

Grayson, H. T., Jr. "Psychosexual Conflict in Adolescent Girls Who Experienced Early Parental Loss by Death." Unpublished doctoral dissertation, Boston University, 1967. (*Dissertation Abstracts,* 1967, *28*[5-B], 2136.)

Green, R., Fuller, M., and Rutley, B. "It Scale for Children and Draw-A-Person Test: 30 Feminine vs. 25 Masculine Boys." *Journal of Personality Assessment,* 1972, *36,* 349-352.

Grossman, B. "Children's 'Ideal Self'—Which Sex? Drawings from Two Mexican Sub-cultures." Paper presented at 85th annual meeting of the American Psychological Association, San Francisco, August 1977.

Hammer, E. F. "Relationship Between Diagnosis of Psychosexual Pathology and the Sex of the First-Drawn Person." *Journal of Clinical Psychology,* 1954, *10,* 168-170.

Hammer, M., and Kaplan, A. M. "The Reliability of the Sex of First Figure Drawn by Children." *Journal of Clinical Psychology,* 1964, *20,* 251-252.

Hassell, J., and Smith, E. W. L. "Female Homosexuals' Concepts of Self, Men, and Women." *Journal of Personality Assessment,* 1975, *39,* 154-159.

Heinrich, P., and Triebe, J. K. "Sex Preferences in Children's Human Figure Drawings." *Journal of Personality Assessment,* 1972, *36,* 263-267.

Hetherington, E. M. "Effects of Father Absence on Personality Development in Adoles-cent Daughters." *Developmental Psychology,* 1972, *7,* 313-326.

James, S. L., Osborn, F., and Oetting, E. "Treatment for Delinquent Girls: The Ado-lescent Self-Concept Group." *Community Mental Health Journal,* 1967, *3,* 377-381.

Jolles, I. "A Study of the Validity of Some Hypotheses for the Qualitative Interpretation of the H-T-P for Children of Elementary School Age: I. Sexual Identification." *Journal of Clinical Psychology,* 1952, *8,* 113-118.

Kettering, W. R. "The Use of Two Projective Drawing Techniques as Indices of Mascu-linity and Femininity with Children of Varying Levels of Intelligence." Unpub-lished doctoral dissertation, University of Pittsburgh, 1965. (*Dissertation Ab-stracts,* 1966, *27*[3-B], 956-957.)

Kokonis, N. D. "Sex Role Identification in Schizophrenia: Psychoanalytic and Role-Theory Predictions Compared." Unpublished doctoral dissertation, Illinois Insti-tute of Technology, 1971. (*Dissertation Abstracts International,* 1971, *32*[3-B], 1849-1850.)

Kokonis, N. D. "Choice of Gender on the DAP and Measures of Sex Role Identification." *Perceptual and Motor Skills,* 1972a, *35,* 727-730.

Kokonis, N. D. "Sex Role Identification in Neurosis: Psychoanalytic-Developmental and Role Theory Predictions Compared." *Journal of Abnormal Psychology,* 1972b, *80,* 52-57.

Kokonis, N. D. "Parental Dominance and Sex Role Identification in Schizophrenia." *Journal of Psychology,* 1973, *84,* 211-218.

Laosa, L. M., and Brophy, J. E. "Effects of Sex and Birth Order on Sex Role Develop-ment and Intelligence in Kindergarten Children." Paper presented at 18th annual meeting of the Southwestern Psychological Association, San Antonio, Texas, April, 1971. (ERIC Document Reproduction Service No. ED 053 403.)

Laosa, L. M., and Brophy, J. E. "Effects of Sex and Birth Order on Sex Role Develop-ment and Intelligence Among Kindergarten Children." *Developmental Psychol-ogy,* 1972, *6,* 409-415.

LaVoie, J. C., and Andrews, R. "Cognitive Determinants of Gender Identity and Con-stancy." Paper presented at 83rd annual meeting of the American Psychological Association, Chicago, September 1975.

LaVoie, J. C., and Andrews, R. "Facial Attractiveness, Physique, and Sex Role Identity in Young Children." *Developmental Psychology,* 1976, *12,* 550-551.

Lebovitz, P. S. "Feminine Behavior in Boys: Aspects of Its Outcome." *American Journal of Psychiatry,* 1972, *128,* 103-109.

LeCorgne, L. L., and Laosa, L. M. "Father Absence in Low-Income Mexican-American

Families: Children's Social Adjustment and Conceptual Differentiation of Sex Role Attributes." *Developmental Psychology,* 1976, *12,* 470-471.

Lefkowitz, M. M. "Some Relationships Between Sex Role Preference of Children and Other Parent and Child Variables." *Psychological Reports,* 1962, *10,* 43-53.

Melikian, L. H., and Wehab, A. Z. "First-Drawn Picture: A Cross-Cultural Investigation of the DAP." *Journal of Projective Techniques and Personality Assessment,* 1969, *33,* 539-541.

Money, J., and Wang, C. "Human Figure Drawings: I. Sex of First Choice in Gender-Identity Anomalies, Klinefelter's Syndrome, and Precocious Puberty." *Journal of Nervous and Mental Disease,* 1966, *143,* 157-162.

Morgenstern, M. "The Psychosexual Development of the Retarded." In F. F. de la Cruz and G. D. LaVeck (Eds.), *Human Sexuality and the Mentally Retarded.* New York: Brunner/Mazel, 1973.

Phelan, H. M. "The Incidence and Possible Significance of the Drawing of Female Figures by Sixth-Grade Boys in Response to the Draw-A-Person Test." *Psychiatric Quarterly,* 1964, *38,* 1-16.

Pustel, G., Sternlicht, M., and Deutsch, M. "Feminine Tendencies in Figure Drawings by Male Homosexual Retarded Dyads." *Journal of Clinical Psychology,* 1971, *27,* 260-261.

Reed, M. R. "A Study of the Masculinity-Femininity Dimension of Personality in 'Normal' and 'Pathological' Groups: An Investigation of Differences in M-F Test Productions of Hospitalized and Nonhospitalized Women." Unpublished doctoral dissertation, Washington University, 1955. (*Dissertation Abstracts,* 1955, *15*[8], 1442-1443.)

Reed, M. R. "The Masculinity-Femininity Dimension in Normal and Psychotic Subjects." *Journal of Abnormal and Social Psychology,* 1957, *55,* 289-294.

Rice, J. H. "The Relationship of Male Sex Role Identification and Self-Esteem to Aggressive Behavior." Unpublished doctoral dissertation, United States International University, 1975. (*Dissertation Abstracts International,* 1974, *35*[6-B], 2997-2998.)

Roback, H. B., Langevin, R., and Zajac, Y. "Sex of Free-Choice Figure Drawings by Homosexual and Heterosexual Subjects." *Journal of Personality Assessment,* 1974, *38,* 154-155.

Rosenberg, E. S. "Some Psychological and Biological Relationships Between Masculinity and Femininity and Field Dependence and Field Independence." Unpublished doctoral dissertation, Northwestern University, 1975. (*Dissertation Abstracts International,* 1976, *36*[12-B], 6453.)

Saarni, C., and Azara, V. "Developmental Analysis of Human Figure Drawings in Adolescence, Young Adulthood, and Middle Age." *Journal of Personality Assessment,* 1977, *41,* 31-38.

Swenson, C. H. "Sexual Differentiation on the Draw-A-Person Test." *Journal of Clinical Psychology,* 1955, *11,* 37-41.

Tolor, A., and Tolor, B. "Children's Figure Drawings and Changing Attitudes Toward Sex Roles." *Psychological Reports,* 1974, *34,* 343-349.

Vroegh, K. "Lack of Sex Role Differentiation in Preschoolers' Figure Drawings." *Journal of Projective Techniques and Personality Assessment,* 1970, *34,* 38-40.

Weider, A., and Noller, P. A. "Objective Studies of Children's Drawings of Human Figures: I. Sex Awareness and Socioeconomic Level." *Journal of Clinical Psychology,* 1950, *6,* 319-325.

Weider, A., and Noller, P. A. "Objective Studies of Children's Drawings of Human Figures: II. Sex, Age, Intelligence." *Journal of Clinical Psychology,* 1953, *9,* 20-23.
Whitaker, L. "The Use of an Extended Draw-A-Person Test to Identify Homosexual and Effeminate Men." *Journal of Consulting and Clinical Psychology,* 1961, *25,* 482-485.

11. FRANCK DRAWING COMPLETION TEST (FDCT)

AUTHOR: Kate Franck

DATE: 1949

VARIABLE: Masculinity-femininity

TYPE OF INSTRUMENT: Projective drawing

DESCRIPTION: The FDCT consists of thirty-six different, simple, abstract line drawings. Each line drawing is inside a square that is two and a quarter inches on a side. Twelve line drawings are printed per page.

PREVIOUSLY ADMINISTERED TO: Ages 5 and older

APPROPRIATE FOR: Ages 5 and older

ADMINISTRATION: The test can be individually or group administered. Respondents are directed to complete the drawings in any manner they choose. Respondents typically complete the test in fifteen minutes, but some will take far longer.

SCORING: It is recommended that the test be scored by a "trained clinician, accustomed to careful scoring and interpretation of projective techniques" (Franck and Rosen, 1949, p. 249). Using criteria (for example, internal elaboration, angularity, closure, roundness) provided in the manual and scoring key, each drawing is scored as either masculine or feminine. The total score is the number of drawings scored feminine. Thus, the total score can range from 0 (all masculine) to 36 (all feminine). Once one gains some experience in scoring, a test can usually be scored in less than ten minutes.

DEVELOPMENT: An item pool consisting of sixty different, simple, abstract line drawings was submitted to 250 college students with instructions to complete the drawings. Completed drawings were examined for such qualities as expansion, closure, and elaboration. The thirty-six items from the pool of sixty that yielded statistically significant differences ($p < .05$) between the manner of completion by men and by women comprise the test.

RELIABILITY: Three raters independently scored the drawings of 150 college men and 150 college women. The interrater reliabilities, computed separately for males and females, ranged from .84 to .90 (Franck and Rosen, 1949). Other studies have reported interrater reliabilities ranging from .66 to .93 (Bieliauskas and Mikesell, 1972; Bieliauskas, Miranda, and Lansky, 1968; Blane and Chafetz, 1971; Child, 1965; D'Andrade, 1973; Fellows and Cerbus, 1969; Franck and Rosen, 1949; Grant and Domino, 1976; Lipsitt and Lelos, 1972; Lipsitt and Strodtbeck, 1967; Reed, 1957; Rosenfeld, 1969; Shepler, 1951; Thompson and others, 1973; Urbina and others, 1970). Some researchers have reported interrater reliability percentages: They range from 76 percent to 100 percent (Blane and Yamamoto, 1970; Lansky and McKay, 1969; Munroe and Munroe, 1971; Wilsnack, 1973).

VALIDITY: Franck and Rosen (1949) administered the scale to 150 college men and 150 college women. The scores for men ranged from 5 to 24; the scores for women ranged from 9 to 28. The difference between the mean scores of men and women was significant (p < .001). Other studies have also reported significant differences between FDCT scores obtained by males and females who were high school age or older (Bezdek and Strodtbeck, 1970; Bieliauskas, Miranda, and Lansky, 1968; Cottle, 1968; Cottle, Edwards, and Pleck, 1970; LeLieuvre and Wise, 1974; Lipsitt and Lelos, 1972; McCarthy, Anthony, and Domino, 1970; Munroe and Munroe, 1971; Shepler, 1951; Urbina and others, 1970). Fellows and Cerbus (1969) obtained data from children ages 7 to 14 and found significant differences between boys and girls only at ages 12 and 13. Furthermore, Lansky and McKay (1969) found no significant differences in FDCT scores between boys and girls in kindergarten; and Munroe and Munroe (1971) found no significant differences between male and female native adult Caribs in British Honduras.

Several studies have investigated the relationship between the FDCT and other measures of masculinity-femininity. Many have found that there is no significant correlation between the FDCT and the Gough Femininity Scale (#36) (Bezdek and Strodtbeck, 1970; Blane and Yamamoto, 1970; Cottle, 1968; Cottle, Edwards, and Pleck, 1970; Engel, 1966; Strodtbeck, Bezdek, and Goldhammer, 1970). Other studies have also found no significant relationship between the FDCT and other masculinity-femininity scales, including: the masculinity-femininity scale of the Minnesota Multiphasic Personality Inventory (#52) (Engel, 1966; McCarthy, Anthony, and Domino, 1970; Reed, 1957; Shepler, 1951); the femininity scale of the California Psychological Inventory (#47) (Kapor-Stanulovic and Lynn, 1972; McCarthy, Anthony, and Domino, 1970); the masculinity-femininity scale of the Strong Vocational Interest Blank (#56) (Engel, 1966; Shepler, 1951); the Attitude Interest Analysis Test (#31) (Engel, 1966; Shepler, 1951); and the Marke-Gottfries Attitude Interest Schedule (#37) (Marke and Gottfries, 1970).

Other studies have reported significant relationships between the FDCT and measures of masculinity-femininity, including the It Scale for Children (#17) (Lansky and McKay, 1969); the femininity scale of the California Psychological Inventory (#47) and the Welsh Figure Preference Test (#59) (Grant and Domino, 1976); the Figure Drawing Test (#10) (Reed, 1957); and an antifeminist scale (Marke and Gottfries, 1970).

NOTES AND COMMENTS: (1) Several studies have modified the instrument by using an abbreviated form of the FDCT consisting of ten or eleven of the original thirty-six stimuli (Bezdek, 1976; Bezdek and Strodtbeck, 1970; Blane and Chafetz, 1971; Blane and Yamamoto, 1970; Cottle, Edwards, and Pleck, 1970; Lipsitt and Lelos, 1972; Lipsitt and Strodtbeck, 1967; Strodtbeck, Bezdek, and Goldhammer, 1970; Thompson and others, 1973; Wilsnack, 1973). From data obtained by item analysis on all thirty-six stimuli, the chosen stimuli were those shown to have the most discriminating power between the sexes. Another abbreviated form consists of the first twelve stimuli on page one of the FDCT (McCarthy, Anthony, and Domino, 1970; and Urbina and others, 1970).

Two studies have varied the instructional set to include standard, same-sex, and opposite-sex instructions (Bieliauskas, Miranda, and Lansky, 1968; LeLieuvre and Wise, 1974). In these studies that varied instructional set, there were no significant differences in scores between females in the three instructional groups. However, for males, the mean score obtained with opposite-sex instructions was significantly more feminine than the mean score obtained with standard instructions.

(2) Scores on the FDCT have been related to numerous other variables, including: creativity (Grant and Domino, 1976; Suter and Domino, 1975; Urbina and others, 1970); esthetic judgment (Child, 1965); family conflict and dominance (Becker and Iwakami, 1969); family interaction and prediction of school performance (Cottle, 1968); sibling constellation (D'Andrade, 1973; Strodtbeck and Creelan, 1968); paternal masculinity-femininity (Grant and Domino, 1976); perceived paternal similarity (Biller and Barry, 1971); father absence (D'Andrade, 1973); contraceptive use (Kapor-Stanulovic and Lynn, 1972); passive-aggressive and paranoid schizophrenic personalities (Butler and Bieliauskas, 1972); various psychotic personalities (Reed, 1957); husbands with pregnancy symptoms (Munroe and Munroe, 1971); feminism (Bieliauskas, 1974); heterosexuality and homo-sexuality (Thompson and others, 1973); juvenile delinquency (Blane and Chafetz, 1971; Rosenfeld, 1969); alcoholism (Wilsnack, 1973); self-concept (Bieliauskas and Mikesell, 1972); independence and dependence (Lansky and McKay, 1969); Japanese heritage (Blane and Yamamoto, 1970); attitudes toward social and political issues (Cottle, Edwards, and Pleck, 1970); willingness to act (Bezdek, 1976; Bezdek and Strodtbeck, 1970; Strodtbeck, Bezdek, and Goldhammer, 1970).

(3) Given the lack of any reliability data other than interrater reliability, and given the lack of established validity, this instrument is not recommended for use in future research, despite the fact that it has been used extensively in the past.

(4) The instrument is reviewed in the *Fifth Mental Measurements Yearbook* (Buros, 1959, entry 136), and is listed in the *Eighth Mental Measurements Yearbook* (Buros, 1978, entry 562).

SOURCE: Australian Council for Educational Research
            Frederick Street
            Hawthorn, Victoria 3122
            Australia

BIBLIOGRAPHY:

Altucher, N. "Conflict in Sex Identification in Boys." Unpublished doctoral dissertation, University of Michigan, 1956. (*Dissertation Abstracts*, 1958, *18*[4], 1487.)
Becker, J., and Iwakami, E. "Conflict and Dominance Within Families of Disturbed Children." *Journal of Abnormal Psychology*, 1969, *74*, 330-335.
Becker, J., and Siefkes, H. "Parental Dominance, Conflict, and Disciplinary Coerciveness in Families of Female Schizophrenics." *Journal of Abnormal Psychology*, 1969, *74*, 193-198.
Bezdek, W. "Sex Identity, Values, and Balance Theory." *Sociometry*, 1976, *39*, 142-153.
Bezdek, W., and Strodtbeck, F. L. "Sex Role Identity and Pragmatic Action." *American Sociological Review*, 1970, *35*, 491-502.
Bieliauskas, V. J. "A New Look at 'Masculine Protest.' " *Journal of Individual Psychology*, 1974, *30*, 92-97.

Bieliauskas, V. J., and Mikesell, R. H. "Masculinity-Femininity and Self-Concept." *Perceptual and Motor Skills,* 1972, *34,* 163-167.

Bieliauskas, V. J., Miranda, S. B., and Lansky, L. M. "Obviousness of Two Masculinity-Femininity Tests." *Journal of Consulting and Clinical Psychology,* 1968, *32,* 314-318.

Biller, H. B., and Barry, W. "Sex Role Patterns, Paternal Similarity, and Personality Adjustment in College Males." *Developmental Psychology,* 1971, *4,* 107.

Blane, H. T., and Chafetz, M. E. "Dependency Conflict and Sex Role Identity in Drinking Delinquents." *Quarterly Journal of Studies on Alcohol,* 1971, *32,* 1025-1039.

Blane, H. T., and Yamamoto, K. "Sexual Role Identity Among Japanese and Japanese-American High School Students." *Journal of Cross-Cultural Psychology,* 1970, *1,* 345-354.

Bombard, J. A. "An Experimental Examination of Penis Envy." Unpublished doctoral dissertation, Wayne State University, 1969. (*Dissertation Abstracts International,* 1971, *32*[5-B] , 2996.)

*Buros, O. K. *The Fifth Mental Measurements Yearbook.* Highland Park, N.J.: Gryphon Press, 1959.

*Buros, O. K. *The Eighth Mental Measurements Yearbook.* Highland Park, N.J.: Gryphon Press, 1978.

Butler, R. P., and Bieliauskas, V. J. "Performance of Paranoid Schizophrenics and Passive Aggressives on Two Masculinity-Femininity Tests." *Psychological Reports,* 1972, *31,* 251-254.

Child, I. L. "Personality Correlates of Esthetic Judgment in College Students." *Journal of Personality,* 1965, *33,* 476-511.

Colson, D. B. "The Interaction of Sex Role Conflict with the Experimental Manipulation of Masculinity-Femininity Test Scores of College Students." Unpublished doctoral dissertation, University of Cincinnati, 1966. (*Dissertation Abstracts,* 1966, *27*[6-B] , 2131.)

Cottle, T. J. "Family Perceptions, Sex Role Identity, and the Prediction of School Performance." *Educational and Psychological Measurement,* 1968, *28,* 861-886.

Cottle, T. J., Edwards, C. N., and Pleck, J. "The Relationship of Sex Role Identity and Social and Political Attitudes." *Journal of Personality,* 1970, *38,* 435-452.

D'Andrade, R. "Father Absence, Identification, and Identity." *Ethos,* 1973, *1,* 440-445.

Engel, I. M. "A Factor-Analytic Study of Items from Five Masculinity-Femininity Tests." Unpublished doctoral dissertation, University of Michigan, 1962. (*Dissertation Abstracts,* 1962, *23*[1] , 307-308.)

Engel, I. M. "A Factor-Analytic Study of Items from Five Masculinity-Femininity Tests." *Journal of Consulting Psychology,* 1966, *30,* 565.

Feldman, R. C. "A Study of Cognitive Style and Some Personality Variables in Relation to the Conceptual Performance of Emotionally Disturbed Adolescents." Unpublished doctoral dissertation, Temple University, 1965. (*Dissertation Abstracts,* 1965, *26*[3] , 1773-1774.)

Fellows, R., and Cerbus, G. "HTP and DCT Indicators of Sexual Identification in Children." *Journal of Projective Techniques and Personality Assessment,* 1969, *33,* 376-379.

Franck, K., and Rosen, F. "A Projective Test of Masculinity-Femininity." *Journal of Consulting Psychology,* 1949, *13,* 247-256.

Gottfries, I., and Marke, S. "A Study of Stick Figures Test: A Measure of Conformance in Role Perception." *Psychological Research Bulletin,* 1968, *8,* 1-17.

Gottfries, I., and Marke, S. "Dimensions of Masculinity-Femininity Related to Other Personality Variables and Some Measures of School Adjustment." *Psychological Research Bulletin,* 1971, *11,* 1-43.

Grant, T. N., and Domino, G. "Masculinity-Femininity in Fathers of Creative Male Adolescents." *Journal of Genetic Psychology,* 1976, *129,* 19-27.

Harrington, C. C. *Errors in Sex Role Behavior in Teenage Boys.* New York: Teachers College Press, 1970.

Hess, J. G. "Sex Role Development in Psychiatrically Disturbed Adolescent Females and Their Parents." Unpublished doctoral dissertation, University of Rhode Island, 1975. (*Dissertation Abstracts International,* 1976, *37*[1-B], 462.)

Jaskar, R. O., and Reed, M. R. "Assessment of Body-Image Organization of Hospitalized and Nonhospitalized Subjects." *Journal of Projective Techniques and Personality Assessment,* 1963, *27,* 185-190.

Kameya, M. M., and Nadelman, L. *Relationship of Masculinity-Femininity to Dependency and Self-Esteem.* 1972. (ERIC Document Reproduction Service No. ED 087 984.)

Kapor-Stanulovic, N., and Lynn, D. B. "Femininity and Family Planning." *Journal of Sex Research,* 1972, *8,* 286-297.

Kettering, W. R. "The Use of Two Projective Drawing Techniques as Indices of Masculinity and Femininity with Children of Varying Levels of Intelligence." Unpublished doctoral dissertation, University of Pittsburgh, 1965. (*Dissertation Abstracts,* 1966, *27*[3-B], 956-957.)

Lansky, L. M. "The Stability Over Time and Under Stress of Conscious and Unconscious Masculinity-Femininity." *American Psychologist,* 1962, *17,* 302-303.

Lansky, L. M. "The Family Structure Also Affects the Model: Sex Role Attitudes in Parents of Preschool Children." *Merrill-Palmer Quarterly,* 1967, *13,* 139-150.

Lansky, L. M., and McKay, G. "Sex Role Preferences of Kindergarten Boys and Girls: Some Contradictory Results." *Psychological Reports,* 1963, *13,* 415-421.

Lansky, L. M., and McKay, G. "Independence, Dependence, Manifest and Latent Masculinity-Femininity: Some Complex Relationships Among Four Complex Variables." *Psychological Reports,* 1969, *24,* 263-268.

LeLieuvre, R. B., and Wise, D. "Obviousness of Two M-F Tests: A Replication and Extension." *Journal of Social Psychology,* 1974, *93,* 143-144.

Lipinski, B. G. "Sex Role Conflict and Achievement Motivation in College Women." Unpublished doctoral dissertation, University of Cincinnati, 1965. (*Dissertation Abstracts,* 1966, *26*[7], 4077.)

Lipsitt, P. D., and Lelos, D. "The Relationship of Sex Role Identity to Level of Ego Development in Habitual Drug Users." *Proceedings of 80th Annual Convention of the American Psychological Association,* 1972, *7,* 255-256.

Lipsitt, P. D., and Strodtbeck, F. L. "Defensiveness in Decision Making as a Function of Sex Role Identification." *Journal of Personality and Social Psychology,* 1967, *6,* 10-15.

McCarthy, D., Anthony, R. J., and Domino, G. "A Comparison of the CPI, Franck, MMPI, and WAIS Masculinity-Femininity Indexes." *Journal of Consulting and Clinical Psychology,* 1970, *35,* 414-416.

McCaulley, M. H. "Dimensions of Masculinity-Femininity in Relation to Field Dependence, Dogmatism, and Other Estimates of Perceptual-Cognitive Differentiation." Unpublished doctoral dissertation, Temple University, 1964. (*Dissertation Abstracts,* 1965, *25*[7], 4259.)

Marke, S., and Gottfries, I. "Measurement of Masculinity-Femininity." *Psychological Research Bulletin,* 1967, *7,* 1-51.

Marke, S., and Gottfries, I. "Measurement of Sex Role Perception and Its Relation to Psychological Masculinity-Femininity." *Psychological Research Bulletin,* 1970, *10,* 1-33.

Miller, D. R., and Swanson, G. E. *Inner Conflict and Defense.* New York: Schocken Books, 1966.

Munroe, R. L., and Munroe, R. H. "Male Pregnancy Symptoms and Cross-Sex Identity in Three Societies." *Journal of Social Psychology,* 1971, *84,* 11-25.

Nadelman, L. *Sex Identity in American Children: Memory, Knowledge, and Preference Tests.* Ann Arbor: University of Michigan, Department of Psychology, 1973.

Nadelman, L. "Sex Identity in American Children: Memory, Knowledge, and Preference Tests." *Developmental Psychology,* 1974, *10,* 413-417.

Nash, L. J. "Relation Between Sexual Object Choice of Women and Ego Development, Neuroticism, and Conscious and Unconscious Sexual Identity." Unpublished doctoral dissertation, Hofstra University, 1976. (*Dissertation Abstracts International,* 1976, *36*[12-B], 6394.)

Preston, G. A. "Parental Role Perceptions and Identification in Adolescent Girls." Unpublished doctoral dissertation, University of Michigan, 1965. (*Dissertation Abstracts,* 1966, *27*[2-B], 612-613.)

Reed, M. R. "A Study of the Masculinity-Femininity Dimension of Personality in 'Normal' and 'Pathological' Groups: An Investigation of Differences in M-F Test Productions of Hospitalized and Nonhospitalized Women." Unpublished doctoral dissertation, Washington University, 1955. (*Dissertation Abstracts,* 1955, *15*[8], 1442-1443.)

Reed, M. R. "The Masculinity-Femininity Dimension in Normal and Psychotic Subjects." *Journal of Abnormal and Social Psychology,* 1957, *55,* 289-294.

Rosenberg, E. S. "Some Psychological and Biological Relationships Between Masculinity and Femininity and Field Dependence and Field Independence." Unpublished doctoral dissertation, Northwestern University, 1975. (*Dissertation Abstracts International,* 1976, *36*[12-B], 6453.)

Rosenfeld, H. M. "Delinquent Acting Out in Adolescent Males and Its Relationship to the Task of Sexual Identification." Unpublished doctoral dissertation, School for Social Work, Smith College, 1967. (*Dissertation Abstracts,* 1968, *28*[10-B], 4301.)

Rosenfeld, H. M. "Delinquent Acting Out in Adolescent Males and the Task of Sexual Identification." *Smith College Studies in Social Work,* 1969, *40,* 1-29.

Rothstein, A. "Depression in Pregnancy as It Relates to Feminine Identification Conflict and Perceived Environmental Support." Unpublished doctoral dissertation, School for Social Work, Smith College, 1971. (*Dissertation Abstracts International,* 1972, *32*[9-A], 5347.)

Sanford, N. *Self and Society: Social Change and Individual Development.* New York: Atherton Press, 1966.

Shepler, B. F. "A Comparison of Masculinity-Femininity Measures." *Journal of Consulting Psychology,* 1951, *15,* 484-486.

Small, A. C. "Sex Role Development in Psychiatrically Disturbed Adolescent Males and Their Parents." Unpublished doctoral dissertation, University of Rhode Island, 1974. (*Dissertation Abstracts International,* 1974, *35*[5-B], 2448-2449.)

Strassburger, F. "Perception and Fantasy: A Study of Sex Differences and Personality

Correlates." Unpublished doctoral dissertation, Stanford University, 1963. (*Dissertation Abstracts,* 1964, *24*[8] , 3417-3418.)

Strodtbeck, F. L., and Creelan, P. G. "The Interaction Linkage Between Family Size, Intelligence, and Sex Role Identity." *Journal of Marriage and the Family,* 1968, *30,* 301-307.

Strodtbeck, F. L., Bezdek, W., and Goldhammer, D. "Male Sex Role and Response to a Community Problem." *Sociological Quarterly,* 1970, *11,* 291-306.

Suter, B. A. "Masculinity-Femininity in Creative Women." Unpublished doctoral dissertation, Fordham University, 1971. (*Dissertation Abstracts International,* 1971, *32*[4-B], 2411.)

Suter, B. A., and Domino, G. "Masculinity-Femininity in Creative College Women." *Journal of Personality Assessment,* 1975, *39,* 414-420.

Thompson, N. L., Jr. "Family Background and Sexual Identity in Male and Female Homosexuals." Unpublished doctoral dissertation, Emory University, 1971. (*Dissertation Abstracts International,* 1971, *32*[3-B] , 1863.)

Thompson, N. L., Jr., Schwartz, D. M., McCandless, B. R., and Edwards, D. A. "Parent-Child Relationships and Sexual Identity in Male and Female Homosexuals and Heterosexuals." *Journal of Consulting and Clinical Psychology,* 1973, *41,* 120-127.

Urbina, S., Harrison, J. B., Schaefer, C. E., and Anastasi, A. "Relationship Between Masculinity-Femininity and Creativity as Measured by the Franck Drawing Completion Test." *Psychological Reports,* 1970, *26,* 799-804.

Webster, H. "Personality Development During the College Years: Some Quantitative Results." *Journal of Social Issues,* 1956, *12,* 29-43.

Wilsnack, S. C. "Sex Role Identity in Female Alcoholism." *Journal of Abnormal Psychology,* 1973, *82,* 253-261.

Winer, F. "The Relationship of Certain Attitudes Toward the Mother to Sex Role Identity." Unpublished doctoral dissertation, New York University, 1961. (*Dissertation Abstracts,* 1962, *22*[11] , 4416.)

Woudenberg, R. A. "The Relationship of Sexual Attitudes, Sexual Stereotypes, Racial-Sexual Stereotypes, and Racial Attitudes." Unpublished doctoral dissertation, Michigan State University, 1973. (*Dissertation Abstracts International,* 1974, *34*[6-B] , 2958.)

Wrchota, R. J. "Oral Passive Aims in Acting-Out Adolescent Girls in Relationship to the Developmental Task of Sexual Identification." Unpublished doctoral dissertation, School for Social Work, Smith College, 1973. (*Dissertation Abstracts International,* 1974, *34*[9-A] , 6114.)

12. GAMES AND ACTIVITIES PREFERENCE LIST (GAP)

AUTHOR: Monroe M. Lefkowitz

DATE: 1962

VARIABLE: Sex role preference

TYPE OF INSTRUMENT: Forced choice

DESCRIPTION: The test consists of eleven pairs of items; each item is the name of a game or play activity.

PREVIOUSLY ADMINISTERED TO: Grades 3 and 4

APPROPRIATE FOR: Ages 7-12

ADMINISTRATION: The test can be group administered. The first pair is written on the blackboard and used to explain how responses are to be made. The children are directed to circle the one item in each pair which they would prefer to do.

SAMPLE ITEMS: Go shooting [versus] Go bowling
Play follow the leader [versus] Play dodgeball

SCORING: The test yields a measure of sex role preference for girls based on the responses to seven pairs of items. The measure of sex role preference for boys is based on responses to nine pairs of items.

Children are labeled as deviant if they respond to at least one pair by selecting the item that was chosen by fewer than 10 percent of the children of their same sex.

DEVELOPMENT: Items were suggested from the studies of Rosenberg and Sutton-Smith (#4) and Brown (#17). In addition, the author added items he deemed appropriate. The eleven pairs of items were given to 432 boys and 403 girls in grades 3 and 4. In any case where one item of a pair was selected by more than 90 percent of the children of a given sex, that pair was assigned to the sex role preference scale for that sex. In nine item pairs, over 90 percent of the boys chose the same item. Thus the sex role preference scale for boys includes nine pairs. In seven pairs of items, over 90 percent of the girls chose the same item. Thus the scale for girls includes seven pairs.

RELIABILITY: Item-total correlations for the seven items on the girls' scale ranged from .40 to .71 with a median of .58. Item-total correlations for the nine items on the boys' scale ranged from .19 to .58 with a median of .41.

VALIDITY: In addition to completing the GAP, 418 boys and 390 girls completed the Figure Drawing (#10). Lefkowitz found that a significantly higher proportion (p < .05) of deviant boys, compared with nondeviant boys, drew the opposite-sex figure first on the Figure Drawing. A higher proportion of deviant girls, compared with nondeviant girls, also drew the opposite-sex figure first, but the results were not significant.

NOTES AND COMMENTS: The scale is also described in *Tests and Measurements in Child Development: Handbook I* (Johnson and Bommarito, 1971, p. 439).

SOURCE: See Lefkowitz, 1962.

BIBLIOGRAPHY:

*Johnson, O. G., and Bommarito, J. W. *Tests and Measurements in Child Development: Handbook I.* San Francisco: Jossey-Bass, 1971.
Lefkowitz, M. M. "Some Relationships Between Sex Role Preference of Children and Other Parent and Child Variables." *Psychological Reports,* 1962, *10,* 43-53.

---

13. GAMES INVENTORY

AUTHORS: John E. Bates and P. M. Bentler

DATE: 1973

VARIABLE: Gender deviance in boys

TYPE OF INSTRUMENT: Checklist

DESCRIPTION: The Games Inventory consists of three scales with a total of sixty-four games and play activities. Scale 1 contains thirty items that are considered feminine unless played by preschoolers or those in the early grades; scale 2 consists of twenty-two items representing masculine, nonathletic games; and scale 3 contains twelve competitive, athletic games.

PREVIOUSLY ADMINISTERED TO: Mothers who rated their sons ages 5-12

APPROPRIATE FOR: Parents of sons ages 5-12

ADMINISTRATION: The child's parent is directed to circle "yes" for items the child regularly plays and "no" for items the child rarely or never plays.

SAMPLE ITEMS: *Feminine, preschool:* play school, sing songs
Masculine, nonathletic: card games, play spaceman
Competitive, athletic: basketball, foot races

SCORING: The individual scales—that is, scales 1, 2, and 3—are scored by counting 1 point for each "yes" response. A total score is obtained by counting 1 point for each "yes" response on scale 1 and 1 point for each "no" response on scales 2 and 3.

DEVELOPMENT: The mothers of 173 normal boys and the mothers of 18 boys referred for gender identification problems completed the Gender Behavior Inventory for Boys

(#14) and a 120-item games inventory. Items on the games inventory that correlated .2 with Factor I, Effeminacy, on the Gender Behavior Inventory and did not correlate that highly with the other two factors of the Gender Behavior Inventory were selected for scale 1 of the Games Inventory. Likewise, items that correlated .2 with Factor II, Extraversion, on the Gender Behavior Inventory and did not correlate that highly with the other two factors of the Gender Behavior Inventory were selected for scale 2 of the Games Inventory. Items were selected for scale 3 if they correlated −.2 with Factor I and +.2 with Factor II of the Gender Behavior Inventory.

RELIABILITY: The Kuder-Richardson reliabilities were .85, .74, and .83 for scales 1, 2, and 3, respectively. For total score, the Kuder-Richardson reliability was .72. Using coefficient θ to measure internal consistency, values of .97, .94, and .93 were obtained for scales 1, 2, and 3, respectively.

VALIDITY: Since the items on the Games Inventory were selected for their relationship to the Gender Behavior Inventory (#14), it was expected that scores on the two measures should be correlated. By using the data for sixty-six boys—who were not involved in the instrument's development—it was found that scale 1 on the Games Inventory correlated .37 (p < .01) with Factor I on the Gender Behavior Inventory; and scale 2 correlated .22 (p < .05) with Factor II. Scale 3 correlated .28 (p < .05) with Factor II, but correlated negatively (nonsignificant) with Factor I. Scale 4, total score on the Games Inventory, correlated significantly with Factors I and II of the Gender Behavior Inventory.

Clinical psychology students rated eighteen boys who had been referred for gender disturbances and for whom there were data on the Games Inventory. They rated the boys on two variables: degree of gender disturbance and extraversion. Ratings on both variables correlated moderately (nonsignificant) with both scales 1 and 2. Clinical ratings of gender disturbance were significantly correlated (p < .01) with both scales 3 and 4.

The scores for the eighteen boys referred for gender disturbance and eighteen matched controls (whose data had not been used in development) were compared. On all four scales, there was a significant difference (p < .05) between the two groups.

NOTES AND COMMENTS: Intercorrelations between the scales suggest that the only orthogonal relationship is between scales 1 and 3.

SOURCE: See Bates and Bentler, 1973.

BIBLIOGRAPHY:

Bates, J. E., and Bentler, P. M. "Play Activities of Normal and Effeminate Boys." *Developmental Psychology,* 1973, *9,* 20-27.

14. GENDER BEHAVIOR INVENTORY FOR BOYS

AUTHORS: John E. Bates, P. M. Bentler, and Spencer K. Thompson

DATE: 1973

VARIABLE: Gender deviance in boys

TYPE OF INSTRUMENT: Rating scale

DESCRIPTION: The scale consists of fifty-five short sentences, each of which describes some behavior. The fifty-five items are grouped into four factors: Feminine Behavior (eighteen items), Extraversion (fourteen items), Behavior Disturbance (seventeen items), and Mother's Boy (six items). Each item is followed by either a five-point scale or an eight-point scale indicating frequency of occurrence. On the five-point scale, the responses range from "always" to "never"; on the eight-point scale, the responses range from "daily" to "once every six months or less."

PREVIOUSLY ADMINISTERED TO: Mothers who rated their sons ages 5-12

APPROPRIATE FOR: Parents of sons ages 5-12

ADMINISTRATION: The parent is directed to indicate, for each item, the response that best describes her son.

SAMPLE ITEMS: *Feminine Behavior:* He is good at imitating females.
　　　　　　　　Extraversion: He likes people.
　　　　　　　　Behavior Disturbance: He acts defiant when given orders.
　　　　　　　　Mother's Boy: He dresses sloppily.

SCORING: Items are objectively scored. Items with five response options can contribute up to 5 points to the score; items with eight response options can contribute up to 8 points to the score. Total scores are obtained for each of the three factors.

DEVELOPMENT: The item pool consisted of 173 items concerning children's play patterns, interests, aggressiveness, mannerisms, relationships with parents, and emotional behavior. Data were obtained from the mothers of 175 normal boys and 15 boys referred for gender identity problems. A factor analysis was performed, and four factors emerged: (I) Feminine Behavior; (II) Extraversion; (III) Behavior Disturbance; and (IV) Mother's Boy. The items loading on these four factors were retained for the scale.

RELIABILITY: Using the data supplied by forty-five mothers, coefficient θ was computed to determine the internal consistency of each of the four scales. The values were .78, .86, .96, and .71 for Factors I-IV, respectively (Bates, Bentler, and Thompson, 1973).

VALIDITY: The scale was administered to the mothers of twenty-three normal boys and twenty-three boys suspected of gender identity problems. The means for the two groups were significantly different ($p < .001$) for Factors I, II, and III. The difference between means was not significant for Factor IV (Bates, Bentler, and Thompson, 1973).

Two clinical psychology students ranked twenty-two boys referred for gender identity problems. The clinicians' rankings were compared with the mothers' responses to the Gender Behavior Inventory. Clinicians' rankings on Factor I correlated .56 with scores on Factor I; clinicians' rankings on Factor II correlated .14 with scores on Factor II; clinicians' rankings on Factor III correlated .02 with Factor III (Bates, Bentler, and Thompson, 1973).

The Games Inventory (#13), a measure of gender deviance in boys, and the Gender Behavior Inventory for Boys were both completed by the mothers of sixty-six boys. Because the items on the Games Inventory were selected for their relationship to the Gender Behavior Inventory, it was expected that scores on the two measures would be correlated. Factor I on the Gender Behavior Inventory correlated .37 ($p < .01$) with scale 1 on the Games Inventory, but it correlated negatively with scale 3; Factor II correlated .22 ($p < .05$) with scale 2 and .28 ($p < .05$) with scale 3. Factors I and II both correlated significantly with the total score on the Games Inventory.

NOTES AND COMMENTS: Correlations among the factors suggested that Factors II and IV may not be independent.

SOURCE: See Bates, Bentler, and Thompson, 1973.

BIBLIOGRAPHY:

Bates, J. E., and Bentler, P. M. "Play Activities of Normal and Effeminate Boys." *Developmental Psychology,* 1973, *9,* 20-27.
Bates, J. E., Bentler, P. M., and Thompson, S. K. "Measurement of Deviant Gender Development in Boys." *Child Development,* 1973, *44,* 591-598.

---

15. GROUP TOY PREFERENCE TEST

AUTHOR: Nicholas J. Anastasiow

DATE: 1963

VARIABLE: Sex role preference

TYPE OF INSTRUMENT: Forced choice picture preference

DESCRIPTION: This is a paper-and-pencil test consisting of forty-five pairs of pictures of toys. There are a total of ten different toys, with each toy being paired with each of the other toys. Half of the toys are considered masculine (soldier, fire engine, gun, blocks, and truck) and half feminine (beads, doll, purse, dishes, and comb and brush). Each picture is placed on the right of the pair about half the time and on the left about half the time. (Perfect balance in terms of right-left position is impossible due to the uneven number of pairs.)

PREVIOUSLY ADMINISTERED TO: Ages 3-10

APPROPRIATE FOR: Ages 3-10

ADMINISTRATION: This is a group administered test in which the children are directed to mark for each pair the toy they would prefer to play with.

SCORING: Five of the pictures comprise the masculine scale and the other five pictures comprise the feminine scale. Each picture has a specified weight assigned to it. The weights for the masculine toy pictures range from zero to four. The weights for the feminine toy pictures range from one to five. For each choice the child makes, she is assigned points equal to the weight assigned to that toy. Masculine toy choices earn points on the masculine scale; feminine toy choices earn points on the feminine scale. Since some item pairs consist of a masculine toy paired with a masculine toy and some item pairs consist of a feminine toy paired with a feminine toy, every child is forced to choose at least some masculine toys and some feminine toys. As a result, each child obtains both a masculine and a feminine score. The maximum masculine score is 80 and the maximum feminine score is 115. If a choice is indicated for each pair, the minimum masculine score is 10 and the minimum feminine score is 20.

DEVELOPMENT: Five masculine toys and five feminine toys were selected that differentiated between boys and girls at the .001 level in Rabban's (1950) research. After the instrument was assembled, it was administered to sixty boys and sixty girls in kindergarten. The total number of times an item was chosen by the inappropriate sex was subtracted from the total number of times it was selected by the appropriate sex. This provided an indication of the relative sex typing of a toy. The difference scores were used to rank order the masculine toys and the feminine toys. Scoring weights were assigned on the basis of these ranks. Thus, the highest scoring weight on the masculine scale was assigned to the toy that had the largest difference score when the number of girls choosing the toy was subtracted from the number of boys choosing the toy.

RELIABILITY: To determine the consistency of the group's choices, fifty-eight boys and fifty-six girls from the group on which the test was developed were retested after a four-month interval. The rank correlation for the toy choices was .96 (Anastasiow, 1963). Test-retest reliability was estimated by using the fall and spring scores obtained by twenty-five boys. The correlation was .81 (Anastasiow, 1963).

VALIDITY: The test was administered to 229 boys ages 5 and 6. Distributions of masculine and feminine scores were constructed and quartile points were identified. Twenty-nine boys were identified as "high masculine" because they satisfied the following criteria: masculine score at or above the third quartile on the masculine distribution, feminine score below the first quartile on the feminine distribution, and no feminine toy choices other than those made when a feminine toy was paired with a feminine toy. Thirty-nine boys were identified as "feminine" because their feminine score was at or above the third quartile on the feminine distribution and their masculine score was below the first quartile on the masculine distribution. Thirty boys were identified as "median" because their scores on both distributions were within one half standard deviation from the mean. The three groups of boys—high masculine, feminine, and median—were administered the Sears Toy Preference Test (#26) and Sears Activity Preference Test (#25) and were rated on masculinity by their teachers. On the Sears Activity Preference Test (#25), feminine boys made feminine choices significantly more often than the high masculine or median groups (p < .001). The following results were obtained on the Sears Toy Preference Test (#26): feminine and median boys selected a feminine toy (before it was paired with a feminine toy) significantly more often than masculine boys; there were no significant differences among the groups in terms of playing with feminine toys. There were no significant differences between the ratings of masculinity assigned to high masculine boys and to feminine boys (Anastasiow, 1963, 1965). Additional information regarding the validity of the instrument can be obtained by looking at the results of Biller's (1967, 1968) study, in which he used this instrument along with the Biller Game Preference Test (#2), which is another measure of sex role preference. Using the data obtained from 186 kindergarten boys, he found that the correlation between the two measures was .75. Biller also used the It Scale (#17) and the Figure Drawing (#10), which he claims are measures of sex role orientation. As he predicted, the correlations between the Group Toy Preference Test and each of the measures of sex role orientation were lower (.10 for Figure Drawing and .23 for It Scale) than the correlation between the two measures of sex role preference.

Biller also used the Biller Sex Role Adoption Rating Scale (#3). The correlation between the Group Toy Preference Test and the rating scale was .29. This is also consistent with Biller's expectation that a sex role preference scale should correlate lower with a measure of sex role adoption than it does with a second measure of sex role preference.

NOTES AND COMMENTS: (1) Anastasiow does not report whether an attempt was made to balance the size, attractiveness, and manipulative potential between masculine-typed and feminine-typed toys.

(2) Some researchers have combined scores from the Group Toy Preference Test with scores on the Biller Game Preference Test (#2) to arrive at an overall sex role preferences score (Biller, 1967, 1968, 1969; Biller, Singer, and Fullerton, 1969; and Flammer, 1971).

(3) Scores on the Group Toy Preference Test have been compared with other variables, including sex (Flammer, 1971; Laosa and Brophy, 1971, 1972); age (Piercy, 1976); intelligence (Biller, 1967, 1968; Piercy, 1976); creativity (Biller, Singer, and Fullerton, 1969); achievement (Anastasiow, 1963, 1965); teacher ratings of school success (Anastasiow, 1963, 1965); self-esteem (Flammer, 1971); parent identification (Flammer, 1971); birth order (Laosa and Brophy, 1971, 1972); father dominance (Biller, 1967, 1968, 1969); father availability (Biller, 1967, 1968); maternal encouragement of assertive, aggressive, and independent behavior (Biller, 1967, 1968); physique (Biller, 1967, 1968); and socioeconomic status (Biller, Singer, and Fullerton, 1969).

SOURCE: See Anastasiow, 1963 or 1965; or ETS Tests in Microfiche (#004293).

BIBLIOGRAPHY:

Anastasiow, N. J. "The Relationship of Sex Role Patterns of First-Grade Boys to Success in School." Unpublished doctoral dissertation, Stanford University, 1963. (*Dissertation Abstracts,* 1964, *25* [1], 278-279.)

Anastasiow, N. J. "Success in School and Boys' Sex Role Patterns." *Child Development,* 1965, *36,* 1053-1066.

Biller, H. B. "An Exploratory Investigation of Masculine Development in Kindergarten-Age Boys." Unpublished doctoral dissertation, Duke University, 1967. (*Dissertation Abstracts,* 1968, *28* [10-B], 4290.)

Biller, H. B. "A Multiaspect Investigation of Masculine Development in Kindergarten-Age Boys." *Genetic Psychology Monographs,* 1968, *78,* 89-138.

Biller, H. B. "Father Dominance and Sex Role Development in Kindergarten-Age Boys." *Developmental Psychology,* 1969, *1,* 87-94.

Biller, H. B., Singer, D. L., and Fullerton, M. "Sex Role Development and Creative Potential in Kindergarten-Age Boys." *Developmental Psychology,* 1969, *1,* 291-296.

Brophy, J. E., and Laosa, L. M. "The Effect of a Male Teacher on the Sex Typing of Kindergarten Children." *Journal Supplement Abstract Service Catalog of Selected Documents in Psychology,* 1973, *3,* 44.

Flammer, D. P. "Self-Esteem, Parent Identification, and Sex Role Development in Pre-school-Age Boys and Girls." *Child Study Journal,* 1971, *2,* 39-45.

Laosa, L. M., and Brophy, J. E. "Effects of Sex and Birth Order on Sex Role Development and Intelligence in Kindergarten Children." Paper presented at 17th annual meeting of the Southwestern Psychological Association, San Antonio, Texas, April 1971. (ERIC Document Reproduction Service No. ED 053 403.)

Laosa, L. M., and Brophy, J. E. "Effects of Sex and Birth Order on Sex Role Development and Intelligence Among Kindergarten Children." *Developmental Psychology,* 1972, *6,* 409-415.

Piercy, P. A. "The Relationship of Cognitive Functioning to the Development of Sex Role in Black Male Children Ages Four to Ten." Unpublished doctoral dissertation, Adelphi University, 1976. (*Dissertation Abstracts International,* 1976, *37*[4-B], 1974.)

*Rabban, M. "Sex Role Identification in Young Children in Two Diverse Social Groups." *Genetic Psychology Monographs,* 1950, *42,* 81-158.

---

16. INDIVIDUAL SEX ROLE PREFERENCE CHECKLIST

AUTHOR: Carol Anne Dwyer

DATE: 1974

VARIABLE: Sex role preference

TYPE OF INSTRUMENT: Checklist

DESCRIPTION: The test consists of forty-six items, each of which is an activity or an object. Ten items relate to reading, ten relate to arithmetic, and the remaining twenty-six relate to other areas. There are three response options per item: L (like), ? (can't decide), and D (dislike).

PREVIOUSLY ADMINISTERED TO: Grades 2, 4, 6, 8, 10, and 12

APPROPRIATE FOR: Ages 7-18

ADMINISTRATION: The test is group administered. The children are directed to circle their response (L, ?, D) for each item. For second graders, the examiner reads each item aloud and allows the children time to respond after each item is read.

SAMPLE ITEMS: Counting change
Reading magazines
Playing football

SCORING: There are three scores from this test: a reading preference score, an arithmetic preference score, and a sex role conformity score. Only the last score is of interest here. In scoring for sex role conformity, the child is assigned points if her/his response was consistent with the response given by the majority of her/his sex.

DEVELOPMENT: This instrument, which was modeled after the Sex Role Standards Questionnaire (#76), was given twice to the same 385 children in grades 2 through 12. In the first administration it was used as a measure of sex standards, and the children were asked to indicate whether boys, girls, or both like each item. The results from this administration were used to determine whether each item should be classified as masculine or feminine when the items were used to measure sex role preference.

RELIABILITY: No data are provided.

VALIDITY: Dwyer compared scores from the Individual Sex Role Preference Checklist with scores from tests of reading and arithmetic achievement. Contrary to prediction, there was no relationship between the scores.

NOTES AND COMMENTS: Given the absence of evidence regarding the reliability and validity of the instrument, there is no basis for using it at this time.

SOURCE: Carol Dwyer
Educational Testing Service
Princeton, New Jersey 08540

BIBLIOGRAPHY:

Dwyer, C. A. "Influence of Children's Sex Role Standards on Reading and Arithmetic Achievement." *Journal of Educational Psychology,* 1974, *66,* 811-816.

17. IT SCALE FOR CHILDREN (ITSC)

AUTHOR: Daniel G. Brown

DATE: 1956

VARIABLE: Sex role preference

TYPE OF INSTRUMENT: Picture preference

DESCRIPTION: The test consists of three parts. Part 1 contains drawings of sixteen toys, eight of which are stereotypically masculine (tractor, dump truck, train engine, rifle, pocket knife, soldiers, earthmover, and racing car) and eight of which are stereotypically feminine (cradle, dishes, doll buggy, necklace, doll, purse, high chair, and baby bath). Part 2 consists of drawings of eight pairs of pictures of objects or people. In each pair, one item is considered masculine (Indian chief, male clothing, airplane parts, shaving articles, mechanical tools, men's shoes, boys playing, and building tools) and one is considered feminine (Indian princess, dress, sewing materials, cosmetic articles, household objects, women's shoes, girls playing, and baking articles). Part 3 consists of four drawings: a girl, a boy, a girl dressed as a boy, and a boy dressed as a girl. In addition, there is a drawing of a child that is intended to be ambiguous as to sex and is referred to as "It." All drawings are in black on 3" x 4" white cards.

PREVIOUSLY ADMINISTERED TO: Ages 3-12; teenage and adult retardates

APPROPRIATE FOR: Ages 3-8

ADMINISTRATION: After the child is seated at a small table, she is shown the "It" figure. Part 1 is administered by displaying all sixteen pictures in front of the child and asking "Which toy would 'It' like the best?" The procedure is repeated until the child has made eight choices. Part 2 is administered by showing the child one pair of pictures at a time. For each pair, the child is asked to indicate which "It" would prefer to do (or be, or have, depending on the nature of the pictures). In Part 3, the child is asked to indicate which one of the four pictures "It" would rather be. Administration time is typically seven to eight minutes.

SCORING: Items are objectively scored but differentially weighted across sections. No explanation is provided for the different item weights. Total scores can range from 0 (all feminine choices on all parts) to 84 (all masculine choices on all parts).

DEVELOPMENT: In constructing the scale, Brown (1956) considered the behavior patterns typically associated with male and female roles in American society. Objects, activities, and people associated with the male role were selected and scored as masculine; objects, activities, and people associated with the female role were selected and scored as feminine. The "It" figure was included to provide an indirect, projective measure of sex role preference. Pilot testing using a more direct approach to elicit sex role preferences suggested that children were likely to respond in terms of social norms rather than their own preferences. The use of the "It" figure was intended to overcome this problem.

RELIABILITY: Brown (1956) used the data obtained from seventy-eight kindergarten boys and sixty-eight kindergarten girls to estimate test-retest reliability. The interval between the two testings was approximately one month. Brown obtained rank-difference coefficients of .69 for boys and .82 for girls.

Other researchers have also determined the test-retest reliability of the ITSC. Borstelmann (1961) obtained data from thirty-two boys and thirty girls, with a median age of 4 years 2 months. The test-retest reliability coefficient was .80 for boys and .64 for girls. Dixit (1971) administered the ITSC on two occasions to a sample of thirty-three girls and forty-five boys, ages 3 to 5, in India. The interval between testings was thirty days. Test-retest reliability was .67 for boys and .72 for girls. Kobasigawa (1959) administered the ITSC on two occasions to 207 Okinawan children with a mean age of 6 years. The interval between testings was one month. Test-retest reliability was .91.

Feinman and Ross (1975) used the data obtained from thirty-eight boys and thirty-nine girls, in preschool through second grade, to determine the homogeneity of the ITSC. They obtained alpha coefficients of .64 for boys and .88 for girls.

Other researchers have estimated the split-half reliability of the ITSC. Using data obtained from 186 five-year-old boys, all enrolled in kindergarten classes, Biller (1968a) calculated the corrected, split-half reliability and obtained a value of .89. Using the data from thirty-four five-year-old kindergarten boys, Biller (1969a) calculated the corrected, split-half reliability to be .83. LaVoie and Andrews (1975) obtained data from seventy middle-class white children, ages 3 through 9. They calculated the corrected, split-half reliability to be .86.

VALIDITY: Using the data obtained from seventy-eight kindergarten boys and sixty-eight kindergarten girls, Brown (1956) found that the mean score for boys ($\overline{X}$ = 66.36) was significantly higher than the mean score for girls ($\overline{X}$ = 38.40, p < .01). Numerous other studies have also found that boys score significantly higher (more masculine) than girls on the ITSC (Biller and Borstelmann, 1965; Borstelmann, 1961; Brown, 1957b; Clark, 1963a; Dixit, 1971; Domash and Balter, 1976; Duryea, 1967; Fling and Manosevitz, 1972; Frueh and McGhee, 1975; Hall and Keith, 1964; Hartup, 1962; Hartup and Zook, 1960; Kobasigawa, 1959; Kohlberg and Zigler, 1967; Lansky and McKay, 1969; Laosa and Brophy, 1972; LaVoie and Andrews, 1975; Montgomery and Landers, 1974; Schell and Silber, 1968; Sher and Lansky, 1968; Thompson and McCandless, 1970; and Ward, 1972). Also, Fling and Manosevitz (1972) found that the mean of the boys' mothers' scores was significantly higher than that of the girls' mothers' scores (p < .001). Similarly the mean of the boys' fathers' scores was significantly higher than that of the girls' fathers' scores (p < .005). Contrary to what is typically found, a study conducted by Ward (1973) did not find significant differences between mean scores for boys and girls.

Despite the fact that boys typically score higher than girls, many studies have shown that girls tend to score in the masculine range, that is, between 42 and 84 (Brown, 1957b; Clark, 1963a; Doll, Fagot, and Himbert, 1973; Domash and Balter, 1976; Fling and Manosevitz, 1972; Frueh and McGhee, 1975; Hall and Keith, 1964; Hartup, Moore, and Sager, 1963; Hetherington, 1965; Kohlberg and Zigler, 1967; Mussen and Rutherford, 1963; Schell and Silber, 1968; Thompson and McCandless, 1970; and Ward, 1972, 1973). Results of these studies suggest that the ITSC may not be an adequate measure of sex role preference in girls.

Biller (1968a) considers the ITSC to be a measure of sex role orientation. He predicted that the correlation between two measures of sex role orientation would be higher than the correlations between a measure of sex role orientation and measures of sex role preference or adoption. Biller tested 186 kindergarten boys with five scales: two measures of sex role orientation (ITSC and Figure Drawing—#10), two measures of sex role preference (Biller Game Preference Test—#2—and Group Toy Preference Test—#15), and one measure of sex role adoption (Biller Sex Role Adoption Ratings—#3). The correlation between the two sex role orientation scores was .58. The correlations between ITSC and each of the other measures were: Biller Game Preference Test = .27; Group Toy Preference Test = .23; Biller Sex Role Adoption Ratings = .11. As can be seen, Biller's prediction was supported.

NOTES AND COMMENTS: (1) The ITSC procedures have been modified in many of the studies where it was used. One of the most popular variations, developed by Lansky and McKay (1963), involves keeping the It figure concealed in an envelope throughout the administration of the test. Respondents are asked to make choices for the child in the envelope, and upon completion of the test, they are asked to guess whether It was a boy or a girl. This modification has been used in numerous studies (Doll, Fagot, and Himbert, 1971, 1973; Domash, 1973; Endsley, 1967; Lansky and McKay, 1969; LaVoie and Andrews, 1975, 1976; Montgomery and Landers, 1974; Sher and Lansky, 1968; Thompson and McCandless, 1970; Ward, 1972, 1973). Another variation of the ITSC that has been extensively used was developed by Biller (1968b). In Biller's modification only the face of the It figure is presented to the child. Research using this method has been done by Biller (1969a, 1969b), Biller, Singer, and Fullerton (1969), Dill and others (1975), Laosa and Brophy (1972), and Radin (1972).

Hartup and Zook (1960) added two different instructional sets to the standard instructions. In one, the It figure was referred to as the same sex as the respondent, and in the other, the examiner used the respondent's name to refer to the It figure. The former instructions were also used by Thompson and McCandless (1970), and both of these instructional sets were used by Hartup, Moore, and Sager (1963).

Many other modifications of the scale have been used: the child makes only same-sex or opposite-sex choices (Reed and Asbjornsen, 1968; Schell and Silber, 1968); the child makes choices directly for herself (Biller and Borstelmann, 1965; Fling and Manosevitz, 1972; Sher and Lansky, 1968); the child draws a picture of a child, which is then used as the projective figure (Summers and Felker, 1970); a blank card is substituted for the It figure, and the child is instructed to pretend that a child named "It" is on the card (Dickstein and Seymour, 1977; Fling and Manosevitz, 1972; Perry and Perry, 1975); neutral (not sex typed) items have been added to the first two parts of the scale (Dickstein and Seymour, 1977); the eight least sex-differentiating pictures have been eliminated from the first part of the scale (Kohlberg and Zigler, 1967; Radin, 1972); when the children are preschoolers, the sixteen pictured toys are presented in four groups of four rather than in one group of sixteen (Hartup, 1962; Hartup and Zook, 1960); the sixteen pictured toys are presented in two groups of eight to preschoolers (Thompson and McCandless, 1970) or retardates (Clark, 1963a, 1963b); paper-and-pencil group administration procedure is used (Duryea, 1967); parents complete the ITSC and indicate which items they prefer for their children (Fling and Manosevitz, 1972).

(2) Comparison of standard ITSC and modified versions: Sher and Lansky (1968) found that preschool girls attributed "boy" to the unconcealed It more than preschool boys attributed "girl" to the unconcealed It (p < .001). Among those children who made an own-sex attribution during the concealed version of the ITSC, girls changed their attributions upon seeing the It figure more than boys changed their attributions (p < .025).

Fling and Manosevitz (1972) studied thirty-two four-year-old children and learned that more children labeled the standard It figure as a boy (p < .001). This finding was not related to the sex of the respondents. In contrast, the imaginary It was not labeled more often as one sex than the other, and its labeling was related to the sex of the respondents (p < .001).

Using the data obtained from sixty-four preschoolers, Schell and Silber (1968) found that although boys had more masculine scores ($\overline{X}$ = 56.0) than girls ($\overline{X}$ = 42.5) when the figure was identified as It, girls had more feminine scores ($\overline{X}$ = 19.8) than boys ($\overline{X}$ = 32.8) when the figure was identified as a "little girl." In the Hartup and Zook (1960) study using preschoolers, girls in the standard ITSC administration group obtained significantly less feminine scores than girls in the group in which the figure was referred to as a girl (p < .01) and girls in the group in which the experimenter used the child's name to refer to the It figure (p < .01). Similarly, boys in the standard administration group obtained less masculine scores than boys in the group in which the It figure was referred to by the child's name (p < .05).

Doll, Fagot, and Himbert (1973) obtained data from 240 girls, ages 6, 9, and 12, and found that scores on the standard version were more masculine than scores on the concealed version (p < .001).

The findings reported above suggest that the It figure does contain masculine cues. Contrary to this evidence, Endsley (1967) found no significant differences for preschoolers between the mean ITSC score on the concealed version and the mean ITSC score on the standard version. Furthermore, based on data from their preschool sample, Reed and Asbjornsen (1968) found that although boys perceived the It figure as ambiguous, girls perceived it as female (p < .02). The correlation between scores on the It-figure and child-drawn figure administrations in the Summers and Felker (1970) study was .842 for boys and .567 for girls. The mean difference in scores on these two administrations was not significant for boys or girls. Sher and Lansky (1968) found no significant difference between means obtained from a group of boys and girls using the concealed version of the ITSC and a group using the standard version. Dickstein and Seymour (1977) found that boys scored significantly higher on the standard It scale than on the modified version with neutral items added (p < .001), and the mean scores for girls on the two scales did not differ significantly. Lansky and McKay (1963) found that for the concealed version of the ITSC, the mean score for boys who guessed that the concealed It was a boy was 58.0, while the mean for boys who guessed It was a girl was 31.3. The difference between these means was statistically significant (p < .002).

Duryea (1967) studied first-grade children by administering the test using standard procedures and then using a group administered procedure. The correlation between the scores obtained using the two procedures was .57 (p < .01). Dill and others (1975) obtained data from ninety-three black children by revealing only the facial features of the It figure. They found that their children obtained significantly higher scores than the black children in the Summers and Felker (1970) study, who used their own child-drawn figures as "It." The girls in the study by Dill and others did not differ significantly from the girls studied by Summers and Felker.

(3) Scores on the ITSC have been related to numerous variables: parental dominance and power (Biller, 1969b; Domash and Balter, 1976; Hetherington, 1965; Laosa and Brophy, 1972); parental encouragement of appropriate sex-typed activities (Biller, 1968a, 1969a; Domash and Balter, 1976; Fling and Manosevitz, 1972; Mussen and Rutherford, 1963; Sears, 1965); parental child-rearing practices (Hartup, 1962; Radin, 1972); parental personality (Mussen and Rutherford, 1963); parent-child trait similarity (Hether-

ington, 1965); father availability (Badaines, 1976; Biller, 1968a, 1968b, 1969a; Hetherington, 1966; Houston, 1973); maternal employment status (Gold and Andres, 1978); sibling constellation (Bigner, 1972; Dixit, 1971; Laosa and Brophy, 1972; Schell and Silber, 1968); intellectual level (Biller, 1968a; Biller and Borstelmann, 1965; Clark, 1963b; Kohlberg and Zigler, 1967; Laosa and Brophy, 1972; Radin, 1972); race (Doll, Fagot, and Himbert, 1971, 1973; Hetherington, 1966; Thompson and McCandless, 1970); socioeconomic status (Hall and Keith, 1964; Thompson and McCandless, 1970); respondent's parental imitation (Hartup, 1962; Hetherington, 1965; Kohlberg and Zigler, 1967; Ward, 1972, 1973); parental identification (Flammer, 1971); parental attachment (Kohlberg and Zigler, 1967); self-esteem (Flammer, 1971); dependence and independence (Lansky and McKay, 1969); risk taking (Montgomery and Landers, 1974); avoidance of inappropriate sex-typed activities (Hartup, Moore, and Sager, 1963); amount of television viewing time (Frueh and McGhee, 1975); creative potential (Biller, Singer, and Fullerton, 1969); facial attractiveness and physique (LaVoie and Andrews, 1976); gender constancy, physical conservation, understanding of gender labels, and parent salience (LaVoie and Andrews, 1975); sex of experimental model (Perry and Perry, 1975); sex of examiner (Borstelmann, 1961; Doll, Fagot, and Himbert, 1971, 1973; Thompson and McCandless, 1970); humor related to sex-inappropriate behaviors (McGhee and Grodzitsky, 1973).

(4) The ITSC has also been translated for use with children in other countries, including: India (Dixit, 1971), Okinawa (Kobasigawa, 1959), and Australia (Perry and Perry, 1975). In these studies, the test was adapted to fit culturally defined masculine or feminine objects and activities.

(5) An advantage to using this instrument is that it has been used extensively in prior research. As a result, there is much information with which findings can be compared. However, attempts to establish the reliability and validity of the instrument have yielded inconsistent results. One should be particularly concerned about using the scale with girls. Furthermore, the eight masculine toys include five vehicles; if the vehicles are considered as one type of toy, there are really only four types of masculine toys. Similarly, the eight feminine toys include five dolls and doll accessories, so the feminine toys might also be considered to include only four types of toys. In the selection of toys, Brown does not indicate whether he attempted to control for the attractiveness of the toys or their manipulative potential. Another criticism is that the drawings accompanying the third part of the instrument are rather bizarre looking.

(6) The ITSC is described and reviewed in the *Sixth Mental Measurements Yearbook* (Buros, 1965, entry 129), is listed in the *Eighth Mental Measurements Yearbook* (Buros, 1978, entry 592), and is described in *Socioemotional Measures for Preschool and Kindergarten Children* (Walker, 1973, pp. 145-146).

SOURCE: Psychological Test Specialists
        P.O. Box 1441
        Missoula, Montana 59801

BIBLIOGRAPHY:

Badaines, J. S. "Identification, Imitation, and Sex Role Preference as a Function of Father Absence and Father Presence in Black and Chicano Boys." Unpublished doctoral dissertation, University of South Carolina, 1972. (*Dissertation Abstracts International,* 1973, *34*[1-B], 403-404.)

Badaines, J. S. "Identification, Imitation, and Sex Role Preference in Father-Present and Father-Absent Black and Chicano Boys." *Journal of Psychology,* 1976, *92,* 15-24.

Bennett, M. C. "Exploratory Study of Masculine-Feminine Choices of Preschool Children." Unpublished doctoral dissertation, Claremont Graduate School and University Center, 1968. (*Dissertation Abstracts,* 1969, *29*[7-B], 2616.)

Bigner, J. J. "The Effects of Sibling Influence on Sex Role Development in Young Children." Unpublished doctoral dissertation, Florida State University, 1970. (*Dissertation Abstracts International,* 1971, *31*[10-B], 6093-6094.)

Bigner, J. J. "Sibling Influence on Sex Role Preference of Young Children." *Journal of Genetic Psychology,* 1972, *121,* 271-282.

Biller, H. B. "An Exploratory Investigation of Masculine Development in Kindergarten-Age Boys." Unpublished doctoral dissertation, Duke University, 1967. (*Dissertation Abstracts,* 1968, *28*[10-B], 4290.)

Biller, H. B. "A Multiaspect Investigation of Masculine Development in Kindergarten-Age Boys." *Genetic Psychology Monographs,* 1968a, *78,* 89-138.

Biller, H. B. "A Note on Father Absence and Masculine Development in Lower-Class Negro and White Boys." *Child Development,* 1968b, *39,* 1003-1006.

Biller, H. B. "Father Absence, Maternal Encouragement, and Sex Role Development in Kindergarten-Age Boys." *Child Development,* 1969a, *40,* 539-546.

Biller, H. B. "Father Dominance and Sex Role Development in Kindergarten-Age Boys." *Developmental Psychology,* 1969b, *1,* 87-94.

Biller, H. B. "Maternal Salience and Feminine Development in Young Girls." *Proceedings of 77th Annual Convention of the American Psychological Association,* 1969c, *4,* 259-260.

Biller, H. B., and Borstelmann, L. J. "Intellectual Level and Sex Role Development in Mentally Retarded Children." *American Journal of Mental Deficiency,* 1965, *70,* 443-447.

Biller, H. B., Singer, D. L., and Fullerton, M. "Sex Role Development and Creative Potential in Kindergarten-Age Boys." *Developmental Psychology,* 1969, *1,* 291-296.

Booth, D. W. "The Effect of Psychological Sexual Identity on Imitation of Aggression in Preschool Children." Unpublished doctoral dissertation, University of Maine, 1971. (*Dissertation Abstracts International,* 1972, *32*[11-B], 6671.)

Borstelmann, L. J. "Sex of Experimenter and Sex-Typed Behavior of Young Children." *Child Development,* 1961, *32,* 519-524.

Bray, R. M. "An Examination and Revision of the Brown 'It Scale for Children.'" Unpublished master's thesis, University of Toronto, 1969.

Broida, H. "Empirical Study of Sex Role Identification and Sex Role Preference in a Selected Group of Stuttering Male Children." Unpublished doctoral dissertation, University of Southern California, 1962. (*Dissertation Abstracts,* 1963, *23*[7], 2626.)

Brophy, J. E., and Laosa, L. M. "The Effect of a Male Teacher on the Sex Typing of Kindergarten Children." *Journal Supplement Abstract Service Catalog of Selected Documents in Psychology,* 1973, *3,* 44.

Brown, D. G. "Sex Role Preference in Young Children." *Psychological Monographs,* 1956, *70* (entire issue).

Brown, D. G. "The Development of Sex Role Inversion and Homosexuality." *Journal of Pediatrics,* 1957a, *50,* 613-619.

Brown, D. G. "Masculinity-Femininity Development in Children." *Journal of Consulting Psychology,* 1957b, *21,* 197-202.

Brown, D. G. "Sex Role Preference in Children: Methodological Problems." *Psychological Reports,* 1962, *11,* 477-478.

Burns, R. A. "The Effect of Father's Absence on the Development of the Masculine Identification of Boys in Residential Treatment." Unpublished doctoral dissertation,
  St. Johns University, 1971. (*Dissertation Abstracts International*, 1972, *32*[7-B],
  4179-4180.)

*Buros, O. K. *The Sixth Mental Measurements Yearbook*. Highland Park, N.J.: Gryphon
  Press, 1965.

*Buros, O. K. *The Eighth Mental Measurements Yearbook*. Highland Park, N.J.: Gryphon
  Press, 1978.

Clark, E. T. "Sex Role Preference in Mentally Retarded Children." *American Journal of
  Mental Deficiency*, 1963a, *67*, 606-610.

Clark, E. T. "Sex Role Preference in Mentally Retarded Females." *American Journal of
  Mental Deficiency*, 1963b, *68*, 433-439.

Dickstein, E. B., and Seymour, M. W. "The Effect of the Addition of Neutral Items on It
  Scale Scores." Paper presented at 23rd annual meeting of the Southwestern
  Psychological Association, Albuquerque, New Mexico, April 1976. (ERIC Docu-
  ment Reproduction Service No. ED 141 711.)

Dickstein, E. B., and Seymour, M. W. "Effect of the Addition of Neutral Items on It
  Scale Scores." *Developmental Psychology*, 1977, *13*, 79-80.

Dill, J. R., Bradford, C. E., Prudent, S., Semaj, L., and Harper, J. "Sex Role Preference in
  Black Preschool Children Using a Modification of the It Scale for Children." *Perceptual and Motor Skills*, 1975, *41*, 823-828.

Dixit, R. C. "Sex Role Preference in Children as a Function of Birth Space." *Psychologia:
  An International Journal of Psychology in the Orient*, 1971, *14*, 175-178.

Doll, P. A., Fagot, H. J., and Himbert, J. D. "Experimenter Effect on Sex Role Preference
  Among Black and White Lower-Class Male Children." *Psychological Reports*,
  1971, *29*, 1295-1301.

Doll, P. A., Fagot, H. J., and Himbert, J. D. "Examiner Effect on Sex Role Preference
  Among Black and White Lower-Class Female Children." *Psychological Reports*,
  1973, *32*, 427-434.

Domash, L. G. "Selected Maternal Attitudes as Related to Sex, Sex Role Preference, and
  Level of Psychological Differentiation of the Five-Year-Old Child." Unpublished
  doctoral dissertation, New York University, 1973. (*Dissertation Abstracts International*, 1973, *34*[6-B], 2925-2926.)

Domash, L. G., and Balter, L. "Sex and Psychological Differentiation in Preschoolers."
  Journal of Genetic Psychology, 1976, *128*, 77-84.

Duryea, W. R. "Sex Role Preference in Children: Individual and Group Administration of
  the It Scale for Children." *Psychological Reports*, 1967, *21*, 269-274.

Endsley, R. C. "Effects of Concealing 'It' on Sex Role Preferences of Preschool Children." *Perceptual and Motor Skills*, 1967, *24*, 998.

Epstein, R. "Verbal Conditioning in Children as a Function of Sex Role Identification,
  Internal Control, and Need for Approval." Unpublished doctoral dissertation,
  Ohio State University, 1961. (*Dissertation Abstracts*, 1962, *22*[7], 2462.)

Epstein, R., and Liverant, S. "Verbal Conditioning and Sex Role Identification in Children." *Child Development*, 1963, *34*, 99-106.

Feinman, S., and Ross, S. L. "Homogeneity Reliability of the It Scale for Children."
  Psychological Reports, 1975, *36*, 415-420.

Flammer, D. P. "Self-Esteem, Parent Identification, and Sex Role Development in Pre-
  school-Age Boys and Girls." *Child Study Journal*, 1971, *2*, 39-45.

Fling, S., and Manosevitz, M. "Sex Typing in Nursing School Children's Play Interests."
  Developmental Psychology, 1972, *7*, 146-152.

Frueh, T., and McGhee, P. E. "Traditional Sex Role Development and Amount of Time Spent Watching Television." *Developmental Psychology,* 1975, *11,* 109.

Gold, D., and Andres, D. "Relations Between Maternal Employment and Development on Nursery School Children." Paper presented at the Canadian Psychological Association Convention, Toronto, June 1976. (ERIC Document Reproduction Service No. ED 135 461.)

Gold, D., and Andres, D. "Relations Between Maternal Employment and Development of Nursery School Children." *Canadian Journal of Behavioral Science,* 1978, *10,* 116-129.

Green, R., Fuller, M., and Rutley, B. "It Scale for Children and Draw-A-Person Test: 30 Feminine vs. 25 Masculine Boys." *Journal of Personality Assessment,* 1972, *36,* 349-352.

Grob, P. "The Relationship of Self-Concept, Sex Role Preference, and Religio-Cultural Background to the Academic Performance of Ten-Year-Olds of Predominantly Middle-Class Backgrounds." Unpublished doctoral dissertation, University of Virginia, 1971. (*Dissertation Abstracts International,* 1972, *32*[8-A], 4348-4349.)

Hall, M., and Keith, R. A. "Sex Role Preference Among Children of Upper and Lower Social Class." *Journal of Social Psychology,* 1964, *62,* 101-110.

Hartup, W. W. "Some Correlates of Parental Imitation in Young Children." *Child Development,* 1962, *33,* 85-96.

Hartup, W. W., Moore, S. G., and Sager, G. "Avoidance of Inappropriate Sex Typing by Young Children." *Journal of Consulting Psychology,* 1963, *27,* 467-473.

Hartup, W. W., and Zook, E. A. "Sex Role Preferences in Three- and Four-Year-Old Children." *Journal of Consulting Psychology,* 1960, *24,* 420-426.

Hernandez, N. M. "Sex Role Development of Preschool Middle- and Lower-Class Mexican-American and Anglo-American Males." Unpublished master's thesis, University of Texas at El Paso, 1974.

Hetherington, E. M. "A Developmental Study of the Effects of Sex of the Dominant Parent on Sex Role Preference, Identification, and Imitation in Children." *Journal of Personality and Social Psychology,* 1965, *2,* 188-194.

Hetherington, E. M. "Effects of Parental Absence on Sex-Typed Behaviors in Negro and White Preadolescent Males." *Journal of Personality and Social Psychology,* 1966, *4,* 87-91.

Houston, H. S. "Familial Correlates of Sex Role Development in Boys: An Exploratory Study." *Personality: An International Journal,* 1970, *1,* 303-317.

Houston, H. S. "Father Absence and the Development of Sex Role." *Australian Journal of Social Issues,* 1973, *8,* 209-216.

Hull, D. M. "Examination of Three Maternal Characteristics in Relationship to Sex Role Development of Father-Present and Father-Absent Children." Unpublished doctoral dissertation, University of Washington, 1975. (*Dissertation Abstracts International,* 1976, *37*[2-A], 807-808.)

Inselberg, R. M., and Burke, L. "Social and Psychological Correlates of Masculinity in Young Boys." *Merrill-Palmer Quarterly,* 1973, *19,* 41-47.

Joshi, A. K. "Sex Role Preferences in Preschool Children from Five Subcultures of the United States." Unpublished doctoral dissertation, Iowa State University, 1969. (*Dissertation Abstracts International,* 1970, *30*[11-B], 5120.)

Keller, E. D. "Parents' Self-Reports, Children's Representations of Parent Behavior, and Masculinity in Young Boys." Unpublished doctoral dissertation, University of Iowa, 1961. (*Dissertation Abstracts,* 1962, *22*[8], 2872.)

Kobasigawa, A. "Sex Role Preference in Okinawan Preschool Children." *Psychologia,*
      1959, *2,* 124-127.
Kohlberg, L., and Zigler, E. "The Impact of Cognitive Maturity on the Development of
      Sex Role Attitudes in the Years 4 to 8." *Genetic Psychology Monographs,* 1967,
      75, 89-165.
Langford, E. P. "The Sex Role of the Female as Perceived by Anglo and Negro Children."
      Unpublished doctoral dissertation, East Texas State University, 1969. (*Disserta-
      tion Abstracts International,* 1970, *30*[7-A], 2803.)
Lansky, L. M. "Some Comments on Ward's (1968) 'Variance of Sex Role Preferences
      Among Boys and Girls.' " *Psychological Reports,* 1968, *23,* 649-650.
Lansky, L. M., and McKay, G. "Sex Role Preferences of Kindergarten Boys and Girls:
      Some Contradictory Results." *Psychological Reports,* 1963, *13,* 415-421.
Lansky, L. M., and McKay, G. "Independence, Dependence, Manifest and Latent Mascu-
      linity-Femininity: Some Complex Relationships Among Four Complex Vari-
      ables." *Psychological Reports,* 1969, *24,* 263-268.
Laosa, L. M., and Brophy, J. E. "Effects of Sex and Birth Order on Sex Role Development
      and Intelligence in Kindergarten Children." Paper presented at 17th annual con-
      vention of the Southwestern Psychological Association, San Antonio, Texas,
      1971. (ERIC Document Reproduction Service No. ED 053 403.)
Laosa, L. M., and Brophy, J. E. "Effects of Sex and Birth Order on Sex Role Develop-
      ment and Intelligence Among Kindergarten Children." *Developmental Psychol-
      ogy,* 1972, *6,* 409-415.
LaVoie, J. C., and Andrews, R. "Cognitive Determinants of Gender Identity and Con-
      stancy." Paper presented at 83rd annual meeting of the American Psychological
      Association, Chicago, September 1975.
LaVoie, J. C., and Andrews, R. "Facial Attractiveness, Physique, and Sex Role Identity in
      Young Children." *Developmental Psychology,* 1976, *12,* 550-551.
Lindsay, H. E. "The Sex Role Classification of School Objects by Selected Second-Grade
      Male Subjects from Contrasting Learning Environments." Unpublished doctoral
      dissertation, Ohio State University, 1974. (*Dissertation Abstracts International,*
      1974, *35*[2-A], 812-813.)
Lynn, R. "Sex Role Preference and Mother-Daughter Fantasies in Young Girls." Unpub-
      lished doctoral dissertation, University of Denver, 1961. (*Dissertation Abstracts,*
      1962, *22*[11], 4084.)
McGhee, P. E. "Television as a Source of Learning Sex Role Stereotypes." Paper pre-
      sented at the biennial meeting of the Society for Research in Child Development,
      Denver, April 1975. (ERIC Document Reproduction Service No. ED 111 528.)
McGhee, P. E., and Grodzitsky, P. "Sex Role Identification and Humor Among Preschool
      Children." *Journal of Psychology,* 1973, *84,* 189-193.
Montemayor, R. "Children's Performance on and Attraction to an Activity as a Function
      of Masculine, Feminine, or Neutral Labels on Sex Role Preference." 1971. (ERIC
      Document Reproduction Service No. ED 068 875.)
Montgomery, G. T., and Landers, W. F. "Transmission of Risk Taking Through Modeling
      at Two Age Levels." *Psychological Reports,* 1974, *34,* 1187-1196.
Motte, C. J. D. "An Investigation of the Masculine Personality as Related to Varying Ex-
      periences with Family Consistency." Unpublished doctoral dissertation, Case
      Western Reserve University, 1969. (*Dissertation Abstracts International,* 1970,
      30[9-B], 4378-4379.)
Munter, L. "Children's Sex Role Patterns and School Success in the Primary Grades."

Unpublished doctoral dissertation, Claremont Graduate School and University Center, 1969. (*Dissertation Abstracts International*, 1970, *30*[11-A], 4835.)

Mussen, P., and Distler, L. "Masculinity, Identification, and Father-Son Relationships." *Journal of Abnormal and Social Psychology*, 1959, *59*, 350-356.

Mussen, P., and Distler, L. "Child-Rearing Antecedents of Masculine Identification in Kindergarten Boys." *Child Development*, 1960, *31*, 89-100.

Mussen, P., and Rutherford, E. "Parent-Child Relations and Parental Personality in Relation to Young Children's Sex Role Preferences." *Child Development*, 1963, *34*, 589-607.

Mussen, P., and Rutherford, E. "Parent-Child Relations and Parental Personality in Relation to Young Children's Sex Role Preferences." In P. Mussen, J. Conger, and J. Kagan (Eds.), *Readings on Child Development and Personality*. New York: Harper & Row, 1965.

Nicholson, C. A., Jr. "A Comparison of Masculine Role Preference of Scholastically Successful and Scholastically Unsuccessful Primary Grade Boys." Unpublished doctoral dissertation, U.S. International University, 1973. (*Dissertation Abstracts International*, 1973, *34*[4-A], 1708-1709.)

Perry, D. G., and Perry, L. C. "Observational Learning in Children: Effects of Sex of Model and Subject's Sex Role Behavior." *Journal of Personality and Social Psychology*, 1975, *31*, 1083-1088.

Piercy, P. A. "The Relationship of Cognitive Functioning to the Development of Sex Role in Black Male Children Ages Four to Ten." Unpublished doctoral dissertation, Adelphi University, 1976. (*Dissertation Abstracts International*, 1976, *37*[4-B], 1974.)

Radin, N. "Father-Child Interaction and the Intellectual Functioning of Four-Year-Old Boys." 1971. (ERIC Document Reproduction Service No. ED 057 909.)

Radin, N. "Father-Child Interaction and the Intellectual Functioning of Four-Year-Old Boys." *Developmental Psychology*, 1972, *6*, 353-361.

Reed, M. R., and Asbjornsen, W. "Experimental Alteration of the It Scale in the Study of Sex Role Preference." *Perceptual and Motor Skills*, 1968, *26*, 15-24.

Rosensweet, M. A. "The Relationship of Masculinity-Femininity of Selected Elementary School Teachers and Other Environmental Factors to the Masculinity-Femininity of Their Students." Unpublished doctoral dissertation, Miami University, 1972. (*Dissertation Abstracts International*, 1972, *33*[1-A], 196.)

Rutherford, E. E. "Familial Antecedents of Sex Role Development in Young Children." Unpublished doctoral dissertation, University of California, Berkeley, 1964. (*Dissertation Abstracts*, 1965, *25*[7], 4252-4253.)

Schell, R. E., and Silber, J. W. "Sex Role Discrimination Among Young Children." *Perceptual and Motor Skills*, 1968, *27*, 379-389.

Sears, R. R. "Development of Gender Roles." In F. A. Beach (Ed.), *Sex and Behavior*. New York: Wiley, 1965.

Sears, R. R., Rau, L., and Alpert, R. *Identification and Child Rearing*. Stanford, Calif.: Stanford University Press, 1965.

Sher, M. A., and Lansky, L. M. "The It Scale for Children: Effects of Variations in the Sex Specificity of the It Figure." *Merrill-Palmer Quarterly*, 1968, *14*, 323-330.

Sugawara, A. I. "Sex Role Discrimination and Preference in Preschool-Aged Children." Unpublished doctoral dissertation, Oregon State University, 1971. (*Dissertation Abstracts International*, 1971, *32*[3-B], 1830-1831.)

Summers, D. L., and Felker, D. W. "Use of the It Scale for Children in Assessing Sex Role

Preference in Preschool Negro Children." *Developmental Psychology,* 1970, *2,* 330-334.

Thomas, P. J. "Sub-Cultural Differences in Sex Role Preference Patterns." Unpublished doctoral dissertation, Western Reserve University, 1965. (*Dissertation Abstracts,* 1966, *26*[11], 6894-6895.)

Thompson, N. L., Jr., and McCandless, B. R. "It Score Variations by Instructional Style." *Child Development,* 1970, *41,* 425-436.

*Walker, D. K. *Socioemotional Measures for Preschool and Kindergarten Children.* San Francisco: Jossey-Bass, 1973.

Ward, W. D. "Sex Role Preference and Parental Imitation Within Groups of Middle-Class Whites and Lower-Class Blacks." *Psychological Reports,* 1972, *30,* 651-654.

Ward, W. D. "Patterns of Culturally Defined Sex Role Preference and Parental Imitation." *Journal of Genetic Psychology,* 1973, *122,* 337-343.

Wright, K. W. "Sex Role Classification of School Objects by Selected Kindergarten and First-Grade Students in Contrasting Learning Environments." Unpublished doctoral dissertation, Ohio State University, 1975. (*Dissertation Abstracts International,* 1976, *36*[8-A], 5169-5170.)

---

18. LAOSA-BROPHY TOY PREFERENCE TEST

AUTHORS: Luis M. Laosa and Jere E. Brophy

DATE: 1971

VARIABLE: Sex role preference

TYPE OF INSTRUMENT: Picture preference

DESCRIPTION: Nine pictures of toys were cut from catalogues and glued to black construction paper. The test includes three feminine toys (dishes, doll, and stove), three masculine toys (fire truck, gas station, and tool set), and three neutral toys (phonograph, puzzle, and Viewmaster).

PREVIOUSLY ADMINISTERED TO: Grade K

APPROPRIATE FOR: Ages 3-6

ADMINISTRATION: The child is shown the array of pictures and asked to select the toy she would like to play with "now." The procedure is repeated until five choices are made.

SCORING: Two points are assigned for each masculine choice, 1 point is assigned for each neutral choice, and 0 points for each feminine choice. The maximum score is 8 (very masculine) and the minimum score is 2 (very feminine).

DEVELOPMENT: No information is provided.

RELIABILITY: No data are provided.

VALIDITY: Although the authors used the Laosa-Brophy Toy Preference Test in conjunction with other sex role measures (It Scale for Children—#17; Group Toy Preference Test—#15; and the Biller Game Preference Test—#2), they failed to report any correlations between the measures. Thus, there is no information regarding the concurrent validity of the instrument.

In a study of kindergarten children (Laosa and Brophy, 1972), it was found that forty-seven boys obtained a mean score of 7.36, whereas forty-six girls obtained a mean score of 2.89. In another study of kindergarten children (Brophy and Laosa, 1973), it was found that forty-eight boys obtained a mean score of 7.37 and forty-eight girls obtained a mean score of 2.87. Neither study reported the significance of the difference between means.

NOTES AND COMMENTS: No evidence is provided that the individual toys are correctly categorized as masculine, feminine, or neutral. The work done by Lippman and Grote (1974; see #19) indicates that the dishes, doll, fire truck, tool set, and phonograph are correctly sex typed.

SOURCE: See Laosa and Brophy, 1971 or 1972.

BIBLIOGRAPHY:

Brophy, J. E., and Laosa, L. M. "The Effect of a Male Teacher on the Sex Typing of Kindergarten Children." *Journal Supplement Abstract Service Catalog of Selected Documents in Psychology*, 1973, *3*, 44.

Laosa, L. M., and Brophy, J. E. "Effects of Sex and Birth Order on Sex Role Development and Intelligence in Kindergarten Children." Paper presented at 17th annual meeting of the Southwestern Psychological Association, San Antonio, Texas, April 1971. (ERIC Document Reproduction Service No. ED 053 403.)

Laosa, L. M., and Brophy, J. E. "Effects of Sex and Birth Order on Sex Role Development and Intelligence Among Kindergarten Children." *Developmental Psychology*, 1972, *6*, 409-415.

*Lippman, M. Z., and Grote, B. H. "Social-Emotional Effects of Day Care. Final Project Report." Washington, D.C.: Office of Child Development, 1974. (ERIC Document Reproduction Service No. ED 110 164.)

19. LIPPMAN-GROTE TOY PREFERENCE TEST

AUTHORS: Marcia Z. Lippman and Barbara H. Grote

DATE: 1974

VARIABLE: Sex role preference

TYPE OF INSTRUMENT: Forced choice picture preference

DESCRIPTION: The test consists of fifteen color pictures of toys, cut from catalogues and encased in plastic. The fifteen pictures include: five masculine toys (football, tool set, train, airplane, and fire engine); five feminine toys (purse, sewing machine, doll house, dishes, and doll); and five neutral toys (camera, Lincoln logs, record player, guitar, and alphabet board). Pictures are grouped into five triads, with each triad including one masculine, one feminine, and one neutral toy.

PREVIOUSLY ADMINISTERED TO: Age 4

APPROPRIATE FOR: Ages 3-6

ADMINISTRATION: The child is shown one triad at a time and asked to indicate which of the three toys she would most like to play with. After the series of five triads is completed, new triads are formed which include a different combination of the pictures but still include one masculine, one feminine, and one neutral toy. In all, there are three sets of five triads used.

SCORING: Responses are objectively scored and equally weighted. The scores range from 0 (all feminine choices) to 30 (all masculine choices).

DEVELOPMENT: Fifteen pictures were cut from catalogues and encased in plastic. The pictures were selected so as to be approximately equal in size, attractiveness, and amount of detail. The fifteen pictures were submitted to five adults who independently sorted them into three groups: masculine, feminine, and neutral. There was 100 percent agreement among the judges.

RELIABILITY: No data are provided.

VALIDITY: Using the data from 198 four-year-olds, Lippman and Grote found a significant difference between the mean obtained by boys and the mean obtained by girls.

NOTES AND COMMENTS: (1) A neutral category of toys was included "to help avoid the overestimation of sex typing which might occur with a forced choice between masculine and feminine toys" (p. 185).
    (2) To complete the scale, children respond to sets of triads three times. The authors felt that this procedure would facilitate discriminating between the extremely sex-typed child and the child who knows the socially appropriate response but is personally attracted to a variety of toys. The latter child would be expected to give sex-appropriate answers on the first set of triads, but on the subsequent sets, she would be ex-

pected to display the diversity of her interests. The authors' assumption on the usefulness of using three sets of triads was not empirically tested.

SOURCE: See Lippman and Grote, 1974.

BIBLIOGRAPHY:

Lippman, M. Z., and Grote, B. H. "Social-Emotional Effects of Day Care. Final Project Report." Washington, D.C.: Office of Child Development, 1974. (ERIC Document Reproduction Service No. ED 110 164.)

---

20. MAY MEASURE OF GENDER IDENTITY

AUTHOR: Robert R. May

DATE: 1966

VARIABLE: Gender identity

TYPE OF INSTRUMENT: Projective storytelling

DESCRIPTION: The measure consists of two pictures: a man and a woman in mid-air doing a trapeze act and a bullfighter standing alone in the ring. The respondent is asked to tell a story about the picture. The stories can be communicated orally or in writing.

PREVIOUSLY ADMINISTERED TO: Preschoolers through adults

APPROPRIATE FOR: Ages 4 and older

ADMINISTRATION: The measure can be either group or individually administered. If it is group administered, the stories are written by the respondents. If it is individually administered, the stories can be written down by the examiner or can be tape recorded.

SCORING: The stories are scored in terms of the number of "enhancement" and "deprivation" statements made and whether those statements occur before or after the "pivotal incident" in the story. "Enhancement," "deprivation," and "pivotal incident" are defined for the scorer (see May, 1966). If the tone of the story is "enhancement" followed by "deprivation," then the total score will be negative; if the tone of the story is "deprivation" followed by "enhancement," then the total score will be positive.

DEVELOPMENT: May (1966) provides a two-and-a-half-page explanation of the theoretical background for positing that males' stories will follow an enhancement-pivotal incident-deprivation sequence and females' stories will follow a deprivation-pivotal incident-enhancement sequence.

May (1966) originally used four pictures to elicit stories. The interrater reliability on one picture was quite low (r = .42), and there were no sex differences in enhancement-deprivation responses for another picture. The remaining two pictures comprise the instrument.

RELIABILITY: Interrater reliability has been reported in two studies. May (1966) administered the scale to 104 college students. He reports interrater reliabilities of .79 and .77 for the two pictures. May (1971) reports an interrater reliability of .89 for a set of sixty-three stories.

In a study of children in grades 3 through 5, May (1971) obtained a correlation of .52 between scores obtained on the two pictures. However, when Saarni (1976) administered the scale to 104 college students and adults, she found the correlation between scores on the two pictures to be only .17.

VALIDITY: May contends that the fact that women score significantly higher on the instrument provides evidence for its construct validity. Women scored significantly higher in several studies (May, 1966, 1969, 1971; Cramer and Bryson, 1973); however, Cramer and Bryson did not find the expected differences among younger children.

Findings regarding the relationship between the May Measure of Gender Identity and the Gough Femininity Scale (#36) are inconsistent. May (1969) reports a nonsignificant correlation for the two measures for women (r = −.10) but a significant correlation for the two measures for men (r = +.78, p < .001). Saarni (1976) reports a correlation of .09 for the trapeze picture and the Gough Femininity Scale and a correlation of .03 for the matador picture and the Gough Femininity Scale. She does not analyze the data according to sex.

NOTES AND COMMENTS: May's system of scoring has been used to analyze stories elicited by pictures other than the ones he used (Cramer and Bryson, 1973; McClelland and Watt, 1968).

SOURCE: See May, 1966 (pictures not included).

BIBLIOGRAPHY:

Cramer, P., and Bryson, J. "The Development of Sex-Related Fantasy Patterns." *Developmental Psychology*, 1973, *8*, 131-134.

May, R. R. "Sex Differences in Fantasy Patterns." *Journal of Projective Techniques and Personality Assessment*, 1966, *30*, 576-586.

May, R. R. "Deprivation-Enhancement Patterns in Men and Women." *Journal of Projective Techniques and Personality Assessment*, 1969, *33*, 464-469.

May, R. R. "A Method for Studying the Development of Gender Identity." *Developmental Psychology*, 1971, *5*, 484-487.

McClelland, D. C., and Watt, N. F. "Sex Role Alienation in Schizophrenia." *Journal of Abnormal Psychology*, 1968, *73*, 226-239.

Saarni, C. I. "Social-Cohort Effect on Three Masculinity-Femininity Instruments and Self-Report." *Psychological Reports*, 1976, *38*, 1111-1118.

Saarni, C. I., Taber, R., and Shaw-Hamilton, L. "The Vicissitudes of Sex Roles Assessment." Paper presented at 53rd annual meeting of the Western Psychological Association, Anaheim, California, April 1973. (ERIC Document Reproduction Service No. ED 084 284.)

Winter, S. "Characteristics of Fantasy While Nursing." *Journal of Personality,* 1969, *37,* 58-72.

---

21. PUPIL PERCEPTIONS TEST (PPT)

AUTHOR: Edward E. Gotts

DATE: 1965

VARIABLES: Masculinity-femininity; knowledge of sex role stereotypes

TYPE OF INSTRUMENT: Alternate choice

DESCRIPTION: The instrument consists of forty one-sentence descriptions of an instrumental or expressive interaction between a child and an adult. In the first twenty items, the adult is a teacher. The content of the second twenty items matches the content of the first twenty items, but the word *parent* is substituted for the word *teacher.* For each item, the respondent is to indicate whether the adult is a man or a woman and whether the child is a boy or a girl. Responses are communicated by having the child place a mark on the face of a boy or a girl and a mark on the face of a man or a woman.

PREVIOUSLY ADMINISTERED TO: Grades 5 and 6

APPROPRIATE FOR: Ages 4-12

ADMINISTRATION: The test is administered orally while the children record their responses on specially designed answer sheets. When the scale is administered to preschoolers through second graders, it should be administered in two parts, with each part administered on a different day. A break after every tenth item is recommended. When respondents are older than second graders, the test can be administered in one session with a short break provided after half of the items are completed.

SAMPLE ITEMS: The teacher is scolding the child for misbehaving on the school grounds.
• Do you think the child is a boy or a girl?
• Do you think the teacher is a man or a woman?
                    The parent is helping the child to find a place to sit down.
• Do you think the child is a boy or a girl?
• Do you think the teacher is a man or a woman?

SCORING: Masculinity-femininity scores are based on the responses to nine of the child choices (boy or girl) and five of the adult choices (man or woman). The choice of a male (boy or man) is assigned a value of 1 and then multiplied by the scoring weight for that item (provided by Gotts). The choice of a female (girl or woman) is assigned a value of 2 and then multiplied by the scoring weight for that item. Blanks are not scored. The scores for the fourteen responses are algebraically summed to yield a total score. A low score is considered masculine; a high score is considered feminine.

DEVELOPMENT: No information is provided on the source or selection of the forty items. Scoring weights and the selection of the fourteen items to be included in the masculinity-femininity score are based on the results of a discriminant analysis applied to the responses from sixty girls and fifty-seven boys in the fifth grade in five ethnically diverse schools.

RELIABILITY: No data are provided for the masculinity-femininity scores. Internal consistency reliability for knowledge of sex role stereotypes was .85 based on responses from children ages 5 to 10 (Gotts, 1965).

VALIDITY: The test was administered to fifth graders from five ethnically diverse schools. Predictions were stated in advance regarding which schools would have the most masculine means. These predictions were based on known characteristics of the ethnic groups. The results obtained from the five schools were consistent with prior predictions.

It was predicted that scores on the PPT should be independent of IQ scores as measured by the California Test of Mental Maturity. The correlations between PPT and nonlanguage IQ were −.12 for both boys and girls; the correlations between PPT and language IQ were −.01 for boys and −.03 for girls. None of the obtained correlations was significant.

A predicted and significant relationship was found between boys' scores on the PPT and anxiety. The finding indicates that boys who are low on masculinity are more likely to be high on anxiety. The relationship did not apply to girls (Gotts, 1968).

Gotts (1965) reports that older children, compared with younger children, demonstrate greater knowledge of sex role stereotypes on the PPT.

NOTES AND COMMENTS: (1) Gott's decision to develop the instrument on children from ethnically diverse backgrounds is both unusual and good. Typically instruments are developed on a rather homogeneous sample with no regard for ethnic differences.

(2) The PPT is described in *Tests and Measurements in Child Development: Handbook II* (Johnson, 1976, pp. 1201-1203).

SOURCE: Edward Gotts
                Appalachia Educational Laboratory, Inc.
                Box 1348
                Charleston, West Virginia 25325

BIBLIOGRAPHY:

Gotts, E. E. "The Pupil Perceptions Test (PPT)." Unpublished manuscript, Appalachia Educational Laboratory, 1965.
Gotts, E. E., and Phillips, B. N. "The Relation Between Psychometric Measures of Anxiety and Masculinity-Femininity." *Journal of School Psychology,* 1968, 6, 123-130.
*Johnson, O. G. *Tests and Measurements in Child Development: Handbook II.* San Francisco: Jossey-Bass, 1976.

22. RABBAN TOY PREFERENCE TEST

AUTHOR: Meyer Rabban

DATE: 1950

VARIABLE: Sex role identification

TYPE OF INSTRUMENT: Toy preference

DESCRIPTION: The test consists of sixteen toys, eight of which were judged appropriate for girls (high chair with doll, baby buggy with doll, doll crib with doll, beads, doll dishes, purse, baby doll, Bathinette with doll) and eight of which were judged appropriate for boys (gun, steamroller, dump truck, auto racer, fire truck, cement mixer, soldiers, rubber knife). All toys are inexpensive and under ten inches in size.

PREVIOUSLY ADMINISTERED TO: Ages 3-8

APPROPRIATE FOR: Ages 3-8

ADMINISTRATION: The child is brought to a room where the sixteen toys are arranged in a prescribed order. The examiner states, "Show me the toy you like best," followed by "Give it to me and I'll put it here." The child is then told "Show me another toy you like." The procedure is repeated until the child has made six choices.

SCORING: One point is assigned for each sex-appropriate toy choice. The maximum score is 6.

DEVELOPMENT: A list of twenty sex-typed toys was compiled by consulting sales-people in toy stores, toy catalogues, trade journals, and popular publications. Children, ages 9 to 11, and graduate students in education (178 males and 203 females) were asked to indicate which of the twenty toys they would purchase for a boy and which for a girl. The recipient of the gift was to be 3 to 6 years old. In compiling the final set of toys for the test, toys for which there was less than 70 percent agreement among the judges were eliminated. Color was controlled for by eliminating two toys and adding two others. Toy size, manipulative interest, and age level interest were considered in selecting toys for the test.

RELIABILITY: Test-retest reliability was estimated for 4- and 5-year-olds using an average test-retest interval of twenty days. Eight correlations were computed: two age levels x two socioeconomic levels x two sexes. Correlations ranged from .50 (4-year-old working-class girls) to .89 (5-year-old working-class boys) (Rabban, 1950).

VALIDITY: Two toys, beads and knife, were selected significantly less often by younger children (ages 3 and 4). On only one toy (steamroller) was there a significant difference between the choices made by working-class children and the choices made by upper-middle-class children. Each toy did differentiate between boys and girls (p < .05) (Rabban, 1950).

NOTES AND COMMENTS: (1) Toys are well described.

(2) Sears Toy Preference Test (#26) is based on and closely related to this test.

(3) The masculine toys include five vehicles and the feminine toys include six dolls. Therefore one might argue that the entire test includes only seven toys: dolls, beads, purse, vehicles, gun, soldiers, and rubber knife.

(4) Melson (1977) asked children to choose six toys from an array of twelve rather than from an array of sixteen.

SOURCE: See Rabban, 1950.

BIBLIOGRAPHY:

Melson, G. F. "Sex Differences in Proxemic Behavior and Personal Space Schemata in Young Children." *Sex Roles,* 1977, *3,* 81-89.
Rabban, M. "Sex Role Identification in Young Children in Two Diverse Social Groups." *Genetic Psychology Monographs,* 1950, *42,* 81-158.

---

23. SANTROCK DOLL PLAY INTERVIEW FOR MASCULINITY-FEMININITY

AUTHOR: John W. Santrock

DATE: 1967

VARIABLE: Masculinity-femininity

TYPE OF INSTRUMENT: Picture preference

DESCRIPTION: The instrument consists of twelve items. Six items are brief vignettes: four describe a situation and ask the respondent to select a man or a woman to go with the vignette; two indicate the preferences of a man and a woman and ask the respondent which adult she would agree with. Of the remaining six items, four ask the respondent to indicate which of two activities she would prefer, and two ask the respondent to express a preference for being masculine or feminine. Each item is accompanied by a pair of pictures. The picture pairs are presented on twelve white cards (15" x 20"). In each pair of pictures, one of the pair represents femininity and the other represents masculinity. A doll that looks like a child and is the same sex as the respondent is also used.

PREVIOUSLY ADMINISTERED TO: Ages 4-12

APPROPRIATE FOR: Ages 3-9

ADMINISTRATION: The instrument is individually administered. The child is shown one pair of pictures, about which the examiner asks a question. The child is asked to place the doll on the picture she prefers as the answer. The procedure is repeated for the twelve pairs of pictures.

SAMPLE ITEMS: The man is in the toy store and the woman is in the toy store. The little boy is with them. The little boy wants to buy a toy. Does he ask the woman, or does he ask the man to buy him a toy?

Would you rather play with dolls or would you rather play with guns?

SCORING: Items are objectively scored and equally weighted. Total scores can range from 0 (no masculine choices) to 12 (all masculine choices).

DEVELOPMENT: No information is provided.

RELIABILITY: No data are provided.

VALIDITY: Santrock (1967) administered the Doll Play Interview for Masculinity-Femininity to sixty lower-class black children, ages 4 to 6. He also administered the Santrock Maternal Interview for Assessing Masculinity-Femininity in Children (#24) to the mothers of the children and administered a measure of aggression and a measure of dependency to the children. The correlations between the Doll Play Interview for Masculinity-Femininity and the other measures were as follows: aggression = .49 (p < .01); dependency = .38 (p < .01); Santrock Maternal Interview for Assessing Masculinity-Femininity in Children (#24) = .73 (p < .01). Using a chi-square test, it was found that boys were significantly more masculine than girls (p < .001).

Wohlford and others (1971) administered the test to sixty-six children and found that boys were more masculine ($\bar{X}$ = 9.42) than girls ($\bar{X}$ = 1.39, p < .001). They also found that scores obtained were significantly correlated with scores on a measure of aggression (r = .335, p < .005) and with scores on the Santrock Maternal Interview for Assessing Masculinity-Femininity in Children (#24) (r = .208, p < .05).

NOTES AND COMMENTS: Santrock's Doll Play Interview for Masculinity-Femininity is one part of a larger doll play instrument that measures aggression and dependency as well as masculinity-femininity.

SOURCE: See Santrock, 1967 (pictures not included).

BIBLIOGRAPHY:

Santrock, J. W. "Father-Absence, Sex Typing, and Identification." Unpublished master's thesis, University of Miami, 1967.

Santrock, J. W. "Paternal Absence, Sex Typing, and Identification." *Developmental Psychology,* 1970, *2,* 264-272.

Santrock, J. W., and Wohlford, P. "Effects of Father Absence: Influence of the Reason for and the Onset of the Absence." *Proceedings of the Annual Convention of the American Psychological Association,* 1970, *5,* 265-266.

Wohlford, P., Santrock, J. W., Berger, S. E., and Liberman, D. "Older Brothers' Influence on Sex-Typed, Aggressive, and Dependent Behavior in Father-Absent Children." *Developmental Psychology,* 1971, *4,* 124-134.

24. SANTROCK MATERNAL INTERVIEW FOR ASSESSING MASCULINITY-FEMININITY IN CHILDREN

AUTHOR: John W. Santrock

DATE: 1967

VARIABLE: Masculinity-femininity

TYPE OF INSTRUMENT: Open-ended questions

DESCRIPTION: The instrument consists of four open-ended questions which require the parent to describe her child.

PREVIOUSLY ADMINISTERED TO: Mothers of children, ages 4-6

APPROPRIATE FOR: Parents of children ages 3-8

ADMINISTRATION: The instrument is individually administered. The entire interview is tape recorded.

SAMPLE ITEM: What type of games does [child's name] play with?

SCORING: Masculinity-femininity scores range from 0 (most feminine) to 3 (most masculine). Specific criteria have been established to allow one to determine the number of points to be assigned to the interview results. Separate criteria are provided for scoring the responses given by mothers of girls and mothers of boys. For example: for a boy to receive a score of 3, he (a) must act like a "real boy," should act like a "real boy" now, (b) must play masculine games only and be rough, (c) must not play with dolls, and must play with boys almost exclusively.

DEVELOPMENT: No information is provided beyond stating that the scale is related to the work of Sears, Maccoby, and Levin (1957).

RELIABILITY: A sample of interviews was scored by two raters. The percentage agreement between the two was 87.5 percent (Santrock, 1967).

VALIDITY: Santrock (1967) administered this instrument along with the Santrock Doll Play Interview for Masculinity-Femininity (#23) and measures of aggression and dependency to sixty lower-class black children, ages 4 to 6. The correlation between the two measures of masculinity-femininity was .73 (p < .01); the correlation between aggression and this instrument was .47 (p < .01); and the correlation between this instrument and the measure of dependency was −.16 (nonsignificant). Using a chi-square test, it was found that boys were significantly more masculine than girls (p < .001).

Wohlford and others (1971) administered this instrument along with an interview measure of aggression to the mothers of sixty-six father-absent, economically disadvantaged black children between the ages of 4 and 6. The correlation between the two measures was .424 (p < .005). The sixty-six children also were scored on the Santrock Doll Play Interview for Masculinity-Femininity (#23); the correlation between the two measures of masculinity-femininity was .208 (p < .05).

NOTES AND COMMENTS: (1) This instrument was incorporated into a maternal interview schedule, which also included measures of the following variables: parent-child relationship, aggression, dependency, and mother-father relationship. The entire interview schedule can be administered in about thirty minutes.

(2) The only evidence regarding the instrument's validity is based on interviews conducted with mothers of black children from low socioeconomic homes. Data are needed to establish the validity of the scale for white children and children from middle economic groups.

SOURCE: See Santrock, 1967.

BIBLIOGRAPHY:

Santrock, J. W. "Father Absence, Sex Typing, and Identification." Unpublished master's thesis, University of Miami, 1967.
Santrock, J. W. "Paternal Absence, Sex Typing, and Identification." *Developmental Psychology,* 1970, *2,* 264-272.
*Sears, R. R., Maccoby, E. E., and Levin, H. *Patterns of Child Rearing.* New York: Harper & Row, 1957.
Wohlford, P., Santrock, J. W., Berger, S. E., and Liberman, D. "Older Brothers' Influence on Sex-Typed, Aggressive, and Dependent Behavior in Father-Absent Children." *Developmental Psychology,* 1971, *4,* 124-134.

---

25. SEARS ACTIVITY PREFERENCE TEST

AUTHORS: Robert R. Sears, Lucy Rau, and Richard Alpert

DATE: 1961

VARIABLE: Sex role preference

TYPE OF INSTRUMENT: Forced choice picture preference

DESCRIPTION: This test consists of eight line drawings of a child engaged in an activity. The pictures vary along three dimensions: child playing versus child helping with adult work; masculine activity versus feminine activity; indoor setting versus outdoor setting (2 x 2 x 2 = 8 drawings). All pictures include a male and a female adult. The eight drawings are presented in twelve specified pairs. Two forms of the test exist: one form shows a boy performing the activity and one form shows a girl performing the activity.

PREVIOUSLY ADMINISTERED TO: Ages 3-8

APPROPRIATE FOR: Ages 3-8

ADMINISTRATION: The child is shown a pair of pictures in which the child depicted is the same sex as the child taking the test. The pictures are described and the child is asked, "Which one do you like to do best?" The procedure is repeated for the twelve pairs of pictures.

SAMPLE ITEM: The child is asked to choose between playing cowboy (with costume, boots, hat, and gun) or taking a doll for a walk in a buggy.

SCORING: One point is assigned each time the child's choice is sex appropriate, that is, a girl chooses a feminine activity or a boy chooses a masculine activity. The maximum score is 8, because only eight of the twelve pairs measure sex role preference. (The remaining four pairs measure age role preference and were not included in any further analysis.)

DEVELOPMENT: No information is provided on scale development beyond indicating that it is adapted from Fauls-Smith Activity Preference Test (#7).

RELIABILITY: Using the data from thirty-two boys and thirty-two girls ranging in age from 3 years 4 months to 5 years 0 months, Borstelmann (1961) obtained test-retest reliabilities of .37 for boys and .38 for girls. These reliabilities were computed on the scores from all twelve pairs of test items.

VALIDITY: For the children tested by Borstelmann (see Reliability), the correlations with the It Scale for Children (#17), a measure of sex role preference, were .28 and .39 for girls, and .26 and .40 for boys. The correlations with Sears Toy Preference Test (#26), a measure of masculinity-femininity, were .44 and .33 for boys and .51 and .09 for girls.

   Sears, Rau, and Alpert (1965) tested twenty-one boys with a mean age of 4 years 9 months and nineteen girls with a mean age of 4 years 10 months. The correlations with each of the other measures were: It Scale for Children (#17) = .13 for girls and .53 for boys; Sears Toy Preference Test (#26) = .69 for girls and .20 for boys; observer rating = .71 for girls and .29 for boys. There is considerable variability in the correlations reported.

NOTES AND COMMENTS: (1) This test is closely related to the Fauls-Smith Activity Preference Test (#7).

   (2) The sex role preference measure (eight pairs of pictures) was interspersed with an age role preference measure (four pairs of pictures). There are no data provided to indicate the reliability and validity of the sex role preference measure when it is given alone.

SOURCE: See Sears, Rau, and Alpert, 1965, pp. 356-358.

BIBLIOGRAPHY:

Anastasiow, N. J. "Success in School and Boys' Sex Role Patterns." *Child Development,*
        1965, *36,* 1053-1066.
Borstelmann, L. J. "Sex of Experimenter and Sex-Typed Behavior of Young Children."
        Child Development, 1961, *32,* 519-524.
Kohlberg, L., and Zigler, E. "The Impact of Cognitive Maturity on the Development of
        Sex Role Attitudes in the Years 4 to 8." *Genetic Psychology Monographs,* 1967,
        75, 89-165.

Sears, R. R. "Development of Gender Role." In F. A. Beach (Ed.), *Sex and Behavior.* New York: Wiley, 1965.

Sears, R. R., Rau, L., and Alpert, R. *Identification and Child Rearing.* Stanford, Calif.: Stanford University Press, 1965.

---

26. SEARS TOY PREFERENCE TEST

AUTHORS: Robert R. Sears, Lucy Rau, and Richard Alpert

DATE: 1961

VARIABLE: Masculinity-femininity

TYPE OF INSTRUMENT: Toy preference

DESCRIPTION: The test consists of seven masculine toys (gun, road scraper, cable car, tugboat, soldier, airplane, dump truck) and seven feminine toys (doll, crib, Bathinette, purse, Baby-tenda, tea set, doll buggy). The toys are positioned in a prescribed order, eight inches apart in a row on the floor.

PREVIOUSLY ADMINISTERED TO: Ages 3-6

APPROPRIATE FOR: Ages 2½-6

ADMINISTRATION: The child is brought to the toys and the experimenter begins by naming each toy for the child. The child is asked to select the toy she "would like to play with most of all." The procedure is repeated until eight choices have been made. The experimenter then gives the child her first-choice toy and the first-chosen sex-inappropriate toy. Taking the remaining toys along, the experimenter leaves the room.

SCORING: Masculinity or femininity is scored by assigning 1 point for each sex-appropriate toy chosen. Maximum score is 7. Satiation is scored by the length of time that elapses before the child tires of playing with her first-choice toy and switches to playing with her first-chosen sex-inappropriate toy.

DEVELOPMENT: The test is based on the Rabban Toy Preference Test (#22). The toys included in this test "were as nearly like those of Rabban (1950) as we could secure" (Sears, Rau and Alpert, 1965, p. 176). All toys selected had to satisfy five criteria: (a) have one moving part, (b) have no more than two possible types of manipulation, (c) be clearly sex typed, (d) be unavailable in the nursery school from which children were selected, and (e) be attractive to preschool children.

RELIABILITY: Using sixty-four children ranging in age from 3 years 4 months to 5 years 0 months, Borstelmann (1961) obtained test-retest correlations of .76 for boys and .62 for girls.

VALIDITY: Borstelmann (1961) tested thirty-two boys and thirty-two girls, ages 3 years 4 months to 5 years 0 months. The correlations with the It Scale for Children (#17), a measure of sex role preference, were .33 and .35 for boys and .25 and .30 for girls. The correlations with the Sears Activity Preference Test (#25), another measure of sex role preference, were .44 and .33 for boys and .51 and .09 for girls.

Sears, Rau, and Alpert (1965) tested twenty-one boys with a mean age of 4 years 9 months and nineteen girls with a mean age of 4 years 10 months. The correlations with each of the other measures were: It Scale for Children (#17) = .03 for girls and boys; Sears Activity Preference Test (#25) = .69 for girls and .20 for boys; observer rating = .36 for girls and .09 for boys. There is considerable variability in the correlations reported.

NOTES AND COMMENTS: (1) This test is closely related to the Rabban Toy Preference Test (#22).

(2) Toys are very well described in Sears, Rau, and Alpert (1965).

(3) Compared with toy selection for other toy preference tests, unusual care was used to select toys for this instrument that would be equated in terms of moving parts, manipulative potential, and attractiveness.

SOURCE: See Sears, Rau, and Alpert, 1965, pp. 358-360.

BIBLIOGRAPHY:

Anastasiow, N. J. "Success in School and Boys' Sex Role Patterns." *Child Development,* 1965, *36,* 1053-1066.
Borstelmann, L. J. "Sex of Experimenter and Sex-Typed Behavior of Young Children." *Child Development,* 1961, *32,* 519-524.
*Rabban, M. "Sex Role Identification in Young Children in Two Diverse Social Groups." *Genetic Psychology Monographs,* 1950, *42,* 81-158.
Sears, R. R. "Development of Gender Role." In F. A. Beach (Ed.), *Sex and Behavior.* New York: Wiley, 1965.
Sears, R. R., Rau, L., and Alpert, R. *Identification and Child Rearing.* Stanford, Calif.: Stanford University Press, 1965.

---

27. SEX ROLE PREFERENCE QUESTIONNAIRE

AUTHOR: Aletha Huston Stein

DATE: 1971

VARIABLE: Sex role preference

TYPE OF INSTRUMENT: Summated rating scale

DESCRIPTION: The scale consists of twenty-five questions, thirteen of which comprise the masculine preference subscale and twelve of which comprise the feminine preference subscale. The questions ask whether the respondent likes certain things, finds certain activities fun, and perceives certain things as interesting. In each question, the "activity" or "thing" is specified as appropriate for one sex. Each question is followed by five response options such as "very interesting," "interesting," "fairly interesting," "a little bit interesting," and "not interesting."

PREVIOUSLY ADMINISTERED TO: Grades 6 and 9

APPROPRIATE FOR: Ages 10-15

ADMINISTRATION: The scale can be self-administered and can be completed in less than fifteen minutes.

SAMPLE ITEMS: *Masculine preference:* How interesting do you think boys' books are?
Feminine preference: How interesting do you think women's magazines are?

SCORING: Items are objectively scored and equally weighted. Item scores are totaled to yield a masculine score and a feminine score.

DEVELOPMENT: An item pool of forty-two items (half masculine and half feminine) was administered to sixty-four children in the sixth grade. An item analysis was performed on the results, and items were selected for the final scale on the basis of satisfying two criteria: (1) high correlation with total score and (2) good discrimination between male and female children.

RELIABILITY: The scale was administered to twenty-six sixth-grade girls and twenty-seven sixth-grade boys on two occasions separated by about six months. The test-retest correlations for boys were .53 on the masculine scale and .52 on the feminine scale. The test-retest correlations for girls were .80 on the masculine scale and .52 on the feminine scale (Stein, 1973).

Item-total correlations were computed separately for thirty-two males and thirty-two females in the sixth grade. On the feminine scale, item-total correlations ranged from .30 to .90 (median = .65) for males and .20 to .90 (median = .65) for females. On the masculine scale, item-total correlations ranged from .00 to .80 (median = .50) for males and .10 to .95 (median = .70) for females (Stein, 1973).

VALIDITY: When the scale was administered to 235 sixth and ninth graders, significant differences were found between the mean scores for boys and for girls (p < .001) on both the masculinity and femininity scales. On the masculine scale, there was a significant difference in the means for older and younger children (p < .05) and a significant Sex x Socioeconomic Status (SES) interaction effect (p < .05). For the feminine scale, there was a significant difference due to SES and a significant Age x SES interaction effect (p < .05) (Stein, 1971).

Stein herself questions the validity of the scale: "The scale was expected to predict children's motivation and effort on sex-typed tasks in two studies. . . . In one study (Stein, Pohly and Mueller, 1971), the masculine and feminine scales did predict some indices of motivation and effort for females but not for males. In the other study (Stein, 1971), there was no relation of either scale to reported motivation on sex-typed tasks" (Stein, 1973, p. 4).

NOTES AND COMMENTS: (1) For the twenty-six female and twenty-seven male sixth graders who completed the scale twice, correlations were computed between their scores on the masculinity and femininity scales. For males, the correlation was .21 on the first test administration and .15 on the second test administration. For females, the correlation was −.28 for the first administration and .05 for the second administration. None of these correlations is significant, suggesting that the scales are independent (Stein, 1973).

(2) The test-retest correlations are unacceptably low. Test-retest correlations should be recomputed using a shorter interval between the two test administrations. This would indicate whether the test is unreliable or whether real changes took place in the respondents due to the long interval between the two test administrations.

(3) The lack of sufficient evidence of validity may be related to the low reliability of the scale, and both may be related to the fact that some of the questions are ambiguous. For example, the item "How much do you dislike mens' chores at home?" is subject to numerous interpretations. "Mens' chores" is very ambiguous.

(4) The scale has also been described in *Tests and Measurements in Child Development: Handbook II* (Johnson, 1976, pp. 631-632).

SOURCE: Aletha Stein
           Human Development and Family Life
           University of Kansas
           Lawrence, Kansas 66045

BIBLIOGRAPHY:

*Johnson, O. G. *Tests and Measurements in Child Development: Handbook II.* San Francisco: Jossey-Bass, 1976.

Stein, A. H. "The Effects of Sex Role Standards for Achievement and Sex Role Preference on Three Determinants of Achievement Motivation." *Developmental Psychology,* 1971, *4,* 219-231.

Stein, A. H. "Sex Role Preference Questionnaire." Unpublished manuscript, University of Kansas, 1973.

Stein, A. H., Pohly, S. R., and Mueller, E. "The Influence of Masculine, Feminine, and Neutral Tasks on Children's Achievement Behavior, Expectancies of Success, and Attainment Value." *Child Development,* 1971, *42,* 195-207.

---

28. SILVERMAN COMPULSIVE MASCULINITY SCALE

AUTHOR: Ira Jay Silverman

DATE: 1970

VARIABLE: Compulsive masculinity

TYPE OF INSTRUMENT: Alternate choice

DESCRIPTION: The instrument contains thirty-two statements regarding "tough" or illegal behavior. For each statement, the boy is to indicate whether the statement is "Like me" or "Not like me."

PREVIOUSLY ADMINISTERED TO: Delinquent boys, ages 14-19

APPROPRIATE FOR: Delinquent males, ages 14-19

ADMINISTRATION: The test can be self-administered, but in order to control for differences in reading ability, Silverman administered it via audio tape. The boys recorded their answers after the tape "read" the statement.

SAMPLE ITEMS: I am known in my neighborhood as a "mean dude."
          I am really hip to the new dance step.

SCORING: Items are objectively scored and equally weighted. Higher scores indicate more compulsive masculinity.

DEVELOPMENT: A review of the literature indicated that compulsive masculinity is composed of two primary dimensions: toughness and sexual athleticism. Items were constructed to assess these two dimensions. The items were reviewed by "several boys from lower-class areas" (Silverman, 1970, p. 36) and some additions and modifications were made as a result of their inputs. A fifty-one-item scale was administered to seventy-four boys in an institution serving delinquent boys. Their responses were subjected to an internal consistency analysis, which resulted in the elimination of nineteen items. The remaining thirty-two items comprise the scale.

RELIABILITY: No data are provided.

VALIDITY: A sample of 284 boys living in an institution for delinquent boys completed the Silverman Compulsive Masculinity Scale and several other instruments. Correlations were computed between the measures. The correlations between the Silverman Compulsive Masculinity Scale and each of the other measures follow: the Lykken Scale, a measure to differentiate sociopaths and nonsociopaths = .39 (p < 01); the Zuckerman Sensation Seeking Scale, a measure reflecting the desire for personally stimulating activities = .20 (p < .01); the Gough Socialization Scale, a measure of tendency toward delinquency = .43 (p < .01); a self-rating of manliness = .01 (nonsignificant); a self-rating of toughness = .18 (p < .01); a self-report measure of prior involvement in deviant activities = .55 (p < .01); and a brief measure of attitudes relating to delinquent behavior = .37 (p < .01) (Silverman, 1970).
      Silverman hypothesized that scores from the Silverman Compulsive Masculinity Scale would be higher (1) for older boys, (2) for black boys, (3) for boys from matriarchal homes, (4) for boys with serious delinquency histories, and (5) for boys placed in an on-the-job training program rather than a vocational education program. His first and third hypotheses were not supported by the data. His second and fifth hypotheses were supported by the data. His fourth hypothesis was essentially supported in that the results from three of the four indicators of delinquency history were in the predicted direction. Silverman does not report the statistical significance of the findings that support any of his hypotheses (Silverman, 1970).

NOTES AND COMMENTS: (1) The scale was developed with delinquent boys and Silverman used the scale with delinquent boys. There is no information that allows one to judge the appropriateness of the scale for nondelinquent boys. In fact, an examination of the item content suggests that the scale may be inappropriate for nondelinquent boys.

(2) Slang is frequently used in the phrasing of the scale items. Anyone unfamiliar with the slang used would be unable to understand the items. Furthermore, since slang frequently changes, the scale has a limited "life-expectancy."

SOURCE: See Silverman, 1970.

BIBLIOGRAPHY:

Silverman, I. J. "Compulsive Masculinity and Delinquency." Unpublished doctoral dissertation, Ohio State University, 1970. (*Dissertation Abstracts International,* 1971, *31*[9-A], 4914-4915.)
Silverman, I. J., and Dinitz, S. "Compulsive Masculinity and Delinquency: An Empirical Investigation." *Criminology,* 1974, *11,* 498-515.

---

29. THE TOY PREFERENCE TEST

AUTHOR: Lenore A. DeLucia

DATE: 1963

VARIABLE: Sex role identification

TYPE OF INSTRUMENT: Forced choice picture preference

DESCRIPTION: The test consists of twenty-four pairs of black-and-white photographs (5" x 7"), each displaying one toy. Four pairs contain a toy with a masculine rating paired with a toy with a feminine rating; ten pairs contain toys that both received masculine ratings; and ten pairs contain toys that both received feminine ratings. There are two forms of the test.

PREVIOUSLY ADMINISTERED TO: Grades K-4

APPROPRIATE FOR: Ages 4-9

ADMINISTRATION: The pairs of photographs are placed on a flannel board, one pair at a time, along with a black-and-white ink drawing of a child who is the same sex as the respondent. The respondent is asked to indicate which one of the pair of toys the child on the flannel board would prefer to play with.

SAMPLE ITEMS: Wheelbarrow—erector set
                          Teddy bear—jump rope

SCORING: One point is scored for each sex-appropriate response; that is, boys receive one point each time they select the toy with the more masculine (lower) rating and girls receive one point each time they select the toy with the more feminine (higher) rating (ratings are explained below). The maximum score is 24.

DEVELOPMENT: Nineteen female and twenty-eight male college students were shown photographs of fifty-two toys and asked to rate them on a nine-point scale, with 9 indicating a very feminine toy, 5 indicating a toy equally appropriate for boys and girls, and 1 indicating a very masculine toy. Using the mean rating of each toy, the toys were listed in rank order. Four toys were eliminated from the original list and the remaining forty-eight toys were divided into two equivalent sets (A and B) of twenty-four toys by assigning every other toy in the ranked list to one set. In each set, a toy is paired with two other toys in the same set. Procedures for determining pairs are not explained.

RELIABILITY: Alternate-form reliability (rho) based on eighteen kindergarten children who responded to sets A and B was .57. Each child was given both sets by the same examiner. Test-retest reliabilities were estimated for kindergarteners (one- to four-week interval), second graders (seven-day interval), and third graders (ten-day interval). Kindergarteners and second graders were tested by a female examiner; third graders were tested by a male examiner. The reliability estimates were .21 and .13 for girls (tested by same-sex examiner) in kindergarten and second grade, respectively. Reliability estimates were .67 and .72 for boys (tested by opposite-sex examiner) in kindergarten and second grade, respectively. In third grade, the reliability for boys (tested by same-sex examiner) was .37, and for girls (tested by opposite-sex examiner) it was .70 (DeLucia, 1963).

Item-total correlations based on the responses from thirty-nine boys in kindergarten through second grade ranged from .18 to .95 with a median of .46. The correlations for a comparable group of girls ranged from −.22 to .72 with a median of .30.

VALIDITY: The mean number of sex-appropriate choices for both boys and girls increased with increasing grade level for kindergarteners, first, second, and third graders. DeLucia (1963) claims that this provides some evidence of validity.

A male examiner gave fourth graders the Toy Preference Test and a modification of the Checklist of Games and Play Activities (#4), a measure of masculinity-femininity. For boys (same-sex examiner), the correlation (rho) was −.13; for girls (opposite-sex examiner), the correlation (rho) was .64 (DeLucia, 1963).

NOTES AND COMMENTS: (1) Further work needs to be done on the effects of the experimenter's sex relative to the respondent's sex.

(2) Though the masculinity-femininity of the toy pairs is balanced, no indication is given as to whether the toys are balanced in other ways. For example, the pairs should be balanced in terms of color, size, and number of moving parts.

(3) Selcer and Hilton (1970) modified the procedure. They showed the child pictures of twenty-four toys and asked the child to select his or her eight favorite toys.

(4) DeLucia (1963) does not indicate what toys are in Set B.

SOURCE: See DeLucia, 1963.

BIBLIOGRAPHY:

DeLucia, L. A. "The Toy Preference Test: A Measure of Sex Role Identification." *Child Development*, 1963, *34*, 107-117.

Marr, J. "Can Training Change Sex Role Stereotypes?" *Psychology,* 1974, *11,* 10-16. (Reprinted in *Psychological Studies,* 1975, *20,* 16-24.)

Selcer, R. J., and Hilton, I. R. *Cultural Differences in the Acquisition of Sex-Roles.* 1970. (ERIC Document Reproduction Service No. ED 077 585.)

---

30. ZUCKER FANTASY PREFERENCE MEASURE

AUTHOR: Robert A. Zucker

DATE: 1968

VARIABLE: Unconscious sex role identity

TYPE OF INSTRUMENT: Open-ended questions

DESCRIPTION: The instrument consists of two open-ended questions, one asking the respondents to name three books or movies that they had "liked very much in the last few years" and one asking the respondents to name three that they had disliked. Next to each book or movie listed, the respondent is asked to provide a one-sentence description of the item listed.

PREVIOUSLY ADMINISTERED TO: Adolescents

APPROPRIATE FOR: Ages 10 and older

ADMINISTRATION: The scale can be self-administered and can be completed in about fifteen minutes.

SCORING: Listed books and movies are scorable if they reflect a masculine theme (sports, adventure/war, or man-machine relationships) or a feminine theme (suffering/hardship, romance, teenage life, or religious/inspirational). The remaining books and movies are considered unscorable and assigned a value of 0. Books and movies that are scorable are assigned a weight of +1 if they are masculine and liked, a score of −1 if they are masculine and disliked, a score of −1 if they are feminine and liked, and a score of +1 if they are feminine and disliked. Item scores are algebraically summed. If the result is positive, the respondent is classified as "masculine"; if negative, the respondent is "feminine"; and if 0, the respondent is classified as "indeterminate."

DEVELOPMENT: Twenty-four categories were developed for classifying books and movies. "In establishing the categories, the intent was to choose psychologically meaningful divisions that were related to the vicarious experience of the reader as he identified with the main figure or figures in the narrative" (Zucker and Fillmore, 1969, p. 426). The instrument was administered to 100 boys and 100 girls in freshman and sophomore high school classes. Their responses were classified according to the twenty-four categories. On seven categories, there was a significant difference in the frequency with which males and females had listed books and movies that fell into the categories. The categories adventure/war ($p < .001$), sports ($p < .001$), and man-machine relationships ($p < .01$) were used significantly more often to classify boys' responses. The categories suffering/hardship ($p < .001$), romance ($p < .001$), teenage life ($p < .001$), and religious/inspirational ($p < .01$) were used significantly more often to classify girls' responses. Thus books and movies falling into these seven categories are scorable on the measure of sex role preference.

RELIABILITY: Two coders independently classified the responses from the validation sample. They agreed on 91 percent of the items scored (Zucker and Fillmore, 1969).

VALIDITY: Respondents were classified as masculine, feminine, or indeterminate. When gender was the criterion, 60 percent of the respondents were correctly classified, 7.5 percent were incorrectly classified, and 32.5 percent were labeled "indeterminate." A point-biserial correlation between gender and the algebraic summation score equaled .62.

NOTES AND COMMENTS: (1) This instrument represents a novel approach to measuring sex role identity, but the specific examples in the coding forms must be regularly updated to be of use.

(2) The authors do not address the issue of how to handle instances in which the respondent has not seen three movies or read three books within the prior few years. Furthermore, if the respondent only read feminine (or masculine) books within the prior few years, then the score would have to be zero. For example, if one read only feminine books, then the three most liked and the three most disliked books would all be feminine, thereby yielding a score of zero.

(3) Rather than measuring unconscious sex role identity, which is what the author claims it measures, the instrument seems to measure sex role preference.

SOURCE: See Zucker and Fillmore, 1969.

BIBLIOGRAPHY:

Zucker, R. A. "Sex Role Identity Patterns and Drinking Behavior of Adolescents." *Quarterly Journal of Studies on Alcohol,* 1968, *29,* 868-884.

Zucker, R. A., and Fillmore, K. M. "Masculinity-Femininity in Fantasy Preferences: An Indirect Approach." *Journal of Projective Techniques and Personality Assessment,* 1969, *33,* 424-432.

Adults

Included in this section are instruments that are appropriate for adults: all are appropriate for persons over age 21 and none is appropriate for persons below age 12. Full descriptions, following the standard format used in this book, are provided for four-teen instruments, and abridged descriptions are provided for fifteen others. Each of these fifteen instruments yields numerous scores, at least one of which is relevant to sex role. The instruments for which abridged descriptions are provided are all described and re-viewed in a *Mental Measurements Yearbook.*

The most frequently used instrument for adults is the Minnesota Multiphasic Per-sonality Inventory (#52), which yields scores for a variety of variables; hence, only an abridged description of it is given here. Of the fully described instruments, the most fre-quently used is the Attitude Interest Analysis Test (#31). Published in 1936, it is also the oldest instrument in this section and hence of questionable value today. Of the newer instruments, the Bem Sex Role Inventory (#32) has been the most frequently used.

Proportionally more is known about the measures described in this section than in many other chapters of this book. Information is provided on the development of all fourteen fully described instruments; data relevant to reliability are provided for twelve; and some information is given regarding the validity of all fourteen. Furthermore, though information is not included here pertaining to the development, reliability, and validity of the fifteen scales with abridged descriptions, the information is available elsewhere.

As was the case with sex role measures intended for children and adolescents, many of these measures highlight the problems previously discussed regarding sex role instruments. Most authors claim that their instruments measure masculinity and feminin-ity rather than masculinity and femininity of a particular aspect of sex role. Also half of the instruments treat masculinity and femininity as though they are the ends of a single continuum rather than separate continua. However, whereas all of the measures for chil-dren and adolescents are assumed to be unidimensional, four of the measures intended for adults yield several scores. That is, some attempt is made for scores to reflect the multi-dimensionality of the underlying variable. The instruments in this section also differ from those intended for children and adolescents in terms of the focus of the item content. The measures for children most often focused on interests; the measures for adults most often focus on personality traits.

As was the case with measures for children, the development of these adult mea-sures highlights the lack of a theoretical basis for instrument development. All fourteen fully described instruments were developed on the basis of an empirical procedure. For seven, actual differences in responses elicited from men and women served as the criterion for item selection. For the other seven, stereotyped conceptions of masculinity and femininity served as the criterion for item selection. As mentioned previously, this empiri-cally based procedure poses many problems, not the least of which is that the instruments become outdated as society's sex role norms change. Furthermore, an empirically based instrument may not be appropriate for a group different from that on which it was devel-oped. Seven of the fourteen instruments that follow were developed on the basis of col-lege students' responses; these instruments may not be appropriate for noncollege popula-tions.

Finally, because the following instruments were all developed solely on an empiri-cal basis, caution should be exercised in interpreting scores from them and questions can legitimately be raised regarding their usefulness.

31. ATTITUDE INTEREST ANALYSIS TEST

AUTHORS: Lewis M. Terman and Catharine Cox Miles

DATE: 1936

VARIABLE: Masculinity-femininity

TYPE OF INSTRUMENT: Multiple choice

DESCRIPTION: There are two forms of the test: Form A (456 items) and Form B (454 items). Each form includes seven subtests which are called "exercises." Exercise 1, entitled "Word Association," includes sixty items on each form. Each item consists of one word followed by four other words. The respondent's task is to indicate which of the four words "seems to go best or most naturally with" the key word. Exercise 2 is entitled "Ink-blot Association" and includes eighteen items on each form. Each item consists of a somewhat ambiguous black-and-white drawing followed by the names of four objects that might be what the picture represents. The respondent is to indicate which word "tells what the drawing makes you think of most." Exercise 3, entitled "Information," includes seventy items on each form. Each item is an incomplete sentence followed by four options for completing the sentence. The respondent is to identify "the word that makes the sentence true." All of the items are factual statements that do have right and wrong answers, though they are not scored on the basis of whether the answer is right or wrong. Exercise 4, entitled "Emotional and Ethical Response," includes 105 items on each of the two forms. This exercise includes six parts. The first four parts ask the respondents to indicate how much of a particular emotion they experience in response to specific things. The emotions are anger (seventeen items), fear (twenty items), disgust (eighteen items), and pity (fifteen items on Form A and fourteen items on Form B). The response options are: very much, much, a little, and none. On the fifth part, the respondent is given a list of twenty-eight items and asked to indicate how wicked or bad each is. The response options are: extremely wicked, decidedly bad, somewhat bad, and not really bad. The last part of Exercise 4 provides pairs of activities and asks the respondents to indicate which of the pair they prefer or that the two activities are liked equally well. Form A has seven items of this type and Form B has eight items. Exercise 5 is entitled "Interests"; it includes 119 items on Form A and 118 items on Form B. For each item, the respondents are to indicate whether they like, are indifferent to, or dislike the item. The items include such things as occupations, games, book titles, artistic subjects, and social activities. Exercise 6, entitled "Personalities and Opinions," includes forty-two items on Form A and forty-one items on Form B. This exercise consists of two parts: the first part asks the respondents to indicate whether they like, dislike, or neither like nor dislike each of a list of famous persons; the second part asks the respondents to indicate whether each of a series of statements is true or false. The statements are a matter of opinion and not fact. Exercise 7, entitled "Introvertive Response," includes forty-two items on each of the two forms. Each item is a question similar to the type typically found on personality tests. The questions are each to be answered "yes" or "no."

PREVIOUSLY ADMINISTERED TO: Ages 12 and older

APPROPRIATE FOR: Ages 12 and older

ADMINISTRATION: The test can be self-administered; it is generally completed in forty to fifty minutes, although occasionally it may take an hour.

SAMPLE ITEMS:

Word Association: POLE: Barber   cat   North   telephone

Ink-blot Association: A picture of a slightly irregular circle with a comparable, but smaller circle inside is followed by the options: dish, ring, target, and tire.

Information: Marigold is a kind of   fabric   flower   grain   stone

Emotional and Ethical Response:
* anger—Being blamed for something you have not done
* fear—Automobiles
* disgust—An unshaven man
* pity—A bee that is drowning
* wickedness—Picking flowers in a public park
* choice of activities—make plans OR carry out plans

Interests: People with loud voices (like, dislike, neither like nor dislike)

Personalities and Opinions: Jane Addams (like, dislike, neither like nor dislike)
                              The face shows how intelligent a person is. (true, false)

Introvertive Response: Do you like most people you know? (yes, no)

SCORING: The test yields a score on each of the seven exercises and a total score. A scoring key is provided which indicates whether each response is scored masculine, feminine, or neutral. In computing scores on the exercises, items are equally weighted. In computing total scores. Exercises 2 and 7 are multipled by one third, Exercises 1, 3, 4, and 6 are multiplied by one, and Exercise 5 is multiplied by two. Total scores for males generally range from +200 to −100 with a mean of +52; total scores for females generally range from +100 to −200 with a mean of −70.

DEVELOPMENT: The development of each exercise will be explained separately. In developing Exercise 1, the Word Association Test, an initial list of 500 words was compiled. Three judges rated the words in terms of their likelihood of eliciting sex differences. On the basis of the judges' ratings, the list was reduced to 200 words. A word association test was developed using 120 of the words from the set of 220 plus an additional 51 words. It was administered to 600 people: 100 males and 100 females in the seventh grade, in the junior year of high school, and in college. Using their responses, 120 words were selected for the final two forms (60 per form) if they "showed sex differences in the same direction for at least three of the four multiple responses in all the groups tested" (Terman and Miles, 1936, p. 25).

In the early stages of developing Exercise 2, the Ink-blot Association Exercise, pretesting was done using sixty blots. The results indicated that drawings with simple outlines were most appropriate for the intended purposes. One hundred new blots were constructed using simple outlines. Pretesting with 100 male and 100 female high school and college students resulted in the elimination of thirty blots. The remaining seventy blots were administered to 460 persons, including seventh graders, high school freshmen, college students, and nonacademic adults. The respondents were given the blots and asked to indicate what it reminded them of. No response alternatives were provided. The responses given were tabulated and "only those responses were retained for scoring which were given by as many as four subjects in at least three of the four groups tested and which showed a sex difference in the same direction for at least three of the four groups" (Terman and Miles, 1936, p. 28). The number of blots was then reduced to fifty by eliminating the twenty blots that produced the least satisfactory results. Response options were added to accompany each blot. The exercise was administered to 600 persons. For the final tests, thirty-six blots were selected: eighteen on each of the two forms.

To develop Exercise 3, the Information Exercise, a pool of 200 items was administered in multiple-choice format to 800 persons, including 100 males and 100 females in each of four groups: seventh graders, high school students, college students, and nonacademic adults. The ninety-one items that differentiated between the sexes in three of the four groups were retained. An additional pool of 491 items was administered to a sample of 200 persons. An analysis of the results suggested that ninety-five items should be retained. The final tests include 140 items (70 on each form) selected from the sets of ninety-one and ninety-five obtained from the earlier testing.

To develop Exercise 4, the Emotional and Ethical Response Exercise, a pool of items was developed. The initial items were developed by faculty and graduate students in psychology who suggested items that they hypothesized would arouse differing degrees of emotional reactions in males and females. As a result of discussions, some items were eliminated, leaving a pool of 218 items. This item pool was administered to 854 persons including eighth graders, high school students, and college students. The responses from these groups were used to select the 195 items for the final scales (Forms A and B). The last part of Exercise 4 was developed on the basis of the responses given by 239 male and 280 female respondents who were asked to indicate their preference on each of forty pairs of items. The fifteen pairs that best differentiated between males and females were selected for Exercise 4.

To develop Exercise 5, the Interests measure, a pool of 456 items was assembled. The item pool included occupations, people, games and amusements, movies, magazines, school subjects, books and literary characters, travel and sightseeing preferences, and special interests. The test was administered to 245 persons, including seventh graders, high school students, college students, and nonacademic adults. The best 170 items were retained for the final instrument. It is not explained how the 170 items were increased to the 237 items that currently comprise this exercise.

In developing Exercise 6, Personalities and Opinions, a pool of 201 items was compiled, including items from existing measures and new items. Some items were selected for the pool because judges had predicted that they would differentiate between males and females. The item pool was administered to more than 100 males and more than 100 females in the seventh grade and in high school and to 50 males and 50 females in college. Only twenty-eight items were found to differentiate between males and females in the three samples. These were retained and were divided between Forms A and B. In addition, sixty items relating to historical characters were administered to fifty males and fifty females in each of four samples. Fifty-five items differentiated between males and females and were retained for the final instrument.

To develop Exercise 7, the Introvertive Response Exercise, eighty-five items were administered to 100 teenage boys and 100 teenage girls. The fifty-one items that differentiated between boys and girls were then administered to 261 seventh graders and 210 high school freshmen. Another pool of forty-seven items was administered to 231 seventh graders and 231 high school students. From these ninety-eight items, the eighty-four that best discriminated between males and females were retained and divided between the two forms of the final instrument.

RELIABILITY: Using several different samples of respondents—including eighth graders, high school students, and college students—split-half reliabilities were computed for single-sex groups and combined-sex groups for each of the seven exercises in the test. The correlations were as follows (Terman and Miles, 1936).

Exercise	Single-sex groups	Combined-sex groups
1	.40	.62
2	.25	.34
3	.50	.68
4	.89	.90
5	.60	.80
6	.54	.64
7	.24	.32

Split-half reliability coefficients for the total score averaged .78 for single-sex groups and .92 for combined-sex groups. Split-half reliability for a total based on Forms A and B combined was .88 for single-sex groups and .96 for combined-sex groups. Alternate-form reliability was .72 for single-sex groups and .90 for combined-sex groups (Terman and Miles, 1936).

VALIDITY: The scores of males and females were significantly different. These significant differences were found when the samples were selected from populations of eighth graders, high school juniors, gifted teenagers, delinquents, English private school children, Japanese adolescents, college sophomores, college athletes, music college students, black college students, prostitutes, and the general adult population (Terman and Miles, 1936).

NOTES AND COMMENTS: (1) The intercorrelations between the exercises are generally low. For example, for a sample of eighth-grade girls, seventeen of the twenty-one correlations are less than or equal to +.20; the highest intercorrelation is between Exercises 3 and 4 (r = .35). For a sample of high school girls, sixteen of the twenty-one correlations are less than or equal to +.20; the highest intercorrelation is between Exercises 4 and 7 (r = .52) (Terman and Miles, 1936).

(2) Terman and Miles (1936) report data on the relationship between scores on the Attitude Interest Analysis Test and numerous other variables: physical measurements, trait ratings, personality indices, achievement measures, age, education, intelligence scores, and occupations. In addition, other researchers have investigated the relationship between scores on the Attitude Interest Analysis Test and other variables, for example, obesity, neuroticism, regional background, and other measures of masculinity-femininity.

(3) Terman and Miles (1936) report the results of a study in which the Attitude Interest Analysis Test was administered to fifty-two college students on three occasions with three different sets of instructions: standard instructions, instructions to answer with the most masculine response possible, and instructions to answer with the most feminine response possible. The results indicated clearly that responses can be faked. However, Terman and Miles point out that the title of the test is deliberately intended to disguise the purpose of the test and respondents do not seem to suspect what the test is actually trying to measure.

(4) Terman and Miles (1936) provide extensive normative data, but the data are quite old.

(5) When this instrument was developed in 1936, it was unusual in terms of the care that went into its development and the extent to which it was empirically constructed. However, it is obviously quite old and a review of the items reveals that many would no longer differentiate between males and females (Lunneborg, 1972). Furthermore, many of the items would be unfamiliar to people today. Nevertheless, it is included here because it has historical import and some researchers are still using the exercises.

(6) This scale has been described and reviewed in *The Third Mental Measurements Yearbook* (Buros, 1949, entry 24).

SOURCE: See Terman and Miles, 1936.

BIBLIOGRAPHY:

Angrilli, A. F. "A Study of the Psychosexual Identification of Preschool Boys." Unpublished doctoral dissertation, New York University, 1957. (*Dissertation Abstracts,* 1958, *19*[4], 874-875.)

Angrilli, A. F. "The Psychosexual Identification of Preschool Boys." *Journal of Genetic Psychology,* 1960, *97,* 329-340.

Barnett, W. L. "Study of an Adult Male Homosexual and Terman-Miles M-F Scores." *American Journal of Orthopsychiatry,* 1942, *12,* 346-351.

Berenberg, A. N. "A Study of the Relationship Between Skills in Certain Cognitive Areas and Certain Patterns Involving Attitudes, Interests, and Identifications in Eighth-Grade Students." Unpublished doctoral dissertation, New York University, 1957. (*Dissertation Abstracts,* 1958, *18*[2], 651-652.)

Bosselman, B., and Skorodin, B. "Masculinity and Femininity in Psychotic Patients: As Measured by the Terman-Miles Interest Attitude Analysis Test." *American Journal of Psychiatry,* 1940, *97,* 699-702.

Botwinick, J., and Machover, S. "A Psychometric Examination of Latent Homosexuality in Alcoholism." *Quarterly Journal of Studies on Alcohol,* 1951, *12,* 268-272.

Burger, F. E., Nemzek, C. L., and Vaughn, C. L. "The Relationship of Certain Factors to Scores on the Terman-Miles Attitude Interest Analysis Test." *Journal of Social Psychology,* 1942, *16,* 39-50.

*Buros, O. K. *The Third Mental Measurements Yearbook.* Highland Park, N.J.: Rutgers University Press, 1949.

Capwell, D. F. "Personality Patterns of Adolescent Girls: II. Delinquents and Nondelinquents." *Journal of Applied Psychology,* 1945, *29,* 289-297.

Carter, L., and Nixon, M. "Ability, Perceptual, Personality, and Interest Factors Associated with Different Criteria of Leadership." *Journal of Psychology,* 1949, *27,* 377-388.

Crummer, M. L. "Sex Role Identification, 'Motive to Avoid Success,' and Competitive Performance in College Women." Unpublished doctoral dissertation, University of Florida, 1972. (*Dissertation Abstracts International,* 1973, *34*[1-B], 408.)

de Cillis, O. E., and Orbison, W. D. "A Comparison of the Terman-Miles M-F Test and the M-F Scale of the MMPI." *Journal of Applied Psychology,* 1950, *34,* 338-342.

Disher, D. R. "Attitude Interest Analysis of Florida State College for Women Students." *Psychological Bulletin,* 1939, *36,* 616.

Disher, D. R. "Regional Differences in Masculinity-Femininity Responses." *Journal of Social Psychology,* 1942, *15,* 53-61.

Durea, M. A., and Bilsky, H. B. "An Exploratory Study of Personality Characteristics in Schizophrenia and Manic-Depressive Psychoses." *Journal of General Psychology,* 1943, *28,* 81-98.

Engel, I. M. "A Factor-Analytic Study of Items from Five Masculinity-Femininity Tests." Unpublished doctoral dissertation, University of Michigan, 1962. (*Dissertation Abstracts,* 1962, *23*[1], 307-308.)

Engel, I. M. "A Factor-Analytic Study of Items from Five Masculinity-Femininity Tests." *Journal of Consulting Psychology,* 1966, *30,* 565.

Farr, R. S. "Personality Variables and Problem Solving Performance: An Investigation of the Relationships Between Field-Dependence-Independence, Sex Role Identification, Problem Difficulty, and Problem Solving Performance." Unpublished doctoral dissertation, New York University, 1968. (*Dissertation Abstracts,* 1969, *29*[8-A], 2561-2562.)

Ferguson, L. W. "The Cultural Genesis of Masculinity-Femininity." *Psychological Bulletin,* 1941, *38,* 584-585.

Fisher, A. C. "The Relationship Between Participation in Selected Sport Activities and Sex Role Orientation of Institutionalized Males." Unpublished doctoral dissertation, Ohio State University, 1970. (*Dissertation Abstracts International,* 1971, *31*[10-A], 5175.)

Fisher, S., and Hinds, E. "The Organization of Hostility Controls in Various Personality Structures." *Genetic Psychology Monographs,* 1951, *44,* 3-68.

Fleming, P. A. D. "Masculinity-Femininity and the Generation Gap as Reflected in University Graduates Twenty Years Ago and Today." Unpublished doctoral dissertation, University of Northern Colorado, 1971. (*Dissertation Abstracts International,* 1972, *32*[10-B], 6028.)

Ford, C. F., and Tyler, L. "A Factor Analysis of Terman and Miles M-F Test." *Journal of Applied Psychology,* 1952, *36,* 251-253.

Franz, J. G. "Social Status and Masculinity-Femininity." Unpublished doctoral dissertation, Ohio State University, 1960. (*Dissertation Abstracts,* 1960, *21*[1], 260.)

Gilkinson, H. "Masculine Temperament and Secondary Sex Characteristics: A Study of the Relationship Between Psychological and Physical Measures of Masculinity." *Genetic Psychology Monographs,* 1937, *19,* 105-154.

Gilkinson, H., and Knower, F. H. "A Study of Standardized Personality Tests and Skill in Speech." *Journal of Educational Psychology,* 1941, *32,* 161-175.

Green, L. "Relationship Between Semantic Differential Measurement of Concept Meanings and Parent-Sex Identification Phenomenon: A Study of the Construct Validity of the Semantic Differential." Unpublished doctoral dissertation, Yeshiva University, 1964. (*Dissertation Abstracts,* 1964, *25*[5], 3100-3101.)

Hardy, V. T. "Relation of Dominance to Nondirectiveness in Counseling." *Journal of Clinical Psychology,* 1948, *4,* 300-303.

Kline, M. V. "A Measure of Mental Masculinity and Femininity in Relation to Hypnotic Age Progression." *Journal of Genetic Psychology,* 1951, *78,* 207-215.

Kokonis, N. D. "Sex Role Identification in Schizophrenia: Psychoanalytic and Role-Theory Predictions Compared." Unpublished doctoral dissertation, Illinois Institute of Technology, 1971. (*Dissertation Abstracts International,* 1971, *32*[3-B], 1849-1850.)

Kokonis, N. D. "Choice of Gender on the DAP and Measures of Sex Role Identification." *Perceptual and Motor Skills,* 1972a, *35,* 727-730.

Kokonis, N. D. "Sex Role Identification in Neurosis: Psychoanalytic-Developmental and

Role Theory Predictions Compared." *Journal of Abnormal Psychology,* 1972b, *80,* 52-57.

Kokonis, N. D. "Parental Dominance and Sex Role Identification in Schizophrenia." *Journal of Psychology,* 1973, *84,* 211-218.

Lamkin, F. D. "Masculinity-Femininity of Preadolescent Youth in Relation to Behavior Acceptability, Tested and Graded Achievement, Inventoried Interests, and General Intelligence." Unpublished doctoral dissertation, University of Virginia, 1967. (*Dissertation Abstracts,* 1968, *28*[7-A], 2558.)

Lee, M. C. "Relationship of Masculinity-Femininity to Tests of Mechanical and Clerical Abilities." *Journal of Applied Psychology,* 1952, *36,* 377-380.

Lefley, H. P. "Masculinity-Femininity in Obese Women." *Journal of Consulting and Clinical Psychology,* 1971, *37,* 180-186.

Lessler, K. J. "The Anatomical and Cultural Dimensions of Sexual Symbols." Unpublished doctoral dissertation, Michigan State University, 1962. (*Dissertation Abstracts,* 1962, *23,* 3976.)

Lunneborg, P. W. "Dimensionality of M-F." *Journal of Clinical Psychology,* 1972, *28,* 313-317.

McCarthy, D., Schiro, F. M., and Sudimack, J. P. "Comparison of WAIS M-F Index with Two Measures of Masculinity-Femininity." *Journal of Consulting Psychology,* 1967, *31,* 639-640.)

Meredith, G. M. "Sex Temperament Among Japanese-American College Students in Hawaii." *Journal of Social Psychology,* 1969, *77,* 149-156.

Milgram, N. A. "Cognitive and Empathic Factors in Role Taking by Schizophrenic and Brain-Damaged Patients." *Journal of Abnormal and Social Psychology,* 1960, *60,* 219-224.

Milgram, N. A. "Role Taking in Female Schizophrenic Patients." *Journal of Clinical Psychology,* 1961, *17,* 409-411.

Milton, G. A. "The Effects of Sex Role Identification upon Problem-Solving Skill." *Journal of Abnormal Social Psychology,* 1957, *55,* 208-212.

Milton, G. A. "The Effects of Sex Role Identification upon Problem-Solving Skill." Unpublished doctoral dissertation, Stanford University, 1958a. (*Dissertation Abstracts,* 1958, *19*[4], 871.)

Milton, G. A. "Five Studies of the Relation Between Sex Role Identification and Achievement in Problem Solving." Technical Report 3. New Haven, Conn.: Yale University, 1958b. (ERIC Document Reproduction Service No. ED 136 078.)

Newton, N. *Maternal Emotions.* New York: Paul B. Hoeber, 1955.

Page, J., and Warkentin, J. "Masculinity and Paranoia." *Journal of Abnormal and Social Psychology,* 1938, *33,* 527-531.

Parker, F. B. "A Comparison of the Sex Temperament of Alcoholics and Moderate Drinkers." *American Sociological Review,* 1959, *24,* 366-374.

Parker, F. B. "Self-Role Strain and Drinking Disposition at a Prealcoholic Age Level." *Journal of Social Psychology,* 1969, *78,* 55-61.

Parker, F. B. "Sex Role Adjustment in Women Alcoholics." *Quarterly Journal of Studies on Alcohol,* 1972, *33,* 647-657.

Parker, F. B. "Sex Role Adjustment and Drinking Disposition of Women College Students." *Quarterly Journal of Studies on Alcohol,* 1975, *36,* 1570-1573.

Pintner, R., and Forlano, G. "Some Measures of Dominance in College Women." *Journal of Social Psychology,* 1944, *19,* 313-315.

Rosenzweig, S. "A Basis for the Improvement of Personality Tests with Special

Reference to the M-F Battery." *Journal of Abnormal and Social Psychology*, 1938, *33*, 476-488.

Sappenfield, B. R. "Test of a Szondi Assumption by Means of M-F Photographs." *Journal of Personality*, 1965, *33*, 409-417.

Sappenfield, B. R., and Balogh, B. "Stereotypical M-F as Related to Two Szondi Test Assumptions." *Journal of Projective Techniques and Personality Assessment*, 1966, *30*, 387-393.

Sebald, H. "Parent-Peer Control and Masculinity-Marital Role Perceptions of Adolescent Boys." Unpublished doctoral dissertation, Ohio State University, 1963. (*Dissertation Abstracts*, 1964, *24*[7], 3003.)

Seward, G. H. "Cultural Conflict and the Feminine Role: An Experimental Study." *Journal of Social Psychology*, 1945, *22*, 177-194.

Shepler, B. F. "A Comparison of Masculinity-Femininity Measures." *Journal of Consulting Psychology*, 1951, *15*, 484-486.

Smith, J. H. "The Relation of Masculinity-Femininity Scores of Sorority Girls on a Free-Association Test to Those of Their Parents." *Journal of Social Psychology*, 1945, *22*, 79-85.

Stanek, R. J. "A Note on the Presumed Measures of Masculinity-Femininity." *Personnel and Guidance Journal*, 1959, *37*, 439-440.

Terman, L. M., and Miles, C. C. *Sex and Personality*. New York: McGraw-Hill, 1936.

Tyler, L., "The Measured Interests of Adolescent Girls." *Journal of Educational Psychology*, 1941, *32*, 561-572.

Walker, E. L. "The Terman-Miles 'M-F' Test and the Prison Classification Program." *Journal of Genetic Psychology*, 1941, *59*, 27-40.

Weiss, P. "Some Aspects of Femininity." Unpublished doctoral dissertation, University of Colorado, 1962. (*Dissertation Abstracts*, 1962, *23*[3], 1083.)

Weitzenhoffer, A. M. "Hypnotic Susceptibility as Related to Masculinity-Femininity." Unpublished doctoral dissertation, University of Michigan, 1956. (*Dissertation Abstracts*, 1956, *17*, 1397.)

Zuckerman, L. "The Relationship Between Sex Differences in Certain Mental Abilities and Masculine-Feminine Sex Identification." Unpublished doctoral dissertation, New York University, 1955. (*Dissertation Abstracts*, 1955, *15*[7], 1251-1252.)

32. BEM SEX ROLE INVENTORY (BSRI)

AUTHOR: Sandra L. Bem

DATE: 1974

VARIABLES: Masculinity, femininity, androgyny, social desirability

TYPE OF INSTRUMENT: Adjective rating scale

DESCRIPTION: The BSRI consists of a list of sixty adjectives: twenty masculine, twenty feminine, and twenty neutral. Respondents are to rate themselves on each adjective using a seven-point rating scale ranging from 1 ("never or almost never true") to 7 ("always or almost always true").

PREVIOUSLY ADMINISTERED TO: Grade 6 and older

APPROPRIATE FOR: Ages 12 and older

ADMINISTRATION: The scale can be self-administered and can be completed in about fifteen minutes.

SAMPLE ITEMS: *Masculine:* acts as a leader
                 Feminine: affectionate
                 Neutral: adaptable

SCORING: The scale yields four scores: masculinity, femininity, androgyny, and social desirability. The masculinity score is the mean of the self-ratings on the twenty masculine items; the femininity score is the mean of the self-ratings on the twenty feminine items. Thus masculinity and femininity scores can range from 1 to 7. Two different procedures can be used to find androgyny scores. The simplest procedure is to subtract the masculinity score from the femininity score. This procedure is recommended by Strahan (1975) and yields results that correlate .98 with results obtained by the more complicated procedure (Bem, 1974). In the more complicated procedure, "the androgyny score is the difference between an individual's masculinity and femininity normalized with respect to the standard deviations of his or her masculinity and femininity scores" (Bem, 1974, p. 158). The social desirability score is the mean of the self-ratings on the neutral items calculated after the ratings on the ten undesirable characteristics are reversed. Scores can range from 1 (describes self in socially undesirable way) to 7 (describes self in socially desirable way).

DEVELOPMENT: A list of 400 personality characteristics was compiled: 200 items were preselected because they seemed to be masculine or feminine in tone; 200 items were preselected because they seemed neutral in tone. The list of 400 items was given to fifty male and fifty female college students with instructions to rate the items. Half the judges were asked to rate the items according to how desirable each characteristic was in a man; half the judges were asked to rate the items according to how desirable each characteristic was in a woman. A seven-point rating scale ranging from "not at all desirable" to "extremely desirable" was used. Twenty items that were judged significantly more desirable for a man than for a woman (p < .05) comprise the masculinity scale. Similarly, twenty items that were judged significantly more desirable for a woman than for a man (p < .05) comprise the femininity scale. Twenty items that were judged to be no more desirable for one sex than for the other comprise the neutral items. Half the neutral items selected were positive personality characteristics and half were negative personality characteristics.

RELIABILITY: Test-retest reliabilities were computed using a test-retest interval of approximately four weeks. The results for twenty-eight college men and twenty-eight college women were: masculinity = .90; femininity = .90; androgyny = .93; and social desirability = .89 (Bem, 1974).
     Coefficient alpha was used to estimate internal consistency for two groups of col-

lege students (n = 723 and n = 194). The results for the two groups, respectively, were: masculinity = .86 and .86; femininity = .80 and .82; androgyny = .85 and .86; and social desirability = .75 and .70 (Bem, 1974).

Tetenbaum (1977) also estimated the internal reliability of the scales. Using the responses from 400 females, he calculated an alpha coefficient of .89 for the masculinity scale and .79 for the femininity scale. Using the responses from 171 males, he calculated an alpha coefficient of .89 on the masculinity scale and .77 on the femininity scale.

VALIDITY: In two groups of college students, males (n = 444 and 117) scored significantly higher ($\overline{X}$ = 4.97 and 4.96) than females (n = 279 and 77, $\overline{X}$ = 4.57 and 4.55) on the masculinity scale (p < .001). Conversely, the college females scored significantly higher ($\overline{X}$ = 5.01 and 5.08) than the college males ($\overline{X}$ = 4.44 and 4.62) on the femininity scale (p < .001) (Bem, 1974). These sex differences on the masculinity and femininity BSRI scales have been substantiated by other studies (Deutsch and Gilbert, 1976; Gaudreau, 1977; Hoffman and Fidell, 1977; Minnigerode, 1976; Nevill, 1975; Powell and Butterfield, 1977a, 1977b). Others have found males to be significantly more masculine than females using the androgyny score (Gaudreau, 1977; Latorre, Endman, and Grossman, 1976; Nevill, 1975; Waters and Pincus, 1976), whereas Cristall and Dean (1976) found no significant differences between graduate males' and females' androgyny scores.

Other studies have contributed evidence regarding the construct validity of the BSRI. Using males and females employed at four job levels, ranging from nonmanagement to upper management, Gaudreau (1975a, 1975b) found nonmanagement females to be significantly more feminine and less masculine than equivalent males, while nonmanagement males did not differ significantly from male and female managers. O'Leary (1977) investigated college students' evaluations of cross-sex behavior and found that the female performers were viewed as significantly more feminine than the male performers, and the male performers were viewed as significantly more masculine than the female performers. Respondents in the Nicoll and Bryson (1977) study rated the adjectives on the BSRI for self, "typical" other sex, and "typical" same sex. Results indicated that responses from both sexes rating the "typical male" differed significantly from responses rating the "typical female." Jordan-Viola, Fassberg, and Viola (1976) obtained data from members of feminist organizations, university women, working women, and nonworking housewives and found that the feminists were significantly more androgynous than the other three groups and that working women were significantly more androgynous than housewives. Furthermore, masculinity and femininity both correlated highly with social desirability for the university women, working women, and housewives, whereas no significant correlations involving social desirability emerged for the feminists. Bender and others (1976) obtained no significant differences between heterosexual and homosexual males and females on the masculinity scale; however, heterosexual females and homosexual males scored significantly higher than heterosexual males and homosexual females on the femininity scale. Shapiro (1977) obtained data from graduate students enrolled in a counseling program and found that both male and female counselors saw the "healthy, well-adjusted female" as significantly more masculine than the "healthy, well-adjusted male." The author states that this represents a reversal of typical findings with this scale.

The correlations between the masculinity-femininity scale of the Guilford-Zimmerman Temperament Survey (#50) and the BSRI masculinity, femininity, and androgyny scales were .11, .04, and .04, respectively, for men and .15, −.06, and −.06, respectively, for women. The correlations between the California Psychological Inventory (#47) masculinity-femininity scale and the BSRI masculinity, femininity, and androgyny scales were −.42, .27, and .50, respectively, for men and −.25, .25, and .30, respectively, for women (Bem, 1974). The correlations between the PRF ANDRO masculinity and femininity scales (#41) and the BSRI masculinity and femininity scales were .68 and .61, respectively, for the combined sexes (Welling, 1975). Finally, a strong positive relationship has been found between androgyny scores and the majority of the scales contained in the Personal Orientation Inventory and the Tennessee Self-Concept Scale (Nevill, 1975).

The correlations between the BSRI and the Personal Attributes Questionnaire (#39), a similar measure of masculinity-femininity, were .75 for males and .73 for females on the Masculinity subscale and .57 for males and .59 for females on the Femininity subscale (Spence and Helmreich, 1978).

NOTES AND COMMENTS: (1) Bem (1977a) compared two methods of classifying respondents, namely the t ratio and a median-split method suggested by Spence, Helmreich, and Stapp (1975). In the median-split method, a person's classification depends on whether she is above the median on masculinity, on femininity, on both masculinity and femininity (androgyny), or on neither masculinity nor femininity (undifferentiated). Bem found that 88 percent of the women and 80 percent of the men who were classified as feminine on the basis of the median split were also classified as feminine or near feminine on the basis of the t ratio. Similarly, 87 percent of the women and 96 percent of the men who were classified as masculine on the basis of the median split were also classified as masculine or near masculine by means of the t ratio. This substantial overlap indicates that the two methods differ little in the way they define masculinity and femininity. However, the two methods of classification do differ in the way they define androgyny: of those subjects classified as androgynous by being above the median on both masculinity and femininity, a substantial proportion failed to be classified as androgynous by means of the t ratio. Furthermore, of those subjects classified as undifferentiated (low on both masculinity and femininity), over half of the men and two-thirds of the women were classified as androgynous on the basis of the t ratio. Thus, Bem recommends differentiating between persons who are high on both masculinity and femininity and persons who are low on both scales, even though the androgyny scores of both types may be equal.

(2) The relationship between masculinity and femininity scores was examined in two groups of college men and two groups of college women (Bem, 1974). For the men, correlations between the two scores were .11 and .02 (n = 444 and 117, respectively); for the women, the correlations were −.14 and −.07 (n = 279 and 77, respectively). These findings, indicating that masculinity and femininity scores are independent, are supported by other studies using the BSRI (Powell and Butterfield, 1977a, 1977b; Whetton and Swindells, 1977).

Correlations were computed between social desirability and each of the other three scores. The findings suggest that masculinity and femininity are related to social desirability (correlations range from .15 to .42), but androgyny is independent of social desirability (correlations range from −.12 to +.12) (Bem, 1974).

(3) Some of the adjective phrases on the scale seem redundant. For example, what is the difference between "self-reliant" and "independent"; between "assertive" and "forceful"; between "acts as a leader" and "has leadership abilities"?

(4) Factor analysis of the BSRI has been the focus of several studies. Gaudreau (1977) based an analysis on the intercorrelations of sixty-four variables, including the sixty BSRI adjectives, sex of respondent, femininity score, masculinity score, and androgyny score. The analysis yielded four factors which were named Femininity, Masculin-

ity, Sex of Subject, and Neutral Maturity. Another study (Moreland and others, in press) found four factors that were nearly identical to Gaudreau's (1977) and labeled them Emotional Expressiveness, Instrumental Activity, Sex of Subject, and Social Immaturity. Tetenbaum (1977) also found four factors that are somewhat similar to those reported by Gaudreau (1977) and Moreland and others (in press) and titled them Assertiveness, Affective Expression, Self-Sufficiency, and Gender Identification. Whetton and Swindells (1977) factor analyzed the BSRI and identified five major factors: Empathy, Power, Honesty, Autonomy, and Neuroticism.

(5) Some researchers using the BSRI have varied the instructions accompanying the inventory. Gilbert, Strahan, and Deutsch (1976) asked respondents to complete the inventory for a "typical" man or woman in society, for a "desirable" man or woman in society, and for the "ideal" man or woman in society. Similarly, Deutsch and Gilbert (1976) asked respondents to complete the inventory for "real" self, "ideal" self, "ideal" other sex, and for belief about other sex's ideal opposite sex. Respondents in the Nicoll and Bryson (1977) study rated the items for themselves, for their beliefs about how a "typical college student" of the other sex would respond, and for their beliefs about how a "typical college student" of their own sex would respond. Watson's (1977) instructions asked respondents to answer for their real self and for their ideal self. Other instructional modifications include responding for the "healthy, well-adjusted" male or female (Shapiro, 1977), for the "healthy, mature, socially competent" adult, male, or female (Gintner, 1976), for an actor or actress crying or evidencing anger (O'Leary, 1977), and for a "good manager" (Butterfield and Powell, 1977; and Powell and Butterfield, 1977a, 1977b).

(6) Scores on the BSRI have been related to a wide range of variables: maternal employment (Hansson, Chernovetz, and Jones, 1977; Klecka and Hiller, 1977); family role differentiation (Klecka and Hiller, 1977); parental expectations for sex-appropriate play behavior and parental sex-typed personality traits (Diepold, 1977); evaluation of cross-sex behavior (O'Leary, 1977); avoidance of cross-sex behavior (Bem and Lenney, 1976); socialization (Allgeier, 1975); occupational role concept (Jordan-Viola, Hosford, and Anderson, 1977); perception of masculinity-femininity in handwriting (Lippa, 1977); ability to match musical selections with paintings (Minnigerode, Ciancio, and Sbarboro, 1976); political ideology (Hershey and Sullivan, 1977); attitudes toward women (Bem, 1977a; Minnigerode, 1976); feminism (Jordan-Viola, Fassberg, and Viola, 1976; Widom, 1977); social conformity (Bem, 1975; Brehony and others, 1977); use of susceptibility to social influence (Falbo, 1975, 1977b); psychological health (Nevill, 1975); personal adjustment (Deutsch and Gilbert, 1976); self-actualization (Cristall and Dean, 1976; Ginn, 1975); sensation-seeking (Waters and Pincus, 1976); empathy (Watson, 1977); need achievement (Latorre, Endman, and Grossman, 1976); self-esteem (Bem, 1977a; Wetter, 1975; Widom, 1977); manifest anxiety (Jordan-Viola, Fassberg, and Viola, 1976); locus of control (Bem, 1977a; Jordan-Viola, Hosford, and Anderson, 1977; Minnigerode, 1976); cognitive complexity (Jordan-Viola, Hosford, and Anderson, 1977); self-disclosure (Bem, 1977a; Bender, 1977; Bender and others, 1976); and nurturance (Bem, Martyna, and Watson, 1976).

SOURCE: See Bem, 1974; or ETS Tests in Microfiche Collection (#001761).

BIBLIOGRAPHY:

Allgeier, E. R. "Beyond Sowing and Growing: The Relationship of Sex Typing to Socialization, Family Plans, and Future Orientation." *Journal of Applied Social Psychology*, 1975, *5*, 217-226.

Anderson, C. L. "Parenting and Perceived Sex Role of Rural Iowa Fathers." Paper presented at the Adult Education Research Conference, Minneapolis, April, 1977. (ERIC Document Reproduction Service No. ED 141 508.)

Banfield, E. E. C. "Women in Middle Management Positions: Characteristics, Training, Leadership Style, Limitations, Rewards, and Problems." Unpublished doctoral dissertation, U.S. International University, 1976. (*Dissertation Abstracts International*, 1976, *34*[4-B], 1952-1953.)

Bem, S. L. "The Measurement of Psychological Androgyny." *Journal of Consulting and Clinical Psychology*, 1974, *42*, 155-162.

Bem, S. L. "Sex Role Adaptability: One Consequence of Psychological Androgyny." *Journal of Personality and Social Psychology*, 1975, *31*, 634-643.

Bem, S. L. "On the Utility of Alternative Procedures for Assessing Psychological Androgyny." *Journal of Consulting and Clinical Psychology*, 1977a, *45*, 196-205.

Bem, S. L. "Psychological Androgyny." In A. G. Sargent (Ed.), *Beyond Sex Roles.* New York: West Publishing, 1977b.

Bem, S. L., and Lenney, E. "Sex Typing and Avoidance of Cross-Sex Behavior." *Journal of Personality and Social Psychology*, 1976, *33*, 48-54.

Bem, S. L., Martyna, W., and Watson, C. "Sex Typing and Androgyny: Further Explorations of the Expressive Domain." *Journal of Personality and Social Psychology*, 1976, *34*, 1016-1023.

Bender, V. L. "Social Sex Role Stereotypes and Sexual Orientation as Related to Self-Disclosure." Paper presented at 85th annual meeting of the American Psychological Association, San Francisco, August 1977.

Bender, V. L., Davis, Y., Glover, O., and Stapp, J. "Patterns of Self-Disclosure in Homosexual and Heterosexual College Students." *Sex Roles,* 1976, *2*, 149-160.

Brehony, K., Augustine, M., Barachie, D., Miller, B., and Woodhouse, W. "Psychological Androgyny and Social Conformity." Paper presented at 85th annual meeting of the American Psychological Association, San Francisco, August 1977.

Burggraf, M. Z. "Holland's Vocational Preference Inventory: Its Applicability to a Group of Technical College Women and the Relationship of Social Level, Self-Concept and Sex Role Identity of the Social Personality Type." Unpublished doctoral dissertation, Ohio University, 1975. (*Dissertation Abstracts International*, 1976, *36*[10-A], 6467-6468.)

Butterfield, D. A., and Powell, G. N. "Evaluations of Leadership Behavior: Do Sex or Androgyny Matter?" Paper presented at 85th annual meeting of the American Psychological Association, San Francisco, August 1977.

Cristall, L., and Dean, R. S. "Relationship of Sex Role Stereotypes and Self-Actualization." *Psychological Reports,* 1976, *39*, 842.

Deutsch, C. J., and Gilbert, L. A. "Sex Role Stereotypes: Effect on Perceptions of Self and Others and on Personal Adjustment." *Journal of Counseling Psychology,* 1976, *23*, 373-379.

Diepold, J. H., Jr. "Parental Expectations for Children's Sex-Typed Play Behavior." Paper presented at 85th annual meeting of the American Psychological Association, San Francisco, August 1977.

Dittman, J. K. "Sex Role Perceptions of North Dakota Vocational Educators. Final Report." Research Series No. 38. Fargo: North Dakota State University, 1976. (ERIC Document Reproduction Service No. ED 131 336.)

Doyle, J. G. "Developmental Aspects of Sex Role Identity in Adolescent Males." Unpublished doctoral dissertation, Catholic University of America, 1976. (*Dissertation Abstracts International*, 1976, *36*[12-B], 6441.)

Duquin, M. E. "Three Cultural Perceptions of Sport." Paper presented at 84th annual meeting of the American Psychological Association, Washington, D.C., September 1976. (ERIC Document Reproduction Service No. ED 137 654.)

Falbo, T. "Sex Role Typing and Sex in the Use of Susceptibility to Influence." Paper presented at 83rd annual meeting of the American Psychological Association, Chicago, August 1975. (ERIC Document Reproduction Service No. ED 119 061.)

Falbo, T. "Multidimensional Scaling of Power Strategies." *Journal of Personality and Social Psychology*, 1977a, *35*, 537-547.

Falbo, T. "Relationships Between Sex, Sex Role, and Social Influence." *Psychology of Women Quarterly*, 1977b, *2*, 62-72.

Gaudreau, P. A. "Investigation of Sex Differences Across Job Levels." Paper presented at 83rd annual meeting of the American Psychological Association, Chicago, August 1975a.

Gaudreau, P. A. "Investigation of Sex Differences Across Job Levels." Unpublished doctoral dissertation, Rice University, 1975b. (*Dissertation Abstracts International*, 1975b, *36*[4-B], 1957.)

Gaudreau, P. A. "Factor Analysis of the Bem Sex Role Inventory." *Journal of Consulting and Clinical Psychology*, 1977, *45*, 299-302.

Gilbert, L. A., Strahan, R. F., and Deutsch, C. J. "Clarification of the Bem Sex Role Inventory." Paper presented at 84th annual meeting of the American Psychological Association, Washington, D.C., September 1976.

Ginn, R. O. "Psychological Androgyny and Self-Actualization." *Psychological Reports*, 1975, *37*, 886.

Gintner, G. G. "Sex Role Stereotypes and the Standard of Mental Health for Males and Females." Unpublished master's thesis, Central Michigan University, 1976.

Gonzalez, T. A. "A Study of the Relationship of the Bem Sex Role Inventory and the Rokeach Dogmatism Scale for Mothers of Preschool Children." Unpublished doctoral dissertation, Ohio University, 1975. (*Dissertation Abstracts International*, 1976, *36*[10-B], 5229-5230.)

Hansson, R. O., Chernovetz, M. E., and Jones, W. H. "Maternal Employment and Androgyny." *Psychology of Women Quarterly*, 1977, *2*, 76-78.

Hardin, J. R. "Psychological Sex Role, Pattern of Need Achievement and Need Affiliation, and Attitudes Toward Women in Undergraduates." Unpublished doctoral dissertation, University of Pennsylvania, 1975. (*Dissertation Abstracts International*, 1976, *36*[12-B], 6355-6356.)

Hershey, M. R., and Sullivan, J. L. "Sex Role Attitudes, Identities, and Political Ideology." *Sex Roles*, 1977, *3*, 37-57.

Hoffman, D. M., and Fidell, L. S. "Characteristics of Androgynous, Undifferentiated, Masculine, and Feminine Middle-Class Women." Paper presented at 85th annual meeting of the American Psychological Association, San Francisco, August 1977.

Hooberman, R. E. "Gender Identity and Gender Role of Male Homosexuals and Heterosexuals." Unpublished doctoral dissertation, University of Michigan, 1975. (*Dissertation Abstracts International*, 1976, *36*[10-A], 6554.)

Horgan, D. D., and Gullo, D. F. "Motherese, Fatherese, Androgynese." Bloomington: Indiana University, 1977. (ERIC Document Reproduction Service No. ED 139 509.)

Jordan-Viola, E., Fassberg, S., and Viola, M. T. "Feminism, Androgyny, and Anxiety." *Journal of Consulting and Clinical Psychology*, 1976, *44*, 870-871.

Jordan-Viola, E., Hosford, R. E., and Anderson, W. R. "Cognitive Complexity, Sex Role

Identity, and Semantic Measurement of Sex-Typed Occupations." Paper presented at 85th annual meeting of the American Psychological Association, San Francisco, August 1977.

Kahn, S. E. "Effects of a Program in Awareness of Sex Role Stereotypes for Helping Professionals." Unpublished doctoral dissertation, Columbia University, 1966. (*Dissertation Abstracts International*, 1975, *36*[4-A], 2027.)

Kinsell-Rainey, L. W. "Achievement and Attribution Patterns as a Function of Sex Role Interpretation: A Comparison of Androgynous and Stereotyped College Women." Unpublished doctoral dissertation, Southern Illinois University, 1976. (*Dissertation Abstracts International*, 1976, *37*[6-A], 3521.)

Kinsell-Rainey, L. W., and Deichmann, J. W. "Sex Differences: An Obsolete Distinction in the Analysis of Classroom Task Approach Patterns." Paper presented at the meeting of the American Educational Research Association, New York, April 1977.

Klecka, C. O., and Hiller, D. V. "Impact of Mothers' Life-Style on Adolescent Gender-Role Socialization." *Sex Roles*, 1977, *3*, 241-255.

Latorre, R. A., Endman, M., and Grossman, I. "Androgyny and Need Achievement in Male and Female Psychiatric Inpatients." *Journal of Clinical Psychology*, 1976, *32*, 233-235.

Lipke, H. J. "The Effects of Model Role, Model Gender, and Subject Expression of Desire to Change on 'Feminine' Females' Imitation of Approach to a Feared Snake." Unpublished doctoral dissertation, St. Louis University, 1976. (*Dissertation Abstracts International*, 1976, *37*[4-B], 1911.)

Lippa, R. "Androgyny, Sex Typing, and the Perception of Masculinity-Femininity in Handwritings." *Journal of Research in Personality*, 1977, *11*, 21-37.

McWay, J. D., Jr. "The Relationship of Sex Role Identification to Psychological Differentiation." Unpublished doctoral dissertation, St. Louis University, 1975. (*Dissertation Abstracts International*, 1976, *37*[4-B], 1916.)

Meyers, J. C. "The Adjustment of Women to Marital Separation: The Effects of Sex Role Identification and of Stage in Family Life, as Determined by Age and Presence or Absence of Dependent Children." Unpublished doctoral dissertation, University of Colorado, 1976. (*Dissertation Abstracts International*, 1976, *37*[5-B], 2516.)

Minnigerode, F. A. "Attitudes Toward Women, Sex Role Stereotyping and Locus of Control." *Psychological Reports*, 1976, *38*, 1301-1302.

Minnigerode, F. A., Ciancio, D. W., and Sbarboro, L. A. "Matching Music with Paintings by Klee." *Perceptual and Motor Skills*, 1976, *42*, 269-270.

Moreland, J. R., Gulanick, N., Montague, E. K., and Harren, V. A. "The Psychometric Properties of the BSRI." Paper presented at 85th annual meeting of the American Psychological Association, San Francisco, August 1977.

Moreland, J. R., Gulanick, N., Montague, E. K., and Harren, V. A. "Some Psychometric Properties of the Bem Sex Role Inventory." *Applied Psychological Measurement*, in press.

Nevill, D. D. "Sex Roles and Personality Correlates." Paper presented at 83rd annual meeting of the American Psychological Association, Chicago, August 1975.

Nicoll, T. L., and Bryson, J. B. "Intersex and Intrasex Stereotyping on the Bem Sex Role Inventory." Paper presented at 85th annual meeting of the American Psychological Association, San Francisco, August 1977.

Olds, L. E. "An Exploratory Study of Androgyny: A Sex Role Construct that Integrates Male and Female Polarities." Unpublished doctoral dissertation, University of

Cincinnati, 1976. (*Dissertation Abstracts International*, 1976, *37*[5-B], 2519-2520.)

O'Leary, J. A. "The Relationship of Sex Role Stereotyping to Self-Reinforcement and Reinforcement of Others." Unpublished doctoral dissertation, Ohio University, 1975. (*Dissertation Abstracts International*, 1976, *36*[10-A], 6481-6482.)

O'Leary, V. E. "Androgynous Men: The 'Best of Both Worlds?' " Paper presented at 85th annual meeting of the American Psychological Association, San Francisco, August 1977.

Ott, T. J. "Androgyny, Sex Role Stereotypes, Sex Role Attitudes and Self-Actualization Among College Women." Unpublished doctoral dissertation, University of Notre Dame, 1976. (*Dissertation Abstracts International*, 1976, *37*[6-A], 3527.)

Powell, G. N., and Butterfield, D. A. "Sex and Sex Role Identification: An Important Distinction for Organizational Research." Paper presented at 85th annual meeting of the American Psychological Association, San Francisco, August 1977a.

Powell, G. N., and Butterfield, D. A. "Sex, Sex Role Identification, and the Good Manager." Paper presented at the meeting of the Academy of Management, Kissimmee, Florida, August 1977b.

Purdy, C. B. "Attitudes Toward the Enjoyment and Value of Mathematics in Relation to Sex Role Attitudes at the Sixth- and Eighth-Grade Levels." Unpublished doctoral dissertation, Boston University School of Education, 1976. (*Dissertation Abstracts International*, 1976, *37*[3-A], 1500.)

Quaranta, B. M. A. "Androgynous, Sex-Typed, and Undifferentiated College Freshmen and Seniors: Their Professional College Choice and Related Characteristics." Unpublished doctoral dissertation, Ohio State University, 1976. (*Dissertation Abstracts International*, 1976, *37*[5-B], 2575-2576.)

Rosenberg, E. S. "Some Psychological and Biological Relationships Between Masculinity and Femininity and Field Dependence and Field Independence." Unpublished doctoral dissertation, Northwestern University, 1975. (*Dissertation Abstracts International*, 1976, *36*[12-B], 6453.)

Shapiro, J. "Socialization of Sex Roles in the Counseling Setting: Differential Counselor Behavioral and Attitudinal Responses to Typical and Atypical Female Sex Roles." *Sex Roles*, 1977, *3*, 173-184.

Shueman, S. A., and Sedlacek, W. E. "An Evaluation of a Women's Studies Program." College Park: Maryland University, 1976. (ERIC Document Reproduction Service No. ED 135 315.)

Singer, T. L. "An Examination of the Sex Role Orientation and Reported Sexual Behavior of Male Drug Addicts in Methadone Maintenance Treatment as Compared with a Stratified Sample of Nonaddicts." Unpublished doctoral dissertation, University of Pittsburgh, 1975. (*Dissertation Abstracts International*, 1976, *36*[9-B], 4673-4674.)

Spence, J. T., and Helmreich, R. L. *Masculinity and Femininity: Their Psychological Dimensions, Correlates, and Antecedents.* Austin: University of Texas Press, 1978.

*Spence, J. T., Helmreich, R. L., and Stapp, J. "Ratings of Self and Peers on Sex Role Attributes and Their Relation to Self-Esteem and Conceptions of Masculinity and Femininity." *Journal of Personality and Social Psychology*, 1975, *32*, 29-39.

Stericker, A. B. "Fear of Success in Male and Female College Students: Sex Role Identification and Self-Esteem as Factors." Unpublished doctoral dissertation, Loyola University of Chicago, 1976. (*Dissertation Abstracts International*, 1976, *36*[11-B], 5819-5820.)

Strahan, R. F. "Remarks on Bem's Measurement of Psychological Androgyny: Alternative Methods and a Supplementary Analysis." *Journal of Consulting and Clinical Psychology,* 1975, *43,* 568-571.

Switkin, L. R. "Self-Disclosure as a Function of Sex Roles, Experimenter-Subject Distance, Sex of Experimenter, and Intimacy of Topics." Unpublished doctoral dissertation, St. Louis University, 1974. (*Dissertation Abstracts International,* 1974, *35*[5-B], 2451.)

Tetenbaum, T. "Masculinity and Femininity: Separate but Equal?" Paper presented at 85th annual meeting of the American Psychological Association, San Francisco, August 1977.

Volgy, S. S. "Sex Role Orientation and Measures of Psychological Well-Being Among Feminists, Housewives, and Working Women." Unpublished doctoral dissertation, University of Arizona, 1976. (*Dissertation Abstracts International,* 1976, *37*[1-B], 533.)

Wakefield, J. A., Jr., Sasek, J., Friedman, A. F., and Bowden, J. D. "Androgyny and Other Measures of Masculinity-Femininity." *Journal of Consulting and Clinical Psychology,* 1976, *44,* 766-770.

Waters, C. W., and Pincus, S. "Sex of Respondent, Respondent's Sex Role Self-Concept, and Responses to the Sensation-Seeking Scale." *Psychological Reports,* 1976, *39,* 749-750.

Watson, N. P. "A Theoretical and Empirical Study of Empathy and Sex Role Differentiation." Unpublished doctoral dissertation, Harvard University, 1976. (*Dissertation Abstracts International,* 1976, *37*[5-B], 2533-2534.)

Watson, N. P. "Empathy and Sex Role Differentiation." Unpublished manuscript. A short version of this paper was presented at 85th annual meeting of the American Psychological Association, San Francisco, August 1977.

Welling, M. A. "A New Androgyny Measure Derived from the Personality Research Form." Paper presented at 83rd annual meeting of the American Psychological Association, Chicago, August 1975.

Wetter, R. E. "Levels of Self-Esteem Associated with Four Sex Role Categories." Paper presented at 83rd annual meeting of the American Psychological Association, Chicago, August 1975.

Whetton, C., and Swindells, T. "A Factor Analysis of the Bem Sex Role Inventory." *Journal of Clinical Psychology,* 1977, *33,* 150-153.

Widom, C. S. "Self-Esteem, Sex Role Identity, and Feminism in Female Offenders." Paper presented at 85th annual meeting of the American Psychological Association, San Francisco, August 1977.

Wittekind, O. S. F., and Olga, M. "Relationships Between Self-Esteem Sex Type and Perceived Competency of 'Male' and 'Female' Attitudes." Unpublished doctoral dissertation, St. Louis University, 1975. (*Dissertation Abstracts International,* 1975, *36*[6-B], 3081.)

Yockey, J. M., Severy, L. J., and Shaw, M. E. "Sex Role Perceptions and Behavior." Paper presented at 84th annual meeting of the American Psychological Association, Washington, D.C., September 1976. (ERIC Document Reproduction Service No. ED 136 121.)

Zeldow, P. B. "Psychological Androgyny and Attitudes Toward Feminism." *Journal of Consulting and Clinical Psychology,* 1976, *44,* 150.

33. FEMININE GENDER IDENTITY SCALE

AUTHORS: Kurt Freund, Ernest Nagler, Ronald Langevin, Andrew Zajac, and Betty Steiner

DATE: 1974

VARIABLE: Feminine gender identity in men

TYPE OF INSTRUMENT: Multiple choice

DESCRIPTION: The test consists of nineteen items, each of which is followed by three to ten response options. Only one response is to be indicated for each item. Twelve items are appropriate for all respondents. The last seven items are to be completed only by nontranssexual homosexual males. Eleven of the first twelve questions concern whether the respondent preferred girls' activities and women's clothing and whether the respondent had wished to be born a girl. These twelve questions refer to when the respondent was between the ages 6 and 17. The last seven questions concern sexual preferences and the desire to be a woman.

PREVIOUSLY ADMINISTERED TO: Heterosexual male college students, alcoholics, and staff of a correctional service; homosexual males from prison hospitals, a gender identity clinic, and homosexual clubs

APPROPRIATE FOR: Males, ages 18 and older

ADMINISTRATION: The scale can be self-administered and can be completed in about ten minutes.

SAMPLE ITEMS: Between the ages of 6 and 12, did you prefer
• to play with boys
• to play with girls
• didn't make any difference
• not to play with other children
• don't remember
                    Since the age of 17, did you put on women's underwear or clothing?
• once a month or more, for at least a year
• (less often, but) several times a year for at least a year
• very seldom did this since age 17
• never did this since age 17

SCORING: For each item, each response option is assigned a predetermined number of points. Scores per item range from 0 to 2. The total score can range from 0 (no feminine gender identity) to 38 (high in feminine gender identity).

DEVELOPMENT: Items with face validity were combined to form the instrument.

RELIABILITY: Using the data from 147 nontranssexual homosexual males, the reliability coefficient (Kuder-Richardson) for the full scale was .93 (Freund and others, 1974c).

Three homosexual groups—androphilic, ephebophilic, and pedophilic—were tested. The intraclass correlation was .85 (Freund and others, 1974a).

Item-total correlations were computed for the 147 nontranssexual homosexual males. The correlations ranged from .28 to .84 (Freund and others, 1974c).

VALIDITY: Sixty-three alcoholics, fifty-three staff of a correction service, and 110 students completed the first twelve questions on the test. These three groups of men were presumed to be heterosexual. There was no overlap between their scores and the scores from thirty-three transsexual homosexual males. The results for 147 nontranssexual males were less clear-cut. The scores of about one third of the nontranssexuals overlapped the scores of the heterosexual men, and only a few nontranssexuals scored as high as the transsexual homosexuals (Freund and others, 1974c).

A discriminant function analysis was performed using the responses of fifty transsexual and 185 nontranssexual homosexuals. No transsexuals were placed in the transsexual category; five transsexuals were placed in the nontranssexual category (Freund and others, 1974b).

NOTES AND COMMENTS: The items on the Feminine Gender Identity Scale are very transparent. The respondent could easily portray any picture of himself that he chose to.

SOURCE: See Freund and others, 1974c.

BIBLIOGRAPHY:

Freund, K., Langevin, R., Laws, R., and Serber, M. "Femininity and Preferred Partner Age in Homosexual and Heterosexual Males." *British Journal of Psychiatry,* 1974a, *125,* 442-446.

Freund, K., Langevin, R., Wescom, T., and Zajac, Y. "Heterosexual Interest in Homosexual Males." *Archives of Sexual Behavior,* 1975, *4,* 509-518.

Freund, K., Langevin, R., Zajac, Y., Steiner, B., and Zajac, A. "The Transsexual Syndrome in Homosexual Males." *Journal of Nervous and Mental Disease,* 1974b, *158,* 145-153.

Freund, K., Nagler, E., Langevin, R., Zajac, A., and Steiner, B. "Measuring Feminine Gender Identity in Homosexual Males." *Archives of Sexual Behavior,* 1974c, *3*(3), 249-260.

Hooberman, R. E. "Gender Identity and Gender Role of Male Homosexuals and Heterosexuals." Unpublished doctoral dissertation, University of Michigan, 1975. (*Dissertation Abstracts International,* 1976, *36*[10-A], 6554.)

Roback, H. B., Langevin, R., and Zajac, Y. "Sex of Free Choice Figure Drawings by Homosexual Subjects." *Journal of Personality Assessment,* 1974, *38,* 154-155.

34. FEMININITY ADJECTIVE CHECK LIST

AUTHOR: Ralph F. Berdie

DATE: 1959 (used 1955)

VARIABLE: Femininity

TYPE OF INSTRUMENT: Adjective checklist

DESCRIPTION: The checklist consists of sixty-one adjectives, forty-six of which are more descriptive of women and fifteen of which are more descriptive of men.

PREVIOUSLY ADMINISTERED TO: College students; black and white adults; homosexuals; schizophrenics

APPROPRIATE FOR: Ages 16 and older

ADMINISTRATION: The respondents are directed to check all adjectives which describe themselves. The usual time to complete the checklist is one or two minutes.

SAMPLE ITEMS: Charming
                Impulsive
                Mild
                Suspicious

SCORING: For each of the feminine items checked, the respondent is given a score of +1; for each of the masculine items checked, the respondent is given a score of −1. Scores can range from −15 (most masculine) to +46 (most feminine).

DEVELOPMENT: A checklist consisting of 148 adjectives was compiled by selecting adjectives from Gough's Adjective Checklist (#45) and from a review of studies of masculinity-femininity. To identify items that differentiated between males and females, the list was given to 200 male and 200 female incoming college students. Adjectives that were selected significantly more often by one sex than by the other were selected for the final instrument. Forty-six items were selected significantly more often (p < .05) by females and fifteen items were selected significantly more often (p < .05) by males.

RELIABILITY: Berdie (1959) used the scores from 200 incoming college men to compute split-half reliability. Using an odd-even split, he obtained a corrected reliability of .49; using a split comparing items in columns one and three with items in columns two and four, he obtained a corrected reliability of .45.

      Berdie (1959) tested ninety-five incoming college men and retested them one day later. He obtained a test-retest correlation of .81.

VALIDITY: Berdie (1959) tested 400 men and 200 women. He found that 5 percent of the men obtained scores above (more feminine) the median for women; he found that 7 percent of the women obtained scores below (more masculine) the median for men.

      Berdie's 400 men represented two different colleges: engineering and liberal arts.

Half of the men in each college were used to develop the instrument. Thus, he had four groups of 100 each. In comparing the means from the four groups, Berdie found that men in liberal arts who were not used to develop the instrument had a significantly higher (more feminine) mean than men in each of the other three groups.

The correlations between scores on the Minnesota Multiphasic Personality Inventory masculinity-femininity scale (#52) and scores on the Femininity Adjective Check List were .44 and .20 for two groups of male freshmen. The correlations between the Strong Vocational Interest Blank masculinity score (#56) and the Femininity Adjective Check List were −.40 and −.22 for two groups of male freshmen (Berdie, 1959).

Berdie (1959) found that the difference between means for 205 men ($\overline{X}$ = 9.1) and 193 women ($\overline{X}$ = 15.6) was significant at the .001 level.

NOTES AND COMMENTS: (1) Berdie (1959) contends that his low split-half reliability coefficients merely reflect that the checklist is measuring a variety of behaviors that are not related to each other. He fails to point out, however, that his higher coefficient on test-retest reliability may reflect memory effects, because only one day elapsed between the two test administrations.

(2) The instrument was developed using the responses of college students; thus it may be inappropriate to administer it to other populations. That is, one cannot assume that the items that were differentially endorsed by incoming male and female college students will be differentially endorsed by other groups. Furthermore, because the instrument was originally developed more than twenty years ago, it is quite possible that even college students would no longer respond differentially to the same items.

(3) The scoring procedure implies that masculinity and femininity are additive. This is a questionable assumption. Furthermore, scores are difficult to interpret because a score of 30 could mean either that the respondent endorsed only thirty feminine adjectives or that the respondent endorsed forty-five feminine adjectives and fifteen masculine adjectives. Should these two different sets of responses really yield identical scores?

(4) Scores are a function of the number of adjectives endorsed. More of the adjectives are classified as feminine. Is it therefore possible that a person who is inclined to endorse more adjectives will get a more feminine score?

(5) The Femininity Adjective Check List has been used to compare people of different races (Cameron, 1971), people of different ages (Cameron, 1968), better functioning schizophrenics with poorer functioning schizophrenics (Ishiyama and Brown, 1965), and homosexual men with nonhomosexuals (Berdie, 1959).

SOURCE: See Berdie, 1959.

BIBLIOGRAPHY:

Berdie, R. F. "A Femininity Adjective Check List." *Journal of Applied Psychology,* 1959, *43,* 327-333.

Cameron, P. "Masculinity-Femininity in the Aged." *Journal of Gerontology,* 1968, *23,* 63-65.

Cameron, P. "Personality Differences Between Typical Urban Negroes and Whites." *Journal of Negro Education,* 1971, *40,* 66-75.

Ishiyama, T., and Brown, A. F. "Sex Role Conceptions and the Patient Role in a State Mental Hospital." *Journal of Clinical Psychology,* 1965, *21,* 446-448.

Siller, J., and Chipman, A. "Response Set Paralysis: Implications for Measurement and Control." *Journal of Consulting Psychology,* 1963, *27,* 432-438.

Stedman, R. E. "The Relationship of Masculinity-Femininity to Perception of Self, Chosen Occupation, and College Teaching Among University Honor Students." Unpublished doctoral dissertation, University of Minnesota, 1963. (*Dissertation Abstracts,* 1963, *24*[3], 1078-1079.)

Taylor, N. T. "Sex, Sex Role, Locus of Control, Achievement Value, and Achievement." Unpublished doctoral dissertation, University of North Carolina at Chapel Hill, 1975. (*Dissertation Abstracts International,* 1975, *36*[6-A], 3529.)

---

35. THE FEMININITY STUDY

AUTHOR: Frederick C. Thorne

DATE: 1968

VARIABLE: Femininity

TYPE OF INSTRUMENT: True-false

DESCRIPTION: The instrument consists of 200 statements representing eleven areas of adjustment: Feminine Social Role (twenty-one items), Female Parent Role (twenty items), Feminine Career Role (thirteen items), Female Homemaker Role (twenty-two items), Female Role Confidence (eighteen items), Female Sex Identification (twenty items), Development and Maturation (twenty items), Sex Drive and Interests (twenty-one items), Promiscuity (twelve items), Homosexuality (eleven items), and Health and Neurotic Conflict (twenty-two items). For each item, the respondent is to indicate whether the statement is true or false as it applies to her. Some items are keyed true and others are keyed false.

PREVIOUSLY ADMINISTERED TO: Females, ages 18-69 including college students, alcoholics, schizophrenics, nuns, nurses, and meatpackers.

APPROPRIATE FOR: Females, age 16 and older

ADMINISTRATION: The instrument is self-administered and can be completed in about one and a quarter hours.

SAMPLE ITEMS: *Feminine Social Role:* I like to go to lots of parties.
                  Female Parent Role: Two children would be enough for me.
                  Feminine Career Role: Marriage is the only career I want.
                  Female Homemaker Role: I don't enjoy housekeeping.
                  Female Role Confidence: I am truly glad I am a woman.
                  Female Sex Identification: My father was weak and I didn't particularly respect him.
                  Development and Maturation: I have such severe menstrual cramps that it often incapacitates me.

> *Sex Drive and Interests:* Sex has always been a problem to me.
>
> *Promiscuity:* I was not [won't be] a virgin when I got [get] married.
>
> *Homosexuality:* It makes me uncomfortable to be the center of atten-

tion.

> *Health and Neurotic Conflict:* People in large groups make me nervous.

SCORING: Items are objectively scored and equally weighted. Scores may be obtained for each of the eleven adjustment areas; or scores may be obtained for factors using the results from one of the factor analyses mentioned below. High scores are always indicative of greater femininity. Before interpreting scores, one should heed Thorne's (1977, p. 9) warning: "At the present stage of research investigation, there are insufficient definitive results to warrant any attempt at scale scoring except that scale scores may suggest important problem areas for further investigation. The examiner should have detailed information about base rate responding and typical factor patterns of the group of which the S is a member. Hopefully, the scale scores will indicate the positivity of the female concept, specific feelings of inadequacy, and role-playing deficiencies."

DEVELOPMENT: "The test items were constructed from actual verbatim comments or responses made by women who were being studied for sex role adjustment problems" (Thorne, 1977, p. 6). The items were intended to concern clinically significant behaviors regardless of whether the behaviors were considered specific to one sex. In order to determine which response (true or false) indicated femininity, Sannito and others (1972) asked five female clinical psychologists and five male psychologists to respond to the items the way they believed a "very feminine" person would. The judges were directed to consider a continuum ranging from "very feminine" to "not very feminine" when responding to the items. If at least seven of the ten judges agreed on the response to the item, this judgment determined the direction of the scoring for the item. All ten judges agreed on the responses for seventy-five items; nine judges agreed on forty-two items; eight judges agreed on thirty-two items; and seven judges agreed on twenty-four items. This left twenty-seven items that failed to meet the criterion for determining the direction of scoring. Sannito and others (1972) eliminated those twenty-seven items from the analysis they performed on the results obtained with the instrument.

RELIABILITY: Eighty-one undergraduate women completed the instrument on two occasions separated by an average interval of 41.2 days. After eliminating the twenty-seven items that failed to satisfy the criterion for determining scoring direction, Sannito and others (1972) estimated the test-retest reliability for each of the eleven subscales. The results were: Feminine Social Role = .88; Female Parent Role = .68; Feminine Career Role = .76; Female Homemaker Role = .85; Female Role Confidence = .84; Female Sex Identification = .78; Development and Maturation = .70; Sex Drive and Interests = .77; Promiscuity = .65; Homosexuality = .78; and Health and Neurotic Conflict = .85.

VALIDITY: Sannito and others (1972) obtained results from several groups of women. They factor analyzed the responses from one group of 200 Roman Catholic undergraduate women and obtained two factors. Factor I was labeled "Delight in Being Feminine"; Factor II was labeled "Enjoyment of Homemaker Role." Sannito and others then compared the mean factor scores from seven groups of women: the 200 women whose responses were used in the factor analysis; thirty-seven undergraduate education majors; forty-two schizophrenics; sixty-five nuns; twenty Jewish undergraduate women; fifteen Roman Catholic undergraduates attending the same eastern college as the Jewish undergraduates; and fifty-eight Protestant undergraduates at the same eastern college. A t test was used to compare all possible pairs of means on each of the two factors. Twenty of the forty-two t tests yielded statistically significant differences ($p < .05$), leading the authors to conclude that the test is able to discriminate between various groups.

NOTES AND COMMENTS: There have been other factor-analytic studies in addition to the one reported above. Pishkin and Thorne (1977) factor analyzed the responses from 31 alcoholic women, 146 college women, and 152 schizophrenic women. They extracted five factors: Heterosexual Social Role Inadaptability, Parental Role Inadaptability, Home-maker Role Inadaptability, General Affective Instability, and Maternal Role Inadaptability. Thorne and Pishkin (1977) performed separate factor analyses on the responses from 31 alcoholic women, 62 female psychology students, 44 female psychology students enrolled at a different university, and 152 schizophrenic women. They identified five factors for each group. For the alcoholics, the factors were labeled High Interpersonal Adaptability, Heterosexual Social Role Inadaptability, Female Role Ambivalence, Female Identification Problems, and Maternal Role Inadaptability. For the 62 female psychology students, the factors were labeled Heterosexual Social Inadaptability, General Female Role Inadequacy, Physical and/or Psychosomatic Disabilities with Low Female Self-Concepts, Positive Female Self-Concepts and Interests, and Emancipated Female Role Concepts. For the 44 female psychology students, the factors were labeled Heterosexual and General Social Inadaptability, Heterosexual Interests and Adaptability, Homosexual Tendencies, Conflictual Sexuality, and Emancipated Female Role Concepts. For the schizophrenics, the factors were labeled Homosexual Conflicts, Heterosexual Adaptability, Rejection of Parental-Caretaker Role, Promiscuity, and Negative Sexual Self-Concepts. Posavac and others (1977) factor analyzed the responses from 512 undergraduate women. Five factors were labeled: Heterosexual Role Insecurity, Rejection of Housework versus Contentment with the Traditional Housewife Role, Physical and Emotional Complaints, Functions Well in Social Situations, and Homemaker Efficiency. Six other factors were described: normal sex role identity, aggressive rejection of the normal parental role, satisfaction with physical appearance, impatience with children, repression of sexuality versus interest in sex and enjoyment of physical contact, and dissatisfaction with parents. On the basis of the diverse outcomes of various factor-analytic studies of the Femininity Study, Thorne (1977, p. 8) states, "The only conclusion to be drawn from such findings is that at this stage of research investigation, every new group should be factor analyzed separately and across time to determine its own specific characteristics. Nothing that resembles a constant feminine 'trait' or 'personality structure' composition can be demonstrated at the present time."

SOURCE: Clinical Psychology Publishing Company
            4 Conant Square
            Brandon, Vermont 05733

BIBLIOGRAPHY:

Pishkin, V., and Thorne, F. C. "A Factorial Structure of the Dimensions of Femininity in Alcoholic, Schizophrenic, and Normal Populations." *Journal of Clinical Psychology*, 1977, *33*, 10-17.
Posavac, E. J., Walker, R. E., Foley, J. M., and Sannito, T. "Further Factor-Analytic Investigation of the Thorne Femininity Study." *Journal of Clinical Psychology*, 1977, *33*, 24-31.

Sannito, T., Walker, R. E., Foley, J. M., and Posavac, E. J. "A Test of Female Sex Iden-
    tification: The Thorne Femininity Study." *Journal of Clinical Psychology*, 1972,
    28, 531-539.
Thorne, F. C. "The Measurement of Femininity." *Journal of Clinical Psychology*, 1977,
    33, 5-10.
Thorne, F. C., and Pishkin, V. "Comparative Study of the Factorial Composition of
    Femininity in Alcoholic, Schizophrenic, and Normal Populations." *Journal of
    Clinical Psychology*, 1977, *33*, 18-23.

---

36. GOUGH FEMININITY SCALE

AUTHOR: Harrison G. Gough

DATE: 1952

VARIABLE: Psychological femininity

TYPE OF INSTRUMENT: True-false

DESCRIPTION: The instrument consists of fifty-eight statements pertaining to a wide variety of topics including interests, self-perceptions, feelings, and thoughts. The respondents are to indicate whether each statement is true or false as it applies to them. Thirty-six statements are phrased so that a response of "true" is indicative of femininity; twenty-two statements are phrased so that a response of "false" is indicative of femininity.

PREVIOUSLY ADMINISTERED TO: Children in grades 2, 5, and 9; high school students; unmarried college students; adults; pregnant wives; husbands of pregnant wives; reformatory inmates; juvenile delinquents; homosexuals; sailors; hospitalized veterans.

APPROPRIATE FOR: Ages 13 and older

ADMINISTRATION: This self-administered instrument can be completed in about half an hour.

SAMPLE ITEMS: I want to be an important person in the community.
            If I get too much change in a store I always give it back.

SCORING: Items are objectively scored and equally weighted. High scores indicate greater femininity.

DEVELOPMENT: An item pool was constructed consisting of 300 items, most of which were originally designed to assess political attitudes. The items were selected for the pool if they were likely to differentiate between males and females but were subtle in terms of what they were measuring. The initial item pool was reduced to 112 items as a result of successive administrations to high school and college students. The 112 items were administered to a sample of 188 high school females and 176 high school males and to a second sample including 270 college females and 301 college males. Only items that successfully differentiated between males and females in both samples were retained for the final instrument.

RELIABILITY: Split-half reliabilities were computed based on the responses from 270 female and 301 male college students used for item selection. The reliability was .88 for females and .86 for males (Gough, 1952). Gough acknowledges that these correlations are probably overestimates of the instrument's reliability because they were based on the same persons who were used for item selection.

VALIDITY: Comparisons of mean scores obtained by the males and females who were used for item selection indicated that females scored significantly higher (more feminine, p < .0001) than males. A comparison of the mean scores obtained by sixty-two college females and sixty-two college males who were not used in item selection again showed that females scored significantly higher (more feminine, p < .001) than males. Similarly, a comparison of mean scores obtained by 408 high school females and 404 high school males not used for item selection showed that females scored significantly higher (more feminine, p < .0001) than males. A thirty-two-item version of the instrument was administered to thirty-eight reformatory inmates known to engage in homosexual behavior and to thirty-eight inmates "matched for age, education, and IQ, but not presenting problems of homosexual behavior" (Gough, 1952, p. 434). The homosexuals scored significantly higher (p < .01) than the nonhomosexuals.

To determine the type of impression made by persons who score high on the test, ten persons with high scores and ten persons with low scores on the Gough Femininity Scale were rated on an adjective checklist by nine staff members at a personality institute. Gough (1952, p. 439) reported that the "adjective 'feminine,' which is included in the original adjective checklist . . . does not itself differentiate between high and low scorers on the . . . femininity scale." High scorers were rated as having such characteristics as accepting, soft, mild, and tolerant; low scorers were rated as self-centered, formal, hard-headed, and cool.

Nichols (1962) administered numerous masculinity-femininity measures, including the Gough Femininity Scale, to 100 men and 100 women. He reports the following correlations with the Gough Femininity Scale: Guilford-Martin Inventory of factors GAMIN (#49) = .48 (p < .005) for females and .47 (p < .005) for males; the masculinity-femininity scale of the Minnesota Multiphasic Personality Inventory (#52) = .28 (p < .005) for females and .33 (p < .005) for males; the femininity scale of the California Psychological Inventory (#47) (which includes a subset of the items on the Gough Femininity Scale) = .79 (p < .001) for females and .80 (p < .001) for males; a masculinity-femininity score from the Heston Personal Adjustment Inventory = .36 (p < .005) for females and .21 (p < .01) for males; the Conventionality subscale from the VC Personality Test Battery (#58) = .36 (p < .005) for females and .43 (p < .005) for males; the Passivity subscale from the VC Personality Test Battery = .31 (p < .005) for females and .05 (nonsignificant) for males; and the Feminine Sensitivity subscale of the VC Personality Test Battery = .52 (p < .005) for females and .45 (p < .005) for males. Based on a factor-analytic study of responses to these scales, Nichols constructed three measures of masculinity-femininity: a Subtle scale, a Stereotype scale, and an Obvious scale (#38). Eight of Gough's items were included on the Stereotype scale and eleven were included on the

Obvious scale. Nichols then correlated scores on the Gough Femininity Scale with each of his three scales. He found a correlation with the Obvious scale of .58 for males and .53 for females; a correlation with the Stereotype scale of .37 for males and .30 for females; and a correlation with the Subtle scale of .10 for males and −.09 for females. These findings suggest that the Gough Femininity Scale is measuring "obvious masculinity-femininity." Nichols also computed a point biserial correlation between sex and scores on the Gough Femininity Scale. He obtained a coefficient of .77.

May (1969) administered the Gough Femininity Scale and the May Measure of Gender Identity (#20) to sixteen men and eighteen women who were equated in terms of age, intelligence, and social class. The correlation between the two scores was −.10 (nonsignificant) for females and +.78 (p < .001) for males.

Rosenfeld (1969) administered the Gough Femininity Scale to forty delinquent boys and forty nondelinquent boys. Consistent with his hypothesis, he found that delinquents scored significantly more masculine (p < .01) than nondelinquents.

Biaggio and Nielsen (1976) administered the Gough Femininity Scale to 108 college women and 71 college men and used the scores to classify respondents as "masculine," "middle," and "feminine." They then compared the three groups on two measures of anxiety. As predicted they found that those classified as feminine were significantly more anxious (p < .01 and p < .05) than those classified as masculine.

Bieliauskas (1974) administered the Gough Femininity Scale to twenty-nine feminists and twenty-nine nonfeminists. There was not a significant difference between the means from the two groups.

Robertson and Cohen (1967) administered the Gough Femininity Scale to eighty-four veterans undergoing "social rehabilitation" in a VA hospital. They found that veterans with a more feminine sex role identification were hospitalized significantly longer (p < .01) than other veterans. They replicated their study with sixty-nine other veterans and obtained the same results.

Strodtbeck, Bezdek, and Goldhammer (1970) administered the Gough Femininity Scale and the Franck Drawing Completion Test (#11), which is another measure of masculinity-femininity, to 356 men. They selected forty men who had extreme scores on the Gough Femininity Scale and forty men who had extreme scores on the Franck Drawing Completion Test. Using the responses from these eighty men on the eleven most discriminating items from the Franck and twenty-four items from the Gough, they obtained a correlation between the two scales of .13.

NOTES AND COMMENTS: (1) The original Gough Femininity Scale as described above contains fifty-eight items. Gough (1966) eliminated twenty items and included the remaining thirty-eight as a subscale on the California Psychological Inventory (#47). Reliability and validity data that pertain to the subscale of the California Psychological Inventory are not reported here. When researchers report using "the Gough scale," it is often unclear whether they are referring to the Gough Femininity Scale as described here, the thirty-eight-item subscale of the California Psychological Inventory, or a modification of one of these two scales. Modifications that shortened the Gough Femininity Scale were used by Bezdek and Strodtbeck (1970), Child (1965), Farley and others (1971), and Strodtbeck, Bezdek, and Goldhammer (1970).

(2) Researchers using the Gough Femininity Scale have reported using it to measure variables other than femininity. For example, it has been used to measure traditional versus nontraditional sex role (Greenspan, 1974), conscious sex role identity (Strodtbeck, Bezdek, and Goldhammer, 1970), "strength of identification with father" relative to

"strength of identification with mother" (Moulton and others, 1966), and awareness of cultural stereotypes (Bieliauskas, 1974).

(3) Strodtbeck, Bezdek, and Goldhammer (1970) factor analyzed responses to a twenty-four-item version of the Gough Femininity Scale. They obtained three factors: Factor I—Admits Feminine Activities (six items); Factor II—Rejects Masculine Occupations (nine items); and Factor III—Accepts Feminine Occupations (nine items).

(4) Scores on the Gough Femininity Scale have been related to the following variables: parenthood (Biaggio and Nielsen, 1976; Bieliauskas, 1974; Biller and Barry, 1971; Miller and Swanson, 1960; Moulton and others, 1966; Siegelman, 1974; and Weller, 1970); achievement motivation and motive to avoid success (Greenspan, 1974); adolescent acting out (Wrchota, 1973); depression (Rothstein, 1971); ego strength (Vaught, 1965); field dependence-independence (Vaught, 1965; Schenkel, 1975); deprivation-enhancement fantasy pattern (May, 1969); pregnancy symptoms in males (Munroe and Munroe, 1971); homosexuality (Siegelman, 1974); sexual identity (Biller and Barry, 1971; Miller and Swanson, 1960); ego-identity status (Schenkel, 1975); openness versus closedness (Biaggio and Nielsen, 1976).

SOURCE: See Gough, 1952.

BIBLIOGRAPHY:

Bezdek, W., and Strodtbeck, F. L. "Sex Role Identity and Pragmatic Action." *American Sociological Review,* 1970, *35,* 491-502.

Biaggio, M. K., and Nielsen, E. C. "Anxiety Correlates of Sex Role Identity." *Journal of Clinical Psychology,* 1976, *32,* 619-623.

Bieliauskas, V. J. "A New Look at 'Masculine Protest.'" *Journal of Individual Psychology,* 1974, *30,* 92-97.

Biller, H. B., and Barry, W. "Sex Role Patterns, Paternal Similarity, and Personality Adjustment in College Males." *Developmental Psychology,* 1971, *4,* 107.

Carmell, D. M., and Johnson, J. E. "Relationship Between Sex Role Identification and Self-Esteem in Early Adolescents." *Developmental Psychology,* 1970, *3,* 268.

Child, I. L. "Personality Correlates of Esthetic Judgment in College Students." *Journal of Personality,* 1965, *33,* 476-511.

Constantinople, A. "Masculinity-Femininity: An Exception to a Famous Dictum." *Psychological Bulletin,* 1973, *80,* 389-407.

Farley, F. H., Hatch, R., Murphy, P., and Miller, K. "Sibling Structure and Masculinity-Femininity in Male Adolescents." *Adolescence,* 1971, *6,* 441-450.

Gough, H. G. "Identifying Psychological Femininity." *Educational and Psychological Measurement,* 1952, *12,* 427-439.

Gough, H. G. "A Cross-Cultural Analysis of the CPI Femininity Scale." *Journal of Consulting Psychology,* 1966, *30,* 136-141.

Greenspan, L. J. "Sex Role Orientation, Achievement Motivation, and the Motive to Avoid Success in College Women." Unpublished doctoral dissertation, Case Western Reserve University, 1974. (*Dissertation Abstracts International,* 1975, *35* [9-A], 5813-5814.)

Landers, D. M. "Sibling-Sex-Status and Ordinal Position Effects on Females' Sport Participation and Interests." *Journal of Social Psychology,* 1970, *80,* 247-248.

Lansky, L. M. "The Stability Over Time and Under Stress of Conscious and Unconscious Masculinity-Femininity." *American Psychologist,* 1962, *17,* 302-303.

Lansky, L. M. "The Family Structure Also Affects the Model: Sex Role Attitudes in Parents of Preschool Children." *Merrill-Palmer Quarterly,* 1967, *13,* 139-150.

Lipsitt, P. D., and Lelos, D. "The Relationship of Sex Role Identity to Level of Ego Development in Habitual Drug Users." *Proceedings of the Annual Convention of the American Psychological Association,* 1972, 7, 255-256.

May, R. R. "Deprivation-Enhancement Patterns in Men and Women." *Journal of Projective Techniques and Personality Assessment,* 1969, *33,* 464-469.

Mikesell, R. H., and Calhoun, L. G. "Sex Role and Need for Approval in Adolescents." *Child Study Journal,* 1971, *2,* 35-37.

Miller, D. R., and Swanson, G. E. *Inner Conflict and Defense.* New York: Holt, Rinehart and Winston, 1960.

Moulton, R. W., Burnstein, E., Liberty, P. G., Jr., and Altucher, N. "Patterning of Parental Affection and Disciplinary Dominance as a Determinant of Guilt and Sex Typing." *Journal of Personality and Social Psychology,* 1966, *4,* 356-363.

Munroe, R. L., and Munroe, R. H. "Male Pregnancy Symptoms and Cross-Sex Identity in Three Societies." *Journal of Social Psychology,* 1971, *84,* 11-25.

Nichols, R. C. "Subtle, Obvious, and Stereotype Measures of Masculinity-Femininity." *Educational and Psychological Measurement,* 1962, *3,* 449-461.

Robertson, R. J., and Cohen, R. D. "Sex Role Identification and Institutional Dependency Among Veterans Undergoing Social Rehabilitation." *Journal of Clinical Psychology,* 1967, *23,* 441-442.

Rosenfeld, H. M. "Delinquent Acting Out in Adolescent Males and the Task of Sexual Identification." *Smith College Studies in Social Work,* 1969, *40,* 1-29.

Rosenfelder, R. "Psychological Correlates of Political Opinion in College Students." Unpublished doctoral dissertation, St. Johns University, 1974. (*Dissertation Abstracts International,* 1975, *35* [8-B], 4152.)

Rothstein, A. "Depression in Pregnancy as It Relates to Feminine Identification Conflict and Perceived Environmental Support." Unpublished doctoral dissertation, Smith College School for Social Work, 1971. (*Dissertation Abstracts International,* 1972, *32* [9-A], 5347.)

Saarni, C. I., Taber, R., and Shaw-Hamilton, L. "The Vicissitudes of Sex Role Assessment." Paper presented at 81st annual meeting of the Western Psychological Association, Anaheim, California, April 1973. (ERIC Document Reproduction Service No. ED 084 284.)

Sanford, N. *Self and Society: Social Change and Individual Development.* New York: Atherton Press, 1966.

Schenkel, S. "Relationship Among Ego Identity Status, Field Independence, and Traditional Femininity." *Journal of Youth and Adolescence,* 1975, *4,* 73-82.

Siegelman, M. "Parental Background of Male Homosexuals and Heterosexuals." *Archives of Sexual Behavior,* 1974, *3,* 3-18.

Strodtbeck, F., Bezdek, W., and Goldhammer, D. "Male Sex Role and Response to a Community Problem." *Sociological Quarterly,* 1970, *11,* 291-306.

Vaught, G. M. "The Relationship of Role Identification and Ego Strength to Sex Differences in the Rod-and-Frame Test." *Journal of Personality,* 1965, *33,* 271-283.

Weller, J. "Sex Differences and Sex Role Identity Differences in Attitudes of College Students Toward Parenthood." Unpublished doctoral dissertation, Columbia University, 1970. (*Dissertation Abstracts International,* 1970, *31* [4-B], 2270.)

Woudenberg, R. A. "The Relationship of Sexual Attitudes, Sexual Stereotypes, Racial-Sexual Stereotypes, and Racial Attitudes." Unpublished doctoral dissertation,

Michigan State University, 1973. (*Dissertation Abstracts International,* 1973, *34*[6-B], 2958.)

Wrchota, R. J. "Oral Passive Aims in Acting-Out Adolescent Girls in Relationship to the Developmental Task of Sexual Identification." Unpublished doctoral dissertation, School for Social Work, Smith College, 1973. (*Dissertation Abstracts International,* 1974, *34*[9-A], 6114.)

---

37. MARKE-GOTTFRIES ATTITUDE INTEREST SCHEDULE (AIS)

AUTHORS: Sven Marke and Ingrid Gottfries

DATE: 1967 (1963)

VARIABLE: Masculinity-femininity

TYPE OF INSTRUMENT: Multiple choice

DESCRIPTION: The scale consists of ten subscales: Occupations, Hobbies, Books, Drawings, Plays, Animals, Disgust, Pity, Fear, and Ethics. The Occupations subscale is a list of fifteen occupations, twelve that are typically preferred by women and three that are typically preferred by men. For each occupation, the respondents are to indicate whether they would like to pursue the occupation. The response options are: like, uninterested, dislike. The Hobbies subscale is a list of twenty hobbies, ten that are typically preferred by women and ten that are typically preferred by men. The respondents are to indicate whether they would like to engage in each hobby. The response options are: like, uninterested, dislike. The Book subscale is a list of sixteen book titles, eleven typically preferred by women and five typically preferred by men. The respondents are asked to indicate whether they would like to read each book. Instructions specify that the respondents should base their judgment solely on the basis of the title and not be concerned if they have never actually heard of the book. The response options are: like, uninterested, dislike. The Drawings subscale is a list of ten items. The respondents are asked to indicate whether they would like to paint a picture of the listed item. Four items are typically preferred by men; six items are typically preferred by women. The response options are: like, uninterested, dislike. The Plays subscale is a list of fifteen play activities. The respondents are to indicate whether as a child they did or did not play each one. The Animals subscale consists of twenty pairs of animals. Each pair consists of one animal typically thought of as possessing feminine characteristics and one animal typically thought of as possessing masculine characteristics. The respondents are told to assume that they could be changed into an animal and pick the one animal in each pair which they would like to be. The Disgust subscale consists of nine questions asking whether the respondent experiences disgust in response to particular situations. The response options are: very strong, strong, moderate, unaffected. The Pity subscale consists of nine questions asking whether the respondent experiences pity in response to particular situations or persons. The response options are: very strong, strong, moderate, unaffected. The Fear subscale consists of a list of fifteen questions that ask whether the respondent experiences fear in response to experiences or objects. The response options are: always, often, sometimes, never. The Ethics subscale consists of very brief descriptions of nineteen behaviors that may or may not be considered objectionable or blameworthy. For each description, the respondents are to indicate whether they view it as: extremely objectionable, decidedly objectionable, somewhat objectionable, or not objectionable.

PREVIOUSLY ADMINISTERED TO: Ages 14 and older

APPROPRIATE FOR: Ages 14 and older

ADMINISTRATION: The instrument is self-administered and can be completed in forty to sixty minutes.

SAMPLE ITEMS: *Occupations:* Airline pilot
                  Hobbies: Work with motors
                  Books: The Daily Life of a Princess
                  Drawings: Tiger
                  Plays: Hop scotch
                  Animals: Leopard-Monkey
                  Disgust: Do you feel disgust at brutality on film or TV?
                  Pity: Do you feel pity for an aged person suffering an incurable disease?
                  Fear: Do you fear becoming lost?
                  Ethics: That boys annoy girls?

SCORING: Specific directions for scoring items are not provided. It is reasonable to assume, however, that items are objectively scored and equally weighted. Scores can be obtained for each of the ten subscales and for three indices: M-F I is labeled Interests and includes the subscales Occupations, Books, and Hobbies; M-F II is labeled Emotions and includes the subscales Disgust, Pity, and Ethics; M-F III is labeled Stereotyped Toughness and includes the subscales Fear, Plays, and Animals.

DEVELOPMENT: A large item pool was constructed, with many items taken from the Attitude Interest Analysis Test (#31), a measure of masculinity-femininity. Items were selected for the following subscales: Occupations (thirty items), Hobbies (forty-two items), Books (thirty items), Drawings (eighteen items), Plays (fifteen items), Animals (twenty-eight items), Disgust (thirteen items), Pity (thirteen items), Fear (sixteen items), Ethics (twenty-five items), Toughness (fourteen items), Emotions (seventeen items), Adjective list (twenty adjectives). A sample of 152 men and 116 women ranging in age from about 16 to 22 completed the lengthy scale. An item analysis was performed on their responses. Items that did not satisfactorily discriminate between males and females were eliminated. Another item analysis was performed by obtaining subscale scores for each respondent. For each subscale, items were eliminated that did not discriminate satisfactorily between those scoring in the upper and lower 25 percent of the distribution of subscale scores. The results of these analyses led the authors to eliminate the last three scales: Toughness, Emotions, and Adjective list. The other ten subscales were retained, but the number of items included on each was reduced. Identification of the three indices, M-F I, M-F II, M-F III, was based on the results of factor analyses (see Notes and Comments below).

RELIABILITY: The ten subscales were administered to about 700 adolescents of an average age of 15. Their responses were used to compute corrected, split-half reliabilities. The results were (Marke and Gottfries, 1967):

Subscale	Males	Females	Total
Occupations	.76	.55	.85
Hobbies	.77	.73	.91
Books	.79	.77	.88
Drawings	.69	.61	.77
Plays	.46	.69	.92
Animals	.81	.75	.86
Disgust	.72	.69	.77
Pity	.82	.70	.79
Fear	.80	.82	.86
Ethics	.87	.75	.84

VALIDITY: The responses from the 700 adolescents were used to cross-validate the scale. To determine if each of the scales differentiated significantly between the sexes, point-biserial correlations were computed between sex and subscale score. The following results were obtained for each subscale: Occupations = .74; Books = .66; Drawings = .59; Hobbies = .81; Plays = .90; Animals = .62; Disgust = .44; Pity = .29; Ethics = .30; Fear = .51; M-F I = .82; M-F II = .38; and M-F III = .78. All correlations were significant at the .001 level. Furthermore, critical ratios comparing the means obtained between males and females were all significant at the .001 level (Marke and Gottfries, 1967).

Correlations between the Franck Drawing Completion Test (#11), a measure of masculinity-femininity, and each of the subscales of the Marke-Gottfries Attitude Interest Schedule were all quite low, ranging from −.13 to +.09 (Marke and Gottfries, 1967).

Correlations were computed between scores on the three indices of the Mark-Gottfries Attitude Interest Schedule and the masculinity-femininity scale of the Minnesota Multiphasic Personality Inventory (#52). The correlations for men were: M-F I = .48; M-F II = .18; M-F III = .27; the correlations for women were M-F I = .58; M-F II = .14; and M-F III = .26. Only the correlations for M-F I were statistically significant (p < .01) (Gottfries and Marke, 1971).

NOTES AND COMMENTS: (1) Separate analyses were computed for males and females using the responses from the sample on which the scale was developed and the sample on which it was cross-validated. Thus, a total of four factor analyses were performed. The first two factors that emerged were quite consistent across sexes and across samples. Factor I was labeled Interests and is "characterized by *preferences for activities* that are usually conventionally interpreted as associated with the sex roles" (Marke and Gottfries, 1967, p. 41). A high masculinity score on the factor is indicative of repudiation of feminine interests and activities. Factor II was labeled Emotions and represents "certain *emotional types of reaction* of almost sensitive kind, such as a tendency to react with feelings of pity, disgust, and moral indignation" (Marke and Gottfries, 1967, p. 41). A high masculinity score on this factor suggests denial of these types of reactions. The third factor was not consistent across sexes and samples and was more difficult to interpret. Marke and Gottfries (1967, p. 41) tentatively labeled it Stereotyped Toughness and state that it represents a "tendency to *describe oneself as tough, aggressive, dominant,* a behavior that in males is usually interpreted as pseudomasculine." Factors I and II correlate .18 (p < .01) for males and .20 (p < .01) for females; Factors I and III correlate .22 (p < .001) for males and .37 (p < .001) for females; Factors II and III correlate .27 (p < .001) for males and .30 (p < .001) for females (Marke and Gottfries, 1967).

(2) Gottfries and Marke (1971) report correlations between each of the three indices (factors) of the scale and numerous measures of personality, teachers' ratings, intelligence, achievement, and adjustment.

(3) In the instructions accompanying the Book subscale, the directions indicate that the respondents need not have read the book in order to indicate whether they would like a book with that title. However, if the respondent has, in fact, read the book, then that respondent may be answering on the basis of the contents of the book. In other words, some persons will be responding solely to the title and others will be responding to the content of the book; thus the stimuli are not identical across respondents.

(4) There are more typically feminine items on the scale than typically masculine items. Would scores differ if there were an equal number of typically masculine and typically feminine items?

(5) The work using this scale was done in Sweden and the scale was administered in Swedish.

SOURCE: See Marke and Gottfries, 1967.

BIBLIOGRAPHY:

Gottfries, I., and Marke, S. "A Study of Stick Figures Test: A Measure of Conformance in Role Perception." *Psychological Research Bulletin,* 1968, *8,* 1-17.
Gottfries, I., and Marke, S. "Dimensions of Masculinity-Femininity Related to Other Personality Variables and Some Measures of School Adjustment." *Psychological Research Bulletin,* 1971, *11,* 1-43.
Hakansson-Zaunders, M., and Uddenberg, N. "Conflicts Regarding Pregnancy and the Maternal Role as Reflected in a Serial Projective Test Instrument." *Psychological Research Bulletin,* 1975, *15,* 1-16.
Marke, S., and Gottfries, I. "Measurement of Masculinity-Femininity." *Psychological Research Bulletin,* 1967, *7,* 1-51.
Marke, S., and Gottfries, I. "Measurement of Sex Role Perception and Its Relation to Psychological Masculinity-Femininity." *Psychological Research Bulletin,* 1970, *10,* 1-33.

38. NICHOLS MASCULINITY-FEMININITY SCALE

AUTHOR: Robert C. Nichols

DATE: 1962

VARIABLE: Masculinity-femininity

TYPE OF INSTRUMENT: Alternate choice

DESCRIPTION: The Nichols Masculinity-Femininity Scale actually consists of three scales: Subtle Scale, Obvious Scale, and Stereotype Scale. The Subtle Scale consists of thirty statements that differentiated between college men and women but were not sex stereotyped by another sample of college students. The Obvious Scale consists of fifty-eight statements that differentiated between college men and women and were correctly sex stereotyped by another sample of college students. The Stereotype Scale consists of sixty-one statements that were sex stereotyped by a sample of college students but did not discriminate between college men and women. In completing the scales, the respondents are to indicate whether each statement is true or false as it applies to them.

PREVIOUSLY ADMINISTERED TO: Grade 9, college students, and married couples

APPROPRIATE FOR: Ages 14 and older

ADMINISTRATION: The three scales are self-administered and can be completed in less than forty-five minutes.

SAMPLE ITEMS: *Subtle Scale:* I hear easily when spoken to.
　　　　　　　　Obvious Scale: I think I would like the work of a dress designer.
　　　　　　　　Stereotype Scale: I can usually find a ready answer for remarks made to me.

SCORING: Items are objectively scored and equally weighted. Separate total scores are obtained for each of the three scales.

DEVELOPMENT: An item pool was formed consisting of all of the items on the masculinity-femininity subscales of the following instruments: Minnesota Multiphasic Personality Inventory (#52), Heston Personal Adjustment Inventory, VC Attitude Inventory (#58), Guilford-Martin Inventory of Factors GAMIN (#49), California Psychological Inventory (#47), and Gough Femininity Scale (#36). Additional items were taken from the Masculinity-Femininity scale of the Strong Vocational Interest Blank (#56) and from the Attitude Interest Analysis Test (#31). This pool of 356 items was administered to 100 college men and 100 college women with instructions to indicate whether each item was true or false as it applied to them. Using their responses, phi coefficients were computed showing the extent to which each item differentiated between men and women. The 356 items were then administered to forty-eight college students with instructions to indicate whether men would be more likely to respond true or false to each item. The items were also administered to sixty-four college students with instructions to indicate whether women would be more likely to respond true or false to each item. Using the responses from these two samples, phi coefficients were computed to indicate the agreement between the stereotypes indicated for men and for women. The Obvious Scale was compiled by selecting items that successfully differentiated between male and female respondents and that were similarly stereotyped by the two stereotyping samples. Items were selected for the Subtle Scale if they successfully differentiated between male and female respondents but were not stereotyped by the stereotyping samples. Items were selected for the Stereotype Scale if they did not differentiate between males and females but were stereotyped by the two stereotyping samples.

RELIABILITY: Kuder-Richardson reliabilities were computed for the sample of 100 college men and 100 college women who completed the 356-item pool. Kuder-Richardson reliabilities were also computed for another sample of 111 college men and 102 college women, and separate reliabilities were computed for males and females in this group. For the Subtle Scale, the reliability was .48 for the sample used in the original development and .14 for the second sample (for the second sample, the reliability was .07 for men and .10 for women). For the Obvious Scale, the reliability was .88 for the original sample and .94 for the second sample (for the second sample, the reliability was .68 for men and .65 for women). For the Stereotype Scale, the reliability for the original sample was .69; for the second sample, the reliability was .71 (for the second sample, the reliability was .66 for men and .70 for women) (Nichols, 1962).

VALIDITY: The second sample, containing 111 college men and 102 college women, was used to cross-validate the scale. For the Subtle Scale, the correlation between sex and score on the scale was .49 for the development sample but .28 on the cross-validation sample. For the Obvious Scale, the correlation with sex was .82 for the development sample and .85 for the cross-validation sample. For the Stereotype Scale, the correlation with sex was .06 for the development sample and .44 for the cross-validation sample. In referring to the correlation obtained by the cross-validation sample on the Stereotype Scale, Nichols (1962, p. 453) points out, "This is considerably higher than was expected and further studies to lower this correlation with sex are needed."

Nichols (1962) reports the correlations between scores on the Obvious, Subtle, and Stereotype Scales and each of the instruments that contributed to the original item pool.

NOTES AND COMMENTS: (1) Nichols (1962) reports the intercorrelations between the Obvious, Subtle, and Stereotype Scales using the data from the development sample and the data from the cross-validation sample. On the development sample, the correlations for females were −.34 between Subtle and Stereotype Scales, −.17 between Subtle and Obvious scales, and .36 between the Stereotype and Obvious Scales. For males, the correlations were −.14 between the Subtle and Stereotype Scales, .11 between the Subtle and Obvious Scales, and .41 between the Stereotype and Obvious Scales. For the cross-validation sample, the correlations for females were −.44 between the Subtle and Stereotype Scales, −.01 between the Subtle and Obvious Scales, and .35 between the Stereotype and Obvious Scales. For males, the correlations were −.49 between the Subtle and Stereotype Scales, −.08 between the Subtle and Obvious Scales, and .19 between the Stereotype and Obvious Scales.

(2) Nichols' idea to develop three scales—Stereotype, Subtle, and Obvious—is creative and intriguing. Unfortunately, the results from the cross-validation sample suggest that he was not very successful. For the Subtle Scale, both the reliability and

validity coefficients were considerably lower for the cross-validation sample than they were for the development sample. Furthermore, the Stereotype Scale items were deliberately selected because they did not discriminate between males and females in the development sample; yet on the cross-validation sample, the correlation between the Stereotype Scale and sex was .44.

(3) The scale has been used with varying instructions. Typically, respondents are asked to respond for themselves. However, Profant (1968) administered the scale to three groups, with each group receiving a different set of instructions. One group was given the typical instructions; one group was asked to answer the way males would answer; and a third group was asked to answer the way females would answer. Starr (1973) asked respondents to answer first for themselves and then the way they believed their spouse would answer.

(4) Scores on the scales have been related to academic major (Profant, 1968) and to creativity (Littlejohn, 1966, 1967).

SOURCE: Chief, Photoduplication Service
Library of Congress
10 First Street S.E.
Washington, D.C. 20540

BIBLIOGRAPHY:

Littlejohn, M. T. "A Comparison of the Responses of Ninth Graders to Measures of Creativity and Masculinity-Femininity." Unpublished doctoral dissertation, University of North Carolina, 1966. (*Dissertation Abstracts,* 1967, *27*[8-A], 2399-2400.)

Littlejohn, M. T. "Creativity and Masculinity-Femininity in Ninth Graders." *Perceptual and Motor Skills,* 1967, *25,* 737-743.

McCaulley, M. H. "Dimensions of Masculinity-Femininity in Relation to Field Dependence, Dogmatism, and Other Estimates of Perceptual-Cognitive Differentiation." Unpublished doctoral dissertation, Temple University, 1964. (*Dissertation Abstracts,* 1965, *25*[7], 4259.)

Nichols, R. C. "Subtle, Obvious, and Stereotype Measures of Masculinity-Femininity." *Educational and Psychological Measurement,* 1962, *22,* 449-461.

Profant, P. M. "Sex Differences and Sex Role Stereotypes as Related to Professional Career Goals." Unpublished doctoral dissertation, Ohio State University, 1968. (*Dissertation Abstracts International,* 1969, *30*[1-B], 388-389.)

Starr, D. L. "Wife Dependency as Related to Marital Adjustment, Masculinity-Femininity and Perceptual Congruence." Unpublished doctoral dissertation, University of Florida, 1973. (*Dissertation Abstracts International,* 1974, *35*[2-B], 1064-1065.)

39. PERSONAL ATTRIBUTES QUESTIONNAIRE (PAQ)

AUTHORS: Janet T. Spence, Robert Helmreich, and Joy Stapp

DATE: 1974

VARIABLES: Sex role stereotypes; masculinity-femininity

TYPE OF INSTRUMENT: Adjective rating scale

DESCRIPTION: The scale consists of two parts. The first part is the Self-Rating scale, which measures masculinity-femininity. The respondents are asked to describe themselves on a series of fifty-five five-point rating scales. The ends of each rating scale are labeled with brief descriptive phrases that are opposite to each other in meaning. There are three subscales: Masculinity, Femininity, and Masculinity-Femininity. The second part is the Stereotype scale, which measures sex role stereotypes. The same fifty-five brief phrases are repeated. However, in this part, a single descriptive phrase which captures the meaning of the opposite descriptive phrases used in the first part (see Sample Item) is placed above the five-point rating scale. The respondent is directed to rate each phrase in terms of whether it is more characteristic of the typical (college) man or typical (college) woman. The five-point rating scale ranges from "much more characteristic of male" to "much more characteristic of female."

PREVIOUSLY ADMINISTERED TO: Junior and senior high school students; college students in the United States (including whites, blacks, and Chicanos), Lebanon, Israel, and Brazil

APPROPRIATE FOR: Ages 12 and older

ADMINISTRATION: The scale is self-administered and can be completed in about thirty to forty-five minutes.

SAMPLE ITEMS:

Self-rating:

       Not at all aggressive A . . . . . B . . . . . C . . . . . D . . . . . E Very aggressive

Stereotype rating:

		Aggressive		
A ------------------- B ------------------- C ------------------- D ------------------- E				
Much more	Slightly	No	Slightly	Much more
characteristic	more	difference	more	characteristic
of male	male		female	of female

SCORING: Five scores are obtained from the PAQ. In all cases, items are objectively scored and equally weighted. On the Stereotype scale, a high score indicates more stereotypic perceptions. On the Self-Rating scale, a high score indicates greater masculinity. In addition to the total score on the Self-Rating scale, three subscale scores are obtained: a Masculinity score (based on twenty-three items), a Femininity score (based on eighteen items), and a Masculinity-Femininity score (based on thirteen items). Respondents who score above the median on both the Masculinity and Femininity subscales are classified as androgynous; respondents who score below the median on both subscales are classified as undifferentiated; respondents who score above the median on only Femininity are classified as feminine; and respondents who score above the median on only Masculinity are classified as masculine.

DEVELOPMENT: The fifty-five items appearing on both parts of the PAQ were selected "more or less arbitrarily" (Spence, Helmreich, and Stapp, 1974, p. 43) from the sixty-six items of the Sex Role Stereotype Questionnaire (#77), which yielded significant sex role stereotypes in the ratings given by both male and female respondents. The determination of the three subscale scores on the Self-Rating scale is also based on research with the Sex Role Stereotype Questionnaire. The twenty-three items that comprise the Masculinity scale "are considered to be socially desirable characteristics for both sexes but . . . males are believed to possess [them] in greater abundance than females (e.g., independence)." The eighteen items that comprise the Femininity scale are "considered to be socially desirable in both sexes but . . . females are believed to possess [them] to a greater degree (e.g., gentleness)." The thirteen items on the Masculinity-Femininity scale are "characteristics whose social desirability appears to vary in the two sexes (e.g., aggressiveness is judged to be desirable in males and nonaggressiveness desirable in females)" (Spence and Helmreich, 1978, p. 19).

RELIABILITY: Thirty-one college students completed the scale on two occasions separated by a thirteen-week interval. Test-retest reliability for men was .92 on the Stereotype scale and .80 on the Self-Rating scale. Test-retest reliability for women was .98 on the Stereotype scale and .91 on the Self-Rating scale. For the three subscales of the Self-Rating scale, test-retest reliabilities varied from .65 to .91 (Spence, Helmreich, and Stapp, 1974).

　　　The PAQ was completed by 248 college men and 282 college women. Internal consistency reliability (alpha) for men was .91 on the Stereotype scale and .73 for the Self-Rating scale. Internal consistency reliability (alpha) for women was .90 on the Stereotype scale and .91 on the Self-Rating scale (Spence, Helmreich, and Stapp, 1974).

　　　Using the data from the 530 college students, item-total correlations were computed for each of the three subscales. The item-total correlations for women ranged from .24 to .70 for the masculinity items, .27 to .55 for the femininity items, and .19 to .64 for the masculinity-femininity items. The item-total correlations for men ranged from .23 to .64 for the masculinity items, .22 to .56 for the femininity items, and .23 to .61 for the masculinity-femininity items (Spence, Helmreich, and Stapp, 1974).

VALIDITY: As mentioned earlier, items selected for the PAQ were those that showed significant sex role stereotypes in prior research using the Sex Role Stereotype Questionnaire. Two groups, one containing 530 college students and one including 164 college students, completed the PAQ. The data indicated statistically significant sex role stereotypes for both sexes on all items (Spence, Helmreich, and Stapp, 1974).

　　　The correlations between the PAQ and the Bem Sex Role Inventory (#32), a similar measure of masculinity-femininity, were .75 for males and .73 for females on the Masculinity subscale and .57 for males and .59 for females on the Femininity subscale (Spence and Helmreich, 1978).

　　　As further evidence of the validity of the PAQ, Spence, Helmreich, and Stapp (1975) report correlations between a measure of social desirability and scores on the

PAQ. The correlations ranged from .08 to .36, and though "some reached statistical significance, their magnitude was unimpressive" (Spence and Helmreich, 1978, p. 34). Spence and Helmreich (1978, p. 35) also report that the relationship between intelligence and PAQ scores is "essentially orthogonal, the correlations ranging from .02 with M [masculinity] to −.12 with F [femininity]."

NOTES AND COMMENTS: (1) The authors of the PAQ have constructed a short form of the PAQ, which includes eight items from each of the three subscales: male-valued items, female-valued items, and sex-specific items. The items were chosen for the short form on the basis of the item-total correlations obtained when the long form was administered. The correlation between the short form of each subscale and the full-length subscale was .90 for each of the three subscales. The correlation between the Total Self-Rating score on the long and short forms was .92. The correlation between the Stereotype scale score on the long and short forms was .94.

(2) Spence and Helmreich (1978) review and summarize the research that has been done using the PAQ.

(3) Spence, Helmreich, and Stapp (1974) provide norms based on the responses from college men and women.

SOURCE: See Spence, Helmreich, and Stapp, 1974; or ETS Microfiche Test Collection (#007795); or Spence and Helmreich, 1978 for short form.

BIBLIOGRAPHY:

Applegarth, L. D. "The Effects of Short-Term Feminist Training of Counselor Trainees." Unpublished doctoral dissertation, Boston University School of Education, 1975. (*Dissertation Abstracts International*, 1976, *36* [8-A], 5031.)

Bender, V. L. "Social Sex Role Stereotypes and Sexual Orientation as Related to Self-Disclosure." Paper presented at 85th annual meeting of the American Psychological Association, San Francisco, August 1977.

Bender, V. L., Davis, Y., Glover, O., and Stapp, J. "Patterns of Self-Disclosure in Homosexual and Heterosexual College Students." *Sex Roles,* 1976, *2,* 149-160.

Mickleson, K. K. "The Effects of Father-Daughter Relationships on the Development of Achievement Orientation and Psychological Androgyny in Females." Unpublished doctoral dissertation, California School of Professional Psychology, 1976. (*Dissertation Abstracts International,* 1976, *37* [6-B], 3085-3086.)

Pasquella, M. J., Mednick, M. T. S., and Murray, S. R. "Causal Attributions for Achievement Outcomes: Sex Role Identity, Sex, and Outcome Comparisons." Paper presented at 85th annual meeting of the American Psychological Association, San Francisco, August 1977.

Spence, J. T., and Helmreich, R. L. *Masculinity and Femininity: Their Psychological Dimensions, Correlates, and Antecedents.* Austin: University of Texas Press, 1978.

Spence, J. T., Helmreich, R. L., and Stapp, J. T. "The Personal Attributes Questionnaire: A Measure of Sex Role Stereotypes and Masculinity-Femininity." *Journal Supplement Abstract Service Catalog of Selected Documents in Psychology,* 1974, *4,* 43-44.

Spence, J. T., Helmreich, R. L., and Stapp, J. T. "Ratings of Self and Peers on Sex Role Attributes and Their Relations to Self-Esteem and Conceptions of Masculinity and Femininity." *Journal of Personality and Social Psychology,* 1975, *32,* 29-39.

Wheeler, E. E., Wheeler, K. R., and Torres-Raines, R. "Women's Stereotypic Roles: A Replication and Standardization of the AWS and PAQ for Selected Ethnic Groups." Paper presented at the Southwestern Social Science Association, Dallas, March 1977. (ERIC Document Reproduction Service No. ED 142 360.)

---

40. PONZO SEX ROLE IDENTITY SCALE

AUTHOR: Zander Ponzo

DATE: 1967

VARIABLE: Sex role identity

TYPE OF INSTRUMENT: Adjective checklist

DESCRIPTION: The instrument consists of 124 adjectives. Sixty-five of the adjectives have been identified as masculine and fifty-nine have been identified as feminine. Three response options accompany each adjective: "Yes, I would generally describe myself as being _____"; "No, I would not generally describe myself as being _____"; and "Sorry, I can't decide on this one" (Ponzo, 1967, p. 145).

PREVIOUSLY ADMINISTERED TO: High school students

APPROPRIATE FOR: Ages 14 and older

ADMINISTRATION: The 124 adjectives are embedded in a list consisting of 271 adjectives. The entire scale can be completed in less than forty-five minutes.

SAMPLE ITEMS: Absent-minded
                Active
                Adaptable (gets used to new situations easily)
                Adventurous

SCORING: A person's score is equal to the number of sex-appropriate choices (that is, sex-appropriate items identified as self-descriptive and sex-inappropriate items identified as not self-descriptive) less the number of sex-inappropriate choices (that is, sex-inappropriate items identified as self-descriptive and sex-appropriate items identified as not self-descriptive). Items for which the response was "Sorry, I can't decide on this one" are not scored. Total scores can range from −124 (all sex-inappropriate choices) to +124 (all sex-appropriate choices).

DEVELOPMENT: Based on a review of the relevant literature, Ponzo selected 271 adjectives from Gough's Adjective Check List (#45). The 271 adjectives were administered to 329 high school seniors with instructions to indicate whether each adjective is more appropriate for describing a teenage boy or a teenage girl. Seven response options accompanied each adjective; the response options ranged from "Definitely more appropriate for the teenage boy" to "Definitely more appropriate for the teenage girl" (Ponzo, 1967, p. 140). Using the combined responses from 149 boys and 180 girls, an analysis was performed to determine which adjectives were perceived as more appropriate for one sex than the other (p < .001); 146 adjectives met this criterion. Analyses were then performed separately for the male respondents and the female respondents to again determine which items were perceived as more appropriate for one sex than the other (p < .05). Twenty-two of the 146 adjectives satisfying the first criterion did not satisfy the second criterion. These were eliminated from the scale. Thus the final scale consists of 124 items which are perceived as more appropriate for one sex (p < .001) when the responses for boys and girls are analyzed together and are also perceived as more appropriate for one sex (p < .05) when responses are analyzed separately for male and female respondents. To determine the test-retest reliability of the responses used to develop the scale, the 271-item checklist was administered a second time seven days later to a subsample of thirty-five boys and forty-six girls. The test-retest reliability (Spearman rank-order correlation) of the 271 adjectives was .936. The test-retest reliability of the 146 adjectives that were perceived as appropriate for one sex (when male and female respondents were considered together) was .950.

RELIABILITY: The scale was administered to forty-four boys and fifty-six girls on two occasions separated by one week. Test-retest reliability was .903 (Ponzo, 1967).

VALIDITY: Ponzo (1967) hypothesized that senior girls in high school would score significantly higher than freshman girls. The hypothesis was supported: freshman girls had a mean of 26.34 and senior girls had a mean of 35.75; the difference was statistically significant (p < .001). Ponzo's hypothesis that college-bound senior girls would score significantly lower than non-college-bound senior girls was not supported by the data. Likewise the hypothesis that college-bound senior boys would score significantly higher than non-college-bound senior boys was not supported by the data.

NOTES AND COMMENTS: (1) Ponzo (1967) looked at the relationship between scores on the Ponzo Sex Role Identity Scale and self-concept of ability, self-expectations, grade point average, academic aptitude, mother's educational level, father's educational level, and mother's work status.

(2) Though persons older than high school age can respond to the items on the scale, there is no evidence to indicate whether the adjectives are correctly sex typed for older persons. Before the scale is used with older persons, some evidence should be obtained to establish the sex typing of the adjectives.

SOURCE: See Ponzo and Strowig, 1973.

BIBLIOGRAPHY:

Ponzo, Z. "Relations Among Sex Role Identity and Selected Intellectual and Nonintellectual Factors for High School Freshmen and Seniors." Unpublished doctoral dissertation, University of Wisconsin, 1967. (*Dissertation Abstracts,* 1967, *28*[A], 2990-2991.)

Ponzo, Z., and Strowig, R. W. "Relations Among Sex Role Identity and Selected Intellectual and Nonintellectual Factors for High School Freshmen and Seniors." *Journal of Educational Research,* 1973, *67,* 137-141.

41. PRF ANDRO SCALE

AUTHORS: Juris I. Berzins, Martha A. Welling, and Robert E. Wetter

DATE: 1974

VARIABLES: Masculinity, femininity, androgyny

TYPE OF INSTRUMENT: True-false

DESCRIPTION: The instrument consists of fifty-six statements: there are twenty-nine items on the masculine scale with nineteen items keyed true and ten keyed false; there are twenty-seven items on the feminine scale, with seventeen items keyed true and ten keyed false. The masculine items relate to "social and intellectual ascendancy, autonomy, and an orientation toward risk"; the feminine items relate to "nurturance, affiliative-expressive concerns, and self-subordination" (Berzins, 1975, p. 5). For each statement, respondents are to indicate whether the statement is true as it applies to them or false as it applies to them.

PREVIOUSLY ADMINISTERED TO: High school and college students, therapists and therapist trainees, alcoholics

APPROPRIATE FOR: Ages 14 and older

ADMINISTRATION: The instrument can be administered in one of two ways. The entire 400-item Personality Research Form (PRF) includes the fifty-six items on the PRF ANDRO scale. Thus one can administer the Personality Research Form and score the fifty-six relevant items. The eighty-five-item Interpersonal Disposition Inventory (IDI) can be administered. It includes the fifty-six items of the PRF ANDRO, twenty items assessing self-esteem, five items from the PRF designed to detect careless responding, and four filler items.

SAMPLE ITEMS:

Masculinity scale: When someone opposes me on an issue, I usually find myself taking an even stronger stand than I did at first.

Femininity scale: When I see someone who looks confused, I usually ask if I can be of any assistance.

SCORING: Each item is objectively scored and equally weighted. A total score is obtained on masculinity (range 0 to 29 with high scores indicative of greater masculinity) and femininity (range 0 to 27 with high scores indicative of greater femininity). A computer program is available from the authors for scoring IDI responses. The computer program provides raw scores, standard scores, and T-scale scores. Four sex role categories are obtained from scores on the masculinity and femininity scales. The median score on each scale determines the division for high versus low scores. Persons who are high on both masculinity and femininity are classified as androgynous; persons who are high on masculinity and low on femininity are classified as masculine typed; persons who are high on femininity and low on masculinity are classified as feminine typed; and persons who are low on both scales are classified as undifferentiated.

Normative data are available for the IDI based on responses from 386 college men and 723 college women (Berzins, Welling, and Wetter, 1977).

DEVELOPMENT: The authors reviewed the 400 items on the PRF to identify items for the PRF ANDRO scale. Items were selected if they were consistent with the rationale that Bem used for item selection and if their content was consistent with the main content themes on the Bem Sex Role Inventory (#32). Bem's rationale "included provisions for (a) separate Masculinity and Femininity scales, (b) items selected on the basis of sex-typed desirability . . . and (c) items with generally positive content" (Berzins, Welling, and Wetter, 1978, p. 127). The main content themes for masculinity on the Bem Sex Role Inventory concern "a dominant-instrumental dimension comprised of themes of social-intellectual ascendancy, autonomy, and orientation toward risk" (Berzins, Welling, and Wetter, 1978, p. 128). For femininity, the themes concern "a nurturant-expressive dimension containing themes of nurturance, affiliative-expressive concerns, and self-sub-ordination" (Berzins, Welling, and Wetter, 1978, p. 128). Applying these criteria, the authors selected sixty-four items, half measuring masculinity and half measuring femininity. On the basis of item analysis performed on the responses from 100 college men and 100 college women, the two scales were shortened to their present length.

RELIABILITY: Internal consistency coefficients (alpha) were estimated from seven different samples. For the masculinity scale, the coefficients ranged from .68 to .79. For the femininity scale, the coefficients ranged from .65 to .70 (Berzins, Welling, and Wetter, 1977).

Test-retest reliability was estimated from the responses of 137 persons. Half completed the IDI in class and three weeks later completed the PRF at home; the other half did the opposite. Test-retest reliability was .81 for both the masculinity and femininity scales (Berzins, Welling, and Wetter, 1977).

VALIDITY: To validate the author's judgment of the sex typing of the items, eighty-seven college students rated the items on the masculinity scale and a different group of ninety college students rated the items on the femininity scale. Raters were directed to indicate, "In American society, how desirable is it for a MAN [alternately, WOMAN] to mark this item TRUE?" (Berzins, Welling, and Wetter, 1978, p. 128). Raters were directed to make normative rather than prescriptive judgments. The items on the masculinity scale had a mean desirability score of 5.35 when the target was a man and 3.29 when the target was a woman; this difference is statistically significant (p < .0001). Similarly, the items on the femininity scale had a mean desirability score of 5.28 when the target was a woman and 3.58 when the target was a man; again the difference was statistically significant (p < .0001) (Berzins, Welling, and Wetter, 1978).

The PRF ANDRO was administered to two samples of respondents: Sample 1 contained 1,160 college students; Sample 2 contained 986 college students. For both samples, and for both the masculinity and femininity scales, the differences between the means for men and women were statistically significant (p < .0001). In every case, the direction of the difference was consistent with what would be expected (Berzins, Welling, and Wetter, 1978).

The authors specified that the masculinity and femininity scales should be independent of each other. To test whether this is in fact the case, they correlated the scores on the two subscales for each of the two samples. For Sample 1, the correlation for the men was −.05 and the correlation for the women was −.16. For Sample 2, the correlation for the men was −.11 and the correlation for the women was −.24 (Berzins, Welling, and Wetter, 1978).

Sample 1 completed the Bem Sex Role Inventory (#32), which measures masculinity-femininity-androgyny, the Marlowe-Crowne Social Desirability Scale, a twenty-item
PRF Desirability Scale, the Bem Sex Role Inventory Desirability scale, a measure of self-
esteem, and a measure of locus of control. Correlations were computed between scores on
the PRF ANDRO masculinity and femininity scales and the Bem Sex Role Inventory masculinity and femininity scales. For women, the correlations were .50 (p < .001) on the
femininity scales and .65 (p < .001) for the masculinity scales. For men, the correlations
were .60 (p < .001) on the masculinity scales and .52 (p < .001) on the femininity scales.
The correlations with the three desirability scales (Bem, PRF, and Marlowe-Crowne) were
"generally positive and low" (Berzins, Welling, and Wetter, 1978, p. 132). For both men
and women, correlations between the PRF ANDRO masculinity scale and the measure of
self-esteem were moderate (women, r = .38, p < .001; men, r = .36, p < .001). No other
correlations involving the PRF ANDRO scales exceeded .30 (Berzins, Welling, and Wetter,
1978).

Seventy-one men and 112 women completed the PRF ANDRO and the Personal
Attributes Questionnaire (#39), which is another measure of masculinity and femininity.
Correlations with the masculinity scale of PRF ANDRO were .57 for men and .42 for
women; correlations with the femininity scale of PRF ANDRO were .56 for men and .46
for women. All correlations were statistically significant (p < .001).

Correlations between scores from the PRF ANDRO scale and older masculinity-
femininity scales tend to be low. A sample of 682 college students completed the PRF
ANDRO and the masculinity-femininity scale of the Omnibus Personality Inventory
(#53). Correlations with the femininity scale from the PRF ANDRO were −.22 for men,
−.16 for women, and −.42 for both sexes combined. Correlations with the masculinity
scale from the PRF ANDRO were .04 for men, .08 for women, and .30 for both sexes
combined. A sample of 206 male alcoholics completed the masculinity-femininity scale
from the Minnesota Multiphasic Personality Inventory (#52) and completed the PRF
ANDRO. Correlations with the masculinity scale were −.06; correlations with the femininity scale were .00 (Berzins, Welling, and Wetter, 1977).

Correlations between the scales of the PRF ANDRO and measures of intellectual
functioning have been low (range = −.13 to +.13) (Berzins, Welling, and Wetter, 1977).

NOTES AND COMMENTS: (1) Berzins, Welling, and Wetter (1977, 1978) have compared
the items and scores from the PRF ANDRO with the items and subscale scores on the
PRF.

(2) A factor analysis of responses to the PRF ANDRO yielded seven interpretable
factors. Four factors include exclusively items from the masculinity scale. These factors
were labeled Social-Intellectual Ascendancy, Autonomy, Orientation Toward Risk, and
Individualism. Two factors included exclusively items from the femininity scale. These
factors were labeled Nurturance and Affiliative-Concerns—Self-Subordination. One factor
included items from both scales and was labeled Helpful Initiative (Berzins, Welling, and
Wetter, 1978).

(3) Though the scale is quite well developed and there is much evidence pertaining to its reliability and validity, most of the research has used college students. As a
result, research should be done to determine whether the scale is equally appropriate for
persons other than college students and what the psychometric properties of the scale are
when it is administered to persons other than college students.

(4) Scores on the PRF ANDRO have been compared with autobiographical variables (Woods, 1975), responses to the Parent Behavior Form (Kelly and Worell, 1975,

1976), self-esteem (Wetter, 1975), and scores on the Interpersonal Check List (Berzins, Welling, and Wetter, 1976).

SOURCE: Juris I. Berzins
    Department of Psychology
    University of Kentucky
    Lexington, Kentucky 40506

BIBLIOGRAPHY:

Berzins, J. I. "New Perspectives on Sex Roles and Personality Dimensions." Paper presented at 83rd annual meeting of the American Psychological Association, Chicago, August 1975.

Berzins, J. I., Welling, M. A., and Wetter, R. E. "Androgynous vs. Traditional Sex Roles and Interpersonal Behavior Circle." Paper presented at 84th annual meeting of the American Psychological Association, Washington, D.C., September 1976.

Berzins, J. I., Welling, M. A., and Wetter, R. E. "The PRF ANDRO Scale: User's Manual" (Revised). Unpublished manuscript, 1977.

Berzins, J. I., Welling, M. A., and Wetter, R. E. "A New Measure of Psychological Androgyny Based on the Personality Research Form." *Journal of Consulting and Clinical Psychology,* 1978, *46,* 126-138.

Kelly, J. A., and Worell, L. "The Relation of Sex Role Categories to Dimensions of Parental Behavior." Paper presented at 83rd annual meeting of the American Psychological Association, Chicago, August 1975.

Kelly, J. A., and Worell, L. "Parent Behaviors Related to Masculine, Feminine, and Androgynous Sex Role Orientations." *Journal of Consulting and Clinical Psychology,* 1976, *44,* 843-851.

Welling, M. A. "A New Androgyny Measure Derived from the Personality Research Form." Paper presented at 83rd annual meeting of the American Psychological Association, Chicago, August 1975.

Wetter, R. E. "Levels of Self-Esteem Associated with Four Sex Role Categories." Paper presented at 83rd annual meeting of the American Psychological Association, Chicago, August 1975.

Woods, M. M. "The Relation of Sex Role Categories to Autobiographical Factors." Paper presented at 83rd annual meeting of the American Psychological Association, Chicago, August 1975.

42. REVISED CONCEPT MEANING MEASURE

AUTHORS: Michael M. Reece; revised by Bert R. Sappenfield

DATE: 1966

VARIABLE: Masculinity-femininity

TYPE OF INSTRUMENT: Semantic differential scale

DESCRIPTION: The instrument consists of thirty-six bipolar scales. If the instrument is intended to measure self-perception of masculinity-femininity, then the concept rated is self. If the instrument is intended to measure perceptions of someone else's masculinity-femininity (for example, husband, wife, mother, father), then the concept rated is that other person. The concepts are rated on seven-point scales.

PREVIOUSLY ADMINISTERED TO: College students

APPROPRIATE FOR: Ages 16 and older

ADMINISTRATION: The scale can be self-administered and can be completed in less than ten minutes.

SAMPLE ITEMS: Vigorous-Languid
                          Individualistic-Conforming
                          Arrogant-Meek

SCORING: Items are objectively scored and equally weighted. Total scores range from 36 (most masculine) to 252 (most feminine).

DEVELOPMENT: One hundred ninety-two subjects used the Concept Meaning Measure to rate photographs of persons (Sappenfield, Kaplan, and Balogh, 1966). The thirty-six items that most successfully differentiated feminine photographs from masculine photographs comprise the Revised Concept Meaning Measure.

RELIABILITY: No data are provided.

VALIDITY: Sappenfield (1968) conducted a series of studies in which different persons rated the following concepts: own wife, own husband, own mother, own father, ideal person of own sex and age, ideal person to marry. In every case, means based on ratings of females were significantly higher (more feminine) than means based on ratings of males. Furthermore, Sappenfield found that when females rated themselves, the means were significantly higher (more feminine) than when males rated themselves ($p < .01$).

For those persons who also completed the masculinity-femininity scale of the Minnesota Multiphasic Personality Inventory (#52), Sappenfield was able to correlate their scores on the two masculinity-femininity measures. He found that correlations were higher for males ($r = .55, .39, .60,$ and $.56$) in the five groups he tested than for females ($r = .43, .31, .29,$ and $.43$). As a result, he concluded that "the Revised CMM may have adequate validity as a test of self-report M-F only for males" (Sappenfield, 1968, p. 95).

In another study, Sappenfield and Harris (1975) altered the Revised Concept Meaning Measure by using a five-point rating scale and scoring only twenty-one of the thirty-six items. They tested thirty-three college males and forty-five college females and found a significant difference ($p < .01$) in their mean self-ratings.

NOTES AND COMMENTS: (1) The original Concept Meaning Measure, which first appeared in the literature in 1964, was intended to assess stereotypes of masculinity and femininity. Four concepts—"typical masculinity," "typical femininity," "ideal masculinity," and "ideal femininity"—were rated on forty-five bipolar scales. In developing the scale, Reece (1964) hypothesized six factors: Form, Emotion, Potency, Tactility, Activity, and Social Behavior. He selected six bipolar scales to represent each of the first five factors, and fifteen bipolar scales to represent Social Behavior. He then administered the scale to forty male and forty female college students and factor analyzed the results. The factor analysis for "typical masculinity" supported the six hypothesized factors. The results for the other three concepts were less clear-cut.

(2) Sappenfield, Kaplan, and Balogh (1966) used only twenty-one bipolar scales and used photographs as the stimuli to be rated.

SOURCE: See Sappenfield, Kaplan, and Balogh, 1966.

BIBLIOGRAPHY:

*Reece, M. M. "Masculinity and Femininity: A Factor-Analytic Study." *Psychological Reports,* 1964, *14,* 123-139.
Sappenfield, B. R. "The Revised CMM as a Test of Perceived M-F and of Self-Report M-F." *Journal of Projective Techniques and Personality Assessment,* 1968, *32,* 92-95.
Sappenfield, B. R., and Harris, C. L. "Self-Reported Masculinity-Femininity as Related to Self-Esteem." *Psychological Reports,* 1975, *37,* 669-670.
Sappenfield, B. R., Kaplan, B. B., and Balogh, B. "Perceptual Correlates of Stereotypical Masculinity-Femininity." *Journal of Personality and Social Psychology,* 1966, *4,* 585-590.

---

43. SMITH MASCULINITY-FEMININITY SCALE

AUTHOR: Henry Clay Smith

DATE: 1968

VARIABLE: Masculinity-femininity

TYPE OF INSTRUMENT: True-false

DESCRIPTION: The instrument consists of twenty items, half of which are more likely to be true of men and half of which are more likely to be true of women. Twelve items concern likes and dislikes; eight items relate to one's perception of one's own personality traits or related behavior; and three items assess attitudes. For each item, the respondents are asked to indicate whether each statement is "true" or "false" as applied to themselves.

PREVIOUSLY ADMINISTERED TO: College students

APPROPRIATE FOR: Ages 16 and older

ADMINISTRATION: The instrument can be self-administered and can be completed in less than ten minutes.

SAMPLE ITEMS: I like ballet performances.
                            I am temperamentally more a skeptic than a believer.

SCORING: Items are objectively scored and equally weighted. Total scores can range from 0 (all masculine responses) to 20 (all feminine responses).

DEVELOPMENT: A pool of 200 items was administered to college students. The twenty items that best discriminated between the responses of male and female college students comprise this instrument.

RELIABILITY: No data are provided.

VALIDITY: The instrument was administered to a sample of ninety-two college students. Mean scores for females ($\overline{X}$ = 16.73) were significantly higher (more feminine) than mean scores for males ($\overline{X}$ = 7.24, p < .001) (Touhey, 1974).

NOTES AND COMMENTS: (1) Three of the twenty items on the instrument warrant criticism. If persons respond "false" to the statement "I control my sexual impulses by instituting prohibitions and restrictions," they might mean either that they use a different procedure to control their sexual impulses or that they simply do not control their sexual impulses. Two other items assume that respondents are familiar with names or terms. Specifically, the item "The European attitude toward mistresses is more sensible than ours" requires that respondents know what the European system is; and "I would rather read *Business Week* than *Atlantic Monthly*" assumes that respondents are familiar with both magazines. These assumptions may be incorrect for some respondents.

(2) The scale has also been used to measure sex role stereotypes by asking subjects to indicate whether a statement would be more characteristic of males or females.

SOURCE: See Smith, 1968, p. 345.

BIBLIOGRAPHY:

Smith, H. C. *Personality Development.* (2nd ed.) New York: McGraw-Hill, 1968.
Touhey, J. C. "Masculinity-Femininity and Accuracy of Sex Role Ascription." *Social Behavior and Personality,* 1974, 2, 40-42.

44. WELLESLEY ROLE ORIENTATION SCALE (WROS)

AUTHOR: Thelma G. Alper

DATE: 1973 (used 1964)

VARIABLE: Sex role preference

TYPE OF INSTRUMENT: Summated rating scale

DESCRIPTION: The scale consists of twenty-four items, seven on each of three subscales (Feminine Traits, Feminine Role Activities, and Male-Oriented Careers) and three filler items (which are not scored). Some items are phrased so that an "agree" response reflects a feminine sex role preference; for other items, a "disagree" response reflects a feminine sex role preference. The women are asked to select their responses to each item from six alternatives: strongly agree, moderately agree, slightly agree, slightly disagree, moderately disagree, or strongly disagree.

PREVIOUSLY ADMINISTERED TO: Female high school and college students

APPROPRIATE FOR: Females, ages 16 and older

ADMINISTRATION: The scale is self-administered and can be completed in about fifteen minutes.

SAMPLE ITEMS:

Feminine Traits: Aggressiveness and drive are valuable personality attributes.

Feminine Role Activities: Just because a woman has chosen a career rather than marriage does not mean that she is less feminine.

Male-Oriented Careers: It is more difficult to have confidence in a female doctor than in a male one.

Filler: All colleges should adopt the honor system.

SCORING: The original scoring procedure assigned 1 point to each item when the feminine response was selected and 0 points when it was not. Scores could range from 0 to 21, with 0 indicating low femininity and 21 indicating high femininity. The new scoring procedure scores each item on the basis of a 7-point scale and sums item scores to yield total scores. Total scores range from 21 (low femininity) to 147 (high femininity).

DEVELOPMENT: College students were asked to write sex-role-relevant statements. An examination of the statements suggested the three categories that are included in the scale: feminine traits, feminine role activities, and male-oriented careers. Other students sorted the statements into three piles: masculine, feminine, and ambiguous (or irrelevant). Ambiguous and irrelevant statements were eliminated and the remaining statements were again sorted. Items on which there was consensus and some filler statements were subjected to a pilot test. Those statements that were uniformly accepted or rejected were eliminated. The remaining twenty-four items comprise the WROS.

RELIABILITY: Split-half reliability was estimated for two groups. The Spearman rho correlations obtained were .58 and .60. Test-retest reliability was estimated based on the results obtained from twenty-five college women who were tested on two occasions, separated by about one semester. The correlation (rho) was .70 (Alper, 1973).

VALIDITY: Twenty-four college women completed the WROS and indicated both preferences and expectations for what they would be doing one year and ten years after college graduation. The data regarding one-year post-graduation plans tended to support the validity of the WROS. Women who scored low (as compared to women who scored high) on the WROS were more likely to be expecting to be involved in a career (p < .10) and were more likely to prefer to be involved in a career (p < .01). There were no differences between high and low scorers in regard to the responses for ten years after graduation (Alper, 1973).

No significant relationships have been found between scores on the WROS and scores on the femininity scale of the California Psychological Inventory (#47) or between scores on the WROS and scores on the Marlowe-Crowne Social Desirability Scale. Correlations between scores on the WROS and scores on the Traditional Family Ideology Scale (#129) have "consistently been positive and highly significant" (Alper, 1973, p. 15).

When WROS scores were used to divide women into traditional and nontraditional groups, the predicted differences in achievement motivation and motive to avoid success have, in general, been found (Alper, 1973, 1974; O'Leary and Hammack, 1975). In other words, traditional women generally show less achievement motivation or greater motive to avoid success than do nontraditional women.

NOTES AND COMMENTS: (1) The WROS should be embedded in the Traditional Family Ideology Scale (#129) when it is given.

(2) Though the scale can be completed by any female over age 16, the content of the statements suggests that they are most appropriate for unmarried college women. Furthermore, the development of the scale as well as reliability and validity is based on responses from college women.

(3) The WROS is intended for research purposes only.

SOURCE: Thelma G. Alper
         51 Harvard Avenue
         Brookline, Massachusetts 02146

BIBLIOGRAPHY:

Alper, T. G. "The Relationship Between Role Orientation and Achievement Motivation in College Women." *Journal of Personality*, 1973, *41*, 9-31.

Alper, T. G. "Achievement Motivation in College Women: A Now-You-See-It-Now-You-Don't Phenomenon." *American Psychologist*, 1974, *29*, 194-203.

Behrens, M. G. "Effects of Global-Analytic Style, Female Role Orientation, and Fear of Success on Problem-Solving Behavior." Unpublished doctoral dissertation, Claremont Graduate School, 1973. (*Dissertation Abstracts International*, 1974, *34*[7-B], 3517.)

Dickstein, L. S., and Brown, N. "Effect of Role Orientation and Instructions Regarding Competition on Cognitive Performance of College Females." *Psychological Reports*, 1974, *34*, 291-297.

O'Leary, V. E., and Hammack, B. "Sex Role Orientation and Achievement Context as Determinants of the Motive to Avoid Success." *Sex Roles,* 1975, *1,* 225-234.

Rodgon, M. M., Gralewski, C., and Hetzel, J. "Maternal Attitudes Toward Sex Roles Related to Children's Attitudes Toward Maternal Roles in Second- and Sixth-Grade Children." Paper presented at the biennial meeting of the Society for Research in Child Development, New Orleans, 1977. (ERIC Document Reproduction Service No. ED 136 935.)

Sturm, S. G. "An Examination of the Motive to Avoid Success, Performance, Locus of Control, and Role Orientation." Unpublished doctoral dissertation, University of Tennessee, 1974. (*Dissertation Abstracts International,* 1975, *35* [8-B] , 4198.)

The fifteen instruments that follow all include several subscales, with at least one subscale indicating sex role adoption, preference, or orientation/identity. Because the purpose of these instruments is broader than just the measurement of sex role and because each is a published test listed in *Tests in Print* and a *Mental Measurements Yearbook,* the instruments are not fully described here; instead abridged descriptions are given. Included in the abridged description is information on how to locate the instrument in *Tests in Print, The Mental Measurements Yearbook,* and *Personality Tests and Reviews.* By referring to these references, one can obtain a description of the instrument, evaluative reviews of it, and a bibliography of the research that used it. The evaluative reviews may appear in the *Mental Measurements Yearbook* or *Personality Tests and Reviews.* The descriptions and bibliographies appear in all three publications. Because bibliographic entries are not repeated in successive editions of a publication or in the different books, it will be necessary to consult all the sources listed to obtain a complete bibliography. Furthermore, the bibliographies will reflect all applications of these instruments, not just those that used the sex role subscale. As a result, readers will have to rely on the title of each bibliographic entry to determine whether it is likely to be relevant to their interests.

The appropriate books to consult for each instrument are given in coded form on the following pages. The code indicates the precise location of information pertinent to each instrument. There are two editions of *Tests in Print*; the roman numeral preceding the colon indicates whether the instrument is listed in the first or second edition; the number following the colon indicates the instrument's entry number. Instruments are listed in all of these publications in numerical order by entry number; page numbers are not necessary. There are eight editions of *The Mental Measurements Yearbook.* The number preceding the colon indicates which edition to consult; the number following the colon is the entry number for the instrument. Since only one edition of *Personality Tests and Reviews* has been published, only the entry number is provided here.

BIBLIOGRAPHY:

Buros, O. K. *The 1938 Mental Measurements Yearbook.* Highland Park, N.J.: Gryphon Press, 1938.

Buros, O. K. *The 1940 Mental Measurements Yearbook.* Highland Park, N.J.: Gryphon Press, 1941.

Buros, O. K. *The Third Mental Measurements Yearbook*. Highland Park, N.J.: Gryphon Press, 1949.

Buros, O. K. *The Fourth Mental Measurements Yearbook*. Highland Park, N.J.: Gryphon Press, 1953.

Buros, O. K. *The Fifth Mental Measurements Yearbook*. Highland Park, N.J.: Gryphon Press, 1959.

Buros, O. K. *The Sixth Mental Measurements Yearbook*. Highland Park, N.J.: Gryphon Press, 1965.

Buros, O. K. *The Seventh Mental Measurements Yearbook*. Highland Park, N.J.: Gryphon Press, 1972.

Buros, O. K. *The Eighth Mental Measurements Yearbook*. Highland Park, N.J.: Gryphon Press, 1978.

Buros, O. K. *Personality Tests and Reviews*. Highland Park, N.J.: Gryphon Press, 1970.

Buros, O. K. *Tests in Print: A Comprehensive Bibliography of Tests for Use in Education, Psychology, and Industry*. Highland Park, N.J.: Gryphon Press, 1961.

Buros, O. K. *Tests in Print II: An Index to Tests, Test Reviews, and the Literature on Specific Tests*. Highland Park, N.J.: Gryphon Press, 1974.

---

45. ADJECTIVE CHECK LIST (ACL)

AUTHORS: Harrison G. Gough and Alfred B. Heilbrun, Jr.

VARIABLE: Masculinity-femininity

APPROPRIATE FOR: Ages 14 and older

NOTES AND COMMENTS: (1) The instrument yields twenty-four other scores: number of adjectives checked, defensiveness, favorable adjectives checked, unfavorable adjectives checked, self-confidence, self-control, lability, personal adjustment, achievement, dominance, endurance, order, intraception, nurturance, affiliation, heterosexuality, exhibition, autonomy, aggression, change, succorance, abasement, deference, and counseling readiness.

(2) Gough and Heilbrun found that 54 of the 300 adjectives on the instrument discriminated significantly between masculine college males and feminine college females. Some users measure masculinity-femininity with these fifty-four adjectives. Other researchers have considered high scores on some subscales to be indicative of masculinity and high scores on other subscales to be indicative of femininity.

(3) The Adjective Check List has also been used to assess sex stereotypes by asking respondents to indicate whether each adjective is more characteristic of males or females.

SOURCE: Consulting Psychologists Press
            577 College Avenue
            Palo Alto, California 94306

TESTS IN PRINT: II:1094

MENTAL MEASUREMENTS YEARBOOK: 7:38, 8:495

PERSONALITY TESTS AND REVIEWS: 4

SUPPLEMENTARY BIBLIOGRAPHY: The references listed below are not included in the bibliographies in *Tests in Print, Mental Measurements Yearbook,* or *Personality Tests and Reviews,* but all describe studies that used the masculinity-femininity scale of the Adjective Check List (ACL).

Benoist, I. R. "An Investigation of the Relationship Between Sex Role Attitudes and Expressive Behavior." Unpublished doctoral dissertation, University of Minnesota, 1974. (*Dissertation Abstracts International,* 1974, *35* [6-B], 3005.)

Biller, H. B., and Kayton, R. "Sex Role Development and Psychopathology in Adult Males." *Journal of Consulting and Clinical Psychology,* 1972, *38,* 208-210.

Heilbrun, A. B., Jr. "Perceived Maternal Attitudes, Masculinity-Femininity of the Maternal Model, and Identification as Related to Incipient Psychopathology in Adolescent Girls." *Journal of General Psychology,* 1964, *70,* 33-40.

Heilbrun, A. B., Jr. "Parent Identification and Filial Sex Role Behavior: The Importance of Biological Context." *Nebraska Symposium on Motivation,* 1973a, *21,* 125-194.

Heilbrun, A. B., Jr. "Parental Identification and Educational Dissatisfaction in Troubled College Students." *Journal of Genetic Psychology,* 1973b, *122,* 183-188.

Heilbrun, A. B., Jr., Kleemeier, C., and Piccola, G. "Developmental and Situational Correlates of Achievement Behavior in College Females." *Journal of Personality,* 1974, *42,* 420-436.

Hess, J. G. "Sex Role Development in Psychiatrically Disturbed Adolescent Females and Their Parents." Unpublished doctoral dissertation, University of Rhode Island, 1975. (*Dissertation Abstracts International,* 1976, *37* [1-B], 462.)

Komarovsky, M. "Cultural Contradictions and Sex Roles: The Masculine Case." *American Journal of Sociology,* 1973a, *78,* 873-884.

Komarovksy, M. "Presidential Address: Some Problems in Role Analysis." *American Sociological Review,* 1973b, *38,* 649-662.

Komarovsky, M. *Dilemmas of Masculinity: A Study of College Youth.* New York: Norton, 1976.

Robinson, B. E. "Sex-Typed Attitudes, Sex-Typed Contingency Behaviors, and Personality Traits of Male Caregivers." Paper presented at the biennial meeting of the Society for Research in Child Development, New Orleans, March 1977. (ERIC Document Reproduction Service No. ED 140 948.)

Small, A., Biller, H. B., and Prochaska, J. O. "Sex Role Development and Parental Expectations Among Disturbed Adolescent Males." *Adolescence,* 1975, *10,* 609-615.

Trader, D. D. "A Study of College Women's Attitudes Toward the Feminine Role." Unpublished doctoral dissertation, University of North Carolina at Greensboro, 1972. (*Dissertation Abstracts International,* 1972, *33* [4-B], 1650.)

Tucker, B. Z. "Feminine Sex Role and Occupational Choice: A Study of Self and Intergroup Perceptions of Three Groups of Women." Unpublished doctoral dissertation, Temple University, 1970. (*Dissertation Abstracts International,* 1971, *31* [11-A], 5783-5784.)

Wakefield, J. A., Jr., Sasek, J., Friedman, A. F., and Bowden, J. D. "Androgyny and

Other Measures of Masculinity-Femininity." *Journal of Consulting and Clinical Psychology,* 1976, *44,* 766-770.

Williams, J. E., and Bennett, S. M. "The Definition of Sex Stereotypes via the Adjective Check List." *Sex Roles,* 1975, *1,* 327-337.

Williams, J. E., Bennett, S. M., and Best, D. L. "Awareness and Expression of Sex Stereotypes in Young Children." *Developmental Psychology,* 1975, *11,* 635-642.

Williams, J. E., Giles, H., Edwards, J. R., Best, D. L., and Daws, J. T. "Sex-Trait Stereotypes in England, Ireland, and the United States." *British Journal of Social and Clinical Psychology,* 1977, *16,* 303-309.

---

46. THE ADJUSTMENT INVENTORY

AUTHOR: Hugh M. Bell

VARIABLE: Masculinity

APPROPRIATE FOR: High school and college students

NOTES AND COMMENTS: The instrument yields five other scores: home, health, submissiveness, emotionality, and hostility.

SOURCE: Consulting Psychologists Press
          577 College Avenue
          Palo Alto, California 94306

TESTS IN PRINT: II:1095

MENTAL MEASUREMENTS YEARBOOK: 1:912, 2:1200, 4:28, 5:30, 6:59

PERSONALITY TESTS AND REVIEWS: 5

47. CALIFORNIA PSYCHOLOGICAL INVENTORY

AUTHOR: Harrison G. Gough

VARIABLE: Femininity

APPROPRIATE FOR: Ages 13 and older

NOTES AND COMMENTS: (1) The instrument yields seventeen other scores: dominance, capacity for status, sociability, social presence, self-acceptance, sense of well-being, responsibility, socialization, self-control, tolerance, good impression, communality, achievement via conformance, achievement via independence, intellectual efficiency, psychological mindedness, and flexibility.

(2) This instrument includes 38 items from the Gough Femininity Scale (#36).

(3) The Personal Values Abstract (#55) is a shortened version of the California Psychological Inventory.

SOURCE: Consulting Psychologists Press
       577 College Avenue
       Palo Alto, California 94306

TESTS IN PRINT: II:1121

MENTAL MEASUREMENTS YEARBOOK: 5:37, 6:71, 7:49, 8:514

PERSONALITY TESTS AND REVIEWS: 27

SUPPLEMENTARY BIBLIOGRAPHY: The references listed below are not included in the bibliographies in *Tests in Print, Mental Measurements Yearbook* or *Personality Tests and Reviews* but all describe studies that used the femininity scale of the California Psychological Inventory.

Barclay, A., and Cusumano, D. R. "Father Absence, Cross-Sex Identity, and Field-Dependent Behavior in Male Adolescents." *Child Development,* 1967, *38,* 243-250.

Becker, J., and Iwakami, E. "Conflict and Dominance Within Families of Disturbed Children." *Journal of Abnormal Psychology,* 1969, *74,* 330-335.

Becker, J., and Siefkes, H. "Parental Dominance, Conflict, and Disciplinary Coerciveness in Families of Female Schizophrenics." *Journal of Abnormal Psychology,* 1969, *74,* 193-198.

Biller, H. B., and Kayton, R. "Sex Role Development and Psychopathology in Adult Males." *Journal of Consulting and Clinical Psychology,* 1972, *38,* 208-210.

Bott, M. M. "The M-F Scale: Yesterday and Today." *Measurement and Evaluation in Guidance,* 1970, *3,* 92-96.

Canty, E. M. "Effects of Women's Studies Courses on Women's Attitudes and Goals." Paper presented at 85th annual meeting of the American Psychological Association, San Francisco, August 1977.

Giordano, A. S. "The Relationship of Sex Role Typing and Socialization to Moral Development." Unpublished doctoral dissertation, University of California, Berkeley, 1974. (*Dissertation Abstracts International,* 1975, *36*[1-B], 492.)

Goldberg, C. "Sex Roles, Task Competence, and Conformity." *Journal of Psychology*, 1974, *86*, 157-164.

Goldberg, C. "Conformity to Majority Type as a Function of Task and Acceptance of Sex-Related Stereotypes." *Journal of Psychology*, 1975, *89*, 25-37.

Gough, H. G. *Manual for the California Psychological Inventory.* Palo Alto, Calif.: Consulting Psychologists Press, 1975.

Helson, R. "Personality of Women with Imaginative and Artistic Interests: The Role of Masculinity, Originality, and Other Characteristics in Their Creativity." *Journal of Personality*, 1966, *34*, 1-25.

Hess, J. C. "Sex Role Development in Psychiatrically Disturbed Adolescent Females and Their Parents." Unpublished doctoral dissertation, University of Rhode Island, 1975. (*Dissertation Abstracts International*, 1976, *37*[1-B], 462.)

Hetherington, E. M. "Effects of Father Absence on Personality Development in Adolescent Daughters." *Developmental Psychology*, 1972, *7*, 313-326.

Jacobs, J. E. "A Comparison of the Relationship Between the Level of Acceptance of Sex Role Stereotyping and Achievement and Attitudes Toward Mathematics of Seventh Graders and Eleventh Graders in a Suburban Metropolitan New York Community." Unpublished doctoral dissertation, New York University, 1974. (*Dissertation Abstracts International*, 1974, *34*[12-A, Pt. 1], 7585.)

Kapor-Stanulovic, N., and Lynn, D. B. "Femininity and Family Planning." *Journal of Sex Research*, 1972, *8*, 286-297.

Kayton, R., and Biller, H. B. "Sex Role Development and Psychopathology in Adult Males." *Journal of Consulting and Clinical Psychology*, 1972, *38*, 208-210.

Komarovsky, M. "Cultural Contradictions and Sex Roles: The Masculine Case." *American Journal of Sociology*, 1973a, *78*, 873-884.

Komarovsky, M. "Presidential Address: Some Problems in Role Analysis." *American Sociological Review*, 1973b, *38*, 649-662.

Littlejohn, M. T. "A Comparison of the Responses of Ninth Graders to Measures of Creativity and Masculinity-Femininity." Unpublished doctoral dissertation, University of North Carolina at Chapel Hill, 1966. (*Dissertation Abstracts*, 1967a, *27*[8-A], 2399-2400.)

Littlejohn, M. T. "Creativity and Masculinity-Femininity in Ninth Graders." *Perceptual and Motor Skills*, 1967b, *25*, 737-743.

McGarty, M. "The Relationship of Sex Role Identification, Locus of Control, and Interpersonal Trust to Susceptibility to Influence." Unpublished doctoral dissertation, Fordham University, 1976. (*Dissertation Abstracts International*, 1976, *37*[5-B], 2514.)

Meyers, J. C. "The Adjustment of Women to Marital Separation: The Effects of Sex Role Identification and of Stage in Family Life, as Determined by Age and Presence or Absence of Dependent Children." Unpublished doctoral dissertation, University of Colorado, 1976. (*Dissertation Abstracts International*, 1976, *37*[5-B], 2516.)

Mussen, P., and Rutherford, E. "Parent-Child Relations and Parental Personality in Relation to Young Children's Sex Role Preferences." *Child Development*, 1963, *34*, 589-607.

Nash, L. J. "Relation Between Sexual Object Choice of Women and Ego Development, Neuroticism, and Conscious and Unconscious Sexual Identity." Unpublished doctoral dissertation, Hofstra University, 1976. (*Dissertation Abstracts International*, 1976, *36*[12-B], 6394.)

Orpen, C., and Low, A. "The Influence of Image Congruence on Brand Preference: An Empirical Study." *Psychology*, 1973, *10*, 4-6.

Peretti, P. O., and Carberry, J. "Sex Role Identification, Conflict, and Psychopathology in Adult Males." *Acta Psychiatrica Belgica,* 1974, *74,* 357-364.

Porter, H. K. "Prison Homosexuality: Locus of Control and Femininity." Unpublished doctoral dissertation, Michigan State University, 1969. (*Dissertation Abstracts International,* 1970, *31*[3-B], 1549.)

Schatzberg, A. F., Westfall, M. P., Blumetti, A. B., and Birk, C. L. "Effeminacy: I. A Quantitative Rating Scale." *Archives of Sexual Behavior,* 1975, *4,* 31-41.

Spence, J. T., and Helmreich, R. "The Attitudes-Toward-Women Scale: An Objective Instrument to Measure Attitudes Toward the Rights and Roles of Women in Contemporary Society." *Journal Supplement Abstract Service Catalog of Selected Documents in Psychology,* 1972a, *2,* 66.

Spence, J. T., and Helmreich, R. "Who Likes Competent Women? Competence, Sex Role Congruence of Interests, and Subjects' Attitudes Toward Women as Determinants of Interpersonal Attraction." *Journal of Applied Social Psychology,* 1972, *2,* 197-213.

Zucker, R. A. "Sex Role Identity Patterns and Drinking Behavior of Adolescents." *Quarterly Journal of Studies on Alcohol,* 1968, *29,* 868-884.

---

48. DYNAMIC PERSONALITY INVENTORY

AUTHOR: T. G. Grygier

VARIABLES: Masculine sexual identification, feminine sexual identification

APPROPRIATE FOR: Ages 15 and older

NOTES AND COMMENTS: The inventory yields thirty-one scores; hypocrisy, passivity, seclusion-introspection, orality, oral aggression, oral dependence, emotional independence, verbal aggression, impulsiveness, unconventionality, hoarding behavior, attention to details, conservatism, submissiveness, anal sadism, insularity, phallic symbol interest, narcissism, exhibitionism, active Icarus complex, passive Icarus complex, sensuality, Icarian exploits, sexuality, tactile impression enjoyment, creative interests, social role seeking, social activity interest, need to give affection, ego defense persistence, and initiative.

SOURCE: NFER Publishing Co. Ltd.
2 Jennings Building
Thames Avenue
Windsor, Berks ENGLAND

TESTS IN PRINT: II:1162

MENTAL MEASUREMENTS YEARBOOK: 6:86, 7:70, 8:539

PERSONALITY TESTS AND REVIEWS: 65

SUPPLEMENTARY BIBLIOGRAPHY: The reference below is not included in the bibliographies in *Tests in Print, Mental Measurements Yearbook,* or *Personality Tests and Reviews,* but it describes a study that used the masculine sexual identification and feminine sexual identification scales of the Dynamic Personality Inventory.

Stringer, P., and Grygier, T. G. "Male Homosexuality, Psychiatric Patient Status, and Psychological Masculinity and Femininity." *Archives of Sexual Behavior,* 1976, *5,* 15-27.

---

49. GUILFORD-MARTIN INVENTORY OF FACTORS GAMIN

AUTHORS: J. P. Guilford and H. G. Martin

VARIABLE: Masculinity-femininity

APPROPRIATE FOR: Ages 15 and older

NOTES AND COMMENTS: This scale yields four additional scores: general activity, ascendance-submission, inferiority feelings, and nervousness.

SOURCE: Sheridan Psychological Services, Inc.
P. O. Box 6101
Orange, California 92667

TESTS IN PRINT: I:171; II:1205

MENTAL MEASUREMENTS YEARBOOK: 3:43, 4:47, 5:63, 6:108

PERSONALITY TESTS AND REVIEWS: 102

SUPPLEMENTARY BIBLIOGRAPHY: The references listed below are not included in the bibliographies in *Tests in Print, Mental Measurements Yearbook,* or *Personality Tests and Reviews,* but they describe studies that used the masculinity-femininity scale of the Guilford-Martin Inventory of Factors GAMIN.

Nichols, R. C. "Subtle, Obvious, and Stereotype Measures of Masculinity-Femininity." *Educational and Psychological Measurement,* 1962, *22,* 449-461.
Oxhorn, J. L. "The Relation of Figure Drawings to Masculine-Feminine Orientation and Academic Achievement." Unpublished doctoral dissertation, Rutgers-The State University, 1965. (*Dissertation Abstracts,* 1966, *27*[2-B], 601-602.)

50. GUILFORD-ZIMMERMAN TEMPERAMENT SURVEY

AUTHORS: J. P. Guilford and Wayne S. Zimmerman

VARIABLE: Masculinity

APPROPRIATE FOR: College students and adults

NOTES AND COMMENTS: (1) This instrument yields nine scores: general activity, restraint, ascendance, sociability, emotional stability, objectivity, friendliness, thoughtfulness, and personal relations.

(2) This instrument represents a revision and condensation of three others, including the Guilford-Martin Inventory of Factors GAMIN (#49).

SOURCE: Sheridan Psychological Services, Inc.
P. O. Box 6101
Orange, California 92667

TESTS IN PRINT: II:1207

MENTAL MEASUREMENTS YEARBOOK: 4:49, 5:65, 6:110, 8:574

PERSONALITY TESTS AND REVIEWS: 104

SUPPLEMENTARY BIBLIOGRAPHY: The references listed below are not included in the bibliographies in *Tests in Print, Mental Measurements Yearbook,* or *Personality Tests and Reviews,* but they describe studies that used the masculinity scale of the Guilford-Zimmerman Temperament Survey.

Arbuthnot, J. "Sex Role Identity and Cognitive Style." *Perceptual and Motor Skills,* 1975, *41,* 435-440.

Goldfarb, J. H. "The Concept of Sexual Identity in Normals and Transvestites: Its Relationship to the Body Image, Self-Concept, and Parental Identification." Unpublished doctoral dissertation, University of Southern California, 1963. (*Dissertation Abstracts,* 1964, *24*[9], 3835-3836.)

Gruenfeld, L., and Arbuthnot, J. "Field Independence as a Conceptual Framework for Prediction of Variability in Ratings of Others." *Perceptual and Motor Skills,* 1969, *28,* 31-44.

Himelstein, P., and Stoup, D. D. "Correlation of Three M-F Measures for Males." *Journal of Clinical Psychology,* 1967, *23,* 189.

Money, J., and Brennan, J. G. "Sexual Dimorphism in the Psychology of Female Transsexuals." *Journal of Nervous and Mental Disease,* 1968, *147,* 487-499.

Money, J., and Primrose, C. "Sexual Dimorphism and Dissociation in the Psychology of Male Transsexuals." *Journal of Nervous and Mental Disease,* 1968, *147,* 472-486.

Murray, J. B. "The M-F Scale of the MMPI for College Students." *Journal of Clinical Psychology,* 1963, *19,* 113-115.

Shemberg, K. M., and Leventhal, D. B. "Masculinity-Femininity and Need for Social Approval." *Journal of Projective Techniques and Personality Assessment,* 1968, *32,* 575-577.

51. KUDER PREFERENCE RECORD-VOCATIONAL

AUTHOR: G. Frederic Kuder

VARIABLE: Masculinity-femininity

APPROPRIATE FOR: Ages 13 and older

NOTES AND COMMENTS: This instrument yields ten additional scores: mechanical, computational, scientific, persuasive, artistic, literary, musical, social service, clerical, and outdoor.

SOURCE: Science Research Associates, Inc.
            259 East Erie Street
            Chicago, Illinois 60611

TESTS IN PRINT: II:2195

MENTAL MEASUREMENTS YEARBOOK: 2:1671, 3:640, 4:742, 5:863, 6:1063, 8:1011

52. MINNESOTA MULTIPHASIC PERSONALITY INVENTORY

AUTHORS: Starke R. Hathaway and J. Charnley McKinley

VARIABLE: Masculinity-femininity

APPROPRIATE FOR: Ages 16 and older

NOTES AND COMMENTS: (1) This instrument yields thirteen other scores: hypochondriasis, depression, hysteria, psychopathic deviate, paranoia, psychasthenia, schizophrenia, hypomania, social, question, lie, validity, and test-taking attitude.
        (2) This instrument has been one of the most frequently used measures of masculinity and femininity. However, recently researchers have become more critical of it because its development was based on empirical procedures (that is, items that differentiated between males and females comprise the masculinity-femininity subscale), and a respondent cannot score high on both masculinity and femininity (that is, one cannot be androgynous).

SOURCE: Psychological Corporation
            304 E. 45th Street
            New York, New York 10017

TESTS IN PRINT: II:1281

MENTAL MEASUREMENTS YEARBOOK: 3:60, 4:71, 5:86, 6:143, 7:104, 8:616

PERSONALITY TESTS AND REVIEWS: 166

SUPPLEMENTARY BIBLIOGRAPHY: The references listed below are not included in the bibliographies in *Tests in Print, Mental Measurements Yearbook,* or *Personality Tests and Reviews,* but they describe studies that used the masculinity-femininity scale of the Minnesota Multiphasic Personality Inventory.

Bernknopf, L. A. "A Comparison of the Responses of Behavior-Disordered and Normal Adolescents on a Masculinity-Femininity Scale and on a Stereotyping Questionnaire." Unpublished doctoral dissertation, University of Georgia, 1975. (*Dissertation Abstracts International,* 1976, *36*[9-A], 5986.)

Bernknopf, L. A. "A Comparison of the Responses of Behavior-Disordered and Normal Adolescents on a Masculinity-Femininity Scale and on a Stereotyping Questionnaire." Paper presented at the Annual International Convention, The Council for Exceptional Children, Chicago, April 1976. (ERIC Document Reproduction Service No. ED 125 208.)

Bott, M. M. "The M-F Scale: Yesterday and Today." *Measurement and Evaluation in Guidance,* 1970, *3,* 92-96.

Buehlmann, B. B. "The Relationship Between Avoidance of Success and Other Selected Characteristics of College Females." Unpublished doctoral dissertation, Illinois State University, 1974. (*Dissertation Abstracts International,* 1974, *35*[3-B], 1376-1377.)

de Cillis, O. E., and Orbison, W. D. "A Comparison of the Terman-Miles M-F Test and the M-F Scale of the MMPI." *Journal of Applied Psychology,* 1950, *34,* 338-342.

Dixit, R. C., and Mathur, M. B. "Loving and Punishing Parental Behavior and Masculinity-Femininity Development in School Girls." *Journal of Psychological Researches,* 1973, *17,* 47-49.

Engel, I. M. "A Factor-Analytic Study of Items from Five Masculinity-Femininity Tests." *Journal of Consulting Psychology,* 1966, *30,* 565.

Freedman, B. E. "Task Performance as a Function of Task Sex Typing." Unpublished doctoral dissertation, Syracuse University, 1974. (*Dissertation Abstracts International,* 1975, *36*[1-B], 440.)

Graham, J. R., Schroeder, H. E., and Lilly, R. S. "Factor Analysis of Items on the Social Introversion and Masculinity-Femininity Scales of the MMPI." *Journal of Clinical Psychology,* 1971, *27,* 367-370.

Klemer, R. H. "Factors of Personality and Experience Which Differentiate Single from Married Women." *Marriage and Family Living,* 1954, *16,* 41-44.

Landers, D. M. "Sibling Sex Status and Ordinal Position Effects on Females' Sport Participation and Interests." *Journal of Social Psychology,* 1970, *80,* 247-248.

Littlejohn, M. T. "A Comparison of the Responses of Ninth Graders to Measures of Creativity and Masculinity-Femininity." Unpublished doctoral dissertation, University of North Carolina at Chapel Hill, 1966. (*Dissertation Abstracts,* 1967, *27*[8-A], 2399-2400.)

Littlejohn, M. T. "Creativity and Masculinity-Femininity in Ninth Graders." *Perceptual and Motor Skills,* 1967, *25,* 737-743.

Manosevitz, M. "Item Analyses of the MMPI M-F Scale Using Homosexual and Heterosexual Males." *Journal of Consulting and Clinical Psychology,* 1970, *35,* 395-399.

Milgram, N. A. "Role Taking in Female Schizophrenic Patients." *Journal of Clinical Psychology,* 1961, *17,* 409-411.

Milton, G. A. "The Effects of Sex Role Identification upon Problem-Solving Skill." *Journal of Abnormal Social Psychology,* 1957, *55,* 208-212.

Newmark, C. S., and Toomey, T. "The M-F Scale as an Index of Disturbed Marital Interaction: A Replication." *Psychological Reports,* 1972, *31,* 590.

Panton, J. H. "A New MMPI Scale for the Identification of Homosexuality." *Journal of Clinical Psychology,* 1960, *16,* 17-21.

Sanford, N. *Self and Society: Social Change and Individual Development.* New York: Atherton Press, 1966.

Sappenfield, B. R. "The Revised CMM as a Test of Perceived M-F and of Self-Report of M-F." *Journal of Projective Techniques and Personality Assessment,* 1968, *32,* 92-95.

Taylor, A. J. W. "A Search Among Borstal Girls for the Psychological and Social Significance of Their Tattoos." *British Journal of Criminology,* 1968, *8,* 170-185.

Webster, H. "Personality Development During the College Years: Some Quantitative Results." *Journal of Social Issues,* 1956, *12,* 29-43.

Winer, F. "The Relationship of Certain Attitudes Toward the Mother to Sex Role Identity." Unpublished doctoral dissertation, New York University, 1961. (*Dissertation Abstracts,* 1962, *22*[11], 4416.)

Wrchota, R. J. "Oral Passive Aims in Acting-Out Adolescent Girls in Relationship to the Developmental Task of Sexual Identification." Unpublished doctoral dissertation, School for Social Work, Smith College, 1973. (*Dissertation Abstracts International,* 1974, *34*[9-A], 6114.)

---

53. OMNIBUS PERSONALITY INVENTORY

AUTHORS: Paul Heist, George Yonge, T. R. McConell, and Harold Webster

VARIABLE: Masculinity-femininity

APPROPRIATE FOR: College students

NOTES AND COMMENTS: This instrument yields fourteen other scores: thinking introversion, theoretical orientation, estheticism, complexity, autonomy, religious orientation, social extroversion, impulse expression, personal integration, anxiety level, altruism, practical outlook, response bias, and intellectual disposition category.

SOURCE: Psychological Corporation
        304 E. 45th Street
        New York, New York 10017

TESTS IN PRINT: II:1302

MENTAL MEASUREMENTS YEARBOOK: 6:150, 7:116, 8:634

PERSONALITY TESTS AND REVIEWS: 184

---

54. PERSONAL PREFERENCE SCALE

AUTHORS: Maurice H. Krout and Johanna Krout Tabin

VARIABLE: Masculine-effeminoid, feminine-masculinoid

APPROPRIATE FOR: Ages 15 and older

NOTES AND COMMENTS: This scale yields eight other scores: active-inactive, sociable-individualistic, permissive-critical, consistent-inconsistent, efficient-inefficient, self-effacing-egocentric, emotionally mature-emotionally immature, and socially mature-socially immature.

SOURCE: Johanna Krout Tabin
162 Park Avenue
Glencoe, Illinois 60022

TESTS IN PRINT: II:1316

MENTAL MEASUREMENTS YEARBOOK: 5:93

PERSONALITY TESTS AND REVIEWS: 194

SUPPLEMENTARY BIBLIOGRAPHY: The references listed below are not included in the bibliographies in *Tests in Print, Mental Measurements Yearbook,* or *Personality Tests and Reviews,* but they describe studies that used the masculine-effeminoid and feminine-masculinoid scales of the Personal Preference Scale.

Kokonis, N. D. "Sex Role Identification in Schizophrenia: Psychoanalytic and Role-Theory Predictions Compared." Unpublished doctoral dissertation, Illinois Institute of Technology, 1971. (*Dissertation Abstracts International,* 1971, *32*[3-B], 1849-1850.)

Kokonis, N. D. "Choice of Gender on the DAP and Measures of Sex Role Identification." *Perceptual and Motor Skills,* 1972a, *35,* 727-730.

Kokonis, N. D. "Sex Role Identification in Neurosis: Psychoanalytic-Developmental and Role-Theory Predictions Compared." *Journal of Abnormal Psychology,* 1972b, *80,* 52-57.

Kokonis, N. D. "Parental Dominance and Sex Role Identification in Schizophrenia." *Journal of Psychology,* 1973, *84,* 211-218.

55. PERSONAL VALUES ABSTRACT

AUTHOR: Harrison G. Gough

VARIABLE: Femininity

APPROPRIATE FOR: Ages 13 and older

NOTES AND COMMENTS: (1) This instrument yields two other scores: modernity, which is a composite of six subscales from the California Psychology Inventory (#47), and socialization.

(2) This instrument is an abstract from the California Psychological Inventory (#47).

SOURCE: Consulting Psychologists Press, Inc.
577 College Avenue
Palo Alto, California 94306

TESTS IN PRINT: II:1317

MENTAL MEASUREMENTS YEARBOOK: 8:642

SUPPLEMENTARY BIBLIOGRAPHY: The reference below is not included in the bibliographies in *Tests in Print* or *Mental Measurements Yearbook,* but it describes a study that used the Femininity scale of the Personal Values Abstract.

Miller, W. B., and Smith, P. J. "Elimination of the Menses: Psychological Aspects." *Journal of Psychiatric Research,* 1975, *12,* 153-166.

---

56. STRONG VOCATIONAL INTEREST BLANK FOR MEN

AUTHOR: Edward K. Strong, Jr.

VARIABLE: Masculinity-femininity

APPROPRIATE FOR: Ages 16 and older

NOTES AND COMMENTS: (1) This test yields eighty-three additional scores, most of which are occupational scales.

(2) It has been replaced by the Strong-Campbell Interest Inventory, which does *not* yield a score for masculinity-femininity.

SOURCE: Stanford University Press
Stanford, California 94305

TESTS IN PRINT: II:2212

MENTAL MEASUREMENTS YEARBOOK: 2:1680, 3:647, 4:747, 5:868, 6:1070, 7:1036

SUPPLEMENTARY BIBLIOGRAPHY: The references listed below are not included in the bibliographies in *Tests in Print* or *Mental Measurements Yearbook,* but they describe studies that used the masculinity-femininity scale of the Strong Vocational Interest Blank for Men.

Altman, S. L. "Women's Career Plans and Maternal Employment." Unpublished doctoral dissertation, Boston University Graduate School, 1975. (*Dissertation Abstracts International,* 1975, *35*[7-B], 3569.)

Angrilli, A. F. "A Study of the Psychosexual Identification of Preschool Boys." Unpublished doctoral dissertation, New York University, 1958. (*Dissertation Abstracts,* 1958, *19*[4], 874-875.)

Angrilli, A. F. "The Psychosexual Identification of Preschool Boys." *Journal of Genetic Psychology,* 1960, *97,* 329-340.

Becker, S. J. "A Comparison of Body Attitudes in Women with Masculine Vocational Interests and Those with Feminine Vocational Interests." Unpublished doctoral dissertation, University of Maryland, 1971. (*Dissertation Abstracts International,* 1972, *32*[9-B], 5421.)

Bilick, J. G. "The Effect of Patient Gender on the Clinical Assessment Process." Unpublished doctoral dissertation, University of Cincinnati, 1972. (*Dissertation Abstracts International,* 1973, *33*[8-B], 3926-3927.)

Eichler, L. S. " 'Feminine Narcissism': An Empirical Investigation." Unpublished doctoral dissertation, Boston University Graduate School, 1973. (*Dissertation Abstracts International,* 1973, *33*[12-B], 6074-6075.)

Gysbers, N. G., Johnston, J. A., and Gust, T. "Characteristics of Homemaker- and Career-Oriented Women." *Journal of Counseling Psychology,* 1968, *15,* 541-546.

Harmon, L. W. "Anatomy of Career Commitment in Women." *Journal of Counseling Psychology,* 1970, *17,* 77-80.

Himelstein, P., and Stoup, D. D. "Correlation of Three M-F Measures for Males." *Journal of Clinical Psychology,* 1967, *23,* 189.

Kennedy, M. J. R. "The Relationship of Locus of Control to Career and Homemaking Vocational Choices and Resistance to Change of High School Girls." Unpublished doctoral dissertation, Catholic University of America, 1974. (*Dissertation Abstracts International,* 1974, *35*[3-A], 1446-1447.)

Klopfer, W. C. "Correlation of Women's M-F Scores on the MMPI and Strong VIB." *Journal of Clinical Psychology,* 1966, *22,* 216.

Lunneborg, P. W. "Dimensionality of M-F." *Journal of Clinical Psychology,* 1972, *28,* 313-317.

Sanford, N. *Self and Society: Social Change and Individual Development.* New York: Atherton Press, 1966.

Steele, C. I. "Sexual Identity Problems Among Adolescent Girls in Institutional Placement." *Adolescence,* 1971, *6,* 509-522.

Sutton-Smith, B., Roberts, J., and Rosenberg, B. G. "Sibling Associations and Role Involvement." *Merrill-Palmer Quarterly,* 1964, *10,* 25-38.

57. STRONG VOCATIONAL INTEREST BLANK FOR WOMEN

AUTHOR: Edward K. Strong, Jr.

VARIABLE: Femininity-masculinity

APPROPRIATE FOR: Ages 16 and older

NOTES AND COMMENTS: (1) This instrument yields eighty additional scores, most of which are occupational scales.

(2) It has been replaced by the Strong-Campbell Interest Inventory, which does *not* yield a score for femininity-masculinity.

SOURCE: Stanford University Press
         Stanford, California 94305

TESTS IN PRINT: II:2213

MENTAL MEASUREMENTS YEARBOOK: 2:1681, 3:649, 5:869, 6:1071, 7:1037

58. VC PERSONALITY TEST BATTERY

AUTHORS: Nevitt Sanford and Harold Webster

VARIABLE: Masculine role, masculine preference

APPROPRIATE FOR: Female college students

NOTES AND COMMENTS: There are two tests in the battery: VC Attitude Inventory and VC Figure Preference Test. The Attitude Inventory yields six additional scores: social maturity, developmental status, impulse expression, dominance and confidence, social integration, and repression and suppression. The Figure Preference Test yields one additional score: complex preference.

SOURCE: Mary Conover Mellon Foundation
         Vassar College
         Poughkeepsie, New York 12601

TESTS IN PRINT: I:312

SUPPLEMENTARY BIBLIOGRAPHY: The references listed below are not included in the bibliographies in *Tests in Print,* but they describe studies that used the masculine role, masculine preference scales of the VC Personality Test Battery.

Greenstein, J. M. "Father Characteristics and Sex Role Identification in a Delinquent Group." Unpublished doctoral dissertation, Rutgers University, 1961. (*Dissertation Abstracts,* 1961, *22*[5], 1716.)

Greenstein, J. M. "Father Characteristics and Sex Typing." *Journal of Personality and Social Psychology,* 1966, *3*, 271-277.

Nichols, R. C. "Subtle, Obvious, and Stereotype Measures of Masculinity-Femininity." *Educational and Psychological Measurement,* 1962, *22*, 449-461.

---

59. WELSH FIGURE PREFERENCE TEST, RESEARCH EDITION

AUTHOR: George S. Welsh

VARIABLE: Male-female

APPROPRIATE FOR: Ages 6 and older

NOTES AND COMMENTS: This test yields twenty-six additional scores, most of which relate to figure-structure preference.

SOURCE: Consulting Psychologists Press, Inc.
577 College Avenue
Palo Alto, California 94306

TESTS IN PRINT: II:1437

MENTAL MEASUREMENTS YEARBOOK: 6:197

PERSONALITY TESTS AND REVIEWS: 287

SUPPLEMENTARY BIBLIOGRAPHY: The references listed below are not included in the bibliographies in *Tests in Print, Mental Measurements Yearbook,* or *Personality Tests and Reviews,* but they describe studies that used the male-female scale of the Welsh Figure Preference Test, Research Edition.

Grant, T. N., and Domino, G. "Masculinity-Femininity in Fathers of Creative Male Adolescents." *Journal of Genetic Psychology,* 1976, *129*, 19-27.

Sanford, N. *Self and Society: Social Change and Individual Development.* New York: Atherton Press, 1966.

4

░ ░ ░ ░ ░ ░ ░ ░ ░ ░

Sex Stereotypes

░ ░ ░ ░ ░ ░ ░ ░ ░ ░ ░ ░ ░ ░ ░ ░ ░ ░ ░ ░

Sex stereotypes are perceptions of persons, objects, activities, or concepts that are based on relatively rigid, oversimplified, and overgeneralized beliefs or assumptions regarding the characteristics of males and females. Sex stereotypes, like all stereotypes, disregard individual differences. Research studies regarding sex stereotypes are very common in the professional literature. However, for the most part, the measuring instruments to assess sex stereotypes are not well developed. Researchers rarely use an empirical procedure for developing the instruments; and if there is a theoretical basis for their development, it is not communicated in the report of the research study. The reliability and validity of the instruments are rarely considered. It appears that researchers either assume that their instruments are reliable and valid or they simply ignore these issues. As a result, most instruments that have been used to measure sex stereotypes have been omitted from this book. For the most part, even those which are included here are not as well developed or as psychometrically sound as instruments in other chapters of the book.

Twenty-five instruments for assessing sex stereotypes satisfied the criteria for inclusion here; that is, information could be obtained regarding their development or reliability or validity, or they had been used extensively. There are twelve instruments for assessing sex stereotypes of personality traits, five for assessing sex stereotypes of occupations, four for assessing sex stereotypes of objects, and four for assessing sex stereotypes of activities. These instruments are intended for respondents covering a wide age span; for example, some are appropriate for children in their preschool years and many are appropriate for adult respondents. The year in which an instrument's use is first reported in the

164

literature ranges from 1948 to 1977, with seventeen originally appearing in the literature after 1970. Of the twenty-five instruments in this chapter, the one that has been used most frequently is the Sex Role Stereotypes Questionnaire (#77). However, as is pointed out later, there are so many variations of this measure that it is more accurate to view it as a procedure rather than as a well-defined instrument.

The instruments vary in terms of how scores are assigned. For some, scores are assigned to respondents. The scores indicate either the extent to which the respondent agrees with commonly held stereotypes, the extent to which the respondent's perceptions are based on sex stereotypes, or the particular stereotypes the respondent holds regarding males and females. With other instruments, no scores are assigned to respondents; instead responses are totaled across respondents, and scores are assigned to personality traits, occupations, activities, "men," or "women."

Included in this chapter are five summated rating scales, five semantic differential scales, seven multiple choice instruments, three alternate choice instruments, three rating scales, a sorting task, and a story completion task. Despite this apparent variation in the types of instruments, there is actually considerable similarity among them. On all of the multiple choice instruments, all of the alternate choice instruments, three of the five summated rating scales, the sorting task, and the story completion task, the task for the respondents is quite similar: the respondents are asked to choose a response indicating either male or female. The instruments vary in terms of whether the response options are presented orally, pictorially, or in writing. They also vary in terms of the exact wording and number of response options; for example, the choices might include "mommy" and "daddy"; or "boys," "girls," and "both boys and girls"; or "Men are much more likely," "Men are somewhat more likely," "Men and women are equally likely," "Women are somewhat more likely," and "Women are much more likely." The instruments also vary in terms of how the respondents' answers are communicated: they may be communicated orally or in writing, or they may be communicated by pointing or sorting. Despite these variations, the essence of the respondents' task—to choose a response indicating either male or female—is the same on fifteen of the twenty-five instruments. Thus, a common way to assess sex stereotypes is to provide the respondent with a set of personality traits, activities, objects, occupations, and so forth and ask the respondent to associate each element of the set with males, females, both, or neither.

Sex stereotypes are also commonly assessed with semantic differential scales. In fact the review of the literature undertaken to select instruments for this book revealed that the semantic differential scale is the most frequently used method for assessing sex stereotypes. Unfortunately, most semantic differential scales described in the literature did not meet the criteria for inclusion in this book. They were developed by selecting concepts of interest to the researcher, choosing bipolar adjective pairs which the researcher felt would be relevant, and ignoring the need to establish reliability and validity. And most of these semantic differential scales were used by one researcher in the conduct of a single research study. Though most semantic differential scales failed to meet the criteria for inclusion, the five semantic differential scales included are quite similar to the omitted ones. Four of the five use words denoting males and females as the concepts to be rated. They vary in terms of how they label the males and females; that is, one scale uses the concept "man"; one uses the concept "average man"; and one uses "typical male" and "ideal male." For the Sex Role Stereotype Questionnaire (#77), users have varied the phrasing of the concepts; for example, for the feminine concept, the most commonly used terms have been "female," "ideal female," and "healthy adult female."

However measured, there are numerous problems associated with assessing sex stereotypes. One problem relates to the lack of content validity. Researchers typically do not define a domain and then sample elements to comprise the set to be rated. As a result, it is difficult to know to what domain the results can generalize. For example, on a measure of sex stereotypes of occupations, researchers are likely to pay insufficient attention to which occupations are selected. Are the selected occupations representative of a particular domain of occupations? Are they balanced in terms of the education necessary for entering the occupations, the prestige associated with the occupations, and the income derived from the occupations? If one wishes to generalize results to occupations in general, then the content validity of the instrument is an important consideration.

Another problem with some sex-stereotype instruments is the ambiguity regarding which perceptions they seek to measure. It is reasonable to assume that respondents may have different stereotypes regarding what is, what ought to be, and what could be. Similarly, respondents are likely to give different responses if they are asked to indicate their own beliefs or if they are asked to indicate their perceptions of what most persons believe. Unless the directions accompanying the instrument make it clear what it is asking, it is difficult for respondents to know how to answer. With different respondents interpreting the directions differently, an unambiguous interpretation of scores is essentially impossible.

Instruments that force respondents to choose between the response "masculine" or the response "feminine" (or equivalent responses) guarantee that respondents will express stereotypes even if they do not believe them. Not only does this lower the validity of the instrument, but it also can frustrate or anger the respondents. There is no way to know what effect this frustration or anger has on the responses given. Only when the instrument allows for the responses "both" and "neither" are respondents free to give their honest perceptions even if they are *not* sex-stereotyped perceptions. There are probably situations in which it is desirable to force respondents to choose between only two alternatives—male and female—but the final choice of response options on any instrument should always reflect a researcher's conscious decision based on what it is intended to measure.

Another problem can arise when respondents are asked to rate something that they do not know or do not understand. It is very rare for researchers investigating sex stereotypes to first ensure that the respondents are familiar with what they are judging. Failure to do this can cause serious problems—especially when the respondents are young children. For example, asking children to sex stereotype the occupations "district attorney" and "philosopher" is likely to elicit random responses.

Unfortunately, most measures of sex role stereotypes are very transparent. Respondents have no doubt about what the instrument is trying to measure, and hence they can easily fake their responses in any way they choose. Similarly, the transparency of the items might lead respondents to give socially desirable answers rather than responding from their honestly felt stereotypes. Since sex stereotypes are less socially acceptable today than they used to be, this creates more of a problem now than it would have ten or twenty years ago. Most researchers have also failed to consider the context in which sex stereotyping is measured. Because the instrument is transparent and respondents can easily "fake" it, the situation and conditions of administration can seriously alter the responses that are elicited. This has already been empirically demonstrated in a study by Hough and Allen (1975; in #68).

In the development of sex-stereotype measures, researchers frequently ask "judges" to stereotype the items to be included on the instrument. Users of the instruments should realize that the judges' opinions may not be valid for different races, different cultural groups, different educational levels, and at different times. Researchers should be alert to the need to cross-validate the opinions of the original judges.

Probably the most serious problem with sex-stereotype measures is that little is known about the relationship between stereotypes expressed on the measures and behavior. Only one study (Diepold, 1977; #63) investigated the relationship between behavior and expressed stereotypes. Diepold found that different results are obtained when children verbally report sex stereotypes of toys and when the children's free-play behavior is observed. Though this problem can be succinctly and easily stated, its solution is far from easy. It will require extensive research to determine the behavioral concomitants of expressed sex stereotypes.

Another problem with research regarding sex stereotypes is the assumption that the measures reflect only *sex* stereotypes; that is, researchers generally interpret the findings using sex-stereotype measures solely in terms of the respondents' stereotypes based on sex. Responses on measures of sex stereotypes of occupations (or activities or personality traits or objects) very likely reflect stereotypes about the occupations (or activities or personality traits or objects) as well as stereotypes about men and women. For example, if one is asked to indicate whether carpentry is a "masculine" or a "feminine" occupation, then the response one gives indicates stereotyped perceptions of carpentry as well as stereotyped perceptions of masculine and feminine. If one's stereotyped perceptions of carpentry are congruent with one's stereotyped perceptions of masculine, then the occupation will be classified as masculine. Typically, experiments designed to change sex stereotypes focus on changing the stereotypes about men and women. Would it not be equally effective to try to change stereotypes about the occupations? And perhaps it would be most effective to change stereotypes about both the sexes and the occupations.

Clearly there are many problems in the study of sex stereotypes. Some of these problems can be corrected by taking greater care in the construction of the instruments; for example, the directions accompanying them should be very specific in terms of what is being asked. Other problems can be corrected only after more research is conducted to answer some crucial questions: To what extent does the environment or context in which the instrument is administered affect responses? What is the difference in the responses that are obtained when only two response options are given—one denoting males and one denoting females—and when respondents are also allowed to answer "neither" or "both"? Do measures of sex stereotypes reflect stereotypes of the object (or activity, occupation, personality trait, and so forth) being judged as well as stereotypes of gender? What is the relationship between admitted stereotypes and behavior?

In general, instruments for assessing sex stereotypes are not psychometrically well developed or sophisticated. Those included in this chapter are probably the best ones presently available. However, even for these measures, there was rarely enough information available to report on their development, provide evidence of their reliability, or demonstrate their validity. In fact, in regard to validity, most often the only evidence was the support or nonsupport of hypotheses tested using the instrument.

60. ACTIVITIES STEREOTYPES SCALE

AUTHORS: Sonia A. Marantz and Annick F. Mansfield

DATE: 1977

VARIABLE: Tendency to sex stereotype adult activities

TYPE OF INSTRUMENT: Multiple choice

DESCRIPTION: The instrument consists of fifty questions, each of which refers to an adult activity. Approximately one third of the items are feminine sex typed, one third are masculine sex typed, and one third are equally appropriate for both sexes. There are approximately equal number of items representing work roles, domestic roles, and recreational activities. For each item, the respondent is asked to indicate whether "ladies," "men," or "both ladies and men" are likely to engage in the activity.

PREVIOUSLY ADMINISTERED TO: Girls, ages 5-11

APPROPRIATE FOR: Ages 5 and older

ADMINISTRATION: For children who are 8 years old or younger, the test is individually administered with items presented orally and responses recorded by the examiner. For those who are at least 9 years old, the test is administered in small groups and answers are recorded by the respondents.

SAMPLE ITEMS: Who goes to work?
                      Who cooks dinner?

SCORING: Items are objectively scored and equally weighted. Total scores range from 0 (completely nonstereotyped responses) to 50 (completely stereotyped responses).

DEVELOPMENT: Eighty-four adults rated the items on the scale. Items are classified as "masculine," "feminine," or "both," depending on the response given by the majority of the adults.

RELIABILITY: Ninety-eight middle-class girls, ages 5-11, completed the scale. The corrected, split-half reliability was .96.

VALIDITY: Using the responses from the ninety-eight girls mentioned above, it was found that on nine items, there was a significant difference ($p < .05$) between the responses of girls whose mothers worked and girls whose mothers did not work. Daughters of working mothers gave less stereotyped responses. On twelve items, there was a significant difference ($p < .05$) between age groups with older girls being less stereotyped in their responses.

      The ninety-eight girls completed the Qualities Stereotypes Scale (#73) (a measure of the tendency to sex stereotype personality traits) and a measure of career stereotypes in addition to completing the Activities Stereotypes Scale. The correlation between scores on the Activities and Qualities Stereotypes Scales was .60 ($p < .001$); the correlation between scores on the Activities Stereotypes Scale and the measure of career stereotypes was .33 (p < .002).

NOTES AND COMMENTS: The scale was empirically developed, has demonstrated excellent reliability, and the data suggest that it is valid. It is recently developed and, with one exception, the items are easy for children to understand.

SOURCE: Annick F. Mansfield
Department of Psychology
New York University
6 Washington Place, Room 1068
New York, New York 10003

BIBLIOGRAPHY:

Marantz, S. A., and Mansfield, A. F. "Maternal Employment and the Development of Sex Role Stereotyping in Five- to Eleven-Year-Old Girls." *Child Development,* 1977, *48,* 668-673.

---

61. BACON-LERNER VOCATIONAL ROLE INDEX

AUTHORS: Carolyn Bacon and Richard M. Lerner

DATE: 1975

VARIABLE: Tendency to sex stereotype occupations

TYPE OF INSTRUMENT: Multiple choice

DESCRIPTION: The instrument includes five masculine occupations (doctor, dentist, lawyer, farmer, and truck driver) and five feminine occupations (librarian, nurse, elementary school teacher, secretary, and telephone operator). The child is asked for each of the ten occupations: "can a boy be a [specific vocation] when he grows up, can a girl be a [specific vocation] when she grows up, or can both a boy and a girl be a [specific vocation] when they grow up?" (Bacon and Lerner, 1975, p. 189). The order of the presentation of the three response alternatives is balanced.

PREVIOUSLY ADMINISTERED TO: Grades 2-6

APPROPRIATE FOR: Ages 5-12

ADMINISTRATION: The instrument is individually and orally administered; the procedure takes between ten and fifteen minutes.

SCORING: Two indexes of vocational role stereotype are obtained. One index is found by counting the number of times a respondent indicates that both sexes could engage in a masculine occupation; the other index is found by counting the number of times a respondent indicates that both sexes could engage in a feminine occupation. Each of the two indexes can range from 0 (all single-sex responses) to 5 (all both-sex responses).

DEVELOPMENT: Occupations were identified as masculine or feminine if, according to U.S. employment tables, at least 85 percent of the workers in the occupation were of one sex; that is, masculine occupations had at least 85 percent male workers and feminine occupations had at least 85 percent female workers. Occupations whose titles specify sex —for example, repairman—were not selected. Beyond stating this restriction, the authors give no information. They do not indicate the number of occupations from which they made their selection, nor do they indicate how occupations were chosen. Furthermore, the source of the specific employment tables and their year of publication are not provided.

RELIABILITY: A sample of thirty girls was tested in second grade and again one year later when they were in third grade. Another sample of thirty girls was tested in fourth grade and again one year later. Test-retest correlations were computed separately for the masculine and feminine indexes. The correlations for the younger group were: masculine index = $-.18$ and feminine index = $-.17$. For the older groups, the test-retest correlations were: masculine index = .52 (p < .01) and feminine index = .38 (p < .05) (Lerner, Vincent, and Benson, 1976).

VALIDITY: Bacon and Lerner (1975) tested second-, fourth-, and sixth-grade girls. For the masculine occupations, they found that older girls scored significantly higher (less stereotyped) than younger girls, and girls whose mothers were employed scored significantly higher (less stereotyped) than girls whose mothers were not employed. The direction of the mean differences was the same for the feminine occupations, but the differences were not significant.

     Lerner, Benson, and Vincent (1976) tested fourth, fifth, and sixth graders. They did not find any significant differences among different ages or between different sexes.

     Lerner, Vincent, and Benson (1976) retested girls in grades three and five who had been tested one year earlier. They found that scores increased significantly for both age groups on the index for masculine occupations and scores increased significantly for the younger sample on the index for feminine occupations. In other words, upon retesting, the girls showed less sex stereotyping.

NOTES AND COMMENTS: (1) For the sample of thirty second-grade girls tested again in third grade, the correlation between the two indexes of vocational role stereotypy was .44 (p < .05) for the first testing and .70 (p < .01) for the retesting. For the sample of thirty fourth-grade girls tested again in fifth grade, the correlation between the two indexes of vocational role stereotypy was .48 (p < .01) for the first testing and .37 (p < .05) for the retesting.

     (2) It is difficult to interpret the test-retest reliability coefficients, because the interval between test and retest was so long. It is quite likely that the low correlations indicate that real changes took place in the respondents' stereotypes and the changes were not equivalent across persons. This seems a reasonable hypothesis given that Lerner, Vincent, and Benson (1976) found that scores generally increased over a year's time. The test-retest reliability of the instrument should be assessed using a shorter interval.

SOURCE: See Bacon and Lerner, 1975.

BIBLIOGRAPHY:

Bacon, C., and Lerner, R. M. "Effects of Maternal Employment Status on the Development of Vocational Role Perception in Females." *Journal of Genetic Psychology*, 1975, *126*, 187-193.
Lerner, R. M., Benson, P., and Vincent, S. "Development of Societal and Personal Vocational Role Perception in Males and Females." *Journal of Genetic Psychology*, 1976, *129*, 167-168.
Lerner, R. M., Vincent, S., and Benson, P. "One-Year Stability of Societal and Personal Vocational Role Perceptions of Females." *Journal of Genetic Psychology*, 1976, *129*, 173-174.

---

62. CHILDREN'S SEX STEREOTYPES OF ADULT OCCUPATIONS

AUTHORS: Candace Garrett Schau, P. L. Ein, L. Tremaine, and Lynne Kahn

DATE: 1977

VARIABLES: Tendency to sex stereotype occupational ability

TYPE OF INSTRUMENT: Summated rating scale

DESCRIPTION: The scale consists of twenty-one occupations: seven are considered typically masculine, seven are considered typically feminine, and seven are considered neutral. The scale can be administered with instructions to indicate either who "can" perform in each occupation or who "should" perform in each occupation. Each occupation is accompanied by five response options which are represented both verbally and pictorially: "only women" is accompanied by a picture of four female heads; "more women than men" is accompanied by a picture of three female heads and one male head; "about the same number of women and men" is accompanied by a picture of two female heads and two male heads; "more men than women" is accompanied by a picture of three male heads and one female head; and "only men" is accompanied by a picture of four male heads.

PREVIOUSLY ADMINISTERED TO: Grades 1-5

APPROPRIATE FOR: Ages 6-12

ADMINISTRATION: The scale can be either individually or group administered. The children are first taught the meaning of the words "can" and "should." Instructions are then given for completing the instrument and using the response options. When the scale itself is given, a one-sentence description of the occupation is given, followed by the question "Who do you think can [or should] be _____?" When both the "can" and "should" questions are given to first or second graders, it takes about forty-five minutes to complete the entire testing process. When both scales are given to third graders or older children, it takes about thirty-five minutes to complete the entire testing process.

SAMPLE ITEMS: Sewing machine operators are people who sew clothing on machines to sell to other people. Who do you think can be a sewing machine operator?

Fire fighters work at putting out fires. Who do you think can be a fire fighter?

SCORING: Several scoring options are available. One method gives each child three scores: masculine stereotypes, feminine stereotypes, and neutral items. To obtain these scores, each item is assigned between 1 and 5 points with 1 point assigned to the response "only women" and 5 points assigned to the response "only men." With this method of scoring, a respondent showing maximum and correct stereotyping would score high on the masculine stereotype score (maximum = 35), low on the feminine stereotype score (minimum = 7) and in the middle on neutral items (middle = 21).

Another method of scoring is to give each respondent a total stereotyping score. This score is found by assigning 1 point to the responses "only women" and "only men," 2 points to the responses "more women than men" and "more men than women," and 3 points to the response "about the same number of women and men." With this method of scoring, a score of 21 would show maximum stereotyping and a score of 63 would show no stereotyping.

The authors recommend a third method of scoring, which also yields a total stereotyping score. In this third method, "reverse the ratings of all jobs that the Census shows are filled by more than 50 percent men" (Schau and Kahn, 1978, p. 4). Scores for all items are then totaled. This method seems to make sense only if the total score is based solely on the responses to the feminine and masculine items. Otherwise, the neutral items would be treated as though they were feminine and it would be impossible to interpret the total score.

DEVELOPMENT: A forty-item version of the instrument was constructed by selecting occupations from the SRA (Science Research Associates) Occupation Kit (1964) to represent three levels of educational requirements: high school completion, post-high school training, and college training. The occupations selected represented three degrees of sex stereotyping: occupations that were filled by at least 75 percent men; occupations that were filled by at least 75 percent women; and occupations that were filled by fewer than 75 percent men and fewer than 75 percent women. This instrument was administered to 355 first, third, and fifth graders. Seven occupations that the children stereotyped as masculine, five that they stereotyped as feminine, and seven that were not stereotyped were included on the present scale. In addition, the authors added to the present instrument two occupations which they believed would be stereotyped as feminine.

A pilot study was conducted with 185 elementary school children to determine the children's ability to handle the response options adequately. In the pilot test, the questions had "concrete referents and correct answers" (Schau and Kahn, 1978, p. 5). The findings from the pilot test suggest that children found it easy to use boxes 1, 3, and 5 (the extreme and neutral responses) correctly. Errors were more frequent when the correct answer was box 2 or 4. This was especially true for first graders, who were still inclined to mark responses in the middle of the instrument, but not necessarily the correct response.

RELIABILITY: Coefficient alphas computed from various applications of this instrument "are consistently in the .90s for both 'can' and 'should' responses" (Schau and Kahn, 1978, p. 4).

The original forty-item version was given to 120 first graders, 110 third graders, and 125 fifth graders. Their responses were scored from 1 to 5, with 1 indicating a reversal of the sex stereotypic response and 5 indicating maximum sex stereotyping. Coefficient alpha was .85 (Garrett, Ein, and Tremaine, 1977).

A sample of 114 children completed a twenty-item version of the scale about one month after they were initially tested. Using a Wilcoxson matched-pairs signed-ranks test, no significant difference was found between the means obtained from the two testings (Garrett, Ein, and Tremaine, 1977). The responses to nineteen of the twenty occupations showed less stereotyping on the retest, but the difference was not significant (Schau and Kahn, 1978).

VALIDITY: The responses of 120 first graders, 110 third graders, and 125 fifth graders were compared with "reality" as reported by the U.S. Census Bureau. The correlation was .95 (Garrett, Ein, and Tremaine, 1977).

NOTES AND COMMENTS: (1) In a summary of the results from research using this scale, Schau and Kahn (1978) report the following: "Children's 'should' responses are more stereotyped than their 'can' responses"; "There are practice effects with use of the scale such that children's attitudes become less stereotyped with each administration of the scale"; "When children respond to 'can' first and then 'should,' both sets of responses are more stereotyped than when they respond to 'should' first and then 'can' " (p. 5).

(2) Two features of this instrument are unusual and notable: the distinction between who "can" and who "should" engage in an occupation; and the presentation of a brief description of the occupation before the respondent is expected to indicate an answer. The can-should distinction and the fact that the two words are explained before the task is begun increase the likelihood that respondents will all interpret the task the same way. The description of the occupations increases the likelihood that no one will misunderstand what is meant by an occupational title.

SOURCE: Candace Garrett Schau
        Department of Educational Foundations
        College of Education
        Albuquerque, New Mexico 87131

BIBLIOGRAPHY:

Garrett, C. S., Ein, P. L., and Tremaine, L. "The Development of Gender Stereotyping of Adult Occupations in Elementary School Children." *Child Development,* 1977, *48,* 507-512.

Kahn, P. L. "The Effect of Role-Reversed Stories on Children's Stereotyping of Occupations." Paper presented at 85th annual meeting of the American Psychological Association, San Francisco, August 1977.

Schau, C. G. "Evaluating the Use of Sex-Role-Reversed Stories for Changing Children's Stereotypes." Paper presented at meeting of the American Educational Research Association, Toronto, Canada, 1978.

Schau, C. G., and Kahn, L. "Children's Sex Stereotypes of Adult Occupations." Unpublished manuscript, 1978.

*Science Research Associates (SRA). *Junior Occupational Briefs.* Palo Alto, Calif.: Science Research Associates, 1964.

---

63. CHILDREN'S SEX-TYPED TOY INSTRUMENT

AUTHOR: John H. Diepold, Jr.

DATE: 1977

VARIABLE: Stereotypes of toys

TYPE OF INSTRUMENT: Multiple choice

DESCRIPTION: The instrument consists of color photographs of twelve toys, one masculine, one feminine, and one neutral for each of the following four types: puzzles, costumes, house sets, and mechanical devices. Three response options are presented in pictorial form: a drawing of four boys' faces, a drawing of four girls' faces, and a drawing of two boys' and two girls' faces. Children may express their responses by pointing to a pictorial response option or by giving a verbal response.

PREVIOUSLY ADMINISTERED TO: Ages 3-5

APPROPRIATE FOR: Ages 3-6

ADMINISTRATION: The child is shown one picture and told: "This is a [toy name]. Who do you think would like to play with this the most?" After each response, the examiner states "So you think that [child's choice] would like to play with the [toy name] the most?"

SAMPLE ITEMS: *Masculine:* football player puzzle
                Feminine: Cinderella puzzle
                Neutral: Jack and Jill puzzle

SCORING: Scores are obtained from all children for each individual toy or for the three categories of toys: masculine, feminine, and neutral.

DEVELOPMENT: Toys were selected to represent four categories with one feminine, one masculine, and one neutral choice per category (see Description). Toys within each category were selected to have the same number of moving parts and to be about equal in size. To validate the initial sex-typing judgments, thirty-four college students indicated their perceptions of the masculinity, femininity, or neutrality of the toys. For each of the twelve toys, there was at least 75 percent agreement among the judges.

RELIABILITY: No data are provided.

VALIDITY: Although the author predicted that children would be consistent in sex typing toys, fifty-two children, ages 3, 4, and 5, did not achieve 75 percent consensus on any one of the twelve toys. However, when item scores were totaled to yield three scores —sex typing of masculine toys, feminine toys, and neutral toys—the means for each of the three scores indicated that children were correctly stereotyping the groups of toys contributing to each score (Diepold, 1977).

NOTES AND COMMENTS: (1) Diepold (1977) video taped the 3-, 4-, and 5-year-old children while they were individually placed in a free-play setting with the twelve toys. Of the three age groups, the 5-year-olds were most likely to play with toys they had labeled as sex inappropriate, and the 3-year-olds were least likely to play with toys they had labeled as sex inappropriate. Diepold's findings indicate that different results are obtained when children are asked their stereotypes of sex typing of toys compared with when they are observed in a free-play situation with the same toys.

(2) This instrument is unusual in that it is well developed and presents a good balance of items; that is, four categories of toys are used and there is one masculine, one feminine, and one neutral toy for each category.

SOURCE: See Diepold, 1977.

BIBLIOGRAPHY:

Diepold, J. H., Jr. "Parental Expectations for Children's Sex-Typed Play Behavior." Paper presented at 85th annual meeting of the American Psychological Association, San Francisco, August 1977.

Garrett, C. S., Cherry, F., Kahn, L., and Diepold, J. H., Jr. "The Effects of Age, Sex, and Adult Presence on Preschool Children's Sex-Typed Toy Play Behavior." Paper presented at 85th annual meeting of the American Psychological Association, San Francisco, August 1977.

---

64. EAGLY-ANDERSON SEX ROLE EQUIVALENCE SCALE

AUTHORS: Alice H. Eagly and Pamela Anderson

DATE: 1974

VARIABLE: Perceptions of who should perform activities necessary for the functioning of the family

TYPE OF INSTRUMENT: Multiple choice

DESCRIPTION: The instrument includes a list of twenty activities that are typically performed by family members. For each activity, the respondent is asked to indicate whether the activity is "appropriate only for female," "appropriate mainly for female," "equally appropriate for both sexes," "appropriate mainly for male," or "appropriate only for male."

PREVIOUSLY ADMINISTERED TO: College students

APPROPRIATE FOR: Ages 10 and older

ADMINISTRATION: The instrument can be self-administered and can be completed in about five minutes.

SAMPLE ITEMS: Cleaning the house (vacuuming, dusting)
                            Mending clothes

SCORING: If the response indicates that the activity should be performed "only" by one sex, 3 points are assigned; if the response indicates that the activity should be performed "mainly" by one sex, 2 points are assigned; if the response indicates that the activity is "equally appropriate" for both sexes, then 1 point is assigned. Total scores can range from 20 (all non-sex-typed responses) to 60 (all sex-typed responses).

DEVELOPMENT: The activities included on the instrument were those that college students had indicated on a pretest were appropriate only for one sex.

RELIABILITY: The responses from 386 college students were used to calculate reliability. Coefficient alpha was .90.

VALIDITY: In addition to completing the Eagly-Anderson Sex Role Equivalence Scale, the 386 college students also completed a measure of attitudes toward the feminist movement, a measure of conservatism, and a measure of liberalism. The correlations between the Sex Role Equivalence Scale and each of the other three measures were all significant ($p < .01$) and in the predicted direction.

A comparison of the means for 250 males and 136 females indicated that males were significantly more opposed to sex role equivalence ($p < .001$).

SOURCE: Alice H. Eagly
                  Department of Psychology
                  University of Massachusetts
                  Amherst, Massachusetts 01003

BIBLIOGRAPHY:

Eagly, A. H., and Anderson, P. "Sex Role and Attitudinal Correlates of Desired Family Size." *Journal of Applied Social Psychology*, 1974, *4*, 151-164.

65. FAY SEX STEREOTYPE SCALE

AUTHOR: Todd L. Fay

DATE: 1971

VARIABLE: Stereotypes of males and females

TYPE OF INSTRUMENT: Semantic differential scale

DESCRIPTION: Five concepts are presented, one per page, with each concept accompanied by twenty-five seven-point semantic differential scales. The concepts used are: self, ideal male, ideal female, typical male, and typical female. Three versions are available: English language, Tagalog-English, and Spanish.

PREVIOUSLY ADMINISTERED TO: College students in the United States, the Philippines, and Colombia

APPROPRIATE FOR: Ages 14 and older

ADMINISTRATION: The scale can be self-administered and can generally be completed in twenty minutes.

SAMPLE ITEMS: (bipolar adjective scales) dependable-undependable
logical-illogical
soft-hard

SCORING: Items are objectively scored and equally weighted. Total scores can range from 25 (totally feminine) to 175 (totally masculine).

DEVELOPMENT: The original pool of scales included forty-eight bipolar adjective pairs. Twelve pairs were eliminated either because they referred to "well-established physical differences between the sexes (e.g., 'short-tall')" (Fay, 1970, p. 14) or because there was a problem translating them from English. Three graduate students in psychology rank ordered the remaining thirty-six pairs in terms of the "differentiatability between the sexes the pairs evoked." The same three judges reported which item of the pair was masculine and which was feminine. There was 100 percent agreement on the latter task. The twenty-five pairs that had the highest average ranks based on their ability to differentiate between the sexes comprise the scale.

RELIABILITY: No data are provided.

VALIDITY: No data are provided.

NOTES AND COMMENTS: (1) Fay (1970, 1975) reports comparisons based on the sex of the rater, the culture of the rater, and the target sex rated.

(2) Research is needed to determine the reliability and validity of the scale. Similarly, research is needed to determine whether the scale is a unifactor or multifactor scale.

(3) It is questionable whether three of the twenty-five bipolar adjective pairs actually represent opposite ends of a continuum: gentle-rough, brave-fearful, and aggressive-timid.

SOURCE: See Fay, 1970.

BIBLIOGRAPHY:

Fay, T. L. "Culture and Sex Differences in Concepts of Sex Role and Self." Unpublished doctoral dissertation, Northwestern University, 1970. (*Dissertation Abstracts International,* 1971, *31* [10-B], 6239.)

Fay, T. L. "Ideal and Typical Males and Females: Stereotypes in Three Cultures." Paper presented at 83rd annual meeting of the American Psychological Association, Chicago, August 1975.

---

66. FEMALE PERSONALITY TRAIT SCALE

AUTHOR: Kenneth Kammeyer

DATE: 1964 (used 1961)

VARIABLE: Tendency to sex stereotype female personality traits

TYPE OF INSTRUMENT: Summated rating scale

DESCRIPTION: The scale consists of eight statements, each of which expresses a stereotype about women as compared with men. Each statement is followed by four response options: agree, agree somewhat, disagree somewhat, and disagree.

PREVIOUSLY ADMINISTERED TO: Female college students and female adults in Israel

APPROPRIATE FOR: Ages 14 and older

ADMINISTRATION: The scale can be self-administered and can be completed in less than three minutes.

SAMPLE ITEMS: Women are more emotional than men.
            Men are better leaders than women.

SCORING: Items are objectively scored and equally weighted. Item scores are summed to yield a total score, which can range from 8 (total agreement with existing stereotypes about women) to 32 (total disagreement with existing stereotypes about women).

DEVELOPMENT: Ideas for items were taken from Komarovsky (1946) and from "the traditional folklore about the differences between males and females" (Kammeyer, 1964, p. 297).

RELIABILITY: No data are provided.

VALIDITY: An item analysis based on the responses given by 209 unmarried college women indicated that all items successfully discriminated between those with total scores in the top 20 percent of the distribution of total scores and those with total scores in the bottom 20 percent of the distribution (Kammeyer, 1964).

The Female Personality Trait Scale and the Feminine Role Behavior Scale (#150), a measure of attitudes toward the roles of women, were both administered to 209 college women. It was hypothesized that the two scales would yield highly related results. It was found that 58 percent of the women who had "modern" attitudes on one scale also had "modern" attitudes on the other scale. Yule's Q for the two scales was .59 (Kammeyer, 1964).

A study was done of 232 unmarried college women. As predicted, it was found that first-born and only-child women were more traditional on the Female Personality Trait Scale (Kammeyer, 1966). The hypothesis that a woman who had an older brother would be more traditional on the Female Personality Scale was not supported (Kammeyer, 1967).

NOTES AND COMMENTS: (1) The scale is short and can be completed quickly. This is an advantage as long as the scale is sufficiently long to yield reliable results. Unfortunately, there are no data regarding the reliability of the scale. If data are gathered that demonstrate that the scale is sufficiently reliable, I would highly recommend it.

(2) Despite the age of the scale—first used in 1961—none of the items appears outdated.

(3) Because every statement mentions men as well as women, the scale could be labeled as a measure of the tendency to stereotype masculine personality traits.

(4) The scale is also described in *Family Measurement Techniques* (Straus, 1969, pp. 159-160; Straus and Brown, 1978, pp. 109-110).

SOURCE: See Kammeyer, 1964, 1966, or 1967.

BIBLIOGRAPHY:

Kammeyer, K. "The Feminine Role: An Analysis of Attitude Consistency." *Journal of Marriage and the Family*, 1964, *26*, 295-305.

Kammeyer, K. "Birth Order and the Feminine Sex Role Among College Women." *American Sociological Review*, 1966, *31*, 508-515.

Kammeyer, K. "Sibling Position and the Feminine Role." *Journal of Marriage and the Family*, 1967, *29*, 494-499.

*Komarovsky, M. "Cultural Contradictions and Sex Roles." *American Journal of Sociology*, 1946, *52*, 184-189.

*Straus, M. A. *Family Measurement Techniques: Abstracts of Published Instruments, 1935-1965.* Minneapolis: University of Minnesota Press, 1969.

*Straus, M. A., and Brown, B. W. *Family Measurement Techniques: Abstracts of Published Instruments, 1935-1974.* Minneapolis: University of Minnesota Press, 1978.

Weller, L., Hazi, O., and Natan, O. "Birth Order and the Feminine Sex Role of Married Women." *Journal of Individual Psychology*, 1975, *31*, 65-70.

67. FERNBERGER STEREOTYPES OF SEX DIFFERENCES

AUTHOR: Samuel W. Fernberger

DATE: 1948

VARIABLE: Tendency to sex stereotype personality traits

TYPE OF INSTRUMENT: Story completion-fixed response alternatives

DESCRIPTION: The instrument consists of a short story containing sixteen blanks. The respondents can insert the word "men," or "women," or leave the item blank if they think neither word or both words should be included. By filling in the blank in the story, the respondents are expressing their perceptions of whether a particular characteristic is more true of men or women.

PREVIOUSLY ADMINISTERED TO: College students

APPROPRIATE FOR: Ages 14 and older

ADMINISTRATION: The instrument can be self-administered and can be completed in about ten minutes.

SAMPLE ITEMS: Excerpts from story: But at times they had troubles, and _____ were usually found to be the cause.

It was also a fact that _____ talked too much and sometimes pretty foolishly.

SCORING: Scoring is objective. All responses are equally weighted. Scores can range from 0 (all items left blank, no stereotyping) to 16 (all items completed, maximum stereotyping).

DEVELOPMENT: The instrument is a slight modification of a "Psychoquiz" that appeared in *Look Magazine* (April 29, 1947).

RELIABILITY: No data are provided.

VALIDITY: Fifty-four graduate students in psychology obtained a lower median score (Median = 8) than 217 undergraduate students in psychology (Median = 14). This finding that undergraduate students reveal more sex stereotypes is interpreted by Fernberger (1948) as a reflection of the fact that graduate students know more about psychology and thus are more aware that many popularly accepted stereotypes have not been empirically demonstrated.

Fernberger (1948) found that college men and women tend to agree in their responses to eleven of the sixteen items.

NOTES AND COMMENTS: (1) The story begins, "Once upon a time, there were two kinds of people, called men and women. They were different in many ways, but in general they liked each other. At least it didn't occur to men or women to try to kill off each other, and neither sex actually declared war on the other" (Neufeld, Langmeyer, and Seeman, 1974, p. 248). This semihumorous introduction does not encourage one to take the task seriously. Furthermore, the introduction clearly indicates that the sexes are different and thus implies that blanks should be completed. The respondent might experience additional "demands" from the story because (a) in order for the story to make sense, the blanks must be completed, and they cannot all be completed with the same response; and (b) in parts of the story, the story seems to be so aligned with existing stereotypes that the respondent might experience an implicit "demand" to comply and provide the "right" answer. Data are needed that compare scores obtained on this instrument with a more direct measure of the stereotypes of the traits included in the story.

(2) The instructions accompanying the instrument tell the respondent, "We would like to see how good a psychologist you are." It is therefore unclear whether the respondents' answers reflect their own stereotypes, or whether their answers indicate their perceptions of how psychologists would respond. An empirical study could demonstrate whether different responses are obtained when the instructions include the statement previously used and when the instructions ask the respondents to indicate their own opinions.

(3) The scoring of the instrument considers only whether an answer is provided, not whether the answer is consistent with prevailing stereotypes. Thus, two persons can obtain the same high score, though one may have given all stereotypic responses and one may have given all counterstereotypic responses. Someone giving all counterstereotypic responses would probably not be responding honestly.

(4) Neufeld, Langmeyer, and Seeman (1974) replicated Fernberger's study. They compared the responses obtained in 1948 with responses obtained in 1970.

SOURCE: See Neufeld, Langmeyer, and Seeman, 1974.

BIBLIOGRAPHY:

Fernberger, S. W. "Persistence of Stereotypes Concerning Sex Differences." *Journal of Abnormal and Social Psychology,* 1948, *43,* 97-101.
Neufeld, E., Langmeyer, D., and Seeman, W. "Some Sex Role Stereotypes and Personal Preferences, 1950 and 1970." *Journal of Personality Assessment,* 1974, *38,* 247-254.

---

68. HOUGH-ALLEN OCCUPATIONAL STEREOTYPES SCALE

AUTHORS: Karen S. Hough and Bem P. Allen

DATE: 1975

VARIABLE: Tendency to sex stereotype occupational ability

TYPE OF INSTRUMENT: Rating scale

DESCRIPTION: The scale consists of twenty-five occupations: fifteen that are stereotypically masculine, four that are stereotypically feminine, and six that are not stereotyped. For each occupation, the respondents are asked to rate how well a typical female and a typical male would perform in the occupation. A five-point rating scale is used with 5 representing maximum capability.

PREVIOUSLY ADMINISTERED TO: Female college students

APPROPRIATE FOR: Ages 14 and older

ADMINISTRATION: The scale can be self-administered and can generally be completed in five to eight minutes.

SAMPLE ITEMS: *Masculine:* commercial airplane pilot
                    Feminine: florist
                    Neutral: artist

SCORING: Scores are not assigned to respondents; they are assigned to "men" and to "women." Item scores range from 1 to 5, with 1 assigned to the least favorable rating and 5 assigned to the most favorable rating. A total rating score is computed separately for ratings of men and ratings of women.

DEVELOPMENT: The occupations were rated for their masculinity and femininity. The outcome showed that they "fall at the appropriate points on the masculine-feminine continuum . . . (p < .001)" (p. 252). No information was provided on who did the rating, how many raters there were, or how the data were analyzed.

RELIABILITY: No data are provided.

VALIDITY: Fourteen female college students were assigned to each of three conditions. In one condition, the females anonymously completed the scale; in a second condition, the females completed the questionnaire while being observed by a female experimenter; in the third condition, the females were led to believe that a machine they were hooked up to could read their minds. The conditions of administration made a difference to the ratings that were obtained. There was a significant sex-by-condition interaction: with the anonymous questionnaire, females were rated more favorably than males; with the female observer, males and females were rated about equally; and when the female respondents believed that their minds could be read, males were rated more favorably than females.

NOTES AND COMMENTS: This instrument is typical—both in terms of its development and in terms of its design—of instruments used to measure sex stereotypes. However, the article from which the instrument was taken is unusual because it demonstrates that responses to sex-stereotype questionnaires cannot be presumed to measure honestly held stereotypes.

SOURCE: See Hough and Allen, 1975.

BIBLIOGRAPHY:

Hough, K. S., and Allen, B. P. "Is the 'Women's Movement' Erasing the Mark of Oppression from the Female Psyche?" *Journal of Psychology*, 1975, *89*, 249-258.

69. MACDONALD SEX ROLE STEREOTYPE SCALE

AUTHOR: A. P. MacDonald, Jr.

DATE: 1974

VARIABLE: Stereotypes of men and women

TYPE OF INSTRUMENT: Semantic differential scale

DESCRIPTION: The instrument consists of two concepts, man and woman, each of which is accompanied by eight seven-point bipolar adjective scales. There are four scales measuring the evaluative dimension and four scales measuring the potency dimension. Each concept is placed on a separate page.

PREVIOUSLY ADMINISTERED TO: College students

APPROPRIATE FOR: Ages 14 and older

ADMINISTRATION: The scale can be self-administered and can be completed in less than five minutes.

SAMPLE ITEMS: *Bipolar adjectives, evaluative:* sociable-unsociable.
              Bipolar adjectives, potency: strong-weak.

SCORING: Items are objectively scored and equally weighted. The scale yields four scores: man evaluative, man potency, woman evaluative, and woman potency. Responses to four bipolar adjective pairs comprise each score.

DEVELOPMENT: The instrument is taken from the work of Pervin and Lilly (1967).

RELIABILITY: Based on the responses from 193 college students, MacDonald reports the following internal consistency (alpha) coefficients: man evaluative = .698, man potency = .298, woman evaluative = .649, and woman potency = .255.

VALIDITY: The Sex Role Survey (#199), a multidimensional measure of support for equality between the sexes, and MacDonald Sex Role Stereotype Scale were both administered to 100 female and 93 male college students. As predicted, individuals who supported equality between the sexes assigned lower potency ratings to Man ($r = -.24$, $p < .01$) and lower evaluative ratings to Man ($r = -.17$, $p < .05$). Furthermore, as predicted, individuals who supported equality between the sexes assigned lower Evaluative ratings to Woman ($r = -.17$, $p < .05$) but higher potency ratings to Woman ($r = .38$, $p < .0001$).

NOTES AND COMMENTS: (1) The original instrument included four bipolar adjective pairs to assess the activity dimension. However, because the internal consistency coefficients were unacceptably low (.096 for Man and .196 for Woman), they were not used in the analyses performed by MacDonald.

(2) Given the low internal consistency (.298 and .255) of the potency dimension, the interpretability of the potency scores is questionable.

SOURCE: See MacDonald, 1974.

BIBLIOGRAPHY:

MacDonald, A. P., Jr. "Identification and Measurement of Multidimensional Attitudes Toward Equality Between the Sexes." *Journal of Homosexuality,* 1974, *1,* 165-182.
MacDonald, A. P., Jr., and Games, R. G. "Some Characteristics of Those Who Hold Positive and Negative Attitudes Toward Homosexuals." *Journal of Homosexuality,* 1974, *1,* 9-27.
*Pervin, L. A., and Lilly, R. S. "Social Desirability and Self-Ideal Self-Ratings on the Semantic Differential." *Educational and Psychological Measurement,* 1967, *27,* 845-853.

---

70. MASTERS-WILKINSON SEX STEREOTYPES OF TOYS SCALE

AUTHORS: John C. Masters and Alexander Wilkinson

DATE: 1976

VARIABLES: Sex stereotypes of toys; agreement with sex stereotypes of toys

TYPE OF INSTRUMENT: Alternate choice

DESCRIPTION: The instrument consists of fifty-two toys laid out on tables. Each toy is accompanied by a card stating the name of the toy and its identification number. The task for each respondent is to indicate whether each toy is more likely to be used by boys or by girls. Adults are asked to rate the toys with reference to children ages 4 to 8.

PREVIOUSLY ADMINISTERED TO: Ages 4, 7, and 8, and adults

APPROPRIATE FOR: Ages 4 and older

ADMINISTRATION: For adults, the instrument can be self-administered, with responses recorded by the respondent. For children, the instrument is individually administered by an examiner, who reads the instructions aloud and records the child's responses. The child's responses can be given orally or by pointing to either a male stick figure or a female stick figure.

SAMPLE ITEMS: Xylophone
            Toy telephone
            Jacks and ball

SCORING: A consensual stereotypy score is found for each toy using the responses from all of the persons who complete the instrument. This score is used to classify the toys into five categories: highly stereotyped for boys, moderately stereotyped for boys, neutral, moderately stereotyped for girls, and highly stereotyped for girls.

In addition, four discriminative stereotyped scores are found for each respondent. The scores indicate "the extent to which an individual gave differential ratings to toys in different categories" (p. 211).

DEVELOPMENT: No information is provided.

RELIABILITY: Six four-year-olds and four adults completed the scale on two occasions, separated by a four-month interval. Test-retest consistency for the toys was figured by considering the proportion of toys similarly classified on the two testings. For the four-year-olds, the test-retest consistency was .64 for neutral toys, .68 for moderately stereotyped toys, and .82 for highly stereotyped toys. For adults, the comparable values were .68, .83, and .91.

Another type of reliability was found by comparing the test-retest consistency of the four-year-olds (within-subjects consistency) with the consistency across subjects. The findings indicated that "four-year-olds were at least as likely to agree with themselves on retesting as they were to agree with other four-year-olds on initial testing" (p. 211).

VALIDITY: Sixteen children, ages 7 and 8, and thirty-six adults completed a continuous scale rating the masculinity-femininity of the fifty-two toys and completed the Masters-Wilkinson Sex Stereotypes of Toys Scale. Responses to the two scales were compared. Twenty-eight adults showed no inconsistencies in the way they rated each toy on the two scales. Only two adults were inconsistent on their responses to more than two toys. Eleven children showed no inconsistency in the way they rated each toy on the two scales, and none was inconsistent on the responses to more than four toys.

Three groups completed the scale: sixteen four-year-olds, sixteen seven- and eight-year-olds, and thirty-six adults. Half of each age group were female. The correlation between the responses given by four-year-olds and by adults was .71; the correlation between the responses given by four-year-olds and by seven- and eight-year-olds was .77; the correlation between responses given by seven- and eight-year-olds and by adults was .94. The correlations between the two sexes were .93 for adults, .90 for 7- and 8-year-olds, and .49 for 4-year-olds.

NOTES AND COMMENTS: Based on the results from Masters and Wilkinson's study of four-, seven-, and eight-year-olds and adults, the toys were stereotyped as follows: eight highly stereotyped for girls, nine moderately stereotyped for girls, twelve highly stereotyped for boys, eleven moderately stereotyped for boys, and twelve neutral.

SOURCE: Dr. John C. Masters
              Department of Child Development
              University of Minnesota
              Minneapolis, Minnesota 55455

BIBLIOGRAPHY:

Masters, J. C., and Wilkinson, A. "Consensual and Discriminative Stereotypy of Sex-Typed Judgments by Parents and Children." *Child Development,* 1976, *47,* 208-217.

71. NASH SEX STEREOTYPING SCALE

AUTHOR: Sharon Churnin Nash

DATE: 1974

VARIABLES: Sex stereotypes of males and females; sex role concept of self; sex role concept of ideal self

TYPE OF INSTRUMENT: Semantic differential scale

DESCRIPTION: This instrument consists of ninety-eight pairs of bipolar adjectives. The adjective pairs are placed at the ends of a sixty-point continuum. For some adjective pairs, the right-hand side of the continuum represents the masculine end, and for other adjective pairs it represents the feminine end. Four concepts are to be rated on the adjective pairs: average man, average woman, self, and ideal self. The four concepts are rated on the same graphic rating scale; that is, when the respondent has completed the scale, there will be four marks on each of the ninety-eight continua.

PREVIOUSLY ADMINISTERED TO: Grades 6 and 9

APPROPRIATE FOR: Ages 12 and older

ADMINISTRATION: The directions for the scale are read aloud as the students follow along with their written copy. The scale can be completed in one hour and fifteen minutes.

SAMPLE ITEMS: Brave-Scared
Running-Sitting
Not at all talkative-Very talkative
Very practical-Very impractical
Very consistent-Not at all consistent

SCORING: Scoring procedures can vary, but the procedure used by Nash is explained here. Each sixth-grade subject receives a mean normalized score for average man, average woman, self, and ideal self based on his or her responses to the thirty-five items that sixth graders had been found to stereotype. Each ninth-grade subject receives three sets of mean normalized scores for average man, average woman, self, and ideal self. One set of scores is based on the thirty-five items that sixth and ninth graders had been found to stereotype; one set is based on the fifty items that ninth graders had been found to stereotype (including the preceding thirty-five items); and one set is based on ten items related to intellectual functioning which the ninth graders stereotyped. In all cases, a higher score indicates a more masculine rating.

DEVELOPMENT: Three hundred eighty kindergarten through eleventh-grade students were given an open-ended task designed to elicit their perceptions of the differences between males and females. Their responses were the basis for many of the bipolar adjectives included on the scale. The remaining adjectives were taken from the Sex Role Stereotype Questionnaire (#77). A total of ninety-eight bipolar adjectives were identified.

Using the responses from a sample of forty-six sixth-grade boys, fifty-nine sixth-grade girls, forty-five ninth-grade boys, and fifty-seven ninth-grade girls, a statistical analysis was performed to determine which items were considered sex stereotyped by each grade and sex. In order to be considered sex stereotyped, an item had to be stereotyped by both boys and girls at a given grade level, and both groups had to stereotype the item in the same direction (masculine or feminine). For the sixth graders, thirty-six items were identified as sex stereotyped. Thirty-five of these items were also sex stereotyped by the ninth graders. (The items stereotyped by the sixth graders but not by the ninth graders are eliminated from analysis.) Fifteen items were sex stereotyped by the ninth graders but not by the sixth graders, giving a total of fifty items stereotyped by the ninth graders. Of the fifty items, ten appeared to be related to intellectual ability.

RELIABILITY: Forty-four sixth graders and thirty-one ninth graders completed a twenty-item version of the scale on two occasions separated by one month. The twenty items included on the scale were selected before items were identified as sex stereotypic. No information is provided to indicate the overlap between the items chosen for the twenty-item scale and the items later identified as sex stereotypic. The responses from the children completing the scale on two occasions were used to compute the test-retest reliability of the scale. For "average male," the correlations range from .667 (sixth-grade boys) to .863 (ninth-grade girls); for "average female," the correlations range from .661 (sixth-grade girls) to .991 (sixth-grade boys); for "self," the correlations range from .473 (sixth-grade boys) to .984 (ninth-grade girls); and for "ideal self," the correlations range from .761 (sixth-grade boys) to .937 (ninth-grade girls) (Nash, 1974).

VALIDITY: The responses from forty-six sixth-grade boys and fifty-nine sixth-grade girls show a significant difference in mean normalized "self" ratings (p < .001); that is, males' self-concept was more masculine and females' self-concept was more feminine. On "ideal self" ratings, however, the difference was not statistically significant (p < .08). The responses from forty-five ninth-grade boys and fifty-seven ninth-grade girls show a significant difference in mean normalized "self" ratings (p < .0001) and mean normalized "ideal self" ratings (p < .0001). Again males score in the more masculine direction and females score in the more feminine direction. This finding was true when scores were based on the thirty-five items stereotyped by both sixth and ninth graders and when scores were based on the fifty items stereotyped by ninth graders. For the ten items related to intellectual functioning, significant differences were found for the ninth graders in terms of both "self" rating (p < .003) and "ideal self" rating (p < .02) (Nash, 1974).

The students referred to above were asked whether they prefer to be boys or girls. Sixth-grade boys who indicated a preference to be a girl scored significantly lower (more feminine) on "self" ratings compared with sixth-grade boys who indicated a preference to be a boy (p < .01). Sixth-grade girls who indicated a preference to be a boy scored significantly higher (more masculine) on "ideal self" ratings compared with girls who indicated a preference to be a girl (p < .01). Ninth-grade girls who indicated a preference to be a boy scored significantly higher (more masculine) on "self" ratings compared with girls who indicated a preference to be a girl (p < .005). No ninth-grade boys indicated a preference to be a girl (Nash, 1974).

NOTES AND COMMENTS: This scale is closely related to the Sex Stereotype Questionnaire (#77) in terms of format, adjectives, and applicability.

SOURCE: See Nash, 1974.

BIBLIOGRAPHY:

Nash, S. R. C. "Conceptions and Concomitants of Sex Role Stereotyping." Unpublished
     doctoral dissertation, Columbia University, 1974. (*Dissertation Abstracts Interna-
     tional,* 1975, *35*[10-B], 5163-5164.)
Nash, S. R. C. "The Relationship Among Sex Role Stereotyping, Sex Role Preference,
     and the Sex Difference in Spatial Visualization." *Sex Roles,* 1975, *1,* 15-32.

---

72. POSITIVE REGARD SCALE

AUTHORS: Shirley Ross and James Walters

DATE: 1973

VARIABLE: Positive regard for women

TYPE OF INSTRUMENT: Summated rating scale

DESCRIPTION: This scale consists of thirty-two statements. Most statements concern
perceptions of the personality traits, ability, and behavior of women in comparison with
men. About one third of the statements are phrased to reflect positive regard for women
and the remaining two thirds are phrased to reflect negative regard for women. Each
statement is accompanied by five response options: strongly agree, mildly agree, undecided, mildly disagree, and strongly disagree.

PREVIOUSLY ADMINISTERED TO: Male college students

APPROPRIATE FOR: Ages 16 and older

ADMINISTRATION: The scale can be self-administered and can be completed in about
ten minutes.

SAMPLE ITEMS: Women perform as well as men under pressure.
                        The majority of women are only interested in a man in terms of what
they can get from him.

SCORING: Items are objectively scored and equally weighted. Total scores can range
from 0 (negative regard for women) to 64 (positive regard for women).

DEVELOPMENT: A pool of sixty-nine items—including items selected from existing scales
and items specifically constructed for this scale—was given to five family-life specialists.
The specialists were asked to identify which items should be deleted, provide suggestions
for modifying the items, and for each item identify the response option that indicated the

most positive regard for women. As a result of the responses from the family-life specialists, twenty-two items were eliminated from the item pool and other items were reworded. The forty-seven-item scale was completed by 122 college men. Chi-square analyses were performed to determine which items significantly differentiated between those
men scoring in the upper and lower quartiles of the distribution of total scores. The
thirty-two items that discriminated between the two quartiles at the .05 level were retained for the scale.

RELIABILITY: The responses from the 122 college men were used to compute the reliability of the scale. The corrected, split-half reliability was .97.

VALIDITY: No data are provided.

NOTES AND COMMENTS: (1) When Ross and Walters compared the responses given by
students classified according to age, class in school, number of sisters, social class, dating
status, church attendance, mother's role (domineering-submissive), perceptions of one's
own masculinity, or preference for dating partner (highly feminine-not highly feminine),
no significant differences were found between means of compared groups. There was a
significant difference between groups classified on the basis of the perceived femininity of
the mother. College men who perceived their mothers as highly feminine showed a more
positive regard for women than did college men who did not perceive their mothers as
highly feminine.

(2) The reliability of the scale is excellent; however, research is needed to establish the validity of the scale.

(3) An examination of the items suggests that the scale actually measures stereotypes of women as compared with men.

SOURCE: See Ross and Walters, 1973.

BIBLIOGRAPHY:

Ross, S., and Walters, J. "Perceptions of a Sample of University Men Concerning
Women." *Journal of Genetic Psychology,* 1973, *122,* 329-336.

---

73. QUALITIES STEREOTYPES SCALE

AUTHORS: Sonia A. Marantz and Annick F. Mansfield

DATE: 1977

VARIABLE: Tendency to sex stereotype personality traits

TYPE OF INSTRUMENT: Multiple choice

DESCRIPTION: The instrument consists of eighteen questions, each of which asks who possesses a particular personality characteristic. Eight questions relate to feminine sex-typed personality traits, seven relate to masculine sex-typed personality traits, and three relate to neutral personality traits. For each question, the respondent is asked to indicate whether the personality trait describes the way ladies are, the way men are, or the way both men and ladies are.

PREVIOUSLY ADMINISTERED TO: Girls, ages 5-11

APPROPRIATE FOR: Ages 6 and older

ADMINISTRATION: For children who are 8 years old or younger, the scale is individually administered, with items presented orally and responses recorded by the examiner. For those who are at least 9 years old, the instrument is administered in small groups and answers are recorded by the respondents.

SAMPLE ITEMS: Who cares more about winning?
                            Who needs more help from other people?

SCORING: Items are objectively scored and equally weighted. Total scores can range from 0 (complete disagreement with existing stereotypes) to 18 (complete agreement with existing stereotypes).

DEVELOPMENT: The eighteen items were rated by twelve adults. The response selected by the majority of adults determined whether an item would be classified as "masculine," "feminine," or "both."

RELIABILITY: Ninety-eight middle-class girls, ages 5 to 11, completed the scale. The corrected, split-half reliability was .79.

VALIDITY: Using the responses from the ninety-eight girls mentioned above, it was found that on four items, there was a significant difference ($p < .05$) between the responses of girls whose mothers worked and girls whose mothers did not work. On one item, there was a significant difference ($p < .05$) between age groups, with the older girls being less stereotyped in their responses.

The ninety-eight girls completed the Activities Stereotypes Scale (#60) (a measure of the tendency to sex stereotype adult activities), a measure of career stereotypes, and the Qualities Stereotypes Scale. The correlation between scores on the Qualities Stereotypes Scale and scores on the Activities Stereotypes Scale was .60 ($p < .001$); the correlation between scores on the Qualities Stereotypes Scale and the measure of career stereotypes was .28 ($p < .005$).

NOTES AND COMMENTS: Despite the fact that Marantz and Mansfield used the instrument with children as young as 5 years old, a review of the items suggests that it is, in fact, too difficult for children that young. It is probably even too difficult for many children as young as age 6. Anyone considering using the instrument with young children should first determine whether the children will be able to comprehend all of the questions.

SOURCE: Annick F. Mansfield
                Department of Psychology

New York University
6 Washington Place, Room 1068
New York, New York 10003

BIBLIOGRAPHY:

Marantz, S. A., and Mansfield, A. F. "Maternal Employment and the Development of Sex Role Stereotyping in Five- to Eleven-Year-Old Girls." *Child Development,* 1977, *48,* 668-673.

---

74. ROLE DISTRIBUTION: CHILDREN'S SERIES

AUTHORS: Ruth E. Hartley and Francis P. Hardesty

DATE: 1964

VARIABLE: Sex stereotypes of children's activities

TYPE OF INSTRUMENT: Multiple choice with pictorial stimuli

DESCRIPTION: The instrument consists of fifty-six pictures, each of which represents an aspect of "play and recreation, peer contacts, participation in parental activities, domestic chores, intrafamily relationships, and 'cultural' activities" (Hartley and Hardesty, 1964, p. 44). Twelve pictures concern places to play; twenty-one pictures concern objects to play with; and twenty-three pictures concern activities, including chores.

PREVIOUSLY ADMINISTERED TO: Ages 5, 8, and 11

APPROPRIATE FOR: Ages 4-12

ADMINISTRATION: The scale is individually administered. The child is shown one picture, which is succinctly described, and is asked "Who mostly plays there [plays with it; does it], boys, or girls, or both, or neither." The procedure is repeated for the fifty-six pictures, which are administered in the following sequence: pictures dealing with places to play, pictures concerning objects to play with, and pictures depicting activities, including chores and services.

SAMPLE ITEMS: *Places:* Playing on playground
Activities: Washing dishes
Objects: Playing with toy trucks

SCORING: No scores are computed. Responses are tallied for each picture included on the scale.

DEVELOPMENT: No information is provided.

RELIABILITY: The responses "both," "neither," or "either" are considered egalitarian. The corrected, split-half reliability for egalitarian responses was .84 (Hartley and Hardesty, 1964).

VALIDITY: Using the responses from 131 children, Hartley and Hardesty (1964) found that there was consensus on the sex attribution of forty-six of the fifty-six items. Of the forty-six items, seventeen were classified as "girls," twenty-three were classified as "boys," and six were classified as "both."

NOTES AND COMMENTS: (1) Hartley and Hardesty (1964) compared the responses within the following four groups: thirty-four males compared with thirty-four females; twenty-eight eight-year-olds compared with twenty-eight 11-year-olds; twenty-eight upper-middle-class children compared with twenty-eight lower-middle-class children; and twenty children with working mothers compared with twenty children with nonworking mothers. The boys and girls differed in their responses to five items. The eight-year-olds and eleven-year-olds differed in their responses to two items. The upper-middle-class and lower-middle-class children differed in their responses to four items. The children of working and nonworking mothers differed in their responses to two items.

(2) The scale is also described in *Tests and Measurements in Child Development: Handbook I* (Johnson and Bommarito, 1971, p. 445).

SOURCE: See Hartley and Hardesty, 1964 (pictures are not included, but items are described).

BIBLIOGRAPHY:

Hartley, R. E., and Hardesty, F. P. "Children's Perceptions of Sex Roles in Childhood." *The Journal of Genetic Psychology,* 1964, *105,* 43-51.
*Johnson, O. G., and Bommarito, J. W. *Tests and Measurements in Child Development: Handbook I.* San Francisco: Jossey-Bass, 1971.

---

75. SEX ATTRIBUTION QUESTIONNAIRE

AUTHORS: Peter B. Zeldow and Roger P. Greenberg

DATE: 1975

VARIABLE: Extent to which people use the sex of another person to explain that other person's behavior

TYPE OF INSTRUMENT: Summated rating scale

DESCRIPTION: The scale consists of forty-eight statements, half of which refer to "he" and half of which refer to "she." Of the twenty-four statements that refer to "he," eight are sex congruent, eight are sex discrepant, and eight are sex neutral. The twenty-four statements that refer to "she" are similarly classified. A statement is considered sex congruent if the sex of the subject (he or she) is consistent with the stereotypic sex appropriateness of the activity mentioned in the statement. A statement is considered sex discrepant if the sex of the subject is opposite to the stereotypic sex appropriateness of the activity. A statement is considered sex neutral if the activity mentioned in the statement is considered equally appropriate for men and women. Each statement is followed by a four-point scale on which the respondent is asked to indicate whether the statement made is "all," "mostly," "somewhat," or "not at all" due to the fact that the person in the statement is a man (for "he" statements) or a woman (for "she" statements).

PREVIOUSLY ADMINISTERED TO: College students

APPROPRIATE FOR: Ages 14 and older

ADMINISTRATION: The scale can be self-administered and can be completed in ten to fifteen minutes.

SAMPLE ITEMS:

Sex congruent-he: He thinks he would like the work of a garage mechanic.

Sex discrepant-he: Sometimes he has the same dream over and over.

Sex neutral-he: He does not read every editorial in the newspaper every day.

Sex congruent-she: She thinks she would like the work of a librarian.

Sex discrepant-she: She thinks she would like to drive a racing car.

Sex neutral-she: She gossips a little at times.

SCORING: Items are objectively scored and equally weighted. Separate scores can be obtained for sex congruent, sex discrepant, and sex neutral items by summing the sixteen items in each category. An overall total is also computed. Higher scores indicate that the respondent is more inclined to use gender as an explanation for behavior.

DEVELOPMENT: The sex-congruent and sex-discrepant items were taken from the Femininity scale of the California Psychological Inventory. Items selected were changed from the first person to the third person. The items selected were known to have been differentially endorsed by men and women. If the item was endorsed more by men, then it would be considered sex congruent when the subject of the statement was a man (he) and sex discrepant when the subject of the statement was a woman (she). The converse is true for statements that were known to be endorsed by more women than men. The sex-neutral items were selected from the Communality scale of the California Psychological Inventory and the Lie scale of the Minnesota Multiphasic Personality Inventory. These items had been shown to be endorsed equally as often by men and women. Again, items were changed from the first person to the third person.

RELIABILITY: The internal consistency of the scale was estimated from the responses of eighty-eight college students. Coefficient alpha for the sex-congruent statements was .899; for the sex-discrepant items it was .836; and for the sex-neutral items it was .909 (Zeldow and Greenberg, 1975). Item-total correlations are reported for each item (Zeldow and Greenberg, 1975); they range from .277 to .830.

VALIDITY: Consistent with their prediction, Zeldow and Greenberg (1975) found that when they tested eighty-eight college students (half male and half female), sex-congruent scores were significantly higher (p < .001) than sex-discrepant or sex-neutral scores.

NOTES AND COMMENTS: The authors cite data from the mid 1960s as evidence that the statements are correctly classified as sex congruent, sex discrepant, or sex neutral. It is quite possible, however, that if data were gathered now, some of the items which were previously differentially endorsed by males and females would no longer elicit differential responses.

SOURCE: See Zeldow and Greenberg, 1975.

BIBLIOGRAPHY:

Greenberg, R. P., and Zeldow, P. B. "Effect of Attitudes Toward Women on Sex Attribution." *Psychological Reports,* 1976, *39,* 807-813.
Zeldow, P. B., and Greenberg, R. P. "The Process of Sex Attribution: Methodology and First Findings." *Sex Roles,* 1975, *1,* 111-120.

---

76. SEX ROLE STANDARDS QUESTIONNAIRE

AUTHORS: Aletha H. Stein and Jancis Smithells

DATE: 1969

VARIABLE: Sex stereotypes of achievement-related activities

TYPE OF INSTRUMENT: Alternate choice

DESCRIPTION: The instrument consists of forty-two items, with seven items from each of six achievement areas: athletic, spatial and mechanical, arithmetic, reading, artistic, and social skills. Six of the seven items in each area describe activities; the seventh is a general item representing the entire area. For elementary-age children, the items are represented by photographs (8" x 10"); for high school age students, the items are represented by verbal descriptions displayed on individual 3" x 5" cards.

PREVIOUSLY ADMINISTERED TO: Grades 2-12

APPROPRIATE FOR: Ages 7-18

ADMINISTRATION: The instrument is individually administered. Elementary school children are shown one picture at a time. The picture is briefly described by the examiner and the child is asked, "Do you think this is a more boyish or a more girlish thing to do?" Responses are recorded by the examiner. For high school age students, the examiner presents the cards, with verbal descriptions, one at a time, and asks, "Do you think this is a more masculine or a more feminine thing to do?" Again responses are recorded by the examiner. The instrument can be completed in about fifteen minutes.

SAMPLE ITEMS: *Athletic:* Playing baseball
                        Spatial and Mechanical: Fixing a broken bike
                        Arithmetic: Counting change
                        Reading: Reading a book
                        Artistic: Drawing
                        Social skills: Being liked by everyone

SCORING: Items are objectively scored and equally weighted. A score is obtained for each of the six areas. Area scores can range from 0 (all masculine responses) to 14 (all feminine responses).

DEVELOPMENT: No information is provided.

RELIABILITY: No data are provided.

VALIDITY: Twenty boys and twenty girls in second, sixth, and twelfth grades completed the instrument. The responses given to the general item in each area were correlated with the total score for each area. The resulting biserial correlations ranged from .74 to .92.

In addition to administering the Sex Role Standards Questionnaire, Stein and Smithells (1969) asked the students to rank order the general item from each of the six areas twice: once on the basis of masculinity and once on the basis of femininity. The rank ordering based on the mean score from the Sex Role Standards Questionnaire can be compared with the average ranks assigned to the six general items. When the general items were ranked on the basis of masculinity, the areas that ranked fifth and sixth were reversed compared with their rank ordering on the basis of the mean scores from the Sex Role Standards Questionnaire. When the general items were ranked on the basis of femininity, the areas that ranked first and second were reversed, and the areas that ranked fifth and sixth were reversed, compared with their rank ordering on the basis of the mean scores from the Sex Role Standards Questionnaire. In those cases where there were reversals in the ranks, the average ranks were very close; that is, when items were ranked on the basis of masculinity, the average ranks were 4.58 and 4.98 for the fifth- and sixth-ranked areas; when items were ranked on the basis of femininity, the average ranks were 5.19 and 5.30 for the first- and second-ranked areas and 1.96 and 2.03 for the fifth- and sixth-ranked areas.

NOTES AND COMMENTS: (1) It appears that scores in the various areas could be greatly affected by the choice of specific items. For example, athletic activities such as football, baseball, and basketball are likely to yield more masculine stereotypes than would activities such as jump rope, relay races, and volleyball. In the absence of any information regarding the development of the instrument, it is impossible to know whether the items were selected to represent a balance of stereotypically masculine and feminine activities. Furthermore, there is no indication whether the authors attempted to select items that were representative of the typical or most commonly engaged in activities representing each area. Some information regarding the content validity of the instrument is needed.

(2) Dwyer (1974) modified the instrument by adding more items, particularly in the areas of reading and arithmetic. She also modified the directions to allow for three

responses: boys, both sexes, and girls. Students were asked to complete the instrument once in terms of which sex would prefer each activity and once in terms of which activities the individual prefers. (See Individual Sex Role Preference Checklist [#16].)

SOURCE: Aletha H. Stein
Human Development and Family Life
University of Kansas
Lawrence, Kansas 66045

BIBLIOGRAPHY:

Dwyer, C. A. "Influence of Children's Sex Role Standards on Reading and Arithmetic Achievement." *Journal of Educational Psychology,* 1974, *66,* 811-816.
Stein, A. H. "The Effects of Sex Role Standards for Achievement and Sex Role Preference on Three Determinants of Achievement Motivation." *Developmental Psychology,* 1971, *4,* 219-231.
Stein, A. H., and Smithells, J. "Age and Sex Differences in Children's Sex Role Standards About Achievement." *Developmental Psychology,* 1969, *1,* 252-259.

---

77. SEX ROLE STEREOTYPE QUESTIONNAIRE

AUTHORS: Paul Rosenkrantz, Susan R. Vogel, Helen Bee, Inge K. Broverman, and Donald M. Broverman

DATE: 1968

VARIABLES: Perceptions of sex role stereotypes; sex role self-concept; social desirability of sex role stereotypes

TYPE OF INSTRUMENT: Semantic differential scale

DESCRIPTION: The instrument consists of 122 bipolar pairs of adjectives or adjective phrases. The 122 pairs include the following: twenty-nine stereotypic male-valued items, twelve stereotypic female-valued items, twenty-five differentiating male-valued items, twenty-three differentiating female-valued items, and thirty-three nondifferentiating items. (The terms *stereotypic, differentiating, nondifferentiating, male-valued,* and *female-valued* are defined below under Development.) Each bipolar adjective pair is placed at the ends of a sixty-point scale.

PREVIOUSLY ADMINISTERED TO: Grade 5 through adult

APPROPRIATE FOR: Ages 10 and older

ADMINISTRATION: The instrument is self-administered. The instructions to the respondent vary according to the purpose for which it is being administered. The usual procedure is to ask respondents to complete the instrument more than once, with a different concept being rated each time it is completed. The concepts that are usually rated are "typical male," "typical female," and "self"; or "ideal male," "ideal female," and "self"; or "healthy adult male," "healthy adult female," and "healthy adult." Quite often one set of rating scales is used to rate three concepts.

SAMPLE ITEMS: Not at all aggressive-very aggressive
Very subjective-very objective
Very talkative-not at all talkative

SCORING: The specific scoring procedures and the number of item pairs scored vary according to the variable being measured and the particular concepts that were rated. When "self" is rated, scores are obtained for individuals; for the other concepts, overall scores are often obtained for each of the traits or for the concepts rather than for individuals. In all scoring procedures, items are objectively scored and equally weighted, although, as stated above, the number of traits contributing to the score varies.

DEVELOPMENT: College students were asked to "list behaviors, attitudes, and personality characteristics which they considered to differentiate men and women" (Rosenkrantz and others, 1968, p. 287). The 122 items that were listed at least twice by the college students comprise the instrument, which was administered to seventy-four college men and eighty college women. Their instructions were to complete it three times, once for each of the following concepts: average adult male, average adult female, and self. The percentage of students rating each trait as more masculine than feminine or more feminine than masculine was computed for the male respondents and again for the female respondents. Any item that was rated in a consistent direction by at least 75 percent of the respondents was classified a *stereotypic* item. Forty-one items were stereotypic items in both the male and female samples. When correlated t tests were performed, the difference between the ratings assigned to the "average adult male" and the "average adult female" were significant at the .001 level for each of the stereotypic items. For the remaining items, correlated t tests were performed to determine the significance of the difference between the ratings assigned to the "average adult male" and the "average adult female." Forty-eight items were rated significantly different (p < .05) in both the sample of college men and the sample of college women. These items are termed *differentiating.* The remaining items are termed *nondifferentiating.*

Seventy-three men and forty-eight women were asked to indicate which pole on each of the 122 pairs was the more socially desirable. In addition thirty-five college men were asked to check, for each item, the place on the sixty-point continuum that represented the most socially desirable response for an adult. On twenty-nine of the forty-one stereotypic items, the masculine pole was the most socially desirable response; on twelve stereotypic items, the feminine pole was the most socially desirable. These twenty-nine and twelve items were labeled *male-valued* and *female-valued,* respectively. On twenty-five of the forty-eight differentiating items, the masculine pole was the most socially desirable response; on twenty-three differentiating items, the feminine pole was the most socially desirable response. Again the items were labeled *male-valued* and *female-valued.*

RELIABILITY: See Validity, below, for information regarding consistency across subjects.

Canty (1977) administered the instrument to seventy-seven college women on two occasions with a three-month interval between test and retest. The college students had been asked to rate males, females, and themselves. Eight measures were defined for each of the three concepts, which allowed for the calculation of twenty-four test-retest reliability coefficients. Only three of the coefficients exceeded .70; the median test-retest reliability was .56.

VALIDITY: The correlation between college women and college men who rated the average adult male was .960; the correlation between college women and college men for their rating on the average adult female was .950 (Rosenkrantz and others, 1968).

The social desirability ratings of the traits were obtained using two different sets of procedures. In one case, seventy-three men and forty-eight women indicated which pole on each trait was more socially desirable (forced choice method); in the other case, thirty-five college men were asked to mark a point on the sixty-point scale that represented the most socially desirable behavior for an adult. The correlation between the two methods of indicating social desirability was .85. Furthermore, the correlation between the responses from men and women who both used the forced choice format was .964 (Rosenkrantz and others, 1968).

Broverman and others (1972) report on scores obtained from 599 men and 383 women, varying in age, marital status, educational level, and religion. They conclude that "although some variation exists from group to group, high consensuality about the differing characteristics of men and women was found on a considerable number of items, and this was independent of age, sex, religion, education level, or marital status" (p. 65).

Factor analyses were performed on four sets of responses: men rating the typical male, women rating the typical male, men rating the typical female, and women rating the typical female. Two factors were extracted from each analysis. "The two factors in all four analyses divided the stereotypic items into those on which the male pole is more socially desirable versus those on which the female pole is more socially desirable" (Broverman and others, 1972, p. 66). This appears to confirm the distinction between male-valued and female-valued items. Based on inspection of the items included in the factor, the authors labeled the male-valued items a *competency cluster*. Based on an inspection of the items included in the other factor, the authors labeled the female-valued items a *warmth and expressiveness cluster*.

Broverman and others (1972) summarize the result from two studies that provide evidence of the construct validity of the instrument. In one study, sixty Catholic mothers of male college students completed the questionnaire. As predicted, "mothers with high competency self-concepts ... were found to have significantly fewer children than mothers who perceived themselves to be low on the competency items (3.12 versus 3.93 children, $p < .025$)" (p. 72). In another study, the questionnaire was completed by twenty-four men and twenty-three women whose mothers were never employed and by thirty-five men and thirty-eight women whose mothers were presently employed. "As expected, daughters of employed mothers perceived significantly smaller differences between men and women than did daughters of homemaker mothers, on both the competency cluster and the warmth-expressiveness cluster. Sons of employed mothers perceived a significantly smaller difference between women and men on the warmth-expressiveness cluster than did sons of homemaker mothers" (p. 74). It was also found that "daughters of employed mothers perceived women less negatively on the competency characteristics than did daughters of homemaker mothers" (p. 74).

Canty (1977) administered the instrument to seventy-seven college women. Based on her results, she questions the content validity of the questionnaire, stating, "In accordance with the guidelines for establishing stereotypic items, the binomial test with $p <$ .001 was applied to the data and not a single item met the criteria for group comparison" (p. 8).

NOTES AND COMMENTS: (1) There is tremendous variation in the number and choice of adjective pairs that researchers have used. There seem to be three standard versions of the instrument: the full-length 122-item version, an 82-item version, and a 38-item version. In addition, there are numerous other versions which differ in length and in the specific items included. As a result, the Sex Role Stereotypic Questionnaire might best be viewed as a procedure rather than as a well-defined instrument.

(2) A frequent application of the instrument is the study of stereotypes of mental health for males and females among mental health professionals and trainees (for example, Anderson and others, 1975; Billingsley, 1976; Broverman and others, 1970; Cowan, 1976; Delk and Ryan, 1975, 1977; Gintner, 1976; Harris and Lucas, 1976; Maslin and Davis, 1975; and Terrill, 1972).

(3) In addition to the concepts mentioned under Administration, the questionnaire has been used to rate numerous other concepts including, for example, black and white adults (O'Leary and Harrison, 1975); women in general, men in general, and men at ages 25, 35, 45, 55, and 65 (Silverman, 1977); adults of each sex, undergraduate students of each sex, graduate students of each sex, married undergraduate students, and married graduate students (Gerber and Balkin, 1977); and medical specialties (Quadagno, 1976).

(4) The Sex Role Stereotype Questionnaire was the basis for the development of the Personal Attributes Questionnaire (#39).

SOURCE: Paul Rosenkrantz
    Department of Psychology
    College of the Holy Cross
    Worcester, Massachusetts 01610

BIBLIOGRAPHY:

Altman, S. L. "Women's Career Plans and Maternal Employment." Unpublished doctoral dissertation, Boston University Graduate School, 1975. (*Dissertation Abstracts International,* 1975, *35* [7-B], 3569.)

Altman, S. L., and Grossman, F. K. "Women's Career Plans and Maternal Employment." *Psychology of Women Quarterly,* 1977, *1,* 365-376.

Anderson, M., and the Feminist Psychology Group. "Sex Role Stereotypes and Clinical Psychologists: An Australian Study." *Australian Psychologist,* 1975, *10,* 325-331.

Angell, M. L., Kadylak, S., and Ginn, R. O. "Feminine Stereotype and the Use of Contraceptives." *Journal of College Student Personnel,* 1975, *16,* 270-272.

Aslin, A. L. "Feminist and Community Mental Health Center Psychotherapists' Mental Health Expectations for Women." Unpublished doctoral dissertation, University of Maryland, 1974. (*Dissertation Abstracts International,* 1975, *35* [11-B], 5630-5631.)

Baruch, G. K. "Feminine Self-Esteem, Self-Ratings of Competence, and Maternal Career Commitment." *Journal of Counseling Psychology,* 1973, *20,* 487-488.

Baruch, G. K. "Sex Role Stereotyping, the Motive to Avoid Success, and Parental Identification: A Comparison of Preadolescent and Adolescent Girls." *Sex Roles,* 1975, *1,* 303-309.

Baruch, G. K. "Girls Who Perceive Themselves as Competent: Some Antecedents and Correlates." *Psychology of Women Quarterly,* 1977, *1,* 38-49.

Bernknopf, L. A. "A Comparison of the Responses of Behavior-Disordered and Normal Adolescents on a Masculinity-Femininity Scale and on a Stereotyping Questionnaire." Unpublished doctoral dissertation, University of Georgia, 1975. (*Dissertation Abstracts International,* 1976, *36* [9-A], 5986.)

Bernknopf, L. A. "A Comparison of the Responses of Behavior-Disordered and Normal Adolescents on a Masculinity-Femininity Scale and on a Stereotyping Questionnaire." Paper presented at the Annual International Convention, The Council for Exceptional Children, Chicago, April 1976. (ERIC Document Reproduction Service No. ED 125 208.)

Billingsley, D. "Sex Role Stereotypes and Clinical Judgments: Negative Bias in Psychotherapy." Paper presented at 84th annual meeting of the American Psychological Association, Washington, D.C., September 1976.

Borod, J. C. "The Impact of a Women's Studies Course on Perceived Sex Differences, Real and Ideal Self-Perceptions, and Attitudes Toward Women's Rights and Roles." Unpublished doctoral dissertation, Case Western Reserve University, 1975. (*Dissertation Abstracts International,* 1976, *36* [8-B], 4127.)

Broverman, I. K., Broverman, D. M., Clarkson, F. E., Rosenkrantz, P. S., and Vogel, S. R. "Sex Role Stereotypes and Clinical Judgments of Mental Health." *Journal of Consulting and Clinical Psychology,* 1970, *34,* 1-7.

Broverman, I. K., Vogel, S. R., Broverman, D. M., Clarkson, F. E., and Rosenkrantz, P. S. "Sex Role Stereotypes: A Current Appraisal." *Journal of Social Issues,* 1972, *28*(2), 59-78.

Burghardt, N. R. "Sex Differences in the Development of Achievement-Related Motives, Sex Role Identity, and Performance in Competitive and Noncompetitive Conditions." Unpublished doctoral dissertation, University of Michigan, 1974. (*Dissertation Abstracts International,* 1975, *35* [7-B], 3549.)

Canty, E. M. "Effects of Women's Studies Courses on Women's Attitudes and Goals." Paper presented at 85th annual meeting of the American Psychological Association, San Francisco, August 1977.

Carlock, C. J., and Martin, P. Y. "Sex Composition and the Intensive Group Experience." *Social Work,* 1977, *22,* 27-32.

Carpeno, L. "Expectations of Male/Female Leadership Styles in an Educational Setting." Unpublished doctoral dissertation, Boston University School of Education, 1976. (*Dissertation Abstracts International,* 1976, *37* [3-B], 1482.)

Clarkson, F. E., Vogel, S. R., Broverman, I. K., and Broverman, D. M. "Family Size and Sex Role Stereotypes." *Science,* 1970, *167,* 390-392.

Cowan, G. "Therapist Judgments of Clients' Sex Role Problems." *Psychology of Women Quarterly,* 1976, *1,* 115-124.

Cowan, G., and Moore, L. "Female Identity and Occupational Commitment." 1971. (ERIC Document Reproduction Service No. ED 056 335.)

Delk, J. L., and Ryan, T. T. "Sex Role Stereotyping and A-B Therapist Status: Who Is More Chauvinistic?" *Journal of Consulting and Clinical Psychology,* 1975, *43,* 589.

Delk, J. L., and Ryan, T. T. "A-B Status and Sex Stereotyping Among Psychotherapists and Patients." *Journal of Nervous and Mental Disease,* 1977, *4,* 253-262.

Dion, K. L. "Women's Reactions to Discrimination from Members of the Same or Opposite Sex." *Journal of Research in Personality,* 1975, *9,* 294-306.

Ellis, L. J., and Bentler, P. M. "Traditional Sex-Determined Role Standards and Sex Stereotypes." *Journal of Personality and Social Psychology,* 1973, *25,* 28-34.

Elman, J., Press, A., and Rosenkrantz, P. "Sex Roles and Self-Concepts: Real and Ideal." *Proceedings of the Annual Convention of the American Psychological Association,* 1970, *5,* 455-456.

Garman, L. G., and Plant, W. T. "Sex Role Stereotypes and Educators' Descriptions of Mature Personality." Paper presented at 54th annual meeting of the Western Psychological Association, San Francisco, April 1974. (ERIC Document Reproduction Service No. ED 109 519.)

Garske, J. P. "Role Variation as a Determinant of Attributed Masculinity and Femininity." *Journal of Psychology,* 1975, *91,* 31-37.

Gerber, G. L., and Balkin, J. "Sex Role Stereotypes as a Function of Marital Status and Role." *Journal of Psychology,* 1977, *95,* 9-16.

Gintner, G. G. "Sex Role Stereotypes and the Standard of Mental Health for Males and Females." Unpublished master's thesis, Central Michigan University, 1976.

Goldberg, P. A. "Prejudice Toward Women: Some Personality Correlates." Paper presented at 80th annual meeting of the American Psychological Association, September 1972. (ERIC Document Reproduction Service No. ED 072 386.)

Goldberg, P. A. "Prejudice Toward Women: Some Personality Correlates." *International Journal of Group Tensions,* 1974, *4,* 53-64.

Goodwin, W. B., Geller, J. D., and Quinlan, D. M. "Attitudes Toward Sex Roles Among A and B Psychotherapists." *Journal of Consulting and Clinical Psychology,* 1973, *41,* 471.

Grossman, S. N. "Sex Role Stereotyping as a Function of Counselors' Judgments." Unpublished doctoral dissertation, University of the Pacific, 1974. (*Dissertation Abstracts International,* 1975, *35*[10-A], 6455.)

Harris, L. H., and Lucas, M. E. "Sex Role Stereotyping." *Social Work,* 1976, *21,* 390-395.

Hoffman, B. R. "Sex Role Perceptions, Sex Role Self-Concepts, and Future Plans of Teenage Girls." Unpublished doctoral dissertation, Boston University Graduate School, 1973. (*Dissertation Abstracts International,* 1973, *34*[4-B], 1749-1750.)

Howell, E. F. "Self-Presentation in Reference to Sex Role Stereotypes as Related to Level of Moral Development." Unpublished doctoral dissertation, New York University, 1975. (*Dissertation Abstracts International,* 1976, *36*[11-B], 5867.)

Huang, L. J. "Sex Role Stereotypes and Self-Concepts Among American and Chinese Students." *Journal of Comparative Family Studies,* 1971, *2,* 215-234.

Johnson, P. I. "The Relationships Between Sex Role Stereotypes and Concepts of Mental Health." Unpublished doctoral dissertation, Arizona State University, 1974. (*Dissertation Abstracts International,* 1974, *34*[10-B], 5195.)

Kravetz, D. F. "Sex Role Concepts of Women." *Journal of Consulting and Clinical Psychology,* 1976, *44,* 437-443.

Lacey, M., and Levinger, G. "Is Conventionality a Determinant of Stereotypy and Self-Disclosure in Close and Casual Relationships?" *Journal Supplement Abstract Service Catalog of Selected Documents in Psychology,* 1975, *5,* 330.

Lavrakas, P. J. "Female Preferences for Male Physiques." *Journal of Research Personality,* 1975, *9,* 324-334.

Lunneborg, P. W. "Trying to Take Sex Role Out of Self-Concept." Paper presented at 83rd annual meeting of the American Psychological Association, Chicago, August 1975.

Maslin, A., and Davis, J. L. "Sex Role Stereotyping as a Factor in Mental Health Standards Among Counselors-in-Training." *Journal of Counseling Psychology,* 1975, *22,* 87-91.

Maxfield, R. B. "Sex Role Stereotypes of Psychotherapists." Unpublished doctoral dissertation, Adelphi University, 1976. (*Dissertation Abstracts International,* 1976, *37*[4-B], 1914.)

Nowacki, C. M., and Poe, C. A. "The Concept of Mental Health as Related to Sex of Person Perceived." *Journal of Consulting and Clinical Psychology,* 1973, *40,* 160.

O'Leary, V. E., and Depner, C. E. "College Males' Ideal Female: Changes in Sex Role Stereotypes." *Journal of Social Psychology,* 1975, *95,* 139-140.

O'Leary, V. E., and Harrison, A. O. "Sex Role Stereotypes as a Function of Race and Sex." Paper presented at 83rd annual meeting of the American Psychological Association, Chicago, August 1975.

Parker, S. R. "The Yin and the Yang: Do Women Managers Have the Best of Both Worlds? A Comparative Study of the Masculinity and Femininity of Managers." Unpublished doctoral dissertation, Louisiana State University and Agricultural and Mechanical College, 1976. (*Dissertation Abstracts International,* 1976, *37*[6-B], 3132-3133.)

Quadagno, J. "Occupational Sex Typing and Internal Labor Market Distributions: An Assessment of Medical Specialties." *Social Problems,* 1976, *23,* 442-453.

Romer, N. "Sex-Related Differences in the Development of the Motive to Avoid Success, Sex Role Identity, and Performance in Competitive and Noncompetitive Conditions." *Psychology of Women Quarterly,* 1977, *1,* 260-272.

Rosenkrantz, P., Vogel, S., Bee, H., Broverman, I., and Broverman, D. M. "Sex Role Stereotypes and Self-Concepts in College Students." *Journal of Consulting and Clinical Psychology,* 1968, *32,* 287-295.

Saarni, C. I. "Social-Cohort Effect on Three Masculinity-Femininity Instruments and Self-Report." *Psychological Reports,* 1976, *38,* 1111-1118.

Saarni, C., and Azara, V. "Developmental Analysis of Human Figure Drawings in Adolescence, Young Adulthood, and Middle Age." *Journal of Personality Assessment,* 1977, *41,* 31-38.

Saarni, C. I., Taber, R., and Shaw-Hamilton, L. "The Vicissitudes of Sex Role Assessment." Paper presented at 53rd annual meeting of the Western Psychological Association, Anaheim, California, April 1973. (ERIC Document Reproduction Service No. ED 084 284.)

Samara, B. M. "Teachers' Conceptions of Children's Sex Roles as Related to Attitudes About the Women's Liberation Movement and Personal Background Data." Unpublished doctoral dissertation, Temple University, 1974. (*Dissertation Abstracts International,* 1974, *35*[6-A], 3532-3533.)

Schwab, J. M. "An Investigation of the Interrelationships of Sex Stereotypy, Perceived Similarity, Sex of Subject, Sex of Object, Actual Sex Similarity, and Empathy." Unpublished doctoral dissertation, University of Notre Dame, 1974. (*Dissertation Abstracts International,* 1975, *35*[7-B], 3650.)

Sibbison, V. H. "Occupational Preferences and Expectations of Rural High School Males and Females: Background, Grade, and Sex Role Correlates." Unpublished doctoral dissertation, Pennsylvania State University, 1974. (*Dissertation Abstracts International,* 1975, *35*[11-A], 7069.)

Silverman, M. "The Old Man as Woman: Detecting Stereotypes of Aged Men with a Femininity Scale." *Perceptual and Motor Skills,* 1977, *44,* 336-338.

Spence, J. T., Helmreich, R., and Stapp, J. "The Personal Attributes Questionnaire: A

Measure of Sex Role Stereotypes and Masculinity-Femininity." *Journal Supplement Abstract Service Catalog of Selected Documents in Psychology,* 1974, *4,* 43-44.

Stericker, A. B., and Johnson, J. E. "Sex Role Identification and Self-Esteem in College Students: Do Men and Women Differ?" *Sex Roles,* 1977, *3,* 19-26.

Strauss, M. D. "Women About Women: A Descriptive Study of the Psychological Impact of the Feminine Sex Role Stereotype." Unpublished doctoral dissertation, University of Texas at Austin, 1971. (*Dissertation Abstracts International,* 1972, *33*[1-A], 401.)

Terrill, M. J. "Sex Role Stereotypes and Conceptions of Mental Health of Graduate Students in Counseling." Unpublished master's thesis, University of Illinois, 1972. (ERIC Document Reproduction Service No. ED 101 255.)

Titus-Maxfield, M. A. "Sex Role Stereotypes of Potential Clinical Psychologists." Unpublished doctoral dissertation, Adelphi University, 1976. (*Dissertation Abstracts International,* 1976, *37*[4-B], 1932.)

Tolor, A., Kelly, B. R., and Stebbins, C. A. "Assertiveness, Sex Role Stereotyping, and Self-Concept." *Journal of Psychology,* 1976, *93,* 157-164.

Vogel, S. R., Broverman, I. K., Broverman, D. M., Clarkson, F. E., and Rosenkrantz, P. S. "Maternal Employment and Perception of Sex Roles Among College Students." *Developmental Psychology,* 1970, *3,* 384-391.

Vogel, S. R., Rosenkrantz, P. S., Broverman, I. K., Broverman, D. M., and Clarkson, F. E. "Sex Role Self-Concepts and Life-Style Plans of Young Women." *Journal of Consulting and Clinical Psychology,* 1975, *43,* 427.

Winkler, A. "Sex and Student Role Stereotypes in Australian University Students." *Australian Journal of Education,* 1976, *20,* 285-291.

Woolever, R. "Expanding Elementary Pupils' Occupational and Social Role Perceptions: An Innovative Federal Project." Paper presented at the meeting of the National Council for the Social Studies, Washington, D.C., November 1976. (ERIC Document Reproduction Service No. ED 133 249.)

---

78. SEX STEREOTYPE MEASURE (SSM)

AUTHORS: John E. Williams, Susan M. Bennett, and Deborah L. Best

DATE: 1973 (revised 1977)

VARIABLE: Awareness of adult-defined sex stereotypes of personality traits

TYPE OF INSTRUMENT: Alternate choice

DESCRIPTION: The Sex Stereotype Measure consists of twenty-four stories, each of which is about three sentences long. Each story describes a person who possesses a sex-stereotyped characteristic. Twelve stories concern stereotypically masculine traits and twelve stories concern stereotypically feminine traits. Each story ends with a question asking who the story is about. All pronouns are plural (for example, they, them) so that the child's answer is not influenced by the wording of the story. Each story is accompanied by two pictures: an adult male and an adult female. The male and female pictures accompanying each story are of the same race and matched on such variables as position and age. To respond to the question at the end of each story, the child is to point to the male or female picture.

The Sex Stereotype Measure II, the revised version, includes thirty-two stories rather than just the twenty-four included in SSM. Again, half the stories concern stereotypically masculine traits and half concern stereotypically feminine traits. SSM II also differs from SSM in terms of the pictorial stimuli used. SSM II uses silhouettes with the head of each figure in profile; the length of the hair and the type of clothing—dress versus pants—provide the gender clues. Thus, each of the thirty-two stories is accompanied by two silhouettes, one male and one female. For half the stories, the male is on the left, and for the other half of the stories, the male is on the right. In the individually administered form, the position of the silhouettes is systematically varied—facing right, facing left, standing, sitting, walking—but the two silhouettes accompanying any one story face the same direction and are in the same position. In the group-administered form, all silhouettes are in the same position.

PREVIOUSLY ADMINISTERED TO: Grades pre-K through 6

APPROPRIATE FOR: Ages 4-12

ADMINISTRATION: The instrument is individually administered to children below the sixth grade. The authors suggest that a female examiner be used with half the children and a male examiner with the other half. This suggestion is based on the fact that examiner's sex was a significant variable in a study of fourth graders. The instrument can be group administered to children in sixth grade. About twenty minutes is required for individual administration of SSM II; slightly longer is required for group administration.

SAMPLE ITEMS:

Stereotypically masculine trait: One of these people is a bully. They are always pushing people around and getting into fights. Which person gets into fights?

Stereotypically feminine trait: One of these people is a gentle person. When they hold puppies, they are careful not to hurt them. Which is the gentle person?

SCORING: Both SSM and SSM II yield three scores: a total stereotyping score, a masculine stereotyping score, and a feminine stereotyping score. The masculine and feminine stereotyping scores are obtained by assigning 1 point each time the child responds to the story by indicating the "correct" figure. Thus, on SSM, the masculine and feminine stereotyping scores can each equal 12, and on the SSM II, the masculine and feminine stereotyping scores can each equal 16. The total score is equal to the sum of the masculine and feminine stereotyping scores.

DEVELOPMENT: To develop the SSM, the 300-item Adjective Check List (#45) was administered to fifty college men and fifty college women with instructions to indicate whether each adjective was more frequently associated with men or with women. If at least 74 percent of the college men and 74 percent of the college women indicated that an adjective was more frequently associated with one sex, the item was classified as a stereotype. There were thirty-three male-stereotyped adjectives and thirty female-stereotyped adjectives. Four judges translated the stereotyped adjectives into a vocabulary appropriate for young children, eliminated evaluative adjectives (for example, cruel), and grouped synonymous words (for example, meek and mild). Twenty-five masculine-typed adjectives were used in developing twelve stories; twenty-four feminine-typed adjectives were used in developing another twelve stories. The twenty-four stories were then given to sixty-two college men and sixty-two college women with instructions to indicate whether each story described a typical male or a typical female. The results from the college students indicate that the stories "were a reasonably accurate representation of the original stereotype adjectives" (Bennett, 1973, p. 17). The pictures selected to accompany the stories were selected from a picture pool that Williams developed for use in measuring racial attitudes of children.

The first draft of the SSM II included all of the items from the SSM plus four additional masculine-stereotyped items and four additional feminine-stereotyped items. The new stories were prepared in the same manner as that described above for the SSM. The thirty-two-item form was administered to 110 college men and women with instructions to indicate whether each story described a typical male or a typical female. All but one of the stories were judged as expected by at least 80 percent of the college students. The one that was not judged satisfactorily was replaced. The pictures were revised for SSM II because "item-picture confounds, which were possible due to the extraneous details presented in the pictures, were suggested in the data" (Williams and Best, 1976, p. 2) when SSM was used.

RELIABILITY: No data are provided.

VALIDITY: The SSM was administered to 284 children in kindergarten, second, and fourth grade. Second graders scored significantly higher ($\overline{X}$ = 15.84, p < .05) than kindergartners ($\overline{X}$ = 14.13), indicating that second graders are more aware of sex stereotypes than are kindergartners. There were no significant differences between second and fourth graders. Masculine stereotyping scores were significantly higher ($\overline{X}$ = 8.29, p < .05) than feminine stereotyping scores ($\overline{X}$ = 6.76) (Bennett, 1973; Williams, Bennett, and Best, 1975). In a similar study of children in the United States, England, and Ireland, using SSM II, similar results were obtained. There was again a significant difference due to age, but in this study knowledge of stereotypes continued to increase after the second grade. And, again, there were significantly higher scores on the masculine stereotypes than on the feminine stereotypes (Best and others, 1977).

McGhee (1975) found that children who watched television often obtained significantly higher scores on the masculine-stereotyped items, the feminine-stereotyped items, and the total score than children who watched television less often.

NOTES AND COMMENTS: (1) Some young children are unable to respond correctly to the instrument. If a child's responses suggest a response set rather than discriminating responses, that child's responses should be discarded. A response set is indicated if all responses are on one side (for example, the right side) or if all responses indicate the same choice (for example, all females).

(2) The SSM II has been used in Ireland and England. Studies are underway in France, the Netherlands, Norway, Germany, Israel, Bolivia, Japan, and New Zealand (Williams and Best, 1976).

(3) Because the authors of the instrument wanted to be certain that pronouns did not provide any gender clues, they used only plural pronouns. As a result, all of the "stories" are grammatically incorrect (see Sample Items). It is possible that this would be distracting to the children.

(4) Two stories that are included on both the SSM and the SSM II can be criticized. For the trait "sophisticated," the story says, "One of these people has such good manners, it makes you sick. They always do everything just right" (Williams and Best, 1976, p. 20). This interpretation of the trait "sophisticated" is not at all consistent with the dictionary definition of the term, which is "Having acquired worldly knowledge or refinement; lacking natural simplicity or naivete" (*American Heritage Dictionary of the English Language,* 1973). Another story, which is intended to reflect the trait "fussy, nagging," states, "One of these people is always fussing at their children about the things they're supposed to do. They never stop fussing, even when you have finished what they say" (Williams and Best, 1976, p. 20). This story might elicit the response "female" because females tend to be associated with children more than males, rather than because females are more likely to be stereotyped as fussy and nagging. This story can be further criticized because the second sentence is grammatically confusing.

(5) Coker (1977) modified the instrument, using ten brief stories and having responses indicated by pointing to a picture of a boy or a girl.

SOURCE: SSM: See Bennett, 1973.
 SSM II: John E. Williams
  Department of Psychology
  Wake Forest University
  Winston-Salem, North Carolina 27109

BIBLIOGRAPHY:

The American Heritage Dictionary of the English Language. Boston: Houghton Mifflin, 1973.

Bennett, S. M. "Children's Recognition of Male and Female Stereotypes: A Developmental Analysis." Unpublished master's thesis, Wake Forest University, 1973.

Best, D. L., Williams, J. E., Cloud, J. M., Davis, S. W., Robertson, L. S., Edwards, J. R., Giles, H., and Fowles, J. "Development of Sex-Trait Stereotypes Among Young Children in the United States, England, and Ireland." Paper presented at the biennial meeting of the Society for Research in Child Development, New Orleans, March 1977. (ERIC Document Reproduction Service No. ED 135 491.)

Coker, D. R. "Development of Gender Concepts in Preschool Children." Paper presented at 85th annual meeting of the American Psychological Association, San Francisco, August 1977.

McGhee, P. E. "Television as a Source of Learning Sex Role Stereotypes." Paper presented at the biennial meeting of the Society for Research in Child Development, Denver, April 1975. (ERIC Document Reproduction Service No. ED 111 528.)

Williams, J. E., Bennett, S. M., and Best, D. L. "Awareness and Expression of Sex Stereotypes in Young Children." *Developmental Psychology,* 1975, *11,* 635-642.

Williams, J. E., and Best, D. L. "Sex Stereotype Measure II and Sex Attitude Measure: General Information and Manual of Directions." Unpublished manuscript, Wake Forest University, 1976.

79. SHINAR OCCUPATIONAL STEREOTYPES QUESTIONNAIRE

AUTHOR: Eva H. Shinar

DATE: 1975

VARIABLE: Sex stereotypes of occupations

TYPE OF INSTRUMENT: Rating scale

DESCRIPTION: The scale consists of 129 occupations, each of which is followed by a seven-point rating scale with the end points labeled "masculine" and "feminine" and the midpoint labeled "neutral."

PREVIOUSLY ADMINISTERED TO: College students

APPROPRIATE FOR: Ages 14 and older

ADMINISTRATION: The scale can be self-administered. Three different sets of instructions for rating the masculinity-femininity of the occupations have been used: (1) respondents have been directed to rate each occupation in terms of its being masculine, feminine, or neutral (vague instructions); (2) respondents have been asked to rate each occupation on the basis of the proportion of each sex employed in it (proportion instructions); and (3) respondents have been asked to rate each occupation on the basis of the personality characteristics of people employed in the occupation (personality-attributes instructions).

SAMPLE ITEMS: Miner
                Theatrical director
                Receptionist

SCORING: Average ratings are obtained for each occupation. Scores are not assigned to persons.

DEVELOPMENT: Occupations were selected for the scale to represent the eight dimensions of Roe's (1956) occupational space: organization, outdoor, general-cultural, service, arts, business-contact, entertainment, and technology. Occupations were selected to represent three levels: professional-managerial, semiprofessional and small business, and skilled occupations.

RELIABILITY: Thirteen subjects completed the scale on two occasions separated by three weeks. They were given the vague instructions (see Administration). Based on the mean ratings assigned to each occupation, the test-retest reliability was found to be .97 (Shinar, 1975).

       The correlation between the mean ratings given by sixty college men and sixty college women was .97 (Shinar, 1975).

VALIDITY: The ratings assigned by respondents in each of three instruction groups (see Administration) were compared. Occupations were rated as significantly more masculine (p < .001) under the proportion instructions. No difference was found between the other two groups (Shinar, 1975).

NOTES AND COMMENTS: Shinar's scale is quite typical of scales used to measure occupational stereotypes. It differs in that it only yields scores for occupations, not scores for the raters.

SOURCE: See Shinar, 1975.

BIBLIOGRAPHY:

*Roe, A. *The Psychology of Occupations.* New York: Wiley, 1956.
Shinar, E. H. "Sexual Stereotypes of Occupations." *Journal of Vocational Behavior,* 1975, *7,* 99-111.

---

80. SILVERN SEX ROLE SCALE

AUTHOR: Louise E. Silvern

DATE: 1976

VARIABLES: Sex role stereotypes; social desirability of sex-typed traits

TYPE OF INSTRUMENT: Multiple choice

DESCRIPTION: There are two parts to the instrument. In the first part, which measures sex role stereotypes, the child is presented with a list of forty-six traits and activities. For each trait or activity, the child is to indicate whether "most people think" that the trait is more characteristic of boys or girls. The second part of the instrument, which measures social desirability of sex-typed traits, presents the child with forty-six sets of five identical stick figures. In each set, the figures are intended to represent varying degrees of a trait. Two verbal descriptors serving as anchor points are presented with each set of stick figures. The child is asked to indicate which "kid you would like best" for each set of five stick figures.

PREVIOUSLY ADMINISTERED TO: Grades 4 and 6

APPROPRIATE FOR: Ages 9 and older

ADMINISTRATION: The instrument can be group administered and can be completed in about an hour.

SAMPLE ITEMS:

Weak: Most people think
• boys are much weaker than girls.

- boys are a little weaker than girls.
- there is no difference between boys and girls.
- girls are a little weaker than boys.
- girls are much weaker than boys.

Mean: Most people think
- boys are much meaner than girls.
- boys are a little meaner than girls.
- there is no difference between boys and girls.
- girls are a little meaner than boys.
- girls are much meaner than boys.

SCORING: Silvern did not obtain scores for each child. Rather, she reported the mean of the responses given by all girls and by all boys to a particular trait.

DEVELOPMENT: A pool of seventy-five items was compiled based on the results from relevant research. Third-grade reading and spelling textbooks were consulted to ensure that the vocabulary in the items would not be too difficult. Thirty-six seventh-grade boys and twenty seventh-grade girls were given the items to determine which would be sex typed. The following criteria were used for determining whether an item was sex typed: (1) a significant difference ($p < .01$) between the classification of the trait as masculine, neutral, or feminine and (2) at least 60 percent of the responses falling on one side of the neutral point with no more than 10 percent falling on the other side of the neutral point. Twenty-six items satisfied both of these criteria. The final form of the instrument includes these twenty-six items, four items that were judged most neutral by the seventh graders, and sixteen filler items. Only the filler items differ on the first and second parts of the scale.

RELIABILITY: No data are provided.

VALIDITY: Silvern used the scale to test two hypotheses: "Boys and girls will judge their own sex more favorably than the opposite sex" and "Girls will judge the female sex role to be more desirable than boys judge the male sex role" (Silvern, 1977, pp. 164, 166). The responses from seventy-five fourth and seventh graders supported the hypotheses. For both boys and girls, the mean social-desirability rating across all traits that they felt described their own sex was significantly higher ($p < .05$ for boys; $p < .001$ for girls) than the mean social-desirability of traits they felt described the opposite sex. The mean of the social desirability ratings that girls assigned to feminine traits was significantly higher ($p < .001$) than the mean of the social-desirability ratings that boys assigned to masculine traits (Silvern, 1977).

NOTES AND COMMENTS: (1) This instrument is unusual in that Silvern took steps to ensure that the vocabulary would be understandable to the respondents; that is, she consulted third-grade reading and spelling textbooks.

(2) Despite the fact that responses obtained supported Silvern's hypotheses, there is some question as to what the first part of the instrument is actually measuring. When we ask about what "most people think," are we measuring sex stereotypes or perceptions of other people's stereotypes? Would different results be obtained if the first part of the instrument asked the respondents to answer in terms of their own beliefs rather than in terms of their perceptions of what other persons believe?

(3) Potential users should consider whether they believe that the second part of the instrument, which asks which "kid you would like best," is really a measure of social desirability. Arguments both pro and con can be made regarding whether "liking best" is the same as "social desirability."

SOURCE: See Silvern, 1977 (filler items and stick figures are not included).

BIBLIOGRAPHY:

Silvern, L. E. "Children's Sex Roles: Femininity Has the Advantage." Paper presented at 56th annual meeting of the Western Psychological Association, Los Angeles, April 1976. (ERIC Document Reproduction Service No. ED 138 895.)
Silvern, L. E. "Children's Sex Role Preferences: Stronger Among Girls than Boys." *Sex Roles,* 1977, *3,* 159-171.

---

81. SIMMONS-TURNER SEX ROLE STEREOTYPES SCALE

AUTHORS: Alan B. Simmons and Jean E. Turner

DATE: 1976

VARIABLE: Tendency to sex stereotype personality traits

TYPE OF INSTRUMENT: Summated rating scale

DESCRIPTION: The scale consists of nineteen adjective phrases that could be used to describe people. The adjective phrases include five masculine-typed desirable adjectives, six feminine-typed desirable adjectives, three masculine-typed undesirable adjectives, three feminine-typed undesirable adjectives, one masculine-typed neutral adjective, and one feminine-typed neutral adjective. There are five response options for each item: "Men are much more likely," "Men are somewhat more likely," "Men and women are equally likely," "Women are somewhat more likely," and "Women are much more likely."

PREVIOUSLY ADMINISTERED TO: Mothers and their children, ages 12-19

APPROPRIATE FOR: Ages 14 and older

ADMINISTRATION: The scale can be self-administered and can be completed in less than ten minutes.

SAMPLE ITEMS: *Masculine, desirable:* To be not easily excited
Feminine, desirable: To be affectionate
Masculine, undesirable: To be dominating
Feminine, undesirable: To be excitable in a crisis

> *Masculine, neutral:* To be aggressive in social situations
> *Feminine, neutral:* To be emotional

SCORING: Items are objectively scored and equally weighted. The responses to the individual items are averaged to yield a "stereotype sumscore." High scores indicate close agreement with prevailing stereotypes.

DEVELOPMENT: College students wrote separate descriptions of "women in general" and "men in general." A total of 240 adjectives were extracted from the written descriptions. The 240 adjectives were then given to another group of students who independently rated each adjective as to whether it was "more likely to be revealed by men" or "more likely to be revealed by women." There were significant differences on the male versus female assignment of 99 adjectives. A third group of students rated the social desirability of the 99 adjectives, and a factor analysis of the responses to the 99 adjectives was also performed. A set of twenty-one items was selected (1) to represent the central attributes revealed in the factor analysis and (2) to yield a balance between socially desirable and socially undesirable traits in males and in females. When the scale of twenty-one items was completed by another sample, it was found that two items were not stereotyped. These two items were eliminated, resulting in a scale of nineteen items.

RELIABILITY: No data are provided.

VALIDITY: The authors do not discuss the issue of validity but do report that there were no significant differences between the responses given by mothers and the responses given by their children.

NOTES AND COMMENTS: (1) The same scale can be used as a measure of sex role self-concept. Each adjective or adjective phrase is inserted into a statement that includes five response options, for example, "In comparison with others of my own sex, I am [much less, somewhat less, equally, somewhat more, or much more] likely to be excitable in a crisis." Each item is assigned a score between 1 and 5, with 5 points assigned to the female-stereotyped response. Item scores are averaged to yield an overall score, in which a high score indicates a feminine self-concept and a low score indicates a masculine self-concept.

(2) Though the scale has been used with children as young as 12 years old, the vocabulary level of some of the descriptive words and phrases may be too difficult for a child that young. Even the recommendation that the scale be used with persons as young as 14 may be questionable. Research is needed to determine empirically the appropriate age level with which this scale can be used.

(3) The authors define the adjective phrases in the journal article, but apparently they did not define them on the scale itself. This can affect the results obtained with the scale, because respondents may not all interpret the adjectives alike. For example, the authors define "emotional" as "to show feelings easily." Without the definition, a respondent might interpret it to mean "cries easily."

(4) The absence of reliability and validity data makes it difficult to evaluate the scale.

SOURCE: See Simmons and Turner, 1976.

BIBLIOGRAPHY:

Simmons, A. B., and Turner, J. E. "The Socialization of Sex Roles and Fertility Ideals: A Study of Two Generations in Toronto." *Journal of Comparative Family Studies,* 1976, *7,* 255-271.

82. STEFFLRE-RESNIKOFF-LEZOTTE OCCUPATIONAL PRESTIGE SCALE

AUTHORS: Buford Stefflre, Arthur Resnikoff, and Lawrence Lezotte

DATE: 1968 (used 1966)

VARIABLE: The effect of sex of worker on occupational prestige

TYPE OF INSTRUMENT: Rating scale

DESCRIPTION: Before a respondent completes the scale, she is directed to establish anchor points for the scale in the following way: She is shown a normal curve with five labeled points: extreme left (A), midway between extreme left and center (B), center (C), midway between center and extreme right (D), extreme right (E). Occupational prestige is explained, as well as how occupational prestige could relate to the normal curve. The respondent is then directed to identify a worker who would fall at each of points A, B, C, D, and E on the normal curve. In other words, she is asked to think of a person who would have the least prestige (point A) and give her a rating of 1. Similarly, she is asked to think of a person who would have the most prestige (point E) and give her a rating of 9. When she indicates the person who would fall at each of the points B, C, and D, she is asked to assign her a rating of 3, 5, and 7, respectively. After the anchor points have been established, the respondent is given a list of twenty workers and asked to assign each one a rating between 1 and 9 using her own anchor points.

There are four forms of the scale: Form A identifies each worker as male; Form B identifies each worker as female; Form C alternates the sex of each worker beginning with a male; and Form D alternates the sex of each worker beginning with a female. A respondent completes only one form of the scale.

PREVIOUSLY ADMINISTERED TO: College students

APPROPRIATE FOR: Ages 16 and older

ADMINISTRATION: The scale can be self-administered and can be completed in about fifteen minutes.

SAMPLE ITEMS: Male architect for leading architectural firm
                          Female bookkeeper for a small manufacturing company

SCORING: The rating assigned by the respondent is the score for that item. No total scores are obtained.

DEVELOPMENT: The model for developing the interval rating scale was taken from Ronning, Stewart, and Stellwagen (1965). Occupations that "might reasonably be filled by either men or by women" (p. 767) were selected for the scale.

RELIABILITY: Test-retest reliability was estimated for thirty-seven college students who completed the scale on two occasions separated by a two-week interval. The test-retest reliability was .91 (Stefflre, Resnikoff, and Lezotte, 1968).

VALIDITY: Occupations were rank ordered according to their average prestige score. The ranking was compared with the results reported by Reiss and others (1961). Rank-order correlations were computed separately for males and for females and also for the two administration times (spring and fall). The correlations ranged from .79 to .82, suggesting that the instrument does measure occupational prestige (Stefflre, Resnikoff, and Lezotte, 1968).

NOTES AND COMMENTS: The authors administered the scale to two different groups of students enrolled in a pupil personnel services course. One group completed the scale during the spring semester and one completed it during the fall semester. The results were not consistent between the two semesters. The authors explain this inconsistency on the basis that their respondents were primarily students entering graduate work in school counseling. For these students, the scale might not be valid. These students might be more likely to be egalitarian in their assignment of occupational prestige, or they might be sufficiently sophisticated to inhibit the expression of their biases.

SOURCE: See Stefflre, Resnikoff, and Lezotte, 1968.

BIBLIOGRAPHY:

*Reiss, A. J., Jr., Duncan, O. D., Hatt, P. K., and North, C. C. *Occupations and Social Status.* New York: Free Press, 1961.
*Ronning, R. R., Stewart, L. H., and Stellwagen, W. R. "An Equisection Scale of Interests: A Preliminary Report." *Journal of Counseling Psychology,* 1965, *12,* 176-181.
Stefflre, B., Resnikoff, A., and Lezotte, L. "The Relationship of Sex to Occupational Prestige." *Personnel and Guidance Journal,* 1968, *46,* 765-772.

83. VENER-WEESE SEX STEREOTYPES OF SEX-LINKED OBJECTS

AUTHORS: Arthur M. Vener and Audray Weese

DATE: 1965

VARIABLE: Ability to correctly stereotype sex-linked objects

TYPE OF INSTRUMENT: Sorting task

DESCRIPTION: The instrument includes forty-four objects, with eleven objects falling into each of four categories: female-stereotyped appearance-related objects; female-stereotyped task-related objects; masculine-stereotyped appearance-related objects; and masculine-stereotyped task-related objects. The objects are all placed in a suitcase. The child is asked to remove the objects, one at a time, and indicate whether each object belongs to a "Mommy" or a "Daddy."

PREVIOUSLY ADMINISTERED TO: Ages 2½-11

APPROPRIATE FOR: Ages 2½-11

ADMINISTRATION: The instrument as described must be individually administered. It could be adapted for paper-and-pencil group administration to children over age 7.

SAMPLE ITEMS: *Female-stereotyped task-related:* iron, dustpan
Female-stereotyped appearance-related: brassiere, lipstick
Male-stereotyped task-related: screw driver, wrench
Male-stereotyped appearance-related: necktie, tennis shoes

SCORING: The number of errors made in classification is counted. Zero to four errors are considered low; five to eight errors are considered medium; and nine to twenty-eight errors are considered high.

DEVELOPMENT: Sixty-three task- and appearance-related objects were selected and sex typed by a panel of four adult judges. The selected objects were pretested on a sample of twenty-five boys and twenty-five girls between the ages of 7 and 11. The objects were placed in a suitcase and each child was directed to indicate whether the object belonged to a "Mom" or a "Dad" or to both. When at least 96 percent of the child judges agreed with the adult judges, the object was retained for the instrument. As a result of applying this criterion, forty-four objects were selected.

RELIABILITY: No data are provided.

VALIDITY: Vener and Weese (1965) administered the instrument to sixty boys and sixty girls between the ages of 2½ and 5 years. As would be expected, younger children made significantly more errors than older children (p < .001).

NOTES AND COMMENTS: The strongest criticism militating against the use of this scale without up-to-date verification of the sex stereotypes of the objects comes from Vener and Weese (1965, p. 50), who stated: "Definitions of the sex-linked appropriateness of cultural paraphernalia do not remain stable from generation to generation in a rapidly changing society such as ours."

SOURCE: See Vener and Weese, 1965.

BIBLIOGRAPHY:

Vener, A. M., and Snyder, C. A. "The Preschool Child's Awareness and Anticipation of Adult Sex Roles." *Sociometry,* 1966, *29,* 159-168.
Vener, A. M., and Weese, A. "The Preschool Child's Perceptions of Adults' Sex-Linked Objects." *Journal of Home Economics,* 1965, *57,* 49-54.

---

84. WORTHY-CRADDICK MASCULINITY-FEMININITY INDEX OF SEXUALLY SYMBOLIC CONCEPTS

AUTHORS: Morgan Worthy and Ray A. Craddick

DATE: 1969

VARIABLE: Sex stereotypes of objects

TYPE OF INSTRUMENT: Semantic differential scale

DESCRIPTION: The instrument consists of eighteen stimulus concepts, eight of which are theoretically feminine and ten of which are theoretically masculine. Each concept is followed by six bipolar adjectives. The adjectives are: hard-soft, small-large, delicate-rugged, masculine-feminine, heavy-light, and weak-strong. The adjective pairs are placed at the ends of seven-point semantic differential scales.

PREVIOUSLY ADMINISTERED TO: College students and psychiatric patients

APPROPRIATE FOR: Ages 14 and older

ADMINISTRATION: The scale can be self-administered and can be completed in fifteen to twenty minutes.

SAMPLE ITEMS: Ship
                        Foot
                        Butterfly

SCORING: Scores are obtained for each concept; typically, no scores are obtained for persons. Items are objectively scored and equally weighted. Higher scores indicate masculine stereotypes. Item scores across the six scales are summed for each person and then averaged across persons. This yields a mean potency score for each concept.

DEVELOPMENT: No data are provided.

RELIABILITY: No data are provided.

VALIDITY: Archer and Burgess (1970) compared mean potency scores for each concept with mean scores on just the masculinity-femininity adjective scale. Given that a score of 4 represents the neutral point on the scale, they specified that a mean rating above 4 on the masculinity-femininity scale classifies the concept as masculine and a mean rating below 4 classifies the concept as feminine. Likewise a mean rating above 24 (4 x 6 concepts = 24) on the potency scale classifies the concept as masculine and a mean rating below 24 on the potency scale classifies the concept as feminine. Using the responses from fifty college students, they found that twelve of the eighteen concepts were classified the same regardless of whether the mean potency score or mean masculinity-femininity score was used to classify the concepts. Six concepts, however, were classified differently depending on whether potency scores or masculinity-femininity scores were used for classification.

Craddick and Worthy (1970) computed the mean masculinity-femininity score and the mean potency score for each concept that had been rated by seventy-two college students. Fourteen of the eighteen concepts were classified the same regardless of which mean score was the basis of the classification; four concepts were classified differently depending on whether masculinity-femininity scores or potency scores were the basis for classification. Craddick and Worthy report a correlation of .74 between masculinity-femininity scores and potency scores.

Brar (1973) looked at the responses from twenty-five female and twenty-five male psychiatric patients. The correlation between the sexes was .971.

NOTES AND COMMENTS: (1) Althouse (1970) followed the general procedure of Worthy-Craddick, but the concepts he used were thirty Freudian sexually symbolic nouns and thirty Jungian sexually symbolic nouns.

(2) The title of the scale, which includes the term "sexually symbolic concepts," may be somewhat misleading. Worthy and Craddick (1969, p. 78) explain that the concepts included on the scale are "presumed to symbolize masculinity or femininity."

(3) Worthy and Craddick (1969) do not provide a rationale for why they presume that their bipolar adjectives, which load on a potency factor (Osgood, Suci, and Tannenbaum, 1957), should measure masculinity-femininity.

SOURCE: See Worthy and Craddick, 1969.

BIBLIOGRAPHY:

Althouse, R. H. "A Semantic Differential Investigation of Sexually Symbolic Concepts: Freud and Jung." *Journal of Projective Techniques and Personality Assessment,* 1970, *34,* 507-512.

Archer, G. S., and Burgess, I. S. "A Further Investigation of Sexually Symbolic Concepts Using the Semantic Differential Technique." *Journal of Projective Techniques and Personality Assessment,* 1970, *34,* 369-372.

Brar, H. S. "Semantic Differential Investigation of Sexually Symbolic Concepts Using a Psychiatric Population." *Journal of Personality Assessment,* 1973, *37,* 260-262.

Craddick, R. A., and Worthy, M. "Reply to Archer and Burgess on Their Investigation of Symbolic Concepts Using the Semantic Differential Technique." *Journal of Projective Techniques and Personality Assessment,* 1970, *34,* 373-374.

*Osgood, C. E., Suci, G. J., and Tannenbaum, P. H. *The Measurement of Meaning.* Urbana: University of Illinois Press, 1957.

Worthy, M., and Craddick, R. A. "Semantic Differential Investigation of Sexually Symbolic Concepts." *Journal of Projective Techniques and Personality Assessment,* 1969, *33,* 78-80.

5

❖ ❖ ❖ ❖ ❖ ❖ ❖ ❖ ❖ ❖ ❖

Sex Role Prescriptions

❖ ❖

The seven instruments contained in this chapter are all intended to assess sex role prescriptions; that is, they can be used to determine which personality traits and behaviors are considered appropriate for women and which are considered appropriate for men. These instruments are closely related to those classified as measuring sex stereotypes. The major difference is that these measure "what ought to be," and the instruments under "Sex Stereotypes" measure "what is." (However, the sex-stereotypes measures might also be used to measure sex role prescriptions by modifying the directions to ask "what ought to be.")

With the exception of one instrument that was first introduced in the literature in 1959, the measures in this chapter have all appeared in the literature since 1970; thus, they are relatively new. None are appropriate for children; the minimum age for respondents is 12 years old. No one instrument in this chapter stands out as being superior to the others, and no instrument stands out as being used frequently or by a variety of researchers.

Because the measures in this chapter are closely related to measures of sex stereotypes, there is overlap in the problems that apply to both types of measures. Problems pertaining to the content validity of the instruments, the transparency of their items, and the behavioral implications of their scores were described in detail in the previous chapter and apply equally to the measures in this chapter.

85. BOTT IDEAL WOMAN QUESTIONNAIRE

AUTHOR: Margaret M. Bott

DATE: 1970

VARIABLE: Perceptions of the ideal woman

TYPE OF INSTRUMENT: True-false

DESCRIPTION: The instrument consists of eighteen items, each of which is an ending to the sentence stem "My ideal woman." For each of the eighteen items, the respondent is asked to indicate whether she believes the item is true or false.

PREVIOUSLY ADMINISTERED TO: Females in grade 11 and college students

APPROPRIATE FOR: Ages 14 and older

ADMINISTRATION: The instrument is self-administered and can be completed in five to ten minutes.

SAMPLE ITEMS: My ideal woman . . . is frightened by the thought of being in an automobile accident.

My ideal woman . . . is very slow in making up her mind.

SCORING: The author does not discuss scoring.

DEVELOPMENT: A pool of 120 items was prepared, including the items from the masculinity-femininity subscale of the Minnesota Multiphasic Personality Inventory (#52), the California Psychological Inventory Femininity Scale (#47), and three Masculinity-Femininity scales from the Vassar College Attitude Inventory (#58). The item pool was administered to eleventh-grade and freshman college women. An analysis of variance was performed on the item frequencies, and fifty items were identified that discriminated at the .05 level. These fifty items were administered to another sample of eleventh-grade females. The eighteen discriminating items (probability level not specified) comprise the Bott Ideal Woman Questionnaire.

RELIABILITY: The instrument was administered to forty-five female and forty-eight male college students. The corrected split-half reliability was .68 for females and .78 for males.

VALIDITY: No data are provided.

NOTES AND COMMENTS: Eleven of the items on the instrument are negative characteristics, and many of those might be considered indicative of neuroticism. Of the remaining seven items, only one might be considered a positive attribute. Thus, in general, the instrument allows respondents to portray a negative or a nonnegative image of their ideal woman, but it does not allow respondents to portray a positive image of their ideal woman.

SOURCE: See Bott, 1970.

BIBLIOGRAPHY:

Bott, M. M. "The M-F Scale: Yesterday and Today." *Measurement and Evaluation in Guidance,* 1970, *3,* 92-96.

---

86. ELLIS-BENTLER TRADITIONAL SEX-DETERMINED ROLE STANDARDS SCALE

AUTHORS: Linda J. Ellis and Peter M. Bentler

DATE: 1973

VARIABLE: Attitudes toward traditional sex role standards

TYPE OF INSTRUMENT: Forced choice

DESCRIPTION: The instrument consists of thirty-eight pairs of statements. The statements comprising each pair refer to controversial behavioral restrictions placed on males and/or females. Each pair includes one statement that reflects approval of traditional sex role standards and one statement that reflects approval of egalitarian standards. The respondents are asked to select the one statement from each pair that best reflects their opinion.

PREVIOUSLY ADMINISTERED TO: College students and parents of preschoolers

APPROPRIATE FOR: Ages 16 and older

ADMINISTRATION: The instrument is self-administered and can be completed in less than half an hour.

SAMPLE ITEMS:

Pair 1: (A) A son should have the use of the family car more often than a daughter. (B) A son and daughter should have the same car privileges.

Pair 2: (A) A man should protect a woman from physical harm, even at his own expense. (B) The man should try to protect himself; the woman should try to protect herself.

SCORING: A person's score is equal to the number of items endorsed that reflect opposition to traditional sex-determined role standards. Scores can vary from 0 (very traditional) to 38 (very nontraditional).

DEVELOPMENT: Seventy-one item pairs were constructed. The item pairs concerned "sex role standards in domestic, social, sexual, legal, educational, and economic areas"

(Ellis and Bentler, 1973, p. 29). A few of the item pairs were adapted from the Belief Pattern Scale for Measuring Attitudes Toward Feminism (#172). All of the item pairs were intended to be "straightforward and controversial, and they represented issues on which the subjects probably had opinions resistant to change" (Ellis and Bentler, 1973, p. 30). The seventy-one item pairs were administered to seventy-six college men and seventy-six college women. Using the responses from these students, ten item pairs were eliminated because of extreme endorsement frequencies. Two factors were extracted from a factor analysis. Since an inspection of the factors indicated that the two factors did not differ in content, the items with the highest loading on each factor were selected for the final instrument.

RELIABILITY: Internal consistency (alpha) reliabilities were computed using the responses from the 152 college students who completed the instrument. The reliability was .91 for women, .88 for men, and .90 for the sexes combined (Ellis and Bentler, 1973).

VALIDITY: Using the data from the same 152 college students, Ellis and Bentler (1973) found that male and female college students who support traditional role standards are more likely to report a difference between their self-perceptions and their perceptions of the opposite sex. Furthermore, for female college students and for males and females considered together, those who support traditional role standards perceive greater differences between males and females.

Contrary to prediction, Falbo (1975) did not find a relationship between scores on this scale and scores on the Bem Sex Role Inventory (#32), a measure of masculinity-femininity-androgyny.

NOTES AND COMMENTS: Mahoney (1975) compared scores that college students obtained on this instrument with scores they obtained on the Rokeach Value Survey.

SOURCE: Peter Bentler
         Department of Psychology
         University of California
         Los Angeles, California 90024

BIBLIOGRAPHY:

Ellis, L. J., and Bentler, P. M. "Traditional Sex-Determined Role Standards and Sex Stereotypes." *Journal of Personality and Social Psychology*, 1973, *25*, 28-34.

Falbo, T. "Sex Role Typing and Sex in the Use of Susceptibility to Influence." Paper presented at 83rd annual meeting of the American Psychological Association, Chicago, August 1975.

Falbo, T. "Multidimensional Scaling of Power Strategies." *Journal of Personality and Social Psychology*, 1977, *35*, 537-548.

Mahoney, J. "An Analysis of the Axiological Structures of Traditional and Proliberation Men and Women." *Journal of Psychology*, 1975, *90*, 31-39.

Thompson, S. K. "The Developmental Usage of Labels in Early Sex Typing and Gender Identification." Unpublished doctoral dissertation, University of California, 1973. (*Dissertation Abstracts International*, 1974, *34*[11-B], 5665.)

Thompson, S. K. "Gender Labels and Early Sex Role Development." *Child Development*, 1975, *46*, 339-347.

87. MASCULINITY-FEMININITY SCALE

AUTHOR: Thomas M. Kando

DATE: 1972

VARIABLE: Attitudes toward traditional sex ascriptions

TYPE OF INSTRUMENT: Summated rating scale

DESCRIPTION: The scale consists of sixty-four statements, each of which is followed by four response options: strongly agree, agree, disagree, strongly disagree. The items can be classified into six areas: attitudinal sex ascriptions (three items), psychological sex ascriptions (nine items), ascriptions of skills and responsibilities based on sex (ten items), occupational sex ascriptions (twenty-four items), structural role ascriptions based on sex (three items), and ascriptions of gender attributes (fifteen items).

PREVIOUSLY ADMINISTERED TO: Males, females, and feminized transsexuals, ages 18 and older

APPROPRIATE FOR: Ages 16 and older

ADMINISTRATION: The scale can be self-administered and can generally be completed in twenty to twenty-five minutes.

SAMPLE ITEMS:

Attitudinal sex ascriptions: Premarital sex relations are more permissible for men than for women.

Psychological sex ascriptions: Men must be bold while women should conform.

Ascriptions of skills and responsibilities based on sex: Men must be better drivers than women.

Occupational ascriptions: Males—medical doctor; Females—nurse [exact wording of statement not provided].

Structural role ascriptions based on sex: Ultimately, a woman should submit to her husband's decisions.

Ascriptions of gender attributes: It should be more important for a woman than for a man to be physically attractive and young.

SCORING: Items are objectively scored and equally weighted. Total scores can range from 64 (little support for sex stereotypes) to 256 (maximum support for sex stereotypes).

DEVELOPMENT: The items were originally suggested from a review of the literature concerning sex roles. The items were selected on the basis of judgment and face validity.

RELIABILITY: Ten college students each completed the test on two occasions separated by a one-week interval. Spearman's rho, computed for the responses of each of the ten students, ranged from .996 to .999 (Kando, 1974).

VALIDITY: Total scores successfully discriminated between men and women (p < .001). Fifty-eight of the sixty-four individual items also successfully discriminated between men and women (Kando, 1974).

Kando (1974) predicted that women, men, and transsexuals would differ in their scores on the Masculinity-Femininity Scale. His prediction was supported in that the seventeen women he tested were the least conservative, the seventeen men were more conservative, and the seventeen transsexuals were the most conservative.

NOTES AND COMMENTS: (1) Apparently, the sixty-four-item Masculinity-Femininity Scale was part of a larger scale consisting of eighty-four items. Information on the other twenty items is not provided.

(2) Kando (1972) administered the scale in two forms. He used the scale as described here, and he also reworded the items to phrase them as facts about oneself (for example, "I know a great deal about politics"). He then used the difference between the masculinity-femininity scores (based on all eighty-four items) and scores on the rephrased version to obtain a measure of role strain.

(3) The scale is also described in *Family Measurement Techniques* (Straus and Brown, 1978, pp. 110-111).

SOURCE: See Kando, 1974.

BIBLIOGRAPHY:

Kando, T. M. "Role Strain: A Comparison of Males, Females, and Transsexuals." *Journal of Marriage and the Family*, 1972, *34,* 459-464.
Kando, T. M. "Males, Females, and Transsexuals: A Comparative Study of Sexual Conservatism." *Journal of Homosexuality*, 1974, *1,* 45-64.
*Straus, M. A., and Brown, B. W. *Family Measurement Techniques: Abstracts of Published Instruments, 1935-1974.* Minneapolis: University of Minnesota Press, 1978.

---

88. NADLER CHIVALRY SCALE

AUTHORS: Eugene B. Nadler and William R. Morrow

DATE: 1959

VARIABLE: Chivalrous attitudes toward women

TYPE OF INSTRUMENT: Summated rating scale

DESCRIPTION: The scale consists of eighteen statements regarding chivalrous behavior toward women. Seventeen of the items are phrased to reflect support for chivalrous behavior toward women. Seven items involve behaviors in which the man shows superficial protection or assistance toward women; six of the items involve behaviors in which men show special deference toward women; and the remaining five items involve support for deference toward women in an abstract sense. Each item is accompanied by six response alternatives ranging from strong agreement to strong disagreement.

PREVIOUSLY ADMINISTERED TO: Male college students

APPROPRIATE FOR: Ages 16 and older

ADMINISTRATION: The scale can be self-administered and can be completed in about six minutes.

SAMPLE ITEMS:

Superficial protection and assistance in conduct toward women: No gentleman should allow a lady to soil her hands with messy work if he can possibly convince her that it is easier for him to do it.

Special deference in conduct toward women: A gentleman should remove his hat and hold it in his hand when a lady enters the elevator in which he is a passenger.

Support for deference toward women in an abstract sense: Although fighting a duel for the honor of a lady is a custom which is not practiced in the modern world, the idea behind this custom should certainly be maintained.

SCORING: Items are objectively scored and equally weighted. Total scores can range from 18 (opposed to chivalry) to 126 (supportive of chivalry).

DEVELOPMENT: A pool of twenty-five items was administered to sixty-two college men. An item analysis was performed comparing responses from men scoring in the upper and lower 25 percent of the distribution of total scores. Items that discriminated poorly were revised or eliminated. This resulted in a scale of eighteen items.

RELIABILITY: The scale was administered to eighty-three college men. The corrected split-half reliability was .86 (Nadler and Morrow, 1959).

VALIDITY: The eighty-three college men also completed three other scales: the Nadler Open Subordination of Women Scale (#191); a measure of ethnocentrism; and a measure of fascism. As predicted the Nadler Chivalry Scale correlated positively with the other three measures. The correlation with Nadler Open Subordination of Women Scale was .35 (p < .01); the correlation with the measure of ethnocentrism was .73 (p < .01); and the correlation with the measure of fascism was .60 (p < .01) (Nadler and Morrow, 1959).

NOTES AND COMMENTS: (1) When Nadler used the scale, it was interspersed with the items from the Nadler Open Subordination of Women Scale (#191); a measure of ethnocentrism; and a measure of fascism.

(2) Most of the items on the scale would be considered obsolete today.

(3) The scale is also described in *Scale for the Measurement of Attitudes* (Shaw and Wright, 1967, pp. 459-461).

SOURCE: See Nadler, 1953; Nadler and Morrow, 1959; or Shaw and Wright, 1967, pp. 460-461.

BIBLIOGRAPHY:

Nadler, E. B. "The Measurement of Chivalrous and Hostile Attitudes Toward Women." Unpublished master's thesis, Western Reserve University, 1953.
Nadler, E. B., and Morrow, W. R. "Authoritarian Attitudes Toward Women, and Their Correlates." *Journal of Social Psychology*, 1959, *49*, 113-123.
*Shaw, M. E., and Wright, J. M. *Scales for the Measurement of Attitudes.* New York: McGraw-Hill, 1967.
Werner, M. E. "A Scale for the Measurement of 'Sexist' Attitudes." Unpublished doctoral dissertation, Columbia University, 1973. (*Dissertation Abstracts International*, 1973, *34*[1-A], 180-181.)

---

89. SEX ROLE SCALE I AND II

AUTHORS: Sven Marke and Ingrid Gottfries

DATE: 1970

VARIABLES: Traditional versus egalitarian sex role prescriptions for boys and girls; traditional versus egalitarian sex role prescriptions for marital partners

TYPE OF INSTRUMENT: Summated rating scale

DESCRIPTION: Sex Role Scale I consists of seven subscales: Division of Home Work, Nursing Interests, Aggressiveness, Preoccupation with Looks, Technical Interests, Antisocial Behaviors, and Emotionality. Each subscale contains a brief description of six activities or emotions. The respondents are directed to think of boys and girls between the ages of 15 and 18 and to indicate for each item whether it is appropriate for boys or for girls. Five response options are provided: appropriate only for boys, appropriate mostly for boys, equally appropriate or inappropriate for boys and girls, appropriate mostly for girls, and appropriate only for girls. Sex Role Scale II consists of five subscales: Division of Home Work, Expressive Leader, Home versus Occupation, Instrumental Leader, and Dominance. Again each subscale contains six items. For these items, the respondents are asked to consider a family consisting of a husband and wife who are both gainfully employed outside the home and two children between the ages of 3 and 8. The respondent is to indicate who is being described in the item. The specific response options are not provided, but they are comparable to the ones provided with Sex Role Scale I.

PREVIOUSLY ADMINISTERED TO: Age 16

APPROPRIATE FOR: Ages 12 and older

ADMINISTRATION: The scales are self-administered and both can be completed within thirty to forty-five minutes.

SAMPLE ITEMS:

SEX ROLE SCALE I

Division of Home Work: Help with the house cleaning at home

Nursing Interests: Interest oneself in an occupation that involves care and upbringing of children

Aggressiveness: Watch films about war and crime

Preoccupation with Looks: Being careless about hair tidiness

Technical Interests: Building model airplanes

Antisocial Behaviors: Mischief making and playing pranks

Emotionality: Not crying when injured

SEX ROLE SCALE II

Division of Home Work: Be the one mostly concerned with washing up

Expressive Leader: Be the one who usually comforts the children when they are upset

Home versus Occupation: Stay home from work when the children are sick

Instrumental Leader: Be the one who mostly tries to teach the children to become independent

Dominance: Be the one to decide in questions of money and economy

SCORING: Items are objectively scored and equally weighted. High scores indicate a more conservative and less egalitarian ideology. Low scores indicate a more liberal or egalitarian ideology. Separate scores are obtained on the two sex role scales and each of the twelve subscales.

DEVELOPMENT: Sex Role Scale I is based on a scale previously used by Rommetveit (1955). Rommetveit's scale includes six subscales: Division of Work, Receptive Interests, Parent-Child Relationships, Preoccupation with Looks, Aggressiveness, and Religious Behavior. In developing Sex Role Scale I, two scales from Rommetveit were omitted—Parent-Child Relationships and Religious Behavior—and three others were added—Emotionality, Sexual Contact Behavior, and Occupations. On the basis of pretesting with 123 males and 149 females, four subscales were retained with slight modifications. The retained subscales were: Division of Home Work, Aggressiveness, Emotionality, and Preoccupation with Looks. Receptive Interests was divided into two subscales: Technical Interests and Nursing Interests. The subscale Antisocial Behavior was added as a supplement to Aggressiveness.

In developing Sex Role Scale II, five subscales were pretested with 123 males and 149 females. The subscales were: Home versus Occupation, Dominance, Division of Home Work, Leisure-Time Habits, and Special Attributes. On the basis of the pretesting, three subscales were retained: Division of Home Work, Home versus Occupation, and Dominance. Two new subscales were added: Instrumental Leader and Expressive Leader.

RELIABILITY: Item analyses based on the responses of 350 boys and 350 girls with an average age of 16 indicated that "the different subscales can be said to fill conventional demands of homogeneity" (Marke and Gottfries, 1970, p. 7).

VALIDITY: Significant differences were found between the responses from 350 males and 350 females on eight of the twelve subscales; the significant differences between sexes were found on Division of Home Work, Nursing Interests, Aggressiveness, Emotionality, Expressive Leader, Home versus Occupation, Instrumental Leader, and Dominance. Females expressed more egalitarian ideology than did males (Marke and Gottfries, 1970).

NOTES AND COMMENTS: (1) The intercorrelations between the twelve subscales were computed using the data from 280 males and 303 females. For males, the intercorrelations range from .11 to .55; for females, they range from .07 to .44 (Marke and Gottfries, 1970).

(2) A factor analysis was performed on the responses from the 700 adolescents. Four factors were labeled: Factor I—Norms concerning home work; Factor II—Norms concerning aggressive behavior; Factor III—Norms concerning dominance in the family; and Factor IV—Norms concerning emotional-sensitive behavior. The factors are not pure; in general, items load on more than one factor. Based on the factor-analytic results, four indexes were developed, with one index corresponding to each of the four factors. Index I contains eighteen items; the remaining three indexes each contain twelve items. A total score for the four indexes is obtained. Marke and Gottfries (1970) report the intercorrelations between the four indices based on the responses from 278 males and 295 females. For males, the intercorrelations range from .35 to .49; for females the intercorrelations range from .35 to .51. They also report the correlation between each of the indexes and total score. For males, the correlations are .80 for Index I, .72 for Index II, .63 for Index III, and .71 for Index IV. For females, the corresponding correlations are .75, .67, .64, and .69. These high correlations indicate that the indexes are not independent of each other. Significant differences were found between the scores of males and females on indexes I, II, and IV. Furthermore, significant differences were obtained between males and females on the Index Total.

Correlations between a measure of antifeminism and scores on the four indexes tended to be low. For females, the correlations were .20 for Index I, .02 for Index II, .12 for Index III, and .00 for Index IV. The corresponding correlations for males were .28, .21, .19, and .18. The correlations between the antifeminism measure and the Index Total was .23 for females and .27 for males. Both are significantly different from zero (p < .01) (Marke and Gottfries, 1970).

(3) The scale was developed and used in Sweden.

SOURCE: See Marke and Gottfries, 1970.

BIBLIOGRAPHY:

Marke, S., and Gottfries, I. "Measurement of Sex Role Perception and Its Relation to Psychological Masculinity-Femininity." *Psychological Research Bulletin,* 1970, *10,* 1-33.

*Rommetveit, R. *Social Norms and Roles.* Oslo, Norway: Akademiskforlag, 1955.

90. SEX-ROLE TRADITIONALISM SCALE

AUTHORS: Zick Rubin and Letitia A. Peplau

DATE: 1973

VARIABLE: Traditional versus nontraditional sex role attitudes

TYPE OF INSTRUMENT: Summated rating scale

DESCRIPTION: The scale consists of ten statements relating to marital roles, parental roles, women and work, social etiquette, and the women's liberation movement. Five statements reflect traditional attitudes and five items reflect nontraditional attitudes. Responses are indicated on a six-point scale ranging from "strongly agree" to "strongly disagree."

PREVIOUSLY ADMINISTERED TO: College students

APPROPRIATE FOR: Ages 16 and older

ADMINISTRATION: The scale is self-administered and can be completed in less than five minutes.

SAMPLE ITEMS: If husband and wife both have full-time jobs, the husband should devote just as much time to housekeeping as the wife should.
    When a couple is going somewhere by car, it's better for the man to do most of the driving.

SCORING: Items are objectively scored. The final score is the mean of the item scores and can range from 1 (nontraditional) to 6 (very traditional).

DEVELOPMENT: No information is provided.

RELIABILITY: The scale was completed by ninety-one dating college couples. For women, coefficient alpha was .83; for men, it was .81 (Peplau, 1976a).

VALIDITY: Peplau (1973) administered the scale to ninety-four dating college couples. She found no significant difference between the scores obtained by men and the scores obtained by women. Hammen and Peplau (1978) administered the scale to thirty-seven college men and thirty-seven college women. They report significant differences ($p < .01$) between the mean obtained by men ($\overline{X} = 33$) and the mean obtained by women ($\overline{X} = 26$). (They scored the scale by summing item scores for each individual rather than by taking the mean item score for each individual.)
    Peplau (1973) administered many other measures along with the Sex Role Traditionalism Scale. She reports that the correlation between responses to a single item measuring attitudes toward the women's liberation movement and scores on the Sex Role Traditionalism Scale was .65 for men ($p < .001$) and .69 for women ($p < .001$). Peplau (1973) also reports a correlation of .48 ($p < .001$) between dating couples' scores on the scale.

NOTES AND COMMENTS: (1) When Peplau (1973, 1975, 1976a, 1976b) used the scale, it included five items measuring romanticism.

(2) A factor analysis was performed on the responses from 147 dating couples. All items loaded on a single factor (Peplau, 1973).

(3) Peplau (1973) compared scores on the Sex Role Traditionalism Scale with measures of numerous other variables, including career orientation, authoritarianism, internality-externality, romanticism, liking, loving, self-ratings of creativity, attractiveness, intelligence, self-confidence, desirability as a date and as a marriage partner, achievement, length of present dating relationship, experience of intercourse with present partner, number of sexual partners, and frequency of church attendance. Kaplan (1976) and Peplau (1975) compared scores on the Sex Role Traditionalism Scale with measures of power in relationships. Hammen and Peplau (1978) compared Sex Role Traditionalism scores with measures of interaction and recall from same-sex and opposite-sex dyads.

SOURCE: See Peplau, 1973.

BIBLIOGRAPHY:

Hammen, C., and Peplau, L. A. "Brief Encounters: Impact of Gender, Sex Role Attitudes, and Partner's Gender on Interaction and Cognition." *Sex Roles,* 1978, *1,* 75-90.

Kaplan, S. L. "The Assertion of Power: Ideals, Perceptions, and Styles." Paper presented at 84th annual meeting of the American Psychological Association, Washington, D.C., September 1976.

Peplau, L. A. "The Impact of Fear of Success, Sex Role Attitudes, and Opposite-Sex Relationships on Women's Intellectual Performance." Unpublished doctoral dissertation, Harvard University, 1973.

Peplau, L. A. "Power in Dating Relationships." In J. Freeman (Ed.), *Women: A Feminist Perspective.* (2nd ed.) Palo Alto, Calif.: Mayfield, 1975.

Peplau, L. A. "Fear of Success in Dating Couples." *Sex Roles,* 1976a, *2,* 249-258.

Peplau, L. A. "Impact of Fear of Success and Sex Role Attitudes on Women's Competitive Achievement." *Journal of Personality and Social Psychology,* 1976b, *34,* 561-568.

---

91. SIMMONS-TURNER SEX ROLE STANDARDS SCALE

AUTHORS: Alan B. Simmons and Jean E. Turner

DATE: 1976

VARIABLE: Sex role standards for males' and females' behavior

TYPE OF INSTRUMENT: Rating scale

DESCRIPTION: The scale consists of eight statements concerning appropriate behavior for males and/or females. Each statement is to be rated on a scale ranging from 10 (disagree strongly) to 50 (agree strongly).

PREVIOUSLY ADMINISTERED TO: Mothers and children

APPROPRIATE FOR: Ages 12 and older

ADMINISTRATION: The scale can be self-administered and can be completed in less than five minutes.

SAMPLE ITEMS: It is all right for a wife to express her opinions, but the husband should always have the final say.
                The father should have the primary responsibility for punishing the children.

SCORING: Each item is assigned the score corresponding to the scale value marked by the respondent. High total scores indicate agreement with a "traditional" role for women.

DEVELOPMENT: No information is provided.

RELIABILITY: The intercorrelations between the items all equaled or exceeded .30.

VALIDITY: In a study conducted in Toronto, Canada, there was a significant difference in the scores obtained by mothers ($\overline{X}$ = 35.7) and their daughters ($\overline{X}$ = 28.6, p < .0005), with the daughters indicating less traditional attitudes. Significant differences were found between members of different religions. Catholic mothers of Italian extraction ($\overline{X}$ = 40.5) were significantly more traditional in their responses than were Protestant mothers of British extraction ($\overline{X}$ = 31.7, p < .05).

SOURCE: See Simmons and Turner, 1976.

BIBLIOGRAPHY:

Simmons, A. B., and Turner, J. E. "The Socialization of Sex Role and Fertility Ideals: A Study of Two Generations in Toronto." *Journal of Comparative Family Studies,* 1976, *7*, 255-271.

6

❖ ❖ ❖ ❖ ❖ ❖ ❖ ❖ ❖ ❖

Children's
Sex Roles

❖ ❖ ❖ ❖ ❖ ❖ ❖ ❖ ❖ ❖ ❖ ❖ ❖ ❖ ❖ ❖ ❖ ❖ ❖ ❖

The eleven instruments in this chapter focus on sex-typed behaviors or personality traits of children. There are only two types of instruments in this chapter: rating scales and summated rating scales. The majority of the scales are fairly new; eight first appeared in the literature after 1970.

Four of these scales are closely related to each other: the Feinman Measure of Disapproval of Appropriate-Sex Behavior (#98), the Feinman Measure of Disapproval of Cross-Sex Behavior (#99), the Feinman Measure of Approval of Cross-Sex and Cross-Age Behavior (#97), and the Feinman Measure of Approval of Appropriate Sex Role and Appropriate Age Role Behavior (#96). The first two are essentially identical except that the gender of the person in each of the items is reversed. The first scale describes behavior in which the subject is doing something that is considered sex appropriate, and the second scale describes the same behaviors but the subject is of the opposite sex, and therefore the behavior is considered sex inappropriate. The last two scales are also parallel to each other, but they are longer than the first two and assess reactions to age-appropriate and age-inappropriate behavior as well as to sex-appropriate and sex-inappropriate behavior. Though the first two scales contain ten items each and the last two contain forty-five items each, there is minimal overlap between the first two and the last two.

Two instruments (#95 and #102) measure attitudes toward female participation in sports. Because sports have traditionally been considered part of the masculine domain, female participation in sports can be classified as cross-sex behavior. Two scales (#93 and #100) assess evaluations of sex-typed traits in children; one refers to boys and one to girls. Two scales (#92 and #101) assess reactions to sex-appropriate or sex-inappropriate behavior in children, and one scale (#94) measures sex role bias in evaluating behavioral descriptions of children.

Perhaps the most striking problem arising in several of the instruments in this chapter is that they elicit logical and rational responses to issues that in actuality tend to be very emotional. More specifically, reactions to cross-sex behavior are probably motivated by unconscious feelings, and persons may have great difficulty in predicting their reactions until they actually confront the situation. Perhaps projective measures would be more effective in tapping unconsciously motivated reactions. Clearly more research is needed to determine what is actually being measured by scales that purport to measure reactions to cross-sex behavior.

---

92. ATKINSON-ENDSLEY PARENT-CHILD INTERACTION SURVEY

AUTHORS: Jean Atkinson and Richard C. Endsley

DATE: 1975

VARIABLE: Parents' reactions to sex-appropriate and sex-inappropriate behavior as described in hypothetical situations involving their offspring

TYPE OF INSTRUMENT: Summated rating scale

DESCRIPTION: The scale consists of fourteen hypothetical situations in which a child's interaction with another person is described. In half the situations the child is behaving in a typically masculine manner, and in the other half the child is behaving in a typically feminine manner. For each of the hypothetical situations, the parent is to indicate (1) how she feels about the child's behavior, (2) whether she would try to change the child's behavior, and (3) how important it is to change (or not change) the child's behavior. A seven-point scale, ranging from "strongly like" to "strongly dislike," is used to indicate feelings about the child's behavior. Desire to change the child's behavior is indicated on a yes-no scale. A seven-point scale, ranging from "very important" to "very unimportant," is used to indicate perceptions of the importance of changing (or not changing) the child's behavior. There are two forms of the test: one in which a son is the subject of each hypothetical situation and one in which a daughter is the subject of each hypothetical situation.

PREVIOUSLY ADMINISTERED TO: Parents of preschoolers

APPROPRIATE FOR: Ages 14 and older

ADMINISTRATION: The scale can be self-administered and can be completed in twenty minutes.

SAMPLE ITEMS:

Typical feminine behavior: After your dinner guests have all arrived, you ask your daughter to come meet them. You have difficulty coaxing her to do so, as she seems hesitant about meeting your guests.

Typical masculine behavior: While you are working in the yard, your daughter and her friends are playing nearby. You hear voices being raised and then see a playmate hit your daughter. Your daughter hits back and the playmate runs home crying.

SCORING: Two scores are obtained for the scale: a Like-Femininity score and an Importance-to-Encourage-Femininity score. The Like-Femininity score is obtained by assigning the maximum number of points (7) to the response indicating liking of feminine behaviors and to the response indicating disliking of masculine behaviors. The Importance-to-Encourage-Femininity score is obtained by assigning 7 points to the response indicating that it was very important to change masculine behaviors and very important not to change feminine behaviors. For both scales, item scores are summed to yield a total score, which can range from 14 to 98.

DEVELOPMENT: The authors of the scale judged whether the hypothetical situation illustrated feminine or masculine behavior.

RELIABILITY: The scale was completed twice by five mothers and five fathers. They completed the scale on two occasions separated by approximately one month. On the Like-Dislike ratings, the average change was .6 points per item for mothers and .7 points per item for fathers. The change in ratings ranged from .4 to 1.0 points for each of the fourteen items. In responding "yes" or "no" to whether they would try to change the child's behavior, mothers were consistent in their responses on sixty-seven out of the possible seventy instances (14 items x 5 mothers = 70). Fathers were consistent on only fifty of the seventy instances, which represents significantly less consistency than shown by the mothers (p < .01). Responses to the yes-no question regarding changing the child's behavior were combined with responses regarding the importance of change (or no change) to yield a fourteen-point scale. Mothers' scores differed by an average of 1.2 points per item on the two testings. Fathers' scores differed by an average of 2.7 points per item.

Item-total correlations were computed for like-dislike responses and total Like-Femininity score. Nine of the fourteen items were significantly correlated with the total score (p < .05). Similarly item-total correlations were computed for the importance-to-change ratings and total Importance-to-Encourage-Femininity score. Ten of the fourteen items were significantly correlated with the total score.

VALIDITY: The correlation was computed between the total score reflecting liking of feminine behaviors and the total score reflecting resistance to change feminine behaviors. The correlation was .78.

NOTES AND COMMENTS: It is indicated above that the scale is appropriate for persons who are 14 years and older. If the scale is used with anyone other than parents of preschoolers, it must be specified in the directions that the child in the stories should be assumed to be a preschooler.

SOURCE: Jean Atkinson
School of Home Economics
Oregon State University
Corvallis, Oregon 97331

BIBLIOGRAPHY:

Atkinson, J., and Endsley, R. C. "Influence of Sex of Child and Parent on Parental Reactions to Hypothetical Parent-Child Situations." *Genetic Psychology Monographs,* 1976, *94,* 131-147.

---

93. BOYS' STEREOTYPE SCALE (BSS)

AUTHOR: Arthur J. Rudy

DATE: 1965

VARIABLE: Evaluation of sex-typed traits in boys

TYPE OF INSTRUMENT: Rating scale

DESCRIPTION: The scale consists of seventy-eight trait-descriptive adjectives and short phrases. Of the seventy-eight items, thirty-five are stereotypically masculine, thirty-five are stereotypically feminine, and eight are neutral. The items are presented in alphabetical order. The respondent is directed to "imagine that someone has just told you that you are a boy who is _____" (Rudy, 1965) and to indicate how desirable the description would be. Seven response options are provided: very desirable, desirable, slightly desirable, neither desirable nor undesirable, slightly undesirable, undesirable, very undesirable.

PREVIOUSLY ADMINISTERED TO: Males, grades 9 and 10

APPROPRIATE FOR: Ages 12 and older

ADMINISTRATION: The scale can be self-administered and can be completed in less than half an hour.

SAMPLE ITEMS: Active
Adorable
Adventurous
Affectionate
Aggressive
Attractive

SCORING: Items are objectively scored and equally weighted. The scale yields two scores: mean desirability score on the Masculine subscale and mean desirability score on the Feminine subscale. The mean desirability score on the neutral items is used "to control for the effects of sex differences in rating tendencies" (Rudy, 1965, p. 40).

DEVELOPMENT: An initial item pool was compiled from a search of the literature and the responses of ninth and tenth graders to an open-ended question requesting a list of adjectives that describe boys. Items that were beyond the comprehension level of typical ninth and tenth graders were eliminated. Three scales were constructed with the remaining items. Each scale was given to a different group of sixty males with instructions to rate each item according to the frequency with which the item is used to describe boys or girls. Five response options were provided: boys almost always, boys more often, both boys and girls, girls more often, girls almost always. Half of the boys in each group completed the scale a second time one week later. Using the responses from these testings, it was determined whether each of the items was sex typed. If at least 65 percent of the boys agreed that the item was masculine (or feminine), and if there was at least 70 percent individual retest agreement regarding the masculinity (or femininity) of the item, then the item was considered sex typed (masculine or feminine). Items were considered neutral if the modal rating was in the central category and if the distribution in the two ends of the continuum was approximately equal.

RELIABILITY: The responses from thirty males who were tested on two occasions, separated by about one week, were used to estimate reliability. The test-retest reliability for the masculine subscale was .82; the test-retest reliability for the feminine subscale was .84 (Rudy, 1965).

VALIDITY: No data are provided.

NOTES AND COMMENTS: This scale was used in conjunction with a similar scale, the Girls' Stereotype Scale (#100). Of the seventy-eight items on the scales, thirty-five are identical on the two scales and forty-three are unique to the Boys' Stereotype Scale.

SOURCE: See Rudy, 1965.

BIBLIOGRAPHY:

Rudy, A. J. "Sex Role Perceptions in Early Adolescence." Unpublished doctoral dissertation, Columbia University, 1965. (*Dissertation Abstracts,* 1966, *26*[10], 6174-6175.)

Rudy, A. J. "Sex Role Perceptions in Early Adolescence." *Adolescence,* 1968-1969, *3,* 453-470.

94. CHASEN DIAGNOSTIC SEX ROLE BIAS SCALE

AUTHORS: Barbara Chasen and Sharon Weinberg

DATE: 1974

VARIABLE: Sex role bias in evaluating behavioral descriptions of children

TYPE OF INSTRUMENT: Rating scale

DESCRIPTION: The scale consists of ten brief case descriptions of "somewhat un-healthy" children between the ages of 8 and 10. Each case is followed by four rating scales: assessment of health/pathology is to be rated on a seven-point scale ranging from "extremely unhealthy" to "extremely healthy"; assessment of the priority of the referral is to be rated on a seven-point scale ranging from "do not see any problem here" to "refer to school psychologist, urgent"; treatment recommended is to be rated on a seven-point scale ranging from "none" to "extensive psychotherapy"; and the prognosis for the child, as an adolescent, if no treatment is provided is to be rated on a seven-point scale ranging from "extremely unhealthy" to "extremely healthy." Half of the cases describe boys and half describe girls. Two cases are included merely to detract respondents from recognizing which variables are being studied. The remaining eight cases vary along the dimensions of activity (defined as aggression and independence) and passivity (defined as nonaggression and dependence). Thus, there is a case describing a male child and a case describing a female child with each of the following dominant characteristics: aggressive, independent, nonaggressive, and dependent.

PREVIOUSLY ADMINISTERED TO: School psychologists

APPROPRIATE FOR: Mental health professionals and trainees, teachers and teacher trainees, other professionals who work with children

ADMINISTRATION: The scale is self-administered and can be completed in about forty-five minutes.

SAMPLE ITEM: *Female, aggressive:* Ethel, 10 years old, gets into frequent fights. She frequently throws things when angry. She breaks things when upset. She is not at all uncomfortable about aggression. She uses very harsh language. She gets angry and hostile when not winning at competitive games, and turns on the winner. She seems to really enjoy beating classmates at games.

SCORING: One score is obtained for each respondent. To find the score, the ratings as-signed to the two active boy cases (aggressive and independent) and to the two passive girls cases (nonaggressive and dependent) are added together; from that sum is subtracted the total of the ratings assigned to the two passive boy cases and the two active girls cases. A negative score indicates stereotypic bias; a positive score indicates counterstereotypic bias.

DEVELOPMENT: Cases were constructed and given to school psychologists with instruc-tions to rank order the cases according to degree of mental health. Initials instead of a child's name were used on each case to eliminate the possibility that the ratings would be affected by the sex of the child. Cases which were consistently ranked as healthier or less healthy than the other cases were changed to make them more equivalent to the other cases in terms of healthiness. All the school psychologists were able to categorize correctly all cases in terms of whether the described child was independent, dependent, aggressive, or nonaggressive. They were also all able to categorize correctly all cases in terms of whether the described child was active or passive. After the cases were rewritten they were given to another sample of five male and five female school psychologists with instructions to rate them on a nine-point scale indicating mental health status. Four additional cases were included to be rated. Two were intended to be descriptions of extremely healthy children and two were intended to be descriptions of extremely unhealthy children. For all cases, initials of children rather than names were again used. The mean ratings for the four extreme cases were different from the means of the eight "somewhat unhealthy" cases. Two of these four cases are included in the final scale but do not contribute to the score. A statistical analysis indicated that there was no difference in the mean ratings assigned to the eight "somewhat unhealthy" cases. Thus, it was concluded that these eight cases represent equivalent degrees of mental health.

RELIABILITY: A sample of ten school psychology students and ten accounting students completed the Chasen Diagnostic Sex Role Bias Scale on two occasions separated by three to four weeks. Using their responses, test-retest reliability was calculated to be .71 (Chasen, 1974).

VALIDITY: To determine if the scale had discriminative validity, it was administered to seventeen female school psychology students, fifteen male medical students, and twenty-one male accounting students. It was predicted that accounting students would show the most sex role bias and school psychology students would show the least. The mean scores fell in the predicted direction, but the differences between means were not significant (Chasen, 1974).

NOTES AND COMMENTS: Scores on the Chasen Diagnostic Sex Role Bias Scale have been related to authoritarianism, sex role attitudes, and sex (Chasen, 1974, 1975; Chasen and Weinberg, 1975).

SOURCE: See Chasen, 1974; or ETS Microfiche Collection (#008000).

BIBLIOGRAPHY:

Chasen, B. G. "Diagnostic Sex Role Bias and Its Relation to Authoritarianism, Sex Role Attitudes, and Sex of the School Psychologist." Unpublished doctoral dissertation, New York University, 1974. (*Dissertation Abstracts International*, 1974, *35*[5-B], 2400.)
Chasen, B. G. "Diagnostic Sex Role Bias and Its Relations to Authoritarianism, Sex Role Attitudes, and Sex of the School Psychologist." *Sex Roles*, 1975, *1*, 355-368.
Chasen, B. G., and Weinberg, S. L. "Diagnostic Sex Role Bias: How Can We Measure It?" *Journal of Personality Assessment*, 1975, *39*, 620-629.

95. CHILDREN'S ATTITUDES TOWARD FEMALE INVOLVEMENT
IN SPORTS (CATFIS)

AUTHOR: Rosemary Selby

DATE: 1975

VARIABLE: Attitudes toward female participation in sports

TYPE OF INSTRUMENT: Summated rating scale

DESCRIPTION: The scale consists of nineteen different statements regarding girls and sports. One item appears twice, giving a total of twenty statements. The majority of the statements relate to whether girls ought to be involved in sports. Nine items are phrased to reflect a positive attitude and eleven items are phrased to reflect a negative attitude. All statements are considered appropriate for persons with a third-grade reading level. Each statement is accompanied by five response alternatives: completely disagree, mostly disagree, not sure, mostly agree, and completely agree.

PREVIOUSLY ADMINISTERED TO: Grades 3-9

APPROPRIATE FOR: Ages 8 and older

ADMINISTRATION: The scale has been orally administered, with responses recorded by the children. About twenty-five minutes should be allowed to explain the directions and administer the scale. The scale could be adapted for paper-and-pencil self-administration.

SAMPLE ITEMS: Girls should find other things to do than play sports.
              Boys should be glad to have girls play on their teams.

SCORING: Items are objectively scored and equally weighted. One score is obtained and is equal to the mean of the item scores. Higher scores indicate more favorable attitudes.

DEVELOPMENT: An item pool consisting of sixty items was constructed based on a search of the relevant literature. Nineteen items were judged to be ambiguous or double barreled and were eliminated. The remaining forty-one items were administered to sixteen third-grade girls and twenty-four third-grade boys. Item-total correlations were computed. The twenty items with the highest correlations (.56 to .79) were selected for the scale.

RELIABILITY: Thirty-three children in the third through sixth grades completed the scale on two occasions. The interval between testings was two weeks. The test-retest correlation was .81 (Selby, 1975).

VALIDITY: The scale was completed by 833 third- through ninth-grade children. As predicted, girls scored significantly higher ($\overline{X}$ = 4.11) than boys ($\overline{X}$ = 2.82, p < .001). It was hypothesized that older children would have less positive attitudes than younger children. This hypothesis was not supported (Selby, 1975).

Eighty-four girls who had participated in a YMCA-sponsored sports program were retested after five months of sports participation. It was hypothesized that their attitudes toward female involvement in sports would become more favorable. This hypothesis was not supported (Selby, 1975). It is possible that these two hypotheses were not supported because they were in fact false. However, it is also possible that the scale is not valid.

NOTES AND COMMENTS: A factor analysis was performed on the responses from the forty children on whom the scale was developed. All items were found to load on the first factor extracted. Factor loadings ranged from .45 to .77.

SOURCE: See Selby, 1975.

BIBLIOGRAPHY:

Selby, R. "Children's Attitudes Toward Females in Sports." Unpublished master's thesis, University of Illinois, 1975.
Selby, R., and Lewko, J. H. "Children's Attitudes Toward Females in Sports: Their Relationship with Sex, Grade, and Sports Participation." *Research Quarterly*, 1976, *47*, 453-463.

---

96. FEINMAN MEASURE OF APPROVAL OF APPROPRIATE SEX ROLE AND APPROPRIATE AGE ROLE BEHAVIOR

AUTHOR: Saul Feinman

DATE: 1977

VARIABLES: Reactions to appropriate sex role behavior; reactions to appropriate age role behavior

TYPE OF INSTRUMENT: Rating scale

DESCRIPTION: The scale consists of forty-five statements: ten statements describe a boy engaged in behavior that is typical for his sex; ten statements describe a boy engaged in behavior that is typical for his age; ten statements describe a girl engaged in behavior that is typical for her sex; ten statements describe a man engaged in behavior that is typical for his age; five statements are filler items that describe women engaged in various behaviors. The respondent is to assume that the children in the items are between the ages of 5 and 10 and that adults are between the ages of 21 and 50. For each item, the respondent is to indicate approval or disapproval of the behavior described by rating the behavior on an eleven-point scale ranging from strong disapproval to strong approval.

PREVIOUSLY ADMINISTERED TO: College students

APPROPRIATE FOR: Ages 10 and older

ADMINISTRATION: The scale can be self-administered and can be completed in about twenty minutes.

SAMPLE ITEMS: *Boy sex-appropriate:* A boy is capable of defending himself if attacked.
　　　　　　　Boy age-appropriate: A boy is carefree.
　　　　　　　Girl sex-appropriate: A girl does not use harsh language.
　　　　　　　Man age-appropriate: A man is able to cook food.

SCORING: Six scores are obtained: Girl Sex Approval, Boy Sex Approval, Total Sex Approval, Boy Age Approval, Man Age Approval, and Total Age Approval. Each score is obtained by summing the ratings of the items contributing to the score. The two Total scores are comprised of twenty items each and can range from 0 (extreme disapproval) to 200 (extreme approval). The remaining four scores are comprised of ten items each and can range from 0 (extreme disapproval) to 100 (extreme approval).

DEVELOPMENT: Fifty-four college students were asked to list traits and behaviors that they thought acceptable and desirable for young boys, young girls, men, and women. The 106 behaviors and traits that were listed for the same category by at least two students comprised a "role expectation instrument." This instrument was administered to a different group of 207 college students with instructions to rate the acceptability/desirability of each item for one of the following categories of persons: adult male, adult female, young boy, or young girl. The responses were used to select ten items for each of four categories: sex appropriate for boys, sex appropriate for girls, age appropriate for boys, and age appropriate for men. The twenty items for the sex role scales were selected so that the average difference between the ratings for boys and girls engaged in masculine-appropriate behaviors was approximately equal to the average difference between the ratings of boys and girls engaged in feminine-appropriate behaviors. Similarly, the twenty items for the age role scales were selected so that the average difference between the ratings of boys and men engaged in behaviors appropriate for men was approximately equal to the average difference between the ratings of boys and men engaged in behaviors appropriate for boys.

RELIABILITY: The scale was administered to fifty-two college students and reliability estimates were calculated. The following values of coefficient alpha were obtained: Girl Sex Approval score = .83; Boy Sex Approval score = .83; Total Sex Approval score = .88; Man Age Approval score = .60; Boy Age Approval score = .70; and Total Age Approval score = .63.

VALIDITY: No data are provided.

NOTES AND COMMENTS: (1) This scale has been used in conjunction with another scale, the Feinman Measure of Approval of Cross-Sex and Cross-Age Behavior (#97). The two measures are very similar, differing only in the sex or age of the subject in each statement.

　　　(2) This scale represents an extension of the Feinman Measure of Disapproval of Appropriate-Sex Behavior (#98).

SOURCE: Saul Feinman, Ph.D.
　　　　　Department of Sociology

University of Wyoming
Laramie, Wyoming 82071

BIBLIOGRAPHY:

Feinman, S. "Effects of Status on Role Expectations and Performance Evaluation." Unpublished manuscript, no date.

---

97. FEINMAN MEASURE OF APPROVAL OF CROSS-SEX AND CROSS-AGE BEHAVIOR

AUTHOR: Saul Feinman

DATE: 1977

VARIABLES: Reactions to inappropriate sex role behavior; reactions to inappropriate age role behavior

TYPE OF INSTRUMENT: Rating scale

DESCRIPTION: The scale consists of forty-five statements: ten statements describe a boy engaged in behavior that is not typical for his sex; ten statements describe a boy engaged in behavior that is not typical for his age; ten statements describe a girl engaged in behavior that is not typical for her sex; ten statements describe a man engaged in behavior that is not typical for his age; five statements are filler items that describe women engaged in various behaviors. The respondent is to assume that the children in the items are between the ages of 5 and 10 and the adults are between the ages of 21 and 50. For each item, the respondent is to indicate approval or disapproval of the behavior described by rating the behavior on an eleven-point scale ranging from strong disapproval to strong approval.

PREVIOUSLY ADMINISTERED TO: College students

APPROPRIATE FOR: Ages 10 and older

ADMINISTRATION: The scale can be self-administered and can be completed in about twenty minutes.

SAMPLE ITEMS: *Girl sex-inappropriate:* A girl is capable of defending herself if attacked.
> *Man age-inappropriate:* A man is carefree.
> *Boy sex-inappropriate:* A boy does not use harsh language.
> *Boy age-inappropriate:* A boy is able to cook food.

SCORING: Six scores are obtained: Girl Sex Approval, Boy Sex Approval, Total Sex

Approval, Boy Age Approval, Man Age Approval, and Total Age Approval. Each score is obtained by summing the ratings of the items contributing to the score. The two Total scores are comprised of twenty items each and can range from 0 (extreme disapproval) to 200 (extreme approval). The remaining four scores are comprised of ten items each and can range from 0 (extreme disapproval) to 100 (extreme approval).

DEVELOPMENT: Fifty-four college students were asked to list traits and behaviors that they thought acceptable and desirable for young boys, young girls, men, and women. The 106 behaviors and traits that were listed for the same category by at least two students comprised a "role expectation instrument." This instrument was administered to a different group of 207 college students with instructions to rate the acceptability/desirability of each item for one of the following categories of persons: adult male, adult female, young boy, or young girl. The responses were used to select ten items for each of four categories: sex inappropriate for boys, sex inappropriate for girls, age inappropriate for boys, and age inappropriate for men. The twenty items for the sex role scales were selected so that the average difference between the ratings for boys and girls engaged in masculine-appropriate behaviors was approximately equal to the average difference between the ratings of boys and girls engaged in feminine-appropriate behaviors. Similarly, the twenty items for the age role scales were selected so that the average difference between the ratings of boys and men engaged in behaviors appropriate for men was approximately equal to the average difference between the ratings of boys and men engaged in behaviors appropriate for boys.

RELIABILITY: The scale was administered to forty-five college students and reliability estimates were calculated. The following values of coefficient alpha were obtained: Girl Sex Approval score = .73; Boy Sex Approval score = .90; Total Sex Approval score = .89; Boy Age Approval score = .72; Man Age Approval score = .79; and Total Age Approval score = .74.

VALIDITY: No data are provided.

NOTES AND COMMENTS: (1) This scale has been used in conjunction with another scale, the Feinman Measure of Approval of Appropriate Sex Role and Appropriate Age Role Behavior (#96). The two measures are very similar, differing only in the sex or age of the subject in each statement.

(2) This scale represents an extension of the Feinman Measure of Disapproval of Cross-Sex Behavior (#99).

SOURCE: Saul Feinman, Ph.D.
            Department of Sociology
            University of Wyoming
            Laramie, Wyoming 82071

BIBLIOGRAPHY:

Feinman, S. "Effects of Status on Role Expectations and Performance Evaluation." Unpublished manuscript, no date.

98. FEINMAN MEASURE OF DISAPPROVAL OF APPROPRIATE-SEX BEHAVIOR (MDASB)

AUTHOR: Saul Feinman

DATE: 1977

VARIABLE: Reactions to appropriate sex role behavior

TYPE OF INSTRUMENT: Rating scale

DESCRIPTION: The scale consists of ten statements, each of which describes a child engaged in behavior that is considered typical for that child's sex. Five items describe behavior enacted by a boy and five describe behavior enacted by a girl. For each sex of actor, there is one item concerning each of the following five areas: dress, play activities, aggressive behavior, helping same-sexed parent, and independence-dependence. The respondent is to assume that the child in the item is between the ages of 3 and 7. The respondent is then to use a seven-point scale to indicate approval or disapproval of the behavior described. A high rating indicates strong disapproval; a low rating indicates strong approval.

PREVIOUSLY ADMINISTERED TO: College students

APPROPRIATE FOR: Ages 10 and older

ADMINISTRATION: The scale can be self-administered. It takes about ten minutes to administer the scale to a group, allowing for distribution and collection of materials and explanation of directions.

SAMPLE ITEMS: A girl plays with baby dolls.
              A boy wears jeans and a sweatshirt while outside the house.

SCORING: Three scores are obtained. A Total Disapproval score is obtained by summing the ratings assigned to each of the ten items. The score can range from 10 (extreme approval of appropriate sex role behaviors) to 70 (extreme disapproval of appropriate sex role behaviors). The ratings assigned to the five items that describe a girl enacting a behavior are summed to yield a Female Disapproval score; the ratings assigned to the five items that describe a boy enacting a behavior are summed to yield a Male Disapproval score. These two scores each have a range from 5 (extreme approval) to 35 (extreme disapproval).

DEVELOPMENT: The MDASB was developed by taking the ten items from the Measure of Disapproval of Cross-Sex Behavior (#99) and reversing the sex of the child mentioned in each item.

RELIABILITY: The MDASB was administered to about eighty-five college students and reliability estimates were calculated. Coefficient alpha was .72 for the Total Disapproval score, .55 for the Female Disapproval score, and .57 for the Male Disapproval score.

VALIDITY: Fifty college students were asked to consider children between the ages of 3 and 8 and to list twenty behaviors that were more likely to be expected from boys than girls and another twenty behaviors that were more likely to be expected from girls than boys. An examination was made of whether college students classified the sex appropriateness or inappropriateness of relevant behaviors in the same direction as they are classified on the MDASB. It was found that for each of the items, at least 80 percent of the relevant behaviors listed by the college students were classified in the same direction as the behavior is classified in the MDASB. For example, "80 percent of the references to independence behavior were those that indicated that such behavior was either appropriate for boys or inappropriate for girls" (p. 11).

NOTES AND COMMENTS: (1) The MDASB has been used in conjunction with another scale, the Feinman Measure of Disapproval of Cross-Sex Behavior (#99). The scales differ from each other in terms of whether the items portray sex-appropriate or sex-inappropriate behavior.

(2) Feinman has developed another pair of measures (#96 and #97) that assess responses to behavior on the basis of the sex and age appropriateness or inappropriateness of the behavior. Along with adding another variable—age—to the scale, the new measures are considerably longer (forty-five items rather than ten items each).

SOURCE: Saul Feinman, Ph.D.
            Department of Sociology
            University of Wyoming
            Laramie, Wyoming 82071

BIBLIOGRAPHY:

Feinman, S. "Why is Cross-Sex-Role Behavior More Approved for Girls than for Boys? The Effect of Status of Behavior and Status of an Actor on Evaluation of Deviant and Conforming Sex Role Behaviors." Paper presented at the meeting of the Midwest Sociological Society, Minneapolis, Minnesota, April 1977.

---

99. FEINMAN MEASURE OF DISAPPROVAL OF CROSS-SEX BEHAVIOR (MDCSB)

AUTHOR: Saul Feinman

DATE: 1972 (revised 1977)

VARIABLE: Reactions to inappropriate sex role behavior

TYPE OF INSTRUMENT: Rating scale

DESCRIPTION: The scale consists of ten statements, each of which describes a child engaged in behavior that is typically assumed to be appropriate for the opposite sex. Five items describe behavior enacted by a boy and five describe behavior enacted by a girl. For each sex of actor, there is one item concerning each of the following five areas: dress, play activities, aggressive behavior, helping opposite-sexed parent, and independence-dependence. The respondent is to assume that the child in the item is between the ages of 3 and 7. The respondent is to use a seven-point scale to indicate approval or disapproval of the behavior described. A high rating indicates strong disapproval; a low rating indicates strong approval.

PREVIOUSLY ADMINISTERED TO: College students

APPROPRIATE FOR: Ages 10 and older

ADMINISTRATION: The scale can be self-administered. It takes about ten minutes to administer the scale to a group, including time for distribution and collection of materials and explanation of directions.

SAMPLE ITEMS: A boy plays with baby dolls.
                        A girl wears jeans and a sweatshirt while outside the house.

SCORING: Three scores are obtained. A Total Disapproval score is obtained by summing the ratings assigned to each of the ten items. The score can range from 10 (extreme approval of cross-sex-role behaviors) to 70 (extreme disapproval of cross-sex-role behaviors). The ratings assigned to the five items that describe a girl enacting a behavior are summed to yield a Female Disapproval score; the ratings assigned to the five items that describe a boy enacting a behavior are summed to yield a Male Disapproval score. These two scores each have a range from 5 (extreme approval) to 35 (extreme disapproval).

DEVELOPMENT: In developing the original MDCSB, items were selected "by choosing behaviors that psychological and sociological research on sex roles and sex differences had indicated were more expected for either boys or girls" (Feinman, 1977, p. 9). In revising the MDCSB, items were reworded "in a more clear-cut, neutral, and unbiased fashion" (Feinman, 1977, p. 10).

RELIABILITY: The MDCSB was administered to 107 college students, and reliability estimates were calculated. Coefficient alpha was .73 for the Total Disapproval score, .63 for the Female Disapproval score, and .67 for the Male Disapproval score (Feinman, 1974).
          The revised MDCSB was administered to about eighty-five college students, and reliability estimates were calculated. Coefficient alpha was .72 for the Total Disapproval score, .45 for the Female Disapproval score, and .72 for the Male Disapproval score (Feinman, 1977).

VALIDITY: Fifty college students were asked to consider children between the ages of 3 and 8 and to list twenty behaviors that were more likely to be expected from boys than girls and another twenty behaviors that were more likely to be expected from girls than boys. An examination was made of whether college students classified the sex appropriateness or inappropriateness of relevant behaviors in the same direction as they are classified on the MDCSB. It was found that for each of the items, at least 80 percent of the relevant behaviors listed by the college students were classified in the same direction as they are classified in the item. For example, "80 percent of the references to independence behavior were those that indicated that such behavior was either appropriate for boys or inappropriate for girls" (Feinman, 1977, p. 11).

NOTES AND COMMENTS: (1) The MDCSB has been used in conjunction with another scale, the Feinman Measure of Disapproval of Appropriate Sex Behavior (#98). The scales differ from each other in terms of whether the items portray sex-appropriate or sex-inappropriate behavior.

(2) Feinman has developed another pair of measures (#96 and #97), which assess responses to behavior on the basis of the sex and age appropriateness or inappropriateness of the behavior. Along with adding another variable—age—to the scale, the new measures are considerably longer (forty-five items rather than ten items each).

(3) This scale is also described in *Tests and Measurements in Child Development: Handbook II* (Johnson, 1976, pp. 817-818).

SOURCE: Saul Feinman, Ph.D.
        Department of Sociology
        University of Wyoming
        Laramie, Wyoming 82071

BIBLIOGRAPHY:

Feinman, S. "Approval of Cross-Sex-Role Behavior." *Psychological Reports,* 1974, *35,* 643-648.
Feinman, S. "Why is Cross-Sex-Role Behavior More Approved for Girls than for Boys? The Effect of Status of Behavior and Status of an Actor on Evaluation of Deviant and Conforming Sex Role Behaviors." Paper presented at the meeting of the Midwest Sociological Society, Minneapolis, Minnesota, April 1977.
*Johnson, O. G. *Tests and Measurements in Child Development: Handbook II.* San Francisco: Jossey-Bass, 1976.

---

100. GIRLS' STEREOTYPE SCALE (GSS)

AUTHOR: Arthur J. Rudy

DATE: 1965

VARIABLE: Evaluation of sex-typed traits in girls

TYPE OF INSTRUMENT: Rating scale

DESCRIPTION: The scale consists of seventy-eight trait-descriptive adjectives and short phrases. Of the seventy-eight items, thirty-five are stereotypically masculine, thirty-five are stereotypically feminine, and eight are neutral. The items are presented in alphabetical order. The respondent is directed to "imagine that someone has just told you that you are a girl who is _____" and to indicate how desirable the description would be. Seven response options are provided: very desirable, desirable, slightly desirable, neither desirable nor undesirable, slightly undesirable, undesirable, very undesirable.

PREVIOUSLY ADMINISTERED TO: Females, grades 9 and 10

APPROPRIATE FOR: Ages 12 and older

ADMINISTRATION: The scale can be self-administered and can be completed in less than half an hour.

SAMPLE ITEMS: Adventurous
Affectionate
Athletic
Big
Bold
Brave

SCORING: Items are objectively scored and equally weighted. The scale yields two scores: mean desirability score on the masculine subscale and mean desirability score on the feminine subscale. The mean desirability score on the neutral items is used "to control for the effects of sex differences in rating tendencies" (Rudy, 1965, p. 40).

DEVELOPMENT: An initial item pool was compiled from a search of the literature and the responses of ninth and tenth graders to an open-ended question requesting a list of adjectives that describe girls. Items that were beyond the comprehension level of typical ninth and tenth graders were eliminated. Three scales were constructed with the remaining items. Each scale was given to a different group of sixty females with instructions to rate each item according to the frequency with which the item is used to describe boys or girls. Five response options were provided: boys almost always, boys more often, both boys and girls, girls more often, girls almost always. Half of the girls in each group completed the scale a second time one week later. Using the responses from these testings, it was determined whether each of the items was sex typed. If at least 65 percent of the girls agreed that the item was masculine (or feminine), and if there was at least 70 percent individual retest agreement regarding the masculinity (or femininity) of the item, then the item was considered sex typed (masculine or feminine). Items were considered neutral if the modal rating was in the central category and if the distribution in the two ends of the continuum was approximately equal.

RELIABILITY: The responses from thirty females who were tested on two occasions, separated by about one week, were used to estimate reliability. The test-retest reliability for the feminine subscale was .91; the test-retest reliability for the masculine subscale was .73 (Rudy, 1965).

VALIDITY: No data are provided.

NOTES AND COMMENTS: This scale was used in conjunction with a similar scale, the Boys' Stereotype Scale (#93). Of the seventy-eight items on the scales, thirty-five are identical on the two scales, and forty-five are unique to the Girls' Stereotype Scale.

SOURCE: See Rudy, 1965.

BIBLIOGRAPHY:

Rudy, A. J. "Sex Role Perceptions in Early Adolescence." Unpublished doctoral dissertation, Columbia University, 1965. (*Dissertation Abstracts,* 1966, *26*[10],
6174-6175.)
Rudy, A. J. "Sex Role Perceptions in Early Adolescence." *Adolescence,* 1968-1969, *3,*
453-470.

---

101. LOWER-KRAIN SEX ROLE SCALE REGARDING CHILDREN

AUTHORS: Deborah Jean Lower and Mark Krain

DATE: 1975

VARIABLES: Attitudes toward children's sex roles, encouragement of egalitarian sex
roles for children, and likelihood that children will display egalitarian sex roles

TYPE OF INSTRUMENT: Summated rating scale

DESCRIPTION: There are three parts to the scale. All three parts include the same nineteen brief descriptions of children engaged in behavior that is not traditional for their sex.
In the first part, the woman is to indicate her feelings in reaction to the situation. The
response options are: I would be very upset by it; I would be somewhat concerned about
it; It would not matter to me; I would be pleased about it; I would be very happy about
it. In the second part, the woman is asked to indicate what she would do in response to
the situation. The response options are: I would take immediate steps to change this; I
would discourage this; I would not do anything about this; I would approve of this; and I
would strongly encourage this. In the third part, the woman is asked to indicate how
likely it is that each of the situations described is or will be true of her children. The
response options are: Very true or probable; Fairly true or probable; Somewhat true or
probable; A little true or probable; and Not true or probable.

PREVIOUSLY ADMINISTERED TO: Nurses

APPROPRIATE FOR: Ages 16 and older

ADMINISTRATION: This scale can be self-administered and can be completed in about
half an hour.

SAMPLE ITEMS: Will, age 13, has stopped playing with his old clique of boy playmates
and now associates more closely with activities of his sister and her friends.
            Vicki, age 14, has no good friends who are girls, but she plays with the
neighborhood boys as they play baseball and touch football.

SCORING: Items are objectively scored and equally weighted. Separate totals are obtained on each of the three parts of the scale.

DEVELOPMENT: No information is provided.

RELIABILITY: Based on the responses from 157 women, internal consistency coefficients (alpha) were computed for each of the three parts. The coefficients were .82, .83, and .94 for parts 1, 2, and 3, respectively. Scale minus item correlation coefficients were computed for each part; that is, each time an item was correlated with the total score, that particular item was eliminated from the calculation of the total score. For the first part, the item-total correlations ranged from .08 to .61; the correlations on the second part ranged from .11 to .60; and the correlations on the third part ranged from .38 to .77 (Lower, 1975).

VALIDITY: Lower (1975, p. 98) hypothesized a relationship between each of the parts of the Lower-Krain Sex Role Scale Regarding Children and women's career commitment as measured by the Lower-Krain Woman's Career Commitment Scale (#155). For the first part, Lower hypothesized "High career commitment is positively related to equalitarian attitudes toward sex roles for children." For the second part, Lower hypothesized "High career commitment is positively related to encouragement of equalitarian sex roles for children." Both hypotheses were supported when women's career commitment was assessed in regard to problems arising with children. For the third part of the scale, Lower hypothesized "High career commitment is positively related to the probability of the woman's children displaying equalitarian sex role behavior." This hypothesis was not supported.

NOTES AND COMMENTS: The authors assume that the reactions elicited by the scale are a function of the children's behavior being sex inappropriate; that is, the children are described as engaged in behaviors that are not traditional for their sex. It is quite possible, however, that some persons would respond to a particular situation the same way regardless of whether the situation involved a boy or a girl. As the scale is presently constructed, there is no way to determine whether the sex of the child in the description is the significant variable affecting the responses elicited.

SOURCE: See Lower, 1975.

BIBLIOGRAPHY:

Krain, M., and Lower, D. "The Relationship of Women's Career Commitment to Their Attitudes Toward Their Children's Sex Role Socialization, to Their Attitudes on Spousal Roles, and to Marital Adjustment." Paper presented at the meeting of the Midwest Sociological Society, St. Louis, Missouri, 1976. (ERIC Document Reproduction Service No. ED 138 855.)
Lower, D. J. "The Relations of Women's Career Commitment and Their Attitudes Regarding the Socialization of Children into Sex Roles, Marital Role Relations, and Marital Adjustment." Unpublished master's thesis, University of Iowa, 1975.

102. MCGEE SCALE OF ATTITUDES TOWARD INTENSIVE COMPETITION FOR GIRLS

AUTHOR: Rosemary McGee

DATE: 1956

VARIABLE: Attitudes toward intensive athletic competition for high school girls

TYPE OF INSTRUMENT: Summated rating scale

DESCRIPTION: The scale consists of seventy items relating to intensive athletic competition for girls. Intensive athletic competition is defined as "team games comparable to tournament basketball games . . . which involve crowds, intense excitement, publicity, and gate receipts" (p. 71). The scale is divided into seven areas: personality development (thirteen items), recreation (nine items), physical development and conditioning (eleven items), public relations (eleven items), health and safety (eight items), skill (six items), and human relations (twelve items). Each statement is accompanied by five response alternatives: strongly agree, agree, neutral or indifferent, disagree, and strongly disagree. Some items are phrased to reflect a positive attitude, and others are phrased to reflect a negative attitude.

PREVIOUSLY ADMINISTERED TO: School administrators, teachers, parents

APPROPRIATE FOR: Ages 12 and older

ADMINISTRATION: The scale can be self-administered and can be completed in twenty to thirty minutes.

SAMPLE ITEMS:

Personality development: Participation in intensive competition develops leadership.

Recreation: Girls should have the same opportunity as boys to enjoy the combative struggle of interscholastic basketball.

Physical development and conditioning: A season of scheduled contests makes undue demands on girls.

Public relations: Participating in intensive competition before crowds of excited spectators makes too much emotional strain for most girls.

Health and safety: Travel arrangements used by most teams are completely adequate for the safety and health of the team.

Skill: Intensive competition meets the challenge of highly skilled players.

Human relations: Interscholastic participation develops responses useful in situations of emergency.

SCORING: Items are objectively scored and equally weighted. Total scores can range from −70 (very negative attitude) to +70 (very positive attitude). Scores can also be obtained for seven subscales corresponding to the seven areas listed above.

DEVELOPMENT: A pool of eighty-two items was constructed based on a survey of the relevant literature. The item pool was given to a group of ninety-four graduate students with two sets of instructions. First, they were directed to indicate on a five-point scale whether each statement reflected a positive or negative attitude toward intense athletic competition. Then they were asked to report their personal opinion on a five-point scale. The first set of responses was used to determine which items to retain on the scale. If fewer than 70 percent of the group agreed on whether the statement was positive or negative, the item was eliminated. Twelve items were eliminated by this criterion. The remaining seventy items comprise the scale.

RELIABILITY: The ninety-four graduate students completed the scale a second time two weeks after they first completed it. The test-retest reliability for the scale was .95.

VALIDITY: The scale was completed by administrators, teachers, and parents in one school district that promoted intensive athletic competition for girls and in two school districts that did not. Significantly more favorable attitudes were expressed by those in the school district that promoted intensive athletic competition for girls. Significant differences were found on each of the seven subscales as well as on the total scale.

NOTES AND COMMENTS: (1) Caution should be exercised regarding the use of this scale, as a few items may not be appropriate for use today.

(2) The procedure for estimating the scale's reliability was questionable. The ninety-four graduate students who completed the scale on two occasions were first asked to indicate whether each statement was positive or negative. This initial task sensitized the respondents to the items; that is, they may have been reacting to their own judgment of the positiveness or negativeness inherent in the items, rather than to the specific content of the items. It seems logical that it is easier to respond consistently to the positive or negative quality of an item than to respond consistently to the specific content of the item. Thus, the procedure used may have led to a spurious correlation.

(3) This scale is also described in *Scales for the Measurement of Attitudes* (Shaw and Wright, 1967, pp. 90-94).

SOURCE: See McGee, 1956; or Shaw and Wright, 1967.

BIBLIOGRAPHY:

McGee, R. "Comparisons of Attitudes Toward Intensive Competition for High School Girls." *Research Quarterly,* 1956, *27,* 60-73.
*Shaw, M. E., and Wright, J. M. *Scales for the Measurement of Attitudes.* New York: McGraw-Hill, 1967.

7

▦ ▦ ▦ ▦ ▦ ▦ ▦ ▦ ▦ ▦ ▦

Gender Knowledge

▦ ▦ ▦ ▦ ▦ ▦ ▦ ▦ ▦ ▦ ▦ ▦ ▦ ▦ ▦ ▦ ▦ ▦ ▦ ▦

The five instruments in this chapter measure gender knowledge; that is, they either measure whether children know their own gender or whether children can correctly identify the gender of other persons. These instruments differ from others in this book in that they are cognitive tests; they are scored on the basis of whether the child gives correct or incorrect answers. All are relatively new; four instruments first appeared in the literature in 1973; one first appeared in 1975. Compared with the instruments in some of the other chapters, relatively little is known about most of these measures. Information regarding development is known for only one instrument (#103), and it has a theoretical rather than an empirical basis. Reliability data are provided for only one instrument (#104), but validity data are provided for all five. These instruments are appropriate for children ranging in age from 16 months to 6 years. Because the intended respondents are so young, all five tests must be individually administered. Three different procedures are used for assessing gender knowledge: #104 and #107 involve asking the child some gender-related questions and recording the child's responses; #105 involves listing words denoting gender and determining whether the child can point to the correct picture for each word; and #103 and #106 require the child to sort pictures based on the gender of the pictured persons.

There are not many instruments available for assessing gender knowledge. Only one gender-knowledge test was found that failed to satisfy the criteria for inclusion in this book. And, as can be seen from reading this chapter, three of the instruments were authored by the same person and used in the same study.

The researcher interested in a gender-knowledge test might select any one of the instruments described here, but for four of the tests, evidence of reliability should be obtained before they are used. The researcher's selection among the five should depend on (1) the precise variable the researcher wishes to measure and (2) the extent to which the researcher is willing to use a test that requires special stimulus materials or apparatus.

---

103. MICHIGAN GENDER IDENTITY TEST (MIGIT)

AUTHORS: University of Michigan Personality and Language Behavior Research Project

DATE: 1973

VARIABLE: Gender identity

TYPE OF INSTRUMENT: Sorting task

DESCRIPTION: The stimuli for this test are colored photographs (3½" x 4½") of four dogs, five balls, four boys, four girls, and the child. Also included are cartoon-like line drawings of a ball, a dog, a boy, and a girl.

PREVIOUSLY ADMINISTERED TO: Ages 16-51 months

APPROPRIATE FOR: Ages 16 months to 5 years

ADMINISTRATION: Administration of the MIGIT typically requires three people: one to administer the test, one to complete the scoring form, and one to take the child's photograph. The adult accompanying the child to the testing session is permitted to be present.

The child's photograph is taken at the beginning of the testing session using a camera capable of instant development. Trial 1 then begins. The child is shown the cartoon-like drawings of the ball and the dog, and asked to identify them by name. If she does not respond correctly, the examiner names the pictures. The child is then given two photographs of dogs and two photographs of balls and asked to identify which are dogs and which are balls. The child can use a variety of modes of response, including sorting, verbal labeling, and so forth. If the child is reluctant to respond, various procedures are tried to encourage responding (see Dull and others, 1975). Upon completion of this trial, trial 2 begins. The child is shown three photographs of balls and two photographs of dogs. Again the child is asked to identify which are balls and which are dogs. This second trial with dogs and balls can be omitted if there is no doubt that the child easily and correctly responded on the first administration of the dog and ball photographs.

Next the child is shown the cartoon-like drawings of the boy and the girl. If the child cannot label them, the examiner does it. For trial 3 the child is shown two photographs of boys and two photographs of girls and asked to identify which are boys and which are girls. Finally, on trial 4, the child is shown two photographs of boys, two photographs of girls, and the child's own photograph. The child is again asked to identify which are girls and which are boys. In all trials, the child is allowed to use any mode of response she chooses. Administration time varies from five to fifteen minutes, depending on the cooperativeness of the child.

SCORING: Performance on this test is considered "perfect" if the child can correctly identify each of the photographs. However, much information in addition to the correctness of response is recorded by the scorer, including mode of response, observations regarding the child's attitudes and behavior, and observations regarding the attitudes and behavior of the adult accompanying the child. A scoring form is provided which facilitates recording all the necessary information.

DEVELOPMENT: The development of the MIGIT was a theoretical rather than empirical procedure. A three-page rationale for the development of the test is provided (see Dull and others, 1975).

RELIABILITY: No data are provided.

VALIDITY: The fact that as children get older a larger proportion of them achieve a perfect score on the MIGIT provides some evidence for the validity of the test. Paluszny and others (1973) tested 106 children between the ages of 16 and 51 months. In reporting their data, they grouped children into three-month intervals by age. They found that after age 27 months, the percentage of children achieving a perfect score increased for each increasing age group.

Paluszny and others also asked, "Are you a little girl or a little boy?" Only two of the children who achieved perfect scores on the MIGIT failed to answer the question correctly. Of those who failed to achieve perfect scores on the MIGIT, sixteen (23 percent) were able to answer the direct question correctly. Thirteen of those sixteen were boys.

Dull and others (1975) report that as age increased the children were able to correctly identify more *successive* photographs. Only nine children (8 percent of 106) exhibited performance in which correct responses were not sequential. This provides evidence that the test does become more difficult in each of the successive trials.

NOTES AND COMMENTS: (1) The authors stress that MIGIT is a research instrument.

(2) The scale is also described in *Tests and Measurements in Child Development: Handbook II* (Johnson, 1976, pp. 617-618).

SOURCE: Dr. A. Z. Guiora
N5714 University Hospital
University of Michigan
Ann Arbor, Michigan 48104

BIBLIOGRAPHY:

Dull, C. Y., Guiora, A. Z., Paluszny, M., Beit-Hallahmi, B., Catford, J. C., and Cooley, R. E. "The Michigan Gender Identity Test (MIGIT)." *Comprehensive Psychiatry,* 1975, *16,* 581-592.
*Johnson, O. G. *Tests and Measurements in Child Development: Handbook II.* San Francisco: Jossey-Bass, 1976.

Paluszny, M., Beit-Hallahmi, B., Catford, J. C., Cooley, R. E., Dull, C. Y., and Guiora, A. Z. "Gender Identity and Its Measurement in Children." *Comprehensive Psychiatry*, 1973, *14*, 281-290.

---

104. SLABY-FREY GENDER CONCEPT TEST

AUTHORS: Ronald G. Slaby and Karin S. Frey

DATE: 1975

VARIABLES: Knowledge of gender identity, gender stability over time, gender consistency across situations

TYPE OF INSTRUMENT: Alternate choice

DESCRIPTION: The test consists of fourteen questions, each of which (except #14) is followed by a counterquestion (see sample items). Nine questions assess knowledge of gender identity; two questions assess knowledge of gender stability over time; and three questions assess knowledge of gender consistency across different situations and motivations. The following equipment is required to administer the test: a man doll and a woman doll (13 cm. tall), a boy doll and a girl doll (8 cm. tall), two color photographs of the face and upper torso of a man, and two color photographs of the face and upper torso of a woman (8 x 8 cm.).

PREVIOUSLY ADMINISTERED TO: Ages 2-6

APPROPRIATE FOR: Ages 2-6

ADMINISTRATION: The test is individually administered. A question is administered orally, and after the child responds the counterquestion is asked. The first eight questions require that the child be shown a doll or photograph while the question is asked.

SAMPLE ITEMS:

Identity: Is this a girl or a boy? (in response to a doll) Is this a [opposite sex of subject's response]?

Stability: When you were a little baby, were you a little girl or little boy? Were you ever a little [opposite sex of subject's response]?

Consistency: If you played [opposite sex of subject] games, would you be a girl or a boy?

SCORING: An item is scored "plus" if both the question and counterquestion are correctly answered. If the question and/or counterquestion is answered incorrectly, the item is scored "minus."

DEVELOPMENT: No information is provided.

RELIABILITY: Slaby and Frey (1975) tested twenty-three boys and thirty-two girls ranging in age from 26 to 68 months. The three sets of questions formed a Guttman scale with a coefficient of reproducibility equal to .98.

VALIDITY: Based on the responses from the fifty-five children tested, Slaby and Frey (1975) report that for each of the three variables measured (that is, gender identity, stability, and consistency), the questions assessing that variable were found to be of approximately equal difficulty. Furthermore, the questions assessing gender consistency were more difficult than those assessing gender stability, which in turn were more difficult than those assessing gender identity. A positive and significant correlation was found between age and stage of gender constancy.

NOTES AND COMMENTS: The use of questions and counterquestions increases the likelihood of detecting random responding or response sets.

SOURCE: See Slaby and Frey, 1975.

BIBLIOGRAPHY:

Coker, D. R. "Development of Gender Concepts in Preschool Children." Paper presented at 85th annual meeting of the American Psychological Association, San Francisco, August 1977.
Slaby, R. G., and Frey, K. S. "Development of Gender Constancy and Selective Attention to Same-Sex Models." *Child Development*, 1975, *46*, 849-856.

---

105. THOMPSON GENDER LABEL IDENTIFICATION TEST

AUTHOR: Spencer Keith Thompson

DATE: 1973

VARIABLES: Ability to match verbal gender labels with appropriate male or female pictures; ability to make sex discriminations based on hair and clothing cues

TYPE OF INSTRUMENT: Alternate choice

DESCRIPTION: The test consists of seventeen pairs of pictures and seventeen pairs of words that denote gender. Each picture pair and each word pair include one masculine and one feminine item.

PREVIOUSLY ADMINISTERED TO: Ages 2-3

APPROPRIATE FOR: Ages 2-4

ADMINISTRATION: The child is seated on the mother's lap in front of an apparatus that can display two pictures on side-by-side screens. Before the actual test is given, the child is given another test that provides practice in the mode of responding and simultaneously tests the child's receptive-language ability. Two training trials are given with the Gender Label Identification Test before the testing actually begins. The examiner asks the child to touch the picture that represents a particular word. If the child's response is correct, a bunny's face above the correct screen and the screen itself light up. The procedure is repeated for the seventeen item pairs on the test. The test is completed in five to ten minutes.

SAMPLE ITEMS: *Word:* man. *Picture:* forty-year-old man with a short haircut, wearing a sport coat and pants.
               Word: lady. *Picture:* thirty-five-year-old lady with hair piled on top of her head, wearing a long dress.

SCORING: The score is the number of correct responses. The maximum score is 34.

DEVELOPMENT: No information is provided.

RELIABILITY: No data are provided. However, test-retest reliability for the receptive-language test, which uses the identical apparatus, was .89 (Thompson, 1973, 1975).

VALIDITY: Scores are reported for eleven boys and eleven girls in each of three age groups: 24 months, 30 months, and 36 months. A significant difference was found between the age groups, with older children scoring higher ($p < .01$). When the scores for boys and for girls were considered separately, there was a consistent increase in mean score with increasing age. This pattern was found for gender nouns, pronouns, same-sex items, and opposite-sex items.
        Correlations were computed for scores on the Thompson Gender Label Identification Test; the Thompson Self-Sort Test (#106), which measures knowledge of own gender; and the Thompson Verbal Gender Questions (#107), which also measures knowledge of own gender. The correlation with the Thompson Self-Sort Test was .55 ($p < .001$), and the correlation with the Thompson Verbal Gender Questions was .56 ($p < .001$) (Thompson, 1973).

NOTES AND COMMENTS: The receptive-language test referred to above is used as a screening device. Any child who fails to demonstrate adequate receptive-language ability should not be expected to complete the Thompson Gender Label Identification Test.

SOURCE: See Thompson, 1973.

BIBLIOGRAPHY:

Thompson, S. K. "The Developmental Usage of Labels in Early Sex Typing and Gender Identification." Unpublished doctoral dissertation, University of California at Los Angeles, 1973. (*Dissertation Abstracts International,* 1974, *34*[11-B], 5665.)
Thompson, S. K. "Gender Labels and Early Sex Role Development." *Child Development,* 1975, *46,* 339-347.

106. THOMPSON SELF-SORT TEST

AUTHOR: Spencer Keith Thompson

DATE: 1973

VARIABLE: Knowledge of own gender

TYPE OF INSTRUMENT: Sorting task

DESCRIPTION: This instrument includes eighteen stimuli: two paper-doll cutouts of girls, two paper-doll cutouts of boys, two photographs of the child to be tested (one full-length picture and one of the head and upper body), six photographs of girls, and six photographs of boys. The latter twelve photographs are of children in the 2- to 3-year age range. The child is to sort all of the pictures according to gender.

PREVIOUSLY ADMINISTERED TO: Ages 2-3

APPROPRIATE FOR: Ages 2-4

ADMINISTRATION: The child is seated on the mother's lap and shown two cardboard boxes. One box is labeled as the bed for girls and one box is labeled as the bed for boys. Using the paper-doll cutouts as training materials, the child is taught to place the girls' cutouts in the girls' bed and the boys' cutouts in the boys' bed. The child is then asked to sort the pictures as they are handed to her. The task can be completed in ten to fifteen minutes.

SCORING: The score is dependent solely on whether the child can correctly sort her own pictures. A maximum of two points is possible.

DEVELOPMENT: No information is provided.

RELIABILITY: No data are provided.

VALIDITY: The test was administered to eleven boys and eleven girls in each of three age groups: 24 months, 30 months, and 36 months. An analysis of variance indicated a significant age effect ($p < .05$), with older children correctly sorting more pictures.

The sixty-six children completing the Thompson Self-Sort Test also completed the Thompson Gender Label Identification Test (#105), which measures gender knowledge, and the Thompson Verbal Gender Questions (#107), which measures knowledge of one's own gender. The correlation between the Thompson Self-Sort Test and the Thompson Gender Label Identification Test was .55 ($p < .001$); the correlation between the Thompson Self-Sort Test and the Thompson Verbal Gender Questions was .34 ($p < .01$) (Thompson, 1973).

NOTES AND COMMENTS: A receptive-language test is used as a screening device. Any child who fails to demonstrate adequate receptive-language ability should not be expected to complete the Thompson Self-Sort Test.

SOURCE: See Thompson, 1973.

BIBLIOGRAPHY:

Thompson, S. K. "The Developmental Usage of Labels in Early Sex Typing and Gender Identification." Unpublished doctoral dissertation, University of California at Los Angeles, 1973. (*Dissertation Abstracts International*, 1974, *34*[11-B], 5665.)
Thompson, S. K. "Gender Labels and Early Sex Role Development." *Child Development*, 1975, *46*, 339-347.

---

107. THOMPSON VERBAL GENDER QUESTIONS

AUTHOR: Spencer Keith Thompson

DATE: 1973

VARIABLE: Knowledge of own gender label and sex category

TYPE OF INSTRUMENT: Alternate choice

DESCRIPTION: This test consists of five gender-related questions.

PREVIOUSLY ADMINISTERED TO: Ages 2-3

APPROPRIATE FOR: Ages 2-4

ADMINISTRATION: The child is asked a question regarding her own gender; after the answer is given, the next question is asked. The test takes about two minutes to administer.

SAMPLE ITEMS: Are you a _____? [The word "boy" or "girl" is inserted so that the question asks about the opposite sex first.]
            Are you going to be a _____? [The word "daddy" or "mommy" is inserted so that the question asks about the opposite sex first.]

SCORING: The number of correct answers is the child's score. The maximum score is 5.

DEVELOPMENT: No information is provided.

RELIABILITY: No data are provided.

VALIDITY: The instrument was administered to eleven boys and eleven girls in each of three age groups: 24 months, 30 months, and 36 months. An analysis of variance indicated a significant age effect (p < .01), with older children correctly responding to more questions.
    The thirty-six children completing the Thompson Verbal Gender Questions also completed the Thompson Self-Sort Test (#106), which measures knowledge of one's own

gender, and the Thompson Gender Label Identification Test (#105), which is another measure of gender knowledge. The correlation between the Thompson Verbal Gender Questions and the Thompson Self-Sort Test was .34 (p < .01); the correlation between the Thompson Verbal Gender Questions and the Thompson Gender Label Identification Test was .56 (p < .001) (Thompson, 1973).

NOTES AND COMMENTS: A receptive-language test is used as a screening device. Any child who fails to demonstrate adequate receptive-language ability should not be expected to complete the Thompson Verbal Gender Questions.

SOURCE: See Thompson, 1973.

BIBLIOGRAPHY:

Thompson, S. K. "The Developmental Usage of Labels in Early Sex Typing and Gender Identification." Unpublished doctoral dissertation, University of California at Los Angeles, 1973. (*Dissertation Abstracts International,* 1974, *34*[11-B] , 5665.)
Thompson, S. K. "Gender Labels and Early Sex Role Development." *Child Development,* 1975, *46,* 339-347.

8

🏛 🏛 🏛 🏛 🏛 🏛 🏛 🏛 🏛 🏛

Marital and
Parental Roles

🏛 🏛 🏛 🏛 🏛 🏛 🏛 🏛 🏛 🏛 🏛 🏛 🏛 🏛 🏛 🏛 🏛 🏛 🏛 🏛

The research relating to marriage and the family is indeed broad. Among other variables, it includes marital happiness, marital adjustment, divorce, parent-child relationships, child-rearing attitudes and philosophies, marital roles, parental roles, and family power. Most aspects of marriage and family research are beyond the scope of this book. Only those instruments that deal specifically with marital and parental *roles* are included here. The reader who is interested in learning about instruments covering a broader range of topics should consult *Family Measurement Techniques: Abstracts of Published Instruments, 1935-1974* (Straus and Brown, 1978), which includes abstracts of, and bibliographies associated with, 813 instruments covering a wide range of topics relevant to the family.

The twenty-three instruments included here measure variables representing four areas: attitudes toward marital roles, perceptions and feelings regarding one's own marital roles or one's parents' marital roles, marital task allocation, and marital power (which includes marital decision making). When two instruments measure the same variable, their scores are not necessarily labeled identically. For example, scores from instruments pertaining to marital role attitudes and the performance of marital roles have been labeled as egalitarian versus male dominant, authoritarian versus democratic, dominant versus egalitarian versus submissive, traditional versus egalitarian, traditional versus companionship,

261

and democratic versus autocratic. There seems to be no general agreement on the terminology, though clearly the authors are trying to describe marital roles in which spouses are equal—labeled egalitarian, democratic, equalitarian, or companionship—and marital roles in which spouses are not equal—termed dominant, authoritarian, submissive, traditional, or autocratic.

There are basically two methods for assessing marital roles: self-report methods and observational methods. All the instruments described here rely on the self-report technique. All can be administered in a paper-and-pencil format, though some have more often been part of an interview schedule. Only three can be administered to persons below age 14, and these three ask about children's perceptions of their parents' marital roles.

Observational measures have generally been omitted from this book, but because they are quite significant in the study of marital roles, a few will be explained here. One observational technique is called SIMFAM, which stands for Simulated Family Activity Measurement (Straus and Tallman, 1971). SIMFAM is "a technique for measuring the power, support, and communication structure of families, and their creativity and problem-solving ability . . . based on direct observation of family interaction during performance of a standard task" (p. 412). The task is a motor task, which is presented in the form of a game. During the playing of the game, the following variables are assessed through direct observation: power, support, communication frequency, communication flow, linguistic ability, problem-solving ability, activity level, and creativity. The observations are used to derive scores on numerous variables, with the particular variables being a function of the purpose of the research. The technique is explained in considerable detail in "SIMFAM: A Technique for Observational Measurement and Experimental Study of Families" (Straus and Tallman, 1971).

Another observational technique for assessing marital roles, in particular marital power, consists of asking married couples to perform independently a task that involves judgment; for example, the spouses might be asked to complete an attitude questionnaire. The spouses are then brought together and asked to reach a consensus on those items for which they had originally responded with different answers. While the spouses discuss the items on which they disagreed, their interactions are observed and systematically recorded. Scoring of this observational technique is based on both process and outcome. (See for example, Murphy, 1976; Olson, 1969; Pienaar, 1969; Roberts, 1975; and Strodtbeck, 1951.)

A third observational technique was developed by Kenkel (1957, 1959, 1961a, 1961b, 1961c), who described the technique as follows: "Each couple was asked to assume that they had received a gift of $300 with the stipulation that none of it could be saved, nor could any of it be used for items they had previously decided to purchase. They were asked to discuss between themselves how to spend the money and in about an half hour to reach agreement on its use. Paper, pencils, and $300 in stage money was furnished in order to help the couple make their trial allocations of the money" (Kenkel, 1961a, p. 352). Systematic observations are recorded during the couples' half hour of discussion time, and these observations provide the basis for the scoring of marital influence and power. These three observational procedures exemplify the observational measures used in marital role research.

The common problems associated with the self-report instruments in this chapter fall under three headings: the dimensionality of the underlying variable(s); the content validity of the measures; and problems associated with reliance on the self-report technique. In general, the authors of these instruments tended to ignore the issue of dimensionality and acted on the assumption that the underlying variables are unidimensional. Is this a tenable assumption? Is it reasonable to speak of attitudes toward or enactment of marital roles, or does it make more sense to speak of a specific aspect of the marital role? Since each spouse occupies many roles within the marriage—for example, a wife's roles may include wage earner, housekeeper, childcare worker, purchasing agent, sex partner, hostess, financial manager, and so on—it seems reasonable that attitudes toward or enactment of marital roles is a multidimensional variable; that is, a respondent could reasonably be expected to support a traditional role for one aspect of the wife's role and simultaneously support an egalitarian role for a different aspect of the wife's role. Furthermore, there is no reason to assume that attitudes toward or enactment of a specific aspect of the marital role is unidimensional. Studies that have already examined the factor structure of marital roles suggest that the marital role scales are multidimensional. For example, Cromwell and Wieting (1975) factor analyzed responses to the Blood-Wolfe Marital Decision-Making Scale (#109). They found that "Using evidence from five samples, looking at both interitem correlations and factor analyses for the respective samples, the results do not support a unidimensional conclusion but indicate a multidimensional pattern. Interitem correlations are generally low, and factor analyses (while yielding disparate solutions) all provide a solution with more than one dimension" (p. 146). Cromwell and Wieting reported different factor structures for males and for females and different factor structures for the various samples that they used. The implication of their results is clear: items on the Blood-Wolfe Marital Decision-Making Scale should not be treated as additive. The instrument is not unidimensional, and the multiple dimensions they found do not cut across gender or across different samples. Another implication of their findings is that factor-analytic studies should be performed for the other instruments in this section, and no assumption should be made that a factor structure established from the responses of one sample will apply to the responses from another sample. Furthermore, separate factor analyses should be performed using the responses from males and the responses from females.

The second problem that applies to many of the instruments in this chapter concerns their content validity. Because spouses and parents occupy many roles within their families, it cannot be assumed that scores reflect all aspects of the marital or parental role. All the instruments in this chapter should have been constructed by first delineating a content domain and then developing items that systematically sample the content domain. Only when this procedure is followed will it be clear to what domain the results can be generalized. Problems relating to content sampling are particularly acute in the measurement of marital or parental role enactment—for example, marital decision making and marital task allocation. Scant attention seems to have been given to balancing the items that are typed "masculine" with those typed "feminine." For example, the amount of effort and time needed to complete the task, the frequency with which the task must be performed, and the importance of the task to the family's functioning should be equivalent on the "stereotypically masculine" and "stereotypically feminine" items included on a measure of task allocation. Similarly, the importance of the decision, the frequency with which the decision must be made, the consequences of a wrong decision, and the extent to which the decision affects the various family members should be equivalent on the "stereotypically masculine" and "stereotypically feminine" items included on a measure of marital decision making. If, for some reasons related to the purpose of the research, it is advisable to include items that are not equivalent, then this should be taken into account in scoring. It simply does not make sense to assign equal weight to "changing a light bulb"—a stereotypically masculine task that is performed infrequently, requires

little investment of time or effort, and can often be neglected with no serious consequences to any members of the family—and "doing the grocery shopping"—a stereotypically feminine task that is performed on a regular basis, requires at least a moderate
investment of time and effort, and must be performed (unless the family members eat
exclusively in restaurants) in order for the family members to survive.

Because the instruments in this chapter rely exclusively on self-report techniques,
there are numerous potential problems. The extent to which social desirability affects
responses is generally unknown. Because current cultural trends regarding marital and
parental roles, especially among college students, favor egalitarian rather than traditional
roles, it is quite possible that responses to these instruments reflect those cultural trends
rather than the respondents' honest beliefs or perceptions. Responding with socially desirable answers rather than with "truth" does not necessarily imply a conscious attempt on
the part of the respondents to distort their answers. As a result, increasing respondents'
motivation or guaranteeing them anonymity does not necessarily eliminate the problem
of eliciting socially desirable, rather than honest, responses. More research is needed to
determine the extent to which these instruments elicit socially desirable responses and to
determine ways to minimize the social desirability response set.

Unique problems are associated with the use of self-report measures to describe
the enactment of marital or parental roles. In order to be able to describe their own role
enactment, respondents must have been aware of their own behavior. Because persons
acted particular ways does not guarantee that they were aware of how they acted. For
example, the assertion of marital power is not necessarily overt; it might be very subtle
and also very complex. As a result, the persons involved may not have been aware of who
was asserting power. Furthermore, even when the persons were aware of the roles they
were enacting at a particular time, there is no guarantee that they will remember them. It
seems reasonable to assume that when persons' role enactments differ from their ideal,
either they are likely to forget totally how they enacted the role or their recollection is
likely to be distorted. Questions concerning aspects of role behavior that are not likely to
occur on a regular basis may require that the persons remember things that happened
months or years prior to completing the instrument. Even if persons were once aware of
and had accurate perceptions of their relevant behaviors, it is quite possible that they no
longer remember them accurately. And even when persons were aware and can remember
how they enacted their roles, certain characteristics of the self-report instrument can
make it very difficult for them to describe accurately their role enactment. For example,
persons do not always enact their roles in the same way. The measures should specifically
state the time period for which answers are desired. If there has been a recent, significant
event that has altered—perhaps temporarily—the roles that the spouses enact, should the
spouses respond on the basis of their behavior prior to the significant event or since the
significant event? For example, if the couple has just had a baby or the wife has just
taken a job out of the home, should answers be based on their roles prior to the significant event, or the roles they are enacting while adjusting to the significant event, or the
roles they expect to enact after their lives assume a regular routine? In the absence of
specific directions regarding the time frame for answers, there is no way to know how
respondents will interpret the items. Furthermore, even if there has been no significant
event in the lives of the couple, they are likely to enact their roles differently at different
times. Expecting the couple to respond based on the frequency with which they have
enacted each role—for example, husband more often than wife or wife more often than
husband—assumes that they can quantify something for which they have kept no records.
It should be clear that what is being measured in these cases are persons' perceptions of
their behavior, not actual reports of their behavior.

Another problem with relying on self-report measures of marital or parental roles is that the responses depend on who is asked the questions. The older studies in this area relied on the wife's responses and assumed that they accurately described the marital roles of both partners. However, Olson and Cromwell (1975) reviewed twelve self-report studies of marital power and reported that eight of them found discrepancies between the responses given by marital partners. In discussing the perceptual biases found in self-report studies of marital power, Olson and Cromwell (1975, p. 144) stated: "husbands tend to overestimate their power, whereas wives tend to underestimate their power in the family.... Other studies ... have found that individuals tend to underestimate their own power and overreport their spouse's power." Clearly no one partner should be relied on to describe the marital roles; perceptions should be obtained from both partners.

Because of all the problems involved in self-report measures of marital and parental roles, researchers have studied the relationship between responses to self-report measures of marital power and results from observational measures that assess marital power (Cromwell, 1972; Kenkel, 1963; Olson, 1969; Olson and Rabunsky, 1972; and Turk and Bell, 1972). In general, they find discrepancies between the results obtained from self-report measures and observational measures. As a result, researchers should consider using both self-report and observational measures when studying marital power. There is no reason to doubt that the findings regarding marital power would also apply to other aspects of marital and parental role enactment; that is, whenever one is studying marital or parental roles, it is probably advisable to use a combination of self-report and observational measures. There are problems with the validity of both types of measures, but their strengths and weaknesses complement each other, and more valid information is likely to be acquired from using them in combination.

BIBLIOGRAPHY:

Cromwell, R. E. "Multivariate Explorations in Marital and Family Power Structure: Toward a Theoretical and Methodological Clarification of Power as a Dependent Variable." Unpublished doctoral dissertation, University of Minnesota, 1972. (*Dissertation Abstracts International,* 1973, *33*[10-A], 5853.)

Cromwell, R. E., and Wieting, S. G. "Multidimensionality of Conjugal Decision-Making Indices: Comparative Analyses of Five Samples." *Journal of Comparative Family Studies,* 1975, *6,* 139-152.

Kenkel, W. F. "Influence Differentiation in Family Decision Making." *Sociology and Social Research,* 1957, *42,* 18-25.

Kenkel, W. F. "Traditional Family Ideology and Spousal Roles in Decision Making." *Marriage and Family Living,* 1959, *21,* 334-339.

Kenkel, W. F. "Dominance, Persistence, Self-Confidence, and Spousal Roles in Decision Making." *Journal of Social Psychology,* 1961a, *54,* 349-358.

Kenkel, W. F. "Husband-Wife Interaction in Decision Making and Decision Choices." *Journal of Social Psychology,* 1961b, *54,* 252-262.

Kenkel, W. F. "Sex of Observer and Spousal Roles in Decision Making." *Marriage and Family Living,* 1961c, *23,* 185-186.

Kenkel, W. F. "Observational Studies of Husband-Wife Interaction in Family Decision Making." In M. B. Sussman (Ed.), *Sourcebook in Marriage and the Family.* (2nd ed.) Boston: Houghton Mifflin, 1963.

Murphy, R. F. "Dimensions of Therapeutic Contracts for Consumers and Providers of Mental Health Services in Arkansas." Unpublished doctoral dissertation, Texas Technological University, 1976. (*Dissertation Abstracts International,* 1976, *37*[5-B], 2517.)

Olson, D. H. "The Measurement of Family Power by Self-Report and Behavioral Methods." *Journal of Marriage and the Family,* 1969, *31,* 545-550.

Olson, D. H., and Cromwell, R. E. "Methodological Issues in Family Power." In R. E. Cromwell and D. H. Olson (Eds.), *Power in Families.* New York: Halsted Press, 1975.

Olson, D. H., and Gravatt, A. E. "Attitude Change in a Functional Marriage Course." *Family Coordinator,* 1968, *17,* 99-104.

Olson, D. H., and Rabunsky, C. "Validity of Four Measures of Family Power." *Journal of Marriage and the Family,* 1972, *34,* 222-234.

Pienaar, W. D. "Dominance in Families." Unpublished doctoral dissertation, University of Kansas, 1969. (*Dissertation Abstracts International,* 1969, *30*[6-B], 2914-2915.)

Roberts, P. L. B. "The Female Image in the Caldecott Medal Award Books." Unpublished doctoral dissertation, University of the Pacific, 1975. (*Dissertation Abstracts International,* 1975, *36*[6-A], 3392.)

Straus, M. A., and Brown, B. W. *Family Measurement Techniques: Abstracts of Published Instruments, 1935-1974.* Minneapolis: University of Minnesota Press, 1978.

Straus, M., and Tallman, I. "SIMFAM: A Technique for Observational Measurement and Experimental Study of Families." In J. Aldous, T. Condon, R. Hill, M. Straus, and I. Tallman (Eds.), *Family Problem Solving.* Hinsdale, Ill.: Dryden Press, 1971.

Strodtbeck, F. L. "Husband-Wife Interaction over Revealed Differences." *American Sociological Review,* 1951, *16,* 468-473.

Turk, J. L., and Bell, N. W. "Measuring Power in Families." *Journal of Marriage and the Family,* 1972, *34,* 215-222.

---

108. ATTITUDES TOWARD THE ROLE OF HUSBAND AND WIFE IN MARRIAGE

AUTHOR: Alver Hilding Jacobson

DATE: 1950

VARIABLE: Support for egalitarian versus male-dominant roles in marriage

TYPE OF INSTRUMENT: Summated rating scale

DESCRIPTION: The scale includes twenty-eight statements pertaining to the roles of husband and wife in marriage. Items relate to such topics as responsibility for decision making, freedom in social activities, responsibility for home and family tasks, and so forth. About three-quarters of the items are phrased to reflect traditional (male-dominant) roles and one quarter are phrased to reflect egalitarian roles. Each statement is accompanied by five response alternatives: strongly agree, agree, uncertain, disagree, and strongly disagree.

PREVIOUSLY ADMINISTERED TO: College students in the United States, Japan, Thailand, and India; adults including nurses, married couples, and divorced couples

APPROPRIATE FOR: Ages 16 and older

ADMINISTRATION: The scale can be self-administered and can be completed in about fifteen minutes.

SAMPLE ITEMS: The husband should decide whether or not to have children.
The wife should take the husband's religion as her own.

SCORING: Items are objectively scored and equally weighted. A total score is obtained that can range from 28 (male dominant) to 140 (egalitarian).

DEVELOPMENT: A pool of sixty items was developed from: (1) the responses given by sixty-two married and divorced persons who were asked "what they thought the husband and wife were expected to do in economic, religious, political, affectional, parent or pre-parent, and day-to-day living situations in their specific marriages and in marriages in general" (Jacobson, 1950, p. 14); and (2) a survey of the relevant literature. The sixty items were given to three judges who were asked to "judge each item on the basis of: the quality of expressing an attitude, relevance to the role of spouses in marriage, clarity, and as nearly as possible, expression in the vernacular" (Jacobson, 1952, p. 147). Based on their responses, the item pool was reduced to fifty items. The fifty-item scale was administered to thirty married couples and thirty divorced couples. The twenty-eight items that best discriminated between those scoring in the upper and lower 25 percent of the distribution of total scores were retained for the final scale.

RELIABILITY: The scale was administered to twenty married couples and twenty divorced couples. Split-half reliability, based on their responses, was .908. The couples completed the scale a second time, twenty days after they first completed it. Test-retest reliability was .794 (Jacobson, 1950).

VALIDITY: The scale was administered to ten persons whom Jacobson (1950) knew to hold conventional attitudes and eleven persons whom Jacobson knew to hold egalitarian attitudes. The traditional group had an average item score of 1.9; the egalitarian group had an average item score of 4.1.

Jacobson (1950, 1951, 1952) hypothesized that "divorced couples exhibit a greater disparity in their attitudes toward the roles of the husband and wife in marriage than do married couples." Using the responses from 100 divorced couples and 100 married couples, Jacobson found that the difference between the means of the divorced couples was approximately four times the size of the difference between the means of the married couples.

Researchers have found sex differences in scale scores, with females reporting more egalitarian views than males (Arkoff, Meredith, and Dong, 1963; Gardiner, 1968; Iwahara, 1964; Jacobson, 1950, 1951, 1952; Kalish, Maloney, and Arkoff, 1966; Sharma, 1971).

NOTES AND COMMENTS: (1) The scale has most frequently been used to study sex differences in attitudes (see Validity above) and ethnic differences in attitudes (Arkoff, Meredith, and Dong, 1963; Arkoff, Meredith, and Iwahara, 1964; Gardiner, 1968; Gardiner, Singh, and D'Orazio, 1974; Iwahara, 1964; Kalish, Maloney, and Arkoff, 1966; and Sharma, 1971). The scale has also been used to study the relationship between attitudes and marital status (Jacobson, 1950, 1951, 1952) and the relationship between attitudes and career commitment (Krain and Lower, 1976; Lower, 1975).

(2) Blood and Hamblin (1958) constructed a Guttman scale to measure changes in authority expectations. The scale includes seven of the items from the Attitudes Toward the Role of Husband and Wife in Marriage Scale. The coefficient of reproducibility for the seven-item Guttman scale averaged .91.

(3) Many of the items are subject to varying interpretations. For example, does the statement, "The husband should decide whether or not to have children" mean that the husband alone should make the decision? If that is what is meant, then it should be clearly stated. Does the statement, "The wife should be free to go out nights by herself" mean that the wife should be free to go out without her husband or without anyone? As the item is presently phrased, a negative response might mean that a woman should never go out totally alone at night because it is not safe. This response reflects attitudes about one's neighborhood more than attitudes about marital roles. The several items that state that a husband should "help" with various aspects of housework or childrearing imply a traditional orientation. Does disagreement with these "helping" statements mean that a husband should be totally uninvolved in these responsibilities, or does it mean that he should assume responsibility for them rather than just helping out with them? Does the statement, "If a husband runs around, so can his wife" refer to sexual activities or to physical exercise (that is, jogging)? "The wife should mend and sew" could be interpreted to mean that the wife should be the only one in the family that does mending and sewing, or it could mean that the wife should mend and sew her own clothes. In other words, agreeing with the statement does not guarantee that one would disagree with the statement "The husband should mend and sew." These are just some of the examples of items that are subject to more than one interpretation.

(4) Attitudes Toward the Role of Husband and Wife in Marriage is described in *Family Measurement Techniques* (Straus, 1969, pp. 153-154; Straus and Brown, 1978, pp. 82-83).

SOURCE: See Jacobson, 1950 or 1951.

BIBLIOGRAPHY:

Arkoff, A., Meredith, G., and Dong, J. "Attitudes of Japanese-American and Caucasian-American Students Toward Marriage Roles." *Journal of Social Psychology,* 1963, *59,* 11-15.

Arkoff, A., Meredith, G., and Iwahara, S. "Male-Dominant and Equalitarian Attitudes in Japanese, Japanese-American, and Caucasian-American Students." *Journal of Social Psychology,* 1964, *64,* 225-229.

Blood, R. O., Jr., and Hamblin, R. L. "The Effect of the Wife's Employment on the Family Power Structure." *Social Forces,* 1958, *36,* 347-352.

Gardiner, H. W. "Attitudes of Thai Students Toward Marriage Roles." *Journal of Social Psychology,* 1968, *75,* 61-65.

Gardiner, H. W., Singh, U. P., and D'Orazio, D. E. "The Liberated Woman in Three Cultures: Marital-Role Preferences in Thailand, India, and the United States." *Human Organization,* 1974, *33,* 413-415.

Iwahara, S. "Marriage Attitudes in Japanese College Students." *Psychologia: An International Journal of Psychology in the Orient,* 1964, *7,* 165-174.

Jacobson, A. H. "A Study of Conflict in Attitudes Toward the Roles of the Husband and the Wife in Marriage." Unpublished doctoral dissertation, Ohio State University, 1950.

Jacobson, A. H. "Conflict in Attitudes Toward the Marital Roles of Husband and Wife." *Washington State University Research Studies,* 1951, *19,* 103-106.

Jacobson, A. H. "Conflict of Attitudes Toward the Roles of the Husband and Wife in Marriage." *American Sociological Review,* 1952, *17,* 146-150.

Kalish, R. A., Maloney, M., and Arkoff, A. "Cross-Cultural Comparisons of College-Student Marital-Role Preferences." *Journal of Social Psychology,* 1966, *68,* 41-47.

Krain, M., and Lower, D. "The Relationship of Women's Career Commitment to Their Attitudes Toward Their Children's Sex Role Socialization, to Their Attitudes on Spousal Roles, and to Marital Adjustment." Paper presented at the meeting of the Midwest Sociological Society, St. Louis, Missouri, 1976. (ERIC Document Reproduction Service No. ED 138 855.)

Lower, D. J. "The Relation of Women's Career Commitment and Their Attitudes Regarding the Socialization of Children into Sex Roles, Marital Role Relations, and Marital Adjustment." Unpublished master's thesis, University of Iowa, 1975.

Sharma, K. L. "Attitudes of Indian Students Toward Marriage Roles." *Journal of Social Psychology,* 1971, *83,* 299-300.

*Straus, M. A. *Family Measurement Techniques: Abstracts of Published Instruments, 1935-1965.* Minneapolis: University of Minnesota Press, 1969.

*Straus, M. A., and Brown, B. W. *Family Measurement Techniques: Abstracts of Published Instruments, 1935-1974.* Minneapolis: University of Minnesota Press, 1978.

---

109. BLOOD-WOLFE MARITAL DECISION-MAKING SCALE

AUTHORS: Robert O. Blood, Jr., and Donald M. Wolfe

DATE: 1958 (used 1955)

VARIABLE: Marital power

TYPE OF INSTRUMENT: Summated rating scale

DESCRIPTION: The scale is introduced with the following statement: "In every family somebody has to decide such things as where the family will live and so on. Many couples talk such things over first, but the final decision often has to be made by the husband or the wife" (Blood and Wolfe, 1960, p. 282). The statement is followed by eight questions that ask which spouse makes the decision in a particular area. The response options are: husband always, husband more than wife, husband and wife exactly the same, wife more than husband, wife always.

PREVIOUSLY ADMINISTERED TO: Married adults in the United States, Greece, Germany, France, Mexico, Kenya, Yugoslavia, Denmark, Puerto Rico, and Turkey; also junior high school girls

APPROPRIATE FOR: Married adults

ADMINISTRATION: The scale is often administered as part of an interview. The response options are written on a card and presented to the respondent so that she may refer to them during the interview. The scale may also be presented as a self-administered instrument. About five minutes are required to complete the scale.

SAMPLE ITEMS: Who usually makes the final decision about what car to get?
                          Who usually makes the final decision about how much money your family can afford to spend per week on food?

SCORING: Items are objectively scored and equally weighted. Typically the mean score for the responses to all the items is found. Care must be used in interpreting mean scores of 3, because they might represent either an egalitarian response to all the items or an equal number of extreme responses.

DEVELOPMENT: The decision items were selected "because they are all relatively important (compared to deciding whether to go to a movie tonight). They are also questions which nearly all couples have to face. (This is why no questions were asked relating to children.)" (Blood and Wolfe, 1960, p. 19). Only items that could affect the entire family were selected; and it was desired that the decisions ranged from "typically masculine to typically feminine" (Blood and Wolfe, 1960, p. 20).

RELIABILITY: Guttman scalogram analysis was applied to the responses from 258 wives and 221 husbands. The coefficient of reproducibility was .86 for husbands and .88 for wives (p < .0001 for both coefficients). Coefficient alpha was computed using the responses from the same persons; the coefficient was .62 (Bahr, 1973).
          Cromwell and Wieting (1975) computed interitem correlations using the data from the following five groups: 731 Detroit wives, 450 French wives, 115 California husbands and wives, 266 Mexican husbands and wives, and 119 Minnesota husbands and wives. The results indicated generally low interitem correlations. For the Detroit wives, the coefficients ranged from −.05 to .21; for French wives, the correlations ranged from 0 to .32. In California, most coefficients were near zero. In Mexico, the correlations ranged from −.17 to .41. For the Minnesota wives, the correlations ranged from −.15 to .35.
          For information regarding the consistency between responses given by pairs of husbands and wives, see Validity.

VALIDITY: Granbois and Willett (1970) administered the scale to 167 married couples. The correlation between responses given by husbands and wives was .353. "A cross-classification of these estimates (grouped into four frequency classes) revealed congruent classification in only 42 percent of the cases. . . . Disagreeing couples were nearly equally divided between those where the wife's estimate exceeded that of the husband (31 percent) and those where the husband's estimate exceeded the wife's (27 percent)" (p. 69). Other researchers have also examined the relationship between the responses given by husbands and those given by wives. Davis (1971) analyzed the responses given by seventy-seven married couples and found the correlation between husband and wife responses to be .15. Wilkes (1975) performed the same analysis on the responses from sixty black couples and obtained a correlation of .31. Turk and Bell (1972) looked at data obtained from 211 families. They found that the difference between the sums obtained by husband-and-wife pairs was significant at the .003 level. "The nature of this difference is that each spouse tends to underreport himself and overreport his marital partner" (p. 217).

Several researchers have compared the results obtained when different measures of marital power are used (Davis, 1971; Turk and Bell, 1972; Wilkes, 1975). In each case, the Blood-Wolfe Marital Decision-Making Scale was one of the measures used. The general conclusion appears to be that different results are obtained when different measures are used; that is, the correlations between the various measures tend to be low.

Centers, Raven, and Rodrigues (1971) compared responses from the Blood-Wolfe Marital Decision-Making Scale with results obtained using a similar format but a different set of questions. They concluded, "The distribution of conjugal power . . . is strongly influenced by the make-up of the sample of decisions employed to reveal it" (p. 271).

NOTES AND COMMENTS: (1) The scale could easily be adapted for unmarried persons, as was done by Klecka and Hiller (1977) in order to measure a person's ideal or future preferences regarding marital power. Furthermore, the scale could be used to measure children's conceptions of the marital power distribution in their parents' marriage.

(2) Cromwell and Wieting (1975) performed separate factor analyses on the responses from five groups who completed the scale: a Detroit group, a French group, a California group, a Mexican group, and a Minnesota group. For no group was one factor sufficient to explain the variance in responses. Cromwell and Wieting (p. 146) conclude: "The advisability of using items discussed here to construct an additive scale is not warranted. It would appear that individual item weights should not be summed to form composite mean scores and those scores used in data analysis because it is impossible to determine which factor or combination of factors contributed to that score. The resultant score does not represent a single variable." They further state (p. 147): "there remains considerable unexplained variation in the respective solutions even when two, three, or four factors are extracted." They also suggest that different factors might be extracted if the responses are elicited from wives as compared with husbands.

(3) Results on the Blood-Wolfe Marital Decision-Making Scale have been related to many other variables. Blood and Wolfe (1960) have related the scores to rural-urban setting, immigrant status, religion, age, education, husband's occupation, income, social status, race, suburban versus urban residence, wife's employment status, and stage in the family life cycle. Other researchers have compared scores on the Blood-Wolfe scale with age (Cromwell, Corrales, and Torsiello, 1973; Green and Cunningham, 1975; Richmond, 1976; Sharp and Mott, 1956; and Weller, 1968); income (Buric and Zecevic, 1967; Cromwell, Corrales, and Torsiello, 1973; Green and Cunningham, 1975; Richmond, 1976; Rodman, 1967; Sharp and Mott, 1956); education (Buric and Zecevic, 1967; Centers, Raven, and Rodrigues, 1971; Cromwell, Corrales, and Torsiello, 1973; First-Dilic, 1974; Fox, 1973; Noordhoek and Smith, 1971; Richmond, 1976; Rodman, 1967; and Weller, 1968); occupation (Beckman and Houser, 1975; Buric and Zecevic, 1967; Centers, Raven, and Rodrigues, 1971; Cromwell, Corrales, and Torsiello, 1973; Fox, 1973; and Rodman, 1967); race (Centers, Raven, and Rodrigues, 1971; Jackson, 1972; and TenHouten, 1970); hometown (Burchinal and Bauder, 1965; and Dietrich, 1975); family size (Campbell, 1970; First-Dilic, 1974; Richmond, 1976; and Weller, 1968); wife's employment status (Aldous, 1969; Buric and Zecevic, 1967; Noordhoek and Smith, 1971; and Safilios-Rothschild, 1970); nationality (Rodman, 1967; and Safilios-Rothschild, 1967, 1969); religion (First-Dilic, 1974); social class (Cromwell, Corrales, and Torsiello, 1973; First-Dilic, 1974; and Gold and Slater, 1958); marital satisfaction or length of marriage (Buric

and Zecevic, 1967; Centers, Raven, and Rodrigues, 1971; First-Dilic, 1974; Michel, 1970; Safilios-Rothschild, 1967; and Weller, 1968); attitudes toward female role (Green and Cunningham, 1975); and relationship to ideal power division (Abbott, 1976).

(4) It is quite common for a researcher to modify the scale by adding, deleting, or modifying items (Abbott, 1976; Aldous, 1969; Aldous and Straus, 1966; Beckman and Houser, 1975; Burchinal and Bauder, 1965; Buric and Zecevic, 1967; Campbell, 1970; Centers, Raven, and Rodrigues, 1971; Cromwell, Corrales, and Torsiello, 1973; Cunningham and Green, 1974; Dietrich, 1975; First-Dilic, 1974; Fox, 1973; Green and Cunningham, 1975; Hadley and Jacob, 1976; Hawkes and Taylor, 1975; Hill, 1965; Klecka and Hiller, 1977; Lamouse, 1969; Michel, 1970; Noordhoek and Smith, 1971; Richmond, 1976; Safilios-Rothschild, 1967, 1969, 1970; Weller, 1968).

(5) Despite the fact that this scale has been used by many researchers in many diverse settings, the psychometric properties of the scale cause one to question its value. Research described above has indicated that the responses are a function of who is responding and what specific set of decision questions they are responding to. The scale has been interpreted as unidimensional, but in fact it has been shown to be multidimensional.

(6) The scale is also described in *Family Measurement Techniques* (Straus, 1969, pp. 41-42; Straus and Brown, 1978, pp. 75-76).

SOURCE: See Blood and Wolfe, 1960; or Granbois and Willett, 1970; or Wilkes, 1975.

BIBLIOGRAPHY:

Abbott, S. "Full-Time Farmers and Weekend Wives: An Analysis of Altering Conjugal Roles." *Journal of Marriage and the Family*, 1976, *38*, 165-174.

Aldous, J. "Wives' Employment Status and Lower-Class Men as Husband-Fathers: Support for the Moynihan Thesis." *Journal of Marriage and the Family*, 1969, *31*, 469-476.

Aldous, J., and Straus, M. A. "Social Networks and Conjugal Roles: A Test of Bott's Hypothesis." *Social Forces*, 1966, *44*, 576-580.

Bahr, S. J. "The Internal Consistency of Blood and Wolfe's Measure of Conjugal Power: A Research Note." *Journal of Marriage and the Family*, 1973, *35*, 293-295.

Beckman, L. J., and Houser, B. B. "Employed Women's Attitudes Toward Women's Liberation, Family Decision Making, and Tasks." Paper presented at 83rd annual meeting of the American Psychological Association, Chicago, August 1975.

Benson, E. E. "Marital Power: A Theoretical Explication and Empirical Exploration of Three Process Models." Unpublished doctoral dissertation, Michigan State University, 1976. (*Dissertation Abstracts International*, 1976, *37*[2-A], 1253-1254.)

Blood, R. O., Jr., and Takeshita, Y. J. "Development of Cross-Cultural Equivalence of Measure of Marital Interaction for U.S.A. and Japan." *Transactions of the Fifth World Congress of Sociology*, 1964, *4*, 333-344.

Blood, R. O., Jr., and Wolfe, D. M. *Husbands and Wives: The Dynamics of Married Living.* Glencoe, Ill.: Free Press, 1960.

Burchinal, L. G., and Bauder, W. W. "Decision Making and Role Patterns Among Iowa Farm and Nonfarm Families." *Journal of Marriage and the Family*, 1965, *27*, 525-530.

Buric, O., and Zecevic, A. "Family Authority, Marital Satisfaction, and the Social Network in Yugoslavia." *Journal of Marriage and the Family*, 1967, *29*, 325-336.

Campbell, F. L. "Family Growth and Variation in Family Role Structure." *Journal of Marriage and the Family*, 1970, *32*, 45-53.

Centers, R., Raven, B. H., and Rodrigues, A. "Conjugal Power Structure: A Reexamination." *American Sociological Review,* 1971, *36,* 264-278.

Corrales, R. G. "Power and Satisfaction in Early Marriage." In R. E. Cromwell and D. H. Olson (Eds.), *Power in Families.* New York: Halsted Press, 1975.

Cromwell, R. E., Corrales, R., and Torsiello, P. M. "Normative Patterns of Marital Decision-Making Power and Influence in Mexico and the United States: A Partial Test of Resource and Ideology Theory." *Journal of Comparative Family Studies,* 1973, *4,* 177-196.

Cromwell, R. E., and Wieting, S. G. "Multidimensionality of Conjugal Decision-Making Indices: Comparative Analyses of Five Samples." *Journal of Comparative Family Studies,* 1975, *6,* 139-152.

Cunningham, I. C. M., and Green, R. T. "Purchasing Roles in the U.S. Family, 1955 and 1973." *Journal of Marketing,* 1974, *38,* 61-64.

Davis, H. L. "Measurement of Husband-Wife Influence in Consumer Purchase Decisions." *Journal of Marketing Research,* 1971, *8,* 305-312.

Dietrich, K. T. "A Reexamination of the Myth of Black Matriarchy." *Journal of Marriage and the Family,* 1975, *37,* 367-374.

Duncan, O. D., Schuman, H., and Duncan, B. *Social Change in a Metropolitan Community.* New York: Russell Sage Foundation, 1973.

First-Dilic, R. "Conjugal Power Relations in the Working Wife's Family in Yugoslavia." *International Journal of Sociology of the Family,* 1974, *4,* 11-22.

Fox, G. L. "Another Look at the Comparative Resources Model: Assessing the Balance of Power in Turkish Marriages." *Journal of Marriage and the Family,* 1973, *35,* 718-730.

Gold, M., and Slater, C. "Office, Factory, Store—and Family: A Study of Integration Setting." *American Sociological Review,* 1958, *23,* 64-74.

Granbois, D. H., and Willett, R. P. "Equivalence of Family Role Measures Based on Husband and Wife Data." *Journal of Marriage and the Family,* 1970, *32,* 68-72.

Green, R. T., and Cunningham, I. C. M. "Feminine Role Perception and Family Purchasing Decisions." *Journal of Marketing Research,* 1975, *12,* 325-332.

Hadley, T. R. "The Measurement of Family Power: A Methodological Study." Unpublished doctoral dissertation, University of Pittsburgh, 1974. (*Dissertation Abstracts International,* 1975, *35* [9-B], 4650.)

Hadley, T. R., and Jacob, T. "The Measurement of Family Power: A Methodological Study." *Sociometry,* 1976, *39,* 384-395.

Hawkes, G. R., and Taylor, M. "Power Structure in Mexican and Mexican-American Farm-Labor Families." *Journal of Marriage and the Family,* 1975, *37,* 807-811.

Hill, R. "Decision Making and the Family Cycle." In E. Shanas and G. F. Streib (Eds.), *Social Structure and the Family.* Englewood Cliffs, N.J.: Prentice-Hall, 1965.

Jackson, J. J. "Marital Life Among Aging Blacks." *Family Coordinator,* 1972, *21,* 21-27.

Kandel, D. B., and Lesser, G. S. "Marital Decision Making in American and Danish Urban Families: A Research Note." *Journal of Marriage and the Family,* 1972, *34,* 134-138.

Klecka, C. O., and Hiller, D. V. "Impact of Mother's Life-Style on Adolescent Gender-Role Socialization." *Sex Roles,* 1977, *3,* 241-255.

Lamouse, A. "Family Roles of Women: A German Example." *Journal of Marriage and the Family,* 1969, *31,* 145-152.

Michel, A. "Wife's Satisfaction with Husband's Understanding in Parisian Urban Families." *Journal of Marriage and the Family,* 1970, *32,* 351-359.

Noordhoek, J., and Smith, Y. "Family and Work." *Acta Sociologica,* 1971, *14,* 43-51.

Richmond, M. L. "Beyond Resource Theory: Another Look at Factors Enabling Women to Affect Family Interaction." *Journal of Marriage and the Family,* 1976, *38,* 257-266.

Rodman, H. "Marital Power in France, Greece, Yugoslavia, and the United States: A Cross-National Discussion." *Journal of Marriage and the Family,* 1967, *29,* 320-324.

Safilios-Rothschild, C. "A Comparison of Power Structure and Marital Satisfaction in Urban Greek and French Families." *Journal of Marriage and the Family,* 1967, *29,* 345-352.

Safilios-Rothschild, C. "Family Sociology or Wives' Family Sociology? A Cross-Cultural Examination of Decision Making." *Journal of Marriage and the Family,* 1969, *31,* 290-301.

Safilios-Rothschild, C. "The Influence of the Wife's Degree of Work Commitment upon Some Aspects of Family Organization and Dynamics." *Journal of Marriage and the Family,* 1970, *32,* 681-691.

Sharp, H., and Mott, P. "Consumer Decision in the Metropolitan Family." *Journal of Marketing,* 1956, *21,* 149-156.

*Straus, M. A. *Family Measurement Techniques: Abstracts of Published Instruments, 1935-1965.* Minneapolis: University of Minnesota Press, 1969.

*Straus, M. A., and Brown, B. W. *Family Measurement Techniques: Abstracts of Published Instruments, 1935-1974.* Minneapolis: University of Minnesota Press, 1978.

TenHouten, W. D. "The Black Family: Myth and Reality." *Psychiatry,* 1970, *33,* 145-173.

Turk, J. L., and Bell, N. W. "Measuring Power in Families." *Journal of Marriage and the Family,* 1972, *34,* 215-222.

Weller, R. H. "The Employment of Wives, Dominance, and Fertility." *Journal of Marriage and the Family,* 1968, *30,* 437-442.

Wilkes, R. E. "Husband-Wife Influence in Purchase Decisions: A Confirmation and Extension." *Journal of Marketing Research,* 1975, *12,* 224-227.

110. BLOOD-WOLFE MARITAL TASK ALLOCATION SCALE

AUTHORS: Robert O. Blood, Jr., and Donald M. Wolfe

DATE: 1958 (used 1955)

VARIABLE: Division of family-oriented tasks among husbands and wives

TYPE OF INSTRUMENT: Multiple choice

DESCRIPTION: The instrument consists of eight questions that ask whether the husband or wife performs specific tasks related to the family. Three tasks are considered typically masculine (repairing things around the house, mowing the lawn, and shoveling the sidewalk); four tasks are considered typically feminine (doing the grocery shopping, getting the husband's breakfast on workdays, straightening the living room for company, and doing the evening dishes); and one task is not sex typed (keeping track of the money and bills). The response options are: husband always, husband more than wife, husband and wife exactly the same, wife more than husband, and wife always.

PREVIOUSLY ADMINISTERED TO: Married adults in the United States, Germany, France, and Belgium

APPROPRIATE FOR: Married adults

ADMINISTRATION: The instrument is usually administered as part of an interview. The response options are written on a card and presented to the respondent so that she may refer to them during the interview. The instrument may also be presented as a self-administered instrument. About five minutes are required to complete it.

SCORING: A Relative Task Participation score is obtained by finding the mean score on all items; the response "wife only" is awarded the maximum number of points in finding the mean. A score for Adherence to Male Roles reflects the extent to which the husband performs the three typically masculine tasks. A score for Adherence to Female Roles reflects the extent to which the wife performs four typically feminine tasks. The combination of the Adherence to Male Roles score and the Adherence to Female Roles score indicates the Adherence to Traditional Sex Roles. A Role Stereotypy score is found by counting the number of tasks that are performed exclusively by the traditional partner. A Role Specialization score reflects the number of tasks performed exclusively by one partner, regardless of whether it is the traditional partner.

DEVELOPMENT: Little information is provided regarding the development of the scale. Blood and Wolfe (1960, p. 49) state, "The questions were chosen because they concern tasks which most families perform." One third of the persons responding to the original measure did not have children; as a result, childcare tasks were deliberately omitted from the list of tasks. In selecting tasks, only those that could theoretically be performed by both partners—that is, both partners would be available to perform the task—were chosen.

RELIABILITY: See the Validity section for information regarding the consistency between responses from husbands and wives. No other type of reliability data are provided.

VALIDITY: Granbois and Willett (1970) report the results of a study in which 167 married couples independently responded to the instrument. The percentage of couples who disagreed in their response to each question varied from 28.9 to 54.5. The correlation between responses of husbands and wives was .61. There was essentially no difference in the number of cases in which the wife's estimate exceeded the husband's and the number of cases in which the husband's estimate exceeded the wife's. Granbois and Willett (1970, p. 70) conclude, "Responses in the aggregate are similar between husbands and wives, but comparison of individual spouses' responses reveals discrepancies about half the time."

Using a modification of the scale, Levinger (1964) obtained responses from sixty married couples and compared the responses given by and for husbands and wives. When Levinger correlated the husband's rating of his wife's performance with the wife's rating of her husband's performance, the correlations for the various items ranged from −.02 to

−.92; when he correlated the husband's rating of his own performance with the husband's rating of his wife's performance, he obtained correlations on the various items ranging from −.30 to −.91; when he correlated the wife's rating of her own performance with her rating of her husband's performance, the correlations ranged from −.10 to −.98.

NOTES AND COMMENTS: (1) The major criticism of this instrument concerns the number and content of the items. The typically masculine tasks do not match the typically feminine tasks in terms of the importance of the task, the frequency with which the task must be performed, and the amount of time the task requires. Furthermore, eight tasks hardly serve to define the totality of husband and wife roles. Finally, the particular set of eight tasks included do not represent any systematic or random sample of a specific domain of tasks. Therefore, it seems inadvisable to generalize beyond these tasks.

(2) Results on the Blood-Wolfe Marital Task Allocation Scale have been related to many other variables. Blood and Wolfe (1960) have related the scores to immigrant status, religion, rural-urban setting, income, social status, intergenerational occupational mobility, wife's employment status, race, and stage in the family life cycle. Other researchers have compared scores on the Blood-Wolfe Scale with husband's employment environment (Gold and Slater, 1958); rural-urban setting (Blood, 1958; Burchinal and Bauder, 1965; and Silverman and Hill, 1967); effects of wife's employment (Aldous, 1969; and Silverman and Hill, 1967); husband's occupational status (Silverman and Hill, 1967); income (Silverman and Hill, 1967); stage in the family life cycle (Silverman and Hill, 1967); family size and spacing of children (Campbell, 1970); professional or nonprofessional status of working wife (Beckman and Houser, 1975); marital satisfaction (Levinger, 1964); wife's satisfaction with husband's understanding (Michel, 1970); and year of administration (Duncan, Schuman, and Duncan, 1973).

(3) It is quite common for a researcher to modify the instrument. The modifications typically consist of deleting, adding, or modifying the specific questions (Aldous, 1969; Aldous and Straus, 1966; Ballweg, 1967; Beckman and Houser, 1975; Burchinal and Bauder, 1965; Campbell, 1970; Danziger, 1974; Lamouse, 1969; Levinger, 1964; Michel, 1970; Silverman and Hill, 1967; Udry and Hall, 1965).

(4) This instrument is also described in *Family Measurement Techniques* (Straus, 1969, pp. 37-38; Straus and Brown, 1978, pp. 97-98).

SOURCE: See Blood and Wolfe, 1960; or Granbois and Willett, 1970; or Silverman and Hill, 1967.

BIBLIOGRAPHY:

Aldous, J. "Wives' Employment Status and Lower-Class Men as Husband-Father: Support for the Moynihan Thesis." *Journal of Marriage and the Family,* 1969, *31,* 469-476.
Aldous, J., and Straus, M. A. "Social Networks and Conjugal Roles: A Test of Bott's Hypothesis." *Social Forces,* 1966, *44,* 576-580.
Ballweg, J. A. "Resolution of Conjugal Role Adjustment After Retirement." *Journal of Marriage and the Family,* 1967, *29,* 277-281.
Beckman, L. J., and Houser, B. B. "Employed Women's Attitudes Toward Women's Liberation, Family Decision Making, and Tasks." Paper presented at 83rd annual meeting of the American Psychological Association, Chicago, August 1975.
Blood, R. O., Jr. "The Division of Labor in City and Farm Families." *Marriage and Family Living,* 1958, *20,* 170-174.

Blood, R. O., Jr., and Takeshita, Y. J. "Development of Cross-Cultural Equivalence of Measure of Marital Interaction for U.S.A. and Japan." *Transactions of the Fifth World Congress of Sociology,* 1964, *4,* 333-344.

Blood, R. O., Jr., and Wolfe, D. M. *Husbands and Wives: The Dynamics of Married Living.* Glencoe, Ill.: Free Press, 1960.

Burchinal, L. G., and Bauder, W. W. "Decision Making and Role Patterns Among Iowa Farm and Nonfarm Families." *Journal of Marriage and the Family,* 1965, *27,* 525-530.

Campbell, F. L. "Family Growth and Variation in Family Role Structure." *Journal of Marriage and the Family,* 1970, *32,* 45-53.

Danziger, K. "The Acculturation of Italian Immigrant Girls in Canada." *International Journal of Psychology,* 1974, *9,* 129-137.

Duncan, O. D., Schuman, H., and Duncan, B. *Social Change in a Metropolitan Community.* New York: Russell Sage Foundation, 1973.

Gold, M., and Slater, C. "Office, Factory, Store—and Family: A Study of Integration Setting." *American Sociological Review,* 1958, *23,* 64-74.

Granbois, D. H., and Willett, R. P. "Equivalence of Family Role Measures Based on Husband and Wife Data." *Journal of Marriage and the Family,* 1970, *32,* 68-72.

Jackson, J. J. "Marital Life Among Aging Blacks." *Family Coordinator,* 1972, *21,* 21-27.

Lamouse, A. "Family Roles of Women: A German Example." *Journal of Marriage and the Family,* 1969, *31,* 145-152.

Levinger, G. "Task and Social Behavior in Marriage." *Sociometry,* 1964, *27,* 433-448.

Michel, A. "Wife's Satisfaction with Husband's Understanding in Parisian Urban Families." *Journal of Marriage and the Family,* 1970, *32,* 351-359.

Silverman, W., and Hill, R. "Task Allocation in Marriage in the United States and Belgium." *Journal of Marriage and the Family,* 1967, *29,* 353-359.

*Straus, M. A. *Family Measurement Techniques: Abstracts of Published Instruments, 1935-1965.* Minneapolis: University of Minnesota Press, 1969.

*Straus, M. A., and Brown, B. W. *Family Measurement Techniques: Abstracts of Published Instruments, 1935-1974.* Minneapolis: University of Minnesota Press, 1978.

Udry, J. R., and Hall, M. "Marital Role Segregation and Social Networks in Middle-Class, Middle-Aged Couples." *Journal of Marriage and the Family,* 1965, *27,* 392-395.

---

111. BUEHLER-WEIGERT-THOMAS CONJUGAL POWER SCALE

AUTHORS: Marilyn H. Buehler, Andrew J. Weigert, and Darwin L. Thomas

DATE: 1974

VARIABLE: Conjugal power

TYPE OF INSTRUMENT: Summated rating scale

DESCRIPTION: Respondents are asked to indicate which of their parents has the "final say" when they disagree on a decision in each of four areas: home furnishings, disciplining children, spending, and religious matters. Five response options, ranging from "father always" to "mother always," are provided.

PREVIOUSLY ADMINISTERED TO: Catholic high school students in the United States, Germany, Spain, Puerto Rico, and Mexico

APPROPRIATE FOR: Ages 8 and older

ADMINISTRATION: The scale can be self-administered and can be completed in about three minutes.

SCORING: Items are objectively scored and equally weighted. Total scores can range from 4 (high maternal power) to 20 (high paternal power).

DEVELOPMENT: No information is provided.

RELIABILITY: The scale was administered to twenty-nine high school girls on two separate occasions. The interval between testings is not specified. Test-retest reliability was calculated for each of the four questions: home furnishings = .79 (excluding the responses from two girls who gave extremely divergent responses); disciplining children = .70; spending = .79; and religious matters = .90 (Buehler, Weigert, and Thomas, 1974).

The scale was administered to adolescents in six cities: New York; St. Paul, Minnesota; Bonn, Germany; San Juan, Puerto Rico; Seville, Spain; and Merida, Mexico. Inter-item correlation coefficients for the six samples ranged from .16 to .30. The authors indicate that "the relatively low consistency coefficients were not judged too harshly, since an effort was made to include decision areas which are allocated differentially to the husband or wife" (Buehler, Weigert, and Thomas, 1974, p. 8).

VALIDITY: The five countries in which the scale was administered were rank ordered according to their degree of industrialization. As predicted, the scale correlated negatively with degree of industrialization; Spearman rank-order correlations = $-.40$ for females and $-.30$ for males.

Correlations were computed between scores on the scale and each of the following variables: husband's occupation, husband's education, wife's employment, wife's education, husband's religiosity, and wife's religiosity. There was no clear trend in the correlations obtained in the various countries.

NOTES AND COMMENTS: (1) The scale was translated into Spanish and German for administration in other countries.

(2) Though the authors claim that the scale measures "conjugal power," it would be more accurate to state that it measures perceptions of conjugal power in four specific areas.

SOURCE: See Buehler, Weigert, and Thomas, 1974.

BIBLIOGRAPHY:

Buehler, M. H., Weigert, A. J., and Thomas, D. L. "Correlates of Conjugal Power: A Five-Culture Analysis of Adolescent Perceptions." *Journal of Comparative Family Studies*, 1974, *5*, 5-16.

Thomas, D. L., and Weigert, A. J. "Determining Nonequivalent Measurement in Cross-Cultural Family Research." *Journal of Marriage and the Family,* 1972, *34,* 166-177.

---

112. CONTROL ROLES ATTITUDES SCALE

AUTHOR: Nathan Hurvitz

DATE: 1958

VARIABLES: Authoritarian versus democratic attitudes in marriage

TYPE OF INSTRUMENT: Summated rating scale

DESCRIPTION: The scale consists of nineteen items related to six aspects of married life: family leadership (four items), working wife (three items), woman's activities outside the home (three items), decisions regarding children (three items), authority of the father in decision making (three items), and the general relationship between men and women (three items). All items are phrased to reflect an authoritarian ideology. Each statement is accompanied by five response options. For some items, the response options are: always, often, occasionally, seldom, and never. For other items, the response options are: strongly agree, agree, undecided, disagree, or strongly disagree.

PREVIOUSLY ADMINISTERED TO: Married couples

APPROPRIATE FOR: Ages 16 and older

ADMINISTRATION: The scale is self-administered and can be completed in about ten minutes.

SAMPLE ITEMS:

Family leadership: If we think of the family as a team, the husband is the captain.

Working wife: The wife should work only if her income is needed by the family.

Woman's activities outside the home: Almost any woman is better off in her home than in a job or profession.

Decisions regarding children: The husband should give the children permission before they drive the car.

Authority of the father in decision making: The husband decides where the family should live.

General relationship between men and women: Women who want to remove the word *obey* from the marriage service don't understand what it means to be a wife.

SCORING: Items are objectively scored and equally weighted. Scores are obtained for each of six subscales: Family Leadership, Working Wife, Woman's Activities Outside the Home, Decisions Regarding Children, Authority of the Father in Decision Making, and General Relationship Between Men and Women; a total score is also obtained. Total scores can vary from 1 (democratic attitudes) to 95 (authoritarian attitudes).

DEVELOPMENT: A pool of eighty-seven statements was compiled and administered to forty-seven married couples. The responses were "reviewed to determine which statements elicited a range of responses and appeared to differentiate between those subjects who held authoritarian attitudes from those who held democratic attitudes" (Hurvitz, 1958, p. 85). Statements for which there was unanimous or near-unanimous agreement on the responses were eliminated. The remaining items were then subjected to successive scalogram analyses until seven scales were identified, with each scale containing three or four items. One subscale, sexual activities outside of the marital relationship, was eliminated because the coefficient of reproducibility was less than .85.

RELIABILITY: The coefficients of reproducibility for each subscale for husbands and wives, respectively, were: Family Leadership = .851 and .854; Working Wife = .911 and .908; Woman's Activities Outside the Home = .901 and .892; Decisions Regarding Children = .863 and .885; Authority of the Father in Decision Making = .847 and .914; and General Relationship Between Men and Women = .891 and .856 (Hurvitz, 1958, 1959).

VALIDITY: No data are provided.

NOTES AND COMMENTS: (1) Hurvitz (1959, p. 240) summarized the limitations of the scale, stating, "The 'Control Roles Attitudes Scale' as it presently exists includes the following [limitations] : the indices of reproducibility are not high; the small number of statements in each area limits the measure of intensity with which attitudes expressing control roles are held; and the special characteristics of the sample studied may negate the value of this scale when used with another population." The sample to which he was referring included 104 middle-class married couples in California.

(2) In regard to scoring, Hurvitz (1958, p. 91) cautions, "Spouses who score high on one subscale may score low on another, and adding their subscale scores may give an incorrect picture of the kinds of attitudes which they hold."

(3) It is generally recommended that about half the items on a scale be phrased to reflect one position and the other half be phrased to reflect the opposite position. Hurvitz violates this recommendation by phrasing all items to reflect an authoritarian ideology.

(4) The scale is also described in *Family Measurement Techniques* (Straus, 1969, pp. 148-149; Straus and Brown, 1978, pp. 81-82).

SOURCE: See Hurvitz, 1958 or 1959.

BIBLIOGRAPHY:

Hurvitz, N. "Marital Roles and Adjustment in Marriage in a Middle-Class Group." Unpublished doctoral dissertation, University of Southern California, 1958.
Hurvitz, N. "A Scale for the Measurement of Superordinate-Subordinate Roles in Marriage." *American Catholic Sociological Review,* 1959, *20,* 234-241.
Hurvitz, N. "Control Roles, Marital Strain, Role Deviation, and Marital Adjustment." *Journal of Marriage and the Family,* 1965, *27,* 29-31.

*Straus, M. A. *Family Measurement Techniques: Abstracts of Published Instruments, 1935-1965.* Minneapolis: University of Minnesota Press, 1969.

*Straus, M. A., and Brown, B. W. *Family Measurement Techniques: Abstracts of Published Instruments, 1935-1974.* Minneapolis: University of Minnesota Press, 1978.

---

113. DAY AT HOME

AUTHOR: P. G. Herbst

DATE: 1952

VARIABLES: Marital task allocation; marital decision making

TYPE OF INSTRUMENT: Alternate choice

DESCRIPTION: Each of the two parts of this instrument consists of thirty-three items. The first part asks which parent/spouse actually performs (does) each of thirty-three home- or family-related tasks. More than one person can be indicated as performing the task. Though response alternatives allow for naming one of the children in the family as the one who performs the task, only responses indicating the husband, wife, or husband and wife are scored. The second part of the instrument asks which parent/spouse is responsible for making the decision regarding the performance of each of the same thirty-three home- or family-related tasks. More than one person can be indicated as responsible for the decision. Again responses other than the husband, wife, or husband and wife are not scored.

PREVIOUSLY ADMINISTERED TO: Ages 10-12 in Australia and the United States; ages 12-13 in New Zealand; ages 8-9 in the United States; adolescents (black and white); and parents

APPROPRIATE FOR: Ages 8 and older

ADMINISTRATION: The scale is self-administered and can be completed in about thirty minutes.

SAMPLE ITEMS: *Performance:* Who sees to it that the children get out of bed at the right time?
  Decision: Who decides at what time you have to get out of bed?

SCORING: Herbst (1952, 1954) describes a rather complex method of scoring for family interaction patterns. However, users of the instrument have obtained a count of the number of times each parent/spouse is mentioned.

DEVELOPMENT: In order to construct items for the scale, Herbst (1952) specified four domains (household duties, child control and care, social activities, and economic activities) and three time periods (the morning until husband has left for work and children have left for school; the daytime while husband and children are gone from home; and the latter part of the day when the husband and children return until they all go to bed). A fourth category was added to the time periods to cover social activities that take place outside of the home on weekends and holidays. Items were selected to cover the four domains and the three time periods plus the social period. Only if the husband and wife could potentially perform the activity was it included in the instrument.

RELIABILITY: No data are provided.

VALIDITY: Rutherford (1969) administered a modified version of the instrument to twenty-five sets of parents. The modified version asked which spouse was responsible for making the decision in regard to twenty-seven issues. Rutherford also obtained a measure of the children's ability to make correct masculine and feminine sex role discriminations. The masculine sex role discrimination score was based on the child's ability to name one of the most (or least) masculine male classmates as most likely to like (dislike) playing masculine games and dislike (like) playing feminine games. The feminine sex role discrimination score was based on the child's ability to name one of the most (or least) feminine female classmates as most likely to like (dislike) playing feminine games and dislike (like) playing masculine games. Rutherford hypothesized that "children whose fathers score high in dominance will score higher in masculine sex role discrimination than will children whose fathers score low in dominance" (p. 188) and "children whose fathers score low in dominance (that is, whose mothers score high in dominance) will score higher in feminine sex role discrimination than will children whose fathers score high in dominance" (p. 188). The first hypothesis was supported; the second was not.

In a study of 324 families, Hoffman (1960) compared scores on a modification of Day at Home with scores on the Traditional Sex Role Ideology Scale (#130), which measures attitudes regarding men's participation in household tasks. As predicted, the father's participation in activities typically associated with the mother was significantly related to scores on the Traditional Sex Role Ideology Scale ($p < .0006$); and the father's participation in all home activities was also significantly related to scores on the Traditional Sex Role Ideology Scale ($p < .0004$). However, contrary to predictions, scores from the modification of Day at Home did not relate to scores on the Male Dominance Ideology Scale (#115), a measure of attitudes toward men holding superordinate positions over women.

NOTES AND COMMENTS: (1) Some of the items are clearly inappropriate for some respondents; for example, items pertaining to chopping wood, setting the table for tea, turning on the wireless, and putting out the milk bottles.

(2) Many researchers have modified the instrument. For example, Hoffman (1960) used a modification to obtain three scores for each parent: task participation, activity control, and power relationship. The first score is based on the "doing" questions; the second score is based on the deciding questions; the last score is based on both sets of questions. If one spouse decides and the other spouse performs an activity, it is considered to reflect the power of the former spouse. King (1964, 1969) used only five items that were modified from Day At Home to measure black adolescents' perceptions of their parents' power structure. Papanek (1969) used Herbst's four domains (household duties, child control and care, social activities, and economic activities) to develop an unspecified number of items to measure degree and direction of marital role specializa-

tion. Hillenbrand (1976) used only the decision-making items to study the effects of father's absence in military families.

(3) Yamamura and Zald (1956, p. 220) evaluated the instrument and concluded that it "is inadequate for most social-psychological problems because of its equation of the functionally significant and insignificant and because it fails to take into account meaningful components of family life such as deference and respect behavior."

(4) The instrument is also described in *Family Measurement Techniques* (Straus, 1969, pp. 129-130; Straus and Brown, 1978, p. 487).

SOURCE: See Herbst, 1952, 1954.

BIBLIOGRAPHY:

Brown, L. B. "The 'Day at Home' in Wellington, New Zealand." *Journal of Social Psychology*, 1959, *50*, 189-206.
Herbst, P. G. "The Measurement of Family Relationships." *Human Relations*, 1952, *5*, 3-35.
Herbst, P. G. "Conceptual Framework for Studying the Family." In O. A. Oeser and S. B. Hammond (Eds.), *Social Structure and Personality in a City*. New York: Macmillan, 1954.
Hillenbrand, E. D. "Father Absence in Military Families." *Family Coordinator*, 1976, *25*, 451-458.
Hoffman, L. N. W. "Some Effects of the Employment of Mothers on Family Structure." Unpublished doctoral dissertation, University of Michigan, 1958. (*Dissertation Abstracts*, 1959, *19*[8], 2179-2180.)
Hoffman, L. N. W. "Effects of the Employment of Mothers on Parental Power Relations and the Division of Household Tasks." *Marriage and Family Living*, 1960, *22*, 27-35.
King, K. B., Jr. "Comparison of Power Structure of the Negro and the White Family by Socioeconomic Class." Unpublished doctoral dissertation, Florida State University, 1964. (*Dissertation Abstracts*, 1964, *25*[4], 2657-2658.)
King, K. B., Jr. "Adolescent Perception of Power Structure in the Negro Family." *Journal of Marriage and the Family*, 1969, *31*, 751-755.
Papanek, M. L. "Authority and Sex Roles in the Family." *Journal of Marriage and the Family*, 1969, *31*, 88-96.
Rutherford, E. E. "A Note on the Relation of Parental Dominance as a Decision Maker in the Home to Children's Ability to Make Sex Role Discriminations." *Journal of Genetic Psychology*, 1969, *114*, 185-191.
*Straus, M. A. *Family Measurement Techniques: Abstracts of Published Instruments, 1935-1965*. Minneapolis: University of Minnesota Press, 1969.
*Straus, M. A., and Brown, B. W. *Family Measurement Techniques: Abstracts of Published Instruments, 1935-1974*. Minneapolis: University of Minnesota Press, 1978.
Taft, R. "Some Subcultural Variables in Family Structure in Australia." *Australian Journal of Psychology*, 1957, *9*, 69-90.
Yamamura, D. S., and Zald, N. M. "A Note on the Usefulness and Validity of the Herbst Family Questionnaire." *Human Relations*, 1956, *9*, 217-221.

114. LU DOMINANCE-SUBMISSION SCALE

AUTHOR: Yi-Chuang Lu

DATE: 1950

VARIABLES: Dominant, egalitarian, and submissive roles in marriage

TYPE OF INSTRUMENT: Multiple-choice and open-ended questionnaire with mixed item types

DESCRIPTION: The instrument consists of sixteen items; eight items relate to personality factors and eight relate to relationship factors. The type of item varies, with some items having fixed response alternatives (two, three, or five options) and some items being open-ended. There are two forms of the instrument: husband's form and wife's form. The only difference between the two forms is minor wording changes; for example, the wife's form asks some questions about "husband," whereas the husband's form asks the same questions about "wife."

PREVIOUSLY ADMINISTERED TO: Married couples

APPROPRIATE FOR: Married couples

ADMINISTRATION: The instrument can be self-administered and can be completed in about ten minutes.

SAMPLE ITEMS: *Relationship items:* My wife [husband] is argumentative. Yes _____. No _____.

   Personality items: Do you lose your temper easily? Yes _____. No _____.

SCORING: A scoring key is provided (Lu, 1950, p. 52). The husband's score is based on responses to eleven items on the husband's form and ten items on the wife's form. Similarly, the wife's score is based on responses to eleven items on the wife's form and ten items on the husband's form. The maximum score for either the husband or the wife is 56 points, which indicates maximum dominance. The scores obtained by the husband and wife are not independent of each other, because responses to certain items simultaneously add points to one spouse's score and subtract points from the other spouse's score. When the difference between the husband's and wife's score is between 0 and 4 points, the couple is classified as "equalitarian"; when the difference between their scores is greater than 4, the couple is classified as "husband more dominant" or "wife more dominant," depending on which spouse has the higher score.

DEVELOPMENT: Twenty-eight relationship items and twenty-three personality items were selected from an engagement schedule for men, an engagement schedule for women, a marriage schedule for men, and a marriage schedule for women (Burgess and Wallin, 1953). The items were selected on the basis that they appeared to be relevant to dominant, egalitarian, and submissive roles in marriage. Couples' responses to the fifty-one items were compared with their response to the question, "Who gives in when disagreements arise between husband and wife?" That is, for ten couples in which both the husband and wife agreed that one or the other spouse was more likely to "give in," responses were compared on each of the fifty-one items. Eight personality items and seven relationship items were found to discriminate between couples in which the husband was dominant (as evidenced by consensus among the couple that the wife is more likely to "give in") and couples in which the wife was dominant. These fifteen items, along with the item "Who gives in when disagreements arise between husband and wife?" (a relationship item), make up the instrument.

RELIABILITY: Kokonis (1971) reports a test-retest reliability coefficient of .64. This was based on pilot work, and no information is given regarding respondents or test-retest interval.

VALIDITY: Lu (1950) compared the scores for forty-two couples with interview information obtained from them. When Lu rated the interview information on dominance, she found that her rating agreed with the classification from the Lu Dominance-Submission Scale for 93 percent of the couples classified as "husband dominant," 71 percent of the couples classified as "equalitarian," and 86 percent of the couples classified as "wife dominant" (n = 14 couples per classification). Lu also reports that for 397 couples, one, two, or three friends rated the dominance of the husband and the wife. The correlation between the scores on the Lu Dominance-Submission Scale and the ratings given by friends was .514 (p < .001).

NOTES AND COMMENTS: Despite the age of this scale, none of the items seems outdated. Furthermore, the item content is such that, except for the last item, respondents would have no idea of the specific variable being measured.

SOURCE: See Lu, 1950 or 1952a.

BIBLIOGRAPHY:

*Burgess, E. W., and Wallin, P. *Engagement and Marriage*. Philadelphia: Lippincott, 1953.
Kokonis, N. D. "Sex Role Identification in Schizophrenia: Psychoanalytic and Role-Theory Predictions Compared." Unpublished doctoral dissertation, Illinois Institute of Technology, 1971. (*Dissertation Abstracts International,* 1971, *32*[3-B], 1849-1850.)
Lu, Y. C. "A Study of the Dominant, Equalitarian, and Submissive Roles in Marriage." Unpublished doctoral dissertation, University of Chicago, 1950.
Lu, Y. C. "Marital Roles and Marriage Adjustment." *Sociology and Social Research,* 1952a, *36*, 364-368.
Lu, Y. C. "Parent-Child Relationship and Marital Roles." *American Sociological Review,* 1952b, *17*, 357-361.
Lu, Y. C. "Predicting Roles in Marriage." *American Journal of Sociology,* 1952c, *58*, 51-55.
Lu, Y. C. "Home Discipline and Reaction to Authority in Relation to Marital Roles." *Marriage and Family Living,* 1953, *15*, 223-225.
Lu, Y. C. "Mother-Child Role Relations in Schizophrenia: A Comparison of Schizophrenic Patients with Nonschizophrenic Siblings." *Psychiatry,* 1961, *24*, 133-142.

115. MALE DOMINANCE IDEOLOGY SCALE

AUTHOR: Lois Wladis Hoffman

DATE: 1958

VARIABLE: Attitudes toward men holding superordinate positions over women

TYPE OF INSTRUMENT: Summated rating scale

DESCRIPTION: The scale consists of four statements that refer to the appropriateness of men being superordinate to women. Three statements refer to the marital relationship; the fourth statement refers to men's authority in general. Each statement is accompanied by four response options: agree a lot, agree, disagree, and disagree a lot.

PREVIOUSLY ADMINISTERED TO: Black and white adults

APPROPRIATE FOR: Ages 14 and older

ADMINISTRATION: This self-administered scale can be completed in about three minutes.

SAMPLE ITEMS: Some equality in marriage is a good thing, but by and large the husband ought to have the main say-so in family matters.

It goes against human nature to place women in positions of authority over men.

SCORING: Items are objectively scored and equally weighted.

DEVELOPMENT: No information is provided.

RELIABILITY: No data are provided.

VALIDITY: Contrary to expectation, Hoffman (1960) found that, in a sample of 324 families, scores on the Male Dominance Ideology Scale did not relate to power scores as measured by a variation of Day at Home (#113). Furthermore, scores did not relate to mother's employment status. It was found, however, that within a sample of nonworking mothers, support for male dominance was associated with low mother power.

For 235 mothers, the correlation between scores on the Male Dominance Ideology Scale and scores on the Traditional Sex Role Ideology Scale (#130) was .37. For a sample of 207 fathers, the correlation was .56 (Hoffman, 1958).

NOTES AND COMMENTS: (1) The lack of information pertaining to the development or reliability of the scale and the lack of evidence supporting its validity all suggest that more work needs to be done with the scale before it is used in further research.

(2) TenHouten (1970) used three of the four items from this scale in addition to six other items and found that the nine items formed a Guttman scale measuring male dominance.

(3) This scale is described in *Family Measurement Techniques* (Straus, 1969, pp. 141-142; Straus and Brown, 1978, p. 80).

SOURCE: See Hoffman, 1958 or 1960.

BIBLIOGRAPHY:

Franck, R. "Value Similarity, Role Expectation, and Cognitive Style as Factors in Marital Adjustment." Unpublished doctoral dissertation, University of Michigan, 1974. (*Dissertation Abstracts International,* 1975, *35*[11-B], 5694-5695.)
Hoffman, L. N. W. "Some Effects of the Employment of Mothers on Family Structure." Unpublished doctoral dissertation, University of Michigan, 1958. (*Dissertation Abstracts,* 1959, *19*[8], 2179-2180.)
Hoffman, L. N. W. "Effects of the Employment of Mothers on Parental Power Relations and the Division of Household Tasks." *Marriage and Family Living,* 1960, *22,* 27-35.
*Straus, M. A. *Family Measurement Techniques: Abstracts of Published Instruments, 1935-1965.* Minneapolis: University of Minnesota Press, 1969.
*Straus, M. A., and Brown, B. W. *Family Measurement Techniques: Abstracts of Published Instruments, 1935-1974.* Minneapolis: University of Minnesota Press, 1978.
TenHouten, W. D. "The Black Family: Myth and Reality." *Psychiatry,* 1970, *33,* 145-173.
Turk, J. L., and Bell, N. W. "Measuring Power in Families." *Journal of Marriage and the Family,* 1972, *34,* 215-222.

---

116. MARITAL PATTERNS TEST

AUTHOR: Anthony Ryle

DATE: 1966

VARIABLES: Dominance in marriage; affection given; affection received

TYPE OF INSTRUMENT: Multiple choice

DESCRIPTION: The instrument consists of twenty-four pairs of statements. Each pair includes a statement referring to the respondent's behavior and a comparable statement referring to the spouse's behavior. For each of the forty-eight statements, the respondent is to indicate whether the statement is true or not true or whether she is uncertain as to whether the statement is true. There are two forms of the scale: husband's and wife's. The content of twenty-two pairs is the same on both forms, but the wording differs slightly so that the pronouns are sex appropriate. Two pairs of statements differ on the two forms.

PREVIOUSLY ADMINISTERED TO: Married couples

APPROPRIATE FOR: Ages 16 and older, married

ADMINISTRATION: The instrument is self-administered and can be completed in less than half an hour.

SAMPLE ITEMS: (Wife's form) (a) I am usually very patient with him.
                              (b) He is usually very patient with me.
                              (a) I hardly ever find fault with him.
                              (b) He hardly ever finds fault with me.

SCORING: Three scores are obtained for the instrument: affection given, affection received, and dominance. The dominance score is based on responses to ten pairs of statements. When the response given for the wife is different from the response given for the husband in a particular pair of statements, the item is scored as dominant. The total dominance score is equal to the number of husband-dominating responses, plus ten, minus the number of wife-dominating responses. Thus a score of 10 represents an egalitarian relationship; a higher score represents a husband-dominant relationship; and a lower score represents a wife-dominant relationship.

DEVELOPMENT: An item pool was compiled including items with face validity. Eight judges classified the items as to whether they indicated acceptance, rejection, domination, or submission. Only items correctly sorted by all judges were retained. After a pilot study in which twenty-five subjects completed the instrument using a card-sorting procedure, a seventy-four-item instrument was compiled and was completed by sixty-four married couples. Their responses were analyzed. Items selected for the affection subscales correlated significantly ($p < .01$) with the subscale score. Items selected for the dominance subscale correlated significantly ($p < .02$) with the subscale score.

RELIABILITY: Using the data from the sixty-four couples, split-half reliability for the dominance subscale was found to be .86. Forty-eight couples completed the instrument a second time about one month later. Test-retest reliability for the dominance subscale was .94 (Ryle, 1966).

A second sample of married couples completed the instrument. One item on the husband's form and one item on the wife's form did not relate significantly with the total subscale score ($p < .05$) (Ryle, 1966).

VALIDITY: In a sample of sixty-four couples, the correlation between the husband's and wife's rating on dominance was .44. Each couple was rated on their marital dominance based on information obtained during an interview. There was no significant relationship between the interview ratings of dominance and the subscale dominance scores. The predicted relationship between dominance scores and scores on the Cornell Medical Index, a measure of neuroticism, was not obtained (Ryle, 1966).

NOTES AND COMMENTS: (1) Though preceding information is given pertaining to the validity of this instrument, it should be emphasized that the information does not demonstrate its validity; rather it should lead one to question the validity. Clearly more research is needed to establish whether this instrument is valid.

(2) Because only the dominance subscale is relevant to the variables considered in this book, no information is provided regarding the scoring, reliability, or validity of the affection subscales. For that information, one should read Ryle, 1966.

SOURCE: See Ryle, 1966.

BIBLIOGRAPHY:

Hall-Smith, P., and Ryle, A. "Marital Patterns, Hostility, and Personal Illness." *British Journal of Psychiatry*, 1969, *115*, 1197-1198.

Ryle, A. "A Marital Pattern Test for Use in Psychiatric Research." *British Journal of Psychiatry*, 1966, *112*, 285-293.

---

117. MARITAL ROLES INVENTORY

AUTHOR: Nathan Hurvitz

DATE: 1958 (revised 1961)

VARIABLES: Role performance and role expectations in marriage

TYPE OF INSTRUMENT: Ranking scale

DESCRIPTION: There are four forms of this scale: two are to be completed by the wife and two are to be completed by the husband. The respondents complete one form for themselves and one form for their spouse. Each form lists eleven roles that the person or spouse might perform. When completing the form for themselves, the respondents are directed to number the statements from 1 to 11 in the order of importance in which the roles or functions are actually performed. When completing the form for their spouses, respondents are directed to number the statements from 1 to 11 in the way they would want their spouse to carry out roles or functions in the family.

PREVIOUSLY ADMINISTERED TO: Married couples

APPROPRIATE FOR: Married couples

ADMINISTRATION: The scales are self-administered. Each person must complete two forms of the scale: one for self and one for spouse. It takes about fifteen minutes to complete the two forms.

SAMPLE ITEMS: *Wife's roles:* I help earn the living when my husband needs my help or when the family needs more money.
I practice the family religion or philosophy.
Husband's roles: I do my jobs around the house.
I am a companion to my wife.

SCORING: Three scores are obtained for each person: Index of Strain, Index of Deviation of Performance, and Index of Deviation of Expectation. The Index of Strain is based on the difference between persons' ranking of their own roles and the ranking assigned to them by their spouse. The Index of Deviation of Performance is based on the difference between the way persons rank their own performance and the modal performance rankings assigned by a comparison group. The Index of Deviation of Expectation is based on the difference between how a person ranks the roles for the spouse and the modal expectation rankings assigned by a comparison group.

DEVELOPMENT: Graduate students and staff members at a family casework agency were asked to list the various roles for a husband and wife. Their lists were combined and duplications were grouped together. From the lists, a preliminary form of the scale was constructed, including fourteen husband roles and thirteen wife roles. The preliminary form was completed by thirty married couples. Based on their responses, a revised form was constructed, including ten husband roles and nine wife roles. No information is provided regarding how the responses to the preliminary test were used in revising the scale. The scale was again revised to include eleven roles for each spouse.

RELIABILITY: No data are provided.

VALIDITY: Hurvitz (1958, 1960b) compared husbands and wives on the three scores from the scale and on a measure of marital adjustment. The following comparisons yielded significant correlations ($p < .05$): husbands' Index of Strain and husbands' marital adjustment ($r = -.22$); husbands' Index of Strain and wives' marital adjustment ($r = -.23$); husbands' Index of Strain and wives' Index of Strain ($r = .20$); husbands' Index of Deviation of Performance and husbands' Index of Strain ($r = .31$); wives' Index of Deviation of Performance and wives' Index of Strain ($r = .39$); husbands' Index of Deviation of Expectation and wives' Index of Strain ($r = .50$); wives' Index of Deviation of Expectation and husbands' Index of Strain ($r = .28$); and husbands' Index of Deviation of Performance and wives' Index of Deviation of Performance ($r = .24$).

NOTES AND COMMENTS: (1) Depending on which of the sources below is consulted for the scale, there may be some variability in the number of items on each form.

(2) Because all of the roles listed on the scale are traditional roles, the scale may not accurately reflect marital roles in families that follow a more contemporary role pattern.

(3) The Marital Roles Inventory is reviewed in *The Sixth Mental Measurements Yearbook* (Buros, 1965, entry 680) and described in *Family Measurement Techniques* (Straus, 1969, pp. 149-150; Straus and Brown, 1978, p. 62).

SOURCE: See Hurvitz, 1958, 1959, 1960b; or
                Western Psychological Services
                12031 Wilshire Boulevard
                Los Angeles, California 90025

BIBLIOGRAPHY:

*Buros, O. K. *The Sixth Mental Measurements Yearbook.* Highland Park, N.J.: Gryphon Press, 1965.
Hooper, D., and Sheldon, A. "Evaluating Newly Married Couples." *British Journal of Social and Clinical Psychology,* 1969, *8,* 169-182.
Hurvitz, N. "Marital Roles and Adjustment in Marriage in a Middle-Class Group." Unpublished doctoral dissertation, University of Southern California, 1958.
Hurvitz, N. "The Index of Strain as a Measure of Marital Satisfaction." *Sociology and Social Research,* 1959, *44,* 106-111.

Hurvitz, N. "The Marital Roles Inventory and the Measurement of Marital Adjustment." *Journal of Clinical Psychology*, 1960a, *16*, 377-380.

Hurvitz, N. "The Measurement of Marital Strain." *American Journal of Sociology*, 1960b, *65*, 610-615.

Hurvitz, N. "The Components of Marital Roles." *Sociology and Social Research*, 1961, *45*, 301-309.

*Straus, M. A. *Family Measurement Techniques: Abstracts of Published Instruments, 1935-1965.* Minneapolis: University of Minnesota Press, 1969.

*Straus, M. A., and Brown, B. W. *Family Measurement Techniques: Abstracts of Published Instruments, 1935-1974.* Minneapolis: University of Minnesota Press, 1978.

---

118. MARRIAGE ROLE EXPECTATION INVENTORY

AUTHOR: Marie S. Dunn

DATE: 1959

VARIABLE: Traditional versus egalitarian marital role orientation

TYPE OF INSTRUMENT: Summated rating scale

DESCRIPTION: The scale consists of seventy-one statements, each accompanied by five response options: strongly agree, agree, undecided, disagree, and strongly disagree. Thirty-seven items reflect a traditional orientation toward the marital role and thirty-four reflect an egalitarian orientation toward the marital role. The items concern seven aspects of the marital role: authority (eleven items), homemaking (eleven items), care of children (twelve items), personal characteristics (eight items), social participation (eleven items), education (eleven items), and financial support and employment (seven items).

There are two forms of the scale: form M (intended for men) and form F (intended for women). The content of the statements is the same on both forms, but the phrasing is changed to make the statement appropriate for the sex of the persons completing the scale. For example, form F contains the statement, "In my marriage I expect that if there is a difference of opinion, my husband will decide where to live." On form M, the statement is worded "In my marriage I expect that if there is a difference of opinion, I will decide where to live."

PREVIOUSLY ADMINISTERED TO: High school students (white, black, and Native American); adolescents from intact families and childcare institutions; college students in the United States and Canada; married couples.

APPROPRIATE FOR: Ages 14 and older

ADMINISTRATION: The scale is self-administered and can be completed in less than forty-five minutes.

SAMPLE ITEMS: (All items are from form M.)

Authority: In my marriage I expect that if there is a difference of opinion, I will decide where to live.

Homemaking: In my marriage I expect that the "family schedule," such as when meals will be served and when television can be turned on, will be determined by my wishes and working hours.

Care of children: In my marriage I expect to leave the care of the children entirely up to my wife when they are babies.

Personal characteristics: In my marriage I expect it will be more important for my wife to be a good cook and housekeeper than for her to be an attractive, interesting companion.

Social participation: In my marriage I expect that it will be my responsibility and privilege to choose where we will go and what we will do when we go out.

Education: In my marriage I expect that it would be undesirable for my wife to be better educated than I.

Financial support and employment: In my marriage I expect that I will decide almost all money matters.

SCORING: Only those items for which the subject responds "strongly agree" or "agree" are scored. A score of +1 is assigned for agreement with an egalitarian statement; a score of −1 is assigned for agreement with a traditional statement. Thus, totals can range from −37 (very traditional) to +34 (very egalitarian). Comparable procedures can be used to obtain a score for each of the seven aspects of the marital role.

DEVELOPMENT: High school students were asked to list five things that a good wife does and five things that a good husband does. An examination of their responses suggested seven areas of relevant behavior: authority patterns, homemaking, care of children, personal characteristics, social participation, education, and financial support or employment. With these seven areas in mind, an item pool consisting of 300 statements was constructed from a review of the literature. A high school teacher and five adolescents reviewed the statements. As a result of their inputs, 176 statements were retained. The 176 statements were judged by thirteen "experts" in the field. The judges were first told which of the seven areas each of the items belonged to. They were then asked to indicate whether each item should be reworded and whether each item should be shifted to a different area. Based on the judges' responses, a preliminary form of the scale, including 128 statements, was prepared; 186 high school students completed the preliminary form of the scale, and an item-discrimination analysis was performed on their responses. Any item that failed to discriminate ($p < .05$) between those scoring in the upper and lower 25 percent of the distribution of total scores was eliminated. Items were selected for the final scale from the remaining items. Selected items represented both male and female roles, represented the seven subscales, and represented both traditional and egalitarian roles.

RELIABILITY: Based on the responses from fifty high school seniors, the corrected split-half reliability was .975 (Dunn, 1959, 1960).

VALIDITY: Dunn (1959) contends that the method of scale development provides evidence of the content validity of the scale.

Dunn (1959) found that based on total scores, more traditional attitudes are held by boys than by girls (p < .01), by rural students than by urban students (p < .05), and by lower-class students than middle- and upper-class students (p < .05). However, there were no significant differences between these groups on any of the subscale scores.

NOTES AND COMMENTS: (1) Several researchers have modified the Marriage Role Expectation Inventory. For example, Weeks and Thornburg (1977) omitted the items dealing with personal characteristics, social participation, and education. They then used the scale with five-year-old children and their parents. The test-retest reliability for children was .96. Hobart (1972, 1973) used a portion of the items from the Marriage Role Expectation Inventory in combination with items from another scale. Geiken (1964) used the Marriage Role Expectation Inventory as the basis for the development of a Family Responsibility Inventory in order to "explore the extent of sharing family homemaking responsibilities in a group of married couples" (p. 349). Geiken's interests were in the areas of authority patterns, childcare patterns, and housekeeping tasks. Gould (1961) used fifty-seven items that were identified through item-analysis procedures. The fifty-seven items had a corrected split-half reliability of .87. Hanley (1967) used Gould's revision.

(2) Scores on the Marriage Role Expectation Inventory have been related to numerous other variables, including sex (Del Campo, 1975; Gould, 1961; Hanley, 1967; Lind, 1971; Moser, 1961; Rooks and King, 1973; Snow, 1971, 1973; Sterrett and Bollman, 1970); age or grade level (Del Campo, 1975; Gould, 1961; Hanley, 1967; Hobart, 1972; Kieren and Badir, 1976; Lind, 1971; Sterrett and Bollman, 1970); religion (Gould, 1961; Hanley, 1967; Hobart, 1972, 1973; Moser, 1961); social status (Gould, 1961; Hanley, 1967; Hobart, 1972, 1973; Moser, 1961; Rooks and King, 1973; Sterrett and Bollman, 1970); intellectual and academic variables (Gould, 1961; Lind, 1971; Moser, 1961; Sterrett and Bollman, 1970); parental variables (Hanley, 1967; Hobart, 1972; Jordan, 1972; Kieren and Badir, 1976; Lind, 1971; Sterrett and Bollman, 1970); family structure and power structure (Hanley, 1967; Hobart, 1972, 1973; Jordan, 1972; Kieren and Badir, 1976; Rooks and King, 1973; Sterrett and Bollman, 1970); marital and dating status (Gould, 1961; Hanley, 1967; Kieren and Badir, 1976); sibling constellation (Del Campo, 1975; Hanley, 1967; Kieren and Badir, 1976; Moser, 1961; Sterrett and Bollman, 1970); educational and occupational aspirations and plans (Gould, 1961; Kieren and Badir, 1976; Lind, 1971); employment status (Jordan, 1972); income (Del Campo, 1975); masculinity-femininity (Hobart, 1972); and scores on the Bardis Familism Scale (Del Campo, 1975; Hanley, 1967; Lind, 1971). The Marriage Role Expectation Inventory has also been used to study the effects of a course on marriage (Rogers, 1964) and to compare married couples seeking counseling with married couples who have not sought counseling (Anderson, 1973a, 1973b).

(3) The Marriage Role Expectation Inventory is reviewed in the *Sixth Mental Measurements Yearbook* (Buros, 1965, entry 685) and described in *Family Measurement Techniques* (Straus, 1969, pp. 84-85; Straus and Brown, 1978, pp. 152-153).

SOURCE: See Dunn, 1959 or 1960; or Lind, 1971.

BIBLIOGRAPHY:

Anderson, E. D. "A Comparative Analysis of Marital Role Expectations of Paired Husbands and Wives Seeking Counseling and Paired Husbands and Wives Not Seeking

Counseling." Unpublished doctoral dissertation, University of North Carolina at Greensboro, 1973a. (*Dissertation Abstracts International,* 1973, *33*[9-A], 5316-5317.)

Anderson, E. D. "Role Incongruency in Marriage and Family Counseling." *Journal of Family Counseling,* 1973b, *1,* 19-21.

*Buros, O. K. *The Sixth Mental Measurements Yearbook.* Highland Park, N.J.: Gryphon Press, 1965.

Del Campo, R. L. "Marriage Role Expectations and Familistic Attitudes of Southern Black Adolescents." Unpublished doctoral dissertation, Florida State University, 1975. (*Dissertation Abstracts International,* 1976, *36*[12-A], 8335.)

Dunn, M. S. "Marriage Role Expectations of Adolescents." Unpublished doctoral dissertation, Florida State University, 1959. (*Dissertation Abstracts,* 1960, *20*[8], 3277-3278.)

Dunn, M. S. "Marriage Role Expectations of Adolescents." *Marriage and Family Living,* 1960, *22,* 99-111.

Geiken, K. F. "Expectations Concerning Husband-Wife Responsibilities in the Home." *Journal of Marriage and the Family,* 1964, *26,* 349-352.

Gould, N. S. "Marriage Role Expectations of Single College Students as Related to Selected Social Factors." Unpublished doctoral dissertation, Florida State University, 1961. (*Dissertation Abstracts,* 1962, *22*[8], 2906.)

Hanley, W. J. "Familistic Attitudes and Marriage Role Expectations: A Study of American College Students." Unpublished doctoral dissertation, Florida State University, 1967. (*Dissertation Abstracts,* 1968, *28*[7-A], 2800.)

Hobart, C. W. "Orientations to Marriage Among Young Canadians." *Journal of Comparative Family Studies,* 1972, *3,* 171-193.

Hobart, C. W. "Egalitarianism After Marriage: An Attitude Study of French- and English-Speaking Canadians." In M. Stephenson (Ed.), *Women in Canada.* Toronto: New Press, 1973.

Jordan, L. F. "A Longitudinal Study of Marriage Role Expectations Concerning Authority and Care of Children." Unpublished doctoral dissertation, Florida State University, 1972. (*Dissertation Abstracts International,* 1972, *33*[6-B], 2681-2682.)

Kidd, G. J. "A Comparison of Teaching Methods in Courtship Courses: Small Discussion Groups vs. Lecture Procedures." Unpublished doctoral dissertation, Utah State University, 1967. (*Dissertation Abstracts,* 1968, *28*[10-A], 4050.)

Kieren, D. K., and Badir, D. R. "Teaching About Marital Roles: Using Research Findings to Design Teaching Strategies." *Alberta Journal of Educational Research,* 1976, *22,* 245-253.

Knaub, P. K. "Marriage and Career Role Expectations: A Longitudinal Study." Unpublished doctoral dissertation, University of Nebraska, 1975. (*Dissertation Abstracts International,* 1976, *36*[8-A], 5581.)

Lind, R. W. "Familistic Attitudes and Marriage Role Expectations of American Indian and White Adolescents." Unpublished doctoral dissertation, Florida State University, 1971. (*Dissertation Abstracts International,* 1972, *32*[9-B], 5288; ERIC Document Reproduction Service No. ED 077 633.)

Moser, A. J. "Marriage Role Expectations of High School Students." *Marriage and Family Living,* 1961, *23,* 42-43.

Rogers, M. S. "Measurable Changes in Marriage Role Expectations: University Level." Unpublished doctoral dissertation, Ohio State University, 1964. (*Dissertation Abstracts,* 1965, *25*[11], 6584.)

Rooks, E., and King, K. "A Study of the Marriage Role Expectations of Black Adolescents." *Adolescence,* 1973, *8,* 317-324.

Sebald, H. "Parent-Peer Control and Masculine Marital Role Perceptions of Adolescent Boys." Unpublished doctoral dissertation, Ohio State University, 1963. (*Dissertation Abstracts,* 1964, *24*[7], 3003.)

Sebald, H. "Parent-Peer Control and Masculine Marital Role Perceptions of Adolescent Boys." *Adolescence,* 1973, *8,* 317-324.

Snow, C. W. "Differential Marriage and Family Perceptions and Attitudes of Adolescents Living in Childcare Institutions and Adolescents Living in Intact Families." Unpublished doctoral dissertation, University of North Carolina at Greensboro, 1971. (*Dissertation Abstracts International,* 1971, *32*[1-B], 413.)

Snow, C. W. "Differential Marriage and Family Perceptions and Attitudes of Adolescents Living in Childcare Institutions and Adolescents Living in Intact Families." *Adolescence,* 1973, *8,* 373-378.

Sterrett, J. E., and Bollman, S. R. "Factors Related to Adolescents' Expectations of Marital Roles." *Family Coordinator,* 1970, *19,* 353-356.

*Straus, M. A. *Family Measurement Techniques: Abstracts of Published Instruments, 1935-1965.* Minneapolis: University of Minnesota Press, 1969.

*Straus, M. A., and Brown, B. W. *Family Measurement Techniques: Abstracts of Published Instruments, 1935-1974.* Minneapolis: University of Minnesota Press, 1978.

Weeks, M. O., and Thornburg, K. R. "Marriage Role Expectations of Five-Year-Old Children and Their Parents." *Sex Roles,* 1977, *3,* 189-191.

---

119. MATERNAL ATTITUDE QUESTIONNAIRE

AUTHOR: Warren B. Miller

DATE: 1977

VARIABLE: Attitudes regarding various aspects of maternity and mothering

TYPE OF INSTRUMENT: Summated rating scale

DESCRIPTION: There are two parts to the scale. The first part contains thirty-two items, each of which is a brief description of an experience associated with being pregnant and having children. The woman is to indicate how desirable each item is. Four response options are provided: very, moderately, slightly, and not. The second part includes twenty-six items. Each item is again a description of an experience associated with being pregnant and having children, but the items are more likely to be considered undesirable. The woman is to indicate how undesirable each item is. The response options are the same as for Part I.

PREVIOUSLY ADMINISTERED TO: Females, ages 18-27

APPROPRIATE FOR: Females, ages 16 and older

ADMINISTRATION: The scale is self-administered and can generally be completed in about half an hour.

SAMPLE ITEMS:

Part I: Taking complete care of a little baby
        Having my family and friends admire me and my baby

Part II: Having a child who takes away my freedom to do other things
         Having a child who makes the house small and crowded

SCORING: Items are objectively scored. A formula is provided for obtaining scores on the various scales. The formula takes account of the individual's mean and standard deviation based on her responses to all the items on the scale. A total of twenty-two scores are obtained: Large Desired Family, Pregnancy Now, Maternal Desire, Ambivalence, Counter Normative Maternity, Premarital Pregnancy, Well-Rounded Maternity, Role-Filling Maternity, Religious Maternity, Pride in Maternity, Other-Oriented Maternity, Past-Oriented Maternity, Marriage-Oriented Maternity, Home Confinement, Need for Birth Planning, Single Parenthood, Maternity Depletion, Pregnancy and Childbirth, Traditional Maternity, Positive Maternal Motivation (based on all items in Part I), Negative Maternal Motivation (based on all items in Part II), and Net Maternal Motivation (the difference between Positive and Negative Maternal Motivation scores). The number of items on a scale ranges from three to thirty-two. The scales are not independent of each other in that a particular item is likely to appear on more than one subscale.

DEVELOPMENT: The items in the scale were written after a review of the relevant literature. Pretesting of the instrument was done with young adult women, and revisions were made to ensure that the instructions and item content could be understood by women with at least some high school education. The items were then administered to the following groups of women: young unmarried women, women attending an infertility clinic, women at an abortion clinic, women attending an antepartum clinic, and women attending a postpartum clinic. The responses from these women were used to develop five scales. The twenty items that best discriminated between women who wanted many children and women who wanted few children comprise the Large Desired Family Scale. The twenty-two items that discriminated between women who were trying to become pregnant and women who were seeking an abortion comprise the Pregnancy Now Scale. The fourteen items that contribute to both the Large Desired Family Scale and the Pregnancy Now Scale comprise the Maternal Desire Scale. The absolute value of the difference between the seven items on the Maternal Desire Scale taken from Part I (desirable items) and the seven items on the Maternal Desire Scale taken from Part II (undesirable items) is the Ambivalence score. Thus, when the woman endorses similar numbers of desirable and undesirable items, she is considered ambivalent. The twenty-eight items that were rarely endorsed by the groups of women described above comprise the Counter Normative Maternity Scale. The thirteen items that discriminated between women who have and have not had a premarital pregnancy comprise the Premarital Pregnancy Scale. The next thirteen scales were developed from factor and cluster analyses of the responses given by the women described above and 966 additional women.

RELIABILITY: Using the responses from 966 women, Kuder-Richardson reliabilities were computed. They ranged from −.16 to +.70, with a median of .36. Forty-six women were tested on two occasions with a four-week interval between testings. Their responses were used to compute the test-retest reliabilities for the scales. The reliabilities ranged from .46 to .88, with a median of about .68.

VALIDITY: No data are provided.

NOTES AND COMMENTS: (1) The means and standard deviations for each of the scales are reported for three groups of women: 324 never-married women, 322 women married for four to six months, and 320 women who bore their first child within the previous four to six months.

(2) The low reliabilities and the absence of data relevant to validity suggest that additional research is needed regarding this scale.

SOURCE: Warren B. Miller
American Institute for Research
P.O. Box 1113
1791 Arastradero Road
Palo Alto, California 94302

BIBLIOGRAPHY:

Miller, W. B. "Manual for Description of Instruments Used in a Research Project on the Psychological Aspects of Fertility Behavior in Women." Unpublished manuscript, American Institute for Research, 1977.

---

120. MINNESOTA SATISFACTION QUESTIONNAIRE–MODIFIED

AUTHORS: D. J. Weiss, R. V. Dawis, G. W. England, and L. H. Lofquist; modified by Richard D. Arvey and Ronald H. Gross

DATE: 1967 (modified 1977)

VARIABLE: Satisfaction with the homemaker role

TYPE OF INSTRUMENT: Summated rating scale

DESCRIPTION: The scale consists of thirteen items taken from the Minnesota Satisfaction Questionnaire. Each item asks how satisfied the respondent is with a particular aspect of the homemaker job. Five response options are provided ranging from "very dissatisfied" to "very satisfied."

PREVIOUSLY ADMINISTERED TO: Women

APPROPRIATE FOR: Persons engaged in performing homemaking tasks

ADMINISTRATION: The scale can be self-administered and can be completed in less than ten minutes.

SAMPLE ITEMS: Being able to keep busy all the time
                          The chance to work alone on the job

SCORING: Items are objectively scored and equally weighted. Total scores can range from 13 (very dissatisfied) to 65 (very satisfied).

DEVELOPMENT: The short form of the original Minnesota Satisfaction Questionnaire contains twenty items. The thirteen items that could relate to the job of the homemaker were selected for this scale.

RELIABILITY: The scale was completed by 118 women. Coefficient alpha was .86 (Arvey and Gross, 1977).

VALIDITY: The 118 women who completed the scale also completed the Attitudes Toward Women Scale (#169) and single items assessing overall satisfaction with the homemaker job, perceived effectiveness in the homemaker role, perception of mobility when at home, perceptions of parental attitudes toward working women, and frequency of church attendance. The correlation between scores on the Minnesota Satisfaction Questionnaire-modified and the single item indicating overall satisfaction with the homemaker job was .70. Scores on the single item were thus included in the overall score for homemaker satisfaction. Correlations between the index of homemaker satisfaction and the other measures were then computed separately for homemakers, job holders, and the combined group. Perceptions of parental attitudes toward working women were not significantly correlated with the index of homemaker satisfaction for any of the groups. The scores on the Attitudes Toward Women Scale were significantly correlated ($p < .01$) for the job holders and the combined group. Women with more liberal attitudes toward women were less satisfied with homemaking. Frequency of church attendance was significantly correlated ($p < .01$) for homemakers and the combined group. Women who attended church more frequently were more satisfied with homemaking. Perception of mobility when at home was positively correlated ($p < .01$) for each of the groups. Perceived effectiveness in the homemaker role was also positively correlated ($p < .01$) with the index of homemaker satisfaction for each of the groups (Arvey and Gross, 1977).

NOTES AND COMMENTS: The original Minnesota Satisfaction Questionnaire is described and reviewed in the *Seventh Mental Measurements Yearbook* (Buros, 1972, entry 1064) and the *Eighth Mental Measurements Yearbook* (Buros, 1978, entry 1052).

SOURCE: See Arvey and Gross, 1977.

BIBLIOGRAPHY:

Arvey, R. D., and Gross, R. H. "Satisfaction Level and Correlates of Satisfaction in the Homemaker Job." *Journal of Vocational Behavior,* 1977, *10,* 13-24.
*Buros, O. K. *The Seventh Mental Measurements Yearbook.* Highland Park, N.J.: Gryphon Press, 1972.

*Buros, O. K. *The Eighth Mental Measurements Yearbook.* Highland Park, N.J.: Gryphon Press, 1978.

Gross, R. H., and Arvey, R. D. "Marital Satisfaction, Job Satisfaction, and Task Distribution in the Homemaker Job." *Journal of Vocational Behavior,* 1977, *11,* 1-12.

---

121. PARENTAL DOMINANCE AND POWER SCALE

AUTHOR: Henry B. Biller

DATE: 1967

VARIABLE: Children's perceptions of parental dominance and power

TYPE OF INSTRUMENT: Alternate choice

DESCRIPTION: The instrument consists of twenty questions, with five questions in each of four areas: decision making, competence, nurturance, and limit setting. The child is expected to answer each question with either "father" or "mother." If the child answers "both" or refuses to answer, the interviewer repeats or rephrases the question in an attempt to elicit a response.

PREVIOUSLY ADMINISTERED TO: Ages 4-6

APPROPRIATE FOR: Ages 3-12

ADMINISTRATION: Because of the ages of the children who have previously completed the instrument, it has been administered orally on a one-to-one basis. However, with older children, it could be adapted for paper-and-pencil group administration.

SAMPLE ITEMS:

Decision-making: Who says which TV program your family watches?

Competence: Who would know how to get into your house if your family were locked out?

Nurturance: Who gives you the most gifts and toys?

Limit setting: Who tells you what time you must be in the house?

SCORING: If the question as initially asked elicits an answer, 4 points are given for the response "father" and 0 points are given for the response "mother." If the question must be repeated or rephrased, 3 points are given for the response "father" and 1 point is given for the response "mother." If the question is still not answered, 2 points are given. A score is obtained for each of the four areas and a total score, Power, is also obtained.

DEVELOPMENT: Questions in the areas of decision making, nurturance, and limit setting were based on the questions asked by Freedheim (1960). Questions regarding competence were added by Biller. "Through pilot work questions were selected and modified so that they were suitable for kindergarten-age children" (Biller, 1967, p. 54).

RELIABILITY: Biller (1969) administered the scale to 186 kindergarten boys. Corrected split-half reliability was .81.

VALIDITY: A study of 186 kindergarten boys (Biller, 1968) indicated that fathers were scored significantly higher on Decision Making (p < .0005), Competence (p < .0005), and Power (p < .0005). Mothers were scored significantly higher on Limit Setting (p < .0005). The hypothesis that boys who perceive their fathers as more powerful would score higher on scales assessing masculinity was supported.

NOTES AND COMMENTS: (1) The method of administration—that is, repeating or rephrasing questions which elicited "both" responses—strongly discourages the expression of egalitarian perceptions.

(2) It is difficult to believe that some of the items measure the variable that Biller claims they measure. For example, one competence item asks who changes burned-out light bulbs. Changing a light bulb hardly represents much competence. Two nurturance items concern giving of material things. One can give many gifts and still fail to be nurturing.

(3) The scale is also described in *Family Measurement Techniques* (Straus and Brown, 1978, p. 73).

SOURCE: See Biller, 1968.

BIBLIOGRAPHY:

Biller, H. B. "An Exploratory Investigation of Masculine Development in Kindergarten-Age Boys." Unpublished doctoral dissertation, Duke University, 1967. (*Dissertation Abstracts,* 1968, *28*[10-B], 4290.)

Biller, H. B. "A Multiaspect Investigation of Masculine Development in Kindergarten-Age Boys." *Genetic Psychology Monographs,* 1968, *78,* 89-138.

Biller, H. B. "Father Dominance and Sex Role Development in Kindergarten-Age Boys." *Developmental Psychology,* 1969, *1,* 87-94.

*Freedheim, D. K. "An Investigation of Masculinity and Parental Role Patterns." Unpublished doctoral dissertation, Duke University, 1960. (*Dissertation Abstracts,* 1961, *21*[8], 2363.)

Laosa, L. M., and Brophy, J. E. "Effects of Sex and Birth Order on Sex Role Development and Intelligence in Kindergarten Children." Paper presented at 17th annual meeting of the Southwestern Psychological Association, San Antonio, Texas, April 1971. (ERIC Document Reproduction Service No. ED 053 403.)

Laosa, L. M., and Brophy, J. E. "Effects of Sex and Birth Order on Sex Role Development and Intelligence Among Kindergarten Children." *Developmental Psychology,* 1972, *6,* 409-415.

*Straus, M. A. *Family Measurement Techniques: Abstracts of Published Instruments, 1935-1965.* Minneapolis: University of Minnesota Press, 1969.

*Straus, M. A., and Brown, B. W. *Family Measurement Techniques: Abstracts of Published Instruments, 1935-1974.* Minneapolis: University of Minnesota Press, 1978.

122. PODELL SCALE OF ATTITUDES REGARDING
FAMILY ROLE OF MEN

AUTHOR: Lawrence Podell

DATE: 1967

VARIABLE: Attitudes regarding the place of occupational success in the role of husband and father

TYPE OF INSTRUMENT: Guttman scale

DESCRIPTION: The scale consists of four statements that concern the relationship between occupational success and being a good husband and father. The respondent indicates whether he agrees or disagrees with each statement.

PREVIOUSLY ADMINISTERED TO: Male college students

APPROPRIATE FOR: Males, ages 16 and older

ADMINISTRATION: This self-administered scale can be completed in less than two minutes.

SAMPLE ITEMS: To be a good father, I should be successful in my occupation.
          To gain the respect of my children, I must achieve a position of respect in my line of work.

SCORING: Respondents are classified as one of five scale types depending on the number of items with which they agree. Scale types 0 and 1 are considered to reflect familial diffuseness; scale types II, III, and IV are considered to reflect familial specificity.

DEVELOPMENT: No information is provided.

RELIABILITY: The coefficient of reproducibility is .942.

VALIDITY: No information is provided.

NOTES AND COMMENTS: (1) Podell defines *specificity* as "orienting to others in terms of their limited relevance as means or conditions in interaction" (p. 492), and he defines *diffuseness* as "responding to others as 'total persons' " (p. 492).
    (2) This scale is also described in *Family Measurement Techniques* (Straus and Brown, 1978, p. 163).

SOURCE: See Podell, 1967.

BIBLIOGRAPHY:

Podell, L. "Occupational and Familial Role Expectations." *Journal of Marriage and the Family,* 1967, *29,* 492-493.

*Straus, M. A., and Brown, B. W. *Family Measurement Techniques: Abstracts of Published Instruments, 1935-1974.* Minneapolis: University of Minnesota Press, 1978.

---

123. PROHIBITION SCALE

AUTHORS: Kurt W. Back, Reuben L. Hill, and J. Mayone Stycos

DATE: 1955

VARIABLE: Activities that husband prohibits for wife

TYPE OF INSTRUMENT: Guttman scale

DESCRIPTION: The scale consists of five activities or behaviors. For each item, wives are to indicate whether their husbands would allow them to engage in the activity or behavior, and husbands are to indicate whether they would allow their wives to engage in the activity or behavior. The five items are listed in order from least likely to be prohibited to most likely to be prohibited.

PREVIOUSLY ADMINISTERED TO: Married adults in Puerto Rico

APPROPRIATE FOR: Married persons

ADMINISTRATION: The scale was part of a lengthy interview. However, it could easily be adapted for paper-and-pencil administration. In a paper-and-pencil format, it could be completed in less than two minutes.

SAMPLE ITEMS: Use make-up
                          Have friendships which husband does not like

SCORING: A scale value is assigned to each item. The minimum scale value is 1 for the item least likely to be prohibited and the maximum scale value is 5 for the item most likely to be prohibited.

DEVELOPMENT: No information is provided.

RELIABILITY: Based on interviews with 1,204 married adults, the coefficient of reproducibility was .952 (Back, Hill, and Stycos, 1955).

VALIDITY: No information is provided.

NOTES AND COMMENTS: (1) Because of the age of this scale, data should be obtained to determine whether the coefficient of reproducibility is still applicable today.

        (2) This scale was used as part of an extensive research project studying fertility control in Puerto Rico.

(3) This scale is also described in *Family Measurement Techniques* (Straus and Brown, 1978, p. 80).

SOURCE: See Hill, Stycos, and Back, 1959, p. 426.

BIBLIOGRAPHY:

Back, K. W., Hill, R. L., and Stycos, J. M. "Interviewer Effects on Scale Reproducibility." *American Sociological Review,* 1955, *20,* 443-446.
Hill, R. L., Stycos, J. M., and Back, K. W. *The Family and Population Control: A Puerto Rican Experiment in Social Change.* Chapel Hill: University of North Carolina Press, 1959.
*Straus, M. A., and Brown, B. W. *Family Measurement Techniques: Abstracts of Published Instruments, 1935-1974.* Minneapolis: University of Minnesota Press, 1978.

---

124. ROLE CONCEPTION INVENTORY

AUTHOR: Annabelle Bender Motz

DATE: 1951

VARIABLE: Traditional versus companionship conceptions of marital roles

TYPE OF INSTRUMENT: Alternate choice

DESCRIPTION: There are four forms of the Role Conception Inventory. Two forms are intended to be completed by husbands: one form concerns the husband's conception of the husband's role, and the other form concerns the husband's conception of the wife's role. Similarly, two forms are intended to be completed by wives: one form concerns the wife's conception of the wife's role, and the other form concerns the wife's conception of the husband's role. Each of the four forms contains twenty-four statements. The respondents are to indicate for each statement whether they agree or disagree with the statement. The twenty-four statements on each form concern six areas: financial support, employment, care of children, education, care of house, and community participation. For each of the six areas, there are four questions: one statement reflects a traditional conception of the role and is phrased as a "personal" statement; another statement also reflects a traditional conception of the role but is phrased as a statement about "people in general"; a third statement reflects a companionship conception of the role and is phrased as a "personal" statement; and a fourth statement also reflects a companionship conception of the role but is phrased as a statement about "people in general." The twelve statements that refer to "wives in general" are identical on the two forms concerning conceptions of the wife's role. Similarly the twelve statements that refer to "husbands in general" are identical on the two forms concerning conceptions of the husband's role. Thus, although the four forms include a total of ninety-six statements (4 × 24 = 96), there are only seventy-two different statements.

PREVIOUSLY ADMINISTERED TO: Married adults

APPROPRIATE FOR: Ages 16 and older, married

ADMINISTRATION: The scale can be self-administered. One form of the scale can be completed in about ten minutes.

SAMPLE ITEMS: (All sample items are taken from the form that wives complete about themselves and all concern the financial support area.)

Traditional, wives in general: The wife should help support the family only when it is absolutely necessary.

Traditional, personal: It would be wrong for me to earn money and help support the family when times are normal.

Companionship, wives in general: Marriage is a partnership in which the wife should share the responsibility of supporting the family with the husband whenever possible.

Companionship, personal: I think it should be my responsibility as much as my husband's to help support the family whenever I am able.

SCORING: A response can be considered "companionship" if the respondent agrees with a statement reflecting a companionship orientation or disagrees with a statement reflecting a traditional orientation. The percentage of companionship responses determines which of the following categories the respondent is placed in: companionship (83-100 percent); moderately companionship (58-75 percent); intermediate (50 percent); moderately traditional (25-41 percent); or traditional (0-16 percent). The responses to only twelve items are used to determine the classification of the respondent. Thus, an individual can be classified on the basis of any of four sets of twelve items: personal statements for same-sex role; personal statements for opposite-sex role; people-in-general statements for same-sex role; or people-in-general statements for opposite-sex role.

DEVELOPMENT: A pool of statements was compiled based on responses to open-ended interview questions. The statements had to satisfy several criteria, such as debatable and unambiguous. The statements were typed on 4" x 6" cards and given to judges who independently responded to the statements three times, classifying the cards according to whether the statement represented the "breadwinner," "helpmate," or "companion-wife" role. Some items were eliminated, and the judges classified the remaining items according to whether the statement referred to financial support, employment, housework, child-care, education, social participation, future goals, or more than one area. Some items were eliminated, and the judges classified the remaining items according to whether the statement reflected an opinion about oneself or about "people in general." The results of the judges' classifications were used to select items for the scale.

RELIABILITY: No data are provided.

VALIDITY: Motz (1951) compared the classification of seventy-five husbands based on their responses to the personal items on the husband's Role Conception Inventory with their responses to a five-point self-rating indicating the extent to which they wished to be the boss of their family. The association between the two measures was "moderate" but significant at the .10 level. A comparable comparison was performed for wives and yielded similar results: a "moderate" relationship significant at the .10 level.

Motz (1951) had outside observers rate the respondents they knew and react to certain statements of the inventory as they believed the ratees would. The degree of agreement between observers and respondents was significant at the .01 level for husbands and the .02 level for wives on the conception of wife's role. The degree of agreement between observers and respondents was significant at the .10 level for both husbands and wives on the conception of husband's role.

NOTES AND COMMENTS: (1) Motz (1952) reports that "certain of the statements have discriminatory value for one group and not for the other" (p. 469). The groups to which she is referring are husbands and wives.

(2) Tobin (1976) constructed a measure of conjugal role definition based on statements concerning the wife's role which were taken from the Role Conception Inventory. Correlation alpha for Tobin's five items was .55.

(3) This scale is also described in *Family Measurement Techniques* (Straus, 1969, pp. 201-202; Straus and Brown, 1978, p. 148).

SOURCE: See Motz, 1951.

BIBLIOGRAPHY:

Brinkman, J. E. "The Relationship Between Marital Integration and the Working Wife-Mother." Unpublished doctoral dissertation, University of Oregon, 1976. (*Dissertation Abstracts International*, 1976, *37*[3-A], 1826-1827.)

Cleland, V., Bass, A. R., McHugh, N., and Montano, J. "Social and Psychological Influences on Employment of Married Nurses." *Nursing Research*, 1976, *25*, 90-97.

Davis, H. L. "An Exploratory Study of Marital Roles in Consumer Purchase Decisions." Unpublished doctoral dissertation, Northwestern University, 1970. (*Dissertation Abstracts International*, 1971, *31*[7-A], 3668.)

Motz, A. B. "Conceptions of Marital Roles in Transition." Unpublished doctoral dissertation, University of Chicago, 1951.

Motz, A. B. "The Role Conception Inventory: A Tool for Research in Social Psychology." *American Sociological Review*, 1952, *17*, 465-471.

Russo, N. F. "Sex and Race Differences in Attitudes Toward Sex Role Behaviors." Paper presented at 80th annual meeting of the American Psychological Association, Washington, D.C., 1971.

*Straus, M. A. *Family Measurement Techniques: Abstracts of Published Instruments, 1935-1965*. Minneapolis: University of Minnesota Press, 1969.

*Straus, M. A., and Brown, B. W. *Family Measurement Techniques: Abstracts of Published Instruments, 1935-1974*. Minneapolis: University of Minnesota Press, 1978.

Tobin, P. L. "Conjugal Role Definitions, Value of Children, and Contraceptive Practice." *Sociological Quarterly*, 1976, *17*, 314-322.

Weil, M. W. "An Analysis of the Factors Influencing Married Women's Actual or Planned Work Participation." *American Sociological Review*, 1961, *26*, 91-96.

Weil, M. W. "The Career-Homemaker Role: New Orientation for Analysis." *Journal of Home Economics*, 1962, *54*, 294-296.

Weil, M. W. "A Study of the Factors Affecting the Role and Role Expectations of Women Participating or Planning to Participate in the Labor Force." Unpublished doctoral

dissertation, New York University, 1959. (*Dissertation Abstracts,* 1966, *27*[4-A],
1125.)

Wise, G., and Carter, D. C. "A Definition of the Role of Homemaker by Two Generations
of Women." *Journal of Marriage and the Family,* 1965, *27,* 531-532.

---

125. SCANZONI SOCIAL POSITION OF HUSBAND SCALE

AUTHOR: John H. Scanzoni

DATE: 1975 (used 1971)

VARIABLES: Support for alterations in husband role; support for institutionalized
equality; support for traditional husband role

TYPE OF INSTRUMENT: Summated rating scale

DESCRIPTION: The scale consists of nine items, each of which is accompanied by five
response alternatives ranging from "strongly agree" to "strongly disagree." Five items
relate to alterations in husband role; all are phrased to reflect a "modern" orientation.
Two items relate to institutional equality; both are phrased to reflect a "modern" orientation. Two items relate to the traditional husband role; both are phrased to reflect a "traditional" orientation.

PREVIOUSLY ADMINISTERED TO: College students and adults

APPROPRIATE FOR: Ages 16 and older

ADMINISTRATION: The scale can be self-administered and can be completed in about
five minutes.

SAMPLE ITEMS:

Alterations in husband role: If her job sometimes requires her to be away from home
overnight, this should not bother him.

Institutionalized equality: If his wife works, he should share equally in household chores
such as cooking, cleaning, and washing.

Traditional husband role: A married man's chief responsibility should be his job.

SCORING: Items are objectively scored and equally weighted. For the five items measuring support for alterations in husband role, the total score can range from 0 (strong support) to 20 (strong opposition). For the two items measuring support for institutional
equality, the total score can range from 0 (strong support) to 8 (strong opposition). For
the two items measuring support for the traditional husband role, the total score can
range from 0 (strong support) to 8 (strong opposition).

DEVELOPMENT: Separate factor analyses were performed for the responses given by men and by women to the nine items of the scale. Three factors emerged and the items loading on each of the three factors comprise each of the three subscales.

RELIABILITY: No data are provided.

VALIDITY: No data are provided.

NOTES AND COMMENTS: (1) The scale was administered to samples of males (n = 167 and 191) and females (n = 199 and 197) in 1971 and 1974. The correlations between support for alterations in the husband role and support for institutionalized equality ranged from .51 to .60. The correlations between support for alterations in the husband role and support for the traditional husband role ranged from −.39 to −.51. The correlations between support for institutionalized equality and support for traditional husband role ranged from −.28 to −.51 (Scanzoni, 1975a).

(2) A factor analysis was performed on the responses to three scales: Social Position of Husband, Social Position of Wife (#127), and Social Position of Mother (#126). Two factors emerged: Factor I contained the subscales measuring support for the traditional wife role, support for the traditional husband role, support for the traditional mother role, and support for the religious legitimation of the mother role; Factor II contained the subscales measuring support for equality between interests of wife and interests of husband and children, support for alterations in husband role, and support for institutionalized equality. The first factor was labeled "junior-partner status" and accounted for 20 percent of the variance. The second factor was labeled "equal-partner status" and accounted for 10 percent of the variance (Scanzoni, 1976a).

SOURCE: See Scanzoni, 1975a, 1975b; p. 36; or 1976b.

BIBLIOGRAPHY:

Scanzoni, J. H. "Sex Roles, Economic Factors, and Marital Solidarity in Black and White Marriages." *Journal of Marriage and the Family,* 1975a, *37,* 130-144.

Scanzoni, J. H. *Sex Roles, Life-Styles, and Childbearing: Changing Patterns in Marriage and the Family.* New York: Free Press, 1975b.

Scanzoni, J. H. "Gender Roles and the Process of Fertility Control." *Journal of Marriage and the Family,* 1976a, *38,* 677-691.

Scanzoni, J. H. "Sex Role Change and Influences on Birth Intentions." *Journal of Marriage and the Family,* 1976b, *38,* 43-58.

126. SCANZONI SOCIAL POSITION OF MOTHER SCALE

AUTHOR: John H. Scanzoni

DATE: 1975 (used 1971)

VARIABLES: Support for the religious legitimation of mother role; support for traditional mother role

TYPE OF INSTRUMENT: Alternate choice

DESCRIPTION: The instrument consists of seven questions. Two questions concern the religious legitimation of the mother role. An affirmative answer to each represents support for the religious legitimation of the mother role. Five questions concern the traditional mother role. Affirmative answers to three questions and negative answers to two questions reflect support for the traditional mother role.

PREVIOUSLY ADMINISTERED TO: College students and adults

APPROPRIATE FOR: Ages 16 and older

ADMINISTRATION: The scale can be self-administered and can be completed in about three minutes.

SAMPLE ITEMS:

Religious legitimation of mother role: Do you believe that the institution of marriage and family was established by God?

Traditional mother role: Do you think that a working mother can establish just as warm and secure relationship with her children as a mother who does not work?

SCORING: Items are objectively scored and equally weighted. For the religious legitimation subscale, a total of 2 (maximum score) indicates a secular orientation. For the traditional mother role subscale, total scores can range from 0 (traditional orientation) to 5 (modern orientation).

DEVELOPMENT: Separate factor analyses were performed for the responses given by men and by women to the seven items of the instrument. Two factors emerged and the items loading on each of the two factors comprise each of the two subscales.

RELIABILITY: No data are provided.

VALIDITY: No data are provided.

NOTES AND COMMENTS: (1) For a sample of 167 men tested in 1971, the correlation between the two subscales was .26. For a sample of 199 women tested in 1971, the correlation between the two subscales was .19. For a sample of 191 men tested in 1974, the correlation between the two subscales was .17. For a sample of 197 women tested in 1974, the correlation between the two subscales was .32 (Scanzoni, 1975a).

(2) A factor analysis was performed on the responses to three scales: Social Position of Mother, Social Position of Wife (#127), and Social Position of Husband (#125). Two factors emerged: Factor I contained the subscales measuring support for the traditional wife role, support for the traditional husband role, support for the traditional mother role, and support for the religious legitimation of the mother role; Factor II contained the subscales measuring support for equality between interests of wife and interests of husband and children, support for alterations in husband role, and support for institutionalized equality. The first factor was labeled "junior-partner status" and accounted for 20 percent of the variance. The second factor was labeled "equal-partner status" and accounted for 10 percent of the variance (Scanzoni, 1976a).

SOURCE: See Scanzoni, 1975b, p. 45; 1976a; or 1976b.

BIBLIOGRAPHY:

Scanzoni, J. H. "Sex Roles, Economic Factors, and Marital Solidarity in Black and White Marriages." *Journal of Marriage and the Family*, 1975a, *37*, 130-144.
Scanzoni, J. H. *Sex Roles, Life-Styles, and Childbearing: Changing Patterns in Marriage and the Family.* New York: Free Press, 1975b.
Scanzoni, J. H. "Gender Roles and the Process of Fertility Control." *Journal of Marriage and the Family*, 1976a, *38*, 677-691.
Scanzoni, J. H. "Sex Role Change and Influences on Birth Intentions." *Journal of Marriage and the Family*, 1976b, *38*, 43-58.

---

127. SCANZONI SOCIAL POSITION OF WIFE SCALE

AUTHOR: John H. Scanzoni

DATE: 1975 (used 1971)

VARIABLES: Support for the traditional wife role; support for equality between interests of wife and interests of husband and children

TYPE OF INSTRUMENT: Summated rating scale

DESCRIPTION: The scale consists of twelve statements, each of which is accompanied by five response alternatives ranging from "strongly agree" to "strongly disagree." Eight items relate to the traditional wife role; all are phrased to reflect a traditional attitude toward the role of women. Four items relate to equality between the interests of wife and interests of husband and children; all are phrased to reflect support for equality between interests.

PREVIOUSLY ADMINISTERED TO: College students and adults

APPROPRIATE FOR: Ages 16 and older

ADMINISTRATION: The scale can be self-administered and can be completed in less than ten minutes.

SAMPLE ITEMS:

Traditional wife: A married woman's most important task in life should be taking care of her husband and children.

Equality: Having a job herself should be just as important as encouraging her husband in his job.

SCORING: Items are objectively scored and equally weighted. Traditional wife role scores can range from 0 (very traditional) to 32 (very modern). Equality scores can range from 0 (support for equality of interests) to 16 (opposition to equality of interests).

DEVELOPMENT: Separate factor analyses were performed for the responses given by men and by women to the twelve items. Two factors emerged; one included eight items and the second included four items. The two factors are the two subscales.

RELIABILITY: No data are provided.

VALIDITY: Scanzoni (1975b) states: "These two dimensions or continua of traditional-ism-modernity appear to have considerable face validity as well as conceptual and the-oretical validity" (p. 30).

NOTES AND COMMENTS: (1) For a sample of 167 men tested in 1971, the correlation between the two subscales was −.63. For a sample of 199 women tested in 1971, the correlation between the two subscales was −.57. For a sample of 191 men tested in 1974, the correlation was −.56. For a sample of 197 women tested in 1974, the correlation between the two subscales was −.58 (Scanzoni, 1975a).

(2) A factor analysis was performed on the responses to three scales: Social Position of Wife, Social Position of Husband (#125), and Social Position of Mother (#126). Two factors emerged: Factor I contained the subscales measuring support for the traditional wife role, support for the traditional husband role, support for the traditional mother role, and support for the religious legitimation of the mother role; Factor II contained the subscales measuring support for equality between interests of wife and interests of husband and children, support for alterations in husband role, and support for institutionalized equality. The first factor was labeled "junior-partner status" and accounted for 20 percent of the variance. The second was labeled "equal-partner status" and accounted for 10 percent of the variance (Scanzoni, 1976a).

SOURCE: See Scanzoni, 1975a; 1975b, p. 28; or 1976b.

BIBLIOGRAPHY:

Scanzoni, J. H. "Sex Roles, Economic Factors, and Marital Solidarity in Black and White Marriages." *Journal of Marriage and the Family,* 1975a, *37,* 130-144.
Scanzoni, J. H. *Sex Roles, Life-Styles, and Childbearing: Changing Patterns in Marriage and the Family.* New York: Free Press, 1975b.
Scanzoni, J. H. "Gender Roles and the Process of Fertility Control." *Journal of Marriage and the Family,* 1976a, *38,* 677-691.

Scanzoni, J. H. "Sex Role Change and Influence on Birth Intentions." *Journal of Marriage and the Family,* 1976b, *38,* 43-58.

---

128. SEARLS SCALE OF MASTERY AND ENJOYMENT OF HOMEMAKING TASKS

AUTHOR: Laura Gilkerson Searls

DATE: 1965

VARIABLES: Self-perception of mastery of homemaking tasks; enjoyment of homemaking tasks

TYPE OF INSTRUMENT: Summated rating scale

DESCRIPTION: There are two parts to the scale. The first part, which measures mastery, describes eighteen tasks typically performed by the homemaker. The tasks represent five general areas of homemaking: family meals (five items); housing and furnishing (three items); family clothing (three items); marketing and budgeting (one item); childcare and family relationships (six items). For each task listed, the woman is to indicate the extent to which she feels she needs improvement in her performance of the task. Four response options are provided: considerable improvement desirable, some improvement desirable, close to ideal, and same as ideal.

   The second part of the scale, which measures enjoyment, includes direct statements of the same eighteen tasks described above. For each task the woman is to indicate the extent of her enjoyment from the task. Four response options are provided: no enjoyment, little enjoyment, moderate enjoyment, and much enjoyment.

PREVIOUSLY ADMINISTERED TO: Female adults

APPROPRIATE FOR: Homemakers

ADMINISTRATION: The scale is self-administered; both parts can be completed in about twenty minutes.

SAMPLE ITEMS:

Mastery: Organizing food preparation and clean-up for efficient use of time and energy.

Enjoyment: Organizing and planning work.

SCORING: Items are objectively scored and equally weighted. Six scores are obtained from the Mastery scale and six scores are obtained from the Enjoyment scale. The six scores from each scale include a total score and a score for each of the five broad areas.

DEVELOPMENT: Weigand (1954) reports the length of time devoted to various homemaking tasks. In constructing this scale, one item was written for each half hour of time that homemakers, according to Weigand, devote to a particular task. Items were written in consultation with home-economics specialists in each of the five areas. The items for the mastery scale were deliberately phrased to reflect a standard of competence. The scale was pretested with twenty-one homemakers who were given instructions to rate their adequacy on each task. Four response options were provided: very inadequate, fairly inadequate, fairly adequate, or very adequate. The results of the pretest indicated that most women rated themselves as "fairly adequate" on most tasks. After the instructions were rephrased and the response options revised, the scale was administered to another sample of thirteen homemakers. The results from this second pretest were more variable, suggesting that the scale was able to "evoke responses differentiating homemakers with varying feelings of competency, or 'perceived mastery of homemaking' " (Searls, 1965, p. 28). The scale used in the second pretest was the final form of the instrument as described above.

RELIABILITY: No data are provided.

VALIDITY: No data are provided.

NOTES AND COMMENTS: (1) Given the absence of reliability and validity data, not much is actually known about this scale. However, its development is unusual in that it represents a systematic approach toward sampling from a content domain.

(2) This scale is also described in *Family Measurement Techniques* (Straus and Brown, 1978, pp. 104-105).

SOURCE: See Searls, 1965.

BIBLIOGRAPHY:

Searls, L. G. "Factors Associated with Differences in Role Emphasis Among a Sample of Margaret Morrison Carnegie College Alumnae Homemakers." Unpublished master's thesis, Carnegie Institute of Technology, 1965.

Searls, L. G. "College Major and the Tasks of Homemaking." *Journal of Home Economics,* 1966, *58,* 708-714.

*Straus, M. A., and Brown, B. W. *Family Measurement Techniques: Abstracts of Published Instruments, 1935-1974.* Minneapolis: University of Minnesota Press, 1978.

*Weigand, E. "The Use of Time by Full-Time and Part-Time Homemakers in Relationship to Household Management." Cornell Agricultural Experiment Station, Memoir 330, July 1954. Cited in I. Gross and E. Crandall, *Management for Modern Families.* New York: Appleton-Century-Crofts, 1954.

129. TRADITIONAL FAMILY IDEOLOGY SCALE (TFI)

AUTHOR: Phyllis E. Huffman

DATE: 1950

VARIABLE: Democratic versus autocratic views of the family

TYPE OF INSTRUMENT: Summated rating scale

DESCRIPTION: The scale consists of forty statements representing four areas: (1) parent-child relationships and child-rearing techniques (fifteen items); (2) husband and wife roles and relationships (eight items); (3) general male-female relationships and concepts of masculinity and femininity (thirteen items); and (4) general values and aims (four items). Each item is accompanied by six response alternatives ranging from strong disagreement to strong agreement. Thirty-four statements reflect an autocratic orientation and six reflect a democratic one.

PREVIOUSLY ADMINISTERED TO: High school students; college students; and adults, including physicians and their wives, neurotics, and psychotics

APPROPRIATE FOR: Ages 14 and older

ADMINISTRATION: The scale can be self-administered and can be completed in less than half an hour.

SAMPLE ITEMS:

Parent-child relationships and child-rearing techniques: A child should not be allowed to talk back to his parents, or else he will lose respect for them.

Husband and wife roles and relationships: Some equality in marriage is a good thing, but by and large the husband ought to have the main say-so in family matters.

General male-female relationships and concepts of masculinity and femininity: A man can scarcely maintain respect for his fiancee if they have sexual relations before they are married.

General values and aims: The family is a sacred institution, divinely ordained.

SCORING: Items are objectively scored and equally weighted. The total score can range from 40 (extremely democratic) to 280 (extremely autocratic). Subscale scores can be obtained for the following: Conventionalism (thirteen items), Authoritarian Submission (fifteen items), Exaggerated Masculinity and Femininity (twenty items), Extreme Emphasis on Discipline (eight items), and Moralistic Rejection of Impulse Life (twelve items). The subscale scores are not independent; some items are included on more than one subscale.

DEVELOPMENT: Item construction was designed to reflect two levels of family ideology —the institutional and the psychological. At the institutional level, the items were designed to consider the following: "(a) The male roles of 'husband' and 'father,' with special reference to the definition of 'masculinity.' (b) The female roles of 'wife' and 'mother,' with special reference to the definition of 'femininity.' (c) Husband-wife and parent-child relationships, with attention to problems of authority and the distribution of power and responsibility; specific child-rearing practices and attitudes; (d) general values, expectations, and moral pressures, especially those relating to sex, aggression, and inter-status relationships" (Levinson and Huffman, 1955, p. 253). At the psychological level, the items were designed to consider the following: "conventionalism, authoritarian sub-mission, exaggerated masculinity and femininity, extreme emphasis on discipline, and moralistic rejection of impulse life" (Levinson and Huffman, 1955, p. 253).

RELIABILITY: The scale was administered to 109 evening college students. The cor-rected split-half reliability was .84 (Huffman, 1950).

VALIDITY: Embedded in the TFI scale administered to evening college students was a ten-item measure of ethnocentrism and a ten-item measure of authoritarianism. The cor-relation between TFI and authoritarianism was .73; the correlation between TFI and ethnocentrism was .65 (Huffman, 1950).

TFI scores have shown the expected relationships with various aspects of religious functioning and with scores on projective questions designed to measure variables related to those measured by the TFI (Levinson and Huffman, 1955).

An item analysis was performed comparing the mean scores on each item obtained by those scoring in the upper and lower quartiles of the distribution of total scores. According to Huffman (1950, p. 32), "twelve of the items did not have adequate dis-criminatory power."

Kenkel (1959) administered the TFI to twenty-five married student couples. He also observed each couple in a decision-making task in which they were to decide how to spend a gift of $300. After comparing performance on the decision-making task with scores on three subscales—Conventionalism, Exaggerated Masculinity and Femininity, and Authoritarian Submission—he concluded that "the personality syndrome measured by the several scales of the Traditional Family Ideology scale does not go far in explaining the roles a husband and wife play in decision making" (p. 338).

Alper (1974) reports that correlations between the Wellesley Role Orientation Scale (a measure of sex role preference, #44) and the TFI are repeatedly positive and highly significant.

NOTES AND COMMENTS: (1) A twelve-item version of the TFI has been constructed. This short form was administered to several groups of college students along with mea-sures of ethnocentrism, authoritarianism, and religious conventionalism. The average cor-relations with the TFI were: authoritarianism = .67; ethnocentrism = .64; and religious conventionalism = .46. Corrected split-half reliability was .92. One group of students completed the scale on two occasions separated by about six weeks. Test-retest correla-tion was .93 (Levinson and Huffman, 1955).

(2) When the Wellesley Role Orientation (#44) is administered, it should be em-bedded in the TFI.

(3) In discussing the TFI, Levinson and Huffman (1955, p. 254) state: "We are *not* committed to the hypothesis that the TFI Scale is necessarily adequate, or even ap-plicable, outside the American middle class. Like any other scale, it is bound, in some degree, to the particular traditions, social pressures, range of available ideological alterna-tives, and idiomatic meanings of the social groupings to which it was originally con-structed."

(4) Some of the items on the TFI include more than a single idea. For example, "A wife does better to vote the way her husband does, because he probably knows more about such things" includes the idea that a woman should vote the way her husband does and the idea that husbands probably know more about the best way to vote. It is quite possible for a person to agree with one of those ideas and disagree with the other, but there is no possible way for the respondent to express agreement with half an item. Similarly, "It doesn't seem quite right for a man to be a visionary; dreaming should be left to women," includes two separate ideas. At least three other items on the scale also include more than a single idea.

(5) The TFI is described in *Tests and Measurements in Child Development: Handbook I* (Johnson and Bommarito, 1971, p. 378), in *Scales for the Measurement of Attitudes* (Shaw and Wright, 1967, pp. 66-67), and in *Family Measurement Techniques* (Straus, 1969, pp. 179-180; Straus and Brown, 1978, pp. 521-522).

SOURCE: See Levinson and Huffman, 1955; or Shaw and Wright, 1967.

BIBLIOGRAPHY:

Alper, T. G. "Achievement Motivation in College Women: A Now-You-See-It-Now-You-Don't Phenomenon." *American Psychologist,* 1974, *29,* 194-203.

Becker, J., Spielberger, C. D., and Parker, J. B. "Value Achievement and Authoritarian Attitudes in Psychiatric Patients." *Journal of Clinical Psychology,* 1963, *19,* 57-61.

Ford, A. M. "Some Correlates of Black Consciousness, Internal-External Control, and Family Ideology Among Afro-American College Students." Unpublished doctoral dissertation, Michigan State University, 1972. (*Dissertation Abstracts International,* 1973, *34*[1-B], 410-411.)

Huffman, P. E. "Authoritarian Personality and Family Ideology." Unpublished master's thesis, Western Reserve University, 1950.

*Johnson, O. G., and Bommarito, J. W. *Tests and Measurements in Child Development: Handbook I.* San Francisco: Jossey-Bass, 1971.

Johnson, R. C. "Occupational Types and Traditional Family Ideology." *Child Development,* 1963, *34,* 509-512.

Johnston, J. R. C. "Family Interaction Patterns and Career Orientation in Late Adolescent Females." Unpublished doctoral dissertation, Boston University, 1973. (*Dissertation Abstracts International,* 1974, *35*[1-B], 509.)

Kahn, C. "Family Ideology as a Factor in Determining Spousal Reactions to a Partner's Psychotherapy." Unpublished doctoral dissertation, Columbia University, 1966. (*Dissertation Abstracts,* 1966, *27*[4-A], 1128.)

Kenkel, W. F. "Traditional Family Ideology and Spousal Roles in Decision Making." *Marriage and Family Living,* 1959, *21,* 334-339.

Kutner, N. G., and Brogan, D. "An Investigation of Sex-Related Slang Vocabulary and Sex Role Orientation Among Male and Female University Students." *Journal of Marriage and the Family,* 1974, *36,* 474-484.

Levinson, D. J., and Huffman, P. E. "Traditional Family Ideology and Its Relation to Personality." *Journal of Personality,* 1955, *23,* 251-273.

Lyles, B. F. D. "Familial Ideological Correlates of Authoritarianism as Related to Internality-Externality in Black Male College Students." Unpublished doctoral dissertation, University of Maryland, 1971. (*Dissertation Abstracts International,* 1971, *32*[6-B], 3621-3622.)

O'Neil, W. M., and Levinson, D. J. "A Factorial Exploration of Authoritarianism and Some of Its Ideological Concomitants." *Journal of Personality,* 1954, *22,* 449-463.

Perino, S. A. "Sex Role Orientation and Perceived IQ as Factors in Marital Adjustment for a Selected Sample of High Intelligence Couples." Unpublished doctoral dissertation, Hofstra University, 1975. (*Dissertation Abstracts International,* 1975, *36*[1-B], 454.)

Price, Q. L. E. "Influence of Sex and Family Life Education on Student Attitude Toward Traditional Family Ideology and Sex Knowledge." Unpublished doctoral dissertation, U.S. International University, 1969. (*Dissertation Abstracts International,* 1971, *31*[11-A], 6161.)

Purdom, J. E. "An Assessment of Sex Role Concepts of Male Physicians and Their Wives." Unpublished doctoral dissertation, University of Cincinnati, 1974. (*Dissertation Abstracts International,* 1975, *35*[8-B], 4151.)

*Shaw, M. E., and Wright, J. M. *Scales for the Measurement of Attitudes.* New York: McGraw-Hill, 1967.

Sibbison, V. H. "Occupational Preferences and Expectations of Rural High School Males and Females: Background, Grade, and Sex Role Correlates." Unpublished doctoral dissertation, Pennsylvania State University, 1974. (*Dissertation Abstracts International,* 1975, *35*[11-A], 7069.)

*Straus, M. A. *Family Measurement Techniques: Abstracts of Published Instruments, 1935-1965.* Minneapolis: University of Minnesota Press, 1969.

*Straus, M. A., and Brown, B. W. *Family Measurement Techniques: Abstracts of Published Instruments, 1935-1974.* Minneapolis: University of Minnesota Press, 1978.

Stryker, S. "Role-Taking Accuracy and Adjustment." *Sociometry,* 1957, *20,* 286-296.

White, P. W. "The Relationship of Family Ideology, Dogmatism, and Religious Attitudes, with Marital Happiness in University Couples." Unpublished doctoral dissertation, East Texas State University, 1975. (*Dissertation Abstracts International,* 1976, *36*[8-A], 5065.)

---

130. TRADITIONAL SEX ROLE IDEOLOGY SCALE

AUTHOR: Lois Wladis Hoffman

DATE: 1958

VARIABLE: Attitudes regarding men's participation in household tasks

TYPE OF INSTRUMENT: Summated rating scale

DESCRIPTION: The scale consists of five statements regarding the role of women and men in performing household tasks. All items are phrased to reflect a traditional ideology. Each statement is accompanied by four response options: agree a lot, agree, disagree, disagree a lot.

PREVIOUSLY ADMINISTERED TO: Female college students; adults

APPROPRIATE FOR: Ages 14 and older

ADMINISTRATION: This self-administered scale can be completed in less than five minutes.

SAMPLE ITEMS: Raising children is much more a mother's job than a father's.
   Except in special cases, the wife should do the cooking and house cleaning, and the husband should provide the family with money.

SCORING: Items are objectively scored and equally weighted.

DEVELOPMENT: No information is provided.

RELIABILITY: No data are provided.

VALIDITY: In a study of 324 families, Hoffman (1960) compared scores on the Traditional Sex Role Ideology Scale with scores on a modification of Day at Home (#113), which measures marital task participation. As predicted, scores on the Traditional Sex Role Ideology Scale were significantly related to (1) the father's participation in activities typically associated with the mother ($p < .0006$) and (2) the father's participation in all home activities ($p < .0004$). Additionally, nonworking women were more likely to endorse a traditional ideology than were working women ($p < .007$) (Hoffman, 1960).
   Angrist (1966) did not find a significant difference between the scores of working and nonworking mothers.
   For 235 mothers, the correlation between scores on the Traditional Sex Role Ideology Scale and scores on the Male Dominance Ideology Scale (#115) was .37. For a sample of 207 fathers, the correlation was .56 (Hoffman, 1958).

NOTES AND COMMENTS: (1) The age of the scale, the absence of reliability data, and the inconsistency in the findings between Hoffman and Angrist all suggest that more information is needed regarding the psychometric properties of the scale before it is used in further research.
   (2) This scale is also described in *Family Measurement Techniques* (Straus and Brown, 1978, p. 109).

SOURCE: See Hoffman, 1958 or 1960; or Angrist, 1966.

BIBLIOGRAPHY:

Angrist, S. S. "Role Conception as a Predictor of Adult Female Roles." *Sociology and Social Research,* 1966, *50,* 448-459.

Franck, R. "Value Similarity, Role Expectation, and Cognitive Style as Factors in Marital Adjustment." Unpublished doctoral dissertation, University of Michigan, 1974. (*Dissertation Abstracts International,* 1975, *35* [11-B], 5694-5695.)

Hoffman, L. N. W. "Some Effects of the Employment of Mothers on Family Structure." Unpublished doctoral dissertation, University of Michigan, 1958. (*Dissertation Abstracts,* 1959, *19* [8], 2179-2180.)

Hoffman, L. N. W. "Effects of the Employment of Mothers on Parental Power Relations and the Division of Household Tasks." *Marriage and Family Living,* 1960, *22,* 27-35.

Muthayya, B. C. "Autocratic-Democratic Attitudes and Achievement Motive." *Journal of Psychological Researches,* 1967, *11,* 32-35.

*Straus, M. A., and Brown, B. W. *Family Measurement Techniques: Abstracts of Published Instruments, 1935-1974.* Minneapolis: University of Minnesota Press, 1978.

9

▦ ▦ ▦ ▦ ▦ ▦ ▦ ▦ ▦ ▦ ▦

Employee Roles

▦ ▦

The sixteen instruments in this chapter all relate to paid employment. They concern: (1) the conditions under which a woman intends to work (answered for "self") or should work (answered in general); (2) the important features of a job for women; (3) perceptions of which jobs are open to women; (4) comparisons between female and male workers; and (5) the effects of males entering female-dominated occupations. Only three instruments pertain to specific employment fields: nursing (#135), university teaching and administration (#136), and home economics (#141); the remaining pertain to employment in general or employment at a particular level, such as supervisory or managerial levels. Consistent with the purpose of this book, instruments that do not relate to sex role issues (for example, if they could be used with both men and women to measure job satisfaction or job performance) have been omitted. The majority of these instruments were fairly recently developed. One originated in 1945; four originated in the 1960s; and the remaining eleven first appeared in the literature in the 1970s. The summated rating scale is the most common procedure used in these instruments; ten of the sixteen are summated rating scales. All instruments in this chapter are intended for adolescents and adults; none is appropriate for persons below the age of 15.

A careful examination of the items on these measures suggests that there is a built-in bias. For example, measures that consider the issue of whether a woman ought to work seem to imply that there is a continuum ranging from "women should not work" to "women have a right to work." No instrument seems to treat the continuum as ranging from "women should not work" to "women should work." Apparently, there is no question about whether men should work, as the literature search done in conjunction with preparing this book revealed no instruments concerning whether men ought to work. However, if such measures were constructed, it is difficult to imagine that they would use the same continuum as is used on measures for women. More likely those for men would assume that the continuum should range from "men have a right not to work" to "men should work." A second example of a built-in bias is reflected in the abundance of items suggesting that women might be inferior or equal to men; there are far fewer items suggesting that women might be superior to men. Furthermore, items that suggest that women might be superior to men usually suggest that the superiority is manifested in traditionally feminine traits, such as nurturance, sensitivity, and understanding.

The major problem with many of the instruments in this chapter is that little is known about the behavioral correlates of the scores. Because self-report measures are particularly susceptible to the social desirability response set, it is important to know whether there are behavioral implications of responses. In other words, it is easy to give lip service to equality of employment opportunity, but how will persons behave when they actually have the opportunity to hire or work with a woman who is not a secretary, teacher, or nurse? Similarly, it is easy for a woman to report whether she does or does not intend to work under particular circumstances, but that is no guarantee of what she will do when she is actually faced with the decision. Longitudinal studies are needed to determine whether scores can accurately predict when women will work. Cross-sectional studies are needed to determine whether there is a relationship between expressed attitudes toward the employment of women and actual behavior in the employment situation. Terborg and Ilgen (1975) correlated scores on the Women as Managers Scale (#144) with performance on an in-basket procedure. Their methods can serve as a model for comparing responses on an attitude measure with behavior in a simulated work setting. However, it is also recommended that studies be conducted to compare responses on the attitude measures with behavior in an actual, as opposed to simulated, work setting.

BIBLIOGRAPHY:

Terborg, J. R., and Ilgen, D. R. "A Theoretical Approach to Sex Discrimination in Traditionally Masculine Occupations." *Organizational Behavior and Human Performance,* 1975, *13*, 352-376.

---

131. BASS-KRUSELL-ALEXANDER SCALE OF ATTITUDES TOWARD WORKING WOMEN

AUTHORS: Bernard M. Bass, Judith Krusell, and Ralph A. Alexander

DATE: 1971

VARIABLE: Attitudes toward women working

TYPE OF INSTRUMENT: Summated rating scale

DESCRIPTION: The scale consists of twenty-one items which load on seven factors: Factor I—Women's Expected Life Role (five items); Factor II—Women's Supervisory Potential (three items); Factor III—Dependability of Women Workers (three items); Factor IV—Deference and Chivalry (two items); Factor V—Women's Emotionality (three items); Factor VI—Women's Ability (two items); Factor VII—Life-Style Advantages of Women (three items). All items are phrased to reflect a negative attitude toward women working. Each item is followed by five response options: strongly agree, agree, uncertain or don't know, disagree, and strongly disagree.

PREVIOUSLY ADMINISTERED TO: Males employed in managerial and staff positions

APPROPRIATE FOR: Ages 16 and older

ADMINISTRATION: The scale can be self-administered and can be completed in ten to fifteen minutes.

SAMPLE ITEMS:

Women's Expected Life Role: The country's children would suffer greatly if most women worked.

Women's Supervisory Potential: Males resent working for a female boss.

Dependability of Women Workers: Pregnancy, menstruation, and home responsibilities make women much less desirable as workers than men.

Deference and Chivalry: Women should always try to build their men up.

Women's Emotionality: Women can't cope with stressful situations like men can.

Women's Ability: Women don't make good scientists or engineers because they inherently lack the mathematical and mechanical skills required.

Life-Style Advantages of Women: Looking, cooking, and smelling good for men are women's major responsibilities for men and result in more than equal rights for women.

SCORING: Items are objectively scored and equally weighted. The total score can range from 21 (positive attitudes toward women working) to 105 (negative attitudes toward women working).

DEVELOPMENT: The twenty-one items referred to above were originally part of a fifty-six-item questionnaire that included forty items reflecting a negative attitude and sixteen items reflecting a positive attitude. The fifty-six items were administered to 174 men in managerial or staff positions. The sixteen items that reflected positive attitudes were "of low estimated reliability" and were considered to add no information beyond what was contained in the forty negatively phrased items. Thus, only the forty negatively phrased items were factor analyzed. Fifteen factors were identified, but only seven of them had more than one item with a loading greater than .40. The seven factors and the twenty-one items that loaded on them comprise the scale as described here.

RELIABILITY: No data are provided.

VALIDITY: No data are provided.

NOTES AND COMMENTS: (1) Personal communication from the author (dated April 18, 1978) indicated that the original set of fifty-six items is no longer available.

(2) Given that the authors demonstrated that the scale is composed of seven factors, there is some question as to the value of obtaining an overall total score. Are the various factors additive?

(3) Phrasing all of the items negatively violates the precept which recommends phrasing half of the items positively and half negatively. Phrasing all of the items in the same direction encourages the emergence of a response set and careless responding.

SOURCE: See Bass, Krusell, and Alexander, 1971.

BIBLIOGRAPHY:

Bass, B. M., Krusell, J., and Alexander, R. A. "Male Managers' Attitudes Toward Working Women." *American Behavioral Scientist,* 1971, *15,* 221-236.

---

132. DESIRE TO WORK SCALE

AUTHOR: Lorraine Dittrich Eyde

DATE: 1962

VARIABLE: Women's work motivation

TYPE OF INSTRUMENT: Summated rating scale

DESCRIPTION: The scale lists seventeen conditions which vary along the following dimensions: marital status (single or married), number of children, ages of children, and adequacy of husband's salary. Using a five-point scale that ranges from "I would (did) not want to work under this condition" to "I would (did) very much want to work under this condition," the woman is to indicate her interest in working given each of the seventeen conditions.

PREVIOUSLY ADMINISTERED TO: College and adult women

APPROPRIATE FOR: Females, ages 16 and older

ADMINISTRATION: This scale is self-administered and can be completed in about ten minutes.

SAMPLE ITEMS: Married; two or more children between 1 month and 2 years; salary of husband not adequate.
　　　　　Married; child(ren) between age 13 and 19.

SCORING: Items are objectively scored. They are differentially weighted according to criterion weights and then summed to yield a total score.

DEVELOPMENT: The seventeen conditions included in the scale were given to thirteen judges with instructions to "rate the magnitude of the 'desire to work' which a woman shows when she works under the described condition" (Eyde, 1962, p. 24). Five response options were provided to the judges. The response options ranged from "Working under such a condition reveals little at all about a woman's 'desire to work.' Almost any woman would work under such a condition" to "When working under such a condition, a woman reveals that she has a very strong 'desire to work.' Few women would want to work under such a condition" (Eyde, 1962, p. 24). The responses from the judges were used to determine the criterion weights for scoring the scale.

RELIABILITY: Eyde (1968) administered the scale to fifty-five women on two occasions: at the time of the first testing, they were college seniors; at the time of the second testing, they had been out of college for five years. The test-retest correlation was .45. Eyde (1968) also administered the scale to another sample of fifty-one women on two occasions: at the time of the first testing, they had been out of college for five years; at the time of the second testing, they had been out of college for ten years. The test-retest correlation was .80.

Richardson (1972) obtained scores from thirty-three college women who completed the scale on two occasions. The test-retest correlation was .86.

VALIDITY: Eyde (1962) administered the Desire to Work Scale to seventy college senior women. Based on total scores, she divided the group into two subgroups: those who scored above the median and those who scored below the median. In addition, Eyde obtained information from each woman regarding fifty-five other variables that might relate to Desire to Work scores. She found that the high-scoring and low-scoring groups could be differentiated on the basis of seven of the variables: amount of dating, mother's care for child, minimum salary, number of hours of outside activity desired, number of different college activities, a rating of "mastery" as a work value; and score on the Dominance-Recognition subscale of the Ranked Work Values Scale (#138). Eyde also administered the Desire to Work Scale to sixty women who had graduated from college five years earlier. She obtained information from each woman regarding sixty-eight other variables that might relate to Desire to Work scores. Dividing the group into halves as described above, she found that fifteen variables differentiated the high-scoring and low-scoring groups: homemaker role; career role; mother's care for child; caretaker—home and child; approval of job; minimum salary; years desired to work after marriage; belief that the respondent would not work because the wife's place is in the home; belief that the respondent would not work because she wants to be an excellent homemaker; belief that the respondent would not work only because of the presence of children; belief that respondent would not work for a variety of reasons; a rating of "interesting" as a work value; and scores on the Interesting, Mastery, and Social subscales of the Ranked Work Values Scale (#138).

Luria (1974) found that women who graduate from college with high scores on the Desire to Work Scale score high on a variety of ability measures, including college grades, College Board scores, high school class rank, and high school IQ score.

Wolkon (1972) divided 147 women into three categories: Homemakers—no evidence of work history; Pioneers—employed in fields not traditionally employing women; and Traditionals—all others. As expected, Pioneers scored significantly higher ($\overline{X}$ = 219.382) than Traditionals ($\overline{X}$ = 167.825), and Traditionals scored significantly higher than Homemakers ($\overline{X}$ = 130.538).

Richardson (1974) obtained measures of fourteen career-orientation variables from a sample of ninety-seven women ranging in age from 19 to 23. She found significant correlations between Desire to Work scores and scores on eight of the remaining thirteen variables. Significant correlations were found between desire to work and extent of work in life plans, importance of career and marriage, value of marriage, value of career, occupational field chosen, level of occupational choice, educational aspirations, and certainty of graduate school plans.

SOURCE: See Eyde, 1962.

BIBLIOGRAPHY:

Eyde, L. D. *Work Values and Background Factors as Predictors of Women's Desire to Work.* Bureau of Business Research Monograph 108. Columbus: Ohio State University, 1962.

Eyde, L. D. "Work Motivation of Women College Graduates: Five-Year Follow-Up." *Journal of Counseling Psychology,* 1968, *15,* 199-202.

Luria, Z. "Recent Women College Graduates: A Study of Rising Expectations." *American Journal of Orthopsychiatry,* 1974, *44,* 312-326.

Richardson, M. S. "Self-Concepts and Role Concepts in the Career Orientation of College Women." Unpublished doctoral dissertation, Columbia University, 1972. (*Dissertation Abstracts International,* 1973, *33*[10-B], 5001-5002.)

Richardson, M. S. "The Dimensions of Career and Work Orientation in College Women." *Journal of Vocational Behavior,* 1974, *5,* 161-172.

Richardson, M. S. "Self-Concepts and Role Concepts in the Career Orientation of College Women." *Journal of Counseling Psychology,* 1975, *22,* 122-126.

Waters, O. P. "Sex Role Attitudes and the Manifest Needs, Vocational Maturity, and Career Orientation of College Women." Unpublished doctoral dissertation, Fordham University, 1976. (*Dissertation Abstracts International,* 1976, *37*[5-A], 2654.)

Wolkon, K. A. "Pioneer vs. Traditional: Two Distinct Vocational Patterns of College Alumnae." *Journal of Vocational Behavior,* 1972, *2,* 275-282.

---

133. DOWDALL WORK APPROVAL FOR WOMEN SCALE

AUTHOR: Jean A. Dowdall

DATE: 1972 (used 1968)

VARIABLE: Approval of wives working under various circumstances

TYPE OF INSTRUMENT: Guttman scale

DESCRIPTION: The scale consists of five questions; each question asks whether wives should work under a particular circumstance. For each question, the respondent is to indicate either "yes," "no," or "unsure." When the scale was originally used, respondents were also asked to indicate how strongly they felt about their answers. However, this information is not used in scoring the scale.

PREVIOUSLY ADMINISTERED TO: Females, ages 15-64

APPROPRIATE FOR: Ages 15 and older

ADMINISTRATION: The scale is part of a lengthy structured interview. It can easily be adapted for use as a self-administered paper-and-pencil measure that could be completed in less than three minutes.

SAMPLE ITEMS: Do you think it is all right for a married woman to have a job instead of only taking care of the house and the children while her husband provides for the family?
                Is it all right for a married woman to have a job outside the home if she has no small children?

SCORING: The score equals the number of "yes" responses. "No" responses and "unsure" responses do not add to the work approval score. Thus, total scores can range from 0 (disapproves of each condition given) to 5 (approves of each condition given).

DEVELOPMENT: The items comprising this scale were originally part of lengthy surveys administered by the Population Research Laboratory of Brown University. An attempt was made to construct a Guttman scale using married women's responses to six questions related to the employment of wives. In constructing the scale, "unsure" responses were combined with "no" responses. The scale values—that is, coefficient of reproducibility, minimum marginal reproducibility, percentage improvement, and coefficient of scalability—were not sufficiently high. With one item eliminated, the scale values were greatly improved: the coefficient of reproducibility was .939; the minimum marginal reproducibility was .812; the percentage improvement was .127; and the coefficient of scalability was .676. Attempts were made to improve on the scale by altering the scoring: for example, "unsure" responses were combined with "yes" responses. However, the scale values as described above were the best obtained. When scale values were computed based on the responses from previously married women and never-married women, the scale values were comparable to the ones listed above for married women. Thus, the final scale consists of five items in which "unsure" responses are treated as "no" responses.

RELIABILITY: The scale values for married women, previously married women, and never-married women, respectively, are: coefficient of reproducibility = .939, .936, .918; minimum marginal reproducibility = .812, .772, .803; percentage improvement = .127, .164, .115; and coefficient of scalability = .676, .718, and .584.

VALIDITY: Dowdall (1974a, p. 126) states, "Whether other measures would more accurately reflect underlying attitudes toward work for married women is not known. The items used here would appear to have at least face validity in that all refer directly to approval and to conditions under which a woman might or might not hold a paid job."

NOTES AND COMMENTS: (1) Dowdall (1972, 1974a, 1974b) has compared scores on the Dowdall Work Approval for Women scale with other variables such as respondent's age, marital status, educational attainment level, religion, nationality, socioeconomic level, number of children, age of youngest child, husband's annual income, and husband's educational attainment.

(2) This scale is also described in *Family Measurement Techniques* (Straus and Brown, 1978, p. 99).

SOURCE: See Dowdall, 1972, 1974a, or 1974b.

BIBLIOGRAPHY:

Dowdall, J. A. "Employment and Sex Role Orientation of Rhode Island Women." Unpublished doctoral dissertation, Brown University, 1972. (*Dissertation Abstracts International*, 1973, *33*[12-A], 7035.)

Dowdall, J. A. "Structural and Attitudinal Factors Associated with Female Labor-Force Participation." *Social Science Quarterly*, 1974a, *55*, 121-130.

Dowdall, J. A. "Women's Attitudes Toward Employment and Family Roles." *Sociological Analysis*, 1974b, *35*, 251-262.

*Straus, M. A., and Brown, B. W. *Family Measurement Techniques: Abstracts of Published Instruments, 1935-1974*. Minneapolis: University of Minnesota Press, 1978.

---

134. EQUALITARIAN SCALE

AUTHORS: H. Greenberg, B. Straight, W. Hassenger, and W. Raska

DATE: 1961

VARIABLE: Attitudes toward women working

TYPE OF INSTRUMENT: Summated rating scale

DESCRIPTION: The scale consists of six questions regarding issues relevant to women working, such as the right of women to work and equality between male and female workers. For five of the questions, the response options range from "strongly agree" to "strongly disagree"; for one item, the response options are "very desirable," "all right," "of little difference," "only in extreme circumstances," and "definitely not."

PREVIOUSLY ADMINISTERED TO: Married women

APPROPRIATE FOR: Ages 16 and older

ADMINISTRATION: The scale can be self-administered and can be completed in about three minutes.

SAMPLE ITEMS: Successful careers and successful homes cannot mix.

In a recession economy, working married women take jobs away from men.

SCORING: Items are objectively scored and equally weighted. Total scores can range from 6 (all extreme egalitarian responses) to 30 (all extreme nonegalitarian responses).

DEVELOPMENT: No information is provided.

RELIABILITY: No data are provided.

VALIDITY: Greenberg and others (1961) analyzed the responses from sixty-eight working women and fifty-eight nonworking women. They found that working women scored significantly higher—more egalitarian ($\overline{X}$ = 16.80)—than nonworking women ($\overline{X}$ = 14.90, $p < .01$).

NOTES AND COMMENTS: (1) Because this scale is quite short, it is important that its reliability be established.

(2) The scale was part of a longer questionnaire.

(3) The scale is also described in *Family Measurement Techniques* (Straus, 1969, p. 114; Straus and Brown, 1978, p. 108).

SOURCE: See Greenberg and others, 1961.

BIBLIOGRAPHY:

Greenberg, H., Straight, B., Hassenger, W., and Raska, W. "Personality Attitudinal Differences Between Employed and Unemployed Married Women." *Journal of Social Psychology*, 1961, *53*, 87-96.

*Straus, M. A. *Family Measurement Techniques: Abstracts of Published Instruments, 1935-1965*. Minneapolis: University of Minnesota Press, 1969.

*Straus, M. A., and Brown, B. W. *Family Measurement Techniques: Abstracts of Published Instruments, 1935-1974*. Minneapolis: University of Minnesota Press, 1978.

---

135. FOTTLER SCALE OF ATTITUDES REGARDING THE MALE NURSE

AUTHOR: Myron D. Fottler

DATE: 1976 (used 1973)

VARIABLE: Attitudes toward male nurses

TYPE OF INSTRUMENT: Summated rating scale

DESCRIPTION: The scale consists of ten statements regarding male nurses. All items in the scale are phrased positively, so that agreement always reflects a positive attitude. Five response options are provided: strongly agree, agree, uncertain, disagree, and strongly disagree.

PREVIOUSLY ADMINISTERED TO: Female nurses

APPROPRIATE FOR: Nurses and other persons familiar with the nursing profession

ADMINISTRATION: The scale can be self-administered and can be completed in less than five minutes.

SAMPLE ITEMS: The male nurse, as head of the household, should be given a larger salary than the female nurse.
Since a man can tolerate more pressure, the male nurse should be expected to assume full responsibility in an emergency situation.

SCORING: Items are objectively scored and equally weighted. The total score can vary from 10 (extremely negative attitude) to 50 (extremely positive attitude).

DEVELOPMENT: No information is provided.

RELIABILITY: No data are provided.

VALIDITY: Fottler hypothesized that (1) "Female nurses hold generally positive attitudes toward the male nurse," and (2) "More positive attitudes toward the male nurse are held by younger, single, better-educated, urban-socialized nurses, those employed in a higher level position outside a hospital, and those having extensive contact with male nurses" (p. 103). He claims that the first hypothesis was supported by the data, but he had no predetermined criterion for "generally positive attitudes" and could have interpreted many different findings to support this hypothesis. The second hypothesis was not supported by the data. Though it is possible that the second hypothesis was, in fact, false, it is also possible that the scale does not validly assess attitudes toward male nurses.

NOTES AND COMMENTS: (1) Four of the ten items on the scale actually measure whether the male nurse is perceived as superior to the female nurse. Thus, very high scores on the scale indicate that the male nurse is seen as superior to the female nurse, and egalitarian attitudes are reflected by scores in the intermediate range (for example, 30-34 total points).
(2) Fottler violates the precept that half of the items on an attitude scale should be phrased positively and half should be phrased negatively.

SOURCE: See Fottler, 1976.

BIBLIOGRAPHY:

Fottler, M. D. "Attitudes of Female Nurses Toward the Male Nurse: A Study of Occupational Segregation." *Journal of Health and Social Behavior,* 1976, *17,* 98-111.

136. KING EQUALITARIAN PERCEPTION SCALE

AUTHOR: Elizabeth Camp King

DATE: 1974

VARIABLES: Perceptions of egalitarianism for women in academia; perceptions of role conflict, advancement possibilities, and career aspirations

TYPE OF INSTRUMENT: Summated rating scale

DESCRIPTION: The scale contains twenty-five statements concerning three areas of egalitarian perceptions: role conflict (fourteen items), advancement possibilities (five items), and career aspirations (six items). Each item is accompanied by five response options: strongly agree, agree, undecided, disagree, and strongly disagree.

PREVIOUSLY ADMINISTERED TO: College faculty and administrators

APPROPRIATE FOR: College faculty and administrators

ADMINISTRATION: This self-administered scale can be completed in about five minutes.

SAMPLE ITEMS:

Role Conflict: It is fine for a woman to work if her children are adequately cared for.

Advancement Possibilities: The possibilities for a woman to be promoted to the next academic rank when eligible are only fair.

Career Aspirations: Professional women can realistically expect to have a life-long career.

SCORING: Items are objectively scored and equally weighted. Four scores are obtained from the scale: Role Conflict, Advancement Possibilities, Career Aspirations, and Total.

DEVELOPMENT: An item pool was developed from a search of the literature. The number of items in the pool was not specified. The item pool was administered to faculty, graduate students, and female professionals (number unspecified). The twenty-five items that best discriminated between those scoring in the upper and lower extremes of the distribution were selected for the final scale.

RELIABILITY: King (1974) reports an interjudge reliability of .693. It is difficult to know what is meant by this correlation. The scale was administered to two panels of judges and the reliability apparently reflects the correlation between the responses given by the two panels.

VALIDITY: No data are provided.

NOTES AND COMMENTS: (1) Four of the twenty-five items on this scale refer specifically to the college situation. The remaining items on the scale would be appropriate for use in noncollege institutions where women hold professional or managerial positions.

(2) The author's suggestion that the three subscale scores can be added to yield a total score is questionable. Responses to items dealing with advancement possibilities reflect perceptions of the institutional setting. Responses to items pertaining to role conflict reflect attitudes. It is quite possible that the respondent will perceive the institutional setting as hostile to women but personally have very favorable attitudes toward women working—that is, believe that working presents little or no role conflict. If these two scores are added together, they will cancel each other out. Thus the total score seems essentially uninterpretable.

(3) Many of the items are ambiguous. For example, "Marriage is an asset for professional women" could elicit a negative response because the respondent believes that marriage is a liability for professional women or because marriage is irrelevant to a woman's profession. The item, "For professional women children are an asset" creates the same ambiguity in interpreting responses. Another example, "Women can live in productive harmony with men filling complementary and supplementary roles," implies that the men will be filling the complementary and supplementary roles. Is that really what the author means? It is unclear what attitudes are expressed when the item "Most women would like to be promoted to an administrative position" is responded to.

SOURCE: See King, 1974; or Sarvas, 1976.

BIBLIOGRAPHY:

King, E. C. "Perceptions of Female Vocational Faculty Members as Seen by Themselves and College Administrators." Unpublished doctoral dissertation, Pennsylvania State University, 1974. (*Dissertation Abstracts International*, 1975, *36*[1-A], 145; ERIC Document Reproduction Service No. ED 096 449.)
Sarvas, A. F. "An Analysis of the Relationship Between Perceptions of Vocational Female Faculty and Administrators Toward Female Faculty in Four Institutional Types. Volume 13, No. 11." University Park: Pennsylvania State University, 1976. (ERIC Document Reproduction Service No. ED 118 993.)

---

137. NAGELY SCALE OF ATTITUDES TOWARD CAREER AND CAREER-RELATED VARIABLES

AUTHOR: Donna L. Nagely

DATE: 1970

VARIABLE: The meaning a woman's career has for her

TYPE OF INSTRUMENT: Semantic differential scale

DESCRIPTION: The scale consists of a single concept, "career," to be rated on seventy seven-point bipolar adjective scales.

PREVIOUSLY ADMINISTERED TO: Adult working women

APPROPRIATE FOR: Employed females

ADMINISTRATION: The scale can be self-administered and can be completed in about ten minutes.

SAMPLE ITEMS: Positive-Negative
Creative-Unimaginative
Outgoing-Subdued
Weak-Strong
Unusual-Ordinary

SCORING: Forty-nine of the seventy items are scored on seven-point scales to yield five scores: Masculine Work Orientation, Career Benefits, Feminine Social Orientation, Stop-Gap Job Orientation, and Women's Liberation Orientation.

DEVELOPMENT: The seventy bipolar adjective pairs were selected to represent the following areas: social desirability, uniqueness, role conflict, activity, social service, creativity, power, comfort, excitement, importance, success, self-enhancement, and stability. The responses from forty working women were factor analyzed and five factors were extracted. The factor names are listed under Scoring.

RELIABILITY: No data are provided.

VALIDITY: The forty subjects who completed this scale also completed two other measures: a projective measure of female role perception and a questionnaire measuring a variety of attitudinal and biographical variables. The factor scores from this scale were essentially independent of the projective measure of female role perception. Factor scores were significantly correlated with questionnaire items with which they logically ought to be correlated (Nagely, 1970).

This scale was completed by twenty women employed in occupations traditionally filled by women and twenty women employed in occupations traditionally filled by men. There were significant differences between the two groups on two factors of the scale: Masculine Work Orientation ($p < .01$) and Women's Liberation Orientation ($p < .01$). No significant differences were found on the other three factors (Nagely, 1970).

NOTES AND COMMENTS: (1) A correlation matrix showing the intercorrelations between the factor scores suggests that Factors I, III, IV, and V (Masculine Work Orientation, Feminine Social Orientation, Stop-Gap Job Orientation, and Women's Liberation Orientation, respectively) are essentially independent, but Factor II (Career Benefits) is highly correlated with Factors I, III, and V.

(2) The directions ask respondents to "make judgments on the basis of what a career means to you." Since the respondents are females, presumably they are rating "woman's career"; however, it is possible they are rating what a "man's career" means to them.

SOURCE: See Nagely, 1970.

BIBLIOGRAPHY:

Nagely, D. L. "A Comparison of College-Educated Working Mothers in Traditional and Nontraditional Occupations." Unpublished doctoral dissertation, Ohio State University, 1970. (*Dissertation Abstracts International,* 1971, *31* [9-A], 4556-4557.)
Nagely, D. L. "Traditional and Pioneer Working Mothers." *Journal of Vocational Behavior,* 1971, *1,* 331-341.

---

138. RANKED WORK VALUES SCALE

AUTHOR: Lorraine Dittrich Eyde

DATE: 1962

VARIABLE: Women's work values

TYPE OF INSTRUMENT: Ranking scale

DESCRIPTION: The scale consists of fourteen sets of six phrases. Each phrase describes a reason why a woman might work. In each set, there is one phrase representing each of six value areas: Dominance-Recognition, Economic, Independence, Interesting-Variety, Mastery-Achievement, and Social. The woman is directed to rank the items in each set by placing a "1" next to the phrase that best describes the reason why she does (or will) work, a "2" next to the phrase that is the second-best description of the reason why she does (or will) work, and so on.

PREVIOUSLY ADMINISTERED TO: College and adult women

APPROPRIATE FOR: Females, ages 16 and older

ADMINISTRATION: The scale is self-administered and can be completed in about fifteen to twenty minutes.

SAMPLE ITEMS: (These six items form one set.)
• Want to use my education
• Want to avoid depending upon others
• Want to help people make decisions
• Want to talk about something other than housework and childcare
• Want money to buy basic things
• Want to be helpful to others

SCORING: The scale yields six scores, one for each value area. A score for each area is obtained by summing the ranks assigned to the fourteen items representing that area.

DEVELOPMENT: Using the responses obtained from an open-ended questionnaire and information gleaned from a review of the relevant literature, eight value areas were identified: dominance over people, different reasons for working for money (economic security), self-development or self-actualization, independence, variety of activities, accomplishment of things by learning and doing, recognition by others, and interpersonal relationships. A pool of 245 items was constructed and given to six judges with instructions to sort the items into eight piles corresponding to the eight value areas. Those items for which at least half the judges agreed to their classification were retained. The retained items were given to raters with instructions to rate them on a five-point scale reflecting the social desirability of the item. Items with median ratings of 1 or 2 (low social desirability) were eliminated. The remaining 159 items included 19 items on the Dominance scale and 20 items on each of the seven other scales. The 159 items were administered to college women with instructions to rate each item on a five-point scale indicating the extent to which the value applies to the respondent. A factor analysis of the responses revealed six value factors (Dominance-Recognition, Economic, Independence, Interesting-Variety, Mastery-Achievement, and Social) and a general factor. Fourteen items representing each of the six specific factors were identified for the scale. In selecting items, an effort was made to hold constant the social desirability levels in each set, match items within each set for their factor loadings on the general factor, and include items with high specific factor loadings.

RELIABILITY: Eyde (1968) administered the scale to fifty-five women on two occasions: at the time of the first testing, they were college seniors; at the time of the second testing, they had been out of college for five years. She also administered the scale to another sample of fifty-one women on two occasions: at the time of the first testing, they had been out of college for five years; at the time of the second testing, they had been out of college for ten years. Test-retest correlations were computed for each subscale. The correlations for the five-year and ten-year alumnae, respectively, were: Dominance-Recognition = .60 and .46; Economic = .38 and .60; Independence = .33 and .35; Interesting-Variety = .25 and .48; Mastery-Achievement = .44 and .68; and Social = .50 and .44.

Wolfe (1969a, 1969b) administered the scale to a sample of forty-eight women on two occasions. The interval between test and retest was not specified. Test-retest correlations on the factors were: Dominance-Recognition = .76; Economic = .81; Independence = .69; Interesting-Variety = .77; Mastery-Achievement = .75; and Social = .52.

VALIDITY: Eyde (1962) administered the Ranked Work Values Scale and the Desire to Work Scale (#132) to seventy college senior women. Based on total scores on the Desire to Work Scale, she divided the group into two subgroups: those who scored above the median and those who scored below the median. Of the six scores on the Ranked Work Values Scale, only one, Dominance-Recognition, differentiated the high scorers from the low scorers. Eyde also administered the Ranked Work Values Scale and the Desire to Work Scale to sixty women who had graduated from college five years earlier. She again used scores on the Desire to Work Scale to divide the group in half. Three scores on the Ranked Work Values Scale differentiated low scorers from high scorers: Interesting-Variety, Mastery-Achievement, and Social.

Eyde (1962) asked the women to use a five-point rating scale to indicate the extent to which each of the items on the Ranked Work Values Scale applied to them. She concluded that the rating method "did not predict Desire to Work as well as did the Ranked Work Value scales" (p. 55).

Wolkon (1972) divided 147 women into three categories: Homemakers—no evidence of work history; Pioneers—employed in fields not traditionally employing women; and Traditional—all others. He found that Homemakers and Pioneers were significantly different on their scores on six of the seven subscales. There was no significant difference on the Interesting-Variety subscale.

NOTES AND COMMENTS: (1) The items contributing to the Independence score reflect an assumption that a working woman has more freedom than a homemaker. For example, "Want to determine what I do" and "Want to avoid being told what to do" both imply that working women have considerable freedom on their jobs. Most persons—men and women—are not free to determine what they do at their job, nor do they avoid being told what to do by accepting employment. These, and similar items, suggest that the scale is really intended for women who are thinking about professional level, supervisory level, or self-employed work situations.

(2) Wolfe (1969a, 1969b) compared scores on the Ranked Work Values Scale with marital status, age, educational attainment, current employment status, career pattern, socioeconomic level, and field of work.

SOURCE: See Eyde, 1962.

BIBLIOGRAPHY:

Eyde, L. D. *Work Values and Background Factors as Predictors of Women's Desire to Work.* Bureau of Business Research Monograph 108. Columbus: Ohio State University, 1962.

Eyde, L. D. "Work Motivation of Women College Graduates: Five-Year Follow-Up." *Journal of Counseling Psychology,* 1968, *15,* 199-202.

Wolfe, H. B. "An Analysis of the Work Values of Women: Implications for Counseling." *Journal of the National Association for Woman Deans, Administrators, and Counselors,* 1969a, *33,* 13-17.

Wolfe, H. B. "Women in the World of Work." Albany: New York State Education Department, 1969b. (ERIC Document Reproduction Service No. ED 055 160.)

Wolkon, K. A. "Pioneer vs. Traditional: Two Distinct Vocational Patterns of College Alumnae." *Journal of Vocational Behavior,* 1972, *2,* 275-282.

---

139. ROCKWOOD-FORD ACCEPTABLE REASONS FOR MARRIED WOMEN WORKING

AUTHORS: Lemo D. Rockwood and Mary E. N. Ford

DATE: 1945 (used 1940)

VARIABLE: Reactions to possible reasons why a married woman might work

TYPE OF INSTRUMENT: Checklist

DESCRIPTION: The instrument consists of the following question: "Under what conditions should married women work outside the home for money?" The question is followed by a list of eight possible conditions, and the respondents are directed to check all of the ones they approve of.

PREVIOUSLY ADMINISTERED TO: College students

APPROPRIATE FOR: Ages 16 and older

ADMINISTRATION: The scale can be self-administered and can be completed in less than two minutes.

SAMPLE ITEMS: During early married life before the arrival of children.
                        If wife's earnings are necessary to make it possible for couple to marry.

SCORING: No scores are obtained.

DEVELOPMENT: The instrument was part of a larger questionnaire which was first administered to college students in 1940. Based on the responses from that administration, no revisions were considered necessary.

RELIABILITY: No data are provided.

VALIDITY: Female respondents approved of more reasons for women working than did male respondents. For four of the seven items, the differences were sufficiently small to be due to chance. However, for three of the items, the differences were "substantial."

NOTES AND COMMENTS: (1) The instrument was included in a questionnaire that requested information in five broad areas: personal information, family background, premarital relations, marriage, and divorce. The entire questionnaire takes about forty minutes to complete.

(2) Rockwood and Ford compared the responses of various subgroups from their samples: men versus women; arts-and-sciences students versus agriculture students versus home-economics students versus hotel students versus engineering students; college juniors versus college seniors; fraternity men versus nonfraternity men; sorority women versus nonsorority women; men from urban areas versus men from rural areas; women from urban areas versus women from rural areas; only child versus oldest, youngest, and middle child; children of farmers versus children of men in other occupations; engaged students versus students who were not engaged.

SOURCE: See Rockwood and Ford, 1945, p. 234.

BIBLIOGRAPHY:

Rockwood, L. D., and Ford, M. E. N. *Youth, Marriage, and Parenthood: The Attitudes of 364 University Juniors and Seniors Toward Courtship, Marriage, and Parenthood.* New York: Wiley, 1945.

140. ST. JOHN SCALE OF BEHAVIOR EXPECTED
OF EMPLOYED WOMEN

AUTHOR: Clinton St. John

DATE: 1965

VARIABLE: Attitudes toward specific behaviors when exhibited by women teachers and other employed women

TYPE OF INSTRUMENT: Summated rating scale

DESCRIPTION: The scale consists of twenty-two brief descriptions of different behaviors with each of the twenty-two behaviors phrased once in terms of teachers and once in terms of "others" (referring to women employed in other occupations). Thus, there is a total of forty-four statements. For each statement, the respondents are asked to indicate whether they approve of women behaving in the way described in the statement. There are five response options: yes, strongly; yes, mildly; undecided; no, mildly; and no, strongly.

PREVIOUSLY ADMINISTERED TO: Parents of school age children

APPROPRIATE FOR: Ages 16 and older

ADMINISTRATION: The instrument can be self-administered and can generally be completed in about six minutes.

SAMPLE ITEMS: Do you approve of women behaving in the following ways?
• Teachers smoking in public
• Others smoking in public
• Teachers running for local political office
• Others running for local political office

SCORING: No scores are obtained.

DEVELOPMENT: Greenhoe (1941) conducted a study of school board members, teachers, and teacher-trainees to determine which behaviors are disapproved for male teachers and which for female teachers. The behaviors selected for St. John's scale included most of those behaviors found by Greenhoe to elicit responses indicative of disapproval.

RELIABILITY: No data are provided.

VALIDITY: Differences were found in the results obtained from fathers as compared with mothers. On five items, fathers expected teachers to behave differently than they expected women employed in other areas to behave. Mothers, on the other hand, expected teachers to behave differently than women employed in other areas on only two items. Furthermore, overall, fathers expect teachers to behave differently than women employed in other occupations (p < .01), but mothers do not.

NOTES AND COMMENTS: Many of the items on the scale are obsolete, and there is likely to be little variability in the responses to them. For example, few people today are likely to disapprove of teachers or other employed women who smoke in private or work after marriage.

SOURCE: See St. John, 1965.

BIBLIOGRAPHY:

*Greenhoe, F. G. *Community Contacts and Participation of Teachers.* Washington, D.C.: American Council on Public Affairs, 1941.
St. John, C. "Opinion of Parents on Certain Behaviors of Women Teachers and Other Employed Women." *Ontario Journal of Educational Research,* 1965, *8*, 23-33.

---

141. SEXIST ATTITUDE INVENTORY

AUTHOR: Angelo Michael Bentivegna

DATE: 1974

VARIABLE: Attitudes toward males entering the home-economics profession

TYPE OF INSTRUMENT: Summated rating scale

DESCRIPTION: The scale consists of forty-six statements concerning such issues as the impact on the field of home economics resulting from men entering the field, preferences for males or females as supervisors in the field of home economics, and perceptions of others' acceptance of males in the field of home economics. Nineteen items are phrased to reflect positive attitudes and twenty-seven items are phrased to reflect negative attitudes. Each statement is accompanied by four response options: strongly agree, agree, disagree, and strongly disagree.

PREVIOUSLY ADMINISTERED TO: Members of the American Home Economics Association (that is, professional home economists)

APPROPRIATE FOR: Ages 16 and older

ADMINISTRATION: The scale can be self-administered and can be completed in less than half an hour.

SAMPLE ITEMS: I believe that when males enter home economics, salaries increase.
I believe that males can assume leadership roles in home economics more easily than in disciplines which are not dominated by women.

SCORING: Items are objectively scored and equally weighted. Total scores can range from 46 (extremely negative attitudes toward males entering the home-economics profession) to 184 (extremely positive attitudes toward males entering the home-economics profession).

DEVELOPMENT: An open-ended questionnaire was administered to 200 faculty and graduate students in the colleges of Education, Human Development, and Engineering of a large university. The questionnaire stated, "Please list below your attitudes, negative and positive, regarding male participation in Home Economics" (Bentivegna, 1974, p. 85). The responses were examined, refined, and compiled into a forty-six-item scale.

RELIABILITY: The responses from eighty graduate students in education and human development were used to compute the internal consistency of the scale. Kuder-Richardson reliability was found to be .996 (Bentivegna, 1974).

VALIDITY: Bentivegna (1974, p. 33) claims that "content validity of the instrument is assumed" because of the way in which the scale was developed.

NOTES AND COMMENTS: (1) Bentivegna (1974) suggests that the scale can be modified to measure attitudes toward males entering any female-dominated profession.

(2) Bentivegna (1974) related scores on the Sexist Attitude Inventory to age, sex, salary, work experience, marital status, professional achievement, professional rank, and professional commitment.

SOURCE: See Bentivegna, 1974.

BIBLIOGRAPHY:

Bentivegna, A. M. "Attitudes of Home-Economics College and University Professionals Toward Males Entering the Field." Unpublished doctoral dissertation, Pennsylvania State University, 1974. (*Dissertation Abstracts International,* 1974, *35*[6-B], 2868.)

Bentivegna, A. M., and Weis, S. F. "Attitudes of Acceptance Toward Males Entering the Home-Economics Profession." *Illinois Teacher of Home Economics,* 1977, *20,* 230-236.

---

142. SITUATIONAL ATTITUDE SCALE FOR WOMEN (SASW)

AUTHORS: Michele H. Herman and William E. Sedlacek

DATE: 1973

VARIABLE: Attitudes toward women in nontraditional sex roles

TYPE OF INSTRUMENT: Semantic differential scale

DESCRIPTION: There are two forms of the instrument. Each form consists of single-sentence descriptions of ten situations, with each situation followed by ten semantic differential scales. The situations are ones in which gender might be a variable affecting the way someone responds to the situation. Nine of the ten situations refer to employment. The two forms of the instrument contain the same ten situations. In Form A, the sex of the subject in each situation is not specified. In Form B, the sex of the subject in nine situations is specified as a woman and the situations are typically thought of as applying to a man; in one situation, the sex of the subject is a man, but the situation is one which is more typical for a woman. Within each form, the semantic differential scales following each situation are comprised of different bipolar adjective pairs. Across forms, the semantic differential scales following each pair of comparable situations are the same.

PREVIOUSLY ADMINISTERED TO: College students and student personnel professionals

APPROPRIATE FOR: Ages 16 and older

ADMINISTRATION: Half of the subjects are given Form A and half are given Form B, but none of the subjects should be aware of the existence of two forms. The scale is self-administered and can be completed in fifteen to twenty minutes.

SAMPLE ITEMS:

Form A: You are stopped for speeding by a police officer.

Form B: You are stopped for speeding by a policewoman.

Bipolar Adjectives: calm-nervous
                                 trusting-suspicious

SCORING: Each semantic differential is a five-point scale. The mean score is computed for each semantic differential scale on each form. Using t tests, the comparable semantic differential scale from Form A is compared with that from Form B. If a significant difference exists, it is concluded to reflect attitudes toward women.

DEVELOPMENT: The scale is modeled after the Situational Attitude Scale, which is a similar instrument designed to measure racial attitudes. The SASW was edited and revised as a result of pilot testing with forty-two college students. More specific information is not provided.

RELIABILITY: No data are provided.

VALIDITY: The authors point out that when comparing forms A and B, "If there are significant differences, they must be attributed to the insertion of the words *female, woman,* etc. in Form B, since all other variables were controlled" (Herman and Sedlacek, 1973a, p. 545). When the instrument was administered to 151 college freshmen, there were significant differences on 32 of the 100 semantic differential scale comparisons.

NOTES AND COMMENTS: (1) The authors assume that differences between responses obtained on the two forms reflect attitudes toward women in nontraditional sex roles. They could test this assumption by adding a third form of the scale in which the gender in each item is specified as male. If the authors' assumption is correct, then there should be no differences between responses when no gender is specified and when the male gender is specified, but there should be differences between responses when female gender is specified and responses when male gender or no gender is specified.

(2) The phrasing of the items on Form B, when the sex is specified as female, calls considerable attention to what is being measured; for example, "You have just met your new woman doctor" and "You are a personnel officer and have just interviewed a woman applicant who appears to be aggressive and bright." Because many of the items sensitize respondents to what is being measured, the scale might be very susceptible to faking or a social desirability response set.

(3) Courtois and Sedlacek (1975) modified the scale. They used a different set of ten situations which were designed to measure attitudes toward women's success.

SOURCE: See Herman and Sedlacek, 1973b.

BIBLIOGRAPHY:

Chapman, T. H. "Simulation Game Effects on Attitudes Regarding Racism and Sexism." Unpublished doctoral dissertation, University of Maryland, 1974a. (*Dissertation Abstracts International,* 1975, *36*[2-A], 700.)

Chapman, T. H. "Simulation Game Effects on Attitudes Regarding Racism and Sexism. Research Report No. 8-74." College Park: University of Maryland, 1974b. (ERIC Document Reproduction Service No. ED 106 392.)

Courtois, C., and Sedlacek, W. E. "Sex Differences in Perceptions of Female Success. Research Report No. 2-75." College Park: University of Maryland, 1975. (ERIC Document Reproduction Service No. ED 122 167.)

Herman, M. H., and Sedlacek, W. E. "Sexist Attitudes Among Male University Students." *Journal of College Student Personnel,* 1973a, *14,* 544-548.

Herman, M. H., and Sedlacek, W. E. "Sexist Attitudes Among Male University Students." College Park: University of Maryland, 1973b. (ERIC Document Reproduction Service No. ED 074 421.)

O'Donnell, R. M. "A Study of Attitudes Held by Student Personnel Professionals Toward Sex Roles." Unpublished doctoral dissertation, University of Maryland, 1973. (*Dissertation Abstracts International,* 1973, *34*[6-A], 3066-3067.)

---

143. TURNER PERCEIVED OCCUPATIONAL DISCRIMINATION AGAINST WOMEN

AUTHORS: Barbara F. Turner and Castellano B. Turner

DATE: 1975

VARIABLE: Perceptions of whether specific occupations are open to women

TYPE OF INSTRUMENT: Multiple choice

DESCRIPTION: The instrument consists of a list of twenty-one high-status, white-collar and professional occupations. For each occupation, the respondent is to answer the following question: "Do you think this field is open to women: (1) On the same basis as to men, (2) Open only to exceptional women, (3) Not open to women?"

PREVIOUSLY ADMINISTERED TO: College freshmen

APPROPRIATE FOR: Ages 16 and older

ADMINISTRATION: The scale can be self-administered and can be completed in about five minutes.

SAMPLE ITEMS: Accountant
               Advertising and marketing
               Business executive

SCORING: Items are objectively scored and equally weighted. Total scores can range from 21 (no perceived discrimination) to 63 (extreme discrimination perceived).

DEVELOPMENT: Seventeen of the twenty-one occupations were taken from a survey administered by the National Opinion Research Center.

RELIABILITY: The scale was administered to 3,031 college freshmen, and a reliability estimate was calculated. Coefficient alpha was .83.

VALIDITY: Using the responses from college freshmen, the correlation between perceived discrimination and actual representation of women in each of the occupations was computed. The correlation based on responses from seventy black female respondents was .85; the correlation based on responses from seventy-five black male respondents was .83; the correlation based on responses from 1,457 white female respondents was .65; and the correlation based on responses from 1,429 white male respondents was .78. An analysis of variance yielded a main effect for sex, with women perceiving significantly more discrimination than men. In addition, there was a significant race x sex interaction and a significant sex x SES interaction.

NOTES AND COMMENTS: This scale was used in conjunction with a parallel measure assessing perceptions of whether specific occupations are open to women.

SOURCE: See Turner and Turner, 1975.

BIBLIOGRAPHY:

Turner, B. F., and Turner, C. B. "Race, Sex, and Perception of the Occupational Opportunity Structure Among College Students." *Sociological Quarterly*, 1975, *16*, 345-360.

144. WOMEN AS MANAGERS SCALE (WAMS)

AUTHORS: Lawrence H. Peters, James R. Terborg, and Janet Taynor

DATE: 1974

VARIABLE: Attitudes toward women as managers in a business organization

TYPE OF INSTRUMENT: Summated rating scale

DESCRIPTION: The scale consists of twenty-one statements, ten of which are phrased to reflect a negative attitude toward women and eleven of which are phrased to reflect a positive attitude toward women. A seven-point rating scale is provided for responding to each item. The response options are: strongly disagree, disagree, slightly disagree, neither disagree nor agree, slightly agree, agree, strongly agree. The twenty-one items represent three factors: Factor I (ten items)—general acceptance of females as managers; Factor II (five items)—"feminine barriers" to full-time, permanent employment; and Factor III (six items)—personality traits usually ascribed to managers.

PREVIOUSLY ADMINISTERED TO: College students and adults

APPROPRIATE FOR: Ages 16 and older

ADMINISTRATION: The scale can be self-administered and can be completed in less than fifteen minutes.

SAMPLE ITEMS:

Factor I: It is less desirable for women than men to have a job that requires responsibility.

Factor II: The possibility of pregnancy does not make women less desirable employees than men.

Factor III: Women are not ambitious enough to be successful in the business world.

SCORING: Items are objectively scored and equally weighted. Item scores are totaled to yield a score for each of the three factors and an overall score. Norms are provided (see Peters, Terborg and Taynor, 1974).

DEVELOPMENT: A pool of fifty-five items was compiled to represent two general areas: (1) "general descriptive traits/behaviors of managers" and (2) "female-specific stereotypes thought to represent barriers to the successful integration of women into managerial positions" (Peters, Terborg and Taynor, 1974, p. 5). Some of the fifty-five items were selected from existing scales, and others were written by the authors. Each of the items was written in two ways: for one form of the item, agreement would reflect a positive attitude; and for the other form of the item, agreement would reflect a negative attitude. Two forms of the test were then constructed. Form A contained the fifty-five items, with half phrased in a positive direction and half phrased in a negative direction. Form B contained each of the fifty-five items phrased in the opposite direction from the phrasing on Form A. A total of 541 college students completed the scale, with about half the students responding to each form. Their responses were analyzed and items were omitted from the final scale "if they (1) consistently failed to differentiate among persons holding significantly different attitudes; (2) consistently elicited different responses depending on the direction of the item stem; (3) did not have a minimum factor loading of .40 on the factors selected from the principle components analysis; or (4) did not distinctly load on any given factor in the principle components analysis" (Peters, Terborg, and Taynor, 1974, p. 11). The twenty-one items not omitted comprise the scale.

RELIABILITY: The corrected split-half reliability for the 541 college students completing the scale was .91 (Peters, Terborg, and Taynor, 1974). The split-half, corrected reliability for a sample of 280 full-time employees was .92 (Terborg and others, 1977).

VALIDITY: Using the results from 541 college students, Peters, Terborg and Taynor (1974) computed separate means for males and females on each of the factor scores and on the total score. In every comparison, means for females were significantly more positive than means for males (p < .01). Matteson (1976) and Terborg and others (1977) also found significant differences between the responses of men and women. Both studies reported that significantly more positive attitudes were expressed by women.

Peters, Terborg, and Taynor (1974) correlated scores on the WAMS with responses to a question asking about attitudes toward the women's rights movement. The correlation for males was .54 (p < .001) and the correlation for females was .42 (p < .001).

Terborg and others (1977) examined the relationship between WAMS and work history of the respondents' mother, views toward the women's rights movement, and degree of career commitment. Male respondents whose mothers worked expressed more favorable attitudes on the WAMS (nonsignificant), and female respondents whose mothers did not work expressed more favorable attitudes (n.s.). The results for the female respondents were not consistent with the authors' predictions. As predicted, views toward the women's rights movement were positively and significantly correlated with scores on WAMS for both male (r = .40, p < .01) and female respondents (r = .19, p < .05). The correlation between the degree of career commitment and WAMS scores (r = −.26, p <.01) was consistent with the prediction that women who had greater career commitment would have more positive attitudes on the WAMS.

Thirty-six college men were given both the WAMS and an in-basket exercise that simulated administrative decision making. The in-basket technique was designed to assess sex discrimination both at the time an employee is being hired and after the employee is on the job. College men who rated the woman as more desirable to hire on the in-basket exercise indicated more favorable attitudes on the WAMS (r = .58; p < .01). None of the other measures from the in-basket technique correlated significantly with WAMS when a woman was the stimulus person for the in-basket exercise (Terborg and Ilgen, 1975).

NOTES AND COMMENTS: (1) Rosen and Jerdee (1975) asserted that the WAMS "appears to be very transparent in terms of social desirability" (p. 152). In a published reply, Ilgen and Terborg (1975) indicated that scores on the WAMS had been correlated with scores on the Marlowe-Crowne Social Desirability Scale. The correlation for the two measures was −.13 (n = 60).

(2) Terborg and others (1977) report that "additional research with the scale, since its initial development suggested that the computation of composite factor scores for each of the three components added little beyond consideration of the summated score to all twenty-one items" (p. 92).

SOURCE: See Peters, Terborg, and Taynor, 1974; or Terborg and others, 1977.

BIBLIOGRAPHY:

Best, L. R. "An Assessment of the Attitudes of a Corporation's Male Managers Toward Women in Business Management." Unpublished doctoral dissertation, University of Toledo, 1975. (*Dissertation Abstracts International,* 1976, *36*[7-B], 3661-3662.)
Garland, H., and Price, K. H. "Attitudes Toward Women in Management and Attributions for Their Success and Failure in a Managerial Position." *Journal of Applied Psychology,* 1977, *62,* 29-33.
Ilgen, D. R., and Terborg, J. R. "Sex Discrimination and Sex Role Stereotypes: Are They Synonymous? No!" *Organizational Behavior and Human Performance,* 1975, *14,* 154-157.
Matteson, M. T. "Attitudes Toward Women as Managers: Sex or Role Difference?" *Psychological Reports,* 1976, *39,* 166.
Peters, L. H., Terborg, J. R., and Taynor, J. "Women as Managers Scale (WAMS): A Measure of Attitudes Toward Women in Management Positions." *Journal Supplement Abstract Service Catalog of Selected Documents in Psychology,* 1974, *4,* 27.
Rosen, B., and Jerdee, T. H. "The Psychological Basis for Sex Role Stereotypes: A Note on Terborg and Ilgen's Conclusions." *Organizational Behavior and Human Performance,* 1975, *14,* 151-153.
Terborg, J. R., and Ilgen, D. R. "A Theoretical Approach to Sex Discrimination in Traditionally Masculine Occupations." *Organizational Behavior and Human Performance,* 1975, *13,* 352-376.
Terborg, J. R., Peters, L. H., Ilgen, D. R., and Smith, F. "Organizational and Personal Correlates of Attitudes Toward Women as Managers." *Academy of Management Journal,* 1977, *20,* 89-100.

---

145. WORLD OF WORK SCALE

AUTHORS: Sylvia L. Lee, Elizabeth M. Ray, Louise Vetter, Lila Murphy, and Barbara J. Sethney

DATE: 1971

VARIABLES: Attitudes toward women and work

TYPE OF INSTRUMENT: Summated rating scale

DESCRIPTION: The scale includes seventy-five items relating to such issues as attitudes toward work after marriage; the role of women in regard to family, men, and work; attitudes toward working with others and being useful in society; the desirability of running one's own life and being independent; and attitudes toward salary, promotions, and employment benefits. Each statement is accompanied by five response alternatives: strongly disagree, disagree, indifferent or don't care, agree, and strongly agree.

PREVIOUSLY ADMINISTERED TO: Females, ages 15-55

APPROPRIATE FOR: Females, ages 15 and older

ADMINISTRATION: This self-administered scale can be completed in about thirty to forty minutes.

SAMPLE ITEMS:

Economic Mobility: I would work after marriage to have money to buy basic things.

Role Security: Woman's place is in the home.

Intrinsic Reward: Working with others would be an important part of a job for me.

Challenge: A chance to work with ideas is the ideal kind of job.

Extrinsic Reward: A job should have good opportunities for promotion.

SCORING: Items are objectively scored and equally weighted. Scores are obtained for each of five factors: Economic Mobility, Role Security, Intrinsic Reward, Challenge, and Extrinsic Reward.

DEVELOPMENT: Based on a review of the literature, nine factors relating to attitudes toward work were hypothesized: "financial reward, suitability for women, advancement and recognition, social service, economic necessity, creativity and challenge, fulfillment, working conditions, and interpersonal relationships" (Lee and others, 1971, p. 5). Fifteen items were identified to represent each of the factors; some items were selected from existing scales and some were written especially for this scale. The responses to the 135 items in the item pool were factor analyzed and seven factors were identified: economic mobility, extrinsic reward, intrinsic reward, acceptance of role, role conflict, self-expression, and creativity. Seventy-five items representing the seven factors were completed by 365 high school girls, and their responses were factor analyzed. Five factors were identified: Factor I, Economic Mobility, concerned a positive attitude toward work after marriage (ten items); Factor II, Role Security, reflected a traditional attitude toward women's role and the relationships between women and family, men, and work (fourteen items); Factor III, Intrinsic Reward, reflected a favorable orientation toward working with others and being useful in society (nine items); Factor IV, Challenge, related to the desirability of making decisions, controlling one's life, and having opportunities (fifteen items); Factor V, Extrinsic Reward, concerned salary, promotion, and benefits (five items). The remaining twenty-two items did not load sufficiently high on any factor to be assigned to that factor. Nevertheless, all seventy-five items comprise the scale.

RELIABILITY: Kuder-Richardson reliabilities are reported for each of the five subscales: Economic Mobility = .817; Role Security = .744; Intrinsic Reward = .804; Challenge = .678; Extrinsic Reward = .711 (Tinsley, 1973).

VALIDITY: No data are provided.

NOTES AND COMMENTS: Using the responses from 365 high school girls, Lee and others (1971) compared scores on the World of Work Scale with respondents' community size, socioeconomic level, and type of high school (academic, comprehensive, or vocational).

SOURCE: See Lee and others, 1971; or Tinsley, 1973.

BIBLIOGRAPHY:

Goldstein, R. L. "Effects of Reinforcement and Female Career Role Models on the Vocational Attitudes of High School Girls." Unpublished doctoral dissertation, Boston University, 1975. (*Dissertation Abstracts International,* 1975, *36*[3-A], 1304.)
Lee, S. L., Ray, E. M., Vetter, L., Murphy, L., and Sethney, B. J. "High School Senior Girls and the World of Work: Occupational Knowledge, Attitudes, and Plans." Columbus: Center for Vocational and Technical Education, Ohio State University, 1971. (ERIC Document Reproduction Service No. ED 047 155.)
Pope, S. K. "Effects of Female Career Role Models on Occupational Aspirations, Attitude, and Personalities of High School Seniors." Unpublished doctoral dissertation, University of Missouri, 1971. (*Dissertation Abstracts International,* 1972, *32*[9-A], 4964-4965.)
Tinsley, J. R. "The Differential Effects of an Audio Program Learning Tape and Open Group Discussion on Women's Attitudes Toward Women and Work." Unpublished doctoral dissertation, University of Missouri at Kansas City, 1973. (*Dissertation Abstracts International,* 1974, *34*[7-A], 3894.)

---

146. YERBY SCALE OF ATTITUDES TOWARD FEMALE SUPERVISORY POTENTIAL

AUTHOR: Janet Yerby

DATE: 1972

VARIABLE: Attitudes toward the supervisory potential of women

TYPE OF INSTRUMENT: Summated rating scale

DESCRIPTION: The scale consists of sixteen statements concerning women in leadership positions and personality characteristics that are related to leadership ability. Responses to the statements are indicated on a seven-point scale with the endpoints labeled "agree" and "disagree."

PREVIOUSLY ADMINISTERED TO: College students

APPROPRIATE FOR: Ages 16 and older

ADMINISTRATION: This self-administered scale can be completed in about ten minutes.

SAMPLE ITEMS: Women have more difficulties than men in being objective about a situation.

                    Men are better problem solvers than women.

SCORING: Items are objectively scored and equally weighted.

DEVELOPMENT: An item pool was constructed from five items taken from Bass's (1971) scale measuring male managers' attitudes toward working women and twenty-four items written by the author after a survey of the relevant literature. The item pool was administered to 227 college students and their responses were factor analyzed. Two factors were extracted. Factor I concerned whether women are potentially capable of being effective in leadership positions compared with men; twelve items loaded on this factor. Factor II concerned whether females are subordinate to males; four items loaded on this factor. The sixteen items loading on Factors I and II comprise the scale. Four of the sixteen items are from Bass's scale and the remaining twelve were written by Yerby.

RELIABILITY: No data are provided.

VALIDITY: No data are provided.

NOTES AND COMMENTS: More information is needed about the psychometric properties of this scale before it is used in further research studies.

SOURCE: See Yerby, 1972.

BIBLIOGRAPHY:

*Bass, B. M., Krusell, J., and Alexander, R. A. "Male Managers' Attitudes Toward Working Women." *American Behavioral Scientist,* 1971, *15,* 228-229.

Yerby, J. "Female Leadership in Small Problem-Solving Groups: An Experimental Study." Unpublished doctoral dissertation, Bowling Green State University, 1972. (*Dissertation Abstracts International,* 1973, *33*[11-A], 6491.)

Yerby, J. "Attitude, Task, and Sex Composition as Variables Affecting Female Leadership in Small Problem-Solving Groups." *Speech Monographs,* 1975, *42,* 160-168.

10

❖ ❖ ❖ ❖ ❖ ❖ ❖ ❖ ❖ ❖

Multiple Roles

❖ ❖ ❖ ❖ ❖ ❖ ❖ ❖ ❖ ❖ ❖ ❖ ❖ ❖ ❖ ❖ ❖ ❖ ❖

The majority of the twenty instruments in this chapter concern two roles for women: the marital/parental role and the employee role. Some contrast the two roles, assessing whether the marital/parental role or the employee role is the preferred role for women. Other instruments pertain to both; that is, some items pertain to the marital/parental role and others pertain to the employee role. It is this focus on both roles that differentiates these instruments from those in the two previous chapters. The titles of the instruments and the names of the variables in this chapter may suggest that the measures belong in other chapters; for example, Sex Role Ideology (#163) would be classified with the instruments measuring attitudes toward a variety of issues if titles were the basis for classification. However, classification was based on an examination of item content.

These instruments are all fairly new; none appeared in the literature prior to 1963, and fifteen out of twenty first appeared in the literature in the 1970s. None are appropriate for children; all require that respondents be at least adolescents. Unlike the instruments in other chapters, many of these are appropriate only for female respondents. It is possible to modify them for use with males by changing the instructions. For example, instead of asking respondents to answer for themselves, respondents can be asked to answer as they would like a particular woman to answer, for example, their mother, wife, or girlfriend; or respondents can be asked to answer as they believe a particular woman or women in general would answer. If modifications are made in the scales, one cannot presume anything about their reliability and validity.

Three instruments in this chapter merit special comment. The Student Attitude Scale (#165) differs from other instruments in that it contrasts intellectual goals or roles for women with traditional roles for women. The Richardson-Alpert Role Perception Scale (#159) and the Richardson-Alpert Role Involvement Scale (#158) differ from the others in that they use a unique procedure: Both scales provide verbal projective cues and ask respondents to write stories based on the cues. However, the stories are not scored. Instead each story is followed by a series of true-false items, and the responses to these objective items provide the basis for the scoring. This combination of a projective and an objective technique seems very promising. The projective portion increases the likelihood of eliciting deeper, less conscious feelings which are reflected in the responses to the objective portion, and the objective portion is a more standardized measure and a convenient and reliable way to score responses from large groups of respondents.

Probably the most serious problem with many of the instruments in this chapter is that they presume unidimensionality when, in fact, the variables being assessed are probably multidimensional. The assumption of multidimensionality seems more reasonable given that the instruments all pertain to more than a single role. Problems pertaining to a social desirability response set and lack of content validity also apply to these measures. However, since these problems have been explicated in the introductions to other chapters, they will not be explained in detail here.

---

147. ALMQUIST-ANGRIST INDEX OF CAREER SALIENCE

AUTHORS: Elizabeth M. Almquist and Shirley S. Angrist

DATE: 1970

VARIABLE: Women's work commitment

TYPE OF INSTRUMENT: Multiple choice

DESCRIPTION: The index consists of three parts. On the first part, the woman is asked to indicate whether she would want to work under each of two conditions: "(1) One child of school age, husband's salary adequate," and "(2) Two or more children of school age, husband's salary adequate." On the second part, the woman is given the following hypothetical situation: "Assume that you are trained for the occupation of your choice, that you will marry and have children, and that your husband will earn enough so that you will never have to work unless you want to. Under these conditions which of the following would you prefer?" The response options are "(1) To participate in clubs or volunteer work; (2) To spend time on hobbies, sports, or other activities; (3) To work part time in your chosen occupation; (4) To work full time in your chosen occupation; (5) To concentrate on home and family; (6) Other, explain briefly." On the third part, the woman is asked to respond to the following: "Fifteen years from now would you like to be . . ." The response options are "(1) A housewife with no children; (2) A housewife with one or more children; (3) An unmarried career woman; (4) A married career woman without children; (5) A married career woman with children" (Almquist and Angrist, 1970, p. 244).

PREVIOUSLY ADMINISTERED TO: Female college students

APPROPRIATE FOR: Unmarried females, ages 16 to 25

ADMINISTRATION: The scale can be self-administered and can be completed in five minutes.

SCORING: The first part is scored as "work oriented" if the respondent indicates that she definitely would or probably would work under both conditions described. The second part is scored as "work oriented" if the respondent selects one of the two options that involve continued employment. The third part is scored as "work oriented" if the respondent selects one of the three options that involve employment. Respondents are classified as work oriented if they score "work oriented" on two of the three parts. Otherwise, they are classified as noncareer oriented.

DEVELOPMENT: No information is provided.

RELIABILITY: No data are provided.

VALIDITY: Almquist and Angrist (1971) stated ten hypotheses. They predicted that work-oriented women: (1) are less often sorority members; (2) date less frequently in both high school and college; (3) are less likely to be married, engaged, or going steady during their senior year in college; (4) are more likely to prefer occupations similar to those preferred by their male peers; (5) are more likely to prefer male-dominated occupations; (6) will have held more jobs and had more varied work experiences; (7) are likely to have working mothers and mothers with higher educational attainment; (8) will have been influenced more by teachers and persons in given occupations and less influenced by family and peer pressure. They predicted that noncareer-oriented women: (9) have fathers with higher occupational status and higher educational attainment and (10) have mothers who are more actively involved in clubs, volunteer work, and leisure activities. These hypotheses were tested using the responses from 110 college women in their senior year. The following hypotheses were supported by the data: 1, 3, 4, 5, 6, 7 (for employment differences, but not for educational attainment differences), 8 and 10. Hypotheses 2 and 9 were not supported.

NOTES AND COMMENTS: (1) Altman (1975) and Altman and Grossman (1977) used a modification of the index.

(2) The items on this instrument are a subset of the items on the Life-Style Index (#153).

SOURCE: See Almquist and Angrist, 1970 or 1971.

BIBLIOGRAPHY:

Almquist, E. M., and Angrist, S. S. "Career Salience and Atypicality of Occupational Choice Among College Women." *Journal of Marriage and the Family,* 1970, *32,* 242-249.

Almquist, E. M., and Angrist, S. S. "Role Model Influences on College Women's Career Aspirations." *Merrill-Palmer Quarterly,* 1971, *17,* 263-279.

Altman, S. L. "Women's Career Plans and Maternal Employment." Unpublished doctoral dissertation, Boston University Graduate School, 1975. (*Dissertation Abstracts International,* 1975, *35* [7-B], 3569.)

Altman, S. L., and Grossman, F. K. "Women's Career Plans and Maternal Employment." *Psychology of Women Quarterly,* 1977, *1,* 365-376.

---

148. CAREER AND MARRIAGE PLANS QUESTIONNAIRE (CMPQ)

AUTHOR: Dana Walter

DATE: 1974

VARIABLES: Career and marriage plans

TYPE OF INSTRUMENT: Summated rating scale

DESCRIPTION: The scale includes eleven statements: ten concern future career and marriage plans; one concerns the opinions of male friends regarding women's liberation. The response options for nine statements are: almost positively not, not likely, equal probability, likely, and almost positive. The remaining two statements are presented in a multiple choice format, but the response options differ.

PREVIOUSLY ADMINISTERED TO: Female college students

APPROPRIATE FOR: Female college students

ADMINISTRATION: The scale can be self-administered and can be completed in less than ten minutes.

SAMPLE ITEMS: After receiving my BA or BS, I plan on going to school but not for a masters or doctorate.

If I were to marry, I would plan on working full time at a job (not counting housekeeping or child rearing) for the major part of my life.

SCORING: Items are objectively scored and equally weighted. Two scores are obtained for each woman: importance of a career in a woman's life and traditional plans and attitudes of a woman.

DEVELOPMENT: A sixteen-item scale, including two open-ended items, was administered to seventy-four junior and senior college women. Their responses were factor analyzed and two factors emerged. Items with loadings of at least +.35 on only one factor contribute to that factor score. Factor I concerns "the importance of a career in a woman's life. Such items as going to graduate school, working full time for the major part of my life, working while the children are small, and the importance of a wife's career in relation to her husband's loaded on this factor" (Walter, 1974, p. 30). Factor II concerns "the more conventional, traditional plans and attitudes of a woman. Items loading on this factor included working right after graduation, getting married, having children, and the perceived attitude of male friends about women's liberation" (Walter, 1974, p. 30).

RELIABILITY: No data are provided.

VALIDITY: For the seventy-four college women on which the scale was developed, scores were obtained for a measure of fear of success, the Attitudes Toward Women Scale (AWS) (#169), grade point average, a self-attractiveness rating, and a male attractiveness rating (that is, the woman's attractiveness was rated by two males). Responses to the AWS were factor analyzed: Factor I concerned vocational and educational equality; Factor II concerned sexual equality in regard to dating and courtship behavior and ladylike behavior. All of the obtained measures were intercorrelated. Factor I of CMPQ correlated significantly with Factor I of AWS ($r = .29$, $p < .05$), with Factor II of AWS ($r = .44$, $p < .01$), and with Factor II of CMPQ ($r = -.28$, $p < .05$). Factor II of CMPQ correlated significantly with Factor II of AWS ($r = -.40$, $p < .01$) and with Factor I of CMPQ (see above). No other correlations involving the CMPQ scores were significant (Walter, 1974).

NOTES AND COMMENTS: The response options are awkwardly phrased.

SOURCE: See Walter, 1974.

BIBLIOGRAPHY:

Walter, D. "Psychological Correlates of Sex Role Behavior." Unpublished master's thesis, California State University at Chico, 1974.
Williams, D., and King, M. "Sex Role Attitudes and Fear of Success as Correlates of Sex Role Behavior." *Journal of College Student Personnel*, 1976, *17*, 480-484.

---

149. FEMININE INTEREST QUESTIONNAIRE

AUTHOR: Warren B. Miller

DATE: 1977

VARIABLE: Modern versus traditional female role orientation

TYPE OF INSTRUMENT: Summated rating scale

DESCRIPTION: The scale consists of thirty-one statements. Most of the statements pertain to a woman in regard to the marital and maternal roles or a woman in regard to a career role. Each statement is accompanied by four response options: agree completely, agree somewhat, disagree somewhat, and disagree completely.

PREVIOUSLY ADMINISTERED TO: Females, ages 18-27

APPROPRIATE FOR: Females, ages 16 and older

ADMINISTRATION: This self-administered scale can be completed in about twenty minutes.

SAMPLE ITEMS: Having a challenging job or career is as important to me as being a wife and mother.
            The best thing a woman can do for her husband is to have happy children and keep a good home.

SCORING: Items are objectively scored. A formula is provided for obtaining scores on the various scales. The formula takes account of the individual's mean and standard deviation based on her responses to all the items on the scale. The scale yields seven scores: Modern-Traditional Role Orientation (twenty-five items), Child Limitation (five items), Career Deterrents (six items), Husband Orientation (six items), Homemaker Dissatisfaction (six items), Child and Home Orientation (six items), and Spouse Role Equality (six items). The scales are not independent of each other in that a particular item is likely to appear on more than one subscale.

DEVELOPMENT: The items on the scale were based on the author's clinical experience with married couples, interviews with women, and a review of the relevant literature. Pretesting of the instrument was done with young adult women, and revisions were made to ensure that the instructions and item content could be understood by women with at least some high school education. The scale was administered to over 150 working mothers, nonworking mothers, and career women. Items that discriminated between nonworking mothers and work-oriented mothers comprise the Modern-Traditional Role Orientation scale. The remaining six scales were based on the results of factor analyses of the women's responses.

RELIABILITY: Using the responses from 967 women, Kuder-Richardson reliabilities were computed for the seven scales. The reliability of the Modern-Traditional Role Orientation scale was .90. The reliabilities of the remaining six scales ranged from .53 to .84. Test-retest reliabilities were computed on the basis of responses from forty-six women who were tested on two occasions with a four-week interval between testings. The test-retest reliability of the Modern-Traditional Role Orientation scale was .93. The test-retest reliabilities of the remaining six scales ranged from .72 to .88.

VALIDITY: No data are provided.

NOTES AND COMMENTS: Means and standard deviations on each of the seven scales are reported for three groups of women: 325 never-married women, 322 women who became married during the previous four to six months, and 320 women who bore their first child during the previous four to six months.

SOURCE: Warren B. Miller
American Institute for Research
P.O. Box 1113
1791 Arastradero Road
Palo Alto, California 94302

BIBLIOGRAPHY:

Miller, W. B. "Manual for Description of Instruments Used in a Research Project on the Psychological Aspects of Fertility Behavior in Women." Unpublished manuscript, American Institute for Research, 1977.
Miller, W. B., and Smith, P. J. "Elimination of the Menses: Psychosexual Aspects." *Journal of Psychiatric Research*, 1975, *12*, 153-166.

---

150. FEMININE ROLE BEHAVIOR SCALE

AUTHOR: Kenneth Kammeyer

DATE: 1964 (used 1961)

VARIABLE: Attitudes toward roles of women

TYPE OF INSTRUMENT: Guttman scale

DESCRIPTION: The scale consists of five statements regarding the roles of women as "college girls," wives, and mothers. Each statement reflects a traditional view of the role of women. Four response options accompany each item: agree, agree somewhat, disagree somewhat, and disagree.

PREVIOUSLY ADMINISTERED TO: College students; female adults in Israel

APPROPRIATE FOR: Ages 14 and older

ADMINISTRATION: The scale can be self-administered and can be completed in about two minutes.

SAMPLE ITEMS: In marriage, the major responsibility of the wife is to keep her husband and children happy.
English is a better major for a college girl than economics.

SCORING: The response options "agree" and "agree somewhat" are both considered favorable responses; the response options "disagree" and "disagree somewhat" are both considered unfavorable responses. The responses to the items are classified into six scale types, each of which reflects the specific items that were favorably responded to. For example, scale type 5 agrees with all items; scale type 4 agrees with all but the "most difficult items," that is, least frequently endorsed; and scale type 0 disagrees with all items. Scale types 3, 4, and 5 are considered "traditional," and scale types 0, 1, and 2 are considered "modern."

DEVELOPMENT: A group of 209 college women were asked to respond to eight items concerning feminine role behavior. Five of the items formed a Guttman scale with the following characteristics: a coefficient of reproducibility of .93; two error patterns including more than 5 percent of the sample (5.7 percent and 5.3 percent); item error ranging from 2.8 percent to 10 percent; largest percent error for a response category of 12.8 percent; and minimum marginal reproducibility of .75.

RELIABILITY: Orcutt (1975) administered the Feminine Role Behavior Scale in 1973, twelve years after Kammeyer had given it. Based on the responses given by 1,096 college students, Orcutt found the coefficient of reproducibility to be .86 and the minimum marginal reproducibility to be .73.

VALIDITY: The Feminine Role Behavior Scale and the Female Personality Trait Scale (#66) were both administered to 209 college women. It was hypothesized that the two scales would yield highly related results. It was found that 58 percent of the women who had "modern" attitudes on one scale also had "modern" attitudes on the other scale. Yule's Q for the two scales was .59 (Kammeyer, 1964).

A study was done of 232 unmarried college women. As predicted, it was found that first-born and only-child women were more traditional on the Feminine Role Behavior Scale (Kammeyer, 1966). The hypothesis that a woman who had an older brother would be more traditional on the Feminine Role Behavior Scale was not supported (Kammeyer, 1967).

From the responses given by 1,096 college students, it was found that college women are more likely than college men to be classified as "modern" on the basis of the Feminine Role Behavior Scale (Orcutt, 1975).

NOTES AND COMMENTS: (1) Orcutt (1975) compared the responses he obtained in 1973 from 1,096 college students with the responses Kammeyer obtained in 1961 from 209 college women. For every item, there was a significant ($p < .001$) decrease in the number of students in 1973 who agreed with the statements. Thus, the more recent respondents have significantly more modern attitudes toward the roles of women.

(2) Scores on the Feminine Role Behavior Scale have been related to numerous other variables, including sex (Orcutt, 1975); year in school (Orcutt, 1975); socioeconomic status (Trader, 1972); position in the family (Kammeyer, 1966, 1967; Trader, 1972; Weller, Hazi, and Natan, 1975); race (Trader, 1972); future life plans (Trader, 1972); parental variables (Kammeyer, 1964; Trader, 1972); personal adjustment (Trader, 1972); student activism (Orcutt, 1975; Orcutt and Inmon, 1974); social life (Kammeyer, 1964); and need for failure (Maxwell and Gonzalez, 1972).

(3) The scale is also described in *Family Measurement Techniques* (Straus, 1969, pp. 159-160; Straus and Brown, 1978, pp. 109-110).

SOURCE: See Kammeyer, 1964, 1966, 1967; or Orcutt, 1975.

BIBLIOGRAPHY:

Kammeyer, K. "The Feminine Role: An Analysis of Attitude Consistency." *Journal of Marriage and the Family*, 1964, *26*, 295-305.

Kammeyer, K. "Birth Order and the Feminine Sex Role Among College Women." *American Sociological Review,* 1966, *31,* 508-515.

Kammeyer, K. "Sibling Position and the Feminine Role." *Journal of Marriage and the Family,* 1967, *29,* 494-499.

Maxwell, P. G., and Gonzalez, A. E. J. "Traditional and Nontraditional Role Choice and Need for Failure Among College Women." *Psychological Reports,* 1972, *31,* 545-546.

Orcutt, J. D. "The Impact of Student Activism on Attitudes Toward the Female Sex Role: Longitudinal and Cross-Sectional Perspectives." *Social Forces,* 1975, *54,* 382-392.

Orcutt, J. D., and Inmon, R. R. "The Impact of Student Activism on Female Sex Role Attitudes: Longitudinal and Cross-Sectional Perspectives." Paper presented at the American Sociological Association, Montreal, Canada, 1974. (ERIC Document Reproduction Service No. ED 094 304.)

*Straus, M. A. *Family Measurement Techniques: Abstracts of Published Instruments, 1935-1965.* Minneapolis: University of Minnesota Press, 1969.

*Straus, M. A., and Brown, B. W. *Family Measurement Techniques: Abstracts of Published Instruments, 1935-1974.* Minneapolis: University of Minnesota Press, 1978.

Trader, D. D. "A Study of College Women's Attitudes Toward the Feminine Role." Unpublished doctoral dissertation, University of North Carolina at Greensboro, 1972. (*Dissertation Abstracts International,* 1972, *33*[4-B], 1650.)

Weller, L., Hazi, O., and Natan, O. "Birth Order and the Feminine Sex Role of Married Women." *Journal of Individual Psychology,* 1975, *31,* 65-70.

---

151. KALEY ATTITUDES TOWARD THE MARRIED PROFESSIONAL WOMAN

AUTHOR: Maureen M. Kaley

DATE: 1971 (used 1967)

VARIABLE: Attitudes regarding the married professional woman's ability to handle home responsibilities

TYPE OF INSTRUMENT: Alternate choice

DESCRIPTION: The instrument consists of six statements, five of which concern the ability of the married professional woman to adequately handle home responsibilities. The sixth question concerns whether the woman works for personal or economic reasons. For each item, the respondent is asked to indicate agree or disagree.

PREVIOUSLY ADMINISTERED TO: Adults in professional occupations

APPROPRIATE FOR: Ages 16 and older

ADMINISTRATION: The scale can be self-administered and can be completed in less than three minutes.

SAMPLE ITEMS: In general, the married professional woman is able to adequately meet her responsibilities to both her family and career.
        In general, the full-time homemaker fulfills her obligations to the family better than the married professional woman who is employed full time.

SCORING: No scores have been obtained. Responses to each item were tallied.

DEVELOPMENT: No information is provided.

RELIABILITY: No data are provided.

VALIDITY: In a study of thirty-five female and twenty-four male married professionals, Kaley (1971) found that professional men and professional women differed significantly in their responses to two of the six questions; women expressed the more positive attitudes. Etaugh (1973) studied the responses from 37 female and 173 male college faculty members. She found a significant correlation between sex and responses on the same two statements for which Kaley reported significant differences; again women expressed the more positive attitudes. Etaugh also found a significant correlation between sex and responses on a third statement, where women again expressed more positive attitudes.

SOURCE: See Kaley, 1971; or Etaugh, 1973.

BIBLIOGRAPHY:

Etaugh, C. F. "Attitudes of Professionals Toward the Married Professional Woman." *Psychological Reports,* 1973, *32,* 775-780.
Kaley, M. M. "Attitudes Toward the Dual Role of the Married Professional Woman." *American Psychologist,* 1971, *26,* 301-306.

---

152. KING-MCINTYRE-AXELSON THREAT FROM WORKING WIVES SCALE

AUTHORS: Karl King, Jennie McIntyre, and Leland J. Axelson

DATE: 1968 (used 1963)

VARIABLE: Perception of whether a working wife is a threat to a marital relationship

TYPE OF INSTRUMENT: Guttman scale

DESCRIPTION: The scale consists of five statements, each of which suggests that a working wife poses a threat to the marital relationship. The respondents indicate whether they agree or disagree with each statement.

PREVIOUSLY ADMINISTERED TO: Black and white ninth graders; husbands

APPROPRIATE FOR: Ages 14 and older

ADMINISTRATION: The scale can be self-administered and can be completed in less than two minutes.

SAMPLE ITEMS: If a working wife earns more than her husband, the husband should feel like a failure.
                    A working wife is likely to become too independent.

SCORING: Each set of responses is assigned a value from 1 to 6. A score of 1 indicates agreement with all the items; that is, a wife's working is perceived as a major threat to the marital relationship. A score of 6 indicates disagreement with all the items; that is, a wife's working is perceived as little threat to the marital relationship. Since this is a Guttman scale, intermediate scores (2, 3, 4, and 5) are assigned so as to minimize error.

DEVELOPMENT: The items on the scale were adapted from Axelson (1963).

RELIABILITY: The scale was administered to 1,055 ninth graders and the responses were subjected to Guttman analysis five times: once for the entire sample and four times for various subsamples. The coefficients of reproducibility ranged from .89 to .90 for the five samples (King, McIntyre, and Axelson, 1968).

VALIDITY: King, McIntyre, and Axelson (1968) tested 1,055 ninth graders. As predicted, they found that children of employed mothers scored higher (less perceived threat) than children of nonworking mothers (p < .0001). Furthermore, as predicted, children of college-educated parents scored higher than children of non-college-educated parents (p value not given). A third prediction supported by the data was that females perceive a wife's employment as less of a threat to the marital relationship than do males. There was, however, an interaction between sex and mother's employment status that indicated that the effect of mother's employment was greater for males than for females. Thus the sex differences did not hold up for children of employed mothers.

NOTES AND COMMENTS: (1) King, Abernathy, and Chapman (1976) altered the response format for the items to allow for five response options ranging from strongly agree to strongly disagree. Scoring procedures were changed so that each item was assigned a value from 1 to 5, with 1 being assigned to the response "strongly agree," and 5 assigned to the response "strongly disagree." Total scores were found for each respondent by taking the average of her item scores.
    (2) Axelson's (1963, 1970) measure is similar but not identical to the King-McIntyre-Axelson Threat from Working Wives Scale.
    (3) The scale is also described in *Family Measurement Techniques* (Straus and Brown, 1978, pp. 101-102).

SOURCE: See King, McIntyre, and Axelson, 1968.

BIBLIOGRAPHY:

Axelson, L. J. "The Marital Adjustment and Marital Role Definitions of Husbands of Working and Nonworking Wives." *Marriage and Family Living,* 1963, *25,* 189-195.

Axelson, L. J. "The Working Wife: Differences in Perception Among Negro and White Males." *Journal of Marriage and the Family,* 1970, *32,* 457-464.

King, K., Abernathy, T. J., Jr., and Chapman, A. H. "Black Adolescents' Views of Maternal Employment as a Threat to the Marital Relationship: 1963-1973." *Journal of Marriage and the Family,* 1976, *38,* 733-737.

King, K., McIntyre, J., and Axelson, L. J. "Adolescents' Views of Maternal Employment as a Threat to the Marital Relationship." *Journal of Marriage and the Family,* 1968, *30,* 633-637.

*Straus, M. A., and Brown, B. W. *Family Measurement Techniques: Abstracts of Published Instruments, 1935-1974.* Minneapolis: University of Minnesota Press, 1978.

---

153. LIFE STYLE INDEX

AUTHOR: Shirley S. Angrist

DATE: 1970 (used 1964)

VARIABLE: Level of career aspiration

TYPE OF INSTRUMENT: Multiple choice

DESCRIPTION: The index consists of eleven questions concerning future educational and occupational plans. Each question is accompanied by five or six response alternatives, with the wording of the response alternatives varying according to the particular question asked.

PREVIOUSLY ADMINISTERED TO: Female college students

APPROPRIATE FOR: Female college students

ADMINISTRATION: The index can be self-administered and can be completed in less than five minutes.

SAMPLE ITEMS: As far as you can tell now, do you plan to continue your education after receiving a bachelor's degree?
• Yes, graduate school
• Yes, professional school
• Yes, other training
• No, I do not plan to continue

Assume that you are trained for the occupation of your choice, that you will marry and have children, and that your husband will earn enough so that

you will never have to work unless you want to. Under these conditions, which of the following would you prefer?
* To participate in clubs or volunteer work
* To spend time on hobbies, sports, or other activities
* To work part time in your chosen occupation
* To work full time in your chosen occupation
* To concentrate on home and family
* Other (explain briefly)

SCORING: The response options are dichotomized into "career orientation" responses and "noncareer interests." Responses reflecting a career orientation are assigned 1 point; responses reflecting noncareer interests are assigned 0 points. A total score is obtained, which can range from 0 (strongly noncareer oriented) to 11 (strongly career oriented).

DEVELOPMENT: A pool of twenty-seven items was constructed, including items regarding educational, occupational, and familial aspirations. The item pool was administered to eighty-seven college women and responses were dichotomized. A 2 x 2 chi-square analysis was performed for each item to compare the relationship between a high or low total score with a career-oriented or noncareer-oriented response on the item. Items for which the chi-square value was significant at the .05 level and for which Yule's Q was at least .42 were retained. Twelve items satisfied these two criteria. An internal consistency analysis indicated that eleven of the twelve items were significantly associated with the total score. These eleven items comprise the instrument.

RELIABILITY: The index was administered to the same eighty-seven college women during the fall semester of each of their four college years. Test-retest coefficients and stability coefficients were found using the procedures described by Heise (1969). Test-retest reliability based on the freshman, sophomore, and junior testings was .79. Test-retest reliability based on the sophomore, junior, and senior testings was .88.

Stability coefficients were .71 between freshman and sophomore years, .89 between sophomore and junior years, and .74 between junior and senior years. The lowest stability coefficient was .37, found between the freshman and senior years (Angrist, 1971-72).

VALIDITY: No data are provided.

NOTES AND COMMENTS: (1) Scores on the Life Style Index have been related to physical health, mental health, and college maladjustment (Angrist, 1970). The instrument has been used as the dependent measure in research regarding the impact of career awareness training (Blimline, 1976; Cooper, 1976).

(2) Cowan and Moore (1971) and Erickson and Nordin (1974) used only two of the eleven questions from the index.

(3) A subset of the items on this instrument comprise the Almquist-Angrist Index of Career Salience (#147).

SOURCE: See Angrist, 1971-72.

BIBLIOGRAPHY:

Angrist, S. S. "Personality Maladjustment and Career Aspirations of Career Women." *Sociological Symposium*, 1970, 5, 1-8.

Angrist, S. S. "Measuring Women's Career Commitment." *Sociological Focus,* 1971-72, *5* (2), 29-39.

Angrist, S. S. "Changes in Women's Work Aspirations During College (or Work Does Not Equal Career)." *International Journal of Sociology of the Family,* 1972a, *2,* 87-97.

Angrist, S. S. "Variations in Women's Adult Aspirations During College." *Journal of Marriage and the Family,* 1972b, *34,* 465-468.

Blimline, C. A. "The Effect of a Vocational Unit on the Exploration of Nontraditional Career Options." *Journal of Vocational Behavior,* 1976, *9,* 209-217.

Cooper, J. F. "Comparative Impact of the SCII and the Vocational Card Sort on Career Salience and Career Exploration of Women." *Journal of Counseling Psychology,* 1976, *23,* 348-352.

Cowan, G., and Moore, L. "Female Identity and Occupational Commitment." Detroit: Wayne State University, 1971. (ERIC Document Reproduction Service No. ED 056 335.)

Erickson, L. C., and Nordin, M. L. "Sex Role Ideologies and Career Salience of College Women. A Preliminary Report." Manhattan, Kan.: Kansas State University, 1974. (ERIC Document Reproduction Service No. ED 095 449.)

*Heise, D. R. "Separating Reliability and Stability in Test-Retest Correlation." *American Sociological Review,* 1969, *34,* 93-101.

Slaughter, P. S. "A Comparison of the Self-Concept, Femininity, and Career Aspirations of College Senior Women Preparing for Typical and Atypical Occupations." Unpublished doctoral dissertation, Mississippi State University, 1976. (*Dissertation Abstracts International,* 1976, *37*[3-A], 1412.)

---

154. LIFE STYLES FOR WOMEN SCALE

AUTHOR: Marie Susan A. Burns

DATE: 1974

VARIABLE: Attitudes toward life styles for women

TYPE OF INSTRUMENT: Summated rating scale

DESCRIPTION: The scale consists of twenty statements concerning the roles of motherhood, marriage, and career woman. Each item is accompanied by five response options: strongly agree, agree, undecided, disagree, and strongly disagree.

PREVIOUSLY ADMINISTERED TO: College students

APPROPRIATE FOR: Ages 16-25, unmarried

ADMINISTRATION: The scale can be self-administered. Women are directed to respond to the items in terms of themselves; men are directed to respond to the items in terms of how they wish their future wife (or living partner) would be. The scale can be completed in about five minutes.

SAMPLE ITEMS: I would have a great deal of difficulty being a mother and housewife 24 hours a day.
It is important to me to function as a professional in my career.

SCORING: Items are objectively scored and equally weighted. Total scores can range from 20 (extreme career orientation) to 100 (extreme homemaker orientation).

DEVELOPMENT: Some items were adapted from items developed by Bartsch (1973), and other items reflect ideas expressed by Bardwick (1971) and Oltman (1971).

RELIABILITY: The scale was completed by ninety-eight female and ninety-five male college students. Coefficient alpha was .829 for males and .889 for females (Burns, 1974).

VALIDITY: For ninety-five male college students, there was a significant negative correlation between scores on the Life Styles for Women Scale and attitudes toward the women's liberation movement ($r = -.40$, $p < .01$). A significant negative correlation between the two scales was also obtained for women ($n = 98$, $r = -.53$, $p < .01$). The difference between means for males ($\overline{X} = 58.50$) and females ($\overline{X} = 51.40$) was significant ($p < .01$), with females expressing attitudes that were more career oriented. Significant correlations were found between scores on the Life Styles for Women Scale and expectations for future spouse. The correlation for males was .30 ($p < .01$) and the correlation for females was $-.26$ ($p < .01$). In other words, "females who tended to picture a living partner as equal or submissive tended to be more career oriented. A male who pictured a living partner equal or dominant tended to have a more career-oriented attitude toward life styles for women" (Burns, 1974, p. 228). There were no significant relationships between scores on the Life Styles for Women Scale and age, term in school, marital or dating status, college major, or expected career (Burns, 1974).

Joesting and Whitehead (1976) administered the scale to college students but did not find significant differences in the scores obtained by males and females. Joesting and Whitehead also administered measures of curiosity and creativity and two measures of egalitarianism (Feminism II Scale [#181] and a scale constructed by Joesting). The only significant correlation involving the Life Styles for Women Scale was obtained with the measure of academic curiosity ($r = -.34$, $p < .01$).

NOTES AND COMMENTS: (1) Questions can be raised about the quality of several items on the scale. For example, it is quite possible that both career-oriented and homemaker-oriented women would agree or disagree with the item, "Being single is a selfish existence." In the absence of evidence, it is difficult to believe that the responses to the statement reflect anything about a woman's career or homemaker orientation. The statement, "I believe in stopping my career when I have a child" is subject to two interpretations. Some respondents may interpret it to mean stopping and never resuming their careers; other respondents may interpret it to mean temporarily interrupting their careers. Several statements on the scale involve more than a single idea; for example, "When I get married, my main interest will be unity in the home. I will put my role as wife and mother first"; and, "I must be working to keep alert and maintain my self-image." It is possible that some respondents will answer "disagree" to the statement "If I don't have children, I will have missed the most important part of my life" because they are reacting to the word *most*. Replacing the word *most* with the word *an* might elicit different responses. The item stated above that ends with the sentence, "I will put my role as wife and mother first" implies that there must be a ranking of roles; is it not possible for the woman to rank her roles as wife/mother and career woman equally?

(2) The scale is also described in *Family Measurement Techniques* (Straus and Brown, 1978, p. 98).

SOURCE: See Burns, 1974.

BIBLIOGRAPHY:

*Bardwick, J. *Psychology of Women.* New York: Harper & Row, 1971.
*Bartsch, K. "Choices for Women." Unpublished manuscript, University Park, Pennsylvania State University, 1973.
Burns, M. S. A. "Life Styles for Women: An Attitude Scale." *Psychological Reports,* 1974, *35,* 227-230.
Joesting, J., and Whitehead, G. I., III. "Equalitarianism, Curiosity, and Creativity: Partial Replication." *Psychological Reports,* 1976, *38,* 369-370.
*Oltman, R. "Women in the Professional Caucuses." *American Journal of Science,* 1971, *15,* 281-302.
*Straus, M. A., and Brown, B. W. *Family Measurement Techniques: Abstracts of Published Instruments, 1935-1974.* Minneapolis: University of Minnesota Press, 1978.

---

155. LOWER-KRAIN WOMAN'S CAREER COMMITMENT SCALE

AUTHORS: Deborah Jean Lower and Mark Krain

DATE: 1975

VARIABLES: Woman's career commitment when husband disapproves of wife's working; woman's career commitment when problems exist with children

TYPE OF INSTRUMENT: Summated rating scale

DESCRIPTION: There are two parts to this scale. The first part, which measures a woman's career commitment when her husband disapproves of her working, asks the woman to assume that she is working and her husband disapproves. The woman is then presented with a series of nine situation-specific courses of action. For each one, the woman is asked to indicate whether she would follow the course of action. The response options are: definitely I would, possibly I would, I probably wouldn't, and I definitely wouldn't. The second part of the scale, which measures a woman's career commitment when there are problems with the children, consists of twelve situations regarding children that might be attributable to the wife's working. The woman is to indicate how likely it is that she would quit her job given each of the situations. Four response options are provided: definitely I would quit, possibly I would quit, I probably wouldn't quit, and I definitely wouldn't quit.

PREVIOUSLY ADMINISTERED TO: Nurses

APPROPRIATE FOR: Females ages 16 and older

ADMINISTRATION: The scale can be self-administered and can be completed in less than ten minutes.

SAMPLE ITEMS:

Part I: I would quit my job if my husband felt we should begin having a family.

Part II: If my child was "hanging around" with the wrong kind of friends

SCORING: Items are objectively scored and equally weighted. Separate scores are obtained for the two parts of the scale.

DEVELOPMENT: The first part of the scale originally consisted of fifteen items. Factor analysis was used to reduce the scale to nine items that loaded on one factor and accounted for 100 percent of the variance. The development of the second part of the scale is not explained.

RELIABILITY: Based on the responses from 157 women, coefficient alpha was .82 for the first part and .89 for the second part. Scale minus item correlation coefficients were computed for each part; that is, each time an item was correlated with the total score, that particular item was eliminated from the calculation of the total score. For the first part, item-total correlations ranged from .36 to .66; for the second part, item-total correlations ranged from .52 to .71 (Lower, 1975).

VALIDITY: Lower (1975, p. 98) stated five hypotheses relating scores on the Lower-Krain Woman's Career Commitment Scale to scores on other instruments. The first three hypotheses were tested by using the Lower-Krain Sex Role Scale Regarding Children (#101). The hypotheses were:

   I. High career commitment is positively related to equalitarian attitudes toward sex roles for children.
  II. High career commitment is positively related to encouragement of equalitarian sex roles for children.
 III. High career commitment is positively related to the probability of the woman's children displaying equalitarian sex role behavior.
  IV. No significant relationship between career commitment and marital adjustment.
   V. High career commitment is negatively related to attitudes toward husband and wife roles as they support equalitarian roles for husband and wife.

Hypothesis III was not supported. The other four hypotheses were supported using the results from only one part of the scale; no hypothesis was supported using the scores from both parts of the scale. Hypothesis IV was supported when career commitment was measured as a function of the husband's disapproval (the first part of the scale); hypotheses I, II, and V were supported when career commitment was measured as a function of problems existing with the children (the second part of the scale).

SOURCE: See Lower, 1975.

BIBLIOGRAPHY:

Krain, M., and Lower, D. J. "The Relationship of Women's Career Commitment to Their Attitudes Toward Their Children's Sex Role Socialization, to Their Attitudes on Spousal Roles, and to Marital Adjustment." Paper presented at the meeting of the Midwest Sociological Society, St. Louis, Missouri, 1976. (ERIC Document Reproduction Service No. ED 138 855.)

Lower, D. J. "The Relation of Women's Career Commitment and Their Attitudes Regarding the Socialization of Children into Sex Roles, Marital Role Relations, and Marital Adjustment." Unpublished master's thesis, University of Iowa, 1975.

---

156. PACE SCALE OF ATTITUDES TOWARD MARRIED WOMEN'S EMPLOYMENT

AUTHOR: Lois W. Pace

DATE: 1970

VARIABLE: Attitudes toward married women working

TYPE OF INSTRUMENT: Summated rating scale

DESCRIPTION: The scale consists of twenty statements, most of which concern the advantages and disadvantages of a married woman working. Half of the statements are phrased to reflect a positive attitude and half are phrased to reflect a negative attitude. Each item is accompanied by five response options: strongly agree, agree, uncertain, disagree, and strongly disagree.

PREVIOUSLY ADMINISTERED TO: Married females

APPROPRIATE FOR: Ages 16 and older

ADMINISTRATION: The scale can be self-administered and can be completed in about ten minutes.

SAMPLE ITEMS: Working outside the home tends to improve one's morale.
A wife should work only if the family needs the money.

SCORING: Items are objectively scored and equally weighted. Total scores can range from 20 (very negative attitudes toward married women working) to 100 (very positive attitudes toward married women working).

DEVELOPMENT: An item pool consisting of thirty-four statements was administered to sixty women. An item analysis was performed comparing the responses from the fifteen women who had the highest total scores with the responses from the fifteen women who had the lowest possible scores. Fifteen items that differentiated at the .001 level between the highest- and lowest-scoring women and five items that differentiated at the .01 level comprise the scale.

RELIABILITY: No data are provided.

VALIDITY: No data are provided.

NOTES AND COMMENTS: Pace administered the scale to 213 adult married women and related their responses to age, employment history, educational attainment, family status, family income, place of residence, satisfaction derived from housework, satisfaction with family income, satisfaction from volunteer service, perceptions of other persons' feelings regarding wife's employment, and occupational status.

SOURCE: See Pace, 1970.

BIBLIOGRAPHY:

Pace, L. W. "A Study of Attitudes of Married Women Toward Married Women's Employ-
      ment." Unpublished manuscript, University of Missouri, 1970. (ERIC Document
      Reproduction Service No. ED 042 989.)

---

157. PAWLICKI-ALMQUIST WOMEN'S LIBERATION SCALE

AUTHORS: Robert E. Pawlicki and Carol Almquist

DATE: 1973

VARIABLE: Attitudes toward the issues advocated by the feminist movement

TYPE OF INSTRUMENT: Summated rating scale

DESCRIPTION: The scale consists of six statements regarding issues advocated by the feminist movement, particularly issues pertaining to marriage and career. Three statements are phrased to reflect positive attitudes and three statements are phrased to reflect negative attitudes. Six response options are offered with each item.

PREVIOUSLY ADMINISTERED TO: Female college students and female adults

APPROPRIATE FOR: Ages 16 and older

ADMINISTRATION: The scale can be self-administered and takes less than three minutes to complete.

SAMPLE ITEMS: Women should not be expected to subordinate their careers to home duties to a greater extent than men.
A woman should be proud to take her husband's name at marriage.

SCORING: Items are objectively scored and equally weighted. Total scores can range from −18 (no support for the positions advocated by the feminist movement) to +18 (complete support for the positions advocated by the feminist movement).

DEVELOPMENT: No information is provided.

RELIABILITY: No data are provided.

VALIDITY: The scale was completed by forty-nine college women and by thirty-six members of the National Organization for Women, a feminist group. As predicted, the college students scored significantly lower ($\overline{X}$ = .88) than the members of the National Organization for Women ($\overline{X}$ = 12.93, p < .001) (Pawlicki and Almquist, 1973).

NOTES AND COMMENTS: The validity data suggest that this scale has potential value as a research tool. However, because it is short, it is especially important that evidence pertaining to its reliability be obtained.

SOURCE: See Pawlicki and Almquist, 1973.

BIBLIOGRAPHY:

Pawlicki, R. E., and Almquist, C. "Authoritarianism, Locus of Control, and Tolerance of Ambiguity as Reflected in Membership and Nonmembership in a Women's Liberation Group." *Psychological Reports,* 1973, *32,* 1331-1337.

Taylor, N. T. "Sex Role, Locus of Control, Achievement Value, and Achievement." Unpublished doctoral dissertation, University of North Carolina at Chapel Hill, 1975. (*Dissertation Abstracts International,* 1975, *36* [6-A], 3529.)

158. RICHARDSON-ALPERT ROLE INVOLVEMENT SCALE

AUTHORS: Mary Sue Richardson and Judith Landon Alpert

DATE: 1978

VARIABLES: Role involvement in work, marital, and parental roles

TYPE OF INSTRUMENT: Projective storytelling and true-false

DESCRIPTION: The instrument includes three verbal projective cues: one concerns the work role; one concerns the marital role; and one concerns the parental role. Standard TAT-type instructions are given, and the respondent is allowed five minutes to write a story in response to the cue. At the end of the allotted five minutes, the respondent is asked to react to twenty-two statements by indicating whether each statement is true or false. The statements refer to the main character in the story just written. The true-false items following each story are identical. Some of the statements are phrased so that a "true" response indicates a high level of role involvement, and others are phrased so that a "true" response indicates a low level of role involvement. The projective portion of the scale is not scored but is included on the assumption that it "taps deeper and/or less stereotypic levels of personality, which then affect responses to objective items" (p. 8).

PREVIOUSLY ADMINISTERED TO: Female college students

APPROPRIATE FOR: Females, ages 16 and older

ADMINISTRATION: Because the story writing must be timed, an examiner must administer the scale. It takes about forty minutes to complete the scale.

SAMPLE ITEMS:

Work role cue: Judy is sitting at a desk in her office.

True-false items: Typically, she gives more than is asked or required of her.
She probably wouldn't be there if she didn't have to be.

SCORING: Items are objectively scored and equally weighted. Item scores are summed to yield three scores: Work Role Involvement, Marital Role Involvement, and Parental Role Involvement. A high score indicates a high level of involvement.

DEVELOPMENT: Fifty college students wrote incidents typical of each of the three roles: work role, marital role, and parental role. Thirteen of the true-false statements were derived from the stories they wrote. The remaining nine statements were taken from the Role Involvement subscale of the Richardson-Alpert Role Perceptions Scale (#159).

RELIABILITY: The scale was administered to seventy college women. Three role involvement scores were obtained for each woman. Using the 210 scores obtained, the alpha coefficient was .91.

VALIDITY: The seventy college women who completed the Richardson-Alpert Role Involvement Scale also supplied the following information: whether they wished to enter into each of the three roles (role choice); when they wished to enter each role they expected to enter (proximity of role entry); their semantic conceptions of each of the three roles (evaluative attitudes); their expected satisfaction from each of the roles during the next five years (role expectations-short term) and during their lifetime (role expectations-long term); what their life plan was; and demographic information including their age, grade point average, father's education, mother's education, and educational aspirations. Correlations were computed between each of these variables and the three role involvement scores. For the Work Role Involvement score, significant correlations were obtained with role choice, role expectations-long term, and mother's education. For the Marriage Role Involvement score, significant correlations were obtained with every one of the six role-related variables and with age. For the Parent Role Involvement score, significant correlations were obtained with evaluative attitudes, role expectations-long term, and life plan.

NOTES AND COMMENTS: (1) Richardson and Alpert (1978) found that the intercorrelations between the three involvement scores were not significant.

(2) Richardson (1978) reports that a new version of the scale with modified instructions is being developed.

(3) This scale is based on and related to the Richardson-Alpert Role Perception Scale (#159).

SOURCE: Mary Sue Richardson
School of Education
New York University
75 South Building
Washington Square
New York, New York 10003

BIBLIOGRAPHY:

*Richardson, M. S. Personal communication, June 1978.
Richardson, M. S., and Alpert, J. L. "Role Involvement in College Women: Work, Marriage, and Parent Roles." Paper presented at 49th annual meeting of the Eastern Psychological Association, Washington, D.C., March 1978.

---

159. RICHARDSON-ALPERT ROLE PERCEPTION SCALE

AUTHORS: Mary Sue Richardson and Judith Landon Alpert

DATE: 1976

VARIABLES: Perceptions of role engagement and competition in work role, marital role, parental role, combined work-marital role, combined work-parental role

TYPE OF INSTRUMENT: Projective storytelling and true-false

DESCRIPTION: The instrument includes five verbal projective cues, one for each of the following roles: work, marriage, parent, work-marriage, and work-parent. Standard TAT-type instructions are given, and the respondent is allowed five minutes to write a story in response to the cue. At the end of the allotted five minutes, the respondent is asked to react to forty statements by indicating whether each statement is true or false. The statements refer to the main character in the story just written. Of the forty statements, ten relate to innovation, ten relate to involvement, ten relate to affectivity, and ten relate to competition. The true-false items following each story are identical. Some of the statements are phrased so that a "true" response yields a high score and other statements are phrased so that a "true" response yields a low score. There are two forms of the scale—one for men and one for women. The only difference is in the gender of the characters in the cues. Men write stories and respond to statements about males; women write stories and respond to statements about females. The projective portion of the instrument is not scored, but is included on the assumption that it "taps deeper levels of personality which subsequently affect responses to the objective scale" (Richardson and Alpert, in press, p. 4).

PREVIOUSLY ADMINISTERED TO: College students

APPROPRIATE FOR: Ages 16 and older

ADMINISTRATION: Because the story writing must be timed, an examiner must administer the scale. It takes about one and a half hours to complete the scale.

SAMPLE ITEMS:

Combined work-parent role cue: Carol, who has just come home from work, greets her young child.

True-false, innovation: She has very little to say about how her day is spent.

True-false, involvement: She seldom feels bored.

True-false, affectivity: She feels discouraged.

True-false, competition: She tries hard to be best.

SCORING: Items are objectively scored and equally weighted. Ten scores are obtained for each person, a role engagement score and a competition score for each of five roles: work, marital, parental, combined work-marital, combined work-parental.

DEVELOPMENT: Ten women (ages 25-35) described incidents typical of each of five role categories: work, marriage, parenting, combined work-marriage, combined work-parenting. An examination of the incidents they provided suggested that four categories could adequately describe them: "(1) Innovation—initiate and enjoy novel and diverse activities; (2) Affectivity—positive emotional tone; (3) Involvement—interest in and engagement in activities; (4) Competition—desire to excel and compete" (Richardson and Alpert, in press, p. 5). In order to verify the representativeness of the categories, thirty college students provided an additional set of typical incidents for each of the five role categories being studied. Their incidents fit the four categories described above. Ten true-false items were constructed for each of the four categories. These forty statements were randomly ordered and given to two researchers with instructions to sort them into the four categories. As a result of their sorting, it was determined that three items had to be revised.

The scale was completed by 134 college students and their responses were factor analyzed. Two factors were extracted. The first factor had high loadings from three sub-scales: Affectivity (−.86), Innovation (.59), and Involvement (.49 and .70 for each of two subsets of items). This factor was labeled Role Engagement. The second factor had high loadings from two subsets of competition items: mild competition (−.77) and intense competition (.58). This factor was labeled Competition.

RELIABILITY: No data are provided.

VALIDITY: The responses from the 134 college students were factor analyzed for each sex separately. The results suggested that each of the four subscales (Innovation, Involvement, Affectivity, and Competition) loaded essentially on different factors; three factors were highly correlated and one factor was independent of the others (Richardson and Alpert, in press).

NOTES AND COMMENTS: (1) The Richardson-Alpert Role Involvement Scale (#158) is based on this scale.

(2) The projective cues used (but not scored) with this scale were also included in other research. Richardson and Alpert (1976a) included pictorial representations of three of the five projective cues (along with another picture, which has no counterpart in the Richardson Role Perception Scale) in a study of women's role perceptions. Respondents were given standard TAT instructions and allowed five minutes to write each story. The stories were scored for the presence of role conflict, conflict themes, and outcome. Alpert and others (1976) used the same five verbal cues used in the Richardson Role Perception Scale. Again standard TAT-like instructions were given and the respondents were allowed five minutes to write each story. The stories were scored for outcome, affect, and the presence of role conflict.

SOURCE: See Richardson and Alpert, in press.

BIBLIOGRAPHY:

Alpert, J. L., Richardson, M. S., Perlmutter, B., and Shutzer, F. "Perceptions of Major Roles by College Students." Paper presented at 84th annual meeting of the American Psychological Association, Washington, D.C., September 1976.

Richardson, M. S., and Alpert, J. L. "Role Perceptions of Educated Adult Women: An Exploratory Study." *Educational Gerontology,* 1976a, *1,* 171-185.

Richardson, M. S., and Alpert, J. L. "Role Perceptions: Variations by Sex and Roles." Paper presented at 84th annual meeting of the American Psychological Association, Washington, D.C., September 1976b.

Richardson, M. S., and Alpert, J. L. "Role Perceptions: Variations by Sex and Roles." *Sex Roles,* in press.

160. RICHARDSON ROLE CONCEPT SCALE

AUTHOR: Mary Sue Richardson

DATE: 1972

VARIABLES: Role discrepancy for self-career woman, ideal woman-career woman, self-homemaker, ideal woman-homemaker, career woman-homemaker (labeled Role Differentiation), and self-ideal woman (labeled Self-Esteem)

TYPE OF INSTRUMENT: Adjective rating scale

DESCRIPTION: The scale consists of fifty-eight adjectives, each followed by a seven-point rating scale. Scale points 1 and 2 are labeled "Not like this"; scale points 3, 4, and 5 are labeled "Somewhat like this"; and scale points 6 and 7 are labeled "Like this." The scale is to be completed four times, once for each of the following four phrases: "I am," "The ideal woman is," "Career women are," and "Homemakers are."

PREVIOUSLY ADMINISTERED TO: Female college students

APPROPRIATE FOR: Females, ages 16 and older

ADMINISTRATION: The scale is self-administered and can be completed in less than forty minutes.

SAMPLE ITEMS: Achieving
Active
Adventurous
Affectionate
Aggressive

SCORING: Discrepancy scores are obtained between the ratings assigned to the adjectives when one concept is being rated and when a second concept is being rated. The sign of the difference between ratings is ignored, so that a larger score indicates greater discrepancy between scores. Discrepancy scores are obtained for the following pairs of concepts: self-career woman, ideal woman-career woman, self-homemaker, ideal woman-homemaker, career woman-homemaker (Role Differentiation), and self-ideal woman (Self-Esteem).

DEVELOPMENT: A pool of 334 adjectives was compiled by selecting adjectives from three existing lists—Gough's Adjective Check List (#45), Bill's Index of Adjustment and Values, and Super's Occupational Trait List—and from interview data obtained with homemakers and career women. The item pool was administered to forty-eight college women with instructions to check adjectives which described (1) the ideal woman, (2) the career woman, and (3) the homemaker. The college women could check as many adjectives as they desired. An adjective was retained when it was checked by at least 80 percent of the respondents as being descriptive of one of the concepts. Applying this criterion, twenty-nine adjectives were retained for the scale, with the majority of the adjectives (twenty-four) being descriptive of the ideal woman. In order to select additional adjectives descriptive of the career woman and homemaker, two new criteria were applied: (1) at least 50 percent of the women had to check the adjective as being descriptive of either the homemaker or the career woman; and (2) there had to be at least a 20 percent difference in the number of women who checked the adjective as being descriptive of one of the concepts and the number who checked the adjective as being descriptive of the other concept. Applying these two criteria, an additional twenty-nine adjectives were selected for the scale. The fifty-eight adjectives selected comprise the scale.

RELIABILITY: Thirty-three women completed the scale on two occasions separated by four weeks. Their responses were used to estimate test-retest reliability. The results were: self-ideal woman = .80; self-career woman = .77; self-homemaker = .82; ideal woman-career woman = .44; ideal woman-homemaker = .86; and career woman-homemaker = .76. Richardson (1972, p. 37) comments on the low reliability for the ideal woman-career woman discrepancy score, stating, "When the subjects of this study were born, there was a major movement to encourage women to return to the home from the world of work. . . . More recently, the literature of the women's liberation movement has stressed the greater desirability of the career role. Given these contrary trends, women can be expected to be somewhat uncertain and perhaps even conflicted about the desirability of the career role. This may be the reason for the relatively low reliability of discrepancy scores based on ratings of the ideal woman and ratings of the career woman."

VALIDITY: Ninety-seven unmarried female college seniors completed the Richardson Role Concept Scale and responded to many questions related to career and work orientation. Richardson (1972, p. 104) found that "women whose self-concepts match their concepts of homemakers are not likely to be career oriented." The correlations between self-homemaker congruence and four indicators of career orientation were all negative and statistically significant (p < .01). However, she also found that "women who perceive themselves as similar to career women do not, as had been expected, have a high level of career orientation." The correlations between self-career woman congruence and the four indicators of career orientation were all nonsignificant.

NOTES AND COMMENTS: Richardson (1972) reports that intercorrelations between the six discrepancy scores range from .16 (correlation between self-homemaker and self-career woman) to .84 (correlation between ideal woman-homemaker and self-homemaker).

SOURCE: See Richardson, 1972; or ETS Tests in Microfiche Collection (#007719).

BIBLIOGRAPHY:

Richardson, M. S. "Self-Concepts and Role Concepts in the Career Orientation of College Women." Unpublished doctoral dissertation, Columbia University, 1972. (*Dissertation Abstracts International,* 1973, *33*[10-B], 5001-5002.)
Richardson, M. S. "Self-Concepts and Role Concepts in the Career Orientation of College Women." *Journal of Counseling Psychology,* 1975, *22,* 122-126.

161. SCALE FOR MEASURING ATTITUDES TOWARD
WORKING WOMEN

AUTHOR: S. Sultan Akhtar

DATE: 1966

VARIABLES: Attitudes toward working women; subscales measuring implications for home and family, personal and social relations, and work and efficiency

TYPE OF INSTRUMENT: Summated rating scale

DESCRIPTION: The scale consists of twenty statements, each of which is followed by three response alternatives: agree, undecided, and disagree. The statements concern three broad areas: home and family (nine items), personal and social relations (seven items), and work and efficiency (four items). Eight of the items are phrased to reflect a positive attitude toward women working, and the remaining twelve items reflect a negative attitude toward women working.

PREVIOUSLY ADMINISTERED TO: Postgraduate college students in India

APPROPRIATE FOR: Ages 16 and older

ADMINISTRATION: The scale can be self-administered and can be completed in about ten to twelve minutes.

SAMPLE ITEMS:

Home and Family: A working wife can give the desired love and affection to her husband.

Personal and Social Relations: Working women are neglectful of their social relations.

Work and Efficiency: It is not possible for women to work with full devotion.

SCORING: Items are objectively scored and equally weighted. Three subscale scores and a total score are obtained.

DEVELOPMENT: Items selected for the scale were those that yielded item-total correlations significant at the .01 level and had high, positive "discriminative values."

RELIABILITY: Split-half reliability coefficients were computed for each of the three subscales. The coefficients ranged from .72 to .89 (Akhtar, Pestonjee, and Farooqi, 1969).

VALIDITY: Akhtar, Pestonjee, and Farooqi (1969) tested 85 female and 111 male college students. There was a significant difference in the overall scores obtained by men ($\overline{X}$ = 26.53) and women ($\overline{X}$ = 29.55, p < .01), with women indicating more favorable attitudes. Of the three subscales, only Personal and Social Relations showed a significant difference (p < .01) between the responses given by men ($\overline{X}$ = 10.91) and women ($\overline{X}$ = 12.61), with women again indicating more favorable attitudes.

NOTES AND COMMENTS: (1) Because the work reported here was originally done in India, the phrasing of some of the items is awkward.

(2) Rao (1976) used ten statements based on the Scale for Measuring Attitudes Toward Working Women. He was interested in measuring female college students' attitudes toward "four main areas of social life: (1) Traditional role of women; (2) Improvement in status; (3) Household duties; and (4) Marital adjustment" (p. 4).

SOURCE: See Akhtar, Pestonjee, and Farooqi, 1969.

BIBLIOGRAPHY:

Akhtar, S. S., Pestonjee, D., and Farooqi, F. "Attitudes Towards Working Women." *Indian Journal of Social Work,* 1969, *30,* 93-97.

Rao, U. A. "A Sociological Study of Occupational Choices of Undergraduate Girl Students." *Indian Journal of Social Work,* 1976, *37,* 1-11.

---

162. SCALE OF ATTITUDES TOWARD A DUAL ROLE FOR WOMEN

AUTHORS: Julia I. Dalrymple, Phyllis K. Lowe, and Helen Y. Nelson

DATE: 1971

VARIABLE: Attitudes regarding the dual role of homemaker and wage earner for women

TYPE OF INSTRUMENT: Summated rating scale

DESCRIPTION: The scale consists of twenty-five items relating to women working. The items cover four areas: the effects that a mother's working has on children (five items); financial contributions from the working wife (five items); the maintenance of home and family relationships (nine items); and the societal implications of working women (six items). Eleven items are phrased to reflect a positive attitude toward women working and fourteen items are phrased to reflect a negative attitude. Each item is accompanied by five response alternatives: strongly agree, mildly agree, undecided, mildly disagree, and strongly disagree.

PREVIOUSLY ADMINISTERED TO: Females, ages 14-20

APPROPRIATE FOR: Ages 14 and older

ADMINISTRATION: The scale is self-administered and can be completed in less than twenty minutes.

SAMPLE ITEMS:

The effects that a mother's working has on children: Working women won't be able to spend enough time with their children.

Financial contributions from the working wife: Things today cost money. It is only reasonable for the wife to work to help get money for the family.

The maintenance of home and family relationships: Working women won't be able to keep a proper and clean home.

Societal implications of working women: If too many married women work there won't be enough jobs for the single girls.

SCORING: Items are objectively scored and equally weighted. A total score is obtained that can range from 25 (extremely negative attitude) to 125 (extremely positive attitude).

DEVELOPMENT: A sample of adolescents was given a questionnaire with open-ended questions designed to measure attitudes regarding the dual role of homemaker and wage earner for women. Their responses were used as the basis for the questions included on the Scale of Attitudes Toward a Dual Role for Women.

RELIABILITY: Test-retest reliability was .85. No information is given regarding the sample or interval between testings. Internal consistency reliabilities were computed for four samples of adolescent girls (n = 135 to 162). The reliability coefficients ranged from .80 to .83.

VALIDITY: Item analyses were performed on the responses from five samples of adolescent girls. For all five samples, twenty-two of the twenty-five items were found to differentiate significantly between those in the upper and lower quartiles of the distribution of total scores. The other three items were found to differentiate significantly between those in the upper and lower quartiles for at least some of the samples.

The responses from adolescent girls to a measure of internality-externality (Rotter's I-E Scale) were used to divide the girls into high and low groups. The high group (more internal) scored significantly higher (more positive toward a dual role for women, p < .01) than the low group (more external).

SOURCE: See Dalrymple, Lowe, and Nelson, 1971.

BIBLIOGRAPHY:

Dalrymple, J. I., Lowe, P. K., and Nelson, H. Y. "Preparation for a Dual Role: Homemaker-Wage Earner, with Adaptations to Inner-City Youth. Final Report, Volume I." New York: Cornell University, 1971. (ERIC Document Reproduction Service No. ED 058 464.)

163. SEX ROLE IDEOLOGY

AUTHOR: Jerzy Piotrowski

DATE: 1971 (used 1967)

VARIABLE: Sex role ideology

TYPE OF INSTRUMENT: Summated rating scale

DESCRIPTION: The scale consists of twenty statements—five statements relating to each of the following: traditional sex role ideology, male dominance ideology, married professional role ideology, and evaluation of married women's work. Fourteen items are phrased to reflect a traditional ideology and six are phrased to reflect an egalitarian ideology. Each item is accompanied by five response alternatives: agree, rather agree, difficult to answer, rather disagree, and disagree.

PREVIOUSLY ADMINISTERED TO: Husbands and wives

APPROPRIATE FOR: Ages 14 and older

ADMINISTRATION: The scale can be self-administered and can be completed in ten to fifteen minutes.

SAMPLE ITEMS:

Traditional sex role ideology: Fathers should not take care of little children.

Male dominance ideology: The woman should work when she wishes it even if her husband is opposed.

Married women professional role ideology: A married woman should not work professionally.

Evaluation of married women's work: A professionally working woman enjoys greater respect.

SCORING: Items are objectively scored and equally weighted. Total scores can range from 20 (very traditional) to 100 (very nontraditional). Scores can also be obtained for each of the four subscales.

DEVELOPMENT: Some items on the scale were adapted from a similar scale used by the Danish National Institute of Social Research in Copenhagen (Noordhoek, 1969). The first ten items on the scale are adaptations of items included in the Traditional Sex Role Ideology Scale (#130).

RELIABILITY: No data are provided.

VALIDITY: For the items pertaining to male dominance ideology, men expressed the most traditional attitudes, nonworking women were less traditional than men, and working women were the least traditional. The same rank ordering occurred on the items pertaining to married women's professional role ideology and evaluation of married women's professional work. Significance tests were apparently not performed by the author, as no probability values are reported (Piotrowski, 1971).

NOTES AND COMMENTS: The scale was designed for use in Poland. As a result, some of the items are awkwardly phrased in English.

SOURCE: See Piotrowski, 1971, pp. 83-84.

BIBLIOGRAPHY:

*Noordhoek, J. A. *Gifte Kvinder i familie og erhverv. (Married Women in Family Life and Social Life.)* Copenhagen: Socialforskningsinstituttet, 1969.
Piotrowski, J. "The Employment of Married Women and the Changing Sex Roles in Poland." In A. Michel (Ed.), *Family Issues of Employed Women in Europe and America.* Leiden: E. J. Brill, 1971.

---

164. SIEGEL-CURTIS WORK ORIENTATION SCALE

AUTHORS: Alberta Engvall Siegel and Elizabeth Ann Curtis

DATE: 1963 (used 1961)

VARIABLE: Women's work orientation

TYPE OF INSTRUMENT: Open-ended questions

DESCRIPTION: The instrument consists of five open-ended questions and a rating assigned by the interviewer. The open-ended questions concern future plans and expectations regarding employment and marriage. The interviewer rating is made on the basis of the interviewer's global impression of the respondent's motivation for work achievement. The rating is made on a five-point scale ranging from "strongly oriented to work, ambitious, interested in achievement through work" to "not at all oriented to work, work is not important to self-satisfaction."

PREVIOUSLY ADMINISTERED TO: Female college sophomores

APPROPRIATE FOR: Females, ages 16 and older

ADMINISTRATION: The questions are orally administered and the responses are tape recorded.

SAMPLE ITEMS: When you think of the future, how does marriage figure in your plans? Suppose you were thinking of marrying a particular man, and you realized that if you married this man it would be impossible for you to continue to work. Would you marry this man?

SCORING: Each interview response is judged to be either "work oriented" or "not work oriented." The interviewer's overall rating is made on a five-point scale, with 1 point indicating strong work orientation. The actual assignment of points to items is not adequately explained by the authors, though it is indicated that total scores can range from 6 (maximum work orientation) to 17 (no work orientation).

DEVELOPMENT: No information is provided.

RELIABILITY: Interrater reliability was determined by having two coders independently score the audio tapes from twenty subjects. The results reported pertain to a larger number of items than comprise this scale. For the eleven items assigned nominal codes (including the five on this scale), interrater agreement ranged from 70 percent to 100 percent. For the nine items assigned ratings (including the one on this scale), the median reliability was rho = .93, with a range of .64 to .99.

Intercorrelations between the six items contributing to the scale ranged from −.07 to +.64. Item-total correlations ranged from .31 to .86, with the highest correlation resulting from the relationship between the interviewer's assigned rating and total score.

VALIDITY: For a sample of forty-six college sophomore women, no significant correlations were obtained between work orientation and the following variables: socioeconomic status, parents' educational level, daughters' perceptions of parents' views on the purpose of college, and daughters' perceptions of parents' attitudes toward the importance of education for daughters. There was, however, a significant correlation between work orientation of the respondent and her mother's work orientation (rho = .35, p < .05).

SOURCE: See Siegel and Curtis, 1963.

BIBLIOGRAPHY:

Siegel, A. E., and Curtis, E. A. "Familial Correlates of Orientation Toward Future Employment Among College Women." *Journal of Educational Psychology*, 1963, *54*, 33-37.

---

165. STUDENT ATTITUDE SCALE

AUTHORS: Elizabeth G. French and Gerald S. Lesser

DATE: 1964

VARIABLE: Value placed on intellectual goals and women's role goals

TYPE OF INSTRUMENT: True-false

DESCRIPTION: The instrument consists of sixty-five statements, each of which refers to "girls" at the particular college the respondent attends. Thirty-four statements pertain to intellectual attainment; thirty-one statements pertain to various aspects of the women's role. For each statement, the woman is to indicate whether the statement is true or false as it applies to the other women attending the same college.

PREVIOUSLY ADMINISTERED TO: Female college students

APPROPRIATE FOR: Female college students

ADMINISTRATION: This self-administered scale can be completed in about forty minutes.

SAMPLE ITEMS:

Intellectual Attainment: By and large, the girls consider finishing college important, and it is rare for a girl to drop out before graduation.

Women's Role: Making new friends is the most important aspect of college to most girls.

SCORING: Items are objectively scored and equally weighted. Two scores are obtained: value placed on intellectual attainment and value placed on women's role success. It is possible for a woman to score high or low on both scales or to score high on one scale and low on the other.

DEVELOPMENT: No information is provided.

RELIABILITY: No data are provided.

VALIDITY: French and Lesser (1964) used the instrument to test a series of hypotheses pertaining to the relationship between achievement motivation/performance and the presence of intellectual and/or women's role values. They had two main hypotheses and several subsidiary hypotheses. The two main hypotheses were: "Achievement motivation scores of subjects who believe they are to be competitively evaluated will be high when the performance to be rated leads to a goal the subjects value, but not otherwise" and "Achievement motivation scores will be positively related to performance when the performance leads to a valued goal, but not otherwise" (French and Lesser, 1964, p. 120). Using the Student Attitude Scale to identify college women with intellectual values and college women with women's role values, the two main hypotheses were supported by the data. Friedrich (1976) was unable to replicate the findings of French and Lesser, but Friedrich introduced several modifications into both the instrument and the procedures.

NOTES AND COMMENTS: (1) Taylor (1967) modified the instrument by phrasing each of the items in the first person. Thus, rather than referring to "girls," Taylor's items referred to "I."

(2) Friedrich also modified the instrument. Instead of phrasing the statements in terms of "girls," the statements were phrased in terms of "10 girls you know best at Cornell." The revised instrument was pretested with 125 college women. As a result of an item-discrimination analysis, five items were eliminated. Ten new items were added, resulting in a sixty-nine-item instrument containing thirty items relating to intellectual values and thirty-nine items relating to women's role values.

SOURCE: Dr. Gerald S. Lesser
            Department of Education
            Harvard University
            Cambridge, Massachusetts 02138

BIBLIOGRAPHY:

Baefsky, P. M. "Self-Sacrifice, Cooperation, and Aggression in Women of Varying Sex
       Role Orientations." Unpublished doctoral dissertation, University of Southern
       California, 1974. (*Dissertation Abstracts International,* 1974, *35*[4-B], 1900.)
Baefsky, P. M., and Berger, S. E. "Self-Sacrifice, Cooperation, and Aggression in Women
       of Varying Sex Role Orientations." *Personality and Social Psychology Bulletin,*
       1974, *1,* 296-298.
French, E. G., and Lesser, G. S. "Some Characteristics of the Achievement Motive in
       Women." *Journal of Abnormal and Social Psychology,* 1964, *68,* 119-128.
Friedrich, L. K. "Achievement Motivation in College Women Revisited: Implications for
       Women, Men, and the Gathering of Coconuts." *Sex Roles,* 1976, *2,* 47-61.
Taylor, S. E. "College Women's Evaluation of Other Women as a Function of Congruence
       of Intellectual or Social Role Motives." *Connecticut College Psychology Journal,*
       1967, *4,* 25-32.

---

166. WHITE INDEX OF ANXIETY OVER MOTHER ROLE

AUTHOR: Lynn C. White

DATE: 1972

VARIABLE: Anxiety regarding aspects of the maternal role caused by mother's absence
from the home

TYPE OF INSTRUMENT: Summated rating scale

DESCRIPTION: The scale consists of five items, each of which asks the mother about the
feelings she has when away from her home and children. Each item refers to a different
aspect of the maternal role. The items are accompanied by five response alternatives ranging from "I always feel greatly disturbed" to "I never feel disturbed." All mothers complete the scale for absences due to nonwork activities, such as social events and volunteer activities. Employed mothers complete the scale a second time for absences due to
work activities.

PREVIOUSLY ADMINISTERED TO: Mothers

APPROPRIATE FOR: Mothers

ADMINISTRATION: The scale can be self-administered and can be completed in about
three minutes.

SAMPLE ITEMS: When you are outside the home and away from your children, how do you feel about leaving your children without your personal supervision?

When you are outside the home and away from your children, how do you feel about the amount of entertaining of your children's friends in your home? (White does not state the items verbatim, so this may not be the exact wording of the questions.)

SCORING: Items are objectively scored and equally weighted. A total score reflecting amount of anxiety is obtained.

DEVELOPMENT: Items were constructed for the scale using inputs from sociologists on their perceptions of which areas of activity are potentially anxiety producing for employed mothers.

RELIABILITY: No data are provided.

VALIDITY: White administered the scale to 124 employed mothers and 396 non-employed mothers. Consistent with her prediction, she found that the percentage of employed mothers experiencing high anxiety about leaving their children for work activities (31.5 percent) was almost twice the percentage of nonemployed mothers who experienced high anxiety about leaving their children for nonwork activities (15.7 percent). Contrary to prediction, White did not find a relationship between age of youngest child and degree of anxiety mothers express about being away from home and children. White hypothesized that "middle-class mothers will be more likely than working-class mothers to express feelings of anxiety about the mother role if the mother is regularly employed" (p. 65). This hypothesis was tested by using mother's educational attainment and family income as indicators of social class. The hypothesis was not supported, and the data were, in fact, opposite to the prediction.

Consistent with prediction, White found a significant relationship between a respondent's father's attitude toward the respondent being employed and the respondent's anxiety. Also consistent with prediction, White found a relationship between a respondent's mother's attitude toward the respondent being employed and the respondent's anxiety. This relationship was more moderate than the relationship with the respondent's father's attitude. Contrary to prediction, White did not find a relationship between husband's attitude toward his wife being employed and the respondent's (wife's) anxiety regarding absences for work-related activities. She did, however, find a moderate relationship for absences due to nonwork activities.

NOTES AND COMMENTS: (1) White obtained two measures of anxiety for working mothers: anxiety due to absences for work-related activities and anxiety due to absences for nonwork activities. The relationship between the two measures of anxiety was significant (gamma = .69, p < .0001).

(2) The absence of reliability data is particularly troublesome because the scale is quite short.

SOURCE: See White, 1972.

BIBLIOGRAPHY:

White, L. C. "Maternal Employment and Anxiety Over Mother Role." *Louisiana State University Journal of Sociology,* 1972, 2, 61-81.

11

■■■■■■■■■■

Attitudes Toward
Women's Issues

■■■■■■■■■■■■■■■■■■■

This chapter contains forty-one instruments, each of which assesses attitudes toward a variety of sex role issues. The items on these measures pertain to dating and courtship, marriage, parenting, childcare, employment, education, politics, legislation, social behavior, sexuality, sex stereotypes, sex discrimination, the feminist movement, abortion, heterosexual relations, religion, and sex role equality. There is considerable variability in the particular combination of issues that any particular instrument contains. However, each instrument includes items pertaining to a subset of the topics mentioned above.

The forty-one instruments in this chapter are quite similar to each other in significant ways. In fact, it is quite easy to describe a modal instrument representative of these measures. The description that follows states in parentheses the number of instruments (out of forty-one) that include each of the modal characteristics. The modal instrument first appeared in the literature after 1970 (thirty-two); is a summated rating scale (thirty-five); has been or can be self-administered (forty-one); has been previously administered to college students (thirty-six); is appropriate for both males and females (thirty-eight); can be administered to persons who are at least sixteen years old (forty); possesses some known reliability (thirty-six); and has been either directly or indirectly validated (thirty-eight). The instruments included here are quite similar to myriad others that have been

383

used to measure attitudes toward a variety of women's issues. However, those omitted did not satisfy the criteria for inclusion; that is, published reports of their use failed to include information regarding their development, reliability, or validity. Eventually some of the omitted instruments may prove to be better measuring instruments than the forty-one included here, but at this time there is insufficient information to evaluate them.

Instruments measuring attitudes toward women's issues are typically developed by constructing an item pool that may include items excerpted from existing attitude measures, items constructed from a review of the relevant literature, and items which the author or persons selected by the author believe will reflect attitudes toward the issues being studied. The item pool is reduced either based on factor-analytic or item-analytic procedures or by the subjective evaluations of persons serving as "judges." Reliability estimates most often reflect the internal consistency of the instruments, though test-retest reliability is also frequently calculated. Authors' claims for the validity of the measure are usually based on (1) significant differences in mean scores of males and females, (2) the ability of the instrument to differentiate between known groups such as members of profeminist and antifeminist groups, or (3) comparisons with scores on other instruments—for example, measures of authoritarianism, ethnocentrism, fascism, and other measures of attitudes toward women's issues.

Though the instruments included here are similar in numerous ways, two warrant special mention: the oldest and the most popular. The oldest instrument is the Belief Patterns Scale for Measuring Attitudes Toward Feminism (#172), which first appeared in the literature in 1936. Despite its age, it typifies attitude measures used today. In fact, the items from the Belief Pattern Scale were included in the initial item pool used to construct several scales developed more recently—for example, Attitudes Toward Women Scale (#169 and #170), Feminism II (#181), FEM Scale (#179), and Sex Role Survey (#199). The Attitudes Toward Women Scale (#169 and #170) is the most popular scale; it has been used by more researchers than any other scale for measuring attitudes toward women's issues.

The most common and significant differences between the various measures of attitudes toward women's issues involve the particular combination of issues they pertain to, the specific items chosen to represent those issues, and the number and names of the scores they yield. Most of the instruments yield an overall total score; many yield sub-scale scores as well. The labels assigned to the end of the attitude continuum also vary. *Emergent, nontraditional, liberal, modern, contemporary, egalitarian,* and *profeminist* are adjectives that refer to one end of the attitude continuum. *Traditional, antifeminist, sexist,* and *conservative* are adjectives that refer to the opposite end of the continuum. The instruments also differ in terms of the variable they claim to measure. The terminology connected with the study of women's issues is unstandardized. As a result, there is tremendous variability in the names that authors assign to the variables they are trying to measure. An examination of item content, validity data, and results from factor-analytic studies provides a better indication of what the instrument is actually measuring than does reading the name of the variable which it purports to measure. Two instruments that claim to measure the same variable may actually be measuring very different variables; conversely, two instruments that claim to be measuring different variables may actually be measuring the same underlying variable.

A vast number of items have been included in instruments that measure attitudes toward women's issues. Though no attempt was made to count the number of different items that appear on the forty-one measures in this chapter, some idea of the number of different items is available from Mason's (1975) paper entitled "Sex Role Attitude Items and Scales from U.S. Sample Surveys." Mason listed over 550 items that appeared on forty-nine instruments used in the United States prior to July 1974 to assess attitudes toward either specific sex role issues or attitudes toward a variety of sex role issues. Of course, many of the items listed by Mason do not appear on the instruments included here, because Mason listed items from all of the instruments she located; her instruments did not have to satisfy any particular criterion.

Though there is tremendous diversity in the items that appear on instruments assessing attitudes toward a variety of women's issues, there is also considerable overlap. For example, the item "The word 'obey' should be removed from the marriage service" appears either verbatim or with slight wording changes on six of the forty-one instruments that follow. Identical items will even appear on instruments that purport to measure different variables.

Many of the problems involved in assessing attitudes toward a variety of women's issues are the same problems involved in any type of attitude assessment. The behavioral concomitants of the expressed attitudes are generally unknown. For the most part, researchers assessing sex role attitudes do not study the behavioral manifestations of the attitudes. Many studies have been published concerning sex role attitudes of particular groups or changes in sex role attitudes over time or following specific experimental treatments designed to alter attitudes. What is needed is research regarding the relationship between verbalized attitudes and behavior.

Another common problem with attitude measures in general, and thus with measures of attitudes toward women's issues, is their susceptibility to faking. One common way in which respondents "fake" answers is to give socially desirable responses rather than their honest attitudes. Giving socially desirable responses or "faking" in some other manner may result from a conscious desire on the part of the respondents to present a distorted picture of themselves. However, faking may also be an unconscious process; that is, attitudes toward women's issues are often so deeply ingrained, and at such an unconscious level, that respondents may be unable to report their honest attitudes merely because they are not cognizant of them. Regardless of the cause of the faking, studies of the relationship between behavior and expressed attitudes would be helpful in determining the extent to which faking affects the responses given on measures of attitudes toward women's issues.

Research is also needed to learn more about the effects that conditions of administration have on expressed attitudes toward women's issues. The sex and attitudes of the administrator of the instrument, the sex composition of the group to which the instruments are administered, and the specific instructions accompanying them are a few of the many variables that might affect the responses given. These issues have been given little attention in previous research.

Few authors of sex role attitude instruments deal with the issue of content validity. That is, they do not construct their instruments to represent systematically a content domain. As a result, it is not clear to what domain the findings generalize. As an example, several instruments purport to measure attitudes toward the issues of the feminist movement. If they measure attitudes toward four or six or even ten issues, can one generalize the findings to all of the issues of the feminist movement? Furthermore, there are many facets to any one issue of the feminist movement. Are these various facets adequately represented by the items on the instrument?

Another problem that applies to some instruments measuring attitudes toward women's issues is the number of underlying factors or dimensions. All too often, authors seem to assume that their instrument is unidimensional. The mere fact that it measures attitudes toward a variety of women's issues makes this assumption suspect. Though authors of many instruments have factor analyzed their results and can describe the factors identified, it is not unusual for researchers to obtain inconsistent results when several factor-analytic studies are conducted for a particular instrument; for example, when an instrument is administered to two groups of persons, it is not uncommon for the factor analysis of one group's responses to yield different factors than the factor analysis of the other group's responses. In general, there is considerable ambiguity and a lack of information regarding the number of factors or dimensions that underlie instruments measuring attitudes toward a variety of women's issues; and there is a lack of clarity regarding the extent to which obtained factors apply equally across different groups. One might conceive of a definitive factor-analytic study that would factor analyze responses to all of the statements from all instruments measuring attitudes toward women's issues. Unfortunately the vast number of items makes this an impractical approach; it would take many hours for respondents to complete such a "super scale." Nevertheless, research is needed to determine the factorial composition of attitudes toward women's issues and to determine the consistency of the factor structure across different groups.

To summarize, the assessment of attitudes toward women's issues will be improved when (1) a standardized terminology is adopted for the variable names so that the label of the variable expresses the same idea to different researchers; (2) the item pool from which the attitude measures are constructed is more systematically developed and adequately defined so that it is clear to what domain results can be generalized; (3) more research is conducted regarding the effects of extraneous situational variables on the attitudes reported, so that researchers will know which variables should be controlled; (4) more data are obtained on the factors underlying the measures so that scores can be more accurately interpreted; and (5) the relationship between behavior and expressed attitudes toward women's issues is investigated.

BIBLIOGRAPHY:

Mason, K. O. "Sex Role Attitude Items and Scales from U.S. Sample Surveys." Unpublished manuscript, 1975. Available from Karen Mason, Population Studies Center, University of Michigan.

---

167. ABDELHALIM SCALE OF ATTITUDES TOWARD RELATIONS BETWEEN THE SEXES

AUTHOR: I. H. Abdelhalim

DATE: 1956

VARIABLE: Attitudes toward relations between the sexes in Egypt

TYPE OF INSTRUMENT: Summated rating scale

DESCRIPTION: The scale consists of twenty-eight statements regarding such issues as sexual relations and sexual freedom, marital relations and marital roles, and attitudes toward women. Some items are phrased to reflect a liberal attitude; some items are phrased to reflect a traditional attitude. Each statement is accompanied by five response options: completely agree, agree, undecided, disagree, and completely disagree.

PREVIOUSLY ADMINISTERED TO: Egyptian college students and adults

APPROPRIATE FOR: Egyptians or persons from similar cultures, ages 16 and older

ADMINISTRATION: This self-administered scale can be completed in about fifteen minutes.

SAMPLE ITEMS: The husband should be the absolute master in the home.
                    Differences in pay between men and women doing the same work should be abolished.

SCORING: Items are objectively scored and equally weighted.

DEVELOPMENT: An item pool including seventy-five statements was administered to a sample of eighty people. Based on their responses, forty-seven items were eliminated: "16 items for being noncontroversial, 4 for duplication of content, 5 for ambiguity and 22 for both low validity and internal consistency" (Abdelhalim, 1956, p. 196). The remaining twenty-eight items comprise the scale.

RELIABILITY: The corrected split-half reliability for the scale was .921.

VALIDITY: No data are provided.

NOTES AND COMMENTS: (1) A factor analysis was performed on the responses from 300 men and women; four factors were identified. Factor I was labeled Alterationism, which is similar to radicalism-conservatism; Factor II was labeled Equality versus Emancipation; Factor III was labeled Matrimosexual versus Sociopolitical Alterationism; and Factor IV was labeled Realism versus Humanism.

(2) The scale was designed for use in Egypt. A large number of the items would not be relevant for use in Western countries because they pertain to issues such as polygamy and the unveiling of women.

SOURCE: See Abdelhalim, 1956.

BIBLIOGRAPHY:

Abdelhalim, I. H. "Factors Related to the Attitudes of Adults Towards Relations Between the Sexes in a Specific Culture." *International Journal of Social Psychiatry*, 1956, *2*, 196-206.

168. ATTITUDES TOWARD FEMINIST ISSUES SCALE (ATFI)

AUTHORS: Patricia B. Elmore, Annette M. Brodsky, and Nancy Naffziger

DATE: 1975

VARIABLES: Attitudes toward nine issues: human reproduction; childcare; politics and legislation; employment; overcoming of self-denigration; marriage and family; consciousness raising in media; religion; and education

TYPE OF INSTRUMENT: Summated rating scale

DESCRIPTION: The scale consists of 120 statements divided among the nine areas listed under Variables as follows: human reproduction—six items, childcare—five items, politics and legislation—sixteen items, employment—fifteen items, overcoming self-denigration—eight items, marriage and family—seventeen items, consciousness raising in media—twelve items, religion—eleven items, and education—thirty items. The response to each item is expressed on the following scale: strongly agree, agree, neutral (neither agree nor disagree), disagree, and strongly disagree. All items are phrased to reflect a positive attitude toward feminist issues.

PREVIOUSLY ADMINISTERED TO: College students

APPROPRIATE FOR: Ages 18 and older

ADMINISTRATION: The scale can be self-administered and can be completed in about thirty minutes.

SAMPLE ITEMS:

Human reproduction: Limiting one's own reproduction is a basic human right.

Childcare: Society has a responsibility toward all children to ensure that they are properly cared for and educated.

Politics and legislation: Sex discrimination should be forbidden in employment.

Employment: The minimum wage act should cover all female employees.

Overcoming self-denigration: Women must redirect their anger away from themselves and other women to the discriminatory laws, politics, and attitudes of our society.

Marriage and family: Marriage should be an equal partnership with shared economic responsibility.

Consciousness raising in media: Feminist views should receive equal time on TV and radio.

Religion: Church bodies should restate theological concepts which contribute to a false view of women.

Education: Prompt action should be taken to ensure that all universities and colleges that are federal contractors end discrimination against women.

SCORING: Items are objectively scored and equally weighted. The scale yields nine sub-scores and an overall score. Low scores are associated with positive attitudes.

DEVELOPMENT: The items were written by paraphrasing the resolutions of the 1970 national convention platform of the National Organization for Women, a feminist organization.

RELIABILITY: The scale was administered to 105 college students, 61 enrolled in an introductory women's studies course and 44 enrolled in an introductory psychology course. The students completed the scale once on the first day of class and again at the end of the course three months later. Test-retest reliabilities were computed for each of the subscores and for the total score. The correlations ranged from .47 to .85, with a median of .80. Internal consistency coefficients (alpha) ranged from .77 to .98, with a median of .91 (Elmore, Brodsky, and Naffziger, 1975).

VALIDITY: Using the sample described above, the means obtained by women's studies students and psychology students were compared. On every subscale and on the total score, women's studies students were significantly ($p < .05$) more positive in their attitudes. Furthermore, for eight of the nine subscales and on total score, women were significantly ($p < .05$) more positive in their attitudes than men. Women were not more positive than men on the Childcare subscale (Elmore, Brodsky, and Naffziger, 1975).

NOTES AND COMMENTS: This scale is probably the longest scale of its type. As a result, it is very comprehensive in its coverage of issues relating to the feminist movement. However, there seems to be overlap between some of the items. For example, four of the five items dealing with childcare relate to daycare centers.

SOURCE: See Elmore, Brodsky, and Naffziger, 1975; or Britton and Elmore, 1976.

BIBLIOGRAPHY:

Britton, V., and Elmore, P. B. "Leadership and Self-Development Workshop for Women: A Research Report." Paper presented at 32nd annual meeting of the American Personnel and Guidance Association, Chicago, April 1976. (ERIC Document Reproduction Service No. ED 124 837.)

Brodsky, A. M., Elmore, P. B., and Naffziger, N. "Development of the Attitudes Toward Feminist Issues Scale." *Measurement and Evaluation in Guidance,* 1976, *9,* 140-145.

Elmore, P. B., Brodsky, A. M., and Naffziger, N. "The Attitudes Toward Feminist Issues Scale: A Validation Study." Paper presented at 31st annual meeting of the American Personnel and Guidance Association, New York, 1975. (ERIC Document Reproduction Service No. ED 109 544.)

169. ATTITUDES TOWARD WOMEN SCALE (AWS)

AUTHORS: Janet T. Spence and Robert Helmreich

DATE: 1972

VARIABLE: Attitudes toward the rights and roles of women in contemporary society

TYPE OF INSTRUMENT: Summated rating scale

DESCRIPTION: The AWS consists of fifty-five statements which can be categorized into six theme areas: (1) vocational, educational, and intellectual roles (seventeen items); (2) freedom and independence (four items); (3) dating, courtship and etiquette (seven items); (4) drinking, swearing, and dirty jokes (three items); (5) sexual behavior (seven items); and (6) marital relations and obligations (seventeen items). Each item is accompanied by four response options: agree strongly, agree mildly, disagree mildly, and disagree strongly.

PREVIOUSLY ADMINISTERED TO: Ages 14 and older

APPROPRIATE FOR: Ages 14 and older

ADMINISTRATION: The scale can be self-administered. If machine-scorable answer sheets are used, verbal instructions are given for completing the identifying information— for example, name, sex, age. The scale can be completed in about forty minutes.

SAMPLE ITEMS:

Vocational, educational, and intellectual roles: Vocational and professional schools should admit the best qualified students, independent of sex.

Freedom and independence: A woman should not expect to go to exactly the same places or to have quite the same freedom of action as a man.

Dating, courtship, and etiquette: Under ordinary circumstances, men should be expected to pay all expenses while they're out on a date.

Drinking, swearing, and dirty jokes: Swearing and obscenity is more repulsive in the speech of a woman than a man.

Sexual behavior: There should be no greater barrier to an unmarried woman having sex with a casual acquaintance than having dinner with him.

Marital relations and obligations: Husbands and wives should be equal partners in planning the family budget.

SCORING: Items are objectively scored and equally weighted. Total scores can range from 0 (extremely conservative) to 165 (extremely liberal). Normative data are provided for college students and their parents (Spence and Helmreich, 1972a).

DEVELOPMENT: A pool of items was prepared, including many items from the Belief Pattern Scale for Measuring Attitudes Toward Feminism (#172). Items were included that described "roles and patterns of conduct in major areas of activity in which men and women were, in principle, capable of being granted equal rights" (Spence and Helmreich, 1972a, p. 3). After some preliminary analyses led to revising, eliminating, and adding items, a seventy-eight-item version of the scale was administered to 1000 college students. Item analyses and factor analyses were performed on the responses. The results of the statistical analyses and some judgmental factors resulted in the elimination of twenty-three items from the scale.

RELIABILITY: Test-retest reliabilities, with an average interval between testings of 3.8 months, were .93 for sixty-one college women and .92 for fifty-two college men (Etaugh, 1975b). Test-retest reliabilities for three groups of college women, with a three-month interval between testings, were .85 (n = 20), .89 (n = 23), and .88 (n = 34) (Canty, 1977).

Corrected split-half reliability based on the responses from 294 college students was .92 (Stein and Weston, 1976). The corrected split-half reliability based on twenty-seven ninth graders was .80 (Grant, 1977). The corrected split-half reliability based on twenty-two ninth graders who were taking the test for the second time was .86 (Grant, 1977).

VALIDITY: Spence and Helmreich (1972a) report data indicating that women score more liberally than men. College women (n = 768, $\overline{X}$ = 98.211) scored significantly higher than college men (n = 713, $\overline{X}$ = 89.261, p < .001). Likewise mothers of college students (n = 292, $\overline{X}$ = 86.5) scored significantly higher than fathers of college students (n = 232, $\overline{X}$ = 81.358, p < .01). Numerous other studies have also found that women score significantly more liberally than men in their attitudes toward women (Albright and Chang, 1976; Beach and Kimmel, 1976; Doyle, 1975; Etaugh, 1975a; Etaugh and Bowen, 1976; Lunneborg, 1974; and Valentine, Ellinger, and Williams, 1975). Only one study reports no such differences, but these results might stem from the fact that the low-SES rural Georgian sample was likely to be very conservative (Grant, 1977).

Spence and Helmreich (1972a) report that college women (n = 768) responded differently (p < .05) from college men (n = 713) on forty-seven of the fifty-five items. On eight of these forty-seven items, women responded in the more traditional direction. Mothers of college students (n = 292) responded differently (p < .05) from fathers of college students (n = 232) on thirty of the fifty-five items. On seven of these thirty items, mothers responded in the more traditional direction. Lunneborg (1974) obtained significant differences (p < .05) between men and women on only nine of the fifty-five items.

Several studies have found that attitudes toward women become more liberal as students proceed through college (Etaugh, 1975b; Etaugh and Bowen, 1976; Stein and Weston, 1976). Etaugh's (1975) findings were not consistent with this finding. Etaugh and Bowen (1976, p. 229) provide evidence to suggest that "more liberal attitudes over the college years may be partly due to drop out." Stein and Weston (1976) found that liberal attitudes toward women related in the expected direction to academic emphasis.

Researchers have compared groups of respondents and obtained results consistent with expectations. Spence and Helmreich (1972a) report that college students scored significantly higher than their parents. Lunneborg (1974) obtained significant differences between samples drawn from the North and from the South of the U.S. Numerous demographic indices (for example, church affiliation, major, grade point average, marital status, race, size of town, mother employed, religiosity, number of children) have significantly predicted AWS scores (Beach and Kimmel, 1976; Etaugh, 1975a).

Further evidence of construct validity derives from the successful results of studies using interventions designed to change attitudes toward women's roles, with these changes being measured with the AWS (Canty, 1977; Fiedler and Loeffler, 1977; Lunne-borg, 1974). One study (Grant, 1977) found no significant change in AWS scores after a women's course was given to twenty-seven ninth graders in a low-SES rural community in Georgia.

Scores on the Belief Pattern Scale for Measuring Attitudes Toward Feminism (#172), which provided the basis for the development of the AWS, were correlated with scores on the AWS. The correlation for thirty-seven men was .86 (p < .01); the correlation for thirty-nine women was .87 (p < .01); and the correlation for the combined group was .87 (p < .01) (Doyle, 1975). The correlation between scores on the AWS and scores on the Equalitarian Sex Role Preference Scale (#178), a measure of attitudes toward male-female sex role equality, was .90 (p < .001) for a sample of thirty boys and thirty girls (Kirsch, Shore, and Kyle, 1976).

NOTES AND COMMENTS: (1) Spence and Helmreich (1972a) factor analyzed the responses from college women, college men, mothers, and fathers. A factor analysis of the responses given by college men yielded three main factors: attitudes relating to "masculine superiority and the patriarchal family"; attitudes relating to "equality of opportunity for women"; and attitudes relating to "social-sexual relationships between men and women." A factor analysis of the responses given by college women yielded two main factors: "attributes of the 'conventional woman' in her relationship to men" and equality of opportunity and ability. Other factor analyses are reported by Walter (1974), Williams and King (1976), and Kahoe and Meadow (1977). The factor analysis of Kahoe and Meadow involved an additional nineteen items not included in the AWS and led to the development of the Kahoe-Meadow Attitudes Toward Women Scale (#189).

(2) At least three of the items on the AWS contain more than a single idea: "Divorced men should help support their children but should not be required to pay alimony if their wives are capable of working"; "Women should worry less about their rights and more about becoming good wives and mothers"; "It is ridiculous for a woman to run a locomotive and for a man to darn socks."

(3) A short form of the AWS has been developed (#170). Spence, Helmreich, and Stapp (1973) recommend that AWS be used when information is wanted on attitudes toward each of the issues represented by the items. They recommend using AWS-short form when one wishes to compare *groups* of persons on whether their attitudes toward women are more traditional or more liberal.

(4) Because the AWS and the AWS-short form (#170) have been used so extensively, more is known about their psychometric properties than is known about most of the instruments in this chapter.

SOURCE: See Spence and Helmreich, 1972a.

BIBLIOGRAPHY:

Abernathy, R. W., Abramowitz, S. I., Roback, H. B., Weitz, L. J., Abramowitz, C., and Tittler, B. "The Impact of an Intensive Consciousness-Raising Curriculum on Adolescent Women." *Psychology of Women Quarterly,* 1977, *2,* 138-148.

Abramowitz, C. V. "Sex Role Related Clinician and Client Effects on Attribution of Parental Responsibility for Child Psychopathology." Unpublished doctoral dissertation, George Peabody College for Teachers, 1975. (*Dissertation Abstracts International,* 1975, *36*[4-B], 1909.)

Abramowitz, C. V. "Blaming the Mother: An Experimental Investigation of Sex Role Bias in Countertransference." *Psychology of Women Quarterly,* 1977, *2,* 24-34.

Adelson, B. M. "Moral Judgment in Women as a Function of Field Independence, Feminist Attitudes, and Subjective Adult Experience." Unpublished doctoral dissertation, New York University, 1975. (*Dissertation Abstracts International,* 1975, *36*[4-B], 1897.)

Albright, D. G., and Chang, A. F. "An Examination of How One's Attitudes Toward Women are Reflected in One's Defensiveness and Self-Esteem." *Sex Roles,* 1976, *2,* 195-198.

Arvey, R. D., and Gross, R. H. "Satisfaction Levels and Correlates of Satisfaction in the Homemaker Job." *Journal of Vocational Behavior,* 1977, *10,* 13-24.

Beach, D., and Kimmel, E. "Attitudes Toward Women: A Comparison Study of Counselor Trainees." *Humanist Educator,* 1976, *14,* 209-220.

Bem, S. L. "On the Utility of Alternative Procedures for Assessing Psychological Androgyny." *Journal of Consulting and Clinical Psychology,* 1977, *45,* 196-205.

Boehm, V. R. "The Competent Woman Manager: Will Success Spoil Women's Lib?" Paper presented at 83rd annual meeting of the American Psychological Association, Chicago, September 1975.

Borod, J. C. "The Impact of a Women's Studies Course on Perceived Sex Differences, Real and Ideal Self-Perceptions, and Attitudes Toward Women's Rights and Roles." Unpublished doctoral dissertation, Case Western Reserve University, 1975. (*Dissertation Abstracts International,* 1976, *36*[8-B], 4127.)

Bowker, L. H., and Croci, A. "A Research Note on the Epidemiology of Attitudes Toward Women at a Liberal Arts College." *Journal Supplement Abstract Service Catalog of Selected Documents in Psychology,* 1974, *4,* 80.

Bowman, P. R. "The Relationship Between Attitudes Toward Women and the Treatment of Activity and Passivity." Unpublished doctoral dissertation, Boston University School of Education, 1976. (*Dissertation Abstracts International,* 1976, *36*[11-B], 3779.)

Bowman, P. R., and Nickerson, E. T. "Effectiveness of a Brief Intervention Strategy in Changing Attitudes Toward Women." Paper presented at the National Association of School Psychologists, Atlanta, January 1975.

Braun, J. S., and Chao, H. M. "Attitudes Toward Women: A Comparison of Asian-Born Chinese and American Caucasians." *Psychology of Women Quarterly,* 1978, *2,* 195-201.

Canty, E. M. "Effects of Women's Studies Courses on Women's Attitudes and Goals." Paper presented at 85th annual meeting of the American Psychological Association, San Francisco, August 1977.

Collins, A. M. "The Attitudes Toward Women Scale: Validity, Reliability, and Subscore Differentiation." Unpublished doctoral dissertation, University of Maryland, 1973. (*Dissertation Abstracts International,* 1974, *34*[11-A], 7325-7326.)

Collins, E. R. "A Role-Playing Workshop as a Facilitation of Change in Attitudes Toward Women." Unpublished doctoral dissertation, Boston University School of Education, 1975. (*Dissertation Abstracts International,* 1976, *36*[8-A], 5036-5037.)

Crawford, J. D. "A Comparative Study of Feminine Role Perception, Selected Personality Characteristics, and Career Development." Unpublished doctoral dissertation, Texas Technological University, 1975. (*Dissertation Abstracts International,* 1976, *36*[11-B], 5756-5757.)

Dorn, R. S. "The Effects of Sex Role Awareness Groups on Fear of Success, Verbal Task

Performance, and Sex Role Attitudes of Undergraduate Women." Unpublished doctoral dissertation, Boston University School of Education, 1975. (*Dissertation Abstracts International*, 1975, *36*[3-A], 1386.)

Doyle, J. A. "Comparison of Kirkpatrick's and Spence and Helmreich's Attitudes Toward Women Scales." *Psychological Reports*, 1975, *37*, 878.

Erickson, V. L. "Psychological Growth for Women: A Cognitive-Developmental Curriculum Intervention." *Counseling and Values*, 1974, *18*, 102-116.

Erskine, C. G. "The Effects of Consciousness-Raising Groups on Sex Role Stereotyping Among College Students." Unpublished doctoral dissertation, University of Iowa, 1974. (*Dissertation Abstracts International*, 1974, *35*[4-A], 1977.)

Etaugh, C. "Biographical Predictors of College Students' Attitudes Toward Women." *Journal of College Student Personnel*, 1975a, *16*, 273-275.

Etaugh, C. "Stability of College Students' Attitudes Toward Women During One School Year." *Psychological Reports*, 1975b, *36*, 125-126.

Etaugh, C., and Bowen, E. "Attitudes Toward Women: Comparison of Enrolled and Nonenrolled College Students." *Psychological Reports*, 1976, *38*, 229-230.

Etaugh, C., and Gerson, A. "Attitudes Toward Women: Some Biographical Correlates." *Psychological Reports*, 1974, *35*, 701-702.

Feild, H. S. "Effects of Sex of Investigator on Mail Survey Response Rates and Response Bias." *Journal of Applied Psychology*, 1975, *60*, 772-773.

Fiedler, L. J., and Loeffler, D. "A Psychological Development Curriculum for Adult Women: Design, Implementation, Assessment." Paper presented at 85th annual meeting of the American Psychological Association, San Francisco, August 1977.

Fischer, G. J. "Probability Learning and Attitudes Toward Women as a Function of Monetary Risk, Gain, and Sex." *Bulletin of the Psychonomic Society*, 1977, *9*, 201-203.

Follingstad, D. R. "Decreasing Conforming Behavior in Women: An Intervention Utilizing Male Support for Females' Abilities and an Exploration of Personality Variables Influencing Levels of Conformity." Unpublished doctoral dissertation, University of Colorado, 1974. (*Dissertation Abstracts International*, 1975, *35*[12-B], 6163-6164.)

Follingstad, D. R., Kilmann, P. R., and Robinson, E. A. "Prediction of Self-Actualization in Male Participants in a Group Conducted by Female Leaders." *Journal of Clinical Psychology*, 1976, *31*, 706-712.

Follingstad, D. R., Robinson, E. A., and Pugh, M. "Effects of Consciousness-Raising Groups on Measures of Feminism, Self-Esteem, and Social Desirability." *Journal of Counseling Psychology*, 1977, *24*, 223-230.

Gackenbach, J. I., and Auerbach, S. M. "Empirical Evidence for the Phenomenon of the 'Well-Meaning Liberal Male.' " *Journal of Clinical Psychology*, 1975, *31*, 632-635.

Gill, M. J. "Self-Esteem and Males' Receptiveness to Persuasion Toward Women's Liberation Ideology." Unpublished doctoral dissertation, Washington State University, 1975. (*Dissertation Abstracts International*, 1975, *36*[2-B], 886-887.)

Gilliam, J. R. "The Status of Texas High School Counselors' Attitudes Toward the Roles of Women." Unpublished doctoral dissertation, East Texas State University, 1975. (*Dissertation Abstracts International*, 1976, *36*[11-A], 7207.)

Goldberg, C. "Women Liberation Scale (WLS): A Measure of Attitude Toward Positions Advocated by Women's Groups." *Journal Supplement Abstract Service Catalog of Selected Documents in Psychology*, 1976, *6*, 13.

Gomes, B., and Abramowitz, S. I. "Sex-Related Patient and Therapist Effects on Clinical Judgment." *Sex Roles*, 1976, *2*, 1-13.

Grant, E. "The Effect of a Two-Week Women's Study on Student Attitudes Toward Women." *Journal of Social Studies Research,* 1977, *1,* 36-42.

Greenberg, R. P., and Zeldow, P. B. "Effect of Attitudes Toward Women on Sex Attribution." *Psychological Reports,* 1976, *39,* 807-813.

Gross, R. H., and Arvey, R. D. "Marital Satisfaction, Job Satisfaction, and Task Distribution in the Homemaker Job." *Journal of Vocational Behavior,* 1977, *11,* 1-13.

Gun, B. R. "A Study of the Effect of a Sex Role Stereotypy Workshop on Education: Students' Attitudes Toward Women." Unpublished doctoral dissertation, Boston University School of Education, 1975. (*Dissertation Abstracts International,* 1975, *36*[5-B], 2522-2523.)

Haas, S. F. "Perceptions of Male and Female Competence as a Function of Sex of Subject and Traditionality of Attitudes Toward Women." Unpublished doctoral dissertation, University of Cincinnati, 1976. (*Dissertation Abstracts International,* 1976, *37*[5-B], 2478.)

Hagen, R. L., and Kahn, A. "Discrimination Against Competent Women." *Journal of Applied Social Psychology,* 1975, *5,* 362-376.

Halas, C. M. "Sex Role Stereotypes: Perceived Childhood Socialization Experiences and the Attitudes and Behavior of Adult Women." *Journal of Psychology,* 1974a, *88,* 261-275.

Halas, C. M. "Sex Role Stereotypes: Perceived Childhood Socialization Experiences and the Attitudes and Behaviors of Mature Women." Unpublished doctoral dissertation, Arizona State University, 1974b. (*Dissertation Abstracts International,* 1974, *35*[3-A], 1499.)

Hardin, J. R. "Psychological Sex Role, Pattern of Need Achievement and Need Affiliation, and Attitudes Toward Women in Undergraduates." Unpublished doctoral dissertation, University of Pennsylvania, 1975. (*Dissertation Abstracts International,* 1976, *36*[12-B], 6335-6356.)

Heath, L., and Gurwitz, S. B. "Self-Presentation and Stereotypes: Is It Smart to Play Dumb?" Paper presented at 85th annual meeting of the American Psychological Association, San Francisco, August 1977.

Helwig, A. A. "Counselor Bias and Women." *Journal of Employment Counseling,* 1976, *13,* 58-67.

Hjelle, L. A., and Butterfield, R. "Self-Actualization and Women's Attitudes Toward Their Roles in Contemporary Society." *Journal of Psychology,* 1974, *87,* 225-230.

Hoffman, D. M., and Fidell, L. S. "Characteristics of Androgynous, Undifferentiated, Masculine, and Feminine Middle-Class Women." Paper presented at 85th annual meeting of the American Psychological Association, San Francisco, August 1977.

Holcomb, L. "Role Concepts and Self-Esteem in Church Women with Implications for Pastoral Counseling." *Journal of Psychology and Theology,* 1975a, *3,* 119-126.

Holcomb, L. "Role Concepts and Self-Esteem in Church Women with Implications for Pastoral Counseling." Unpublished doctoral dissertation, Syracuse University, 1974. (*Dissertation Abstracts International,* 1975b, *35*[11-A], 7057-7058.)

Howell, E. F. "Self-Presentation in Reference to Sex Role Stereotypes as Related to Level of Moral Development." Unpublished doctoral dissertation, New York University, 1975. (*Dissertation Abstracts International,* 1976, *36*[11-B], 5867.)

Hunt, P. L. "Female Childcare Workers: Their Feminine Identity Congruence, Attitudes Toward Women, Self-Actualization, and Marital Status." Unpublished doctoral dissertation, Indiana State University, 1975. (*Dissertation Abstracts International,* 1976, *36*[7-A], 4262.)

Joesting, J. "Personality Correlates of Sexism and Antisexism in College Students." *College Student Journal*, 1976, *10*, 194-196.

Johnson, R. W., and MacDonnell, J. "The Relationship Between Conformity and Male and Female Attitudes Toward Women." *Journal of Social Psychology*, 1974, *94*, 155-156.

Kahn, S. E. "Effects of a Program in Awareness of Sex Role Stereotypes for Helping Professionals." Unpublished doctoral dissertation, Arizona State University, 1975. (*Dissertation Abstracts International*, 1975, *36*[4-A], 2027.)

Kahoe, R. D., and Meadow, M. J. "Three Dimensions of Sexist Attitudes: Differential Relationships with Personality Variables." Paper presented at 85th annual meeting of the American Psychological Association, San Francisco, August 1977.

Kilmann, P. R., Follingstad, D. R., Price, M. G., Rowland, K. F., and Robinson, E. A. "Effects of a Marathon Group on Self-Actualization and Attitudes Toward Women." *Journal of Clinical Psychology*, 1976, *32*, 154-157.

Kilpatrick, D. G., and Smith, A. D. "Validation of the Spence-Helmreich Attitudes Toward Women Scale." *Psychological Reports*, 1974, *35*, 461-462.

Kirsch, P. A., Shore, M. F., and Kyle, D. G. "Ideology and Personality: Aspects of Identity Formation in Adolescents with Strong Attitudes Toward Sex Role Equalitarianism." *Journal of Youth and Adolescence*, 1976, *5*, 387-401.

Lavrakas, P. J. "Female Preference for Male Physiques." *Journal of Research in Personality*, 1975, *9*, 324-334.

Levy, S. J., and Doyle, K. M. "Attitudes Toward Women in a Drug Abuse Treatment Program." *Journal of Drug Issues*, 1974, *4*, 428-434.

Loo, R., and Logan, P. "Investigation of the Attitudes Toward Women Scale in Western Canada." *Canadian Journal of Behavioral Sciences*, 1977, *9*, 201-204.

Lunneborg, P. W. "Validity of Attitudes Toward Women Scale." *Psychological Reports*, 1974, *34*, 1281-1282.

McKenna, V. V. "Parental Attitudes and Personality." Paper presented at 85th annual meeting of the American Psychological Association, San Francisco, August 1977.

Marchbanks, J. I. B. "A Comparison of Honors-Program and Nonhonors-Program Females and Males with Emphasis on Traditional-Feminine and Nontraditional-Modern Female Role Characteristics." Unpublished doctoral dissertation, Washington State University, 1975. (*Dissertation Abstracts International*, 1975, *36*[2-A], 708-709.)

Marshak, W. P., Gillman, D. C., and Nelson, L. D. "Cadet Attitudes During the Admission of Women to the United States Air Force Academy." Paper presented at 85th annual meeting of the American Psychological Association, San Francisco, August 1977.

Miller, J. H. "Differential Treatment of Women and Men in Comprehensive Community Mental Health Centers." Unpublished doctoral dissertation, Florida State University, 1975. (*Dissertation Abstracts International*, 1976, *37*[1-B], 470.)

Minnigerode, F. A. "Attitudes Toward Homosexuality: Feminist Attitudes and Sexual Conservatism." *Sex Roles*, 1976a, *2*, 347-352.

Minnigerode, F. A. "Attitudes Toward Women, Sex Role Stereotyping, and Locus of Control." *Psychological Reports*, 1976b, *38*, 1301-1302.

Pomerantz, S., and House, W. C. "Liberated Versus Traditional Women's Performance Satisfaction and Perceptions of Ability." *Journal of Psychology*, 1977, *95*, 205-211.

Scott, R., Richards, A., and Wade, M. "Women's Studies as Change Agent." *Psychology of Women Quarterly*, 1977, *1*, 377-379.

Smith, A. D., Kilpatrick, D. G., Sutker, P. B., and Marcotte, D. B. "Male Student Professionals: Their Attitudes Toward Women, Sex, and Change." *Psychological Reports,* 1976, *39,* 143-148.

Speizer, J. J. "An Evaluation of the Changes in Attitudes Toward Women Which Occur as a Result of Participation in a Women's Studies Course." Unpublished doctoral dissertation, Boston University School of Education, 1975. (*Dissertation Abstracts International,* 1975, *36*[3-A], 1404.)

Spence, J. T., and Helmreich, R. L. "The Attitudes Toward Women Scale: An Objective Instrument to Measure Attitudes Toward the Rights and Roles of Women in Contemporary Society." *Journal Supplement Abstract Service Catalog of Selected Documents in Psychology,* 1972a, *2,* 66.

Spence, J. T., and Helmreich, R. L. "Who Likes Competent Women: Competence, Sex Role Congruence of Interests, and Subjects' Attitudes Toward Women as Determinants of Interpersonal Attraction." *Journal of Applied Social Psychology,* 1972b, *2,* 197-213.

Spence, J. T., and Helmreich, R. L. *Masculinity and Femininity: Their Psychological Dimensions, Correlates, and Antecedents.* Austin: University of Texas Press, 1978.

Spence, J. T., Helmreich, R. L., and Stapp, J. "A Short Version of the Attitudes Toward Women Scale (AWS)." *Bulletin of the Psychonomic Society,* 1973, *2,* 219-220.

Spence, J. T., Helmreich, R. L., and Stapp, J. "Likability, Sex Role Congruence of Interest, and Competence: It All Depends on How You Ask." *Journal of Applied Social Psychology,* 1975a, *5,* 93-109.

Spence, J. T., Helmreich, R. L., and Stapp, J. "Ratings of Self and Peers on Sex Role Attributes and Their Relation to Self-Esteem and Conceptions of Masculinity and Femininity." *Journal of Personality and Social Psychology,* 1975b, *32,* 29-39.

Stanley, G., Boots, M., and Johnson, C. "Some Australian Data on the Short Version of the Attitudes Toward Women Scale (AWS)." *Australian Psychologist,* 1975, *10,* 319-323.

Staten, B. J. "The Effect of Counselor Gender and Sex Role Attitudes on Change of Female Clients' Sex Role Attitudes." Unpublished doctoral dissertation, University of Southern California, 1974. (*Dissertation Abstracts International,* 1975, *35*[10-A], 6470.)

Stein, S. L., and Weston, L. C. "Attitudes Toward Women Among Female College Students." *Sex Roles,* 1976, *2,* 199-202.

Taylor, S. P., and Smith, I. "Aggression as a Function of Sex of Victim and Male Subject's Attitude Toward Women." *Psychological Reports,* 1974, *35,* 1095-1098.

Tipton, R. M. "Attitudes Toward Women's Roles in Society and Vocational Interests." *Journal of Vocational Interests,* 1976, *8,* 155-165.

Tipton, R. M., Bailey, K. G., and Obenchain, J. P. "Invasion of Males' Personal Space by Feminists and Nonfeminists." *Psychological Reports,* 1975, *37,* 99-102.

Trail, B. M. "Comparison of Attitudes Toward Women and Measures of Interests Between Feminist, Traditional Female, and Male University Students." Unpublished doctoral dissertation, Texas A & M University, 1975. (*Dissertation Abstracts International,* 1976, *36*[8-B], 4236.)

Trilling, B. A. "Factors Related to Women's Prejudice Against Women." Unpublished doctoral dissertation, Fordham University, 1975. (*Dissertation Abstracts International,* 1976, *36*[8-B], 4183-4184.)

Tyrrell, L. A. A. "Sex Role Attitudes of Young and Returning Female Community College Students." Unpublished doctoral dissertation, University of Michigan, 1976. (*Dissertation Abstracts International,* 1976, *37*[6-A], 3368-3369.)

Valentine, D., Ellinger, N., and Williams, M. "Sex Role Attitudes and the Career Choices of Male and Female Graduate Students." *Vocational Guidance Quarterly,* 1975, *24,* 48-53.

Volgy, S. S. "Sex Role Orientation and Measures of Psychological Well-Being Among Feminists, Housewives, and Working Women." Unpublished doctoral dissertation, University of Arizona, 1976. (*Dissertation Abstracts International,* 1976, *37*[1-B], 533.)

Wallace, D. H., and Barbach, L. G. "Preorgasmic Group Treatment." *Journal of Sex and Marital Therapy,* 1974, *1,* 146-154.

Walter, D. "Psychological Correlates of Sex Role Behavior." Unpublished master's thesis, California State University at Chico, 1974.

Wheeler, E. E., Wheeler, K. R., and Torres-Raines, R. "Women's Stereotypic Roles: A Replication and Standardization of the AWS and PAQ for Selected Ethnic Groups." Paper presented at the Southwestern Social Science Association/Southwestern Sociological Association, Dallas, March 1977.

Widom, C. S. "Self-Esteem, Sex Role Identity, and Feminism in Female Offenders." Paper presented at 85th annual meeting of the American Psychological Association, San Francisco, August 1977.

Williams, D., and King, M. "Sex Role Attitudes and Fear of Success as Correlates of Sex Role Behavior." *Journal of College Student Personnel,* 1976, *17,* 480-484.

Wysocki, S. R. "Differential Effects of Three Group Treatments on Self-Actualization and Attitudes Toward the Sex Roles of Women." Unpublished doctoral dissertation, University of Southern California, 1975. (*Dissertation Abstracts International,* 1976, *36*[11-A], 7316.)

Zeldow, P. B. "Psychological Androgyny and Attitudes Toward Feminism." *Journal of Consulting and Clinical Psychology,* 1976, *44,* 150.

Zuckerman, D. M. "Challenging the Traditional Female Role: An Exploration of Women's Attitudes and Career Aspirations." Unpublished doctoral dissertation, Ohio State University, 1976. (*Dissertation Abstracts International,* 1977, *38*[8-B], 3923-3924.) (ERIC Document Reproduction Service No. ED 134 878.)

Zuckerman, D. M. "Sex Role Attitudes and Life Goals of Technical College and University Students." Unpublished manuscript, 1978. Available from Diana Zuckerman, Yale University.

---

170. ATTITUDES TOWARD WOMEN-SHORT FORM (AWS-SHORT FORM)

AUTHORS: Janet T. Spence, Robert Helmreich, and Joy Stapp

DATE: 1973

VARIABLE: Attitudes toward the rights and roles of women in contemporary society

TYPE OF INSTRUMENT: Summated rating scale

DESCRIPTION: The AWS-short form consists of twenty-five statements taken from the AWS (#169). Each statement is accompanied by four response options: agree strongly, agree mildly, disagree mildly, and disagree strongly.

PREVIOUSLY ADMINISTERED TO: Ages 12 and older

APPROPRIATE FOR: Ages 12 and older

ADMINISTRATION: The scale is self-administered and can be completed in about fifteen minutes.

SAMPLE ITEMS: Swearing and obscenity are more repulsive in the speech of a woman than of a man.

Women should take increasing responsibility for leadership in solving the intellectual and social problems of the day.

SCORING: Items are objectively scored and equally weighted. Item scores are summed to yield a total score, which can range from 0 (extremely conservative) to 75 (extremely liberal). Normative data for college students and their parents are provided (Spence, Helmreich, and Stapp, 1973).

DEVELOPMENT: The full-length Attitudes Toward Women Scale (#169) was administered to 241 female and 286 male college students. Using their total AWS scores, the students were divided into quartiles and a separate item analysis was performed for each sex. The twenty-five items that best discriminated among quartiles for each sex and that had the highest item-total correlations were selected for the Attitudes Toward Women Scale-Short Form.

RELIABILITY: Stanley, Boots, and Johnson (1975) estimated the internal-consistency reliability of the AWS short form. For ninety-nine girls between the ages of 12 and 16, coefficient alpha was .81; for seventy-two women, coefficient alpha was .82; for sixty-two female and eighty-eight male college students, coefficient alpha was .89.

Spence, Helmreich, and Stapp (1973) report item-total correlations ranging from .31 to .73 for college students and .14 to .70 for parents of college students.

VALIDITY: Correlations between the full-length AWS and AWS short form were .968 for 286 college men, .969 for 241 college women, .956 for 292 mothers of college students, and .963 for 232 fathers of college students (Spence, Helmreich, and Stapp, 1973).

Spence, Helmreich, and Stapp (1973) found that college women (n = 241, $\overline{X}$ = 50.26) scored significantly higher than college men (n = 286, $\overline{X}$ = 44.80, p < .001). Likewise, they found that mothers of college students (n = 292, $\overline{X}$ = 41.86) scored significantly higher than fathers of college students (n = 232, $\overline{X}$ = 39.22, p < .001). Other studies have also demonstrated that men score more traditionally than women on the AWS short form (Heath and Gurwitz, 1977; Helwig, 1976; Minnigerode, 1976b; and Zuckerman, 1976). Spence, Helmreich, and Stapp (1975b) did not find significant differences between college men and women.

Kilpatrick and Smith (1974) found that members of the National Organization for Women, a feminist group, scored significantly higher (p < .001) on AWS-short form than college women and mothers of college women. Stanley, Boots, and Johnson (1975) administered the AWS short form to five groups of women: a women's political group, college women, housewives, members of a women's religious fellowship, and a "Country Women's Association." The results rank ordered the five groups in the expected direction, and the differences between each of the successive groups were significant (p < .05).

Spence, Helmreich, and Stapp (1975b) report significant correlations between scores on the AWS short form and scores on the Personal Attributes Questionnaire (#39), a measure of masculinity-femininity. Minnegerode (1976b) found that the AWS short form correlated significantly with a measure of sexual liberalism-conservatism. Boehm (1975, p. 7) reports data showing that women managers who scored higher in nontraditional attitudes toward women also significantly more often endorsed a "nontraditional relatively high-risk style of resolving role conflict by responding outside of the stereotypical characteristics of both roles."

Both Halas (1974a) and Spence, Helmreich, and Stapp (1975a) report that different results are obtained when AWS short form is used to measure attitudes than when projective techniques are used to measure attitudes.

NOTES AND COMMENTS: (1) Spence, Helmreich, and Stapp (1973) recommend that AWS-short form be used when one wishes to compare *groups* of persons on whether their attitudes toward women are more traditional or more liberal. They recommend that AWS (#169) be used when information is wanted regarding attitudes toward each of the issues represented by the items.

(2) A simplified version of the AWS appropriate for use with teenagers was developed by Stanley, Boots, and Johnson (1975). When given to sixty-two female and eighty-eight male college students, no significant differences were found between the simplified version and the AWS short form.

(3) Spence, Helmreich, and Stapp (1973) factor analyzed the scale and obtained one factor that accounted for 68 percent of the variance for females and 69 percent of the variance for males.

(4) Stanley, Boots, and Johnson (1975) factor analyzed the responses from three groups: ninety-nine girls between the ages of 12 and 16; seventy-two women, including political activists, housewives, members of a religious group, and members of a Country Women's Association; and sixty-two college women. Seven factors were obtained for the college women, and the factors were "virtually impossible" to interpret. Four factors, similar in structure, were obtained for the first two groups. The strongest factor, Puritan Ethic, involved the "ideal expectations about behavior of women being more moral and upright than that of men" (p. 322). The other three factors were labeled Equality of Women with Men; Family and Social Role; and Equal Freedom of Action.

SOURCE: See Spence, Helmreich, and Stapp, 1973; or ETS Tests in Microfiche Collection (#007199).

BIBLIOGRAPHY:

See the bibliography accompanying Attitudes Toward Women (#169).

171. AUTONOMY FOR WOMEN INVENTORY

AUTHOR: Catherine Cameron Arnott

DATE: 1971

VARIABLE: Attitude toward self-determination for women

TYPE OF INSTRUMENT: Summated rating scale

DESCRIPTION: The inventory consists of ten statements; five reflect a positive attitude and five reflect a negative attitude toward self-determination for women. Responses are indicated on a four-point scale: strong agreement, mild agreement, mild disagreement, and strong disagreement.

PREVIOUSLY ADMINISTERED TO: Adults

APPROPRIATE FOR: Ages 16 and older

ADMINISTRATION: The scale can be self-administered and can be completed in less than five minutes.

SAMPLE ITEMS: The word "obey" should be removed from the marriage service.
              Girls should be trained to be homemakers and boys for an occupation suited to their talents.

SCORING: Items are objectively scored and equally weighted. Total scores can range from 10 points (strongly negative) to 70 points (strongly positive). Arnott (1971) classified respondents on the basis of their total scores: 10-25 was considered conservative, 33-47 was considered average, and 55-70 was considered liberal.

DEVELOPMENT: An item pool was compiled based on a search of the relevant literature. Ten doctoral candidates in sociology acted as judges and were asked to rate twenty-seven items in terms of whether the items expressed a strongly negative, negative, neutral, positive, or strongly positive attitude toward autonomy. The items on which the judges generally agreed that a strongly positive or strongly negative attitude was being expressed comprise the scale.

RELIABILITY: The scale was administered to fifteen college students on two occasions separated by about six weeks. The correlation between the two testings was .78 (Arnott, 1971).

VALIDITY: Arnott (1971) administered a version of the scale to two groups of women: members of a women's liberation group and members of the Women's Christian Temperance Union, a conservative group. A comparison of the means obtained by the two groups yielded statistically significant results (p < .0005). The women's liberation group expressed more positive attitudes toward autonomy for women (Arnott, 1971).
    Arnott (1973) administered the scale to members of the National Organization for Women (liberal group) and to participants in Fascinating Womanhood classes (conserva-

tive group). The mean of the liberal group ($\overline{X}$ = 62.4) was significantly different from the mean of the conservative group ($\overline{X}$ = 27.3, p < .001).

Greenhouse and Rosenthal (1974) administered the scale to 223 women and 146 men. They found that women were significantly more favorable than men toward autonomy for women (p < .001), and persons under age 30, compared with persons over age 30, were significantly more favorable toward autonomy for women (p < .01).

Green and Cunningham (1975) used the Autonomy for Women Inventory to classify women into three groups: conservatives, moderates, and liberals. As predicted, "Husbands of liberal wives were perceived as making fewer purchasing decisions on their own than was the case for husbands of either moderate or conservative wives" (p. 331).

NOTES AND COMMENTS: (1) Greenhouse and Rosenthal (1974) offered respondents only two response options: yes or no. They scored the scale by assigning 1 or 2 points to each response.

(2) An examination of the items makes it difficult to believe that the scale is actually measuring attitudes toward autonomy for women. The scale might more accurately be described as measuring attitudes toward women's issues.

(3) This scale is also described in *Family Measurement Techniques* (Straus and Brown, 1978, p. 107).

SOURCE: See Arnott, 1972; or Greenhouse and Rosenthal, 1974.

BIBLIOGRAPHY:

Arnott, C. C. "Commitment and Congruency in the Role Preference of Married Women: An Interpersonal Approach." Unpublished doctoral dissertation, University of Southern California, 1971. (*Dissertation Abstracts International*, 1972, *33*[3-A], 1246.)

Arnott, C. C. "Husbands' Attitude and Wives' Commitment to Employment." *Journal of Marriage and the Family*, 1972, *34*, 673-684.

Arnott, C. C. "Feminists and Antifeminists as 'True Believers.' " *Sociology and Social Research*, 1973, *57*, 300-306.

Green, R. T., and Cunningham, I. C. M. "Feminine Role Perception and Family Purchasing Decisions." *Journal of Marketing Research*, 1975, *12*, 325-332.

Greenhouse, P., and Rosenthal, E. "Attitudes Toward Women's Rights to Self-Determination." *Journal of Family Counseling*, 1974, *2*, 64-70.

*Straus, M. A., and Brown, B. W. *Family Measurement Techniques: Abstracts of Published Instruments, 1935-1974*. Minneapolis: University of Minnesota Press, 1978.

172. BELIEF PATTERN SCALE FOR MEASURING ATTITUDES TOWARD FEMINISM-FORM A

AUTHOR: Clifford Kirkpatrick

DATE: 1936

VARIABLE: Attitudes toward feminism

TYPE OF INSTRUMENT: Checklist

DESCRIPTION: The instrument consists of eighty items. There are ten feminist and ten antifeminist statements in each of four areas: economic, domestic, political-legal, and conduct and social status. Respondents are to place a check mark next to each statement they agree with. If they feel strongly about a statement they agree with, two check marks should be placed next to the statements. There are three forms of the scale: A, B, and C.

PREVIOUSLY ADMINISTERED TO: Ages 11-82; English, French, German, Moroccan, and American college students

APPROPRIATE FOR: Ages 16 and older

ADMINISTRATION: The scale is self-administered and can be completed in thirty to forty minutes.

SAMPLE ITEMS:

Economic: Women have the right to compete with men in every sphere of economic activity.

Domestic: A woman who refuses to bear children has failed in her duty to her husband.

Political-legal: A husband should have the right to dispose of family property as he may please.

Conduct and social status: The use of profane or obscene language by a woman is no more objectionable than the same usage by a man.

SCORING: Items are objectively scored and equally weighted. Five scores are obtained: a total score and a score for each of the four areas. The total score can range from −40 (strongly antifeminist) to +40 (strongly profeminist). Scores in each of the four areas can range from −10 (strongly antifeminist) to +10 (strongly profeminist).

DEVELOPMENT: From relevant literature, ten specific issues were identified in each of four areas: economic, domestic, political-legal, and conduct and social status. An item pool was constructed to represent the forty issues identified. Many items in the pool "were adapted from a list of the 86 official resolutions of feminist organizations" (Kirkpatrick, 1936b, p. 422). The statements were given to thirteen judges who were instructors and graduate students in sociology. The responses of the judges to the eighty statements were as follows: "(1) All of the 13 judges agreed on the Feminist-Antifeminist classification for 72 statements, and 12 of the judges agreed on the classification for the remaining 8. (2) All of the 13 judges agreed on the subcategory classification for 66 statements, 12 judges for 10 statements, and 11 for 4 statements. (3) All of the 13 judges agreed on the classification according to subheading for 71 of the statements, and 2 of the judges agreed on the remaining 9" (Kirkpatrick, 1936b, p. 423).

RELIABILITY: Fifty-nine students completed the scale on two occasions separated by one week. Test-retest reliability was .85. Forms A and B of the scale were completed by 217 college students. Alternate-form reliability was .89. Ninety-six college men completed Forms A and C of the scale. Alternate-form reliability was .94 (Kirkpatrick, 1936b).

Each of the three forms of the test was constructed to meet the same specifications, that is, one profeminist and one antifeminist statement for each of the ten issues in each of the four areas. Therefore each item on Form A has a counterpart on Forms B and C. For the 217 college students who completed Forms A and B, rank-order correlations were computed between the proportion of students accepting comparable statements on the two forms. For females, the correlation was .75; for males the correlation was .58 (Kirkpatrick, 1936b).

VALIDITY: Kirkpatrick (1936b) contends that the method of scale construction provides evidence of the content validity of the scale. In order to determine whether the scale discriminates between groups with opposing views, it was completed by eighty-eight feminists and fifty-six Lutheran ministers. Since no statistical tests were performed to determine the significance of the difference between groups, one must rely on subjective judgment to evaluate the difference. Nevertheless, the data strongly suggest that the scale can differentiate between the two groups. For example, on total score, the feminist group obtained a mean of 22.66, while the Lutheran ministers obtained a mean of .71. Similarly, in the sample of 217 college students, males had a mean score of 6.1, while females had a mean score of 16.8 (Kirkpatrick, 1936b).

Roper and Labeff (1977) obtained completed scales from 282 college students. They found that female students ($\overline{X}$ = 23.3) scored significantly higher than male students ($\overline{X}$ = 15.1, p < .05); students' mothers ($\overline{X}$ = 17.1) scored significantly higher than students' fathers ($\overline{X}$ = 13.0, p < .05); female students scored significantly higher than mothers of students (p < .05); male students scored significantly higher than fathers of students (p < .05); female students scored significantly higher than fathers of students (p < .05); and male students scored higher (nonsignificant) than mothers of students. These differences, based on data collected in 1974, were all consistent with the differences found by Kirkpatrick, whose findings were based on data collected in 1934. Kirkpatrick, however, did not report the significance of the differences.

Doyle (1975a) administered this scale and the Attitudes Toward Women Scale (#169) to thirty-seven college men and thirty-nine college women. The correlation between scores on the two scales was .86 for college men, .87 for college women, and .87 for men and women combined.

NOTES AND COMMENTS: (1) Doyle (1976) administered the Belief Pattern Scale for Measuring Attitudes Toward Feminism to 150 college students. He compared his results with the results obtained approximately forty years earlier by Kirkpatrick. Doyle concluded, "It appears that a substantial profeminist attitudinal shift has occurred among contemporary university females and males alike over the past forty years" (p. 400). Thus, the mean scores obtained by Kirkpatrick are lower than the mean scores that are obtained when the scale is used today.

(2) Researchers have investigated the relationship between scores on the Belief Pattern Scale for Measuring Attitudes Toward Feminism and numerous other variables, including sex (Doyle, 1975a, 1975b; Gold and Andres, 1976, 1978; Kirkpatrick, 1936a, 1936d, 1936f; Neiman, 1954; Roper and Labeff, 1977); age (Kirkpatrick, 1936a, 1936f; Neiman, 1954; Roper and Labeff, 1977); parental variables (Kirkpatrick, 1936a; Seward, 1945; Tyler, 1941); socioeconomic status (Tyler, 1941); marital adjustment (Kirkpatrick, 1939); sex and sexuality (Seward, 1945); education (Kirkpatrick, 1936a; Roper and Labeff, 1977); religion (Seward, 1945); intelligence (Seward, 1945; Tyler, 1941); mother's employment (Gold and Andres, 1976, 1978; Seward, 1945); masculinity-femininity scores (Seward, 1945; Tyler, 1941); nationality (Brotman and Senter, 1968); racism (Morado, 1973); political attitudes (Fowler, Fowler, and Van de Riet, 1973); self-actualizing beliefs (Doyle, 1975b); and sex composition of the group in which the scale is completed (Shomer and Centers, 1970).

(3) The Belief Pattern Scale for Measuring Attitudes Toward Feminism is the oldest scale measuring a variety of issues. Despite its age, many items are still relevant today. As a result, it has served as the basis for the development of many similar scales, with the best known and most frequently used being the Attitudes Toward Women Scale (#169).

(4) MacDonald (1974, p. 166) wrote a searing critique of the Belief Pattern Scale: "Many of the items are dated in content and wording, no information is available concerning the extent to which scores might be affected by social desirability response bias, the instrument treats attitudes toward equal rights as unidimensional, and the wording is often too sophisticated for administration to children and adults with low reading abilities. Also, the items tend to be culture bound, rendering them inadvisable for use in cross-cultural research." Many of these criticisms are equally applicable to many other scales for measuring attitudes toward a variety of sex role issues.

(5) The Belief Pattern Scale for Measuring Attitudes Toward Feminism is also described in *Family Measurement Techniques* (Straus, 1969, pp. 167-168; Straus and Brown, 1978, p. 111) and *Scales for the Measurement of Attitudes* (Shaw and Wright, 1967, pp. 278-287).

SOURCE: See Kirkpatrick, 1936b; or Shaw and Wright, 1967, p. 280.

BIBLIOGRAPHY:

Brotman, J., and Senter, R. J. "Attitudes Toward Feminism in Different National Student Groups." *Journal of Social Psychology,* 1968, *76,* 137-138.

Doyle, J. A. "Comparison of Kirkpatrick's and Spence and Helmreich's Attitudes Toward Women Scales." *Psychological Reports,* 1975a, *37,* 878.

Doyle, J. A. "Self-Actualization and Attitudes Toward Women." *Psychological Reports,* 1975b, *37,* 899-902.

Doyle, J. A. "Attitudes Toward Feminism—Forty Years Later." *Sex Roles,* 1976, *2,* 399-400.

Fowler, M. G., Fowler, R. L., and Van de Riet, H. "Feminism and Political Radicalism." *Journal of Psychology,* 1973, *83,* 237-242.

Gold, D., and Andres, D. "Relations Between Maternal Employment and Development of Nursery School Children." Paper presented at the Canadian Psychological Association Convention, Toronto, June 1976. (ERIC Document Reproduction Service No. ED 135 461.)

Gold, D., and Andres, D. "Relations Between Maternal Employment and Development of Nursery School Children." *Canadian Journal of Behavioral Science,* 1978, *10,* 116-129.

Kirkpatrick, C. "A Comparison of Generations in Regard to Attitudes Toward Feminism." *Journal of Genetic Psychology,* 1936a, *39,* 343-361.

Kirkpatrick, C. "The Construction of a Belief-Pattern Scale for Measuring Attitudes Toward Feminism." *Journal of Social Psychology,* 1936b, *7,* 421-437.

Kirkpatrick, C. "Content of a Scale for Measuring Attitudes Toward Feminism." *Sociology and Social Research,* 1936c, *20,* 512-526.

Kirkpatrick, C. "An Experimental Study of the Modification of Social Attitudes." *American Journal of Sociology,* 1936d, *41,* 649-656.

Kirkpatrick, C. "Inconsistency in Attitudinal Behavior with Special Reference to Attitudes Toward Feminism." *Journal of Applied Psychology,* 1936e, *20,* 535-552.

Kirkpatrick, C. "The Measurement of Ethical Inconsistency in Marriage." *International Journal of Ethics,* 1936f, *46,* 444-460.

Kirkpatrick, C. "A Methodological Analysis of Feminism in Relation to Marital Adjustment." *American Sociological Review,* 1939, *4,* 325-334.

Lilly, R. "Psychodynamics of the Attitudes of Ex-Service Men Toward Feminism." *American Psychologist,* 1947, *2,* 413.

Lott, B. E. "Who Wants the Children? Some Relationships Among Attitudes Toward Children, Parents, and the Liberation of Women." *American Psychologist,* 1973, *28,* 573-582.

*MacDonald, A. P., Jr. "Identification and Measurement of Multidimensional Attitudes Toward Equality Between the Sexes." *Journal of Homosexuality,* 1974, *1,* 165-182.

Morado, C. "Racism and Sexism: An Investigation of Common Traits." Unpublished doctoral dissertation, Boston University Graduate School, 1973. (*Dissertation Abstracts International,* 1973, *34*[4-B], 1729-1730.)

Neiman, L. J. "The Influence of Peer Groups upon Attitudes Toward the Feminine Role." *Social Problems,* 1954, *2,* 104-111.

Roper, B. S., and Labeff, E. "Sex Roles and Feminism Revisited: An Intergenerational Attitude Comparison." *Journal of Marriage and the Family,* 1977, *39,* 113-118.

Seward, G. H. "Cultural Conflict and the Feminine Role: An Experimental Study." *Journal of Social Psychology,* 1945, *22,* 177-194.

*Shaw, M. E., and Wright, J. M. *Scales for the Measurement of Attitudes.* New York: McGraw-Hill, 1967.

Shomer, R. W., and Centers, R. "Differences in Attitudinal Responses Under Conditions of Implicitly Manipulated Group Salience." *Journal of Personality and Social Psychology,* 1970, *15,* 125-132.

*Straus, M. A. *Family Measurement Techniques: Abstracts of Published Instruments, 1935-1965.* Minneapolis: University of Minnesota Press, 1969.

*Straus, M. A., and Brown, B. W. *Family Measurement Techniques: Abstracts of Published Instruments, 1935-1974.* Minneapolis: University of Minnesota Press, 1978.

Tyler, L. "The Measured Interests of Adolescent Girls." *Journal of Educational Psychology,* 1941, *32,* 561-572.

173. BELIEFS ABOUT EQUAL RIGHTS SCALE (BAERS)

AUTHORS: Leonard I. Jacobson, Carole L. Anderson, Mark S. Berletich, and Kenneth W. Berdahl

DATE: 1976

VARIABLE: Beliefs about equal rights for men and women

TYPE OF INSTRUMENT: True-false

DESCRIPTION: The instrument consists of twenty-eight statements, sixteen of which are phrased to reflect a negative attitude toward equality between the sexes and twelve of which are phrased to reflect a positive attitude. For each statement, the respondents are to indicate whether they believe the statement is true or false.

PREVIOUSLY ADMINISTERED TO: College students and adults

APPROPRIATE FOR: Ages 16 and older

ADMINISTRATION: The scale can be self-administered and can be completed in about ten minutes.

SAMPLE ITEMS: I would vote for a man rather than a woman for a political position.
I believe that the liberation of women will also benefit men.

SCORING: Items are objectively scored and equally weighted. Total scores can range from 0 (strongly opposed to equality between the sexes) to 28 (strongly in favor of equality between the sexes).

DEVELOPMENT: Fifty-nine items that were judged to have content validity were selected from a pool of seventy-five items. The fifty-nine items were administered to college students, and an item analysis was performed of their responses. The thirty-six items that had item-total correlations significant at the .05 level were administered to another group of college students. Using the responses from this sample, twenty-eight items had item-total correlations significant at the .01 level. These twenty-eight items comprise the scale.

RELIABILITY: Kuder-Richardson reliability based on the responses from sixty-three college students was .86.
Item-total correlations for the BAERS all were significant at the .02 level. The median point biserial correlation was .48.

VALIDITY: BAERS and the Attitudes Toward Women Scale (#169) were both administered to sixty-three college students. The correlation between the two measures was .14 (nonsignificant), suggesting that they are measuring different variables.
When the BAERS was administered to a sample of 110 college students, it was found that the mean score for women ($\overline{X}$ = 19.66) was significantly higher than the mean score for men ($\overline{X}$ = 16.30, p < .003). Furthermore, when the means for these male and female college students were compared with the means obtained from male and female

members of the National Organization for Women (NOW), a feminist organization, significant differences were found. The mean for men in NOW ($\bar{X}$ = 24.38) was significantly higher than the mean for college men (p < .001), and the mean for women in NOW ($\bar{X}$ = 26.00) was significantly higher than the mean for college women (p < .001). These results are all consistent with predictions.

NOTES AND COMMENTS: (1) The instrument's authors contend that BAERS differs from other measures because it considers attitudes toward both men and women, whereas other scales are concerned only with attitudes toward women. As evidence that attitudes toward sex roles is a "multidimensional phenomenon," they cite the nonsignificant correlation between BAERS and AWS (#169). An examination of the items included on BAERS suggests that they are in fact not different from the items included on many other instruments in this chapter.

(2) Many of the items on this instrument violate established guidelines for phrasing attitude statements. For example, "Sons should be encouraged to become 'strong men' and daughters should be encouraged to become 'pretty girls' " is a statement that includes more than a single idea; the statement "Leadership of our country and communities should remain in the hands of men" assumes that the respondent perceives that leadership is already in the hands of men; the statement "If a husband is offered a good job in one city and the wife a good job in another city, the family should move in every case to the husband's job," violates the guideline that recommends avoiding "universals"—that is, statements that involve "always" or "never."

SOURCE: See Jacobson, Anderson, Berletich, and Berdahl, 1976.

BIBLIOGRAPHY:

Jacobson, L. I., Anderson, C. L., Berletich, M. S., and Berdahl, K. W. "Construction and Initial Validation of a Scale Measuring Beliefs About Equal Rights for Men and Women." *Educational and Psychological Measurement,* 1976, *36,* 913-918.

---

174. BROWN-HELLINGER SCALE OF ATTITUDES TOWARD WOMEN

AUTHORS: Caree Rozen Brown and Marilyn Levitt Hellinger

DATE: 1975

VARIABLE: Contemporary versus traditional attitudes toward women

TYPE OF INSTRUMENT: Summated rating scale

DESCRIPTION: The scale consists of twenty-nine statements concerning women in regard to such issues as marital roles, maternal roles, sexuality, and personality. Traditional attitudes are reflected in eighteen statements; contemporary attitudes are reflected in eleven statements. Each statement is accompanied by seven response options: strongly agree, agree, mildly agree, undecided, mildly disagree, disagree, and strongly disagree.

PREVIOUSLY ADMINISTERED TO: Psychiatrists, psychiatric residents, psychiatric nurses, social workers, and psychologists

APPROPRIATE FOR: Ages 16 and older

ADMINISTRATION: The scale can be self-administered and can be completed in less than ten minutes.

SAMPLE ITEMS:

Contemporary: A woman is capable of handling the responsibilities of a career, marriage, and family simultaneously.

Traditional: The wife who proves to be the better breadwinner should use extraordinary tact in handling her situation.

SCORING: Items are objectively scored and equally weighted. Two mean scores are obtained: the mean of the contemporary items and the mean of the traditional items. A contemporary-traditional ratio is obtained by dividing the contemporary mean score by the traditional mean score.

DEVELOPMENT: The items included on the scale "were selected from a review of a larger sample of items by social work professors and students. Subsequently, a pilot test was conducted for the purpose of purifying and testing the questionnaire" (p. 268). No additional information is provided.

RELIABILITY: Fifteen graduate students completed the scale on two occasions separated by a one-week interval. Test-retest reliability based on their responses was .757. Corrected split-half reliability based on the responses from 177 people was .564.

VALIDITY: The authors stated three a priori hypotheses: (1) "Therapists have attitudes toward women that tend to be more traditional than contemporary"; (2) Female therapists tend to have attitudes toward women that are more contemporary than those of male therapists"; and (3) "Social workers tend to have attitudes toward women that are more contemporary than those of other therapists" (p. 267). The responses from 274 therapists were used to test the hypotheses. The data failed to support hypotheses 1 and 3. Hypothesis 2 was supported (p < .05).

SOURCE: See Brown and Hellinger, 1975.

BIBLIOGRAPHY:

Brown, C. R., and Hellinger, M. L. "Therapists' Attitudes Toward Women." *Social Work*, 1975, *20*, 266-270.

175. CENTERS SCALE OF ATTITUDES TOWARD WOMEN

AUTHOR: Richard Centers

DATE: 1963

VARIABLE: Attitudes toward women

TYPE OF INSTRUMENT: Alternate choice and multiple choice

DESCRIPTION: The instrument consists of twelve questions regarding women or women in comparison to men. There are two response alternatives for each of ten items, but the response alternatives are not the same for each question. There are three response alternatives for the other two questions.

PREVIOUSLY ADMINISTERED TO: Adults

APPROPRIATE FOR: Ages 16 and older

ADMINISTRATION: The scale was administered as part of an interview. It could easily be adapted for self-administration. As a self-administered measure, it could be completed in five minutes.

SAMPLE ITEMS: Do you approve or disapprove of women having the same educational advantages as men?
                    Which are more extravagant, men or women?

SCORING: Items are objectively scored and equally weighted. Total scores can range from 12 (very positive attitudes toward women) to 36 (very negative attitudes toward women).

DEVELOPMENT: The scale was developed by the "usual trial-and-error procedure of collating a large number of possible items and, by pretesting, eliminating those unsuitable for use in a survey while retaining the most promising ones for this type of inquiry" (p. 82). The final survey contained twenty-five items, but thirteen were eliminated from the analysis because they had unsuitable intercorrelations.

RELIABILITY: Centers presents a correlation matrix showing the intercorrelations between the twelve items. They range from .01 to .60.

VALIDITY: The Centers Scale of Attitudes Toward Women was administered along with a measure of authoritarianism to a sample of 750 adults. The correlation between the two measures was .23 ($p < .001$) for male respondents and .25 ($p < .001$) for female respondents. No significant differences between mean scores were found when contrasting groups based on age, education, race, socioeconomic status, social class identification, marital status, and occupation.

SOURCE: See Centers, 1963.

BIBLIOGRAPHY:

Centers, R. "Authoritarianism and Misogyny." *Journal of Social Psychology*, 1963, *61*, 81-85.

---

176. CRITELLI SEX ROLE TRADITIONALITY SCALE

AUTHOR: Joseph W. Critelli

DATE: 1975

VARIABLE: Attitudes toward traditional or nontraditional sex roles

TYPE OF INSTRUMENT: Summated rating scale

DESCRIPTION: There are two forms of this scale: a Female Sex Role Traditionality Scale and a Male Sex Role Traditionality Scale. The female form includes forty-seven items covering fourteen areas: child rearing (three items); household duties (four items); male dominance (four items); Women's Liberation Movement (three items); female career importance (three items); emotional behavior, stereotypical female behaviors (five items); desire for a home and family (three items); male chauvinism (three items); body care (two items); dating behavior (four items); sexual behavior (three items); preferences for achievement versus housewife role (five items); dominance or initiative in sexual behavior (two items); and reactions to popular media personalities (three items). The male form includes thirty-four items covering ten areas: child rearing (three items); household duties (five items); male dominance (five items); Women's Liberation Movement (three items); female career importance (three items); desire for a housewife (two items); male chauvinism (three items); reactions to popular media personalities (three items); status relations with women in work situations (four items); and reactions to women's sexual liberation (three items). Twenty-two items are identical on the two scales. Each item is accompanied by five response options: agree, tend to agree, neither agree nor disagree, tend to disagree, and disagree.

PREVIOUSLY ADMINISTERED TO: College students

APPROPRIATE FOR: Ages 16 and older

ADMINISTRATION: The scale is self-administered and can be completed in about twenty minutes.

SAMPLE ITEMS:

Male Sex Role Traditionality: I don't like to hear women using foul language.

Female Sex Role Traditionality: I would rather be popular with men than good in school.

SCORING: Items are objectively scored and equally weighted. Scores can be obtained for the individual subscales (fourteen scores for females and ten scores for males) or for the three factors (see Notes and Comments below).

DEVELOPMENT: An item pool was developed by selecting items from existing measures of sex role attitudes and adding new items constructed by the author. In identifying items for the item pool, the following definitions were kept in mind: "Traditionality is . . . a sex role orientation with males and females each having their own distinct set of appropriate behaviors and responsibilities. Nontraditionality is . . . an absence of distinctions between male and female role behaviors" (Critelli, 1977, p. 4). The item pool was administered to 400 college students with the same five-point scale used in the final form of the scales. Using the intercorrelations between the items and a subjective judgment of the item content, items were grouped into subscales. The grouping of items was performed separately for males and for females. Subscales that did not have a correlation of at least .40 with total scores were eliminated. This resulted in fourteen subscales retained for females and ten subscales retained for males.

RELIABILITY: The corrected split-half reliability for both the male and female forms was .93 (Critelli, 1975).

VALIDITY: No data are provided.

NOTES AND COMMENTS: (1) Factor analyses were performed for the subscale scores. For the Male Sex Role Traditionality Scale, three factors were extracted to account for the ten subscale scores. The factors were labeled "desire for a traditional family life, with separate household roles and the male in control," "women's liberation movement," and "status relations with females in achievement or work-related situations" (Critelli, 1975, p. 80). Likewise, three factors were extracted to account for the fourteen subscale scores on the Female Sex Role Traditionality Scale. The factors were labeled "a general nontraditionality, with a minimum of role differences in both household and achievement situations," "dominance-subordinance in male-female relations, especially in sexual behavior," and "reactions to traditional female stereotypes, especially with respect to being overemotional and wanting to settle down" (Critelli, 1975, p. 82).

(2) Critelli indicates that subscale scores can be obtained, and the subscales are comprised of few items; therefore it is important to have data on the reliability of the subscales. Given how short the subscales are, it is quite likely that they are not very reliable.

(3) Critelli (1975) compared scores from the Critelli Sex Role Traditionality Scale with scores from measures of romantic attraction, physical attractiveness, friendship, emotional intensity, and self-disclosure.

SOURCE: See Critelli, 1975.

BIBLIOGRAPHY:

Critelli, J. W. "Romantic Attraction and Verbal Communication as a Function of Sex Role Traditionality." Unpublished doctoral dissertation, University of Illinois, 1975. (*Dissertation Abstracts International*, 1975, *36*[5-B], 2520.)

Critelli, J. W. "Romantic Attraction as a Function of Sex Role Traditionality." Paper presented at 85th annual meeting of the American Psychological Association, San Francisco, August 1977.

---

177. ENGELHARD ATTITUDES TOWARD WOMEN

AUTHOR: Patricia Auer Engelhard

DATE: 1969

VARIABLE: Emergent versus traditional attitudes toward women

TYPE OF INSTRUMENT: Summated rating scale

DESCRIPTION: There are two forms of the scale: a long form and a short form. The long form contains sixty-eight statements concerning attitudes toward the overall role of women, child rearing, discriminatory practices, education for women, and the nature of work for women. Half of the items are phrased to reflect traditional attitudes and half are phrased to reflect emergent (contemporary) attitudes. The short form includes eighteen statements that concern the same topics. Seven items are phrased to reflect emergent attitudes and eleven items are phrased to reflect traditional attitudes. The eighteen statements on the short form are all included on the long form. Each statement on both forms is accompanied by five response options: strongly disagree, mildly disagree, equally agree and disagree, mildly agree, and strongly agree.

PREVIOUSLY ADMINISTERED TO: College students and guidance counselors

APPROPRIATE FOR: Ages 16 and older

ADMINISTRATION: Both forms can be self-administered. The long form can be completed in about half an hour; the short form can be completed in about ten minutes.

SAMPLE ITEMS: A woman who works full time cannot possibly be as good a mother to her grade-school-age children as one who stays at home.
There should be a sex advantage to boys, other things being equal, on the granting of graduate fellowships.

SCORING: Items are objectively scored and equally weighted. On the long form, total scores can range from 68 (very traditional attitudes) to 340 (very emergent attitudes). On the short form, total scores can range from 18 (very traditional attitudes) to 90 (very emergent attitudes). In addition, on the short form, three factor scores may be obtained: (I) Working Mother, (II) Sex Role Definition, and (III) Societal Impact.

DEVELOPMENT: In developing the original scale, about one quarter of the items were taken from existing instruments and the remaining items resulted from pilot studies. To develop the short form, a factor analysis was performed on the responses obtained from guidance counselors who completed the long form of the scale. The "data suggested that the most prominent attitude dimensions of the survey could be efficiently measured with 18 of the original 68 items" (Engelhard, Jones, and Stiggins, 1976, p. 366).

RELIABILITY: Eckstein and Eckstein (1974) calculated the split-half reliability of the scale and obtained estimates ranging from .70 to .94. Engelhard, Jones, and Stiggins reported internal consistency reliability for each of the three factor scores: Factor I = .88; Factor II = .74; and Factor III = .69.

VALIDITY: As would be expected, female counselors scored significantly higher (more emergent attitudes) than male counselors (p < .001) (Engelhard, 1969). Results obtained by Otto (1973) and by Engelhard, Jones, and Stiggins (1976) confirmed this finding.

NOTES AND COMMENTS: A factor analysis performed on data obtained in 1968 yielded three factors. A factor analysis performed on data obtained in 1971 yielded the same three factors. Factor I was labeled Working Mother and "reflects the expected impact of working on the mothering of school-age and pre-school-age children" (Engelhard, Jones, and Stiggins, 1976, p. 366). Factor II was labeled Sex Role Definition and "reflects attitudes regarding roles assigned to the sexes" (Engelhard, Jones, and Stiggins, 1976, p. 366). Factor III was labeled Societal Impact and "focuses on the perceived utility of women's special talents" (Engelhard, Jones, and Stiggins, 1976, p. 366).

SOURCE: Full-length scale: Patricia Engelhard
                                    Edina-West Secondary School
                                    6754 Valley View Road
                                    Edina, Minnesota 55435

BIBLIOGRAPHY:

Eckstein, D., and Eckstein, J. "Investigating Emerging Attitudes Toward Women." 1974. (ERIC Document Reproduction Service No. ED 137 653.)
Engelhard, P. A. "A Survey of Counselor Attitudes Toward Women." Unpublished master's thesis, University of Minnesota, 1969.
Engelhard, P. A., Jones, K. O., and Stiggins, R. J. "Trends in Counselor Attitude About Women's Roles." *Journal of Counseling Psychology,* 1976, *23,* 365-372.
Otto, K. M. "Attitudes of Selected High School Counselors Toward Women." Unpublished master's thesis, Mankato State College, Minnesota, 1973.

178. EQUALITARIAN SEX ROLE PREFERENCE SCALE

AUTHOR: Patricia Anne Kirsch

DATE: 1974

VARIABLE: Attitudes toward male-female sex role equality

TYPE OF INSTRUMENT: Summated rating scale

DESCRIPTION: The scale consists of twenty-five statements about women, women's roles, and stereotyped views of men and women. All statements are phrased so that agreement indicates a traditional attitude. Each statement is accompanied by five response options: strongly agree, agree, neither agree nor disagree, disagree, and strongly disagree.

PREVIOUSLY ADMINISTERED TO: Ages 16-20; adults

APPROPRIATE FOR: Ages 14 and older

ADMINISTRATION: The scale can be self-administered and can be completed in about fifteen minutes.

SAMPLE ITEMS: Girls must be more concerned with clothing and appearance than boys. It is best that men rather than women control the world.

SCORING: Items are objectively scored and equally weighted. High scores indicate support for egalitarianism.

DEVELOPMENT: The development of the scale is not described except that the author states, "This investigator wrote a series of typical stereotyped statements commonly verbalized by people with conservative views of women's role and chose 25 of the statements" (Kirsch, 1974, p. 33).

RELIABILITY: Test-retest reliability was computed on the basis of the responses from seventeen adults who were tested on two occasions separated by a six-week interval. The test-retest correlation was .98 (Kirsch, 1974). Sixteen boys and girls, ages 16 to 20, completed the scale on two occasions separated by a six-week interval. Test-retest reliability was .98 (Kirsch, Shore, and Kyle, 1976).

VALIDITY: Seventeen adults who completed the scale were asked to answer the question, "Would you describe your attitudes toward the Women's Liberation Movement in one word as primarily for or against?" Scores on the Equalitarian Sex Role Preference Scale correlated .92 with "for" and "against" responses.

Consistent with their hypothesis, Kirsch, Shore, and Kyle (1976) found a highly significant relationship between very high or very low scores on the scale and the personality traits of flexibility and autonomy. This finding applied to both adolescent boys and adolescent girls, but the relationship was stronger for the girls. The authors state, "This result may also be considered a measure of validity since sex role equality concerns would be assumed to be more highly valued by girls because of the efforts made to appeal to women in the Women's Movement" (Kirsch, Shore, and Kyle, 1976, p. 392).

NOTES AND COMMENTS: (1) By phrasing all of the statements so that agreement indicates a traditional attitude, Kirsch encourages an acquiescent response set. It is advisable to phrase about half of the items to reflect one attitude and the other half of the items to reflect the opposite attitude.

(2) The interpretation of responses to two of the items is particularly difficult. The items state, "Little girls are made of 'sugar and spice and everything nice' " and "Little boys are made of 'frogs and snails and puppy dog tails.' " Could agreement mean that the respondent agrees that this is what the saying is? Does disagreement mean that the respondent believes that little girls (or boys) are all made of the same thing, but it is something better (or something worse) than what is presented in the item? Could disagreement mean that the respondent does not believe that little girls (or boys) are made of anything nonhuman?

(3) Because the scale has previously been used with males as well as females, the recommendation was made above that the scale is appropriate for persons over age 14. However, it is not clear how one item on the scale, "My physical appearance is my most important asset," can apply to both male and female respondents.

SOURCE: See Kirsch, 1974; or Kirsch, Shore, and Kyle, 1976.

BIBLIOGRAPHY:

Kirsch, P. A. "Adolescent Identity Formation and Attitudes Toward Women and Sex Role Equality." Unpublished doctoral dissertation, University of Maryland, 1974. (*Dissertation Abstracts International*, 1974, *35* [6-B], 3022.)
Kirsch, P. A., Shore, M. F., and Kyle, D. G. "Ideology and Personality: Aspects of Identity Formation in Adolescents with Strong Attitudes Toward Sex Role Equalitarianism." *Journal of Youth and Adolescence*, 1976, *5*, 387-401.

---

179. FEM SCALE

AUTHORS: Eliot R. Smith, Myra Marx Ferree, and Frederick D. Miller

DATE: 1975

VARIABLE: Attitudes toward feminism

TYPE OF INSTRUMENT: Summated rating scale

DESCRIPTION: The scale consists of twenty statements, some phrased to reflect positive attitudes toward feminism and some phrased to reflect negative attitudes toward feminism. The statements pertain to such issues as marital roles, maternal roles, and stereotyped views of women's personality traits. Each statement is followed by five response options ranging from "strongly agree" to "strongly disagree."

PREVIOUSLY ADMINISTERED TO: College students

APPROPRIATE FOR: Ages 16 and older

ADMINISTRATION: The scale can be self-administered and can be completed in about five to ten minutes.

SAMPLE ITEMS: Women have the right to compete with men in every sphere of activity.
                      As head of the household, the father should have final authority over his children.

SCORING: Items are objectively scored and equally weighted. Total scores can range from 20 to 100, with higher scores indicating more support for feminism.

DEVELOPMENT: An item pool consisting of forty-one items adapted from the Belief Pattern Scale for Measuring Attitudes Toward Feminism (#172) and sixteen new items was administered to thirty-nine college students using two different sets of instructions. First the students were told to indicate "agree" or "disagree" for each item. Then they were asked to complete the scale again and role play a "strong antifeminist" (half the subjects) or a "strong profeminist" (half the subjects). If five or more respondents failed to support the majority's interpretation of the direction of the item, the item was eliminated. Nine items were eliminated by this criterion. From the remaining forty-eight items, twenty-seven were selected on the basis of good face validity and their success in discriminating between respondents. Most of the items selected had marginal distributions less extreme than 80 percent to 20 percent so as to provide good variability. The twenty-seven-item version was administered to another sample of college students, and their responses were factor analyzed. A single factor labeled Feminism was extracted, and items with loadings below +.40 were eliminated. Twenty items remained on the final version of the scale.

RELIABILITY: Smith, Ferree, and Miller (1975) report a reliability of .91 based on the responses given by 100 college students. Singleton and Christiansen (1977) also report a reliability of .91 (coefficient alpha) using the responses from a sample of 283 college students who were racially and chronologically heterogeneous.

VALIDITY: The correlation between the twenty-item version and the twenty-seven-item version was .973 (Smith, Ferree, and Miller, 1975).

To assess the construct validity of the scale, 100 college students completed the twenty-seven-item version and four other scales. As predicted, scores on the FEM correlated significantly and positively with a measure of activism in the women's liberation movement ($r = +.392$, $p < .01$) and with a measure of identification with the women's liberation movement ($r = +.629$, $p < .01$). Also as predicted, the correlation between the FEM scale and the Rotter I-E Scale was nonsignificant. The students also completed a measure of perceptions of whether the world is a just place. As predicted, scores on the FEM scale were negatively correlated ($r = -.238$, $p < .05$) with the Just World Scale (Smith, Ferree, and Miller, 1975).

To obtain further information regarding the construct validity of the scale, Singleton and Christiansen (1977) administered it along with three other measures to 288 college students. The interrelationships between the measures were all significant and in the predicted direction. The FEM scale correlated negatively with a measure of racial prejudice ($r = -.462$, $p < .001$), negatively with a measure of dogmatism ($r = -.506$, $p <$

.001), and positively with the Singleton-Christiansen Identification with the Women's Movement (#234) (r = +.638, p < .001).

As a further check on validity, Singleton and Christiansen (1977) administered the scale to groups that could logically be expected to differ in their responses. The authors predicted that mean scores would be ranked, from highest to lowest scores, in the following order: National Organization for Women (a profeminist group), female college students, male college students, and Fascinating Womanhood (an antifeminist group). The results were consistent with predictions and the differences between means for adjacent groups were all significant at the .001 level.

NOTES AND COMMENTS: (1) A factor analysis of the twenty-seven-item version suggested the existence of a single factor that accounted for 29.7 percent of the total variance. A factor analysis of the twenty-item version suggested the same single factor, which now accounted for 37.7 percent of the total variance. The factor was labeled Feminism (Smith, Ferree, and Miller, 1975). Singleton and Christiansen (1977) factor analyzed the twenty-item version and found essentially identical results. They extracted a single factor which accounted for 38 percent of the total variance.

(2) Singleton and Christiansen (1977) suggested that users might be interested in a shorter version of the FEM scale. They computed the reliability of a ten-item version, including only the ten items with the highest factor loadings, and found the reliability to be .88. The correlation between the twenty-item version and the ten-item version was .96. They also computed the reliability of a five-item version, including only the five items with the highest factor loadings, and report the reliability to be .81. The correlation between the five-item version and the twenty-item version was .93.

(3) This scale first appeared in the literature fairly recently. The scale is particularly well developed, has good internal consistency reliability, and evidence of its validity has been obtained. For all these reasons, it is worth considering this scale for use in further research.

SOURCE: See Smith, Ferree, and Miller, 1975.

BIBLIOGRAPHY:

Krulewitz, J. E. "Determinants of Rape Judgments: Rapist's Force and Subjects' Sex Role Attitudes." Paper presented at 85th annual meeting of the American Psychological Association, San Francisco, August 1977.

Singleton, R., Jr., and Christiansen, J. B. "The Construct Validation of a Short-Form Attitudes Toward Feminism Scale." *Sociology and Social Research,* 1977, *61,* 294-303.

Smith, E. R., Ferree, M. M., and Miller, F. D. "A Short Scale of Attitudes Toward Feminism." *Representative Research in Social Psychology,* 1975, *6,* 51-56.

180. FEMINISM BEHAVIOR SCALE

AUTHOR: Diane R. Follingstad

DATE: 1977

VARIABLE: Attitudes toward feminism

TYPE OF INSTRUMENT: Summated rating scale

DESCRIPTION: The scale includes fourteen questions regarding behavior and attitudes related to feminist issues. Each question is accompanied by four response options which vary to match the wording of the question.

PREVIOUSLY ADMINISTERED TO: Female college students

APPROPRIATE FOR: Ages 16 and older

ADMINISTRATION: The scale is self-administered and can be completed in about ten minutes. When females complete the scale, they are to answer the questions for themselves; when males complete the scale, they are to answer as they would want a woman (for example, their girlfriend or wife) to answer.

SAMPLE ITEMS: Do you solicit and accept chivalrous attentions from men, such as opening doors?
• Definitely
• Somewhat
• Slightly
• No
                    Do you plan to work even if you marry a man who could support both of you?
• Definitely
• Probably
• Possible
• No

SCORING: Items are objectively scored and equally weighted. Total scores can range from 14 (profeminist) to 56 (antifeminist).

DEVELOPMENT: The items on the scale were judged "by several independent judges as behaviors indicative of a profeminist viewpoint" (p. 225).

RELIABILITY: Test-retest reliability (interval unspecified) was .79.

VALIDITY: Follingstad, Robinson, and Pugh (p. 225) report that "the items significantly discriminated between members of several feminist organizations and members of conservative organizations." However, they do not provide the data to substantiate their claim.

NOTES AND COMMENTS: This scale differs from most scales measuring attitudes toward a variety of issues in that about one third of the items on this scale have behavioral referents.

SOURCE: Diane Follingstad
                  Department of Psychology
                  University of South Carolina
                  Columbia, South Carolina 29208

BIBLIOGRAPHY:

Follingstad, D. R., Robinson, E. A., and Pugh, M. "Effects of Consciousness-Raising Groups on Measures of Feminism, Self-Esteem, and Social Desirability." *Journal of Counseling Psychology,* 1977, *24,* 223-230.

---

181. FEMINISM II SCALE

AUTHOR: Judith Ann Dempewolff

DATE: 1972

VARIABLE: Attitudes toward women

TYPE OF INSTRUMENT: Summated rating scale

DESCRIPTION: The scale consists of fifty-six statements concerning women, especially in relation to the aims of the feminist movement. Some items reflect positive attitudes; other items reflect negative attitudes. Each of twenty-eight items has a "mate" that deals with the same content but is phrased in the opposite direction. Each statement is accompanied by four response options: agree very much, agree a little, disagree a little, and disagree a lot. Short forms of the scale, consisting of twenty-eight items, have also been developed (see Notes and Comments below).

PREVIOUSLY ADMINISTERED TO: Ages 13 and older

APPROPRIATE FOR: Ages 13 and older

ADMINISTRATION: The scale is self-administered and can be completed in less than half an hour.

SAMPLE ITEMS: It is better to have a man as a boss or supervisor than a woman.
                              Women should feel free to compete with men in every sphere of economic activity.

SCORING: Items are objectively scored and equally weighted. Total scores can range from 56 (very negative attitudes toward women) to 224 (very positive attitudes toward women).

DEVELOPMENT: A pool of eighty items was constructed, including many items adapted or excerpted from the Belief Pattern Scale for Measuring Attitudes Toward Feminism (#172). The item pool was administered to 106 college men and 119 college women. Separate factor analyses were performed on the responses from men and from women. The resulting factor structures were sufficiently similar that it was decided that later factor analyses would be done on the responses from males and females combined. First, however, eleven items were eliminated from further analysis. Items were eliminated because they had very skewed distributions—that is, very few positive responses or very few negative responses; they had low correlations with other items; or they had at least twenty negative correlations with other items. Two additional factor analyses were performed on the combined responses from males and females. The results of these factor analyses led to the selection of the fifty-six items that comprise the scale.

RELIABILITY: Using the responses from the 225 college students, internal consistency reliability was estimated by using the mean intercorrelation for all items and the Spearman Brown formula. The reliability was .961 (Dempewolff, 1972, 1974a). Using the responses from another sample of 156 college students, the equivalent-halves reliability for the full scale was .976 (Dempewolff, 1972).

VALIDITY: In order to validate the Feminism II scale, the original eighty-item pool was administered to sixty-eight persons who belonged to groups that would suggest they held positive attitudes toward women and to eighty-six persons who belonged to groups that would suggest they held negative attitudes toward women. The full eighty-item pool was administered because the validation study was conducted simultaneously with the development study; however, only responses to items selected for the Feminism II scale were included in the analysis concerning the scale's validity. A two-way analysis of variance indicated significant main effects for sex and group membership and no significant interaction. Those belonging to groups whose members are likely to have positive attitudes toward women ($\overline{X}$ = 193.88) scored significantly higher than those belonging to groups whose members are likely to have more negative attitudes toward women ($\overline{X}$ = 152.74, p < .001). Furthermore, women ($\overline{X}$ = 181.23) scored significantly higher than men ($\overline{X}$ = 160.04, p < .001) (Dempewolff, 1972).

NOTES AND COMMENTS: (1) One of the last factor analyses led to six factors (Dempewolff, 1972): Factor I concerns equal ability and freedom for women in the political, intellectual, and economic spheres. It deals with issues of "competence, privileges, responsibilities, and leadership for women" (p. 43). Factor II concerns "traditional customs and conduct for women" (p. 46). Factor III is concerned with the traditional role of women and their role in the family. Factor IV deals with "woman's lack of ability and fitness to handle objective legal and business affairs" (p. 46). Factor V is concerned with equality between the sexes in regard to home responsibilities, school admissions, and employment. Factor VI concerns "economic equality for women" (p. 49). In all of the factor analyses performed, the first factor accounted for a high proportion of the variance.

(2) Two short forms of the scale have been developed, with each short form consisting of half the items on the scale. In constructing the short forms, items were assigned in such a way that one of the "mates" from each pair appears on each form of the scale,

and mean scores for each half would be approximately equal. The short forms were each administered to a different group of twenty-five college students. Two weeks later, each group completed the short form they had not previously completed. The correlation between the two forms was .92 (Dempewolff, 1974a).

(3) Dempewolff (1972, 1974b) compared scores on the Feminism II Scale and numerous other variables, including religion, mother's education, father's education, parents' occupations, mother's prior work history, mother's satisfaction with work, family income, birth order, and number and sex of siblings. Other researchers also compared scores on the Feminism II Scale with other variables, including ego development (Blumhagen, 1974); dogmatism (Whitehead and Tawes, 1976); empathy (Manley, 1976); locus of control (Manley, 1976); conformity (Ditmar, Mueller, and Mitchell, 1975); introversion-extraversion (Ditmar, Mueller, and Mitchell, 1975); and various demographic variables (Manley, 1976; Whitehead and Tawes, 1976).

(4) Klecka and Hiller (1977) modified the scale but do not specify what the modification was.

SOURCE: See Dempewolff, 1972.

BIBLIOGRAPHY:

Blumhagen, G. K. O. "The Relationship Between Identity and Feminism." Unpublished doctoral dissertation, Washington University, 1974. (*Dissertation Abstracts International*, 1975, *36*[1-A], 545.)

Coughlin, F. E. "Religious and Lay Graduate Students in Training for Helping Roles in New York State: A Study of Self-Concept and Attitudes Toward Feminism and Sexuality." Unpublished doctoral dissertation, Catholic University of America, 1976. (*Dissertation Abstracts International*, 1976, *36*[9-B], 4682-4683.)

Dempewolff, J. A. "Feminism and Its Correlates." Unpublished doctoral dissertation, University of Cincinnati, 1972. (*Dissertation Abstracts International*, 1973, *33*[8-B], 3913-3914.)

Dempewolff, J. A. "Development and Validation of a Feminism Scale." *Psychological Reports*, 1974a, *34*, 651-657.

Dempewolff, J. A. "Some Correlates of Feminism." *Psychological Reports*, 1974b, *34*, 671-676.

Ditmar, F., Mueller, N., and Mitchell, J. "Females' Attitudes Toward Feminism and Their Conformity in Heterosexual Groups." Paper presented at 83rd annual meeting of the American Psychological Association, Chicago, September 1975.

Joesting, J. "Personality Correlates of Sexism and Antisexism in College Students." *College Student Journal*, 1976, *10*, 194-196.

Joesting, J., and Whitehead, G. I., III. "Egalitarianism, Curiosity, and Creativity: Partial Replication." *Psychological Reports*, 1976, *38*, 369-370.

Klecka, C. O., and Hiller, D. V. "Impact of Mothers' Life-Style on Adolescent Gender-Role Socialization." *Sex Roles*, 1977, *3*, 241-255.

Manley, B. "Feminist Orientation as Related to Empathy, Locus of Control, and Demographic Variables: A Study of Women." Unpublished doctoral dissertation, California School of Professional Psychology, 1976. (*Dissertation Abstracts International*, 1976, *37*[2-B], 977-978.)

Michaelson, B. L. "Vocational Interests, Self-Concepts, and Attitudes Toward Feminine Roles as Related to the Educational and Vocational Choice of College Women."

Unpublished doctoral dissertation, Temple University, 1974. (*Dissertation Abstracts International,* 1974, *35* [6-B] , 2994.)

Whitehead, G. I., III., and Tawes, S. L. "Dogmatism, Age, and Educational Level as Correlates of Feminism for Males and Females." *Sex Roles,* 1976, *2,* 401-405.

---

182. FEMINIST ORIENTATION SCALE

AUTHORS: Morton A. Lieberman, Nancy Solow, Gary R. Bond, and Janet Reibstein

DATE: 1978

VARIABLE: Attitudes toward feminist issues

TYPE OF INSTRUMENT: Guttman scale

DESCRIPTION: The scale consists of the sentence stem "How do you feel about:" followed by seven items. Each item represents an issue advocated by the feminist movement. Four response options accompany each item: strongly approve, moderately approve, moderately disapprove, and strongly disapprove.

PREVIOUSLY ADMINISTERED TO: Women belonging to a consciousness-raising group

APPROPRIATE FOR: Ages 16 and older

ADMINISTRATION: This self-administered scale can be completed in less than five minutes.

SAMPLE ITEMS: How do you feel about public daycare?
How do you feel about abortion on demand?

SCORING: The score equals the number of items that are strongly or moderately approved of.

DEVELOPMENT: No information is provided.

RELIABILITY: Using the responses from seventy-three women, the coefficient of reproducibility was found to be .93, and the coefficient of scalability was .51 (Bond, personal communication, 1978).

VALIDITY: No information is provided.

NOTES AND COMMENTS: (1) Thirty-two women who were participating in a consciousness-raising group completed the scale at the beginning and ending of the group. No significant differences were found in scores as a result of participation in the group.

(2) The scale has been used as part of a lengthy questionnaire including numerous other measures.

SOURCE: Gary R. Bond
          Department of Behavioral Sciences
          University of Chicago
          5848 So. University Avenue
          Chicago, Illinois 60637

BIBLIOGRAPHY:

Bond, G. R. Personal communication, 1978.
Lieberman, M. A., Solow, N., Bond, G. R., and Reibstein, J. "The Therapeutic Impact of Women's Consciousness-Raising Groups." *Archives of General Psychiatry,* 1979, *36,* 161-168.

---

183. FOX INDEX OF SEX-ROLE-RELATED ATTITUDES

AUTHOR: Greer Litton Fox

DATE: 1977 (used 1974)

VARIABLE: Attitudes toward traditional sex roles for men and women

TYPE OF INSTRUMENT: Summated rating scale

DESCRIPTION: The scale consists of sixteen items that assess attitudes in five areas: five items measure "M-F status," which is defined as awareness and commitment to change the differences in status between men and women; two items measure "Hemmaman," which is defined as support for men participating in domestic tasks; three items measure "Malehead," which is defined as support for men being head of the household; two items measure "Altlife," which is defined as interest in alternative life-styles; and four items measure "Marriage," which is defined as support for traditional marriage and family structure. Nine items are phrased to reflect positive attitudes and seven are phrased to reflect negative attitudes. For each item, the respondents are asked to indicate the extent of their agreement with the statement.

PREVIOUSLY ADMINISTERED TO: College students

APPROPRIATE FOR: Ages 16 and older

ADMINISTRATION: The scale can be self-administered and can be completed in less than ten minutes.

SAMPLE ITEMS:

M-F status: Women should get together to discuss the problems common to most women relative to men.

Hemmaman: Fathers should spend as much time in child rearing as mothers.

Malehead: The man should be more responsible for the economic support of the family than the woman.

Altlife: Two women can love each other and have a relationship as fulfilling as one between a woman and a man.

Marriage: The nuclear family (husband, wife, child) is necessary for meeting basic human needs.

SCORING: Items are objectively scored and equally weighted. Five subscale scores and a total score are obtained. Lower scores indicate greater sex role traditionality.

DEVELOPMENT: No information is provided.

RELIABILITY: No data are provided.

VALIDITY: The scale was completed by 683 sexually active single college students. Fox reports, "For most items the differences between the sexes are not large" (p. 274). She does not indicate whether any of the differences are statistically significant. Fox hypothesized that female students with nontraditional sex role attitudes and an internal locus of control would be more likely to use contraceptives. She found that for those with internal locus of control, the correlation between sex role attitudes and contraceptive use was significant for four subscale scores (the exception was Hemmaman) and for Total score. However, the largest correlation was .25. Fox's data failed to support the hypothesis that female students with an external locus of control and traditional sex role attitudes would be unlikely to use contraceptives.

NOTES AND COMMENTS: (1) The five subscale scores were constructed on an intuitive basis. To validate the clustering, a factor analysis was performed. Three factors were extracted: Factor I was dominated by M-F status items; Factor II was dominated by Malehead items; and Factor III was dominated by Altlife and Marriage items.

(2) There are so few items on each subscale that the need for reliability information is crucial. It is quite likely that the subscale scores are not very reliable.

(3) Fox indicates in the text of the article that the scale consists of seventeen items. However, the appendix only describes sixteen items. Furthermore, Fox omits several important items of information from the article. The number and wording of response options are not included; the exact number of points per item is omitted; and the exact wording of each statement is not given. Despite these omissions, potential users can make some reasonable assumptions which allow them to use the scale.

SOURCE: See Fox, 1977.

BIBLIOGRAPHY:

Fox, G. L. "Sex Role Attitudes as Predictors of Contraceptive Use Among Unmarried University Students." *Sex Roles,* 1977, *3*, 265-283.

184. GILBERT-WARNER-CABLE SCALE OF ATTITUDES
TOWARD WOMEN'S LIBERATION ISSUES

AUTHORS: Albin R. Gilbert, John R. Warner, and Dana G. Cable

DATE: 1975

VARIABLE: Attitudes toward issues advocated by the women's liberation movement

TYPE OF INSTRUMENT: Alternate choice

DESCRIPTION: The instrument concerns twelve issues advocated by the women's liberation movement (WLM). Each issue is represented by four items: (1) a statement expressed
in the first person singular that supports the position advocated by the WLM; (2) a statement expressed in the third person singular that supports the position advocated by the
WLM; (3) a statement expressed in the first person singular that opposes the position
advocated by the WLM; and (4) a statement expressed in the third person singular that
opposes the position advocated by the WLM. This yields a total of forty-eight statements,
which are presented in random order. For each item, the respondent has to indicate
whether she agrees or disagrees with the statement.

PREVIOUSLY ADMINISTERED TO: Female college students

APPROPRIATE FOR: Females, ages 16 and older

ADMINISTRATION: The instrument can be self-administered and can be completed in
fifteen to twenty minutes.

SAMPLE ITEMS:

First person, supports: I have been enraged at being considered inferior because I am a
woman.

Third person, supports: Sarah J. is mad that some people have regarded her as "only a
woman."

First person, opposes: It does not bother me at all that some "chauvinists" consider
women to be inferior.

Third person, opposes: Priscilla M. does not mind at all the fact that some men consider
themselves to be superior to women.

SCORING: There are three scores derived from this instrument: a Self-Report score, a
Women's Liberation score, and a Consistency score. The Self-Report score is a count of
the number of first person supporting statements that the respondent agrees with. The
score can range from 0 to 12. The Women's Liberation score represents the number of
times the respondent selects the response that is consistent with the position advocated
by the WLM—that is, the number of times the respondent agrees with supporting statements and disagrees with opposing statements. This score can range from 0 to 48. A Consistency score is found for each issue by counting the number of statements (out of the
four) for which the respondent's answer was consistent with a response she gave to the

first person supporting statement. The maximum score for an issue is 4, given when the responses to all four items are consistent with each other (two agree responses and two disagree responses). The minimum score for an issue is 1, given when the responses to the other three items contradict the response given to the first person supporting item. Total scores can range from 12 to 48.

DEVELOPMENT: The issues to be included on the instrument were suggested by sociology majors at West Virginia Wesleyan College.

RELIABILITY: No data are provided.

VALIDITY: The instrument was administered to college women at two colleges: 104 women at West Virginia Wesleyan College and 128 women at Hood College. It was predicted that Hood women would be more supportive of the issues advocated by the women's liberation movement. The hypothesis was supported both when Self-Report scores were the dependent variable ($p < .01$) and when Women's Liberation scores were the dependent variable ($p < .01$) (Gilbert, Warner, and Cable, 1975).

Along with administering this instrument to the college women, another measure (Tavris, 1971) purporting to assess comparable attitudes was also administered. The correlation with Self-Report scores was +.70 ($p < .001$); the correlation with Women's Liberation scores was +.48 ($p < .001$) (Gilbert, Warner, and Cable, 1975).

NOTES AND COMMENTS: (1) The authors found that the Consistency scores for those with high Self-Report scores were significantly higher ($p < .01$) than the Consistency scores for those with low Self-Report scores.

(2) The authors do not present any data to indicate why this method of asking the same question from four different perspectives is superior or even equal to the more common method of asking a question just once. They also do not demonstrate the equivalency of the four items composing the tetrad.

SOURCE: Albin R. Gilbert
             Department of Psychology
             West Virginia Wesleyan College
             Buckhannon, West Virginia 26201

BIBLIOGRAPHY:

Gilbert, A. R., Warner, J. R., and Cable, D. G. "Probing into the Face Value of Women's Liberation Attitudes." *Psychologische Beitrage,* 1975, *17,* 519-526.
*Tavris, C. "Woman and Man." *Psychology Today,* 1971, *4,* 82-88.

185. HAWLEY SEX ROLE SCALE

AUTHOR: Peggy Hawley

DATE: 1968

VARIABLE: Attitudes toward women

TYPE OF INSTRUMENT: Summated rating scale

DESCRIPTION: The scale consists of thirty-five statements intended to assess whether one perceives sex roles as dichotomous or androgynous. There are seven statements representing each of five factors: Woman as Partner, Woman as Ingenue, Woman as Homemaker, Woman as Competitor, and Woman as Knower. Some statements are phrased to reflect a "modern" viewpoint, and other statements are phrased to reflect a "traditional" viewpoint. Each statement is accompanied by six response alternatives: very strongly agree, strongly agree, agree, disagree, strongly disagree, and very strongly disagree.

PREVIOUSLY ADMINISTERED TO: Grades 10-12; college students; adult women

APPROPRIATE FOR: Ages 14 and older

ADMINISTRATION: The scale is self-administered and can be completed in about twenty minutes.

SAMPLE ITEMS:

Woman as Partner: Women should share the responsibilities and privileges of life equally.

Woman as Ingenue: Women should be slightly illogical, as this makes them "delightfully feminine."

Woman as Homemaker: Women should never let outside interests or activities interfere with their domestic duties.

Woman as Competitor: Modern woman is too competitive.

Woman as Knower: It is just as important to educate daughters as to educate sons.

SCORING: Items are objectively scored and equally weighted. Six scores are obtained: one for each of the five factors and an overall score. High scores indicate support for androgynous roles; low scores indicate support for dichotomous roles.

DEVELOPMENT: An item pool was constructed of 150 items drawn from a variety of sources, including relevant literature and existing instruments. From the 150 items, 80 were selected that covered four topics: women's use of their intelligence, women's competitiveness, sexual aspects of women's behavior, and the wife's role. After the items were reviewed by twenty judges and necessary revisions were made, the items were administered to thirty-three women with instructions to respond as they believed significant men in their lives would respond. Their responses were factor analyzed and six factors were identified. Factor I is labeled Woman as Partner and concerns "division of responsibility, power, and labor between the sexes in work and the conjugal relationship" (Hawley,

1971, p. 195). Factor II is labeled Woman as Ingenue and concerns "woman in her most dependent state, as a possession, a decorative item, and a sex symbol" (Hawley, 1971, p. 195). Factor III is labeled Woman as Homemaker and concerns an "emphasis on the traditional role as keeper of the home" (Hawley, 1971, p. 195). Factor IV is labeled Woman as Competitor and concerns "woman's right to compete, with implications for the man-woman relationship" (Hawley, 1971, p. 195). Factor V is labeled Woman as Knower and concerns "appropriate ways of knowing, for instance, the assumption that women are naturally intuitive and men naturally rational" (Hawley, 1971, p. 195). The sixth factor was a sexual dimension and was eliminated from the scale because it was presumed irrelevant to the original use planned for the scale. Seven items were selected to represent each of the five factors. Each item selected had a loading of at least .45 on the relevant factor.

RELIABILITY: The responses from eighty-six women were used to compute the internal consistency of the scales. The women completed the scale by indicating their perceptions of how men would respond to the statements. The values of coefficient alpha were: Woman as Partner = .75; Woman as Ingenue = .73; Woman as Homemaker = .77; Woman as Competitor = .83; and Woman as Knower = .80 (Hawley, 1968, 1971). Sixty-five high school counselors and 2,229 female high school students completed the scale, indicating their personal responses to the statements. The internal consistency of the total score (coefficient alpha) was .93 for the counselors and .86 for the girls (Hawley, 1975).

VALIDITY: Hawley (1968, 1971) found that homemakers and women engaged in feminine careers scored significantly differently from women engaged in careers usually pursued by men. Hawley also found that married women's scores were significantly different from unmarried women. Hawley (1972) replicated the findings regarding differences between different career groups but failed to replicate the findings concerning differences between married and unmarried women.

Kaplan and Goldman (1973) administered a modified form of the scale to forty-nine college men and fifty-three college women. About half of each group were asked to respond as though they were the average woman and half were asked to respond as though they were the average man. The results indicated that college students perceive women as different from men in their attitudes toward woman's role. More specifically, men were expected to have more traditional attitudes than women.

NOTES AND COMMENTS: (1) Using the responses from eighty-six women, Hawley (1968) computed the intercorrelations between the five scales. The correlations ranged from .515 (Woman as Knower and Woman as Ingenue) to .712 (Woman as Partner and Woman as Competitor). Based on data obtained from 186 college women, Hawley (1970) reports intercorrelations between the scales ranging from .37 (Woman as Ingenue and Woman as Partner) to .68 (Woman as Homemaker and Woman as Competitor).

(2) The scale has been used to measure women's perceptions of men's attitudes (Hawley, 1968, 1970, 1971, 1972). To use the scale for this purpose, each statement begins with "Men think" or "Significant men in my life think."

(3) The exact wording of the items varies depending on which of the sources below is consulted.

SOURCE: See Hawley, 1968, 1970, or 1975.

BIBLIOGRAPHY:

Hawley, P. "The Relationship of Women's Perceptions of Men's Views of the Feminine Ideal to Career Choice." Unpublished doctoral dissertation, Claremont Graduate School, 1968. (*Dissertation Abstracts,* 1969, *29* [8-A], 2523.)

Hawley, P. "The Relationship of Women's Perceptions of Men's Views of the Feminine Ideal to Career Choice." San Diego: San Diego State College, 1970. (ERIC Document Reproduction Service No. ED 046 031.)

Hawley, P. "What Women Think Men Think: Does It Affect Their Career Choice?" *Journal of Counseling Psychology,* 1971, *18*, 193-199.

Hawley, P. "Perceptions of Male Models of Femininity Related to Career Choice." *Journal of Counseling Psychology,* 1972, *19*, 308-313.

Hawley, P. "The State of the Art of Counseling High School Girls. Final Report. Fels Discussion Paper No. 89." New York: Ford Foundation, 1975. (ERIC Document Reproduction Service No. ED 128 744.)

Jennings, J. E. "The Relationship Between Locus of Control and Career Preference to Academic Achievement and Perceptions of the Feminine Ideal Held by Men Significant in the Lives of Senior High School Girls." Unpublished doctoral dissertation, St. Johns University, 1973. (*Dissertation Abstracts International,* 1973, *34* [6-A], 3063-3064.)

Kaplan, R. M., and Goldman, R. D. "Stereotypes of College Students Toward the Average Man's and Woman's Attitudes Toward Women." *Journal of Counseling Psychology,* 1973, *20*, 459-462.

Turner, B. F. "Socialization and Career Orientation Among Black and White College Women." Paper presented at 80th annual meeting of the American Psychological Association, Honolulu, September 1972. (ERIC Document Reproduction Service No. ED 074 412.)

---

186. HYMER WOMEN'S LIBERATION MOVEMENT ATTITUDE SCALE

AUTHOR: Sharon Hymer

DATE: 1972

VARIABLE: Sex role attitudes

TYPE OF INSTRUMENT: Summated rating scale

DESCRIPTION: There are two forms of this scale, with each form containing thirty statements regarding such issues as personality traits of men and women, stereotypes of members of the feminist movement, attitudes regarding working women, prescriptions for the wife's role, and implications of the feminist movement. About two thirds of the items are phrased to reflect traditional attitudes and one third are phrased to reflect nontraditional attitudes. Each statement is accompanied by five response options: strongly disagree, disagree, neutral or undecided, agree, and strongly agree.

PREVIOUSLY ADMINISTERED TO: College students and adults

APPROPRIATE FOR: Ages 16 and older

ADMINISTRATION: The scale can be self-administered. One form can be completed in about fifteen minutes. Researchers may use either one or both forms.

SAMPLE ITEMS: Women should have as much sexual freedom as men.
There is something wrong with a woman who doesn't want children.

SCORING: Items are objectively scored and equally weighted. Total scores can range from 30 (traditional attitudes) to 150 (nontraditional attitudes).

DEVELOPMENT: An eighty-six-item scale was developed and administered to ninety-three college students. Sixty items discriminated (p < .0001) between those obtaining the highest and lowest total scores. The sixty items were divided into two forms, with thirty items on each form.

RELIABILITY: Eighty-four college students and adults completed both forms of the scale. The alternate form reliability was .93 (Hymer, 1972).

VALIDITY: The eighty-four persons who completed the scale included medical students, churchgoers, law students, and members of the National Organization for Women (NOW), a feminist organization. It was expected that the means of the various groups would differ significantly; and it was predicted that the ordering of the means from most traditional to least traditional would be consistent with the sequence in which the groups are named above. The results indicated that the means were consistent with the predictions. It was also found that churchgoers were significantly (p < .001) more traditional than members of NOW; medical students were more traditional than law students, but the difference between means was not significant; medical students were significantly (p < .001) more traditional than members of NOW; and churchgoers were significantly (p < .01) more traditional than law students (Hymer, 1972).

SOURCE: See Hymer, 1972; or Chasen, 1974.

BIBLIOGRAPHY:

Chasen, B. G. "Diagnostic Sex Role Bias and Its Relation to Authoritarianism, Sex Role Attitudes, and Sex of the School Psychologist." Unpublished doctoral dissertation, New York University, 1974. (*Dissertation Abstracts International*, 1974, *35*[5-B], 2400.)

Chasen, B. G. "Diagnostic Sex Role Bias and Its Relation to Authoritarianism, Sex Role Attitudes, and Sex of the School Psychologist." *Sex Roles*, 1975, *1*, 355-368.

Hymer, S. "The Relationship Between Attitudes Toward the Women's Liberation Movement and Mode of Aggressive Expression Among Women." Unpublished master's thesis, Yeshiva University, 1972.

Hymer, S., and Atkins, A. "Relationship Between Attitudes Toward the Women's Liberation Movement and Mode of Aggressive Expression in Women." *Proceedings of the 81st Annual Convention of the American Psychological Association*, 1973, *8*, 173-174.

187. INVENTORY OF FEMININE VALUES

AUTHOR: Alexandra Botwinik Fand (revised by Anne Steinmann)

DATE: 1955 (revised 1968)

VARIABLE: Attitudes toward the feminine role

TYPE OF INSTRUMENT: Summated rating scale

DESCRIPTION: The scale consists of thirty-four statements pertaining to the needs, rights, and responsibilities of women in regard to men, children, and life in general. Half of the statements concern an other- or family-oriented woman—that is, "a person who conceives of herself as the counterpart, the 'other' of the man (and children) in her life and realizes herself indirectly by fostering their fulfillment" (Fand, 1955, p. 30). The other half of the statements concern a self-oriented woman—that is, a woman "as having embraced the main achieving orientation of our culture and . . . striving to fulfill herself directly by realizing her own potentialities" (Fand, 1955, p. 30). Some items are phrased positively and some are phrased negatively. Each statement is accompanied by five response options: strongly agree, agree, no opinion/don't know, disagree, and strongly disagree.

For thirty-three of the thirty-four statements, the content on the original version and the revised version of the scale is essentially the same. The phrasing of the items is different, however; in general, the phrasing on the revised version is more succinct. One statement on the revised version is completely different from the original version.

There are five forms of the revised version. The forms measure woman's self-perception, woman's perception of woman's ideal woman, woman's perception of man's ideal woman, man's perception of man's ideal woman, and man's perception of woman's ideal woman. The content of the items on the five forms is essentially identical. The order of the items is varied, and the phrasing of the items on the forms to be completed by males is slightly different.

PREVIOUSLY ADMINISTERED TO: Junior and senior high school students; college students; adults in the United States, England, Czechoslovakia, Brazil, Greece, Israel, France, India, Finland, Germany, Austria, the Philippines, Peru, Argentina, Mexico, Japan, Iran, and Turkey

APPROPRIATE FOR: Ages 14 and older

ADMINISTRATION: When Fand (1955) used the inventory, she asked that it be completed four times: the women were asked to indicate (1) their own opinion, (2) their perceptions of how the ideal woman would respond; (3) their perceptions of how the average woman would respond; and (4) their perceptions of how a woman most men would like to marry would respond.

Steinmann and Fox (1976a) recommend that three forms of the scale be administered to women: women should be asked for their own opinions (self-perception), their perceptions of how the ideal woman would respond, and their perceptions of how man's ideal woman would respond. When the scale is used with men, Steinmann recommends using two forms: men should be asked for their perceptions of how the ideal woman would respond and their perceptions of how a woman's ideal woman would respond.

SAMPLE ITEMS: An ambitious and responsible husband does not like his wife to work.
A woman who works cannot possibly be as good a mother as the one who stays home.

SCORING: Items are objectively scored and equally weighted. On the revised version, scores range from −68 to +68. Low scores (negative) indicate a greater other-orientation (more traditional); high scores indicate a greater self-orientation (more liberal). On the original version, scoring is exactly opposite to that of the revised version.

DEVELOPMENT: An item pool was developed consisting of twenty items written so that agreement would reflect an other-orientation and twenty items written so that agreement would reflect a self-orientation. The items were given to six judges with instructions to indicate whether other-oriented women or self-oriented women were likely to endorse each statement. Three items were eliminated because at least two judges disagreed on which type of woman was more likely to endorse the items. The remaining thirty-seven items were administered to twenty-one women. The women were asked to complete the scale four times, giving their own opinions, their opinions of the ideal woman, the average woman, and man's ideal woman. Seven response options were provided ranging from "strongly agree" to "strongly disagree." As a result of the pretest, some items were re-phrased and three items were eliminated. The eliminated items were those that did not discriminate between other- and self-oriented women. The remaining thirty-four items constituted the original version of the scale. In order to allow for the use of machine-scorable answer sheets, five response options rather than seven are used with the scale.

RELIABILITY: Fand (1955) administered the scale to eighty-five college women. The corrected split-half reliability was .81 for self and .85 for ideal woman. Inagaki (1967) used a Japanese translation of the scale with 289 college women in Japan. The corrected split-half reliability was .66 for self-perception, .68 for ideal self, and .73 for man's ideal.

VALIDITY: In discussing the validity of the scale, Fand (1955, p. 39) states, "the items . . . have face validity" and "they have been submitted to validation by seven judges and whenever a controversy as to the validity of an item arose, it was either modified until it met everybody's satisfaction or else eliminated." In addition, Fand interviewed eighteen college women who had completed the Inventory of Feminine Values. Using scores obtained on the inventory, the women were classified into one of six categories. Based on information obtained during the interview and without knowing the scores from the inventory, Fand classified the women into the six groups. Fand was correct or one group off in the placement of fifteen of the eighteen women.

Steinmann (1957, 1963) administered the Inventory of Feminine Values to eleven college women and also interviewed them. She reports (1957, p. 330): "In general, the material in the interviews supported the statistical findings from the [inventory]."

NOTES AND COMMENTS: (1) Steinmann and Fox present detailed results from the ad-ministration of the scale to fifteen samples containing 1,094 women (1966a), fifteen samples containing 1,655 women (1976a), and seven samples containing 500 women and 329 men (1976b). Voss and Skinner (1975) present data comparing the responses from a sample of women tested in 1969 and another sample of women tested in 1973.

(2) Closely related to this scale is the Inventory of Masculine Values, which con-tains statements pertaining to the needs, rights, and responsibilities of men. There is also a special version of the inventory appropriate for junior and senior high school students.

The instrument is entitled Developmental Inventory of Feminine Values. The substance of the statements, the response options, and the scoring are comparable to the adult-level Inventory of Feminine Values.

(3) Scores on the Inventory of Feminine Values have been related to many other variables, including personality factors (Abelew, 1974; Blumhagen, 1974; Cohn, 1975; Fand, 1955; Fox, 1975; Gump, 1972; Howe, 1972; Hunt, 1975; Jabury, 1967; Meyers, 1976; Ott, 1976; Porter, 1967; Powell, 1975; Powell and Reznikoff, 1976; Putnam and Hansen, 1972; Ratliff, 1975; Romano, 1975; and Waters, 1976); sex (Barrett, 1975; Cohn, 1975; Howe, 1972; and Steinmann and Fox, 1970, 1974); age (Steinmann, 1961; and Steinmann, Doherty, and Fox, 1970); race (Bonner, 1974; Fox, 1975; Gump, 1975; Slotkin, 1976; and Steinmann and Fox, 1970); religion (Steinmann, Doherty, and Fox, 1970, and Williams, 1970); occupational variables (Altman and Grossman, 1977; Eichler, 1973; Feulner, 1973; Ginn, 1968; Howe, 1972; Jabury, 1967; McKenzie, 1971; Powell, 1975; Powell and Reznikoff, 1976; Putnam and Hansen, 1972; Tucker, 1970; and Waters, 1976); intellectual and social achievement factors (Abelew, 1974; Doherty and Culver, 1976; Gump, 1972; Heilbrun, Kleemeier, and Piccola, 1974; Miles, 1976; Phillips, 1974; Powell, 1975; Powell and Reznikoff, 1976; Thurber, 1976; and Turner, 1974); marital and dating status (Cohn, 1975; Hipple, 1976; Howe, 1972; Hunt, 1975; Rappaport, Payne, and Steinmann, 1970a, 1970b; Voss and Skinner, 1975; Weissman, 1974; and Williams, 1970); life plans (Phillips, 1974; and Porter, 1967); familial variables (Abelew, 1974; Altman and Grossman, 1977; Barrett, 1975; Ginn, 1968; Levine, 1976; Steinmann, 1958; and Steinmann and Fox, 1974); and sex role variables (Gill, 1974; Hunt, 1975; Ott, 1976; and Steinmann and Fox, 1974).

(4) Porter (1967; see also Gump, 1972) modified the Inventory of Feminine Values. Using the original inventory as a starting point, Porter altered eight items slightly, eliminated ten items, and added fifteen items. She then administered the scale and factor analyzed the results. Seven factors were labeled: Factor I—Identity Derived Through Traditional Roles; Factor II—Woman's Role Is Submissive; Factor III—Need for Individualistic Achievement and Satisfactions; Factor IV—Home Oriented, Duty to Children Stressed; Factor V—Traditional Role Implies Some Relinquishing of Needs for Personal Fulfillment; Factor VI—Sense of Autonomy and Heightened Independence; and Factor VII—Family Inadequate to Completely Fulfill Needs. The revised scale was used by other researchers (for example, Gump, 1972, 1975; Powell and Reznikoff, 1976; Thurber, 1976).

(5) This scale is also described in *Family Measurement Techniques* (Straus, 1969, pp. 97-98; Straus and Brown, 1978, p. 113). It is also described and reviewed in *The Eighth Mental Measurements Yearbook* (Buros, 1978, entry 607).

SOURCE: For the original scale, see Fand, 1955.

For the revised scale and the Developmental Inventory, write to:
Maferr Foundation, Inc.
140 West 57th Street
New York, New York 10019
See also Steinmann and Fox, 1974.
For the modified scale, see Gump, 1972.

BIBLIOGRAPHY:

Abelew, T. "Sex Role Attitudes, Perceptual Style, Mathematical Ability, and Perceived Parental Child Rearing Attitudes in Adolescents." Unpublished doctoral dissertation, Fordham University, 1974. (*Dissertation Abstracts International*, 1974, *35*[3-B], 1439.)

Altman, S. L. "Women's Career Plans and Maternal Employment." Unpublished doctoral dissertation, Boston University Graduate School, 1975. (*Dissertation Abstracts International*, 1975, *35*[7-B], 3569.)

Altman, S. L., and Grossman, F. K. "Women's Career Plans and Maternal Employment." *Psychology of Women Quarterly*, 1977, *1*, 365-376.

Barrett, B. "Sex, Birth Order, and Family Composition as Related to the Sex Role Perceptions of Male and Female College Students." Unpublished doctoral dissertation, Rutgers University, The State University of New Jersey, 1975. (*Dissertation Abstracts International*, 1976, *36*[8-B], 4125.)

Bartok, M. A. R. "An Investigation of Selected Attitudes and Personality Characteristics as They Relate to Career Commitment in College Educated Women." Unpublished doctoral dissertation, University of Pittsburgh, 1975. (*Dissertation Abstracts International*, 1976, *36*[9-A], 5816-5817.)

Blumhagen, G. K. O. "The Relationship Between Female Identity and Feminism." Unpublished doctoral dissertation, Washington University, 1974. (*Dissertation Abstracts International*, 1975, *36*[1-A], 545.)

Bonner, F. "Black Women and White Women: A Comparative Analysis of Perceptions of Sex Roles for Self, Ideal Self and Ideal Male." *The Journal of Afro-American Issues*, 1974, *2*, 237-247.

*Buros, O. K. *The Eighth Mental Measurements Yearbook*. Highland Park, N.J.: Gryphon Press, 1978.

Cohn, A. R. "Self-Concept and Role Perceptions as Correlates of Marital Satisfaction." Unpublished doctoral dissertation, Illinois Institute of Technology, 1975. (*Dissertation Abstracts International*, 1976, *36*[7-B], 3569.)

Depner, C. E., and O'Leary, V. E. "Understanding Female Careerism: Fear of Success and New Directions." *Sex Roles*, 1976, *2*, 259-268.

Doherty, E. G., and Culver, C. "Sex Role Identification, Ability, and Achievement Among High School Girls." *Sociology of Education*, 1976, *49*, 1-3.

Eichler, L. S. "Feminine Narcissism: An Empirical Investigation." Unpublished doctoral dissertation, Boston University Graduate School, 1973. (*Dissertation Abstracts International*, 1973, *33*[12-B], 6074-6075.)

Fand, A. B. "Sex Role and Self Concept: A Study of the Feminine Sex Role as Perceived by Eighty-Five College Women for Themselves, Their Ideal Woman, the Average Woman, and Men's Ideal Woman." Unpublished doctoral dissertation, Cornell University, 1955. (*Dissertation Abstracts International*, 1955, *15*, 1135-1136.)

Feulner, P. N. "Women in the Professions: A Social-Psychological Study." Unpublished doctoral dissertation, Ohio State University, 1973. (*Dissertation Abstracts International*, 1974, *34*[8-A, Pt. 2], 5309.)

Fox, D. J., Steinmann, A., and Losen, S. M. "The Impact of Sex Education on the Sex Role Perceptions of Junior High School Students." *International Mental Health Research Newsletter*, 1974, *16*, 13-14.

Fox, L. L. W. "A Comparative Analysis of Internal-External Locus of Control and Sex Role Concepts in Black and White Freshman Women." Unpublished doctoral dissertation, East Texas State University, 1975. (*Dissertation Abstracts International*, 1976, *36*[8-A], 5143-5144.)

Gill, M. K. "Psychological Femininity of College Women as It Relates to Self-Actualization, Feminine Role Attitudes, and Selected Background Variables." Unpublished doctoral dissertation, St. Johns University, 1974. (*Dissertation Abstracts International*, 1976, *36*[11-A], 7206-7207.)

Ginn, F. W. "Career Motivation and Role Perception of Women as Related to Parental Role Expectation and Parental Status Discrepancy." Unpublished doctoral dissertation, Catholic University of America, 1968. (*Dissertation Abstracts*, 1969, *29*[12-B], 4845.)

Gump, J. P. "Sex Role Attitudes and Psychological Well-Being." *Journal of Social Issues*, 1972, *28*, 79-92.

Gump, J. P. "Comparative Analysis of Black Women's and White Women's Sex Role Attitudes." *Journal of Consulting and Clinical Psychology*, 1975, *43*, 858-863.

Hanson, J. C. "Feminine Role Values and Personality Factors Among Women's Liberation Members, College Women Seeking Personal Counseling, and Other College Women." Unpublished doctoral dissertation, Kent State University, 1974. (*Dissertation Abstracts International*, 1975, *35*[10-A], 6456-6457.)

Heilbrun, A. B., Jr. "Parent Identification and Filial Sex Role Behavior: The Importance of Biological Context." *Nebraska Symposium on Motivation*, 1973, *21*, 125-194.

Heilbrun, A. B., Jr., Kleemeier, C., and Piccola, G. "Developmental and Situational Correlates of Achievement Behavior in College Females." *Journal of Personality*, 1974, *42*, 420-436.

Hipple, J. L. "Perceptual Differences in Concepts of the Ideal Woman." *The School Counselor*, 1975, *22*, 180-186.

Hipple, J. L. "Perceptual Differences Between Married and Single College Men for Concepts of Ideal Woman." *Adolescence*, 1976, *11*, 579-583.

Hoar, C. A. "Field Dependence, Level of Ego Development, and Female Sex Role Perceptions of Alcoholic and Nonalcoholic Women." Unpublished doctoral dissertation, George Washington University, 1976. (*Dissertation Abstracts International*, 1976, *37*[8-A], 5701.)

Howe, R. R. "Relationships Between Female Role Concepts and Anxiety Among Employed and Nonemployed Mothers of Preschool-Age Children." Unpublished doctoral dissertation, Wayne State University, 1972. (*Dissertation Abstracts International*, 1973, *33*[12-A], 7037-7038.)

Hunt, P. L. "Female Childcare Workers: Their Feminine Identity Congruence, Attitudes Toward Women, Self-Actualization, and Marital Status." Unpublished doctoral dissertation, Indiana State University, 1975. (*Dissertation Abstracts International*, 1976, *36*[7-A], 4262.)

Inagaki, T. "A Cross-Cultural Study of the Feminine Role Concept Between Japanese and American College Women." *Psychologia*, 1967, *10*, 144-154.

Jabury, D. E. "Identity Diffusion as a Function of Sex Roles in Adult Women." Unpublished doctoral dissertation, Michigan State University, 1967. (*Dissertation Abstracts*, 1968, *28*[12-B], 5207-5208.)

Kalka, B. S. "A Comparative Study of Feminine Role Concepts of a Selected Group of College Women." Unpublished doctoral dissertation, Oklahoma State University, 1967. (*Dissertation Abstracts*, 1968, *28*[12-A], 4822.)

Kaplan, A. B. "Some Relationships Between Influenceability and the Role of Women." Unpublished doctoral dissertation, University of Chicago, 1972.

Kincaid, M. B. "Effects of a Group Consciousness-Raising Program on the Attitudes of Adult Women." Unpublished doctoral dissertation, Arizona State University, 1973. (*Dissertation Abstracts International*, 1973, *34*[3-A], 1082-1083.)

Kincaid, M. B. "Changes in Sex Role Attitudes and Self-Actualization of Adult Women Following a Consciousness-Raising Group." *Sex Roles*, 1977, *3*, 329-336.

Lesser, E. K. "Counselor Attitudes Toward Male and Female Students: A Study of 'Helpers' in Conflict." Unpublished doctoral dissertation, University of Rochester, 1974. (*Dissertation Abstracts International,* 1975, *36* [2-A], 708.)

Lesser, E. K. "Are We Still Sexist? A Recent Study of Counselor Attitudes." *The School Counselor,* 1976, *24,* 84-92.

Levine, R. L. "Patterns of Perceived Mothering and Its Relationship to Body Image, Guilt, and Feminine Values in College Women." Unpublished doctoral dissertation, Adelphi University, 1976. (*Dissertation Abstracts International,* 1976, *37* [4-B], 1909.)

McKenzie, S. P. "A Comparative Study of Feminine Role Perceptions, Selected Personality Characteristics, and Traditional Attitudes of Professional Women and Housewives." Unpublished doctoral dissertation, University of Houston, 1971. (*Dissertation Abstracts International,* 1972, *32* [10-A], 5615-5616.)

Meyers, J. C. "The Adjustment of Women to Marital Separation: The Effects of Sex Role Identification and of Stage in Family Life, as Determined by Age and Presence or Absence of Dependent Children." Unpublished doctoral dissertation, University of Colorado, 1976. (*Dissertation Abstracts International,* 1976, *37* [5-B], 2516.)

Miles, I. G. "Competitive Achievement Performance in Women as a Function of Achievement Motivation, Sex Role Attitudes, and Sex Appropriateness of the Achievement Task in Intra- and Inter-Sex Competitive Situations." Unpublished doctoral dissertation, Catholic University of America, 1976. (*Dissertation Abstracts International,* 1976, *36* [12-B], 6449-6450.)

Ott, T. J. "Androgyny, Sex Role Stereotypes, Sex Role Attitudes, and Self-Actualization Among College Women." Unpublished doctoral dissertation, University of Notre Dame, 1976. (*Dissertation Abstracts International,* 1976, *37* [6-A], 3527.)

Phillips, W. E. "The Motive to Achieve in Women as Related to the Perception of Sex Role in Society." Unpublished doctoral dissertation, University of Maryland, 1974. (*Dissertation Abstracts International,* 1975, *35* [9-A], 5934.)

Porter, J. "Sex Role Concepts, Their Relationship to Psychological Well-Being and to Future Plans in Female College Seniors." Unpublished doctoral dissertation, University of Rochester, 1967. (*Dissertation Abstracts,* 1967, *28* [5-A], 1903.)

Powell, B. "Role Conflict and Symptoms of Psychological Distress in College-Educated Women." Unpublished doctoral dissertation, Fordham University, 1975. (*Dissertation Abstracts International,* 1975, *36* [3-B], 1453.)

Powell, B., and Reznikoff, M. "Role Conflict and Symptoms of Psychological Distress in College-Educated Women." *Journal of Consulting and Clinical Psychology,* 1976, *44,* 473-479.

Putnam, B. A., and Hansen, J. C. "Relationship of Self-Concept and Feminine Role Concept to Vocational Maturity in Young Women." *Journal of Counseling Psychology,* 1972, *19,* 436-440.

Rappaport, A. F., Payne, D., and Steinmann, A. "Marriage as a Factor in the Dyadic Perception of the Female Sex Role." *Psychological Reports,* 1970a, *27,* 283-284.

Rappaport, A. F., Payne, D., and Steinmann, A. "Perceptual Differences Between Married and Single College Women for the Concepts of Self, Ideal Woman, and Man's Ideal Woman." *Journal of Marriage and the Family,* 1970b, *32,* 441-442.

Ratliff, C. L. "A Discriminant Analysis of Selected Personality Factors and Attitudes of Two Groups of Mature Women: Homemaker-Students and Homemakers." Unpublished doctoral dissertation, New York University, 1975. (*Dissertation Abstracts International,* 1976, *36* [12-B], 6452.)

Romano, N. C. "Relationships Among Identity Confusion and Resolution, Self-Esteem, and Sex Role Perceptions in Freshman Women at Rutgers University." Unpublished doctoral dissertation, Rutgers University, The State University of New Jersey, 1975. (*Dissertation Abstracts International,* 1976, *36*[10-A], 6487.)

Slotkin, J. H. "Role Conflict Among Selected Anglo and Mexican-American Female College Graduates." Unpublished doctoral dissertation, University of Arizona, 1976. (*Dissertation Abstracts International,* 1976, *37*[3-A], 1825-1826.)

Staten, B. J. "The Effect of Counselor Gender and Sex Role Attitudes on Change of Female Clients' Sex Role Attitudes." Unpublished doctoral dissertation, University of Southern California, 1974. (*Dissertation Abstracts International,* 1975, *35*[10-A], 6470.)

Steinmann, A. G. "The Concept of the Feminine Role in the American Family: A Study of the Concept of the Feminine Role of 51 Middle-Class American Families. Vols. I and II." Unpublished doctoral dissertation, New York University, 1957. (*Dissertation Abstracts,* 1958, *19,* 899-900.)

Steinmann, A. G. "Lack of Communication Between Men and Women." *Marriage and Family Living,* 1958, *20,* 350-352.

Steinmann, A. G. "The Vocational Roles of Older Married Women." *Journal of Social Psychology,* 1961, *54,* 93-101.

Steinmann, A. G. "A Study of the Concept of the Feminine Role of 51 Middle-Class American Families." *Genetic Psychology Monographs,* 1963, *67,* 275-352.

Steinmann, A. G. "Guidance Personnel and the College Man." *Personnel Journal,* 1966, *45,* 294-299.

Steinmann, A. G. "Female Role Perception as a Factor in Counseling." *Journal of the National Association of Women Deans and Counselors,* 1970, *34,* 27-33.

Steinmann, A. G. "Cultural Values, Female Role Expectancies, and Therapeutic Goals: Research and Interpretation." In V. Franks and V. Burtle (Eds.), *Women in Therapy: New Psychotherapies for a Changing Society.* New York: Brunner/Mazel, 1974.

Steinmann, A. G. "Female and Male Concepts of Sex Roles: An Overview of Twenty Years of Cross-Cultural Research." Paper presented at 83rd annual meeting of the American Psychological Association, Chicago, August 1975.

Steinmann, A. G., Doherty, M. A., and Fox, D. J. "Perceptions of Women Religious Regarding the Female Role." *National Catholic Guidance Conference Journal,* 1970, *15,* 43-54.

Steinmann, A. G., and Fox, D. J. *1955-1966 Manual for the Interpretation of the Maferr Inventory of Feminine Values.* New York: Maferr Foundation, 1966a.

Steinmann, A. G., and Fox, D. J. "Male-Female Perceptions of the Female Role in the United States." *Journal of Psychology,* 1966b, *64,* 265-276.

Steinmann, A. G., and Fox, D. J. "Male and Female Physicians' Perceptions of Ideal Feminine Roles." *Journal of the American Medical Women's Association,* 1967, *22,* 184-188.

Steinmann, A. G., and Fox, D. J. "Specific Areas of Agreement and Conflict in Women's Self-Perception and Their Perception of Men's Ideal Woman in Two South American Urban Communities and an Urban Community in the United States." *Journal of Marriage and the Family,* 1969, *31,* 281-289.

Steinmann, A. G., and Fox, D. J. "Attitudes Toward Women's Family Role Among Black and White Undergraduates." *Family Coordinator,* 1970, *19,* 363-368.

Steinmann, A. G., and Fox, D. J. *The Male Dilemma.* New York: Jason Aronson, 1974.

Steinmann, A. G., and Fox, D. J. *1967-1973 Manual for the Interpretation of the Maferr Inventory of Feminine Values.* New York: Maferr Foundation, 1976a.

Steinmann, A. G., and Fox, D. J. *1973-1976 Manual for the Interpretation of the Maferr Inventory of Feminine Values.* New York: Maferr Foundation, 1976b.

Steinmann, A. G., and Jurich, A. P. "The Effects of a Sex Education Course on the Sex Role Perceptions of Junior High School Students." *Family Coordinator,* 1975, *24,* 27-31.

Steinmann, A. G., Levi, J., and Fox, D. J. "Self-Concept of College Women Compared with Their Concept of Ideal Woman and Men's Ideal Woman." *Journal of Counseling Psychology,* 1964, *11,* 370-374.

Stone, J. M. "Value Characteristics of Mature Women Students Related to Enrollment in a Women's Studies Reentry Program." Unpublished doctoral dissertation, U.S. International University, 1975. (*Dissertation Abstracts International,* 1976, *36* [6-B], 3131.)

*Straus, M. A. *Family Measurement Techniques: Abstracts of Published Instruments, 1935-1965.* Minneapolis: University of Minnesota Press, 1969.

*Straus, M. A., and Brown, B. W. *Family Measurement Techniques: Abstracts of Published Instruments, 1935-1974.* Minneapolis: University of Minnesota Press, 1978.

Thurber, S. "The Achievement Motivation-Performance Relationship as Moderated by Sex Role Attitudes." *Educational and Psychological Measurement,* 1976, *36,* 1075-1077.

Tucker, B. Z. "Feminine Sex Role and Occupational Choice: A Study of Self and Intergroup Perceptions of Three Groups of Women." Unpublished doctoral dissertation, Temple University, 1970. (*Dissertation Abstracts International,* 1971, *31* [11-A], 5783-5784.)

Turner, M. E. L. "Sex Role Attitudes and Fear of Success in Relation to Achievement Behavior in Women." Unpublished doctoral dissertation, Fordham University, 1974. (*Dissertation Abstracts International,* 1974, *35* [5-B], 2451-2452.)

Unger, R. K., and Krooth, D. M. "Female Role Perception and Attitudes Toward Competence as Related to Activism in Housewives." Paper presented at 82nd annual meeting of the American Psychological Association, New Orleans, August 1974. (ERIC Document Reproduction Service No. ED 103 729.)

Voss, J. H., and Skinner, D. A. "Concepts of Self and Ideal Woman Held by College Women: A Replication." *Journal of College Student Personnel,* 1975, *16,* 210-213.

Waters, O. P. "Sex Role Attitudes and the Manifest Needs, Vocational Maturity, and Career Orientation of College Women." Unpublished doctoral dissertation, Fordham University, 1976. (*Dissertation Abstracts International,* 1976, *37* [5-A], 2654.)

Weissman, E. I. "The Relationship Between the Marital Status, Feminine Identity Conflict, and Self-Actualization of Women Doctoral Students." Unpublished doctoral dissertation, Boston University School of Education, 1974. (*Dissertation Abstracts International,* 1974, *35* [6-A], 3441.)

Williams, C. C. "Feminine Role as Perceived by Women Teacher Trainees." Unpublished doctoral dissertation, Arizona State University, 1972. (*Dissertation Abstracts International,* 1972, *33* [3-A], 980.)

Williams, J. A. M. "Sex Role Conflict and Academic Achievement: A Study of Superior Women Students." Unpublished doctoral dissertation, University of Illinois at Urbana-Champaign, 1970. (*Dissertation Abstracts International,* 1971, *31* [12-A], 6419-6420.)

188. INVENTORY OF MASCULINE VALUES

AUTHORS: Anne Steinmann and David J. Fox

DATE: 1966

VARIABLE: Attitudes toward the masculine role

TYPE OF INSTRUMENT: Summated rating scale

DESCRIPTION: The scale consists of thirty-four statements pertaining to the needs, rights, and responsibilities of men in regard to women, children, and life in general. Half of the statements concern a family-oriented man—a man "who sees his own satisfactions as no more important than those of his wife and family, one who sees his family responsibilities as taking precedence over any personal potential professional or occupational activity" (Steinmann and Fox, 1976, p. 2). The other half of the statements concern a self-oriented man—"one who considers his own satisfactions more important than those of his wife and family and one who wishes family roles and responsibilities to place no obstacles to his realization of ambition and ability" (Steinmann and Fox, 1976, p. 2). Some items are phrased positively and some items are phrased negatively. Each statement is accompanied by five response options: strongly agree, agree, no opinion/don't know, disagree, and strongly disagree.

There are five forms of the scale: man's self-perception, man's perception of man's ideal man, man's perceptions of woman's ideal man, woman's perceptions of woman's ideal man, and woman's perception of man's ideal man. The content of the items on the five forms is essentially identical. The order of the items is varied, and the phrasing of the items on the forms to be completed by women is slightly different.

PREVIOUSLY ADMINISTERED TO: Junior and senior high school students; college students; adults in the United States, England, Czechoslovakia, Brazil, Greece, Israel, France, Finland, Germany, Austria, the Philippines, Peru, Argentina, Mexico, Japan, Iran, and Turkey

APPROPRIATE FOR: Ages 15 and older

ADMINISTRATION: When the scale is administered to men, it is recommended that three forms be used. First men should be asked to respond in terms of their own opinions; then men should be asked to indicate their perceptions of how the ideal man would respond; and finally they should be asked to indicate their perceptions of how a woman's ideal man would respond. When the scale is administered to women, it is recommended that two forms be used. First a woman should be asked to indicate her opinions of how the ideal man would respond, and then she is asked to indicate her opinions of how a man's ideal man would respond. One form of the scale can be completed in about fifteen minutes.

SAMPLE ITEMS: A father's place is in the home when he is not at work.
              To be successful, a man needs his wife's encouragement.

SCORING: Items are objectively scored and equally weighted. Scores can range from −68 to +68. Low (negative) scores indicate a greater family orientation; high scores indicate a greater self-orientation.

DEVELOPMENT: Although no information is provided regarding the development of the scale, it is apparent that it was developed from the Inventory of Feminine Values (#187). Both scales contain thirty-four statements. Thirty-one of the statements on the Inventory of Feminine Values seem to have a counterpart on the Inventory of Masculine Values. Some of those thirty-one statements are worded identically on the two forms; some are worded slightly differently to reflect the gender differences in the persons being rated; and some ideas are stated differently because a family-oriented woman is oriented toward home and family, whereas a family-oriented man is oriented toward family and also must hold a job.

RELIABILITY: The corrected, split-half reliability is .86 (Steinmann and Fox, 1976).

VALIDITY: In discussing the validity of the scale, Steinmann and Fox (1976, p. 3) state: "The items have face validity in that they are statements with generally accepted connotations, but they have also been submitted to validation by seven judges, who agreed on the nature of the categorization as family- or self-oriented." However, since this same statement appears in the manual for the Inventory of Feminine Values (#187), I suspect that it was actually the items on the Inventory of Feminine Values which were evaluated by the seven judges.

NOTES AND COMMENTS: (1) Steinmann and Fox (1976) present detailed results from the administration of the scale to twelve American samples including a total of 911 men and 1,543 women.

(2) There are special versions of the scales appropriate for junior and senior high school students. The instrument is entitled Developmental Inventory of Masculine Values. The substance of the statements, the response options and the scoring are comparable to the adult-level Inventory of Masculine Values.

(3) The scale is described and reviewed in *The Eighth Mental Measurements Yearbook* (Buros, 1978, entry 608).

SOURCE: Maferr Foundation, Inc.
      140 West 57th Street
      New York, New York 10019
      See also Steinmann and Fox, 1974.

BIBLIOGRAPHY:

Abelew, T. "Sex Role Attitudes, Perceptual Style, Mathematical Ability and Perceived Parental Child Rearing Attitudes in Adolescents." Unpublished doctoral dissertation, Fordham University, 1974. (*Dissertation Abstracts International*, 1974, 35[3-B], 1439.)

Barrett, B. "Sex, Birth Order, and Family Composition as Related to the Sex Role Perceptions of Male and Female College Students." Unpublished doctoral dissertation, Rutgers University, 1975. (*Dissertation Abstracts International*, 1976, 36[8-B], 4125.)

*Buros, O. K. *The Eighth Mental Measurements Yearbook*. Highland Park, N.J.: Gryphon Press, 1978.

Cohn, A. R. "Self-Concept and Role Perceptions as Correlates of Marital Satisfaction." Unpublished doctoral dissertation, Illinois Institute of Technology, 1975. (*Dissertation Abstracts International,* 1976, *36*[7-B], 3569.)

Fox, D. J., Steinmann, A. G., and Losen, S. M. "The Impact of Sex Education on the Sex Role Perceptions of Junior High School Students." *International Mental Health Research Newsletter,* 1974, *16,* 13-14.

Lesser, E. K. "Counselor Attitudes Toward Male and Female Students: A Study of 'Helpers' in Conflict." Unpublished doctoral dissertation, University of Rochester, 1974. (*Dissertation Abstracts International,* 1975, *36*[2-A], 708.)

Lesser, E. K. "Are We Still Sexist? A Recent Study of Counselor Attitudes." *The School Counselor,* 1976, *24,* 84-92.

Steinmann, A. G., and Fox, D. J. *The Male Dilemma.* New York: Jason Aronson, 1974.

Steinmann, A. G., and Fox, D. J. *Manual for the Interpretation of the Maferr Inventory of Masculine Values.* New York: Maferr Foundation, 1976.

Steinmann, A. G., Fox, D. J., and Farkas, R. "Male and Female Perceptions of Male Sex Roles." *Proceedings of the 76th Annual Convention of the American Psychological Association,* 1968, *3,* 421-422.

Steinmann, A. G., and Jurich, A. P. "The Effects of a Sex Education Course on the Sex Role Perceptions of Junior High School Students." *Family Coordinator,* 1975, *24,* 27-31.

---

189. KAHOE-MEADOW ATTITUDES TOWARD WOMEN SCALE

AUTHORS: Richard D. Kahoe and Mary Jo Meadow

DATE: 1977

VARIABLES: Attitudes toward traditional roles for men and women; attitudes toward economic and social equality between the sexes; attitudes toward an improved position or fewer obligations for men

TYPE OF INSTRUMENT: Summated rating scale

DESCRIPTION: The scale consists of thirty-two items representing three subscales: Antitraditionalism measures attitudes toward traditional roles for men and women (twelve items); Female Liberation measures attitudes toward economic and social equality between the sexes (eleven items); and Male Liberation measures attitudes toward an improved position or fewer obligations for men (nine items). On the Antitraditionalism scale, all items are phrased to reflect a traditional attitude; on the Female Liberation scale, ten of the eleven items are phrased to reflect a positive attitude toward equality between the sexes; and on the Male Liberation scale, eight of the nine items are phrased to reflect a positive attitude toward an improved position for men. Each item is accompanied by four response options: agree strongly, agree mildly, disagree mildly, and disagree strongly.

PREVIOUSLY ADMINISTERED TO: College students

APPROPRIATE FOR: Ages 16 and older

ADMINISTRATION: The scale is self-administered and can be completed in less than fifteen minutes.

SAMPLE ITEMS:

Antitraditionalism: Many women in the women's liberation movement are radicals who really don't know what is best for themselves.

Female Liberation: Women should take increasing responsibility for leadership in solving the intellectual and social problems of the day.

Male Liberation: Special attentions like standing up for a woman when she comes into a room or giving her a seat on a crowded bus are outmoded and should be discontinued.

SCORING: Items are objectively scored and equally weighted. A score is obtained for each of the three subscales. For each score, a higher value indicates a more liberal attitude.

DEVELOPMENT: Nineteen items designed to measure attitudes toward women and the fifty-five item version of the Attitudes Toward Women Scale (#169) were combined into a single scale and administered to 354 college students from two colleges. Separate factor analyses were performed on the responses from the students at each college. Three comparable factors were extracted from both factor analyses. The three subscales described here represent the factors extracted. Items that loaded heavily on each of the factors comprise the items on each of the scales.

RELIABILITY: No data are provided.

VALIDITY: An analysis was made of some of the personality correlates of the scores obtained by the 354 college students. For both men and women, it was found that liberal sex role attitudes were positively correlated with a measure of internal locus of control and negatively correlated with measures of dogmatism and authoritarianism.

NOTES AND COMMENTS: (1) There is considerable overlap between the items on the Kahoe-Meadow Attitudes Toward Women Scale and the Spence and Helmreich Attitudes Toward Women Scale (#169). Of the twelve items on the Antitraditionalism scale, seven appear on Spence and Helmreich's scale; of the eleven items on the Female Liberation scale, eight appear on Spence and Helmreich's scale; and of the nine items on the Male Liberation scale, seven items appear on Spence and Helmreich's scale.

(2) One significant difference between the Kahoe-Meadow Attitudes Toward Women Scale and the Spence and Helmreich Attitudes Toward Women Scale is that the Kahoe-Meadow scale yields three subscale scores but no total score, and the Spence and Helmreich scale yields a total score but no subscale scores.

(3) For men, the average intercorrelation between the three subscales was .34; for women, it was .50.

SOURCE: Richard D. Kahoe
    Route 1, Box 31
    Wheatfield, Indiana 46392

BIBLIOGRAPHY:

Kahoe, R. D., and Meadow, M. J. "Three Dimensions of Sexist Attitudes: Differential
    Relationships with Personality Variables." Paper presented at 85th annual meeting
    of the American Psychological Association, San Francisco, August 1977.

---

190. MATTHEWS ATTITUDES TOWARD CAREER AND MARRIAGE SCALE

AUTHOR: Esther Matthews

DATE: 1960

VARIABLE: Attitudes toward career and marriage for women

TYPE OF INSTRUMENT: Summated rating scale

DESCRIPTION: The scale consists of fifty-seven statements representing fourteen areas: college, career, and time of marriage (peer focus) (four items); time of dating and marriage (parent focus) (six items); attitudes toward children (four items); attitudes toward home-making (four items); women's perceptions of women's attitudes toward the expression of women's intelligence and its implications (six items); women's perceptions of boys' attitudes toward the expression of girls' intelligence (four items); women's perceptions of men's attitudes toward the expression of girls' intelligence and its implications (seven items); women's feeling of inferiority to men (three items); attitudes toward equality of the sexes (two items); women's acceptance of the role of wife and mother and rejection of career (ten items); desirability of having children (two items); acceptance of feminine jobs for women (two items); acceptance of sex differences (two items); and career dominance over marriage (one item). Each statement is accompanied by six response options: agree very much, agree pretty much, agree a little, disagree a little, disagree pretty much, and disagree very much.

PREVIOUSLY ADMINISTERED TO: Females, ages 11-26

APPROPRIATE FOR: Ages 11 and older

ADMINISTRATION: The scale is self-administered and can be completed in about thirty minutes.

SAMPLE ITEMS:

College, career, and time of marriage (peer focus): Girls should go to college mainly to prepare for a profession.

Time of dating and marriage (parent focus): Parents should let their children decide when to marry.

Attitudes toward children: It is fun to take care of children.

Attitudes toward homemaking: All girls should take home economics in junior and senior high school.

Women's perceptions of women's attitudes toward the expression of women's intelligence and its implications: Most women think it's hard to get married if they have a career.

Women's perceptions of boys' attitudes toward the expression of girls' intelligence: Boys don't like smart girls.

Women's perceptions of men's attitudes toward the expression of girls' intelligence and its implications: Hardly any man would want to be a bachelor.

Women's feelings of inferiority to men: Most parents feel a son's education is the most important.

Attitudes toward equality of the sexes: Girls should have as many chances in life as boys.

Women's acceptance of the role of wife and mother and rejection of career: A woman's true happiness lies in her home and family.

Desirability of having children: If couples do not have children they should adopt some.

Acceptance of feminine jobs for women: Women should seek feminine jobs.

Acceptance of sex differences: Men and women think differently.

Career dominance over marriage: A woman with a successful career ought to delay marriage.

SCORING: Items are objectively scored and equally weighted. Scores are obtained for each of the fourteen scales, and an overall total score is computed. Low scores indicate a greater marriage orientation compared with career orientation.

DEVELOPMENT: A scale consisting of seventy-one items was completed by 1,247 females between the ages of 11 and 26. Intercorrelations were computed between each of the items for each of three age groups: junior high school girls, senior high school girls, and adults. Based on the intercorrelation matrices, fifty-one items representing fourteen scales were identified for the final scale.

RELIABILITY: No reliability estimates are provided. However, Matthews (1960) presents correlation matrices showing the intercorrelations between all of the items for each of three age groups: junior high school girls, senior high school girls, and adult women.

VALIDITY: Matthews (1960) tested three hypotheses using the Matthews Attitudes Toward Career and Marriage Scale: "Attitudes toward career and marriage change as a girl ages"; "Attitudes toward marriage and career will vary according to the high school curriculum girls elect or have elected in the past"; and "Attitudes toward marriage and career will vary according to the life plans girls express" (p. 137). All three hypotheses were supported by the data.

NOTES AND COMMENTS: Because the subscale scores are based on so few items, it is especially important that the reliability of each of the scores be determined. It would not be surprising if many of the subscales were quite unreliable.

SOURCE: See Matthews, 1960.

BIBLIOGRAPHY:

Matthews, E. "The Marriage-Career Conflict in Girls and Women." Unpublished doctoral dissertation, Harvard University, 1960.
Matthews, E., and Tiedman, D. V. "Attitudes Toward Career and Marriage and the Development of Life-Style in Young Women." *Journal of Counseling Psychology,* 1964, *11,* 375-384.

---

191. NADLER OPEN SUBORDINATION OF WOMEN SCALE

AUTHORS: Eugene B. Nadler and William R. Morrow

DATE: 1957

VARIABLE: Attitudes toward women

TYPE OF INSTRUMENT: Summated rating scale

DESCRIPTION: The scale consists of twenty statements concerning women and/or men. The phrasing of all items reflects a negative attitude toward women. Five items assess support for social policies that restrict women and encourage their subordination to men; five items assess perceptions of the alleged inferiority of women; four items assess perceptions of the alleged narrowness of women's outlook; and six items assess perceptions of the alleged offensiveness of women. Each of the twenty items is accompanied by six response alternatives ranging from strong agreement to strong disagreement.

PREVIOUSLY ADMINISTERED TO: College students

APPROPRIATE FOR: Ages 16 and older

ADMINISTRATION: The scale can be self-administered and can be completed in less than ten minutes.

SAMPLE ITEMS:

Restrictive policies: It goes against nature to have a woman as foreman or boss over men.

Alleged inferiority: Because of their inborn limitations, women have contributed but little to the discoveries and inventions of civilization.

Alleged narrowness: A major fault that women have is their personal vanity, as shown by the exaggerated importance they attach to minute details of dress and grooming.

Alleged offensiveness: Constant petting and cuddling have the same cheapening effect on a woman as that produced on merchandise which through repeated handling has become faded and rumpled.

SCORING: Items are objectively scored and equally weighted. The total score can range from 20 (very positive attitudes) to 140 (very negative attitudes).

DEVELOPMENT: A pool of twenty-five items was administered to sixty-two college men. An item analysis was performed in which the responses from men scoring in the upper 25 percent of the distribution of total scores were compared with the responses from men scoring in the lower 25 percent of the distribution of total scores. Items that discriminated poorly were revised or eliminated, resulting in a scale of twenty items.

RELIABILITY: The scale was administered to eighty-three college men, and a reliability estimate was calculated. The corrected split-half reliability was .83 (Nadler and Morrow, 1959).

VALIDITY: The eighty-three college men completed three other scales: the Nadler Chivalry Scale (#88), which is a measure of chivalrous attitudes toward women; a measure of ethnocentrism; and a measure of fascism. As predicted, the Nadler Open Subordination of Women Scale correlated positively with the other three measures. The correlation with the Nadler Chivalry Scale was .35 (p < .01); the correlation with the measure of ethnocentrism was .45 (p < .01); and the correlation with the measure of fascism was .66 (p < :01) (Nadler and Morrow, 1959).

NOTES AND COMMENTS: (1) Fourteen of the statements each include two ideas. A respondent might agree with one idea expressed in the statement but disagree with the other idea. This makes the statements difficult to respond to and the scores difficult to interpret.

(2) The scale items were interspersed with the items from the Nadler Chivalry Scale (#88), a measure of ethnocentrism, and a measure of fascism when Nadler administered them.

(3) Nadler (1953) originally titled the scale the Hostility Scale.

(4) The scale is also described in *Scales for the Measurement of Attitudes* (Shaw and Wright, 1967, pp. 458-459).

SOURCE: See Nadler, 1953; Nadler and Morrow, 1959; or Shaw and Wright, 1967, p. 459.

BIBLIOGRAPHY:

Nadler, E. B. "The Measurement of Chivalrous and Hostile Attitudes Toward Women." Unpublished master's thesis, Western Reserve University, 1953.

Nadler, E. B., and Morrow, W. R. "Authoritarian Attitudes Toward Women and Their Correlates." *Journal of Social Psychology*, 1959, *49*, 113-123.

*Shaw, M. E., and Wright, J. M. *Scales for the Measurement of Attitudes.* New York: McGraw-Hill, 1967.

Werner, M. E. "A Scale for the Measurement of 'Sexist' Attitudes." Unpublished doctoral dissertation, Columbia University, 1973. (*Dissertation Abstracts International*, 1973, *34*[1-A], 180-181.)

192. OSMOND-MARTIN SEX ROLE ATTITUDE SCALE

AUTHORS: Marie Withers Osmond and Patricia Yancey Martin

DATE: 1975 (used 1972)

VARIABLE: Sex role attitudes

TYPE OF INSTRUMENT: Summated rating scale

DESCRIPTION: The scale consists of thirty-two statements regarding women and/or men. The statements cover four areas: familial roles (eight items), extrafamilial roles (five items), stereotypes of males and females (ten items), and social change issues related to sex roles (eight items). Eighteen items are phrased to reflect traditional attitudes, and fourteen items are phrased to reflect modern attitudes. Each statement is accompanied by five response options ranging from "strongly agree" to "strongly disagree."

PREVIOUSLY ADMINISTERED TO: College juniors and seniors

APPROPRIATE FOR: Ages 16 and older

ADMINISTRATION: The scale can be self-administered and can be completed in about fifteen minutes.

SAMPLE ITEMS:

Familial Roles: Women with children in grammar school should, if at all possible, stay at home rather than work.

Extrafamilial Roles: I would feel uncomfortable if my immediate supervisor at work was a woman.

Stereotypes: Women generally prefer light conversations over rational discussions.

Social Change: Unlike the race riots, the "battle between the sexes" will never involve violence on any large scale.

SCORING: Items are objectively scored and equally weighted. A total score is obtained that can range from 32 (very modern) to 160 (very traditional).

DEVELOPMENT: A pool of items was given to ten faculty members in various areas of the social sciences, with instructions to indicate whether each item reflected a modern or traditional attitude. There was unanimous agreement on the classification of the thirty-two items that comprise the scale.

RELIABILITY: An estimate of reliability was calculated from the responses of 480 college students. Coefficient alpha was .88.

VALIDITY: In addition to completing the Osmond-Martin Sex Role Attitude Scale, the 480 college students responded to two relevant questions: "(a) How great a need do you feel there is to 'do something' about sexism in our society? and (b) To what extent do you feel that the 'social roles of men and women in the modern world' should be a vital issue of concern to most people in our society" (p. 746). For thirty of the thirty-two items on the attitude scale, there was a significant (p < .001) correlation in the predicted direction with the responses to these two items.

College men (n = 225) obtained more traditional scores (median = 80) than did college women (n = 255, median = 72). No indication is given as to whether the difference between the medians was statistically significant.

An item analysis was performed on the responses given by 480 college students. Thirty-one of the items discriminated significantly (p < .001) between those scoring in the highest quartile and those scoring in the lowest quartile of the distribution of total scores.

A factor analysis was performed on the responses from the 480 college students and six factors were extracted. Four of the factors were essentially the same as the four areas the scale was designed to cover: familial roles, extrafamilial roles, stereotypes of males and females, and social change issues related to sex roles. A fifth factor concerned familial and extrafamilial aspects of the male role; a sixth factor concerned performance-related stereotypes of females.

SOURCE: See Osmond and Martin, 1975.

BIBLIOGRAPHY:

Osmond, M. W., and Martin, P. Y. "Sex and Sexism: A Comparison of Male and Female Sex Role Attitudes." *Journal of Marriage and the Family,* 1975, *37*, 744-758.

---

193. PACES-CLARKE ATTITUDES SCALE

AUTHORS: James Paces and Gerald Clarke

DATE: 1976

VARIABLES: Sex role conception; family orientation

TYPE OF INSTRUMENT: Summated rating scale

DESCRIPTION: The scale consists of thirty-seven statements regarding dating, marriage, family life, and women's roles. For thirty-two items, there are five response options: strongly agree, agree, undecided, disagree, and strongly disagree. For the last five items, the respondent is to indicate either "yes," "undecided," or "no."

PREVIOUSLY ADMINISTERED TO: Grades 9-12

APPROPRIATE FOR: Ages 12 and older

ADMINISTRATION: The scale can be self-administered and can be completed in about ten minutes.

SAMPLE ITEMS:

Sex Role Conception: Raising children is more a mother's job than a father's.

Family Orientation: Remaining single is an excellent way to live.

SCORING: Items are objectively scored and equally weighted. Two summary scores are obtained: one for Sex Role Conception and one for Family Orientation.

DEVELOPMENT: A pool of seventy items was administered to sixty high school students. Based on their responses, thirty-three items were eliminated. The item selection results were cross-validated by administering the scale to 500 students. The responses from 200 of the students were factor analyzed, and two factors were extracted: Sex Role Conception and Family Orientation.

RELIABILITY: No data are provided.

VALIDITY: As predicted, women had more liberal sex role attitudes and were more pro-family in their orientation than men. Contrary to prediction, Sex Role Conception scores were not related to parents' educational level or to mother's employment status. The correlation between Sex Role Conception scores and Family Orientation scores was essentially .00. A measure of knowledge of courtship and family life was also given to high school students. Contrary to expectation, there was very little relationship between knowledge scores and attitude scores.

NOTES AND COMMENTS: The items comprising the Sex Role Conception score could be used without the items measuring Family Orientation. However, first there should be some research conducted to determine the psychometric properties of the Sex Role Conception items when used alone.

SOURCE: Anthony Penna
        Associate Director
        Carnegie Education Center
        Schenley Park
        Pittsburgh, Pennsylvania 15213

BIBLIOGRAPHY:

Angrist, S. S., Mickelsen, R., and Penna, A. N. "Variations in Adolescents' Knowledge and Attitudes About Family Life: Implications for Curriculum Design." *Adolescence,* 1976, *11,* 107-126.

194. PETERSON WOMEN'S LIBERATION SCALE

AUTHOR: M. J. Peterson

DATE: 1975

VARIABLE: Attitudes toward issues associated with the feminist movement

TYPE OF INSTRUMENT: Summated rating scale

DESCRIPTION: The scale consists of fifteen items. Ten items are statements relating to beliefs about men and women. Response options are: strongly agree, agree, neutral, disagree, or strongly disagree. The remaining items are phrases describing issues advocated by the feminist movement. Response options are: strongly approve, approve, neutral, disapprove, or strongly disapprove. The majority of items are phrased to reflect a positive attitude toward the issues associated with the feminist movement.

PREVIOUSLY ADMINISTERED TO: Female college students

APPROPRIATE FOR: Females, ages 16 and older

ADMINISTRATION: The scale can be self-administered and can be completed in about five minutes.

SAMPLE ITEMS:

Agree-disagree: Almost all men are unconscious sexists.

Approve-disapprove: Abortion on demand by women

SCORING: Items are objectively scored and equally weighted. Total scores can range from 15 (strong support for the issues) to 75 (no support for the issues).

DEVELOPMENT: To construct a pool of items, some items were taken from Tavris (1971) and other items were written for this instrument. The item pool was administered to two groups of women: a feminist group and a conservative church group. The fifteen items that discriminated between the two groups comprise the scale.

RELIABILITY: Split-half reliability coefficients ranged between .89 to .96 (Peterson, 1975).

VALIDITY: The scale was completed by 160 college women. The respondents were divided into three groups on the basis of their responses: high, medium and low. The three groups differed in terms of mother's education ($p < .01$) but not in terms of their own career expectations or whether their mothers worked (Peterson, 1975).

SOURCE: See Peterson, 1975.

BIBLIOGRAPHY:

Peterson, M. J. "The Asymmetry of Sex Role Perceptions." *Sex Roles,* 1975, *1,* 267-282.

*Tavris, C. "Woman and Man: A *Psychology Today* Questionnaire." *Psychology Today,*
1971, *4,* 82.

---

195. SARUP SCALE OF ATTITUDES TOWARD FEMINISM (ATF)

AUTHOR: Gian Sarup

DATE: 1976

VARIABLE: Attitudes toward feminism

TYPE OF INSTRUMENT: Summated rating scale

DESCRIPTION: The scale consists of eighteen statements relating to women's rights, roles, and abilities, and the feminist movement. Half of the items are phrased positively and half are phrased negatively. Each statement is accompanied by five response options: strongly agree, agree, undecided, disagree, and strongly disagree.

PREVIOUSLY ADMINISTERED TO: High school students, college students, and adults

APPROPRIATE FOR: Ages 14 and older

ADMINISTRATION: The scale is self-administered and can be completed in ten minutes.

SAMPLE ITEMS: Often because of their sex women are prevented from achieving their goals.
Women's liberation advocates are on an ego trip.

SCORING: Items are objectively scored and equally weighted. Total scores can range from 18 (antifeminist) to 90 (profeminist).

DEVELOPMENT: An item pool consisting of thirty-nine statements was given to six high school students, fifty-three college students, and fourteen employed adults. Based on the responses from these people, items were selected for the final scale to satisfy two criteria: satisfactory discrimination between the highest and lowest quartiles of the distribution of total scores; and a balance of positively and negatively phrased items. The correlation between scores on the final eighteen-item version of the scale and scores on the thirty-nine-item pool was .97 (p < .001).

RELIABILITY: The corrected, split-half reliability coefficient equaled .95 when the scale was administered to seventy-three persons from high school age through adult.

VALIDITY: The scale was completed by 128 persons including high school students, college students, and adults. As predicted, women (n = 59, $\overline{X}$ = 65.10) scored significantly more profeminist than men (n = 69, $\overline{X}$ = 54.27, p < .001). The correlation between gender and ATF scores was .43 (p < .001).

Respondents also completed a thirteen-item measure of authoritarianism. When the respondents were divided into three groups based on their authoritarianism scores, significant differences (p < .001) were found on the ATF scores. The correlation between authoritarianism scores and ATF scores was −.52 (p < .001). Consistent with Sarup's prediction, higher authoritarianism scores were associated with a more antifeminist attitude.

NOTES AND COMMENTS: (1) Of the eighteen statements on the scale, one is a double-barreled statement, two are awkwardly phrased, and one is excessively wordy.

(2) The thirteen-item authoritarianism scale was embedded in the ATF scale when the scales were used.

SOURCE: Microfiche Publications
      P.O. Box 3513
      Grand Central Station
      New York, New York 10017

BIBLIOGRAPHY:

Sarup, G. "Gender, Authoritarianism, and Attitudes Toward Feminism." *Social Behavior and Personality,* 1976, *4,* 57-64.

---

196. SCHMIDT SEX ROLE ATTITUDE SCALE

AUTHOR: Lanalee Carol Schmidt

DATE: 1973

VARIABLE: Sex role attitudes

TYPE OF INSTRUMENT: Summated rating scale

DESCRIPTION: The scale consists of fifty-five statements relating to various aspects of women's roles, including, for example, marital roles, maternal roles, sexual roles, and employee roles. Each statement is followed by the phrase "I feel that I . . ." and five response options: strongly agree, somewhat agree, no opinion, somewhat disagree, strongly disagree. Some items are phrased to reflect traditional attitudes, and others are phrased to reflect egalitarian attitudes.

PREVIOUSLY ADMINISTERED TO: Females

APPROPRIATE FOR: Ages 16 and older

ADMINISTRATION: This self-administered scale can be completed in about half an hour.

SAMPLE ITEMS: In a marriage, the husband is mainly responsible for the financial support of the family. I feel that I . . .
                    Women should initiate intimate interaction with men if they wish to. I feel that I . . .

SCORING: Items are objectively scored and equally weighted. High total scores indicate traditional attitudes.

DEVELOPMENT: A fifty-nine-item pool was compiled and administered as part of a longer instrument to a sample of ten women who identified themselves as traditionalists and ten women who were associated with the feminist movement. The fifty-five items that differentiated between known feminists and known traditionalists were retained for the final form of the scale. Furthermore, the twenty women were asked to indicate whether each statement should be classified as "Feminist," "Ambiguous," or "Traditional." Only items on which there was unanimous agreement among the twenty "judges" and the author were retained for the final scale.

RELIABILITY: The preliminary form of the scale, consisting of fifty-nine items, was administered to a sample of twenty women on two occasions about three weeks apart. Test-retest reliability was .975 (Schmidt, 1973). After the women completed the scale the first time, they were asked to classify each statement as "Feminist," "Ambiguous," or "Traditional." This is likely to have had an effect on the test-retest reliability of the scale.

VALIDITY: When the responses from sixty-one women were used to dichotomize the women into "Traditionalists" and "Feminists," a significant relationship between women's employment status and sex role attitudes was found. Traditionalists were more likely to be not working and feminists were more likely to be working (Schmidt, 1973).

NOTES AND COMMENTS: Schmidt (1973) related scores on the Schmidt Sex Role Attitude Scale to a number of demographic variables, including, for example, number of years married, age, age of children, employment status, educational attainment, and birth order.

SOURCE: See Schmidt, 1973.

BIBLIOGRAPHY:

Nixon, M. "Sex Role and Life-Styles of Professional Women." Unpublished doctoral dissertation, University of Alberta, 1975.
Nixon, M., and Gue, L. R. "Women Administrators and Women Teachers: A Comparative Study." *Alberta Journal of Educational Research*, 1975, *21*, 196-206.
Schmidt, L. C. "Sex Roles Attitudes and Changing Life-Styles of Professional Women." Unpublished doctoral dissertation, University of Alberta, 1973.

197. SEX ROLE EQUALITY INVENTORY (SREI)

AUTHOR: Clinton J. Jesser

DATE: 1974 (used 1972)

VARIABLE: Attitudes toward women and women's issues

TYPE OF INSTRUMENT: Summated rating scale

DESCRIPTION: The scale consists of forty-eight statements regarding women and women's issues, such as perceptions of discrimination against women, issues related to male-female relationships, sex differences, female sexuality, employment issues, feminist movement issues, and marital and maternal role issues. About half the items reflect a positive attitude and half reflect a negative attitude. Each item is accompanied by six response options: strongly agree, agree, mildly agree, mildly disagree, disagree, or strongly disagree.

PREVIOUSLY ADMINISTERED TO: Unmarried female college students

APPROPRIATE FOR: Females, ages 16 and older

ADMINISTRATION: The scale can be self-administered and can be completed in about fifteen minutes.

SAMPLE ITEMS: There are far too many places and activities in our society which un-necessarily use distinctions between male and female.
          The belief that women cannot make as good supervisors or executives as men is totally a myth.

SCORING: Items are objectively scored and equally weighted. Total scores can range from 0 to 240.

DEVELOPMENT: The statements were originally selected from the literature regarding "women in society" and suggestions made by students and faculty. The items were pre-tested for understandability. The results of the pretest were used to revise the original scale.

RELIABILITY: No data are provided.

VALIDITY: No data are provided.

NOTES AND COMMENTS: (1) Jesser factor analyzed the scale. He found that most items loaded on a single factor, which he did not title.
          (2) In reporting the results of his research, Jesser did not use responses to all the items in the scale. Rather he totaled individuals' scores on eleven items of the scale. The eleven items he chose were those that had marginals no more extreme than 37 percent and 63 percent when the three "agree" responses were grouped together and the three "disagree" responses were grouped together. Jesser referred to the score on the eleven

items as the Feminism score. He then compared various groups on their Feminism scores and reported the following: "High feminism was found among (1) a larger proportion of social science majors compared to education majors, (2) a larger proportion of respondents identifying themselves as politically liberal, (3) those favoring sex role change, (4) those perceiving employer discrimination against women, and (5) those believing that women are prevented from getting a good job because of lack of drive" (p. 57).

(3) One item on the scale—"For their own good, women must always make their sexual favors scarce"—is subject to numerous interpretations. The term "sexual favors" has different meanings to different persons.

SOURCE: Clinton Jesser
          Department of Sociology
          Northern Illinois University
          DeKalb, Illinois 60115

BIBLIOGRAPHY:

Jesser, C. J. "A Dim Light on the Way to Damascus: Selective Feminism Among College Women." *Youth and Society,* 1974, *6*, 49-62.

---

198. SEX ROLE ORIENTATION SCALE

AUTHORS: Donna Brogan and Nancy G. Kutner

DATE: 1976

VARIABLE: Sex role ideology

TYPE OF INSTRUMENT: Summated rating scale

DESCRIPTION: The scale consists of thirty-six statements, each of which is followed by six response alternatives: strongly agree, moderately agree, agree slightly more than disagree, disagree slightly more than agree, moderately disagree, and strongly disagree. Twenty of the thirty-six items are phrased to reflect traditional attitudes, and the other sixteen items are phrased to reflect nontraditional attitudes. The item content is designed to measure attitudes toward (1) traditional, sex-based division of labor in marriage, (2) traditional, sex-based power structure, (3) traditional and nontraditional employment of men and women, (4) traditional and nontraditional political status of women, (5) sex role socialization of children, and (6) stereotypes of sex role related behavior, such as dress and morals.

PREVIOUSLY ADMINISTERED TO: College students, graduate nursing students, married and dating couples

APPROPRIATE FOR: Ages 16 and older

ADMINISTRATION: The scale can be self-administered and can be completed in about twenty minutes.

SAMPLE ITEMS:

Sex-based division of labor in marriage: The husband should take primary responsibility for major family decisions, such as the purchase of a home or car.

Sex-based power structure: In groups that have both male and female members, it is appropriate that top leadership positions be held by males.

Employment of men and women: A woman whose job involves contact with the public, e.g., salesperson or teacher, should not continue to work when she is noticeably pregnant.

Political status of women: It is all right for women to hold local political offices.

Sex role socialization of children: The idea of young girls participating in Little League competition is ridiculous.

Stereotypes of sex role related behavior: It is more important for a woman to keep her figure and dress becomingly than it is for a man.

SCORING: Items are objectively scored and equally weighted. Total scores can range from 36 (most traditional) to 216 (most nontraditional).

DEVELOPMENT: The authors compiled an item pool of fifty-three statements, some of which were taken from existing scales and some of which were written by the authors of this scale. The fifty-three-item scale was completed by 298 persons, and their responses were used to perform an item analysis. Items whose item-total correlations equaled or exceeded .50 were selected for the scale. Forty items satisfied this criterion. Four of the forty items were eliminated because they were judged to be ambiguously phrased. For each of the remaining thirty-six items, further analysis was done by dividing the respondents into six groups depending upon the response given (for example, strongly agree, moderately agree) to the particular item. Mean total scores for the six groups were then compared. By this criterion, "all thirty-six items appeared to satisfactorily discriminate among subjects" (p. 35).

RELIABILITY: Corrected split-half reliability based on data obtained from 298 respondents equaled .95. Item-total correlations ranged from .50 to .74.

VALIDITY: To provide evidence of the construct validity of the scale, the authors report the following findings, which are consistent with findings reported in previous research: (1) female graduate students scored significantly higher (more nontraditional) than female undergraduates, who scored significantly higher than male undergraduates; (2) younger males scored significantly higher than older males (the direction of the difference was the same for females, but the difference was not statistically significant); (3) there were significant differences in scores for different religious groups, with Catholics being the most traditional and respondents reporting "no religion" being the most nontraditional; and (4) there were significant correlations between child-rearing ideology and sex role ideology.

NOTES AND COMMENTS: Despite the author's claim that the scale measures sex role

ideology, an examination of the items suggests that the scale is actually measuring attitudes toward women and women's roles.

SOURCE: See Brogan and Kutner, 1976.

BIBLIOGRAPHY:

Brogan, D., and Kutner, N. G. "Measuring Sex Role Orientation: A Normative Approach." *Journal of Marriage and the Family,* 1976, *38,* 31-40.

---

199. SEX ROLE SURVEY (SRS)

AUTHOR: A. P. MacDonald, Jr.

DATE: 1973

VARIABLE: Attitudes regarding equality between the sexes

TYPE OF INSTRUMENT: Summated rating scale

DESCRIPTION: The scale is a multidimensional measure consisting of sixty-three statements concerning women and/or men. The statements pertain to equality between the
sexes in employment situations and in the home, in the performance of social and
domestic work, and in respect to traditionally sex-appropriate behavior. Each statement is
accompanied by six response options: I agree very much, I agree on the whole, I agree a
little, I disagree a little, I disagree on the whole, and I disagree very much.

PREVIOUSLY ADMINISTERED TO: Ages 14-73

APPROPRIATE FOR: Ages 14 and older

ADMINISTRATION: The scale can be self-administered and can be completed in half an
hour.

SAMPLE ITEMS:

Equality in Business and the Professions: The entry of women into the business world in
direct competition with men should be discouraged.

Sex-Appropriate Behavior: A woman who refuses to bear children has failed in her duty
to her husband.

Social-Domestic Work: Women have the right to compete with men in every sphere of
economic activity.

Power in the Home: As head of the household the father should have the final authority
over his children.

SCORING: Items are objectively scored and equally weighted. The scale yields five scores: Equality in Business and the Professions, Sex-Appropriate Behavior, Social-Domestic Work, Power in the Home, and an overall Total score.

DEVELOPMENT: An initial item pool, consisting of 169 items, and the Marlowe-Crowne Social Desirability Scale were administered to 100 college students. Items that had a significant correlation ($p < .05$) with the Marlowe-Crowne and items that failed to correlate significantly ($p < .01$) with the Total score were eliminated. This left 140 items, which were administered to 133 college students. The responses were factor analyzed, and six factors were extracted for each sex. Sixty-three items were identified that loaded highest on a given factor for the overall sample and had a loading of at least +.40 for each sex separately. The sixty-three items were administered to 639 individuals ranging in age from 14 to 73 years, and their responses were factor analyzed. Four factors were identified, and these four factors comprise the subscales mentioned above.

RELIABILITY: The sixty-three-item SRS was administered to 193 college students. Internal consistencies (alpha) were computed for each subscale score, for the total sample and for each sex separately: for Equality in Business and the Professions, total sample = .941, males = .825, and females = .890; for Sex-Appropriate Behavior, total sample = .849, males = .825, and females = .869; for Social-Domestic Work, total sample = .850, males = .854, and females = .832; for Power in the Home, total sample = .855, males = .879, and females = .807; for Total score, total sample = .962, males = .961, and females = .944 (MacDonald, 1974a).

VALIDITY: In order to provide evidence of the construct validity of the scale, several a priori hypotheses were tested using the responses from the 193 college students. It was predicted that scores on the female form of a measure of premarital sexual permissiveness would correlate positively with scores on the Sex-Appropriate Behavior subscale. The hypothesis was supported; significant correlations were found for males ($r = .23, p < .05$), for females ($r = .39, p < .001$), and for the total sample ($r = .30, p < .0001$).

It was hypothesized that scores on the SRS would correlate negatively with Evaluative and Potency ratings of Man, negatively with Evaluative ratings of Woman, and positively with Potency ratings of Woman. (The ratings of Man and Woman were based on results from the MacDonald Sex Role Stereotype Scale [#69].) Obtained correlations were significant and in the predicted direction for male respondents and total respondents on the total SRS scores. Obtained correlations were in the predicted direction for female respondents, but they were significant only on the Potency ratings of Woman. The results for the various subscale scores were not consistently supportive of the hypotheses.

It was hypothesized that scores on the SRS would correlate negatively with a measure of cognitive rigidity, positively with a measure of tolerance for ambiguity, and negatively with a measure of authoritarianism. As predicted, the correlations with cognitive rigidity were significant and negative for male respondents and total respondents on each of the subscales of the SRS and on the total SRS scores. The results for female respondents were inconsistent. As predicted, the correlations between SRS scores and a measure of authoritarianism were negative and significant for males and total respondents on all subscales of the SRS and on total SRS scores. Significant negative correlations were obtained for female respondents on three of the four subscales and on the total SRS scores. As predicted, significant positive correlations were found for males, for females, and for total respondents between a measure of tolerance for ambiguity and each of the subscales and total SRS scores.

Significant differences were found between the responses of 93 male and 100 female college students on three of the four subscales and on total SRS scores. Female respondents were more supportive of equality between the sexes. Only on the Sex-Appropriate Behavior subscale were there no significant differences between the sexes (MacDonald, 1974a).

NOTES AND COMMENTS: (1) This scale is well developed; the reliability data suggest that it is internally consistent; and there are data to provide some evidence for the validity of the scale. As a result, this scale is recommended for use in further research.

(2) MacDonald (1974a) recommends using a fifty-three-item version of the SRS. He has also identified a twenty-item version based on factor loadings and inter-item correlations. However, he cautions that the psychometric properties of the twenty-item version are unknown. MacDonald further suggests that researchers with special interests can use the eleven-item unidimensional measure of support for Equality in Business and the Professions or the nine-item unidimensional measure of support for Sex-Appropriate Behavior.

(3) Factor loadings are provided for each item for male respondents, female respondents, and total respondents (MacDonald, 1974a).

(4) MacDonald and others (1973) and MacDonald (1974b) used a variation of SRS.

SOURCE: See MacDonald, 1974a; or ETS Tests in Microfiche collection (#007496).

BIBLIOGRAPHY:

MacDonald, A. P., Jr. "Identification and Measurement of Multidimensional Attitudes Toward Equality Between the Sexes." *Journal of Homosexuality,* 1974a, *1,* 165-182.

MacDonald, A. P., Jr. "The Importance of Sex Role to Gay Liberation." *Homosexual Counseling Journal,* 1974b, *1,* 169-180.

MacDonald, A. P., Jr., and Games, R. G. "Some Characteristics of Those Who Hold Positive and Negative Attitudes Toward Homosexuals." *Journal of Homosexuality,* 1974, *1,* 9-29.

MacDonald, A. P., Jr., Huggins, J., Young, S., and Swanson, R. A. "Attitudes Toward Homosexuality: Preservation of Sex Morality or the Double Standard?" *Journal of Consulting and Clinical Psychology,* 1973, *40,* 161.

Weinberger, L. E., and Millham, J. "Attitudinal Homophobia and Support of Traditional Sex Roles." Submitted for publication, 1978.

200. SINGER WOMEN'S LIBERATION SCALE

AUTHOR: Jack N. Singer

DATE: 1974

VARIABLE: Attitudes toward the issues advocated by the feminist movement

TYPE OF INSTRUMENT: Summated rating scale

DESCRIPTION: The scale consists of six statements regarding the feminist movement and the positions it advocates. Three items are phrased to reflect positive attitudes and three reflect negative attitudes. Five response options are offered with each item.

PREVIOUSLY ADMINISTERED TO: College students

APPROPRIATE FOR: Ages 16 and older

ADMINISTRATION: The scale can be self-administered and completed in less than three minutes.

SAMPLE ITEMS: Women should be satisfied with maintaining a good house and raising the children.
Women should hold positions of responsibility.

SCORING: Items are objectively scored and equally weighted. Total scores can range from 0 (no support for the positions advocated by the feminist movement) to 24 (strong support for the positions advocated by the feminist movement).

DEVELOPMENT: No information is provided.

RELIABILITY: The internal consistency (alpha) of the scale was computed on the responses given by college students. The coefficient was .79.

VALIDITY: The scale was completed by college men and women at both the freshman and senior level. Significant differences were found between men and women ($p < .01$), with women's responses being more supportive of the issues advocated by the feminist movement. Furthermore, senior college students scored significantly higher ($p < .01$) than freshman college students.

SOURCE: See Singer, 1974.

BIBLIOGRAPHY:

Singer, J. N. "Sex and College Class Differences in Attitudes Toward Autonomy in Work." *Human Relations,* 1974, *27,* 493-499.

201. SOCIAL ORDER SCALE (SOS)

AUTHORS: Leonard Worell and Judith Worell

DATE: 1977

VARIABLE: Attitudes regarding the issues raised by the feminist movement

TYPE OF INSTRUMENT: Summated rating scale

DESCRIPTION: The scale consists of fourteen items, half of which are phrased to reflect positive attitudes regarding feminist issues and half of which are phrased to reflect negative attitudes. The first seven items are statements regarding women and women's roles. Each item is followed by six response alternatives: strongly agree, moderately agree, slightly agree, slightly disagree, moderately disagree, and strongly disagree. The second group of seven items are phrases, each of which is followed by six response alternatives: strongly approve, moderately approve, slightly approve, slightly disapprove, moderately disapprove, and strongly disapprove.

PREVIOUSLY ADMINISTERED TO: College students

APPROPRIATE FOR: Ages 16 and older

ADMINISTRATION: The scale can be self-administered and can be completed in less than ten minutes.

SAMPLE ITEMS:

Agree-disagree: At the present time, both men and women have equal opportunities in education and employment.

Approve-disapprove: The U.S. constitutional Equal Rights Amendment for women.

SCORING: Items are objectively scored and equally weighted. Total scores can range from 14 (opposed to the positions advocated by the feminist movement) to 84 (supportive of the positions advocated by the feminist movement).

DEVELOPMENT: An eighty-item questionnaire concerning demographic data, experiences with sexual discrimination, cultural roles of men and women, and descriptions of platform planks supported by women's activist groups was administered to a sample of 979 college students. Twenty items were identified that related to the platforms of the feminist movement. An item analysis was performed on the twenty items, using "I strongly approve of the Women's Liberation Movement" as the criterion measure. Seventeen items were selected from this item analysis. Another sample of 350 college students completed the items and an item analysis was done using their responses. Fourteen items correlated at least +.40 with the total score as the criterion. These fourteen items comprise the scale.

RELIABILITY: Thirty subjects completed the scale on two occasions separated by a two-week interval. Test-retest reliability was .86. An item analysis was performed; item-total correlations averaged .59.

VALIDITY: The authors stated six directional hypotheses regarding differences to be expected between supporters and opposers of the feminist movement: (1) opposers score higher on authoritarianism; (2) opposers are concrete rather than abstract in their thinking; (3) opposers rely on external cues or sources of approval; (4) opposers are external on a locus of control measure; (5) opposers score lower on a measure of autonomy; (6) opposers score higher on a measure of anxiety or harm avoidance. To test these hypotheses, persons scoring in the upper quartile on the SOS were labeled as supporters of the feminist movement, and persons scoring in the lower quartile were labeled as opposers of the feminist movement. Five of the six hypotheses were supported by the data. Hypothesis 4 was not supported.

NOTES AND COMMENTS: The authors recommend the scale for research purposes only.

SOURCE: Judith Worell
        Department of Educational Psychology and Counseling
        University of Kentucky
        Lexington, Kentucky 40506

BIBLIOGRAPHY:

Worell, J., and Worell, L. "Support and Opposition to the Women's Liberation Movement: Some Personality and Parental Correlates." *Journal of Research in Personality,* 1977, *11,* 10-20.

---

202. WERNER SEXIST ATTITUDE SCALE

AUTHOR: Marie E. Werner

DATE: 1973

VARIABLE: Sexist attitudes

TYPE OF INSTRUMENT: Summated rating scale

DESCRIPTION: The scale consists of sixteen statements; half reflect a positive attitude and half reflect a negative attitude. The items relate to the social and psychological aspects of sex roles (five items), the economic and occupational aspects of sex roles (six items), and the familial and moral aspects of sex roles (five items). Four response options accompany each item: strongly agree, agree, disagree, and strongly disagree.

PREVIOUSLY ADMINISTERED TO: College students and adults

APPROPRIATE FOR: Ages 16 and older

ADMINISTRATION: The scale is self-administered and can be completed in ten minutes.

SAMPLE ITEMS:

Socio-Psychological issues: It is unfair to guard the morals of women more closely than those of men.

Economic-Occupational issues: Housework should be a paid profession for either men or women.

Familial-Moral issues: Women should be able to find satisfaction in traditional female roles.

SCORING: Items are objectively scored and equally weighted. A total score is obtained, which can range from 16 (not sexist) to 64 (very sexist).

DEVELOPMENT: Based on a review of the literature, the author constructed a pool of 165 items covering the following topics: marital relations, divorce, birth control, parental roles, marital roles, legal issues, employment, education, social issues, and psychological issues. The items were independently reviewed by a panel of eight judges, who were asked to indicate which items were irrelevant and whether relevant items were phrased positively or negatively. A revision of the scale using their responses left 108 items in the pool. These items were administered to two groups of subjects: one presumed to be "sexist" and one presumed to be "antisexist." Items for which 60 percent of the "sexist" subjects chose a response on one end of the continuum and 60 percent of the "antisexist" subjects chose a response on the opposite end of the continuum were retained. This left thirty-nine items. These thirty-nine items, along with seven items selected from other scales, were administered to 33 college men and 288 college women. Their responses were factor analyzed, and three factors emerged. Factor I, labeled Socio-Psychological, measures "attitudes towards women's social interaction patterns in society as well as their presumed psychological and emotional functioning" (p. 133). Factor II, labeled Economic-Occupational, concerns "employment behavior and patterns of domestic responsibility" (p. 134). Factor III, labeled Familial-Moral, concerns issues that relate to the functioning of the family unit, including moral issues. In addition to the factor analysis, an item analysis was performed comparing the responses from college students in the highest and lowest quartiles of the distribution of total scores. All items discriminated between the two groups at the .001 level. From the thirty-nine items subjected to factor and item analyses, sixteen items were selected for the final scale. The items selected represent the three factors identified in the factor analysis, include a cross section of topics, and include an equal number of positively and negatively phrased items.

RELIABILITY: No reliability data are presented for the sixteen-item final form of the scale. Reliability data are presented for the thirty-nine-item scale that was factor analyzed. Thirty-two college students completed the scale on two occasions separated by four weeks. Test-retest reliability was .962. Split-half reliability was computed for the 321 subjects who completed the scale. The corrected split-half reliability for the total scale was .91. The corrected split-half reliabilities for the three factors were: Factor I = .87; Factor II = .79; and Factor III = .63 (Werner, 1973).

VALIDITY: The author claims content and face validity for the scale on the basis of the way it was constructed.
      Correlations were computed between scores on the Werner Sexist Attitude Scale and each of the following: each of two items from the Open Subordination of Women

Scale (#191), which is a measure of attitudes toward women; one item from a measure of political and economic conservatism; one item measuring ethnocentrism; each of two items measuring fascism; and one item measuring chivalry. Correlations were computed separately for each of the three factors on the Werner Sexist Attitude Scale and for the total score on the scale. All correlations were significant (p < .001) except for two items that did not correlate significantly with Factor II. The nonsignificant correlations were obtained for one item from the Open Subordination of Women Scale and one item measuring fascism (Werner, 1973).

Gilliam (1975) administered the Werner Sexist Attitude Scale and the Attitudes Toward Women Scale-Short form (#170) to 376 high school counselors. The correlation between scores on the two scales was .62. Gilliam also reports that male counselors' attitudes were significantly more sexist (p < .01) than female counselors' attitudes.

NOTES AND COMMENTS: Werner (1973) reports the relationship between scores on the Werner Sexist Attitude Scale and each of the following variables: sex, race, religion, marital status, employment pattern of mothers, source of parental income, mother's education, participation in civil rights organizations, and attitudes toward feminist issues. Gilliam (1975) compared scores obtained by high school counselors in terms of the counselors' sex, age, marital status, ethnic background, high school size, and attendance at conferences.

SOURCE: See Werner, 1973.

BIBLIOGRAPHY:

Gilliam, J. R. "The Status of Texas High School Counselors' Attitudes Toward the Roles of Women." Unpublished doctoral dissertation, East Texas State University, 1975. (*Dissertation Abstracts International,* 1976, *36*[11-A], 7207.)
Werner, M. E. "A Scale for the Measurement of 'Sexist' Attitudes." Unpublished doctoral dissertation, Columbia University, 1973. (*Dissertation Abstracts International,* 1973, *34*[1-A], 180-181.)

---

203. WILLIAMS SEX ROLE ATTITUDE SCALE

AUTHOR: David L. Williams

DATE: 1976

VARIABLE: Traditional versus egalitarian sex role attitudes

TYPE OF INSTRUMENT: Summated rating scale

DESCRIPTION: The scale contains thirty-eight statements. The majority of the statements concern the rights and responsibilities of men and women, especially in terms of male-female relationships. Some items reflect a traditional attitude toward sex roles and others reflect an egalitarian attitude. For each item, there are five response options: strongly agree, agree, neutral, disagree, and strongly disagree.

PREVIOUSLY ADMINISTERED TO: College students

APPROPRIATE FOR: Ages 16 and older

ADMINISTRATION: The scale is self-administered and can be completed in less than twenty minutes.

SAMPLE ITEMS: If a woman is seriously dating a man, he has the right to expect her to stop dating other men.

The woman should be the more sentimental and emotional one in a relationship.

SCORING: Items are objectively scored and equally weighted. One total score is obtained.

DEVELOPMENT: An item pool of seventy items was compiled, including sixteen items taken from the Traditional Family Ideology Scale (#129). A preliminary analysis indicated the presence of a single factor, so items were selected to maximize internal consistency. A total of thirty-eight items, including sixteen from the Traditional Family Ideology Scale, were found to be highly internally consistent. These thirty-eight items comprise the scale.

RELIABILITY: The responses from 820 persons were used to compute the internal consistency of the scale. Coefficient alpha was .94 (Williams, 1976). It appears that the internal consistency of the scale was computed from the same responses that were used to select the items for the scale.

VALIDITY: Williams (1976) conducted an experiment for which he selected sixty-four male and sixty-four female college students as subjects. All subjects scored in either the upper third or lower third of the distribution of total scores on the Williams Sex Role Attitude Scale. During the experiment, one male and one female subject comprised a dyad in which one played the role of buyer for a chain of retail stores and the other played the role of a wholesale distributor of small appliances. The task facing the dyad was to agree on prices for several small appliances. Williams observed the process of the negotiations and recorded the outcome. He reports that several of his observations provide evidence of the validity of the scale. Traditional females, compared with egalitarian females, made significantly more statements that requested a reaction from their male opponents. Williams (1976, p. 93) states that this "could be viewed as reflecting a greater concern for the male's satisfaction with his outcomes." Egalitarian females, compared with traditional females, were more competitive; that is, they made significantly more statements indicating an unwillingness to make further concessions, and they made significantly more statements indicating strong rejection of the proposals offered by their opponents. For males, however, Williams reports a lack of evidence of the validity of the scale. The only significant difference between traditional and egalitarian males was that egalitarian males made more statements indicating strong rejection of the proposals offered by their opponents. Williams (1976, p. 93) claims that this contradicts "the traditional role for the male as more dominating than the egalitarian role."

Williams (1976, p. 94) claims that additional evidence of the scale's validity is apparent from the finding that "compatible dyads achieved better outcomes and used more of the heuristic trial-and-error approaches in doing so." This outcome occurred only when the experimenter was female.

Furthermore, Williams (1976, p. 94) reports that "males rated as more likable females who held similar sex role attitudes and females rated their own behavior during the negotiations as more attractive when their sex role attitudes were compatible with their opponent's sex role attitudes."

NOTES AND COMMENTS: Though Williams (1976, p. 16) reports "preliminary samples indicated a single large factor for the complete set of items," he does not provide any data to substantiate his statement. An examination of the thirty-eight items of the scale makes it difficult to accept the veracity of his statement.

SOURCE: See Williams, 1976.

BIBLIOGRAPHY:

Mullick, B., and Lewis, S. A. "Sex Roles, Loving, and Liking: A Look at Dating Couples' Bargaining." Paper presented at 85th annual meeting of the American Psychological Association, San Francisco, August 1977.
Williams, D. L. "The Effects of Sex Role Attitudes on Integrative Bargaining." Unpublished master's thesis, Wayne State University, 1976.

---

204. WOMEN'S LIBERATION IDEOLOGY SCALE

AUTHORS: Jean Goldschmidt, Mary M. Gergen, Karen Quigley, and Kenneth J. Gergen

DATE: 1974

VARIABLE: Attitudes toward issues advocated by the feminist movement

TYPE OF INSTRUMENT: Summated rating scale

DESCRIPTION: The scale consists of twelve statements relating to issues associated with the feminist movement, including, for example, employment issues, marital and maternal issues, abortion, and daycare centers. Four statements are phrased to reflect a positive attitude toward the issues, and eight statements are phrased to reflect a negative attitude. Each statement is accompanied by five response options ranging from "strongly agree" to "strongly disagree."

PREVIOUSLY ADMINISTERED TO: Female college students; adults, ages 24-50

APPROPRIATE FOR: Ages 16 and older

ADMINISTRATION: The scale can be self-administered and can be completed in about five minutes.

SAMPLE ITEMS: There should be legislative restrictions on abortion.
Community daycare centers should be established nationally.

SCORING: Items are objectively scored and equally weighted. Total scores can range from 12 (no support for the issues advocated by the feminist movement) to 60 (strong support for the issues advocated by the feminist movement).

DEVELOPMENT: A pool of twenty items was administered to members of a feminist organization at a university; the items were also administered to a random sample of women from the same university. Twelve items that successfully discriminated between the members and nonmembers were selected for the final version of the scale.

RELIABILITY: The average item-total correlation for the twelve items was .67 (Goldschmidt and others, 1974).

VALIDITY: In addition to administering the Women's Liberation Ideology Scale to a group of 448 college women, Goldschmidt and others (1974) administered a measure of activism in the women's movement. There was a significant relationship between the two measures. "Among the sixty lowest scoring women on the scale, fifty had taken no part in women's liberation activities. Among the thirty highest scorers, only four had taken no part" (p. 612).

Chapman and Gadfield (1976) administered the Women's Liberation Ideology Scale to fifteen women, each of whom rated herself on the extent to which she was a "liberated woman." The correlation between the two measures was .84 (p < .001). Chapman and Gadfield also administered a scale which they constructed to measure support for feminist ideology. Though they provide no description of their scale, they do report that the correlation between the two measures of attitudes toward feminist ideology was .85 for women and .95 for men.

Marecek and Frasch (1977) tested college women at the junior and senior level using the Women's Liberation Ideology Scale and a measure of locus of control. As they predicted, "external" women scored significantly lower than "internal" women on the Women's Liberation Ideology Scale.

SOURCE: See Goldschmidt and others, 1974.

BIBLIOGRAPHY:

Chapman, A. J., and Gadfield, N. J. "Is Sexual Humor Sexist?" *Journal of Communication,* 1976, *26,* 141-153.
Goldschmidt, J., Gergen, M. M., Quigley, K., and Gergen, K. J. "The Women's Liberation Movement: Attitudes and Action." *Journal of Personality,* 1974, *42,* 601-617.
Marecek, J., and Frasch, C. "Locus of Control and College Women's Role Expectations." *Journal of Counseling Psychology,* 1977, *24,* 132-136.

205. WOMEN'S LIBERATION SCALE (WLS)

AUTHOR: Carlos Goldberg

DATE: 1975

VARIABLE: Attitudes toward positions advocated by the feminist movement

TYPE OF INSTRUMENT: Summated rating scale

DESCRIPTION: The WLS consists of fourteen statements relating to issues advocated by the feminist movement, including, for example, employment and educational opportunities, daycare centers, abortion, lesbianism, and equality between the sexes. Each item is followed by four response options: strongly agree, agree, disagree, and strongly disagree. All of the items are phrased to reflect a positive attitude toward the positions advocated by the feminist movement. For half of the items, the "strongly agree" response appears as the first response option; for the other half of the items, the "strongly disagree" response appears as the first response option.

PREVIOUSLY ADMINISTERED TO: College students

APPROPRIATE FOR: Ages 16 and older

ADMINISTRATION: The scale can be self-administered and can be completed in five to ten minutes.

SAMPLE ITEMS: In general, the activities of women's liberation groups will have a very good influence in our society.
           Women should be given the same consideration as men when both are applying for the same job.

SCORING: Items are objectively scored and equally weighted. Total score can range from 14 (negative attitude toward the issues of the feminist movement) to 56 (positive attitude toward the issues of the feminist movement).

DEVELOPMENT: No information is provided.

RELIABILITY: The reliability coefficient for males is .65, and for females it is .75. Item-total correlations are reported separately for each sex. For males, they range from .20 to .60 with a median of .40; for females, they range from .28 to .70 with a median of .48 (Goldberg, 1976).

VALIDITY: The scale was administered to 102 college men and 102 college women. Women ($\overline{X}$ = 41.08) scored significantly higher than men ($\overline{X}$ = 37.52, p < .001). Similar results were obtained with other samples: mean for men = 37.94, mean for women = 40.94 (p < .01). Furthermore, female members of the National Organization for Women, a feminist organization ($\overline{X}$ = 51.10), scored higher than female nonmembers ($\overline{X}$ = 41.25, p < .01).

The WLS and the Attitudes Toward Women Scale (#169) were completed by forty college men and forty college women. The correlation between the two scales was .60 for men and .65 for women (p < .001 for each sex) (Goldberg, 1976).

NOTES AND COMMENTS: (1) Goldberg (1976) performed separate factor analyses on the responses from each sex. Five factors were identified for each sex. The first factor, which was the same for both sexes, concerned general equality between the sexes. The remaining factors differed for the two sexes: "For males, the second factor deals with institutions that would facilitate equality for women; the third factor reflects educational equality; the fourth factor is related to change of traditional sex roles; and the fifth factor deals with occupational equality. For females, the second factor is related to occupational equality; the third factor represents facilitating institutions; the fourth factor reflects equal responsibilities, and the fifth factor deals with sexual liberation" (p. 4).

(2) Reversing the order of the response options (that is, putting "strongly agree" first for some items and "strongly disagree" first for other items) could prove very confusing to respondents and lead them to record some responses incorrectly.

(3) Goldberg (1976) provides normative data separately for college men and college women.

SOURCE: See Goldberg, 1976.

BIBLIOGRAPHY:

Goldberg, C. "Conformity to Majority Type as a Function of Task and Acceptance of Sex-Related Stereotypes." *Journal of Psychology,* 1975, *89,* 25-37.

Goldberg, C. "Women's Liberation Scale (WLS): A Measure of Attitude Toward Positions Advocated by Women's Groups." *Journal Supplement Abstract Service Catalog of Selected Documents in Psychology,* 1976, *6,* 13.

206. WOUDENBERG ATTITUDES ABOUT WOMEN SCALE

AUTHOR: Roger A. Woudenberg

DATE: 1973

VARIABLES: Adherence to traditional masculinity-femininity stereotypes; perceptions of women as "good" or "bad"

TYPE OF INSTRUMENT: Summated rating scale

DESCRIPTION: The scale consists of twenty-four items on two subscales: Adherence to traditional masculinity-femininity stereotypes (fifteen items) and perceptions of women as "good" or "bad" (nine items). Of the items measuring adherence to traditional masculinity-femininity stereotypes, one item concerns feminism, one item concerns feminine men, one item concerns women and men, and the remaining twelve items concern stereotypic views of women. Of the items measuring perceptions of women as "good" or "bad," one item concerns men, one item concerns the relationship between sex and "technique," and the remaining seven items concern women and sexuality. With the exception of one item on the latter scale, items on both scales are all phrased to reflect a traditional stereotype. All items are accompanied by the following five response alternatives: strongly agree, agree, undecided, disagree, and strongly disagree.

PREVIOUSLY ADMINISTERED TO: College men

APPROPRIATE FOR: Ages 16 and older

ADMINISTRATION: The scale can be self-administered and can be completed in about fifteen minutes.

SAMPLE ITEMS:

Adherence to traditional masculinity-femininity stereotypes: Although women play a part in many important jobs today, women's proper place is still in the home.

Perceptions of women as "good" or "bad": Any woman openly looking for sex is not much better than a prostitute.

SCORING: Items are objectively scored and equally weighted. Two subscale scores are obtained. Lower scores indicate more traditional attitudes.

DEVELOPMENT: A sex attitude scale was constructed of 100 items. The scale included twenty items on each of five rationally devised subscales. Two of the five subscales are those described here. Using the responses from 350 college men, a cluster analysis was performed for 90 of the 100 items (two items had to be eliminated from each subscale due to the limitations of the computer program). The cluster analysis was performed using the procedures of Tryon and Bailey (1970). The results of the analysis indicated which items would be included on each of the two subscales of the Woudenberg Attitudes About Women Scale.

RELIABILITY: Using the responses from 350 college men, internal consistency reliabilities were computed. Coefficient alpha for adherence to traditional masculinity-femininity stereotypes was equal to .88; for perceptions of women as "good" or "bad," the coefficient was equal to .82 (Woudenberg, 1973).

VALIDITY: In addition to completing the Woudenberg Attitudes About Women Scale, the college men also completed the Gough Femininity Scale (#36) and the Franck Drawing Completion Test (#11), both measures of masculinity-femininity. For the adherence to traditional masculinity-femininity stereotypes, the correlation was $-.15$ ($p < .01$) with the Gough Femininity Scale and $-.07$ with the Franck Drawing Completion Test. For the perceptions of women as "good" or "bad," the correlation was $-.02$ with the Gough Femininity Scale and .03 with the Franck Drawing Completion Test (Woudenberg, 1973).

The study for which this scale was constructed obtained measures on forty-eight variables for each subject. The intercorrelation matrix for the forty-eight variables provides data that could be interpreted as relating to the validity of the scale (Woudenberg, 1973).

NOTES AND COMMENTS: (1) The correlation between the two subscales was .64 (Woudenberg, 1973).

(2) These two subscales were embedded in a 100-item survey. Furthermore, when the survey was administered, it was one of ten instruments used with the subjects. No information is provided regarding the use of these two subscales in the absence of the other instruments.

SOURCE: See Woudenberg, 1973.

BIBLIOGRAPHY:

*Tryon, R. C., and Bailey, D. E. *Cluster Analysis.* New York: McGraw-Hill, 1970.
Woudenberg, R. A. "The Relationship of Sexual Attitudes, Sexual Stereotypes, Racial-Sexual Stereotypes, and Racial Attitudes." Unpublished doctoral dissertation, Michigan State University, 1973. (*Dissertation Abstracts International,* 1973, *34*[6-B], 2958.)
Woudenberg, R. A. "The Relationship of Sexual Attitudes, Attitudes About Women, and Racial Attitudes in White Males." *Sex Roles,* 1977, *3,* 101-110.

---

207. ZATLIN SCALE OF AGREEMENT WITH THE FEMINIST MOVEMENT

AUTHOR: Carole Zatlin

DATE: 1972

VARIABLE: Attitudes toward feminist movement issues

TYPE OF INSTRUMENT: Alternate choice

DESCRIPTION: The instrument contains twenty questions, most of which pertain to issues regarding the feminist movement. Half of the questions are phrased so that agreement represents a liberal or change-oriented attitude; the remaining half are phrased so that agreement represents a conservative attitude. Respondents are expected to react to each question by circling either "yes" or "no."

PREVIOUSLY ADMINISTERED TO: Women

APPROPRIATE FOR: Ages 16 and older

ADMINISTRATION: The instrument can be self-administered and can be completed in ten minutes.

SAMPLE ITEMS: Do you think a woman can combine a career and homemaking successfully?

Is marriage the most satisfying career for a woman?

SCORING: Items are objectively scored and equally weighted. High scores indicate a more liberal attitude.

DEVELOPMENT: The items were taken from a Gallup Opinion Index (September 1970) and several publications associated with the feminist movement.

RELIABILITY: Test-retest reliability was computed from the responses of thirty-three college students. The interval between the test and retest was not specified. The correlation was .85 (Zatlin, 1972; Zatlin, Storandt, and Botwinick, 1973).

VALIDITY: Zatlin (1972) administered the instrument to four groups of women: (1) twenty-nine women between the ages of 35 and 50 who were enrolled in college to obtain a bachelor's degree; (2) twenty-seven women between the ages of 18 and 25 who were also enrolled in college to obtain a bachelor's degree; (3) twenty-six women between the ages of 35 and 50 who had obtained a bachelor's degree before the age of 25 and were not enrolled in college at the time the instrument was completed; and (4) twenty-five women between the ages of 35 and 50 who had never been enrolled in college. An analysis of variance performed on the means of the four groups indicated that the means were significantly different (p < .0001). The group means were then compared by t tests, and the results indicated that the first group was significantly more liberal than the last group and the first group was significantly more conservative than the second group. Though Zatlin did not state any a priori hypotheses, these results seem quite consistent with what one would expect: middle-aged women enrolled in college are more liberal than middle-aged women who have never attended college, but middle-aged women enrolled in college are less liberal than young adult women enrolled in college.

NOTES AND COMMENTS: Because the instrument seems to cover a variety of content areas ranging from whether men should be dominant in marital relations to whether marijuana should be legalized, some information on internal consistency is greatly needed.

SOURCE: See Zatlin, 1972.

BIBLIOGRAPHY:

Gallup Opinion Index. Report No. 63, September 1970.

Zatlin, C. E. "Personality and Values of Women Continuing Their Education After Thirty-Five Years of Age." Unpublished master's thesis, Washington University, 1972.

Zatlin, C. E., Storandt, M., and Botwinick, J. "Personality and Values of Women Continuing Their Education After Thirty-Five Years of Age." *Journal of Gerontology,* 1973, *28,* 216-221.

12

■ ■ ■ ■ ■ ■ ■ ■ ■ ■ ■

Somatic and Sexual Issues

■ ■

Included in this chapter are seventeen instruments, five pertaining to abortion, four pertaining to sexuality, two pertaining to menstruation, two pertaining to body perception, and one pertaining to each of the following: contraception, pregnancy, menopause, and somatic androgyny. The dates on which the instruments first appeared in the literature vary considerably, with one first appearing in the 1940s, one in the 1950s, eight in the 1960s, and seven in the 1970s. Although some of the instruments have previously been part of an interview schedule, all can be adapted for paper-and-pencil administration. No instrument in this chapter is appropriate for persons below the age of 13, and some require that respondents be at least 16 years old. Females can complete all of the instruments; however, only six are also appropriate for male respondents. Some of the instruments that are not appropriate for male respondents can be adapted for use with males by changing items from first person to third person. For example, instead of phrasing an item as "I would have an abortion if . . . ," the item could be phrased as "Women should be able to have an abortion if . . ." Another procedure for adapting the instruments involves changing the instructions to ask males to answer as they would wish or believe a particular woman would answer, for example, their wife, mother, or ideal woman. Of course if an instrument is adapted, it would be necessary to determine its reliability and validity for males. One should not presume that an instrument would be equally reliable or valid for males and females—especially because males would be completing an instrument essentially different from that completed by females.

There is some overlap between the five abortion instruments, in that each of them includes at least some items describing conditions that might lead a woman to seek an abortion. The respondent is asked to indicate either whether she would seek an abortion given the described condition or whether an abortion is legally or morally justifiable given the described condition. The shortest of the abortion measures is the Attitudes Toward Abortion Scale (#211), which contains only six items, all of which concern the conditions under which an abortion would be acceptable. The items refer to the cause of the pregnancy (rape), the physical effects of bearing the child (danger to the mother's life; deformed child), the mother's marital status, and the child being unwanted (generally not wanted; financial hardship). All thirteen items on the Abortion Standard Scale (#209) also concern the conditions under which an abortion would be acceptable. On this instrument the statements are all phrased in the first person, and with one exception the conditions are different from those listed on the Attitudes Toward Abortion Scale. Most of the conditions on the Abortion Standard Scale refer to the social and emotional effects that the pregnancy would have on the pregnant girl. The word *girl* is used deliberately here because, unlike the items on the other abortion scales, these items seem most appropriate for pregnant teenagers. Seven of the twenty-five items on the Abortion Scale (#208) refer to conditions under which an abortion is acceptable; five of the seven items overlap the items on the Attitudes Toward Abortion Scale. The Abortion Scale also includes statements concerning the morality of abortion in general, the point in the pregnancy at which abortion should be permitted, and the social implications of abortion. The fifteen-item Maxwell Attitudes Toward Abortion Scale (#216) contains only three items concerning conditions under which an abortion may be acceptable. The remaining items are prescriptive statements regarding the moral and legal status of abortion. The Zammuner Attitudes Toward Abortion Scale (#224) is the longest and most comprehensive of the abortion measures. It includes fifty-eight statements, which cover a variety of topics including medical-physical issues; individual, family, and social issues; and ethical and legal issues. Six statements pertain to conditions under which an abortion is acceptable; four of the six overlap the items on the Attitudes Toward Abortion Scale.

Though abortion instruments have been related to prior behavior (for example, promiscuity, sexual experience, prior abortion), they have not been used to predict future behavior. Research is needed to determine if responses to an abortion instrument can predict whether a woman will become sexually active with a variety of partners, whether she will be careless about using birth control, whether she will have an unwanted pregnancy, and whether she will ever obtain an abortion.

Of the four instruments concerning sexuality, one measures sexual arousability (#222), two assess guilt feelings concerning sexual matters (#218 and #219), and one concerns sexual self-control and satisfaction (#223). There is very little overlap among these instruments.

The McHugh-Wasser Scale of Attitudes Toward Menstruation (#214) assesses a variety of feelings and attitudes towards menstruation. The Menstrual Distress Questionnaire (#217) is much more limited in scope; it concerns the extent to which a woman experiences a variety of different physiological and psychological symptoms during menstruation. The Neugarten-Kraines Menopausal Symptoms Scale (#220) is similar to the Menstrual Distress Questionnaire in its focus on symptomatology. However, as the title implies, the Neugarten-Kraines scale focuses on the symptomatology accompanying menopause rather than menstruation.

Only two of the other five instruments in this chapter measure the same variable; the Objective Rating Scale (#221) and the Body Image Projective Test (#212) both assess a woman's perception of her own body. Though both are authored by the same persons, were used in the same research, and are intended to measure the same variable, they are very different in terms of procedures, and scores obtained on the two measures are not highly correlated.

The remaining instruments in this chapter measure attitudes toward pregnancy (#215), attitudes toward contraception (#213), and somatic androgyny (#210). The items on these instruments are completely unrelated to each other and to the other instruments in this chapter.

In general, there are not many measures of somatic and sexual issues. As indicated above, for some variables, there was only a single instrument that satisfied the criteria for inclusion in this book; that is, only one included information regarding the development or reliability or validity of the instrument or only one that had been used extensively by a variety of researchers. For other variables, there were no instruments that satisfied the criteria for inclusion. For example, there are no instruments here concerning breast feeding or the experience of having a baby and none assessing attitudes or feelings regarding menopause. Furthermore, none are appropriate for persons below age 13, though doubtlessly children have feelings and attitudes regarding their bodies, their own sexuality, and sexuality in general. Thus, research is needed not only to improve existing instruments but also to develop new ones that can measure additional variables and can be used with persons of different ages.

---

208. ABORTION SCALE

AUTHOR: Panos D. Bardis

DATE: 1972

VARIABLE: Attitudes toward abortion

TYPE OF INSTRUMENT: Summated rating scale

DESCRIPTION: The scale consists of twenty-five statements regarding abortion. All statements are phrased in the liberal direction. The response options are: strongly disagree, disagree, undecided, agree, and strongly agree.

PREVIOUSLY ADMINISTERED TO: Ages 18-65

APPROPRIATE FOR: Ages 16 and older

ADMINISTRATION: The scale can be self-administered and can be completed in about fifteen minutes.

SAMPLE ITEMS: Abortion is all right during the first three months of pregnancy.
Abortion is not murder.

SCORING: Items are objectively scored and equally weighted. Total scores can range from 0 (extremely conservative regarding abortion) to 100 (extremely liberal regarding abortion).

DEVELOPMENT: A pool of 1,500 statements regarding abortion was compiled. The items were suggested by the author of the scale and members of "a large and highly heterogeneous group of native Americans" (Bardis, 1972b, p. 100) and were culled from newspapers, journal articles, short publications, and books. On the basis of "preliminary tests" (which are not described), the author identified the forty-six statements that were the "best" (which is not defined) candidates for a scale to measure attitudes toward abortion. An item-discrimination analysis was performed on the responses given by 100 persons to the forty-six items. Using the results from this analysis, twenty-five items were selected for the final scale.

RELIABILITY: Bardis (1972b) reports corrected split-half reliabilities of .97, .91, and .96 based on three different groups of thirty subjects. Bardis also reports a test-retest reliability of .93 for a sample of thirty subjects, but he provides no information on the test-retest interval.

VALIDITY: Bardis (1972b) reports the results from eight comparisons providing evidence for the validity of the scale: (1) forty Catholics scored significantly lower ($\overline{X}$ = 33.97) than forty Protestants ($\overline{X}$ = 71.50, p < .001); (2) in another sample, forty-five Catholics scored significantly lower ($\overline{X}$ = 37.22) than forty-five Protestants ($\overline{X}$ = 69.03, p < .001); (3) fifty females scored significantly lower ($\overline{X}$ = 55.28) than fifty males ($\overline{X}$ = 64.59, p < .001); (4) in another sample, forty-two females scored significantly lower ($\overline{X}$ = 50.62) than forty-two males ($\overline{X}$ = 62.12, p < .005); (5) thirty-five persons with fewer than fourteen years of education scored significantly lower ($\overline{X}$ = 51.92) than thirty-five persons with at least fourteen years of education ($\overline{X}$ = 60.27, p < .005); (6) in another sample, twenty-five persons with fewer than fourteen years of education scored significantly lower ($\overline{X}$ = 50.51) than twenty-five persons with at least fourteen years of education ($\overline{X}$ = 63.44, p < .001); (7) forty males who were at least 30 years old scored significantly lower ($\overline{X}$ = 63.48) than forty males below age 30 ($\overline{X}$ = 74.06, p < .001); and (8) forty-five females below age 30 scored significantly lower ($\overline{X}$ = 52.91) than forty-five females who were at least 30 years old ($\overline{X}$ = 60.67, p < .01). Bardis contends that all of these results are in the predicted direction.

NOTES AND COMMENTS: (1) Bardis violates the precept that recommends that half the items on an attitude scale should be phrased positively and half should be phrased negatively. He defends himself by saying it "was justified by tests involving two equivalent forms, one mixed and the other unmixed, of the final scale, both of which gave extremely similar results" (Bardis, 1972b, p. 101). He gives no information on the "tests" he performed or the specific results he obtained.

(2) Bardis fails to provide sufficient information at several crucial points in his article. He does not explain how the 1,500-item pool was reduced to 46 items; he provides no information regarding the 100 persons used for the item-discrimination analysis;

he does not give demographic information for each of the samples used to test reliability and validity (though he does give a global description of all samples he used); he does not explain how any of his samples were selected, which is particularly intriguing because he had equal sample sizes for each comparison; and he does not report the interval that elapsed between test and retest for his reliability estimate.

(3) The scale is described in *Family Measurement Techniques* (Straus and Brown, 1978, p. 133).

SOURCE: See Bardis, 1972b.

BIBLIOGRAPHY:

Bardis, P. D. "Abortion and Public Opinion: A Research Note." *Journal of Marriage and the Family,* 1972a, *34,* 111.

Bardis, P. D. "A Technique for the Measurement of Attitudes Toward Abortion." *International Journal of Sociology of Family,* 1972b, *2,* 98-104.

*Straus, M. A., and Brown, B. W. *Family Measurement Techniques: Abstracts of Published Instruments, 1935-1974.* Minneapolis: University of Minnesota Press, 1978.

---

209. ABORTION STANDARD SCALE

AUTHORS: Alfred M. Mirande and Elizabeth L. Hammer

DATE: 1974

VARIABLE: Conditions under which an abortion would be acceptable for oneself

TYPE OF INSTRUMENT: Guttman scale

DESCRIPTION: The scale consists of thirteen statements, each of which describes a condition under which one might consider having an abortion. Each item is accompanied by three "agree" responses (strong, medium, and slight) and three "disagree" responses (strong, medium, and slight).

PREVIOUSLY ADMINISTERED TO: Unmarried female college students

APPROPRIATE FOR: Unmarried females, ages 16 and older

ADMINISTRATION: The scale can be self-administered and can be completed in less than five minutes.

SAMPLE ITEMS: I would have an abortion if I felt that I could not emotionally cope with being pregnant.

I would have an abortion for any reason that was important to me.

SCORING: Items are objectively scored and equally weighted. Total scores can range from 0 (disagreement with all statements; opposed to abortion for oneself) to 13 (agreement with all statements; supportive of abortion for oneself).

DEVELOPMENT: An item pool was compiled of twenty-seven statements describing conditions that might lead one to seek an abortion. Pretest results indicated that fifteen of the twenty-seven items formed a Guttman scale. When the scale was administered to college women at schools in Virginia and North Dakota, the first two items were eliminated from analysis because their marginal frequencies exceeded 20 percent.

RELIABILITY: The coefficient of reproducibility for the thirteen-item Guttman scale was .91 for a sample of single college women in Virginia and .92 for a sample of single college women in North Dakota; the minimal marginal reproducibility was .63 in Virginia and .68 in North Dakota.

VALIDITY: Mirande and Hammer hypothesized that "the more permissive the standards for acceptance of premarital sex, the greater the acceptance of abortion" (p. 487) and "the greater the number of times in love, the greater the acceptance of abortion" (p. 488). Both hypotheses were supported in samples of unmarried college women in Virginia and North Dakota.

NOTES AND COMMENTS: (1) The use of the scale is restricted to unmarried females, because items are phrased in the first person, and many items imply that the respondent is unmarried; for example, "I would have an abortion if I did not want to marry the boy who got me pregnant." The items could be phrased in the third person so as to be appropriate for any respondents to indicate attitudes toward abortion for unmarried women. Of course, one would have to empirically determine whether the items still form a Guttman scale.

(2) This scale is also described in *Family Measurement Techniques* (Straus and Brown, 1978, pp. 139-140).

SOURCE: See Mirande and Hammer, 1974.

BIBLIOGRAPHY:

Mirande, A. M., and Hammer, E. L. "Premarital Sexual Permissiveness and Abortion: Standards of College Women." *Pacific Sociological Review,* 1974, *17,* 485-503.
*Straus, M. A., and Brown, B. W. *Family Measurement Techniques: Abstracts of Published Instruments, 1935-1974.* Minneapolis: University of Minnesota Press, 1978.

210. ANDROGYNIC PATTERNS OF BODY FORM-RATING PROFILE

AUTHORS: Nancy Bayley and Leona M. Bayer

DATE: 1946

VARIABLE: Somatic androgyny

TYPE OF INSTRUMENT: Rating scale

DESCRIPTION: The rating profile lists eight aspects of body form to be rated from rear-view photographs. These include surface modeling, four aspects of trunk contours (shoulder girdle, waistline, hip flare, and buttocks), and three aspects of leg patterns (thigh form, interspace, and muscle bulge). A five-point rating scale is used to rate each item; response options are: hyper-masculine, masculine, intermediate, feminine, and hyper-feminine. A verbal description indicates, for each item, the meaning of each point on the rating scale. Distinctions should be made between intermediate ratings reflecting asexuality (undifferentiated) to bisexuality (showing both masculine and feminine characteristics). The rating profile also lists supplementary criteria on which the subject can be rated. These include penis size or breast size, body hair density, pubic pattern, and strength.

PREVIOUSLY ADMINISTERED TO: Ages 16-18

APPROPRIATE FOR: Ages 16-24

ADMINISTRATION: The first eight items on the rating scale can be completed from nude, rear-view photographs. The rater should be trained in the use of the scale.

SCORING: The range of points assigned to each of the first eight items is 1 to 5, with 1 assigned to a rating of hyper-masculine and 5 assigned to a rating of hyper-feminine. The sum of the ratings assigned to the first eight items is the androgyny score. Totals of 8-12 are considered hyper-masculine; 13-19 are masculine; 20-25 are intermediate; 26-34 are feminine and 35-40 are hyper-feminine.

DEVELOPMENT: To identify somatic characteristics that differentiated between males and females, pilot work was done with sixteen girls and twenty boys. Nude photographs of the subjects were taken and used to rate different aspects of the bodies. This was done by covering all parts of the photograph except the specific attribute to be rated. The Androgynic Patterns of Body Form-Rating Profile includes only those items on which there was considerable agreement between raters and consistent differences between male and female subjects.

RELIABILITY: Four raters independently rated photographs of older adolescents. Using the total androgyny score, correlations between each of the possible pairs of raters (six pairs) who rated seventy-seven boys ranged from .72 to .82 with a median correlation of about .77; correlations for the ratings of seventy-nine girls ranged from .74 to .83 with a median of about .78; correlations for the ratings of a different set of thirty-one girls ranged from .59 to .79 with a median of about .65.

Item-total correlations were computed for the ratings of seventy-seven boys and seventy-nine girls. For boys the item-total correlations ranged from .52 to .72. For girls, they ranged from .35 to .82.

VALIDITY: Bayley and Bayer (1946, p. 454) report that "all of the twelve cases for whom all four raters agree that there were marked asexual or bisexual characteristics have androgyny scores in the intermediate range." Additionally, "there were eighteen girls and fifteen boys . . . who evidently have builds which exhibit in all respects definite or strong differentiation appropriate for their sex" (p. 455). These adolescents obtained scores toward the ends of the distribution.

NOTES AND COMMENTS: Bayley and Bayer report the relationship between somatic androgyny scores, height, weight, and strength.

SOURCE: See Bayley and Bayer, 1946.

BIBLIOGRAPHY:

Bayley, N. and Bayer, L. M. "The Assessment of Somatic Androgyny." *American Journal of Physical Anthropology*, 1946, *4*, 433-461.

---

211. ATTITUDES TOWARD ABORTION SCALE

AUTHORS: See Notes and Comments (1).

DATE: 1965

VARIABLE: Attitudes toward abortion

TYPE OF INSTRUMENT: Alternate choice

DESCRIPTION: The scale consists of six possible reasons why a woman might consider an abortion. For each reason, the respondent is to indicate approval or disapproval of an abortion.

PREVIOUSLY ADMINISTERED TO: Ages 18 and older

APPROPRIATE FOR: Ages 16 and older

ADMINISTRATION: The items are usually orally administered as part of a larger questionnaire. They could easily be given in a paper-and-pencil format and responded to in about three minutes.

SAMPLE ITEMS: If the pregnancy seriously endangered the woman's health?
If the woman believed the child would be deformed?

SCORING: Scoring procedures vary. Users have counted the number of "yes" responses; counted the number of "no" responses; assigned Guttman-scale-type numbers; or simply tallied the responses given by a large group to each item.

DEVELOPMENT: No information is provided.

RELIABILITY: A sample of 440 women was given an oral interview, including the Attitudes Toward Abortion Scale, on two occasions separated by three months. The percentage of persons giving the same response on the two occasions was computed separately for each of the six questions. The percentage ranged from 81 percent to 93 percent. The percentage of women giving identical responses to all six items on the two occasions was 53 percent (Ryder and Westoff, 1971).

     Hendershot and Grimm (1974) report that the six items form a Guttman scale with a coefficient of reproducibility of .94.

VALIDITY: No data are provided.

NOTES AND COMMENTS: (1) This scale has been used in Gallup polls, National Opinion Research Center polls, and polls conducted in conjunction with the National Fertility Studies. It is not clear from the literature who is actually responsible for writing the questions.

     (2) This scale has been modified by some users by including additional items or deleting some items.

     (3) Responses to the items on this scale have been compared with indicators of many other variables, including religion and religiosity (Balakrishnan and others, 1972; Blake, 1971; Bogen, 1974; Clayton and Tolone, 1973; Hedderson and others, 1974; Hendershot and Grimm, 1974; Hertel, Hendershot, and Grim, 1974; Renzi, 1975; Rosen and others, 1974; Rossi, 1966, 1967; Ryder and Westoff, 1971; Westoff, Moore, and Ryder, 1969; Westoff and Ryder, 1977); education (Balakrishnan and others, 1972; Blake, 1971; Hedderson and others, 1974; Hendershot and Grimm, 1974; Rosen and others, 1974; Rossi, 1967; Ryder and Westoff, 1971; Westoff, Moore, and Ryder, 1969; Westoff and Ryder, 1977); age (Balakrishnan and others, 1972; Blake, 1971; Hedderson and others, 1974; Hendershot and Grimm, 1974; Hertel, Hendershot, and Grimm, 1974; Rosen and others, 1974; Ryder and Westoff, 1971; Westoff, Moore, and Ryder, 1969; Westoff and Ryder, 1977); geography, including rural/urban background, size of hometown, region of country (Balakrishnan and others, 1972; Blake, 1971; Ryder and Westoff, 1971; Westoff, Moore, and Ryder, 1969); income (Balakrishnan and others, 1972; Hedderson and others, 1974); sex (Clayton and Tolone, 1973; Hedderson and others, 1974; Hendershot and Grimm, 1974; Hertel, Hendershot, and Grimm, 1974; Rosen and others, 1974; Rossi, 1967); race (Hedderson and others, 1974; Hendershot and Grimm, 1974; Hertel, Hendershot, and Grimm, 1974; Rosen and others, 1974; Ryder and Westoff, 1971; Westoff, Moore, and Ryder, 1969; Westoff and Ryder, 1977; Zelnik and Kantner, 1975); occupational and career information (Hedderson and others, 1974; Hendershot and Grimm, 1974; Hertel, Hendershot, and Grimm, 1974; Ryder and Westoff, 1971; Westoff, Moore, and Ryder, 1969; Westoff and Ryder, 1977); family size (Balakrishnan and others, 1972; Renzi, 1975; Ryder and Westoff, 1971; Westoff, Moore, and Ryder, 1969); marital status (Hendershot and Grimm, 1974; Zelnik and Kanter, 1975); contraceptive attitudes, practices, and failures (Balakrishnan and others, 1972; Ryder and Westoff, 1971; Westoff, Moore, and Ryder, 1969); political orientation (Rossi, 1966, 1967); socioeconomic level

(Ryder and Westoff, 1971; Westoff, Moore, and Ryder, 1969); and whether one has had an abortion (Bogen, 1974).

SOURCE: See Ryder and Westoff, 1971; or Hendershot and Grimm, 1974.

BIBLIOGRAPHY:

Balakrishnan, T. R., Ross, S., Allingham, J. D., and Kantner, J. F. "Attitudes Toward Abortion of Married Women in Metropolitan Toronto." *Social Biology*, 1972, *19*, 35-42.

Blake, J. "Abortion and Public Opinion: The 1960-1970 Decade." *Science*, 1971, *171*, 540-549.

Bogen, I. "Attitudes of Women Who Have Had Abortions." *Journal of Sex Research*, 1974, *10*, 97-109.

Clayton, R. R., and Tolone, W. L. "Religiosity and Attitudes Toward Induced Abortion: An Elaboration of the Relationship." *Sociological Analysis*, 1973, *3*, 26-39.

Hedderson, J., Hodgson, L. G., Bogan, M., and Crowley, T. "Determinants of Abortion Attitudes in the United States in 1972." *Cornell Journal of Social Relations*, 1974, *9*(2), 261-276.

Hendershot, G. E., and Grimm, J. W. "Abortion Attitudes Among Nurses and Social Workers." *American Journal of Public Health*, 1974, *64*, 438-441.

Hertel, B., Hendershot, G. E., and Grimm, J. W. "Religion and Attitudes Toward Abortion: A Study of Nurses and Social Workers." *Journal for the Scientific Study of Religion*, 1974, *13*, 23-34.

Kantner, J. F. "American Attitudes on Population Policy: Recent Trends." *Studies in Family Planning*, 1968, *30*, 1-7.

Renzi, M. "Ideal Family Size as an Intervening Variable Between Religion and Attitudes Toward Abortion." *Journal for the Scientific Study of Religion*, 1975, *14*, 23-27.

Rosen, R. A. H., Werley, H. H., Ager, J. W., and Shea, F. P. "Health Professionals' Attitudes Toward Abortion." *The Public Opinion Quarterly*, 1974, *38*, 159-173.

Rossi, A. S. "Abortion Laws and Their Victims." *Trans-Action*, 1966, *3*(6), 7-12.

Rossi, A. S. "Public View on Abortion." In A. F. Guttmacher (Ed.), *The Case for Legalized Abortion Now*. Berkeley: Diablo Press, 1967.

Ryder, N. B., and Westoff, C. F. *Reproduction in the United States*. Princeton, N.J.: Princeton University Press, 1971.

Westoff, C. F., Moore, E. C., and Ryder, N. B. "The Structure of Attitudes Toward Abortion." *Milbank Memorial Fund Quarterly*, 1969, *47*, 11-38.

Westoff, C. F., and Ryder, N. B. *The Contraceptive Revolution*. Princeton, N.J.: Princeton University Press, 1977.

Zelnik, M., and Kantner, J. F. "Attitudes of American Teenagers Toward Abortion." *Family Planning Perspectives*, 1975, *7*, 89-91.

212. BODY IMAGE PROJECTIVE TEST

AUTHORS: Valerie V. Hunt and Mary Ellen Weber

DATE: 1960

VARIABLE: Woman's perception of her own body

TYPE OF INSTRUMENT: Picture preference

DESCRIPTION: The test booklet consists of eighty-two pages, with each page displaying four nude female silhouettes. There are forty-two pages showing lateral views followed by forty pages showing anterior views. Three questions are to be answered for each page: "What looks most like me?" "What would I least like to look like?" and "What would I most like to look like?" It is not necessary that the questions be answered with three different silhouette choices.

PREVIOUSLY ADMINISTERED TO: Female college students

APPROPRIATE FOR: Females, ages 16 and older

ADMINISTRATION: The test is self-administered and can be completed in less than one hour.

SCORING: Scoring of the test is not well explained, but appears to be a function of the length and contour of the body parts in the silhouettes chosen.

DEVELOPMENT: Seven anterior-view nude female silhouettes were prepared. Three were normal contour (short, average height, and tall), two were thick contour (short and tall), and two were thin contour (short and tall). Each of the silhouettes was subdivided into three parts: arms, torso, and hips-legs. The "parts" were recombined to form seventy-three new silhouettes. Combined with the original seven silhouettes, there were a total of eighty anterior silhouettes. Three nude female lateral silhouettes of average height were prepared: a thick contour, an average contour, and a thin contour. Each silhouette was subdivided into four parts: shoulders, breasts, abdomen, and hips-legs. The "parts" were recombined to form eighty-one silhouettes, which in addition to the original three silhouettes yielded a total of eighty-four lateral silhouettes. Selection of silhouettes to be presented on each page was random, but certain restrictions were made. For anterior silhouettes, no more than two silhouettes on a page could have the same length and same contour for any body part; for lateral silhouettes, no more than two silhouettes on a page could have the same contour for any part.

RELIABILITY: Each page of silhouette pictures was included in the booklet twice to allow for an estimate of reliability for each of the body parts. For the item "What looks most like me," correlations ranged from .81 to .96; for the item "What I would least like to look like," correlations ranged from .70 to .95; for the item "What I would most like to look like," correlations ranged from .68 to .92.

VALIDITY: Fifty female college students completed the Body Image Projective Test and the Objective Rating Scale (#221). The fifty responses to "What looks most like me" on the Body Image Projective Test were correlated with responses to "What I look like" on the Objective Rating Scale. Correlations for each of the nine subscales (body parts) ranged from .10 to .40. Only two correlations (lateral view-abdomen, and lateral view-hips-legs breadth) were significant ($p < .05$).

NOTES AND COMMENTS: The low correlations between the Body Image Projective Test and the Objective Rating Scale (#221) suggest that more research is needed to determine which of the two measures is more valid.

SOURCE: See Hunt and Weber, 1960. (Silhouette drawings are described but only a sample is displayed.)

BIBLIOGRAPHY:

Hunt, V. V., and Weber, M. E. "Body Image Projective Test." *Journal of Projective Techniques,* 1960, *24,* 3-10.

---

213. CONTRACEPTIVE ATTITUDE QUESTIONNAIRE

AUTHOR: Warren B. Miller

DATE: 1977

VARIABLE: Attitudes regarding contraception

TYPE OF INSTRUMENT: Summated rating scale

DESCRIPTION: The scale consists of sixty-four statements, each of which is followed by four response options: agree completely, agree somewhat, disagree somewhat, disagree completely. The statements concern contraception in general, specific forms of contraception, and feelings regarding becoming pregnant.

PREVIOUSLY ADMINISTERED TO: Females, ages 18-27

APPROPRIATE FOR: Females, ages 16 and older

ADMINISTRATION: The scale is self-administered and can generally be completed in thirty to forty minutes.

SAMPLE ITEMS:

Contraception in general: It is primarily the woman's responsibility to take contraceptive precautions.

Specific forms of contraception: Tubal ligation (sterilization of the woman by surgery) is a desirable contraceptive method once the woman has had all the children she wants.

Feelings regarding becoming pregnant: It can be exciting to take a chance on getting pregnant.

SCORING: Items are objectively scored. A formula is provided for obtaining scores on the various scales. The formula takes account of the individual's mean and standard deviation based on her responses to all the items on the scale. The instrument yields scores on nineteen scales: condom, rhythm, withdrawal, foam, IUD, abortion, tubal ligation, oral contraception, premarital sex, chance taking, contraceptive shame, male contraceptive preference, coitus-dependent aversion—short, coitus-dependent aversion—long, ineffective contraceptive acceptance, somatic effects aversion, pill satisfaction, pregnancy wish, and female contraceptive preference. The number of items comprising a subscale ranges from two to ten. The subscales are not independent of each other, in that an item is likely to contribute to more than one score.

DEVELOPMENT: Pretesting of the instrument was done with young adult women, and revisions were made to ensure that the instructions and item content could be understood by women with at least some high school education. The scale was then administered to 200 women, who were also interviewed. Based on the responses of these women, items were selected for the individual criterion scales (the first eight subscales listed above) if they discriminated between those women who were willing to use a particular method of contraception and those who were not. Items were selected for the Premarital Sex subscale if they discriminated between those college women (n = 150) who were sexually active and those who were not.

The scale was then administered to 1,000 women, ages 17-27, and their responses were used to develop the remaining ten scales, using "factoral analytic and correlational cluster techniques."

RELIABILITY: Using the responses from 965 women, Kuder-Richardson reliabilities were computed for each of the nineteen scales. Reliabilities ranged from .04 to .63 with a median of .34. Test-retest reliabilities were computed for each of the nineteen scales, using the responses from forty-six women retested after a four-week interval. Correlations ranged from .49 to .91 with a median of .70.

VALIDITY: No data are provided.

NOTES AND COMMENTS: Means and standard deviations on each of the nineteen scales are presented for the following groups: 323 never-married women; 322 women married for four to six months; 320 women who bore their first child within the previous four to six months.

SOURCE: Warren B. Miller
        American Institute for Research
        P.O. Box 1113
        1791 Arastradero Road
        Palo Alto, California 94302

BIBLIOGRAPHY:

Miller, W. B. "Manual for Description of Instruments Used in a Research Project on the Psychological Aspects of Fertility Behavior in Women." Unpublished manuscript, American Institute for Research, 1977.

214. MCHUGH-WASSER SCALE OF ATTITUDES TOWARD MENSTRUATION

AUTHORS: Gelolo McHugh and Judith K. Wasser

DATE: 1959

VARIABLE: Attitudes toward menstruation

TYPE OF INSTRUMENT: Thurstone attitude scale

DESCRIPTION: The scale consists of forty-eight statements regarding menstruation. The respondent is to indicate the statements she agrees with.

PREVIOUSLY ADMINISTERED TO: Female college students

APPROPRIATE FOR: Females who menstruate

ADMINISTRATION: The scale can be self-administered and can be completed in less than thirty minutes.

SAMPLE ITEMS: Menstruation is a normal biological function to me.
            I feel that menstruation has an essential purpose.

SCORING: The score is the median scale value for the items endorsed by the respondent. A high score indicates a positive attitude.

DEVELOPMENT: Two hundred college women were asked a series of open-ended questions designed to elicit attitudes toward menstruation. From their answers, forty-eight different attitude statements were identified. Fifty-eight female graduate students in mental hygiene were asked to rate the statements of an eleven-point scale ranging from 1, "a most negative attitude toward menstruation from a mental hygiene point of view," to 11, "a most positive or 'good' attitude from a mental hygiene point of view." Eleven female professional psychologists and mental hygienists were also asked to rate the items on an eleven-point scale. Median ratings were computed separately for each group of raters. The median ratings provide the scale values for scoring the scale.

RELIABILITY: No data are provided.

VALIDITY: No data are provided.

NOTES AND COMMENTS: (1) McHugh and Wasser (1959) report the development but not the use of the scale.

(2) Because the scale was developed about twenty years ago, and because attitudes toward and laymen's knowledge of menstruation may have changed considerably since then, one should not assume that the scale values for scoring are still valid today.

(3) Some of the items on the scale can be justifiably criticized. For example, "I feel older and more serious when I menstruate" includes more than a single idea. A woman might feel older but not more serious, or vice versa. "I don't mind mentioning menstruation to dates" is ambiguous. *Mentioning* a topic is different from discussing it;

furthermore talking about menstruation in the abstract is different from indicating that one is presently menstruating. It is not clear what is meant by the term *mentioning* as used above.

(4) Though the scale could be completed by any menstruating female, some of the items might seem very silly to an adult woman; for example, "When I am menstruating, I am ashamed in front of boys" or "Menstruation makes me resent being a girl."

(5) This scale is also described in *Scales for the Measurement of Attitudes* (Shaw and Wright, 1967, pp. 138-140).

SOURCE: See McHugh and Wasser, 1959; or Shaw and Wright, 1967, pp. 138-140.

BIBLIOGRAPHY:

Dunham, F, Y. "Timing and Sources of Information About, and Attitudes Toward, Menstruation Among College Females." *Journal of Genetic Psychology,* 1970, *117,* 205-217.

Levitt, E. E., and Lubin, B. "Some Personality Factors Associated with Menstrual Complaints and Menstrual Attitude." *Journal of Psychosomatic Research,* 1967, *11,* 267-270.

McHugh, G., and Wasser, J. K. "Application of the Thurstone-Chave Attitude Rating Technique to Attitude Toward Menstruation." *Psychological Reports,* 1959, *5,* 677-682.

*Shaw, M. E., and Wright, J. M. *Scales for the Measurement of Attitudes.* New York: McGraw-Hill, 1967.

---

215. MATERNAL ATTITUDE TO PREGNANCY INSTRUMENT (MAPI)

AUTHORS: Abram Blau, Joan Welkowitz, and Jacob Cohen

DATE: 1964

VARIABLE: Attitudes toward pregnancy

TYPE OF INSTRUMENT: Summated rating scale

DESCRIPTION: There are two forms of the scale: one in English and one in Spanish. Each form consists of forty-eight statements regarding "the mother's ability to carry the fetus to term; anxious anticipation, ambivalence, or negative feelings regarding the health of the fetus and coming baby; negative feelings, depression, fatigue, and nausea during pregnancy; and attitudes to breast feeding" (p. 324). Each item is accompanied by four response options. In English, the response options are: strongly agree, agree, disagree, and strongly disagree. Appropriate translations are made in the Spanish form. Some items are phrased to reflect a positive attitude and others are phrased to reflect a negative attitude.

PREVIOUSLY ADMINISTERED TO: Female adults

APPROPRIATE FOR: Ages 16 and older

ADMINISTRATION: The scale can be self-administered and can be completed in about twenty minutes.

SAMPLE ITEMS: (Factor numbers refer to factors on the English-language version. See Development for an explanation of the factors.)

Factor I: Most women feel sick to their stomachs for the first three months of their pregnancy.

Factor II: You can love a baby before it is actually born.

Factor III: Most women want to be awake during labor.

Factor IV: At least half the babies born in the U.S. are not "planned."

SCORING: Items are objectively scored and equally weighted. The scale yields four factor scores and a total score. Total scores can range from 48 to 192. High scores are indicative of positive attitudes.

DEVELOPMENT: *English Version:* Items were written on the basis of clinical findings and ratings from a prior relevant study by the scale's authors. The scale was completed by 337 postpartum women, and their responses were factor analyzed. Factor I (twenty-two items) concerned "a feeling of well-being during pregnancy and an acceptance of pregnancy, labor, and delivery without fear" (p. 326). Factor II (nine items) regarded "exaggerated feelings of well-being during pregnancy, pride of the pregnancy, positive maternal feelings to the child, and positive attitudes toward her doctor" (p. 326). Factor III (four items) related to "an unusual concern about the delivery and birth, a desire for active participation in the delivery, and a positive interest in breast nursing" (p. 326). Factor IV (eleven items) related to positive feelings toward the baby.

Spanish Version: The English version was translated by a Spanish psychiatrist and retranslated by another psychiatrist into English. The items were then discussed with bilingual women to correct any errors in translation. The Spanish version was completed by 110 Spanish-speaking prepartum mothers, and their responses were factor analyzed. Four factors emerged, but they differed from the four factors on the English version. Factor I (sixteen items) concerned "a positive response to pregnancy, labor, and delivery, and a sense of competence regarding handling the infant" (p. 326). Factor II (eight items) "reflected the woman's desire to participate actively in labor and breast feeding, a feeling of looking well during pregnancy, and lack of concern about her postnatal figure" (p. 326). Factor III (sixteen items) concerned anxiety about the pregnancy, about her husband's love, and about the condition of the baby as well as negative feelings about the state of pregnancy. Factor IV (ten items) concerned positive feelings about the pregnancy, rejection of the notion that pregnancy is a bad time, positive feelings about handling the baby, and the belief that it is common not to love the baby at first.

RELIABILITY: The responses from 145 postpartum women were used to compute the internal consistency reliability. Coefficient alpha was .80. Internal consistency reliabilities were computed for each of the factor scores. Based on responses from 337 women who completed the English version, the correlations were: Factor I = .78; Factor II = .65; Factor III = .51; and Factor IV = .55. Based on responses from 110 women who completed the Spanish version, the correlations were: Factor I = .79; Factor II = .58; Factor III = .72; and Factor IV = .68.

VALIDITY: No data are provided.

NOTES AND COMMENTS: All items are phrased in the third person. Therefore, it would be more accurate to say that the scale measures perceptions of women's attitudes toward pregnancy. In the absence of any validity data, one cannot conclude that a woman who is reporting her perceptions of how "most women" feel is actually revealing her own attitudes toward pregnancy.

SOURCE: See Blau, Welkowitz, and Cohen, 1964.

BIBLIOGRAPHY:

Blau, A., Welkowitz, J., and Cohen, J. "Maternal Attitude to Pregnancy Instrument." *Archives of General Psychiatry,* 1964, *10,* 324-331.

---

216. MAXWELL ATTITUDES TOWARD ABORTION SCALE (ATA)

AUTHOR: Joseph W. Maxwell

DATE: 1970 (used 1968)

VARIABLE: Attitudes toward abortion

TYPE OF INSTRUMENT: Summated rating scale

DESCRIPTION: The scale consists of twelve statements relating to abortion. Ten items pertain to whether abortion should be permitted or forbidden. Eight items are phrased to reflect a positive attitude toward abortion, and four items are phrased to reflect a negative attitude toward abortion. Each item is accompanied by five response alternatives.

PREVIOUSLY ADMINISTERED TO: College students

APPROPRIATE FOR: Ages 16 and older

ADMINISTRATION: The scale can be self-administered and can be completed in less than five minutes.

SAMPLE ITEMS: Abortion should be left up strictly to the individual.
              Abortion should be treated legally as a form of murder.

SCORING: Items are objectively scored and equally weighted. Total scores can range from 12 (conservative attitude) to 60 (liberal attitude).

DEVELOPMENT: No information is provided.

RELIABILITY: A group of twenty-four college students were tested on two occasions separated by about four weeks. The test-retest reliability of the scale was estimated to be .80.

VALIDITY: A group of 323 undergraduates completed the Attitudes Toward Abortion Scale, indicated whether they would want an abortion in the event of an unwanted pregnancy, and gave themselves a self-rating on their attitude toward abortion. "Subjects who indicated they would desire an abortion revealed an extremely liberal attitude by their ATA scores" (p. 250). Furthermore, those who rated themselves as conservative generally obtained conservative scores on the scale (median = 35); those who rated themselves as moderate generally obtained moderate scores (median = 43); and those who rated themselves as liberal generally obtained liberal scores (median = 48).

SOURCE: See Maxwell, 1970.

BIBLIOGRAPHY:

Maxwell, J. W. "College Students' Attitudes Toward Abortion." *Family Coordinator,* 1970, *19,* 247-252.

---

217. MENSTRUAL DISTRESS QUESTIONNAIRE (MDQ)

AUTHOR: Rudolph H. Moos

DATE: 1968

VARIABLE: Menstrual cycle symptomatology

TYPE OF INSTRUMENT: Rating scale

DESCRIPTION: The scale consists of forty-six symptoms that might be associated with a woman's menstrual cycle. Each symptom is accompanied by a six-point rating scale, ranging from "no experience of the symptom" to "an acute or partially disabling experience of the symptom." There are two forms of the scale. On Form M, separate ratings are recorded for (1) the time during menstrual flow, (2) the week preceding menstrual flow, and (3) the remainder of the menstrual cycle. On Form T, ratings are made only for the symptoms experienced on the day the scale is being completed.

PREVIOUSLY ADMINISTERED TO: Females who have menstruated

APPROPRIATE FOR: Females who have menstruated

ADMINISTRATION: The scale can be self-administered and takes about five minutes to complete.

SAMPLE ITEMS: Muscle stiffness
Insomnia
Cold sweats
Crying
Affectionate
Chest pains

SCORING: Individual item scores, which range from 1 (no experience of symptom) to 6 (an acute or partially disabling experience of the symptom), can be totaled to yield scores on each of eight symptom groups.

DEVELOPMENT: A list of forty-seven symptoms was compiled from the review of the relevant research and the results of interviews with women. Three control symptoms (buzzing or ringing in ears, numbness or tingling in hands or feet, feelings of suffocation) were taken from the Blatt Menopausal Index (see #220; Neugarten and Kraines, 1965) and included among the forty-seven symptoms. In previous research, these control symptoms were found to be frequently endorsed by menopausal women but infrequently endorsed by women in the 20-30 age range.

The scale was completed by 839 student wives for their most recent cycle and for their worst menstrual cycle. Their responses were factor analyzed, resulting in eight symptom groups: pain, concentration, behavioral change, autonomic reactions, water retention, negative affect, arousal, and control. One item was eliminated because it did not consistently fall on any one factor.

RELIABILITY: Kuder-Richardson reliabilities have been computed for each of the sub-scales on both Forms A and T. The reliabilities for Form A, based on a sample of 839 women, ranged from .53 to .89 (Moos, 1977). The reliabilities for Form T, based on a sample of fifty women, ranged from .56 to .94 (Kleinsasser, 1975). Markum (1976) administered the scale to forty-seven women using standard instructions and to another forty-seven women using instructions that masked the purpose of the scale. She computed split-half reliabilities for each group on each subscale based on two methods of splitting the scale—odd-even and random—and obtained split-half reliabilities ranging from .74 to .98.

VALIDITY: In summarizing the research related to the psychometric properties of the MDQ, Moos (1977, p. 35) states: "The subscales show good internal consistency and intercycle stability, although more information is needed on the latter since substantial variability in menstrual cycle symptom complaints may occur in the same woman over time. The MDQ shows no effects of memory or of the particular phase a woman is in when filling it out on reports of symptom severity. There is little or no evidence of instrument deterioration, indicating that Form T is suitable for longitudinal investigations of stability and change in menstrual cycle symptomatology. In addition, the fact that a woman knows that the MDQ is requesting information about her experiences during the menstrual cycle seems to make relatively little difference on symptom reports."

NOTES AND COMMENTS: (1) Several researchers have modified the MDQ. Favreau (1974) and Wilcoxon, Schrader, and Sherif (1976) have modified the scale for use with men. Ruble, Brooks, and Clarke (1976) asked college women to complete the scale "as if" they were at a specific phase of their menstrual cycle, and they asked premenarcheal girls to indicate what symptoms they expected to experience when they began menstruating. Seagull (1973) revised the MDQ to phrase items in terms of observable behaviors so that a woman could be rated by her friends. And as mentioned earlier, Markum (1976) disguised the purpose of the scale.

(2) Moos (1977) provides a very comprehensive review of the research that has been published using the MDQ.

SOURCE: See Moos, 1968 for the items; for a copy of the manual, write to:
Rudolph Moos
Department of Psychiatry and Behavioral Sciences
Stanford University
Stanford, California 94305

BIBLIOGRAPHY:

Berry, C., and McGuire, F. "Menstrual Distress and Acceptance of Sexual Role." *American Journal of Obstetrics and Gynecology,* 1972, *114,* 84-87.

Brockway, J. "Prediction of Premenstrual Symptomatology Using the Moos Menstrual Distress Questionnaire." Unpublished doctoral dissertation, University of Iowa, 1975. (*Dissertation Abstracts International,* 1976, *36* [12-B], 6371.)

Englander-Golden, P., Whitmore, M. R., and Dienstbier, R. A. "Menstrual Cycle as Focus of Study and Self-Reports of Moods and Behaviors." *Motivation and Emotion,* 1978, *2,* 75-86.

Favreau, O. "Menstrual Cycles and Sex Differences." Unpublished manuscript, 1974.

Golub, S. "The Magnitude of Premenstrual Anxiety and Depression." *Psychosomatic Medicine,* 1976a, *38,* 4-12.

Golub, S. "The Effect of Premenstrual Anxiety and Depression on Cognitive Function." *Journal of Personality and Social Psychology,* 1976b, *34,* 99-104.

Gough, H. G. "Personality Factors Related to Reported Severity of Menstrual Distress." *Journal of Abnormal Psychology,* 1975, *84,* 59-65.

Gruba, G., and Rohrbaugh, M. "MMPI Correlates of Menstrual Distress." *Psychosomatic Medicine,* 1975, *37,* 265-273.

Kleinsasser, J. "The Premenstrual Syndrome and Its Correlation to Personality Characteristics." Unpublished doctoral dissertation, University of South Dakota, 1975. (*Dissertation Abstracts International,* 1976, *36* [8-A], 5152.)

Lederman, M. "Menstrual Cycle and Fluctuation in Cognitive-Perceptual Performance." Unpublished doctoral dissertation, Boston University, 1974. (*Dissertation Abstracts International,* 1975, *35* [3-B], 1388.)

Markum, R. "Assessment of the Reliability of and the Effect of Neutral Instructions on the Symptom Ratings on the Moos Menstrual Distress Questionnaire." *Psychosomatic Medicine,* 1976, *38,* 163-172.

Miller, W. B., and Smith, P. J. "Elimination of the Menses: Psychosocial Aspects." *Journal of Psychiatric Research,* 1975, *12,* 153-166.

Moos, R. "The Development of a Menstrual Distress Questionnaire." *Psychosomatic Medicine,* 1968, *30,* 853-867.

Moos, R. "A Typology of Menstrual Cycle Symptoms." *American Journal of Obstetrics and Gynecology,* 1969, *103,* 390-402.

Moos, R. "Menstrual Distress Questionnaire Manual." Unpublished manuscript, Social Ecology Laboratory, Department of Psychiatry and Behavioral Sciences, Stanford University, Stanford, California, 1977.

Moos, R., Kopell, B., Melges, F., Yalom, I., Lunde, D., Clayton, R., and Hamburg, D. "Fluctuations in Symptoms and Moods During the Menstrual Cycle." *Journal of Psychosomatic Research,* 1969, *13,* 37-44.

*Neugarten, B. L., and Kraines, R. J. "Menopausal Symptoms in Women of Various Ages." *Psychosomatic Medicine,* 1965, *27,* 266-273.

Paige, K. "Women Learn to Sing the Menstrual Blues." *Psychology Today,* 1973, *7,* 41-46.

Parlee, M. "Stereotypic Beliefs About Menstruation: A Methodological Note on the Moos Menstrual Distress Questionnaire and Some New Data." *Psychosomatic Medicine,* 1974, *36,* 229-240.

Ruble, D., Brooks, J., and Clarke, A. "Research on Menstrual-Related Psychological Changes: Alternative Perspectives." Paper presented at the Conference on Bio-psychological Factors Influencing Sex Role Related Behaviors, Northampton, Massachusetts, October 1976.

Seagull, E. "An Investigation of Personality Differences Between Women with High and Low Premenstrual Tension." Unpublished doctoral dissertation, Michigan State University, 1973. (*Dissertation Abstracts International,* 1974, *34*[9-B], 4675.)

Silbergeld, S., Brast, N., and Noble, E. "The Menstrual Cycle: A Double-Blind Study of Symptoms, Mood, and Behavior, and Biochemical Variables Using Enovid and Placebo." *Psychosomatic Medicine,* 1971, *33,* 411-428.

Tarpin, J. "The Effect of the Modification of Sexual Attitudes on Premenstrual Distress." Unpublished doctoral dissertation, University of Miami, 1975. (*Dissertation Abstracts International,* 1976, *36*[9-B], 4712.)

Voda, A. "Correlations Among Physiological Indicators, Physical Signs, and Subjective Complaints in Premenstrual Edema." Unpublished doctoral dissertation, University of Arizona, 1976. (*Dissertation Abstracts International,* 1977, *37*[3-B], 1133.)

Wilcoxon, L., Schrader, S., and Sherif, C. "Daily Self-Reports on Activities, Life Events, Moods, and Somatic Changes During the Menstrual Cycle." *Psychosomatic Medicine,* 1976, *38,* 399-417.

---

218. MOSHER F-C INVENTORY—FORM F

AUTHOR: Donald L. Mosher

DATE: 1968

VARIABLES: Sex-guilt, hostility-guilt, and morality-conscience in women

TYPE OF INSTRUMENT: Forced choice

DESCRIPTION: The instrument consists of seventy-eight sentence stems. Each sentence stem is accompanied by two possible endings: one ending reflects a guilty response and one ending reflects a nonguilty response. The respondent is to indicate which of the two endings is more true of her. The Sex-Guilt Scale consists of thirty-nine items; the Hostility-Guilt Scale consists of twenty-two items; and the Morality-Conscience Scale consists of seventeen items.

PREVIOUSLY ADMINISTERED TO: Female college students

APPROPRIATE FOR: Females, ages 16 and older

ADMINISTRATION: The scale can be self-administered and can be completed in about thirty minutes.

SAMPLE ITEMS: *Sex-guilt:* If in the future I committed adultery . . .
        A. I hope I would be punished very deeply.
        B. I hope I enjoy it.
      Hostility-guilt: If I killed someone in self-defense . . .
        A. I would be glad to be alive.
        B. I would be a murderer.
      Morality-conscience: I punish myself . . .
        A. very infrequently
        B. when I do wrong and don't get caught.

SCORING: A scoring key is provided that indicates the weight (ranging from −2 to +2) for each response to each item. Three scores are obtained by summing the item scores for the items contributing to each scale. Scores on sex-guilt can range from −61 to +64. Scores on hostility-guilt can range from −33 to +33. Scores on morality-conscience can range from −24 to +27. In each case, the higher the score, the more the guilt.

DEVELOPMENT: The Mosher Incomplete Sentences Test (MIST) is a sentence completion test designed to measure three aspects of guilt: sex-guilt, hostility-guilt, and morality-conscience. Using responses to the MIST, a pool of 809 statements was constructed. It included 276 items to measure sex-guilt, 266 items to measure hostility-guilt, and 271 items to measure morality-conscience. The item pool was administered to 100 college women with instructions to indicate which items they agreed with and which items they disagreed with. Scores were obtained on each of the three subscales, and an item analysis was performed for each subscale using the responses from those scoring in the upper and lower 27 percent of the distribution of scores. The item analysis indicated that 362 items differentiated the two extreme groups at the .05 level of significance. Items were eliminated from the 362 differentiating items if more than 75 percent of the respondents scoring in the upper and lower 27 percent answered the item identically. This left 110 items measuring sex-guilt, 77 items measuring hostility-guilt, and 71 items measuring morality-conscience. From this pool, seventy-eight guilty and seventy-eight nonguilty responses to the same seventy-eight item stems were selected for the scale.

RELIABILITY: Mosher (1968) reports the following reliabilities for the three subscales: sex-guilt = .95; hostility-guilt = .76; and morality-conscience = .84.

VALIDITY: Mosher (1968) administered the following instruments to sixty-two college women: the Mosher F-C Inventory; the Mosher "G" Inventory (#219), a true-false measure of guilt that yields the same three subscale scores as the Mosher F-C Inventory; the

MIST, a sentence completion measure of guilt that also yields the same three scores; the Marlowe-Crowne Social Desirability Scale; and the Edwards Social Desirability scale. After the women had completed all the scales, they were readministered the two guilt inventories with instructions to respond to the items in the way that would create the most favorable impression. The correlations between the forced choice and the true-false measures of guilt were as follows: sex-guilt = .86; hostility-guilt = .90; and morality-conscience = .86. All were significant at the .01 level. The correlations between the forced choice and incomplete-sentences measures of guilt were as follows: sex-guilt = .64; hostility-guilt = .67; and morality-conscience = .56. Again, all were significant at the .01 level. The correlations between the scores on the forced choice measure of guilt and each of the two measures of social desirability were nonsignificant, suggesting that scores on the Mosher F-C Inventory do not simply reflect social desirability.

Correlations were computed between scores on the forced choice measure of guilt obtained under the two sets of instructions: standard and favorable impression. None of the correlations was significant. Furthermore, t tests were performed comparing the means obtained on each of the three scores under each of the two sets of instructions. The three t tests all indicated statistically significant differences (p < .01), with scores obtained under standard instructions falling about 10 points higher than scores obtained under instructions to create a favorable impression. This finding suggests that, in general, respondents are not merely trying to create a favorable impression with their answers.

NOTES AND COMMENTS: (1) The Mosher F-C Inventory is closely related to the Mosher "G" Inventory (#219), a true-false measure that yields the same three scores.

(2) The Mosher F-C Inventory measures "the personality disposition of guilt rather than the feeling state of guilt" (Mosher, 1968, p. 690).

(3) Mosher does not discuss the issue of whether the presence of the hostility-guilt and morality-conscience items affects responses to the sex-guilt items. Research is needed to determine whether scores on the sex-guilt items would differ if the items were presented alone, that is, without the items from the other two guilt subscales. Likewise scores on the hostility-guilt and morality-conscience subscales might be affected by the presence of items from other subscales.

(4) A comparable scale is available for males.

SOURCE: Donald Mosher
             University of Connecticut
             Storrs, Connecticut 06268

BIBLIOGRAPHY:

Mosher, D. L. "Measurement of Guilt in Females by Self-Report Inventories." *Journal of Consulting and Clinical Psychology,* 1968, *32,* 690-695.
Mosher, D. L. "Sex Differences, Sex Experience, Sex Guilt, and Explicitly Sexual Films." *Journal of Social Issues,* 1973, *29,* 95-112.
Mosher, D. L., and Abramson, P. R. "Subjective Sexual Arousal to Films of Masturbation." *Journal of Consulting and Clinical Psychology,* 1977, *45,* 796-807.
Mosher, D. L., and Cross, H. J. "Sex Guilt and Premarital Sexual Experiences of College Students." *Journal of Consulting and Clinical Psychology,* 1971, *36,* 27-32.
Mosher, D. L., and Greenberg, I. "Females' Affective Responses to Reading Erotic Literature." *Journal of Consulting and Clinical Psychology,* 1969, *33,* 472-477.

219. MOSHER "G" INVENTORY—FORM F

AUTHOR: Donald L. Mosher

DATE: 1968

VARIABLES: Sex-guilt, hostility-guilt, and morality-conscience in women

TYPE OF INSTRUMENT: True-false

DESCRIPTION: The instrument consists of 150 statements: fifty relate to sex-guilt, fifty relate to hostility-guilt, and fifty relate to morality-conscience. For each statement, the respondent is to indicate whether the statement is true or false as applied to her. On the Sex-Guilt Scale and on the Hostility-Guilt Scale, twenty-five items are keyed true and twenty-five items are keyed false. On the Morality-Conscience Scale, thirty-one items are keyed true and nineteen items are keyed false.

PREVIOUSLY ADMINISTERED TO: Female college students

APPROPRIATE FOR: Females, ages 16 and older

ADMINISTRATION: The scale can be self-administered and can be completed in less than forty-five minutes.

SAMPLE ITEMS:

Sex-guilt: If I had sex relations, I would feel all right, I think.

Hostility-guilt: After a childhood fight, I felt ashamed of myself.

Morality-conscience: When I tell a lie, I know it's not very serious.

SCORING: A scoring key is provided that indicates the weight (ranging from −2 to +2) for each item. The key also indicates which scale each item is scored on. Three scores are obtained by summing the item scores for the fifty items contributing to each scale. Scores on sex-guilt and hostility-guilt can range from −38 to +38, with a high score indicating more guilt. Scores on morality-conscience can range from −25 to +49, with a high score again indicating more guilt.

DEVELOPMENT: The Mosher Incomplete Sentences Test (MIST) is a sentence completion test designed to measure three aspects of guilt: sex-guilt, hostility-guilt, and morality-conscience. Using responses to the MIST, a pool of 809 statements was constructed. It included 276 items to measure sex-guilt, 266 items to measure hostility-guilt, and 271 items to measure morality-conscience. The item pool was administered to 100 college women with instructions to indicate which items they agreed with and which items they disagreed with. Scores were obtained on each of the three subscales, and an item analysis was performed for each subscale using the responses from those scoring in the upper and lower 27 percent of the distribution of scores. The item analysis indicated that 362 items differentiated the two extreme groups at the .05 level of significance. Items were eliminated from the 362 differentiating items if more than 75 percent of the respondents scoring in the upper and lower 27 percent of the distribution of total subscale scores answered the item identically. This left 110 items measuring sex-guilt, 77 items measuring hostility-guilt, and 71 items measuring morality-conscience. From this remaining pool of items, fifty were selected for each of the three subscales.

RELIABILITY: Mosher (1968) reports the following reliabilities for the three subscales: sex-guilt = .95; hostility-guilt = .86; and morality-conscience = .92.

VALIDITY: Mosher (1968) administered the following scales to sixty-two college women: the Mosher "G" Inventory; the Mosher F-C Inventory (#218), a forced choice measure of guilt that yields scores on the same three subscales as the Mosher "G" Inventory; the Mosher Incomplete Sentences Test, a sentence completion measure of guilt that also yields the same three subscale scores; the Marlowe-Crowne Social Desirability scale; and the Edwards Social Desirability scale. After the women had completed all the scales, they were readministered the two guilt inventories with instructions to respond to the items in the way that would create the most favorable impression. The correlations between the true-false and forced choice measures of guilt were as follows: sex-guilt = .86; hostility-guilt = .90; and morality-conscience = .86. All were significant at the .01 level. The correlations between the true-false and incomplete-sentences measures of guilt were as follows: sex-guilt = .73; hostility-guilt = .63; and morality-conscience = .52. All were significant at the .01 level. The correlations between the scores on the true-false measure of guilt and each of the two measures of social desirability were nonsignificant, suggesting that scores on the Mosher "G" Inventory do not simply reflect social desirability.

Correlations were computed between scores on the true-false measure of guilt obtained under the two sets of instructions: standard and favorable impression. Only one of the three correlations was significant ($p < .01$); the significant correlation was found for hostility-guilt. Furthermore, t tests were performed comparing the means obtained on each of the three scores under each of the two sets of instructions. The three t tests all indicated statistically significant differences ($p < .01$), with scores obtained under standard instructions falling about 10 points higher than scores obtained under instructions to create a favorable impression. These results suggest that, in general, respondents completing the scale are not trying to create a favorable impression by their answers.

NOTES AND COMMENTS: (1) The Mosher "G" Inventory is closely related to the Mosher F-C Inventory (#218), a forced choice measure that yields the same three scores.

(2) The Mosher "G" Inventory measures "the personality disposition of guilt rather than the feeling state of guilt" (Mosher, 1968, p. 690).

(3) Mosher does not discuss the issue of whether the presence of the hostility-guilt and morality-conscience items affects responses to the sex-guilt items. Research is needed to determine whether scores on the sex-guilt items would differ if the items were presented alone, that is, without the items from the other two guilt subscales. Likewise scores on the hostility-guilt and morality-conscience subscales might be affected by the presence of items from other subscales.

(4) A comparable scale is available for males.

SOURCE: Donald Mosher
           University of Connecticut
           Storrs, Connecticut 06268

BIBLIOGRAPHY:

Mosher, D. L. "Measurement of Guilt in Females by Self-Report Inventories." *Journal of Consulting and Clinical Psychology*, 1968, *32*, 690-695.
Mosher, D. L., and Abramson, P. R. "Subjective Sexual Arousal to Films of Masturbation." *Journal of Consulting and Clinical Psychology*, 1977, *45*, 796-807.

---

220. NEUGARTEN-KRAINES MENOPAUSAL SYMPTOMS SCALE

AUTHORS: Bernice L. Neugarten and Ruth J. Kraines

DATE: 1965

VARIABLE: Presence of menopausal symptoms

TYPE OF INSTRUMENT: Checklist

DESCRIPTION: The instrument consists of twenty-eight symptoms that are sometimes associated with menopause. The symptoms represent three areas: somatic (twelve items), psychosomatic (five items), and psychological (eleven items). Each woman is to check all symptoms she experiences.

PREVIOUSLY ADMINISTERED TO: Females, ages 13-64

APPROPRIATE FOR: Females, ages 13 and older

ADMINISTRATION: The instrument has been used as part of an interview or it can be self-administered. It can be completed in less than ten minutes.

SAMPLE ITEMS: *Somatic:* Hot flushes
Psychosomatic: Tired feelings
Psychological: Irritable and nervous

SCORING: Four scores are obtained: a count of the total number of symptoms checked and counts of the symptoms checked in each of the three categories. A subset of eleven items on the checklist, entitled the Blatt Menopausal Index, is scored by weighting the checked items according to their presumed diagnostic significance.

DEVELOPMENT: The symptoms were selected for the checklist based on an extensive literature review and the results of preliminary interviews. The final instrument contains symptoms "most often reported by clinicians and by women themselves as being typical of frequent complaints at menopause" (Neugarten and Kraines, 1965, p. 267).

RELIABILITY: The instrument was administered to a sample of forty women on two occasions. The interval between test and retest varied from one to six months. Test-retest reliability for the total number of checked symptoms was .79; test-retest for the Blatt Menopausal Index was .70.

VALIDITY: The instrument was administered to a sample of 460 women ranging in age from 13 to 64 years. The women were divided into six groups: ages 13-18, ages 20-29, ages 30-44, ages 45-54 pre- or postmenopausal, ages 45-54 menopausal, and ages 55-64. Five scores were obtained for each woman: Blatt Menopausal Index score, Somatic score, Psychosomatic score, Psychological score, and Total score. On the Blatt Menopausal Index, the Somatic score, and the Psychosomatic score, the menopausal group scored significantly higher (more symptoms checked) than each of the other five groups (p < .05). On the total score, the menopausal group scored significantly higher (p < .05) than all groups except the adolescent (ages 13-18) group. On the Psychological score, only the older group (ages 55-64) scored significantly lower (p < .05) than the menopausal group.

SOURCE: See Neugarten and Kraines, 1965.

BIBLIOGRAPHY:

Neugarten, B. L., and Kraines, R. J. "Menopausal Symptoms in Women of Various Ages." *Psychosomatic Medicine,* 1965, *27,* 266-273.

---

221. OBJECTIVE RATING SCALE

AUTHORS: Valerie V. Hunt and Mary Ellen Weber

DATE: 1960

VARIABLE: Woman's perception of the size of her own body parts

TYPE OF INSTRUMENT: Rating scale

DESCRIPTION: The scale lists nine body parts with three response options (less than normal, normal, more than normal) for the woman to communicate "what I look like."

PREVIOUSLY ADMINISTERED TO: Female college students

APPROPRIATE FOR: Females, ages 16 and older

ADMINISTRATION: The scale can be self-administered and can be completed in less than five minutes.

SAMPLE ITEMS: Torso length
                        Abdomen size

SCORING: No composite score is obtained.

DEVELOPMENT: No information is provided.

RELIABILITY: One hundred college women completed the scale on two occasions separated by a two-month interval. Test-retest reliabilities for the nine body parts ranged from .77 to .97.

VALIDITY: Fifty women who completed the Objective Rating Scale also completed the Body Image Projective Test (#212), another measure of a woman's perception of her own body. Responses to "What I look like" on the Objective Rating Scale were correlated with responses to "What looks most like me" on the Body Image Projective Test. The correlations for each of nine subscales (body parts) ranged from .10 to .40. Only two correlations (lateral view-abdomen and lateral view-hips-legs breadth) were statistically significant (p < .05).

NOTES AND COMMENTS: (1) The study from which this scale was taken was conducted to develop the Body Image Projective Test (#212).

(2) The low correlations between the Objective Rating Scale and the Body Image Projective Test (#212) suggest that more research is needed to determine which of the two measures is more valid.

SOURCE: See Hunt and Weber, 1960.

BIBLIOGRAPHY:

Hunt, V. V., and Weber, M. E. "Body Image Projective Test." *Journal of Projective Techniques,* 1960, *24,* 3-10.

---

222. SEXUAL AROUSABILITY INVENTORY (SAI)

AUTHORS: Emily Franck Hoon, Peter W. Hoon, and John P. Wincze

DATE: 1976

VARIABLE: Sexual arousability in women

TYPE OF INSTRUMENT: Summated rating scale

DESCRIPTION: The scale consists of twenty-eight brief descriptions of experiences that might be sexually arousing. The items represent five factors: Foreplay, Erotic Visual and Verbal Stimuli, Breast Stimulation, Preparation for and Participation in Intercourse, and Genital Stimulation. For each description, the respondent is to indicate "how sexually aroused you feel when you have the described experience, or how sexually aroused you think you would feel if you actually experienced it." Seven response alternatives are provided, ranging from "adversely affects arousal: unthinkable, repulsive, distracting" to "always causes sexual arousal; extremely arousing."

PREVIOUSLY ADMINISTERED TO: Females, ages 17-48

APPROPRIATE FOR: Females who have engaged in sexual intercourse

ADMINISTRATION: The scale can be self-administered in a paper-and-pencil format and can be completed in about fifteen minutes. Alternatively, it can be administered in a card-sort format, with the respondent sorting the items into seven piles corresponding to the response alternatives provided for the paper-and-pencil form of the scale.

SAMPLE ITEMS:

Foreplay: When a loved one kisses you passionately

Erotic visual and verbal stimuli: When you read a pornographic or "dirty" story

Breast stimulation: When a loved one fondles your breasts with his/her hands

Preparation for and participation in intercourse: When you have intercourse with a loved one

Genital stimulation: When a loved one stimulates your genitals with mouth and tongue

SCORING: Each item is assigned between -1 and $+5$ points, with -1 assigned to the response "adversely affects arousal" and $+5$ assigned to the response "extremely arousing." The total score, which is the algebraic sum of the item scores, has a maximum value of 140 indicating maximum arousability.

DEVELOPMENT: An item pool was developed by consulting relevant literature. After the item pool was revised by six clinical psychologists who made suggestions for additions and modifications, it consisted of 131 descriptions of sexual activities and situations. One hundred fifty-one women rated the items on the degree to which they were or were not sexually arousing. Two sets of twenty items were identified on the basis of item-total correlations and correlations with four criterion variables. The criteria included (1) awareness of sexually induced physiological changes; (2) satisfaction with present state of sexual responsiveness; (3) frequency of sexual intercourse; and (4) amount of sexual intercourse prior to marriage. Three successive factor analyses were performed, and the twenty-eight items that best represented five factors were identified. The five factors were: Foreplay, Erotic Visual and Verbal Stimuli, Breast Stimulation, Preparation for and Participation in Intercourse, and Genital Stimulation.

RELIABILITY: The scale was administered to two samples of women: 151 comprise the validation sample; 134 women comprise the cross-validation sample. Coefficient alpha for the two samples was .91 and .92. The corrected split-half coefficient for each sample was .92. Forty-eight of the women in the cross-validation sample completed the test a second time eight weeks after they first completed it. Test-retest reliability was .69.

VALIDITY: Using the data obtained from the cross-validation sample, correlations were computed between scores on the SAI and each of the four criteria originally used to select items. The correlations were: awareness of sexually induced physiological changes = .57; satisfaction with present state of sexual responsiveness = .24; frequency of sexual intercourse = .43; and amount of sexual intercourse prior to marriage = .34. All correlations were significant at the .01 level. In addition, scores for the cross-validation sample were significantly correlated with amount of education ($r = .17$, $p < .05$), number of sexual partners ($r = .33$, $p < .01$), frequency of orgasm from masturbation ($r = .23$, $p < .01$), frequency of orgasm during intercourse ($r = .32$, $p < .01$), and scores on the Bentler Heterosexual Experience Scale ($r = .42$, $p < .01$).

A sample of fifteen women referred for sex-dysfunction therapy also completed the scale. Their scores were significantly different ($p < .001$) from the scores obtained by the cross-validation sample (the means of the two groups are not given).

NOTES AND COMMENTS: (1) With the exception of three items that refer to breast stimulation, the scale could be administered to males.

(2) Either of two fourteen-item forms can be used in place of the twenty-eight-item scale. Correlations between each of the fourteen-item forms and the full-length form are .94 and .95.

(3) The scale was developed and cross-validated on the responses from middle- and upper-middle class North American women; therefore the authors caution that additional data are necessary to establish the reliability and validity of the scale for other groups of women.

(4) The authors recommend the scale for use as a diagnostic tool to identify sexual dysfunction, as an assessment tool to evaluate the success of sex therapy, and as a research tool.

(5) Norms are provided based on the responses from 285 women.

SOURCE: See Hoon, Hoon, and Wincze.

BIBLIOGRAPHY:

Hoon, E. F., Hoon, P. W., and Wincze, J. P. "An Inventory for the Measurement of Female Sexual Arousability: The SAI." *Archives of Sexual Behavior,* 1976, *5,* 291-300.

---

223. SEXUAL ATTITUDE QUESTIONNAIRE

AUTHOR: Warren B. Miller

DATE: 1977

VARIABLES: Sexual regulation, sexual satisfaction

TYPE OF INSTRUMENT: Summated rating scale

DESCRIPTION: The Sexual Attitude Questionnaire contains thirty-one items: nineteen items are intended to measure Sexual Regulation (control, inhibition, and regulation exerted over one's own sexuality); and twelve items are intended to measure Sexual Satisfaction (satisfaction with sexual experiences). Some items are phrased to reflect the presence of sexual regulation and other items are phrased to reflect the absence of sexual regulation. Likewise, some items are phrased to reflect sexual satisfaction and other items are phrased to reflect sexual dissatisfaction. Each item is accompanied by four response alternatives: agree completely, agree somewhat, disagree somewhat, and disagree completely.

PREVIOUSLY ADMINISTERED TO: Females, ages 18-27

APPROPRIATE FOR: Females, ages 16 and older

ADMINISTRATION: The scale can be self-administered and can be completed in less than fifteen minutes.

SAMPLE ITEMS:

Sexual Regulation: I think it is a good idea for a woman to experiment sexually before she gets married.

Sexual Satisfaction: A woman needs sex in her life in order to be content.

SCORING: Items are objectively scored. The formula provided for obtaining scores takes account of the individual's mean and standard deviation based on her responses to all the items on the scale. A score is obtained for Sexual Regulation and for Sexual Satisfaction. In addition, subscale scores are obtained measuring orgasm proneness, dutiful sex, sex antihedonia, sex eagerness, sex shame, and tense sexuality. The various scores are not independent of each other; that is, the same item appears on more than one subscale.

DEVELOPMENT: The items in the scale were written after a review of the relevant literature. Pretesting of the instrument was done with young adult women, and revisions were made to ensure that the instructions and item content could be understood by women with at least some high school education. The scale was then administered to 230 married and unmarried women who were also interviewed. Based on the responses of these women, items were selected for the Sexual Regulation scale if they successfully discriminated between women who were high and women who were low in the control, inhibition, and regulation they exert over their sexuality. Items were selected for the Sexual Satisfaction scale if they successfully discriminated between women who experienced considerable satisfaction from their sexual experiences and women who experienced little satisfaction from their sexual experiences. Using the responses from about 1,200 women, cluster and factor analyses were performed. As a result, eight internally consistent subscales were developed. Two of these subscales each consist of subsets of the two main scales: Sexual Regulation and Sexual Satisfaction. The labels of the remaining six subscales are given above (see Scoring); each contains between four and six items.

RELIABILITY: Using the responses from 965 women, Kuder-Richardson reliabilities were computed for each of the scales. The reliability for Sexual Regulation was .83; the reliability for Sexual Satisfaction was .57. The reliabilities for the remaining subscales ranged from .24 to .89. Test-retest reliabilities were computed using the responses from forty-six women retested after a four-week interval. The reliability of the Sexual Regulation scale was .91; the reliability for the Sexual Satisfaction scale was .78. The test-retest reliabilities for the remaining subscales ranged from .72 to .91.

VALIDITY: No data are provided.

NOTES AND COMMENTS: (1) The seven most discriminating items from the Sexual Regulation scale comprise a "short form" Sexual Regulation scale. The Kuder-Richardson reliability of the scale was .83; the test-retest reliability of the scale based on a four-week test-retest interval was .89. The six most discriminating items from the Sexual Satisfaction scale comprise a "short form" Sexual Satisfaction scale. The Kuder-Richardson reliability of the scale was .40; the test-retest reliability of the scale based on a four-week test-retest interval was .81.

(2) Means and standard deviations on each of the scales are presented for the following groups: 324 never-married women; 322 women married for four to six months; and 319 women who bore their first child within the previous four to six months.

SOURCE: Warren B. Miller
American Institute for Research
P.O. Box 1113
1791 Arastradero Road
Palo Alto, California 94302

BIBLIOGRAPHY:

Miller, W. B. "Manual for Description of Instruments Used in a Research Project on the Psychological Aspects of Fertility Behavior in Women." Unpublished manuscript, American Institute for Research, 1977.

---

224. ZAMMUNER ATTITUDES TOWARD ABORTION SCALE

AUTHOR: Vanda L. Zammuner

DATE: 1976

VARIABLE: Attitudes toward abortion

TYPE OF INSTRUMENT: Summated rating scale

DESCRIPTION: The scale consists of fifty-eight statements, each of which is accompanied by a seven-point response scale ranging from "I very much agree" to "I very much disagree." Twenty-six items reflect a proabortion or liberal attitude; thirty-two items reflect an antiabortion or conservative attitude. The items consider the relationship between abortion and each of the following: ethical values, conceptions of women, the family, birth-control methods, and the potential infant.

PREVIOUSLY ADMINISTERED TO: High school age and older in Italy, England, and the United States

APPROPRIATE FOR: Ages 16 and older

ADMINISTRATION: The scale can be self-administered and can generally be completed in less than thirty minutes.

SAMPLE ITEMS:

Ethical values: Abortion is murder.

Conceptions of women: A woman is the only person who has the right to decide whether or not to have an abortion, since it is she who has the babies.

The family: Abortion should not be allowed as it tends to undermine the fundamental social institution, the family.

Birth control methods: Birth control should only be achieved by the prevention of conception.

Potential infant: Children have the right to be born, wanted, and loved.

SCORING: Items are objectively scored and equally weighted. Total scores can range from 58 (proabortion) to 406 (antiabortion).

DEVELOPMENT: One hundred fifteen Italians responded to a series of items (the exact number of items was not given) relating to attitudes toward abortion. Their responses were factor analyzed and item-total correlations were computed. The results of these analyses were used to select fifty-eight items for the final scale. The specific criteria for selecting items for the final scale were not explained.

RELIABILITY: No data are provided.

VALIDITY: Respondents completed a semantic differential for the following concepts: abortion, authority, child, god, woman, family, social approval, birth-control methods, nonconformist, protest, unmarried mother, sex, tradition, man, pregnancy, marriage, and morals. The results were used as a criterion for establishing the concurrent validation of the attitude scale. Correlations between semantic-differential scores and subscale scores (see Notes and Comments for an explanation of the subscales) were reported for nine subsamples of Italians (for example, high school students, married working women, medical students). The correlations were reported for seven concepts. Of the 189 correlations (3 subscales × 9 subsamples × 7 concepts = 189), seventy-nine were significant (p < .05). (See Zammuner, 1976, p. 111, for the significant correlations.)

NOTES AND COMMENTS: (1) Five factors emerged from a factor analysis of the responses from 217 Italians. A subscale on each of three factors was interpreted. Subscale items had a loading of at least .35 on one factor and zero or near zero loading on the other factors. Subscale A on Factor I is labeled "moral . . . as it refers to the prevailing customs in a given culture, to the principles governing conduct, with respect to the good and bad categories, which have been traditionally assumed as the ethical norms of social life" (1976, p. 86). Subscale B on Factor II is labeled "social because it takes into account medical, personal, and emotional considerations which refer to abortion considered in a social context" (1976, p. 86). Subscale C on Factor III is labeled "operative in the sense that, given effective birth-control methods, resort to abortion would no longer be a problem. At the same time this factor expresses the woman's right to actually choose motherhood" (1976, p. 86).

Five factors also emerged from a factor analysis of the response from 143 British and American subjects. Again, a subscale on each of three factors was interpreted. Subscale D on Factor I is labeled "eudemonistic, in the sense that it seems to express the concept that the individual should be happy and harmoniously balanced between his rights and his duties" (1976, p. 87). Subscale E on Factor V is labeled "traditionalist," and relates to "concern for social change" (1976, p. 87). Subscale F on Factor II is labeled "need for responsibility dimension, in an individual's behaviour towards birth control and therefore towards sexuality" (1976, p. 88).

(2) The scale is available in English and Italian.

SOURCE: See Zammuner, 1976.

BIBLIOGRAPHY:

Zammuner, V. L. "Costruzione e validazione di una scala di atteggiamento nei confronti dell'aborto." ("Construction and Validation of a Scale of Attitudes Toward Abortion.") Unpublished doctoral dissertation, University of Padua, 1975.

Zammuner, V. L. "Attitudes Toward Abortion: A Pilot Cross-Cultural Comparison." *Giornale Italiano di Psicologia,* 1976, *3,* 75-116.

13

※ ※ ※ ※ ※ ※ ※ ※ ※ ※

Unclassified

※ ※ ※ ※ ※ ※ ※ ※ ※ ※ ※ ※ ※ ※ ※ ※ ※

This chapter contains instruments that are relevant to women's issues but are not appropriate to any of the prior chapters. Each of the eleven instruments in this chapter measures a different variable.

---

225. ALLEN ANTIFEMININITY IN MEN SCALE

AUTHOR: Dean A. Allen

DATE: 1954

VARIABLE: Antifemininity in men, which is defined as "intolerance for tenderness, passivity, and anything hinting at femininity *in men,* together with admiration for a rough, aggressive, strong-willed supermasculinity" (p. 591).

TYPE OF INSTRUMENT: Summated rating scale

DESCRIPTION: The scale consists of twenty-five statements regarding personality traits and behaviors advocated for men (one item refers to women). All items are phrased so that agreement reflects support for the stereotypic "he-man." Six response options accompany each item: agree very strongly, agree pretty much, agree a little, disagree a little, disagree pretty much, and disagree very strongly.

PREVIOUSLY ADMINISTERED TO: Male college students

APPROPRIATE FOR: Ages 16 and older

ADMINISTRATION: The scale can be self-administered and can be completed in ten to twelve minutes.

SAMPLE ITEMS: A man should not let his decisions be influenced by women.
I despise softness and lack of will power in men.

SCORING: Items are objectively scored and equally weighted. The total score can range from −75 (supportive of "femininity" in men) to +75 (opposed to "femininity" in men).

DEVELOPMENT: A scale consisting of thirty items was constructed and administered to college men. An item analysis comparing the responses from high-scoring and low-scoring men indicated that all items discriminated in the predicted direction. However, five items were eliminated because they were judged to discriminate inadequately and "were felt to add little to the total scale" (p. 591).

RELIABILITY: No data are provided.

VALIDITY: The Allen Antifemininity in Men Scale and a measure of authoritarianism were both administered to ninety-five college men. The correlation between the two scales was .70 (p < .001).

NOTES AND COMMENTS: (1) When the scale was used, the antifemininity items were interspersed with items from the measure of authoritarianism and some neutral items.
     (2) Questions can be raised regarding the meaning or usefulness of some items. For example, what does it mean to disagree with the statement "I really have little sympathy for a man who gets discouraged easily"? Does it mean "I have much sympathy" or "I have no sympathy?" Furthermore, because sympathy has such a limited meaning, it is absurd to conclude that a person who has little or even no sympathy for a man who gets discouraged is critical of that man. It is not at all clear how the item "A strong person tends not to show his feelings" relates to the variable being measured. The item does not specify a "strong man"; it simply refers to a "strong person." Allen indirectly acknowledges these problems when he states, "No claim is made for the excellence of the questionnaire items constructed for this investigation; some could doubtless be made to operate more efficiently by rephrasing, and the reader may feel that important aspects of 'antifemininity in men' have been overlooked" (p. 592).

SOURCE: See Allen, 1954.

BIBLIOGRAPHY:

Allen, D. A. "Antifemininity in Men." *American Sociological Review,* 1954, *19,* 591-593.

226. CHAMELEON SYNDROME INDEX (FEMALE FORM)

AUTHORS: Bernard C. Rosen and Carole S. Aneshensel

DATE: 1976

VARIABLES: Chameleon syndrome, including sex role stereotypes, perception of sex role reward structure, and sex role behavior

TYPE OF INSTRUMENT: Multiple choice

DESCRIPTION: The "chameleon syndrome" is defined as "an accommodative response to an environment perceived as hostile to inappropriate sex role behavior" (p. 605). There are three parts of the Chameleon Syndrome Index. The first part concerns sex role stereotypes and asks the adolescent to indicate for each of three descriptions whether it is more like a boy or more like a girl. There are five response options: a lot more like a boy, a little more like a boy, like both equally, a little more like a girl, and a lot more like a girl. The second part concerns perceptions of the sex role reward structure and asks adolescents to indicate for each of five behaviors whether members of the opposite sex would "like you more or like you less" if the respondent engaged in the described behavior. There are four response options: like me a lot more, like me a little more, like me a little less, and like me a lot less. The third part concerns sex role behavior and asks the adolescent to indicate how often she engages in each of six behaviors. The response options are: never, seldom, sometimes, and often.

PREVIOUSLY ADMINISTERED TO: Grades 7-12

APPROPRIATE FOR: Ages 12-18

ADMINISTRATION: The scale can be self-administered and can be completed in about eight minutes.

SAMPLE ITEMS:

Sex Role Stereotypes: Are the following more like a boy or more like a girl? Do things they don't want to do just to make others like them.

Perception of Sex Role Reward System: If you did the following things, would a person your age of the opposite sex like you more or like you less? If you won in a game or sport you were playing with them.

Sex Role Behavior: How often do you do the following: Act dumber than you really are.

SCORING: Items are objectively scored. Three subscores and a total score are obtained. For each subscore, a high score indicates that the respondent attributes chameleon-like behavior to her own sex or to herself. A total score is obtained by converting each subscore to a z score by using the mean and standard deviation of that subscore obtained by all respondents. The three z scores are summed to yield the total score.

DEVELOPMENT: Material acquired through personal interviews provided the basis for the design of the questionnaire. Several preliminary drafts of the questionnaire were pretested in small groups and in classrooms. More specific information is not provided.

RELIABILITY: Reliability was calculated using the responses from 3,049 seventh through twelfth graders. Coefficient alpha for the total score was .52.

VALIDITY: As predicted, the mean score for 1,397 females ($\overline{X}$ = 1.22) was significantly higher than the mean score for 1,343 males ($\overline{X}$ = −1.19, p < .0005).

NOTES AND COMMENTS: The correlations between the three subscores are all positive and low. The correlation between Sex Role Behavior and Perception of the Sex Role Reward Structure was .10; the correlation between Sex Role Behavior and Sex Role Stereotypes was .21; and the correlation between Perception of the Sex Role Reward Structure and Sex Role Stereotypes was .07. Because the correlations were based on such a large sample (n = 3,049), they are all statistically significant (p < .001).

SOURCE: See Rosen and Aneshensel, 1976.

BIBLIOGRAPHY:

Rosen, B. C., and Aneshensel, C. S. "The Chameleon Syndrome: A Social-Psychological Dimension of the Female Sex Role." *Journal of Marriage and the Family,* 1976, *38,* 605-617.

---

227. FRENCH TEST OF INSIGHT

AUTHOR: Elizabeth G. French

DATE: 1958

VARIABLES: Women's role achievement motivation; classic achievement motivation

TYPE OF INSTRUMENT: Projective storytelling

DESCRIPTION: The test consists of ten single-sentence descriptions of different women's behavior. The woman completing the instrument is asked to write out an explanation for each of the ten behaviors described. Imagery dealing with "marriage, heterosexual popularity, social leadership, excellence in feminine skills, civic leadership, etc." (Friedrich, 1976b, p. 1) is considered to reflect women's role achievement motivation.

PREVIOUSLY ADMINISTERED TO: Female college students

APPROPRIATE FOR: Females, ages 16 and older

ADMINISTRATION: The instrument can be self-administered. No indication is given whether there is a limit to the time allowed for writing responses.

SAMPLE ITEMS: Sue frequently organizes groups or committees.
                        Carol gives lots of parties.

SCORING: As is typical for projective tests, scoring is based on subjective judgment. Friedrich (1976b) has published a scoring manual to facilitate scoring of the written responses. They are scored for both women's role achievement motivation and classic achievement imagery.

DEVELOPMENT: The French Test of Insight was originally intended to measure achievement need and affiliation need. In 1964, French and Lesser used the scale to measure women's role achievement motivation.

RELIABILITY: Analysis of variance procedures were used to estimate interrater reliability. The coefficients ranged from .86 to .98 (Friedrich, 1976a, 1976b).

VALIDITY: No data are provided.

NOTES AND COMMENTS: (1) Very little is actually known about the use of this instrument to measure women's role achievement motivation. No rationale is provided for its development; the only reliability data refer to interrater reliability; and no data are provided regarding validity. The only reason the instrument satisfied the criterion for inclusion here is that the interrater reliability data are provided.

    (2) For a more complete bibliography of studies that used the French Test of Insight simply to measure classic achievement motivation, see Chun, Cobb, and French (1975, p. 136, entry F-20).

SOURCE: See Friedrich, 1976b.

BIBLIOGRAPHY:

*Chun, K. T., Cobb, S., and French, J. R. P., Jr. *Measures for Psychological Assessment.* Ann Arbor: University of Michigan Press, 1975.
French, E. G., and Lesser, G. S. "Some Characteristics of the Achievement Motive in Women." *Journal of Abnormal and Social Psychology,* 1964, *68,* 119-128.
Friedrich, L. K. "Achievement Motivation in College Women Revisited: Implications for Women, Men, and the Gathering of Coconuts." *Sex Roles,* 1976a, *2,* 47-61.
Friedrich, L. K. "Guide for the Scoring of Intellectual n Achievement Imagery and Woman's Role n Achievement Imagery for the French Test of Insight." *Journal Supplement Abstract Service Catalog of Selected Documents in Psychology,* 1976b, *6,* 110-111.

228. HOLLENDER-LUBORSKY-SCARAMELLA NEED FOR BODY CONTACT SCALE

AUTHORS: Marc H. Hollender, Lester Luborsky, and Thomas Scaramella

DATE: 1969

VARIABLE: Need for being held (cuddled)

TYPE OF INSTRUMENT: Rating scale

DESCRIPTION: The scale consists of ten statements, nine of which are followed by five response options: never, almost never, sometimes, almost always, and always. For one item, the response options are: usually absent, diminished, unchanged, increased, or much increased. The statements concern reactions to being held, reactions to not being held, situations in which being held is desired, and methods used to arrange to be held. All statements are phrased so that one with a great desire to be held would choose the last response option ("always" or "much increased").

PREVIOUSLY ADMINISTERED TO: Females, ages 18-59, admitted to the psychiatric service of a hospital

APPROPRIATE FOR: Females, ages 18 and older

ADMINISTRATION: The scale can be self-administered and can be completed in less than five minutes.

SAMPLE ITEMS: When you are upset, it is comforting for you to have someone hold you.
            If you are NOT held when you desire closeness you feel tense.

SCORING: Items are objectively scored and equally weighted. Total scores can range from 10 (no need for being held) to 50 (great need for being held).

DEVELOPMENT: No information is provided.

RELIABILITY: Internal consistency was computed for the responses given by thirty-nine women admitted to a hospital's psychiatric service. The correlation was .82. Eighteen of the women completed the scale again one day to two weeks after they first completed it. Test-retest reliability was .84.

VALIDITY: No data are provided.

NOTES AND COMMENTS: The scale was embedded in a longer questionnaire.

SOURCE: See Hollender, Luborsky, and Scaramella, 1969.

BIBLIOGRAPHY:

Hollender, M. H., Luborsky, L., and Scaramella, T. J. "Body Contact and Sexual Entice-ment." *Archives of General Psychiatry,* 1969, *20,* 188-191.

229. MALE THREAT FROM FEMALE COMPETENCE (MTFC)

AUTHOR: Joseph H. Pleck

DATE: 1973

VARIABLE: Extent to which males are likely to perceive female competence as threatening

TYPE OF INSTRUMENT: Sentence completion

DESCRIPTION: The instrument consists of three sentence stems embedded in a twenty-one-item sentence-completion task. The respondent is to complete each sentence item.

PREVIOUSLY ADMINISTERED TO: Male college students

APPROPRIATE FOR: Ages 14 and older

ADMINISTRATION: The scale can be self-administered. The set of twenty-one stems can be completed in about twenty minutes.

SAMPLE ITEMS: When Rob learned that Linda got the highest grade in the class, he . . .
          When Ellen began to do the job, Chuck . . .

SCORING: Each sentence completion is classified as threatened (2 points), neutral (1 point), or positive (0 points). A scoring manual is available (Pleck, 1973) which provides guidelines and examples to facilitate scoring. Scores for the three items are summed. Scores between 0 and 2 are considered low; scores between 3 and 6 are considered high.

DEVELOPMENT: No data are provided.

RELIABILITY: The scale was administered to ninety-five college men. The intercorrelations between the three items were positive but low: .024, .155, and .254. Only the last one was statistically significant ($p < .05$). Overall internal consistency, as measured by coefficient alpha, was .33. The sentence completions were independently scored by two persons. They agreed on the scoring of 98 percent of the sentence completions. In no case did they ever disagree by more than 1 point (Pleck, 1973).

VALIDITY: Pleck (1973) administered the following measures to college men: a scrambled-words task, the MTFC, a word-generation task, a measure of female threat from male competence, a TAT-type measure of fear of success, a ten-item measure of sex role traditionalism, and two "reaction questionnaires," which followed the scrambled-words task and the word-generation task. The word-generation task was completed either under cooperative or competitive instructions. After reporting mixed results on four hypotheses, Pleck concludes: "Findings on two measures, future task preference and performance (qualified by the unanticipated heightened performance of positive males in the cooperative condition) . . . validate the construct Male Threat from Female Competence" (p. 146).

　　　Pleck found significant correlations between MTFC and two other measures: a measure of female threat from male competence ($r = .32$, $p < .05$) and a measure of fear of success ($r = .26$, $p < .05$). Neither of these two measures, however, was significantly correlated with performance under either cooperative or competitive conditions, nor were they significantly correlated with future task preference under either condition.

Scores on measures of sex role traditionalism, preference for wife working, and attitudes toward women's liberation were not significantly correlated with scores on MTFC, nor were they significantly correlated with measures of performance on future task preference. Pleck (1973, p. 151) therefore concludes that "MTFC has convergent validity in predicting male performance in the experiment . . . and future task preference. Further, MTFC has discriminant validity, with respect both to other projective measures scored for negative or conflictful [sic] fantasy and to other sex role attitude measures."

NOTES AND COMMENTS: (1) Embedding the three scored sentences in a twenty-one-item sentence completion task reduces the likelihood that respondents will guess the real purpose of the instrument.

(2) The low intercorrelations between the items and the low internal consistency reliability raises a question as to whether these three items are measuring the same construct.

SOURCE: See Pleck, 1973.

BIBLIOGRAPHY:

Pleck, J. H. "Male Threat from Female Competence: An Experimental Study in College Dating Couples." Unpublished doctoral dissertation, Harvard University, 1973. (*Dissertation Abstracts International,* 1974, *34*[12-B, pt. 1], 6221.)

Pleck, J. H. "Male Threat from Female Competence." *Journal of Consulting and Clinical Psychology,* 1976, *44,* 608-613.

---

230. MOTIVATIONS FOR JOINING CONSCIOUSNESS-RAISING GROUPS

AUTHORS: Morton A. Lieberman and Gary R. Bond

DATE: 1976

VARIABLE: Motivations for joining consciousness-raising groups

TYPE OF INSTRUMENT: Summated rating scale

DESCRIPTION: The scale consists of twenty possible reasons why a woman might join a consciousness-raising group. The reasons represent six general motivations: interest in women's issues (three items), help seeking (six items), social needs (three items), political activation (three items), sexual awareness (three items), and curiosity (two items). Each potential reason is accompanied by four response alternatives: very important, important, somewhat important, and not important.

PREVIOUSLY ADMINISTERED TO: Women who had joined consciousness-raising groups

APPROPRIATE FOR: Females who have been or are members of a consciousness-raising group

ADMINISTRATION: The scale is self-administered and can be completed in less than fifteen minutes.

SAMPLE ITEMS:

Interest in women's issues: To share thoughts and feelings about being a woman

Help seeking: To get relief from things or feelings troubling me

Social needs: To make friends

Political activation: To expand political awareness

Sexual awareness: To explore my sexual feelings toward men

Curiosity: To do something different

SCORING: Six scores are obtained, one for each subscale. The score represents the mean of the responses to each item on the particular subscale.

DEVELOPMENT: A thirty-three-item scale was completed by 1,669 women and their responses were factor analyzed. The six factors that emerged are the six subscales. The items loading on each of the subscales comprise the total scale. All factor loadings for selected items exceeded .59.

RELIABILITY: No data are provided.

VALIDITY: The Political Activation score was positively related to prior involvement in political organizations and a self-report measure of political ideology as "radical." Help-Seeking scores correlated with measures of psychological distress (Bond and Lieberman, in press).

NOTES AND COMMENTS: (1) This scale was part of a lengthy questionnaire that included numerous scales.

(2) Because the subscales are very short, it is important that the reliability of the various subscales be determined.

(3) Of the six items on the Help-Seeking subscale, five items seem to be almost redundant: "To get relief from things or feelings troubling me"; "To solve personal problems"; "To get help"; "To deal with current life problems"; and "To solve long-term problems."

SOURCE: See Lieberman and Bond, 1976.

BIBLIOGRAPHY:

Bond, G. R. Personal communication, 1978.
Bond, G. R., and Lieberman, M. A. "The Role and Function of Women's Consciousness-Raising: Self Help, Psychotherapy, or Political Activation?" In C. L. Heckerman (Ed.), *Women and Psychotherapy: Changing Emotions in Changing Times,* in press.
Lieberman, M. A., and Bond, G. R. "The Problem of Being a Woman: A Survey of 1,700 Women in Consciousness-Raising Groups." *Journal of Applied Behavioral Science,* 1976, *12,* 363-379.
Lieberman, M. A., Solow, N., Bond, G. R., and Reibstein, J. "The Psychotherapeutic Impact of Women's Consciousness-Raising Groups." *Archives of General Psychiatry,* 1979, *36,* 161-168.

---

231. PERCEIVED DISCRIMINATION INDEX

AUTHORS: Morton A. Lieberman, Nancy Solow, Gary R. Bond, and Janet Reibstein

DATE: 1978

VARIABLE: Experience of discrimination as a woman

TYPE OF INSTRUMENT: Multiple choice

DESCRIPTION: The instrument consists of the item stem "Have you personally experienced discrimination as a woman in:" followed by six endings to the sentence. For each sentence ending, the women are to choose from one of three response alternatives: definitely, perhaps/was subtle, no/never.

PREVIOUSLY ADMINISTERED TO: Women belonging to a consciousness-raising group

APPROPRIATE FOR: Females, ages 18 and older

ADMINISTRATION: The scale is self-administered and can be completed in about three minutes.

SAMPLE ITEMS: Have you personally experienced discrimination as a woman in career counseling (high school or college)?
Have you personally experienced discrimination as a woman in college (admissions, fellowships, school loans, etc.)?

SCORING: The score is equal to the sum of the items checked "definitely."

DEVELOPMENT: No information is provided.

RELIABILITY: The internal consistency (alpha) coefficient based on the responses from seventy-three women was .69 (Bond, personal communication, 1978).

VALIDITY: No data are provided.

NOTES AND COMMENTS: (1) The scale was originally part of a lengthy questionnaire which included numerous scales.

(2) The specific items on the scale refer to career counseling, college, employment, and credit and loan applications. In order for the scale to be applicable to respondents who have not had all of these experiences, the response option "not applicable" should be added. Otherwise the response "no" is ambiguous. It might mean that the person has been involved in the activity but did not experience discrimination, or it might mean that the person has never been involved in the activity and therefore could not possibly have been discriminated against.

(3) Although each item contributes equally to the total score, there is not a balance in the item content. One item applies to career counseling in high school or college; one item applies to college admissions, fellowships, and school loans; three items apply to employment situations; and one item applies to obtaining credit and loans. Obviously then, discrimination in employment situations contributes more heavily to the total score.

(4) The question, "Have you personally experienced discrimination in obtaining credit, loans, etc.?" may be confusing. What does "etc." refer to?

SOURCE: Gary R. Bond, Ph.D.
     Department of Behavioral Sciences
     University of Chicago
     5848 S. University
     Chicago, Illinois 60637

BIBLIOGRAPHY:

Bond, G. R. Personal communication, 1978.

Lieberman, M. A., Solow, N., Bond, G. R., and Reibstein, J. "The Psychotherapeutic Impact of Women's Consciousness-Raising Groups." *Archives of General Psychiatry*, in press.

---

232. ROSEN-LA RAIA INDEX OF MODERNITY IN WOMEN

AUTHORS: Bernard C. Rosen and Anita L. La Raia

DATE: 1972

VARIABLE: Modernity in women

TYPE OF INSTRUMENT: Summated rating scale

DESCRIPTION: There are two forms of the scale: a long form consisting of thirty items and a short form consisting of twelve items. Each form contains items in four areas: (1) Family Structure contains items regarding extended family ties, marital decision making, and marital communication (long form = nine items, short form = four items); (2) Perception of Sex Role contains items regarding attitudes toward women (long form = six items, short form = three items); (3) Socialization-Values and Goals contains items regarding attitudes and aspirations concerning children (long form = eight items, short form = two items); and (4) Activistic Values contains items regarding life plans and the future (long form = six items, short form = three items). Some items on the scale are phrased as questions with several response alternatives; other items are phrased as statements accompanied by four response options ranging from "strongly agree" to "strongly disagree." These latter items are all phrased to reflect a traditional orientation.

PREVIOUSLY ADMINISTERED TO: Married women in South America

APPROPRIATE FOR: Married females

ADMINISTRATION: The items on the scale were originally part of an interview. However, the final scale could easily be self-administered. The long form could be completed in less than fifteen minutes.

SAMPLE ITEMS:

Family Structure: A person should seek a job near his parents even if it would mean losing an opportunity.

Perception of Sex Role: As a rule, women are less intelligent than men.

Socialization-Values and Goals: Regardless of what you would like, how much schooling do you think your son will be able to complete?

Activistic Values: All that a man should wish in life is a secure job, not very difficult, that would enable him to purchase a home.

SCORING: Scoring is not clearly explained. The authors state: "The factor-weighted responses of individuals were summed and a standardized modernity score produced for the respondent. . . . The higher the score, the more modern the woman" (p. 355).

DEVELOPMENT: Interviews were conducted with 816 women in Brazil. Items included in the interviews that appeared relevant to a modernity index were identified, and the responses were recorded to follow a standard format. The items were then factor analyzed. The long form was constructed by selecting the thirty items with loadings of at least .25 on the first factor extracted. This factor accounted for 20 percent of the variance. The short form was constructed by selecting representative items from each of the four areas on the long form. Typically the items selected for the short form had the highest factor loadings.

RELIABILITY: No data are provided.

VALIDITY: The correlation between the long and the short form was .92. Rosen and La Raia hypothesized that scores on the subscales would correlate positively with level of education, number of memberships in voluntary organizations, level of participation in the labor force, and educational and occupational status of husband; and they hypothesized that scores would correlate negatively with family size. All correlations were significant (p < .01) and in the predicted direction. The correlations they obtained were (short-form correlations are given in parentheses): wife's educational level = .67 (.59); husband's educational level = .64 (.56); husband's occupational status = .58 (.52); number of memberships in voluntary organizations = .47 (.41); status of labor-force participation = .35 (.36); actual family size = −.35 (−.32); and preferred family size = −.21 (−.16). Furthermore, as predicted, Rosen and La Raia found that scores were directly related to the degree of industrialization in the community where the women had resided for most of their lives (p < .001).

NOTES AND COMMENTS: The authors do not report any information regarding the use of the scale itself. All of their data come from individual interviews in which the scale questions were embedded. Furthermore, when the questions were part of the interview, they did not necessarily appear in the same form or with the same response options as they appear on the scale as described here.

SOURCE: See Rosen and La Raia, 1972.

BIBLIOGRAPHY:

Rosen, B. C., and La Raia, A. L. "Modernity in Women: An Index of Social Change in Brazil." *Journal of Marriage and the Family,* 1972, *34,* 353-360.

---

233. SANGER-ALKER FEMINIST IDEOLOGY SCALE

AUTHORS: Susan Phipps Sanger and Henry A. Alker

DATE: 1972

VARIABLE: Feminist ideology

TYPE OF INSTRUMENT: Forced choice

DESCRIPTION: The instrument consists of sixteen pairs of statements. For each pair, the respondents are to indicate which of the two statements they agree with. Thirteen pairs of statements concern women and employment, discrimination, and heterosexual relations. In each pair, one statement indicates that the individual is responsible for the problem or solution described, and one statement indicates that social forces or group pressure is responsible for the problem or solution described. Of the remaining three pairs, one concerns sports, one concerns child rearing, and one concerns war.

PREVIOUSLY ADMINISTERED TO: Female college students

APPROPRIATE FOR: Ages 16 and older

ADMINISTRATION: The scale can be self-administered and can be completed in about ten minutes.

SAMPLE ITEMS: (a) The best way to handle problems of discrimination against women is for each individual woman to make sure she gets the best training possible for what she wants to do. (b) Only if women pull together in women's rights groups and activities can anything be done about discrimination against them.

(a) It's lack of skills and abilities that keeps many women from getting a job. It's not just because they are women. When a woman is trained to do something, she is able to get a job. (b) Many qualified women can't get a good job; men with the same skills wouldn't have any trouble.

SCORING: For each pair of statements, the choice of one of the statements earns the respondent 1 point and the choice of the other statement earns 0 points. Total scores can range from 0 (strong opposition to feminist ideology) to 16 (strong support for feminist ideology).

DEVELOPMENT: A group of ninety-six women, including fifty women active in feminist organizations and forty-six "controls," completed a lengthy questionnaire including Rotter's I-E scale, seventeen items specially designed to measure feminist ideology, a portion of the Marlowe-Crowne Social Desirability Scale, a set of questions concerning women's liberation, and two pages requesting background material. A factor analysis was performed on the responses, and three factors were extracted. The first factor included thirteen of the seventeen items designed to measure feminist ideology, two filler items from Rotter's I-E scale, and one general item. These sixteen items comprise the Sanger-Alker Feminist Ideology Scale.

RELIABILITY: No data are provided.

VALIDITY: The mean score from the women active in feminist organizations ($\overline{X}$ = 14.00) was compared with the mean score from the control group ($\overline{X}$ = 7.98). The difference was significant ($p < .01$) in the expected direction: women active in feminist organizations are more supportive of feminist ideology.

NOTES AND COMMENTS: (1) The factor analysis yielded two additional factors: Personal Control and Protestant Ethic Ideology.

(2) No information is provided regarding the use of the Sanger-Alker Feminist Ideology Scale alone—that is, when it is not embedded in other scales.

SOURCE: Henry A. Alker
            Department of Psychology
            Cornell University
            Ithaca, New York 14853

BIBLIOGRAPHY:

Sanger, S. P., and Alker, H. A. "Dimensions of Internal-External Locus of Control and the Women's Liberation Movement." *Journal of Social Issues,* 1972, *28*(4), 115-129.

---

234. SINGLETON-CHRISTIANSEN IDENTIFICATION WITH THE WOMEN'S MOVEMENT

AUTHORS: Royce Singleton, Jr. and John B. Christiansen

DATE: 1977

VARIABLE: Identification with the women's liberation movement

TYPE OF INSTRUMENT: Multiple choice

DESCRIPTION: The instrument consists of seven questions, each of which is followed by three response options: yes, no, and don't know or not applicable. The questions are all phrased in such a way that an affirmative response indicates positive identification with the women's liberation movement.

PREVIOUSLY ADMINISTERED TO: College students

APPROPRIATE FOR: Ages 16 and older

ADMINISTRATION: The scale can be self-administered and can be completed in about two minutes.

SAMPLE ITEMS: Do you basically support the goals of the Women's Movement, as you understand these goals?
                    Would you sign a petition supporting a women's cause?

SCORING: Items are objectively scored and equally weighted. Total scores can range from 0 (no identification with the women's movement) to 14 (strong identification with the women's movement).

DEVELOPMENT: No information is provided.

RELIABILITY: No data are provided.

VALIDITY: The Singleton-Christiansen Identification with the Women's Movement scale was given to 283 college students along with the FEM scale (#179), a measure of attitudes toward feminism. As predicted, the correlation between the two measures was significant and positive ($r = +.638$, $p < .001$) (Singleton and Christiansen, 1977).

NOTES AND COMMENTS: The authors' attempts to identify a Guttman scale from the items were unsuccessful. They were unable to produce satisfactory coefficients of reproducibility or minimal marginal reproducibility (Singleton, 1978).

SOURCE: Royce Singleton, Jr.
         Department of Sociology
         College of the Holy Cross
         Worcester, Massachusetts 01610

BIBLIOGRAPHY:

Singleton, R., Jr. Personal communication, June 1978.
Singleton, R., Jr., and Christiansen, J. B. "The Construct Validation of a Short-Form Attitudes Toward Feminism Scale." *Sociology and Social Research,* 1977, *61,* 294-303.

---

235. WALLIN WOMEN'S NEIGHBORLINESS SCALE

AUTHOR: Paul Wallin

DATE: 1953 (used 1948)

VARIABLE: Women's knowledge of and friendliness with neighbors

TYPE OF INSTRUMENT: Guttman scale

DESCRIPTION: The scale consists of twelve questions that ask about one's familiarity or friendliness with one's neighbors. "Neighborhood" is defined for respondents as "all homes within one block in any direction from the block where you live" (p. 243). "Neighbor" is defined as "any person living that distance from you" (p. 243).

PREVIOUSLY ADMINISTERED TO: Adult women under age 60

APPROPRIATE FOR: Ages 18 to 60 living in an urban or suburban community

ADMINISTRATION: The scale was originally administered as an interview. The questions can be open ended or accompanied by fixed response alternatives. Also, the scale could easily be adapted for self-administration with fixed response alternatives. The number of alternatives accompanying each question would vary. In self-administered form, the scale could be completed in less than ten minutes.

SAMPLE ITEMS: How many of your best friends who live in your neighborhood did you get to know since you or they moved into the neighborhood?
         Do you and any of your neighbors go to movies, picnics, or other things like that together?

SCORING: The answers to eleven of the twelve questions are dichotomized into "greater neighborliness" and "lesser neighborliness." For one question, the answers are trichotomized. The total score can range from 0 (minimum neighborliness) to 13 (maximum neighborliness).

DEVELOPMENT: An item pool was constructed using suggestions from students in a sociology class and members of a sociology staff and by taking items from another study regarding neighborhoods. A fourteen-item interview scale was administered to 381 women in Palo Alto, California, and 252 women in San Francisco. For the San Francisco sample, it was found that thirteen items formed a Guttman scale with a coefficient of reproducibility of .917. The fourteenth item produced nonscale types and was eliminated. The remaining thirteen items were analyzed using the responses from the Palo Alto sample. When the sample was restricted to women under age 60, twelve items formed a Guttman scale with a coefficient of reproducibility of .924. These twelve items comprise the scale.

RELIABILITY: No data are provided.

VALIDITY: No data are provided.

SOURCE: See Wallin, 1953.

BIBLIOGRAPHY:

Edelstein, A. S., and Larsen, O. N. "The Weekly Press' Contribution to a Sense of Urban Community." *Journalism Quarterly,* 1960, *37,* 489-498.

Fava, S. F. "Suburbanism as a Way of Life." *American Sociological Review,* 1956, *21,* 34-37.

Greer, S. "Urbanism Reconsidered: A Comparative Study of Local Areas in a Metropolis." *American Sociological Review,* 1956, *21,* 19-25.

Larsen, O. N., and Edelstein, A. S. "Communication, Consensus, and the Community Involvement of Urban Husbands and Wives." *Acta Sociologia,* 1960, *5,* 15-30.

Wallin, P. "A Guttman Scale for Measuring Women's Neighborliness." *American Journal of Sociology,* 1953, *59,* 243-246.

Index of
Instrument Titles

Index of Names*

Abbott, S., 272
Abdelhalim, I. H., *386*, 387
Abelew, T., 434, 441
Abernathy, R. W., 392
Abernathy, T. J., Jr., 358, 359
Abramowitz, C., 392, 393
Abramowitz, S. I., 392, 394
Abramson, P. R., 496, 499
Adelson, B. M., 393
Adelson, J., *40*, 41
Ager, J. W., 483
Akhtar, S. S., *374*, 375
Albright, D. G., 391, 393
Aldous, J., 266, 271, 272, 276
Alexander, R. A., *320*, 322, 347
Alker, H. A., *520*, 521
Allen, B. P., 166, *181*, 182
Allen, D. A., *508*, 509
Allgeier, E. R., 108

Allingham, J. D., 483
Almquist, C., *366*, 367
Almquist, E. M., *349*, 350, 351
Alper, T. G., *145*, 146, 314, 315
Alpert, J. L., *368*, *369*, 370, 371
Alpert, R., 73, *85*, 86, *87*, 88
Althouse, R. H., 216
Altman, S. L., 161, 199, 350, 351, 434, 435
Altucher, N., 50, 125
Anastasi, A., 14, 17, 54
Anastasiow, N. J., *59*, 60, 61, 86, 88
Anderson, C. L., 109, *407*, 408
Anderson, E. D., 293, 294
Anderson, M., 199
Anderson, P., *175*, 176
Anderson, W. R., 108, 110
Andres, D., 68, 71, 405
Andrews, R., 30, 31, 46, 65, 66, 68, 72
Aneshensel, C. S., *510*, 511
Angell, M. L., 199

*An italicized number indicates that the person authored an instrument appearing on that page.

Index of
Variables Measured